D1707878

Sanctuaries *of* Earth, Stone, and Light

The Southwest Center Series

Joseph C. Wilder, editor

Sanctuaries *of* Earth, Stone, and Light

The Churches of Northern New Spain, 1530–1821

Gloria Fraser Giffords

The University of Arizona Press • Tucson

Unless otherwise noted, all photographs are by the author.

The University of Arizona Press

Library of Congress Cataloging-in-Publication Data

Giffords, Gloria Fraser, 1938–
Sanctuaries of earth, stone, and light : the churches of northern New Spain, 1530–1821 / Gloria Fraser Giffords.
p. cm.
Includes bibliographical references and index.
ISBN 978-0-8165-2589-8 (hardcover : alk. paper)
1. Catholic church buildings—Mexico, North.
2. Architecture, Spanish colonial—Mexico, North.
3. Catholic church buildings—Southwest, New.
4. Architecture, Spanish colonial—Southwest, New.
I. Title.
NA5256.N67G54 2007
726.50972'1—dc22 2007009881

Publication of this book is made possible in part by a grant from the Southwest Center of the University of Arizona.

The Southwest Center Series list is on page 463.

Designed by William Benoit, Simpson & Convent.

Manufactured in the United States of America on acid-free, archival-quality paper.

12 11 10 09 08 07 6 5 4 3 2 1

This work is dedicated to the five most influential women in my life:
my mother, Thora Elnora Ackard Fraser Clifton (1910–1994),
my aunt, Ethel Florence Ackard (1891–1994),
my sister, Ruth-Joyce Fraser Vacin (1935–1972)

Gratia vobis et pax.
Rev. 1:4

and especially to my two daughters, Melissa Kay and Gabrielle Dee.

If I had been a more adept student
I could have learned even more from them.

Que Vivan las Mujeres!

Contents

Preface

Any number of books and articles have been written about the construction and relevant furnishings of Spanish colonial churches within the boundaries of the area referred to as northern New Spain. In most cases, however, these churches are examined and treated in isolation, ignoring the fact that they were part of a larger network and were built to the explicit requirements of the Catholic Church and the architectural and decorative precepts of a specific time and place. Furthermore, because of the abundance and generally higher aesthetic quality of religious structures and furnishings in central and southern Mexico, the north's offerings tend to be regarded as less significant. By way of correcting these misperceptions, I conceived this book with two goals in mind—to serve as a thoughtful, wide-ranging introduction to the churches of northern New Spain; and to heighten awareness of the many influences that came to bear upon the art, architecture, and furnishings of those churches during the colonial or viceregal period.

Thirty years as a practicing art conservator, specializing in polychrome statuary and in oil paintings on all types of supports, have given me a special "eye," one that sees an image or object as a veil to be looked beyond and analyzed. Preferring, whenever possible, to explore the actual sites, their contents, and their archives, I visited, in the course of my research, every viceregal mission, cathedral, and parochial structure in the United States, most of those in northern Mexico, and perhaps hundreds of other churches throughout Mexico, Central and South America, and Spain. I gained valuable insights from exploring still other colonial churches in East Asia (Goa, Macao, and the Philippines), as well as mosques and secular buildings in North Africa and Turkey.

In this volume I discuss some topics in detail, while giving others a more general treatment—reflecting my expertise or personal bias, on the one hand, and the abundance or paucity of actual examples and documentary evidence, on the other. In my view an introductory work should encourage curiosity and exploration. It is my hope that readers will find this to be true for *Sanctuaries of Earth, Stone, and Light.*

A few words about the general layout of this work: information on a church building's architectural elements appears in chapter 5: "The Church Building," whereas information on its architectural details and decoration is presented in chapter 6: "Details and Motifs." There are always a few items, of course, that defy logic. I considered altars and baptismal fonts to be furnishings, even though some were incorporated into the buildings' architecture; they are discussed in chapter 7: "Furnishings," while holy water fonts or stoups are discussed in chapter 5, in accordance with the Church's policy since the thirteenth century.

I have tried to strike a workable balance between text and illustrations, deliberately omitting some descriptive text in the hope that readers will find well-chosen illustrations more directly instructive. Although the text focuses on materials or objects directly associated with religious buildings and institutionalized religion, there are numerous instances, some illustrated, where the identical form, function, material, and technique of manufacture apply to items of personal religious observance.

While keeping jargon to a minimum, I did not hesitate to use precise, succinct technical terms where there were no suitable nontechnical equivalents. I made every effort to use the most common terms, but acknowledge that other terms may be correct and locally accepted. Equivalent terms in Spanish (and occasionally, Latin and French) and their etymology are provided for many of the items to help clarify an idea or add a mnemonic device.

Readers unfamiliar with the basic terms and concepts of church architecture, Spanish colonial art, Christian symbolism and iconography, and the basic history of northern New Spain would be well served by consulting Nikolaus Pevsner, John Fleming, and Hugh Honour, *A Dictionary of Architecture;* Vicente Medel Martínez, *Vocabulario arquitectónico ilustrado;* Manuel Toussaint, *Colonial Art in Mexico* (translated from the Spanish by Elizabeth Wilder Weismann); Gertrude Sill, *A Handbook of Symbols in Christian Art;* Juan Ferrando Roig, *Iconografía de los santos;* and Peter Gerhard, *The North Frontier of New Spain.* Listed at book's end, along with primary and secondary sources, are books and articles for further reading and research, as well as a selection of recordings of Spanish colonial church music.

ACKNOWLEDGMENTS

I am particularly grateful to Federico McAninch, retired curator of the Arizona Historical Society and specialist in Spanish colonial Church matters; to Yvonne Lange, director emeritus of the Museum of International Folk Art, Santa Fe, and specialist in iconography; to Jorge Olvera, specialist in Spanish viceregal history, art, and architecture; and to Richard Brooks Jeffery, specialist in adobe and Moorish architecture, for generously sharing their time, research, and expertise, for their meticulous reading of a number of chapters, for their invaluable comments and corrections, and for bringing to my attention bibliographical sources of which I had been unaware.

My thanks to Michael Drewes Marquardt and Craig Russell for their comments on the music section in chapter 7, and again to Craig for his wise observations and contributions to bibliographic and discographic entries for that chapter; to Charles Polzer, SJ, for his enthusiastic assistance in archival matters; to Bernard Fontana for his helpful advice and for providing many important scholastic contacts; to Robert Geibner for an early reading of passages pertaining to architecture; to Helen Lucero and Donna Pierce for first reading and recommending the manuscript for publication; to Kieran McCarty, OFM, for information concerning the Franciscans and their history and vestments; to Keith McElroy for his helpful comments on earlier drafts; and to Ewing Waterhouse for sharing his research on Spanish colonial architecture.

I examined photographs or drawings in the archives of the Library of Congress, Washington, DC; University of Texas, Institute of Texas Culture in San Antonio; Pál Kelemen Collection, Arizona State Museum Library, University of Arizona, Tucson; Benson Latin American Collection, Harry Ransom Humanities Research Center, and the Architectural Drawings Collection, University of Texas at Austin; Texas State Library, Austin; and the Southwest Museum, Pasadena, California. I sifted through and read documents in the original and on microfilm at Documentary Relations of the Southwest, Arizona State Museum; and the University of Arizona Library, both in Tucson; Bancroft Library, University of California at Berkeley; the Benson Latin American Collection, University of Texas, Austin; Old Spanish Missions Research Library, Our Lady of the Lakes University, San Antonio, Texas; the Archivo General y Público de la Nación, Mexico, DF; and the Archivo General de las Indias, Sevilla. I acknowledge with gratitude the assistance given me by the staffs of these institutions.

Debra Beaumont lent her skills and enthusiasm in assisting me to search for and copy hundreds of church inventories on microfilm at Documentary Relations of the Southwest; son-in-law Robert Giffords performed many of the same duties at the Bancroft Library. Wanda Turnley in the Rare Books and Prints section of the Benson Latin American Collection, Tom Shelton at the University of Texas's Institute of Texas Culture, and John Anderson in the Texas State Library archives were not only extremely cooperative, but provided valuable leads and suggestions.

My very special thanks to Elizabeth D. Lonergan, who first took my manuscript in hand, for her sensitive, thoughtful reading; to Harriet J. Mann, for her meticulous vetting of text, endnotes, and sources and for her lucid floor plans; to Meredith L. Milstead, for the excellent line drawings that grace these pages; to Raoul E. Erickson, for his generous loan of and technical assistance concerning digital equipment; to my editor, Jeffrey H. Lockridge, for bringing much-needed focus to a manuscript that had grown far beyond a publishable size; and to Elizabeth Shaw for her encouragement, enthusiasm, and wise counsel. Braced by Jeff's exquisite blends of coffee in our many sessions at Liz's oak dining table, we were able to nip, tuck, and set aside, yet preserve and polish the best of what I wanted to say.

But especially to my husband Spencer J. Giffords who has never once balked at or questioned my suggestion to visit some out-of-the-way locale and who would either join me in the church's interior looking at every single painting or sculpture on display or convince the priest or sacristan to allow me access to the sacristy, store rooms, choir loft, bell towers and roof; or would sit outside with a cigar chatting with the local men, women and children, acquiring information concerning popular beliefs and customs. There's probably a crown waiting for him somewhere.

Sins of omission or commission are solely mine. In anticipation of a revised edition, I invite constructive criticism and suggestions for corrections or additions.

Sanctuaries *of* Earth, Stone, and Light

CHAPTER 1

SCOPE AND FOCUS

Northern New Spain comprises part or all of the Spanish viceregal provinces of Nueva Vizcaya, Nuevo León, Nuevo México, Nueva Galicia, Coahuila, Texas, Sonora, Sinaloa, Nuevo Santander, and Baja and Alta California as they existed from 1535 to 1821.[1] The region is bounded on the west by the Pacific Ocean, between the 22nd and 42nd parallels, and on the east by roughly the 100th meridian and the Gulf of Mexico. Its northern limit—the effective limit of occupation or settlement under Spanish and Mexican governments—roughly follows the northern boundary of Mexico at the time it declared its independence from Spain, from the Pacific Ocean east across California, Nevada, Utah, Wyoming, and south halfway through Colorado, and then angles off through the southwestern tip of Kansas, to include part of the Oklahoma panhandle and almost all of Texas. Its southern limit, a poorly defined line subject to varying political and cultural interpretations, begins near the boundary between the Mexican states of Sinaloa and Nayarit on the west, swings north and east in a crescent along the southern boundary of the state of Durango, through the northern part of the states of Zacatecas and San Luis Potosí, and then along the southern boundary of the state of Tamaulipas to the Gulf of Mexico (figure 1.1).

Scattered over many thousands of square miles, sparse populations of indigenous, Spanish, and mestizo peoples clustered mostly along rivers or around presidios and mining centers. The region was wracked by nearly constant warfare between those defending the missions, settlements, and mines and the native peoples resisting colonization. In the north, the harshness of the terrain and climate, the problem of effectively defending clergy and civilians against hostile natives, and the absence of a coherent political strategy were compounded by the general lack of readily exploitable mineral wealth to provide few incentives for settlement. (Large finds of silver and gold within the present boundaries of

1.1. Northern New Spain at its furthermost boundaries superimposed on the present Mexican and U.S. states.

the United States were not discovered in viceregal times). In the south, despite the presence of several rich mineral finds, a larger population, denser settlement, and closer proximity to sources of goods not produced locally, hostile Indians and the rugged frontier life again hampered development.

The region's boundaries on the north, northwest, and east were drawn more in response to the threat of foreign encroachment than out of a desire to develop new population centers. Without the promise of great riches or the menace of other countries, the capital-based vice-regents could not justify prolonged, expensive military and missionary efforts. Boundaries between the region's political and ecclesiastical divisions, on the other hand, were shifted time and again, as military, mining, agricultural, missionary, and settlement activities waxed and waned over the almost three-hundred-year period.

In the early decades of the sixteenth century, there had been several exploratory attempts (*entradas*) along the coasts. By 1550, inland exploration had taken place through present-day Arizona, New Mexico, Texas, and Kansas, as well as along the coasts of what would later become Baja and Alta California. The central plateau of Mexico, through which some of the earliest expeditions passed, was settled first. Spaniards were reported to be living in Culiacán (Sinaloa) by 1536. Although missionaries accompanied the early explorers as chaplains, conversion of the natives at this time was difficult if not impossible. Consequently, there were few enduring structures built before the seventeenth century. During the period 1530 to 1821, Spain claimed these lands and administered them through colonial governments. After the War of Independence these lands were considered Mexico's until the United States obtained portions of them through purchase, treaty, or war.

Although artistic influences in northern New Spain were mostly Spanish, including many contemporaneous European styles adjusted to the sensitivities of the Spanish colonists and the local artisans, Islamic—and even some Oriental—influences can also be discerned in the region's religious architecture, furnishings, vestments, or ornamentation. There is a natural inclination on the part of many of us to compare the structures, furnishings, and decorations of northern frontier churches with their rich and often opulent counterparts in central and southern Mexico. This is only reasonable: art appreciation, in general, is taught using examples that most completely characterize a particular type or style. Central and southern Mexico are home to numerous complete and excellent examples of baroque, for instance, with its exaggerated, dramatic visual effects and often lavish decorations. In the far north such opulence was the exception and was most often associated with isolated sites of mineral wealth. Yet the simpler churches in early settlements and missions of northern New Spain—as well as their vestments, ornaments, and religious images, and the portable items with which the priests conducted Mass, Baptisms, and other rites—also merit attention. These much more modest structures clearly reflect their styles' manifestos, and in their simple and even sparce manner often tell the observer far more about arrangement of space, proportion, and construction than do the churches to the south, for all their polychrome, gilding, swirls, and angles. Many of the sixteenth-century structures were temporary and have either totally disappeared or are visible only as mounds of rubble; others were incorporated within later structures. Examination of extant structures begins with seventeenth-century missions of present-day New Mexico and Arizona and with mission and diocesan churches dating back to the same era in the modern Mexican states of Durango, Chihuahua, San Luis Potosí, and Zacatecas.[2]

As areas of New Spain's northern frontier became more secure or were at least explored, the population increased and more ambitious and permanent structures were constructed. Most of the material available for examination dates from the mid-seventeenth century, with the bulk falling within the eighteenth century and the first two decades of the nineteenth. Comparatively few examples remain of the objects referred to in the inventories of church properties in the seventeenth and eighteenth centuries. When early buildings were destroyed or abandoned, their furnishings were also destroyed or moved to other locations and later forgotten or absorbed at the new sites. As a result, definite conclusions about types, quality, or even general appearances of furnishings from this time cannot be drawn with certainty. Nevertheless, intelligent assumptions can be made from objects of comparable age still extant in other regions, including central and southern Mexico and Spain.

Despite the almost constant hostilities with various Indian groups, the vast distances over which it was necessary to transport people and supplies, and the arid, torturous terrain, colonization of northern New Spain proceeded. A flurry of mining activity throughout the central northern plateau attracted settlers, merchants, craftsmen, and government officials. Generous land grants were given for ranches in surrounding areas, and gradually the settlements grew, attracting still others, while missionary and military efforts led the way to pacification and settlement of areas that lacked mining interests.

Besides diocesan clergy ministering to the needs of settlers and miners, missionaries from several different orders were active in northern New Spain. One of the two most significant was the Franciscan Order. Active in north central New Spain from the mid-sixteenth century, Franciscans were involved by 1520 in the southern part of Nueva Galicia, then an enormous frontier province, which would later be divided into the provinces of northern New Spain. From 1530 to 1580, the Franciscans pushed northward, carrying their missionary work to what would later become the provinces of Nuevo León and Coahuila and still later Nuevo Santander (Tamaulipas), and founding the first mission on the south slope of the Sierra de Tamaulipa in the late 1550s.

Accompanying Don Francisco de Ibarra on his expedition north to Nueva Vizcaya (Chihuahua and Durango) from Zacatecas in 1554, Franciscans were present at the founding of Nombre de Dios in 1562, as well as Durango (Durango) in 1563. Under the direction of the Custodia de San Francisco de Zacatecas (founded in 1566), they established five *conventos* in Nueva Vizcaya. Franciscan missionaries left behind at Pueblo Indian settlements in New Mexico in 1582 and soon killed by the Indians were replaced by other missionaries, who traveled there with Don Juan de Oñate in 1598, establishing a mission by 1616. Before the Pueblo Revolt of 1680, the order had twenty-five missions in the province of Nuevo México (comprising most of the modern state of New Mexico and parts of Arizona and Texas), and they returned in force when the area was recolonized after 1693. Although the provinces of Nuevo León and Nueva Vizcaya (parts of which later became the province and then the state of Coahuila) did not receive their first Franciscan missionary until 1594, there were Franciscans sporadically in Saltillo at the end of the sixteenth century.

Franciscans were also active in Texas near present-day El Paso and along the Rio Grande by 1659 and farther east around San Antonio three decades later, with their most concerted efforts beginning in the early eighteenth century. (The Franciscan missions along the Rio Grande in today's western Texas and eastern Chihuahua are considered part of the province of Nuevo México.) To the west, Franciscans took over the Jesuit missions of Baja California in 1768, and the following year established their first mission in Alta California, where they would remain until their missions were converted to diocesan use, their last mission being founded there in 1823.

The other religious order with a significant presence in northern New Spain was that of the Jesuits, who arrived at the Villa de Sinaloa in 1590 to found the first of a chain of missions stretching northward through Sonora and the Pimería Alta; they established missions in Baja California as early as 1697. Jesuits had an almost complete monopoly over missionary work among the local Indians until 1767, when they were expelled from every Spanish dominion by decree of Charles III. They were active in Nueva Vizcaya after 1594, establishing schools and a college in Guadiana (the present-day city of Durango) and working among the Tepehuanes from the late 1590s in Guanaceví (Durango) and among the Tarahumaras from 1610 at Satevó (Chihuahua).

Upon the Jesuits' expulsion in 1767, Franciscans assumed most of their duties and posts in Sonora, Sinaloa, Durango, Coahuila, and Baja California, and some Jesuit missions were converted to diocesan use.[3] Dominicans replaced Franciscans in some of the former Jesuit locations in Baja California in 1772, completing missions left unfinished and later also founding some of their own. While they had no significant presence in seventeenth-century Nueva Vizcaya, with neither conventos nor a clearly defined mandate, Dominicans were assigned to work among the Indians in the barrios of Sombrerete (Zacatecas) in 1684, and began construction of the impressive Church of Santo Domingo and its convento there in 1741.

Other religious groups such as the Augustinians and the Hospitaliers of Saint John of God provided hospitals and medical treatment at mining centers in Nueva Vizcaya such as Durango (Durango), Sombrerete (Zacatecas), and Parral (Chihuahua) during the seventeenth and eighteenth centuries. Augustinians also played their part as missionaries in the district of Tampico (later called Nuevo Reino de León, then Nuevo Santander, and now Tamaulipas), founding a convent in Santiesteban in 1540. Carmelites also played a brief, but nonmissionary, role in northern New Spain (see "Orders" in chapter 9).

The missionary endeavor among the Indians was originally intended to serve the short-term educational goals of converting various native peoples (thereby saving their souls) and training them in practical skills, to make them a productive part of Spanish colonial society, after which the missions were to be disbanded and the Indians integrated into colonial society. The Spanish government, for its part, used the mission system as a means of pacifying the Indians, promoting colonial settlement, and creating buffer zones against foreign influences. Criticism of the missions and pressure to convert them to diocesan use began with competition for Indian labor and lands. Missionaries expressed their fears that, once separated from their protection, the Indians would be exploited and their lands taken from them by the non-Indians. Secular authorities countered that the missionaries were the exploiters, that economic development was being impeded due to the lack of available Indian labor, and that the missions were a dubious investment, considering the expense of maintaining the system and the scant monetary return. The exemption of the mission districts from the royal tribute and the ecclesiastical *diezmo* (tithe) served to justify creation of diocesan parishes—in which both Indians and Spaniards would be subject to tithe and tribute. After the War of Independence in 1821 and the establishment of the Republic of Mexico, missions not previously converted to diocesan use were greatly weakened by the lack of financial and military support. As an emerging nation, Mexico simply could not afford continued sponsorship of missionary efforts. Funds were needed elsewhere; the break from Spain resulted not only in the loss of royal patronage but also in the expulsion of many Spanish friars. The forced conversion of mission to diocesan churches was complete by the 1830s. The missionary system was bankrupt, morally as well as financially. The progressive deterioration of the Franciscan Order, the vacuum created by the expulsion of the Jesuits, the general loss of the missionary spirit and discipline, and the pervasive corruption throughout much of Mexico at this time can be regarded either as causes or as effects of this bankruptcy.

Although mission activities, and even construction, continued at some sites after Mexico broke away from Spain, these were of little consequence. Many of the missions simply melted into the earth, their charges drifted away, and their property was claimed by or sold to others.[4] Thus Mexico's independence from Spain in 1821 has been chosen as a logical cutoff date for this study.

For reasons I shall explore in the chapters to follow, the churches of northern New Spain were rarely built, decorated, or furnished without departing, sometimes significantly, from original plans or styles. Protracted building projects, during which architects, *maestros de obras*, and supervising clerics were repeatedly replaced, created ample opportunities for varying opinions and solutions. Then, too, religious rituals and accoutrements, in theory undeviating, were in practice often modified to accommodate economic constraints, shifts of emphasis within ceremonies, and specific needs of particular groups.

Over the course of my field research, I came to appreciate northern New Spain as a microcosm of architectural styles and material culture affected by five continents, a region that over the centuries and as the result of different personal and national ambitions gave rise to a wide variety of artistic expressions in objects as large as an entire building and as small as a ceramic tile or a clamshell full of pigments. I came to see in these objects the sometimes subtle, sometimes clear impress of the religious, social, and artistic traditions of Europe from the start of the Christian era through the nineteenth century, of the Muslim countries ringing the Mediterranean from the seventh through fifteenth centuries, and of northern New Spain's indigenous peoples from before European contact. It also became increasingly obvious that mission churches were the creations of three distinctly different groups: the clergy, who served as spiritual and intellectual directors, although there were also priests who took part in the physical building effort; the maestros and maestros de obras, imported craftsmen who served as architects, skilled labor, and overseers; and the Indians, who served as workmen and artisans.

In northern New Spain, it was the Spanish priests, soldiers, and bureaucrats who "made" history through their written records. Whether out of fear, conceit, ignorance, prejudice, or any combination of these, they slanted and sometimes distorted their accounts to suit themselves or their audiences. Persisting well beyond even the most carefully recited tales, their written records have come to be accepted as fact.

But the church buildings, decorations, and furnishings of northern New Spain serve as other records, records in stone, tile, wood, and adobe that have much to tell those who can read them. Although there will always be debate over the "civilization" and consequent destruction of native cultures by Spanish colonizers and clergy, the surviving churches of northern New Spain bear silent witness to the concentrated efforts of priests, parishioners, and converts to build and beautify structures that would serve as foci for religious and social life. They mark the introduction of Catholicism, on the one hand, and the replacement and even extirpation of indigenous religions and traditions, on the other. Their furnishings and decorations signal the arrival and expression of European technology in the form of manufactured goods as well as architectural, artistic, mining, and agricultural methods.

For the observant, types of materials used or changes in materials or floor plans midproject may indicate the rise or decline of a particular group's skills, interest in, or financial support of a particular church. The quality of workmanship evident in its construction, decoration, and furnishing serves as an excellent indicator of local prosperity or the generosity of wealthy benefactors. A change in the arrangement of furnishings within a church or in emphasis upon a certain altar or religious figure may point to a change in the liturgy or in the importance attached to that figure, whose presence or prominence may, in turn, signal the appearance or ascendance of a particular group, a special concern within the community, a change from regular to diocesan clergy or from one religious order to another, or even a subtle reinterpretation of Church doctrine or policy. A church abandoned or rarely visited by clergy may tell one story, a church whose building and religious figures have been well cared for by its congregation another, while a church destroyed may tell an altogether different story.

Brief exposure to churches in their original settings, however, cannot tell the whole tale. When viewing the existing monuments, cut off as they are from their original purpose and from the animating counterreformational impulse of the Church Militant, many looted and melting away like so many sand castles, it is hard to fully grasp the role they once played. The mysteries of their physical and metaphysical significance are woven into a complicated tapestry of religious institutions, ritual, dogma, nuances of certain words at certain times, and more secular matters—contracts, funding arrangements, agreements between artists and their guilds, and complex divisions of labor.

For any number of reasons, styles achieve popularity, inevitably peak, and then fade, although years later, renewed interest in a style may result in its revival. The ebb and flow of styles in Mexico (as well as in all other countries) has caused much original art, furnishings, and even complete buildings to be destroyed or "restored" beyond recognition (in what my good friend Jorge Olvera liked to characterize as "barbaric renewal"). Indeed, the drive to replace the old with the fresh and novel has destroyed far more in this regard than all of Mexico's political conflicts and wars.

Besides outright neglect and the periodic discarding of furnishings and decorations, conflicts between encroaching settlers, miners, soldiers, and priests, on the one hand, and the indigenous peoples, on the other; political revolutions; and social upheavals have understandably resulted in the loss of much material. Throughout the province of Nuevo México, for example, church furnishings were almost totally destroyed and church buildings severely damaged in the Pueblo Rebellion of 1680. Revolution and civil war from 1910 to about 1928, the closing of the churches in 1926, and President Calles's banning of religious services in the same year resulted in enormous destruction and wholesale dispersal of church property. Indeed, the neglect and abuse these buildings and their furnishings have suffered in modern times probably exceed any misuse they would have experienced in earlier periods under "normal" circumstances. For these reasons, eyewitness accounts by colonial travelers and church inventories by clergy provide invaluable information.

Because it is often impossible to know, for example, precisely what the original paintings, sculptures, or furnishings in a church were, who created them, or even what condition they were in at a particular time, generalities are sprinkled throughout this work. Certainties abound as well, however, such as the function of ecclesiastical elements, most Catholic rituals and dogmas, and the physical shapes and sizes dictated by official Church policy or tradition. Furthermore, using influences and antecedents, styles can be categorized, dates roughly assigned, and origins traced. Intriguing always are the departures from established patterns and methods and the variations they produce. No two churches are exact copies, nor are any two façades or *retablos* (altar screens). While finances, availability of materials, skills, and effort expended are predominant factors, the quirky human factor makes itself clearly felt in the ingenious, surprising, and often playful ways they come together.

CHAPTER 2

STYLES

Not only do we look at things from different angles, but with other eyes; we do not seek to find them identical.

—BLAISE PASCAL

Originality is not newness, but genuineness.

—JOHN RUSKIN

The appreciation of styles and aesthetics in the church art and architecture of northern New Spain requires a certain broadness of taste and understanding on the part of the viewer. Deviating aspects within an example are sometimes the result not of good or bad taste, but of economic, social, and technical conditions that outweighed the prevailing and accepted artistic modes. There is a wide enough variety of examples in northern New Spain, even in their ruined or altered states, to enable the viewer to discern stylistic differences and to evaluate technical success. Discerning individuals will also find themselves appreciating the ephemeral qualities of ingenuity, sincerity, and vitality that many examples exhibit there.

What becomes immediately clear, however, is that we cannot use a single standard to judge the structures and their decoration, even for those of a given style. Indeed, at a deeper level, we must ask ourselves, just what is a "style"? What is its importance besides mere formula? How did certain styles influence or reflect a culture? What needs did they satisfy, or what beliefs did they reinforce?[1] Closely tied to these questions are others: How did a particular style begin? What were the circumstances or influences that encouraged its acceptance, persistence, modification, and, finally, its demise?

Our restless and curious human nature demands change, if only for the sake of novelty. Given the same artistic conundrum, any number of individuals would come up with as many solutions. Factoring into the final result are local needs related to space, climate, available types of material and technical assistance—as well as the educational and ethnic background of the "client," the architect, and the master mason, builder, or contractor (maestro de obra).[2] There are hundreds of examples throughout New Spain, and scores in northern New Spain, that could be used to elucidate the manifold products of these factors.

We can appreciate the extent of Spanish influence when we realize that most of the art and architecture on both sides of the Atlantic is virtually indistinguishable. Sevilla occupied, both economically and culturally, the strategic position of "puerto y puerta de las Indias" (port and gateway to the Indies) for more than two hundred years, from the end of the fifteenth century until 1717, when the Casa de Contratación—Spain's central colonial office, charged with managing all economic and commercial matters in her colonies—was moved to Cádiz, thus ending the Sevillan monopoly on New World commerce. Throughout this time, Sevilla served as the center for exportation of art and artistic ideals. Paintings of popular religious themes certain to be in demand in the New World were rolled up, packed in cases, and brokered through an agent or the ship's captain, who would try to get the best possible price and return the proceeds to the artist on the return voyage.[3] Flemish and Italian artists and architects came to work for Sevilla's wealthy ecclesiastical and secular patrons. The presence of these foreigners was extremely important for the artistic and technical enrichment of local artists and craftsmen, some of whom were to seek their fortunes in the New World.[4]

Because northern New Spain might be considered a microcosm of the Spanish aesthetic, we need to relate its art and architecture to those of central and southern New Spain as well as of Spain itself, rather than examining them in isolation. In central and southern New Spain, the Spaniards found many Indian communities that prized discipline and were accustomed to prolonged building projects. Moreover, the highly developed cultures and complex bureaucracies of these communities could take advantage of the advanced technologies imported from Europe. At the time of the Conquest, such values, customs, and institutions were lacking among the Indians of northern New Spain, where the rugged terrain, harsh climate, limited natural resources, and sparse populations of hunter-gatherers or semisedentary tribes militated against development of a large artisan class. Here, artistic traditions of the indigenous populations centered mostly around utilitarian or small cult objects and the embellishment of personal items or self. With these limitations in mind, the imposing structures and complexes produced by native labor and skills under the direction of the missionaries in northern New Spain, especially in seventeenth-century Nuevo México, are all the more worthy of our respect and admiration.

As trade routes to the north increased and as areas became more populated, blacksmiths, masons, carpenters, and weavers were more generally dispersed,[5] accounting for a repertory of Spanish forms and innovations from central New Spain adapted for use on the frontier. The extremely conservative artistic mentality of that time, most probably shaped by fear of the Inquisition on the part of both artist and client, valued predictability and strict adherence to acceptable styles and themes.

On the other hand, the remoteness from important trade, cultural, or religious centers; the lack of special religious significance for most sites in northern New Spain; and a dearth of architects or artisans capable of creating exact copies almost ensured that architecture, decoration, and furnishings would be simplified, and the finer touches more often lost. But even though impoverished isolation did not engender radical originality, it often gave rise to ingenious approaches to design, construction, and decoration. In the case of baroque decoration, whose exuberance can be overwhelming, the "watered-down" frontier examples created by naive or provincial artists (and sometimes called "frontier baroque") manage to capture the essence of the style, allowing the viewer to clearly examine its basics without too much distraction.

The aesthetic history of Mexico, like that of any other country, cannot be strictly segmented into distinct periods of styles. First, the lag between the inception of a style in a creative center and its gradual filtering out to peripheral settlements varied with distance from the center, as did the resistance of provincial settlers to change. Second, because stylistic formulas developed for European and Spanish modes did not always exactly apply to the New World, they sometimes had to be qualified, used in a general way, stretched, or truncated. Third, these formulas were sometimes interpreted by unsophisticated craftspeople superficially as decorative surface treatments, with little or no appreciation for their original rationale. Finally, completion of ambitious structures often extended from one century into the next.[6] All four of these considerations make it impossible to assign precise or unqualified stylistic designations to structures, or even to precisely date the beginning or end of any style.

Mudéjar, Gothic, plateresque, Renaissance, mannerist, baroque, rococo, and neoclassical elements or principles are present in northern New Spain, ranging from fully developed aesthetic movements to little more

2.1. Main façade, San Francisco Xavier del Bac, near Tucson, Arizona, early twentieth century. The unfinished bell tower is missing its dome as well as a coating of plaster. (Private collection, photographer unknown)

than decorative motifs. Although on occasion a single style was to inspire a complete example in architecture, more often, elements appear commingled with those of other periods. Significantly, there are no exact duplicates among structures and only occasionally among designs. Simplified or intricate floor plans, special provisions for lighting or defense, a preference for the number of bell towers, or certain motifs and arrangements of elements on a façade or in a *retablo* (altar screen) may have been favored by individual architects, master masons, or religious orders, but there is always enough variety to make each example unique.

Comparing measurements, decorative details, materials, and techniques for the Pimería Alta missions of San Francisco Xavier del Bac near Tucson (Arizona; figure 2.1) and La Purísima Concepción de Nuestra Señora de Caborca (Sonora; figure 2.2), the latter completed ten years after the Tucson church, reveals enough similarities to attribute both to a similar plan and probably the same architect or master masons.[7] Indeed, the churches resemble each other more closely than do any other two in northern New Spain.[8] Nevertheless, there are also significant differences between them, very likely the result of different artisans and workers, the need to adapt to different sites, and perhaps also the desire for novelty.

Likewise, there are enough similarities in plan, profile, and particular architectural features among the missions of Alta California and Nuevo México to make them readily identifiable as a group, yet also enough differences to make each one unique.

At the southernmost limit of northern New Spain, the parochial church of Nuestra Señora del Rosario de Charcas (Santa María de Charcas; figure 2.3) displays a similar profile to the chapel of La Tercera Orden in the city of San Luis Potosí (both in the state of San Luis Potosí); they both have an oval form above the main portal and a rectangular form above this, with fluted pilasters flanking the door and framing three niches above and to the side of the rectangular and oval shapes. Although the two lateral niches are placed differently on these two

2.2. La Purísima Concepción de Nuestra Señora de Caborca, Sonora, 1892, private collection. The arched arcade to the left was the convento, which was completely destroyed in the flood of 1914. (Photo by William Dinwiddie)

façades (halfway up the side of the top niche versus close to the entablature of the main portal), each placement is appropriate for the width of its church and in harmony with the bell towers and other parts of the church exterior. Although the façades also differ in the amount of detail and in the molding profiles of their oculi, the stamp of a favored decorative scheme is undeniable. Both churches are Franciscan and are less than eighty miles apart; their size and façade treatment directly reflect the importance of their individual sites.

At the time of the Conquest of Mexico, Spanish art and architecture were beginning a new epoch of development. With the reign of Isabel and Ferdinand at the end of the fifteenth century, Spain evolved a late medieval style heavily dependent on the Gothic. Developing from this was the plateresque—a national style of applied decoration that appeared with designs based first on the Gothic and later on the Italian High Renaissance. Around 1550, Philip II became involved in directing the course of Spanish architecture. The style he encouraged reflected and expressed the dignity of imperial Spain and can best be seen in the work of the architect Juan de Herrera, entrusted with finishing the Escorial in 1572. The severe style of Philip II signaled the arrival of the ideal of Greco-Roman form and proportions, while elsewhere in Europe the Renaissance—drawing on the same inspiration—was metamorphosing into mannerism and later, the baroque. Although it is debatable whether there was a "true Renaissance" in Spain, what did develop stylistically was transmitted to New Spain via drawings, etchings, and sculpture; the Italian Renaissance pattern books of Giacomo Barozzio Vignola, Sebastiano Serlio, and Andrea Palladio; and, most important, the rediscovered and newly published ten books on architecture of Roman urban planner Vitruvius.[9]

2.3. *Main façade, Nuestra Señora del Rosario de Charcas, San Luis Potosí, 1984.*

Italian and French editions of the Latin text were available in Spain by 1565. The speed with which this information was assimilated can be seen in Vitruvius's influence on New Spain's town ordinances dated 1573.

These flowed from the Laws of the Indies, formulated after a great deal of thought by King Philip II and the engineers and architects advising him; the more the ordinances were modified and reinterpreted, the more dependent they became on Vitruvius. Towns were to be planned—and *casas reales* (royal administrative offices), hospitals, and other buildings and enterprises to be sited—from the perspectives of beauty, health, spaciousness, defense, commerce, and even comfort. Streets, for example, were to be oriented and laid out based on local temperatures and prevailing winds.[10] The ordinances dictated the size, shape, and placement of plazas and arcades. Cathedrals and churches were to be erected in isolated areas, preferably on raised grounds, where they could be seen and venerated from all sides.[11]

Specific architectural examples of Serlio's influence include the temple "El Pocito" in Villa Madero, on the outskirts of Mexico City (see figure 3.4a), inspired by the plan of the temple of Baco from Serlio's *Third Book*, and the Metropolitan Cathedral of Morelia (Morelia), whose construction plans quote his work as a source.[12] Serlio's Arch of Triumph in the *Fourth Book* also served as a model for the design of the portal of the church at the former convento of Tecali (Puebla).

The baroque style was also transplanted to the New World by many of the same means, and in particular by emigrating artists and architects. Of crucial importance in this regard was the system of apprenticeship, where a youngster was trained by a master in a particular art or trade. The master was responsible for the physical and spiritual care of his pupil, who sometimes lived with the master's family, and in return was entitled to the fruits of his pupil's labor for a certain amount of time. It was not unusual for a former apprentice or assistant to marry the master's daughter. To keep trade secrets in the family, or to consolidate and control a trained labor pool, dynasties of artists and artisans were created. This is particularly evident in the early history of Mexican painting.[13] It was also not unusual for sons of artists or craftsmen of one art or trade to apprentice under masters of another. Through intermarriage and cross-apprenticeship, social and economic ties between families of artists and artisans were formed, strengthened, protected, and—in many notable instances—carried over to New Spain.[14]

As a consequence of natural geographic barriers, the policies of the Spanish state, and the conservative Hispanic temperament, styles unfolded in northern New Spain well after they had appeared in most parts of Europe. However troubled her relations may have been with her European neighbors, Spain was far from isolated. The Italian and Flemish artists and artisans who arrived in Sevilla, and their Spanish counterparts working in Italy, strongly influenced her culture, and these influences were then conveyed to her territories in the New World.[15]

Both colonial and some native influences are to be seen in the religious art and architecture of New Spain. "Colonial" work in New Spain is understood as craftsmanship that remains true to its Spanish models, although it may undergo subtle to pronounced changes when sifted through the hands of amateur or native builders. While there are some original inventions in New Spain concerning architectural formulas, as well as some uniquely New World motifs, technical innovations, and structural specializations, for the most part, Spanish examples provided the precedents. Early church paintings in northern New Spain were very likely executed using native methods for preparing pigments, paint binders, and surfaces.[16] "Native" styles are most often to be seen in the auxiliary painting or carving in missionary churches, especially in decorative motifs portraying native plants or animals. Despite the close attention paid to native contributions to ensure that nothing heretical was included, unless the priest was fully conversant with local traditions and legends, elements of the previous culture's beliefs and religion were likely to creep in.

Within New Spain after the Conquest and into the closing decades of the sixteenth century, a combination of styles existed: Gothic systems of ribbing and window traceries; medieval monastic, fortresslike churches; mudéjar treatment of ceilings, doorways, and doors with its sense of geometrical aesthetics; delicate plateresque traceries and ornaments on façades and retablos; cities laid out on Renaissance plans; and in the frescoes on convent walls, classical influences from northern European and Italian Renaissance prints and engravings. After about 1570, mannerist schemes appear in the architecture and decoration of the cathedrals of Puebla, Mexico City, and Guadalajara. Artists imported from Spain and Flanders provided important direction in sculpture and painting.

Early baroque innovations began to appear in art and architecture by the end of the sixteenth century and continued into the late eighteenth century. The founding of the Academy of San Carlos in Mexico City in 1785 brought the neoclassical mode then coming into its own in Europe to New Spain via imported instructors, original paintings, plaster casts of classical statuary, engravings, and so on. Note that while I rely on developments in painting and architecture to illustrate changes in styles and fashions, sculpture, textiles, clothing, furniture, and ecclesiastical accoutrements were subject to the same changes and have many of the same distinctive characteristics, although, as always, there are subtle differences among regions throughout every period.

Mudéjar

An Arabic word of fourteenth-century origin designating a Muslim permitted to live among Christians in Spain after the Reconquest in exchange for a tribute, *mudéjar* applies to a specific style of architecture that flourished mostly throughout the southern part of Spain from the thirteenth century until the sixteenth. The mudéjar style is characterized by the use of Moorish building techniques, aesthetics, and ornamentation—as practiced by mudéjares.

Beginning with the Moorish conquest of most of Spain in AD 711 and continuing through almost 800 years of occupation by different Islamic dynasties, the Islamic contributions to the sciences, arts, crafts, and architecture in Spain cannot be too strongly emphasized.[17] The caliphates of Moorish Spain had their greatest and most lasting impact in the province of Andalucía (important later in the conquest of and trade with the New World), and under them, Córdoba, Sevilla, and Granada were at different times world centers of culture.

Mudéjar has become a catchall term for a variety of Hispano-Moorish features, materials, and techniques, especially in Mexico, where it is used to describe an aesthetic philosophy; decorative treatments of brick, tile, and wood; and certain window or arch shapes. Although the mudéjar style dates back to the twelfth century in Spain and arrives in New Spain with the first Spaniards, its vocabulary and respect for the inherent qualities of materials have endured to the present day. In northern New Spain, we encounter these in rubble-filled walls; flat-roofed, post-and-beam construction; ogee and mixtilinear arches (features shared with Gothic); stepped or pyramidal crenellations; patios with fountains, running water, or ponds; molded or carved ornamental plaster and stucco, including carved pilaster friezes and bands around windows and doors; decorative use of stones pressed into mortar joints and of fired brick forming patterns, profiles, or textures on walls; and glazed polychrome tiles (or painted facsimiles) along walls or embedded in church domes and fountains. We see them also in fluting or goring on arches and domes; in the *alfarje* (elaborate pieced woodwork) appearance of carved and painted beams and corbels; in the *artesonado* (paneled and inlaid) doors, shutters, and furniture; and in the strongly Moorish pavilion-and-shed roofs over apses and naves of sixteenth-century churches in Mexico City—still a distinctive feature of sixteenth- and seventeenth-century churches in the state of Chiapas and in Cuba, Colombia, Ecuador, Peru, Bolivia, the province of Andalucía, and North Africa. In Mexico, however, almost all these sixteenth-century roofs and alfarje ceilings were replaced with domes and barrel vaults as the baroque established itself there. (See discussion of artesonado and alfarje in "Ceilings" under "Techniques," "Decorative Work," in chapter 4.)

There is something almost subliminal in Islamic decorative art and architecture—a sensual and refined sense of beauty, an acknowledgment and respect for material, and, especially, a geometric order inspired by the metaphysical and cosmological symbolism of the circle and square. Here, based on mathematical forms, shapes are combined to reflect celestial archetypes within the mind and soul as well as the cosmos. Islamic art and architecture would powerfully influence the Renaissance concept of anthropometry, in which the proportional ideals for painting, sculpture, and architecture were to express the physical perfection of the human form.

To travel across northern New Spain is to witness the impact that the Moorish architecture of North Africa—via Andalucía—had on the design and construction of this region's churches.[18] We can see this in the distinctive fortified appearance of numerous seventeenth- and eighteenth-century churches, for example, San Miguel Arcángel in Santa Fe (New Mexico) and San Bonaventura (Chihuahua).[19] The churches of Andalucía, with their crenellations, polygonal apses, buttresses, and small, easily defendable windows, influenced these structures either directly or indirectly through the sixteenth-century churches of central New Spain.[20]

Even though the shapes, forms, sizes, and purposes of the early Christian churches differed from native expressions, the need to solve similar problems of defense, heat, and light using essentially the same materials gave rise to architectural similarities between the dwellings of the Pueblo Indians and the churches and conventos of Nuevo México—and indeed, between these and arid-land, sun-dried mud structures the world over. If, however, we look at the details of the churches of Nuevo México (and some in Nueva Vizcaya and the Pimería Alta), we can clearly trace their lineage to Andalucía and from there back to the *ksar* structures of North Africa, especially Morocco.

Throughout the arid Islamic world, a vast expanse of many nations and frequently warring factions, structures were fortified in appearance and function to ensure the safety and privacy of extended families and clans. Lacking quarriable stone, builders used sun-dried mud (adobe) to form walls and roofs. They covered the buildings' surfaces with plaster, molded and painted to resist erosion and to give their buildings a finished and aesthetically pleasing look. Lacking large trees for beams or ample wood of any size, they made their rooms narrower; artisans fitted smaller pieces of wood together to form elaborate and complicated ceilings, doors, shutters, and pieces of furniture. To guard against the relentless sun and ever-threatening marauders, walls were made thick and windows

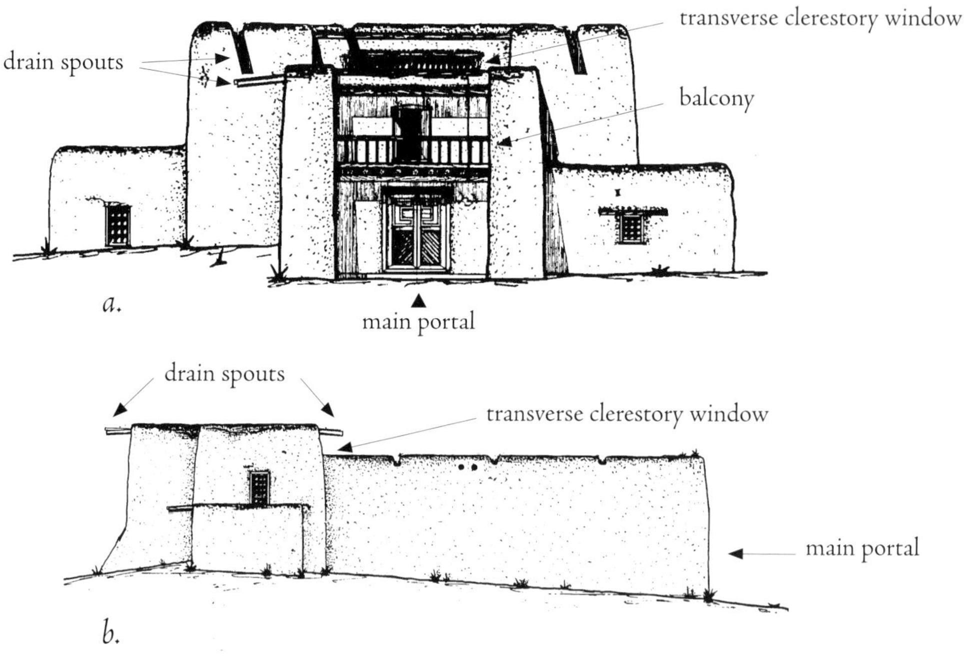

2.4. San José de la Gracia, Las Trampas, New Mexico: a. south elevation; b. east elevation. (Courtesy of Historic American Building Survey)

small and high above the ground, producing cool, easily defendable interiors.

All these features were brought by the Moorish conquerors to Andalucía, where they became part of the building vernacular of southern Spain; from there, they were transplanted to New Spain to serve the same ends. Among the extant churches of northern New Spain, the most important structural detail reflecting this lineage is the transverse clerestory, found in virtually every church in Nuevo México (figure 2.4a–b) and in some churches of Nueva Vizcaya and the Pimería Alta, and admirably suited to the fortresslike churches of northern New Spain. In the traditional clerestory, upper stage windows run the length of the nave, typically on both sides. In the transverse clerestory, by contrast, a horizontal window runs across and above the nave either at the beginning of the transept crossing or just before the sacristy, choir, sanctuary, or apse. Just as the carefully aligned windows or wall slots of the mosque directed light onto the North African Muslim's focus of devotion—the *mihrab*—so the transverse clerestory, placed carefully above the nave, directed light onto the sacred focus of the Christian church—the main altar, located at the rear wall of the apse.

Decorative details reflecting the same lineage—the alfarje and artesonado traditions of Andalucía and North Africa—are numerous. We can see them in the carved and painted beams (*vigas*) and impost blocks or corbels (*zapatas*) of church interiors throughout northern New Spain; in the perpendicular or diagonal arrangement of split and adze-hewn chunks of wood (*tablas*) or slender peeled poles (*savinas* or *latias*) between the beams of Nuestra Señora de Guadalupe in Ciudad Juárez (Chihuahua; figure 2.5) and in many of the churches of the Pimería Alta and Nuevo México; and in the carved and beveled panels of the massive church doors and window shutters throughout northern New Spain. They are also present in the carved and molded plaster decoration on the main frontispiece and niches of San Pedro y San Pablo de Tubutama (Sonora; see figure 2.24); in the *ajaraca*[21] effects at El Templo de los Cinco Señores in Santander Jiménez (Tamaulipas; figure 2.6); and in mixtilinear door frames such as those at San Ignacio de Loyola de Kadakaaman (Baja California Sur; figure 2.7).

Gothic

Responding to medieval aesthetics, the Gothic style of art and architecture flourished in parts of Europe from

2.5. Soffit of choir loft, Nuestra Señora de Guadalupe, Ciudad Juárez, Chihuahua, 1988.

2.6. Main façade, El Templo de los Cinco Señores, Santander Jiménez, Tamaulipas, 1996.

2.7. Mixtilinear door frame, main portal, San Ignacio de Loyola de Kadakaaman, San Ignacio, Baja California Sur, 1986. Originally built by Jesuit missionaries, San Ignacio was turned over to the Dominican Order to administer after the Jesuit expulsion in 1767. Note the stylized symbol of the Dominican Order that was added over the door.

2.8. "Spanish Gothic" ruin, La Purísima Concepción de Quari, Salinas National Monument, New Mexico, 2002. View from the nave toward the apse. Notice the entrances to the transepts on either side of the nave and the empty slots that supported wood ceiling beams and rafters.

about 1200 to 1500. Gothic architecture is characterized by balanced vertical thrusts in stone masonry; visible ribs and vaulting that both delight the eye and provide support for the delicate structure; pointed arches; stained glass windows; and stone tracery. "Gothic" was first used as a derisive term by the art critic Giorgio Vasari (1511–1574) to describe what he considered to be the barbaric art produced between the Middle Ages and the Renaissance. Vasari contrasted the barbarism of Gothic to the refinement of classical Greek and Roman models, a biased estimate blindly accepted by art historians for the next two centuries.

Spanish Renaissance art and architecture curiously overlaid newer elements on older Gothic ones, which hung on in Spain far longer than in the rest of Europe. However, both styles would be pushed aside by those of the Counter-Reformation—mannerism and, later, the baroque.

"Gothic" calls forth images of immense interior spaces, lofty ceilings with ribbed or fan vaulting, magnificent

2.9. North façade, San Francisco Javier de Vigge-Biaundó, Baja California Sur, 1987. The uneven surface on the wall to the very left indicates other structures were originally attached to and enclosing the south side of the church complex.

stained glass windows, fantastic gargoyles, and dramatic flying buttresses. These are not present in northern New Spain. Rather, the structures built during the first half of the seventeenth century in the province of Nuevo México are "Spanish Gothic" in their aesthetic (figure 2.8), with the fortresslike vertical profiles, small rectangular windows, and polygonal naves so evocative of the parochial and monastery churches of medieval Spain and mid-sixteenth-century central New Spain. All these features attest, according to some historians, to the friars' nostalgic desire to emulate earlier missionary efforts and to present their Faith in its simplest and most basic form.

On the other hand, in what has been called "Gothic Survival," builders used genuinely Gothic elements to evoke the structures of the fifteenth century.[22] Thus, clustered columns with rings and bases can be found along the nave of the Dominican church San Francisco de Borja de Adac (Baja California Norte), built perhaps as late as 1801 (after the Jesuit adobe structure was abandoned); in the ogee doorways of the former Jesuit church San Francisco Javier de Vigge-Biaundó (Baja California Sur; figure 2.9); and in a doorway between the nave and the mortuary chapel at San Carlos Borromeo de Carmelo de Monterey in Carmel (California; begun in 1793). Indeed, the baptistery ceiling of San Carlos Borromeo even has plastered elements simulating a tierceron vault (figure 2.10). Other Gothic elements—crenellations, cusped arches, crockets, ornamental zoomorphic spouts, and lancet windows—were incorporated into other later styles and used in the nineteenth-century neo-Gothic style.

2.10. Tierceron vault, baptistery ceiling, San Carlos Borromeo de Carmelo de Monterey, Carmel, California. Photo by Joe Decker, 2006.

Plateresque

Derived from the Spanish word *platero* (silversmith), "plateresque" is used to describe delicate decoration, much like filigree, and refers to a type of surface treatment that has no function except to enliven. It therefore contradicts one of the basic rules of architecture—to "decorate construction and not construct decoration."[23] Its lavish use of ornamental motifs was popular in Spain during the sixteenth century and is considered a manifestation of the Spanish Renaissance. Instead of defining a distinct style, plateresque combines elements from a variety of styles to vaguely tie a surface together: mudéjar, Gothic, and Renaissance design motifs are commingled as though in a loosely thrown net. This superficial ornamentation does not define a function, the shape of a building, or its parts; and its unstructured arrangement of decoration does not even pretend to be self-supporting or in proportion to the juxtaposed parts. Plateresque can be seen in the frontispieces of sixteenth-century Augustinian monasteries in central New Spain, at Yuriria (Guanajuato) and Acolman (México), and strictly speaking, the term should be reserved for that period. In northern New Spain, however, we encounter a plateresque mood in the rambling and strewn decoration of the mid- to late-eighteenth-century church main frontispiece of San Sebastián in Concordia (Sinaloa; figure 2.11), in patches of symbolic elements on the main frontispiece of San Xavier near Tucson (Arizona; finished 1797; see figure 2.1), and in the side frontispieces of the Cathedral of Chihuahua (Chihuahua; figure 2.12). The fantastic beasts from which the water spouts on the Church of San Juan de Dios (Durango, Durango) emerge can also trace their origins to plateresque and Renaissance lexicons (see figure 6.33).

Renaissance

Lasting from the fourteenth through the sixteenth centuries in most parts of Europe, the Renaissance is usually credited with the revival of art and letters under the influence of classical models. The Renaissance ideals of clarity and unity in composition, stability, poise, balance between masses and space, and use of classical orders in definite manners were first developed in central Italy during this rebirth of learning at the close of the Middle Ages. The style did not arrive in Spain until almost the end of the High Renaissance, as it was changing into what is now called mannerism; certain of its ideals and artistic criteria accompanied the first Spanish priests, builders, and artists to the New World.

The approximate dates for the Renaissance style in New Spain are from 1521 to 1600, and the most significant examples of such architecture are found in central and southern New Spain, namely, in the modern states of Puebla, Morelia, Hidalgo, Tlaxcala, Michoacán, Oaxaca, and México, center of the earliest evangelization and largest native population. Even where churches, convents, palaces, hospitals, schools, and civic works were constructed with elements immediately identifiable as Renaissance, however, these were often hybridized or combined with late Gothic, plateresque, mudéjar, mannerist, and *tequitqui* (indigenous-style) elements and thereby acquired a distinctive quality.

2.11. Main façade, San Sebastián, Concordia, Sinaloa, 1979.

2.12. A retablo exterior, east frontispiece, Catedral de Chihuahua, 2000.

Thus, New Spain had few examples of complete or pure Renaissance art or architecture, and, because it was settled so late, northern New Spain had none.

Instead, the Renaissance style made its influence known in other ways. Certain columns (to include herms, atlantes, and caryatids), pediments, and urn-shaped finials suggestive of the Renaissance were used as architectural accents from the seventeenth through the twentieth centuries.[24] And although now sadly missing or in desperate need of repair, the painted and coffered ceilings that are such magnificent features of Renaissance churches in Italy and Spain once graced the Chihuahuan churches Santa Rosa de Lima de Cusihuiriáchic and San Felipe y Santiago de Janos.[25] Indeed, Santa María de las Cuevas (also Chihuahua) may have the only extant Renaissance ceiling in all of northern New Spain (see figure 6.19).

Mannerism

In its primary sense, an acceptance of a manner rather than its significance, "mannerism" designates an artistic style that first appeared in Italy in the late fifteenth century, spread throughout Europe, and lasted in Spain until about the first decades of the seventeenth century. Coinciding with the later Renaissance, this international, subjective style arose out of the clash between the Renaissance, on the one hand, and the Reformation and Counter-Reformation, on the other. Preparing the way for the baroque, mannerism was an attempt on the part of artists and architects to infuse new meaning into the Renaissance ideal. In architecture, it may refer either to the use of motifs in deliberate opposition to their original meaning or to a pure and undeviating classicism. In painting and sculpture, harmony, restraint, and reason give way to a tortured spiritual disquiet, excess, and emotion. The search for realism is pushed to the point where objects appear unrealistic: bodies are elongated and twisted, colors are jewel-like, and perspective is controlled to such a degree that the picture plane becomes flattened.

Mannerism's appearance in the art and architecture of New Spain derives in large part from influences exerted by the architectural treatise of Vignola; Serlio's engravings; imported Flemish engravings of that period; the Flemish painter Simón Pereyns (working in New Spain 1556–1590); and imported Spanish paintings by Alonso Sanchez Coello (1531–1588), Luis de Morales (ca. 1520–1585), and Antonio Moro (ca. 1520–1575). According to Jorge Manrique, mannerism lasted in New Spain from 1570–1580 until 1640–1650. New Spain's leading mannerist painters include Luis Juárez (fl. 1600–1632), Alonso López de Herrera (1579–1650, also referred to as "el divino Herrera") and Baltasar de Echave Ibía (fl. 1610–1640, sometimes referred to as "Echave the younger").[26] (See "Baroque," later in this chapter, for other designations concerning mannerist painting.)

Spanish mannerist (late Renaissance) architecture bears the strong impress of architect Juan de Herrera (ca. 1530–1590), who brought back to Spain from his travels in Italy a severe and majestic form, austere and architecturally correct. A hallmark of the Herreran style is an elongated pyramid with a ball on its apex crowning a pilaster or baluster, and this motif is occasionally included along with other designs in later periods in New Spain.[27] Although Herrera's work at the Escorial, and especially his designs for the Palace of Aranjuez, the Exchange in Sevilla, and the Cathedral of Valladolid, strongly influenced the plan and design of the Cathedrals of Mexico City and Puebla, the Herreran style never enjoyed great popularity in New Spain.[28] Nor, except in isolated motifs more than a hundred years after its eclipse in Spain, would the style ever reach the northern frontier of New Spain. Thus, we can see Herrera's influence on the *remate* (pediment, or attic) of the main frontispiece of San Francisco Javier de Batuc (Sonora; reassembled and on display in Pitic outside Hermosillo; begun in 1741; finished ca. 1760; figure 2.13) and elsewhere in regionally modified forms, as on the north façade of San Francisco Javier de Vigge-Biaundó (Baja California Sur; built 1744–1758; see figure 2.9) and the mannerist treatment of the late-seventeenth-century south and main portals at San José de Parral (Chihuahua; figure 2.14). For the most part, however, this wealthy, vigorous new nation, caught up in the Counter-Reformation, rejected purist mannerism, embracing instead the opulence of the plateresque and, later, the exuberant richness of the baroque.

Baroque

Derived from a jeweler's term for a rough or imperfect pearl and, by extension, later meaning whimsical, grotesque, or odd, "baroque" designates a style of art and architecture that flourished in Europe and the New World from the

2.13. Main frontispiece (reassembled), San Francisco Javier de Batuc, Pitic, Sonora, 1978. The austerity of the suppressed piers and their unadorned bases and capitals is somewhat relieved by the tritóstilo columns on either side of the small niche in the upper story.

2.14. Portal de la Virgen (south portal), San José de Parral, Chihuahua, 1982.

Counter-Reformation through the eighteenth century. Now recognized as a distinct artistic movement rather than the degeneration of the Renaissance, baroque has been subdivided according to country and, in New Spain, further subdivided according to time period, locality, or use of certain architectural elements.[29]

Baroque owes its dispersal in large part to the Church's attempt to recapture her straying flock with explosive drama and brilliance and, in the New World, to dazzle and astound the native populations. Chiefly promoted by the Jesuits, baroque was essentially an art in defense of the Faith, "a theological art carrying an intense spiritual message."[30] The importance of defending Catholicism against the Protestant attack on the Eucharist, the infallibility of the pope, the saints' intercession, and Mary's immaculateness helped mold an artistic movement that triumphantly praised God and his servants. Everything was viewed in terms of conquest, and art reflected this with outbursts of emotion, drama, and zeal.

Baroque paintings regularly feature various saints: in defense of the Eucharist (Mary Magdalen in penance or other saints either receiving Communion or identified by a chalice—for example, Barbara); in defense of the papacy (the Fathers of the Church); and in defense of virtues like charity (Saint John of God). To these are added miraculous visitations and images of ecstasy. The new devotion of the Guardian Angel, begun in the sixteenth century, became stronger as Martin Luther and John Calvin attacked it. Furthermore, the age of the Counter-Reformation was an age of martyrdom. Jesuits, for example, decorated their refectories or studies with scenes of torture and death, extolling their martyred brothers.

The reader should be advised that "baroque" has become loosely and generously applied to all New World architecture having any extravagantly rich decoration from the late sixteenth through the eighteenth centuries, and from the 42nd north parallel to the 40th south. For our purposes, baroque will be understood broadly—as a style of the sixteenth through eighteenth centuries (and into the early nineteenth century along the northern frontier) in which classical forms and ornaments were arranged or manipulated to provide the viewer with the utmost illusion of movement, visual excitement, and emotional involvement. All stages of the baroque can be seen in northern New Spain in painting, sculpture, and architecture.

No matter what their form or medium, baroque works express certain distinctive characteristics. There is an inseparability of structure from ornament and an attempt to amaze the viewer. Animation effects are based on light and shadow, the sudden and unexpected; composition, on the dissolution of unity, rather than equal balance. Scenes are often highly charged with emotion, depicting moments and poses of exaggerated dramatic intensity. Baroque art displays most, if not all, of the following: richness of decoration, illusionary effects, extreme realism, intense contrasts between light and shadow, and the use of diagonal or oblique axes, spirals, and inverted pyramids in dynamic arrangements of space and mass. Summarizing Anthony Blunt, European baroque architects preferred curves to straight lines, and complex forms to simple and symmetrical ones. They preferred the oval to the circle because it eliminated static balance and could be used in countless combinations and variations. Implied movement in baroque art was extended to the actual walls, as most clearly seen in frontispieces, which were frequently treated like sculpture. Painting, architecture, and sculpture were often combined to create a fusion of the arts and trompe l'oeil that contributed to the desired shock effect.[31]

Colonial baroque art of the Americas followed in European footsteps. In its ultimate expression, columns are twisted or turned into inverted pyramids; gold leaf is lavishly used; and real hair, jewelry, bone teeth, glass eyes, and garments are incorporated into sculpture. The line between painted ornamentation and architectural features is blurred and lost. All in all, the viewer is invited to become involved in the emotional impact of the whole, rather than dwell on any one part. Unlike the more introspective, intellectual Renaissance, baroque was the result of "a religious fervor which sometimes produced works of commanding spiritual power," and it readily took root in the New World, especially in New Spain, where it flourished and evolved.[32]

Baroque architecture in New Spain has several stages and local derivations. In the beginning it was influenced by the severity of the Herreran Renaissance-mannerist style. As the style progressed, however, the exuberance of religious feelings produced architecture and sculpture of extreme complication and overwhelming opulence. Baroque buildings or retablos in central New Spain can generally be dated with reasonable certainty by the appearance of particular architectural developments or the arrival of particular artists having distinctive trademarks.[33] In the provincial areas of northern New Spain, on the other hand, we need also to consider the qualifying factors mentioned earlier in this chapter.

Early baroque innovations began to appear in New Spain by the end of the sixteenth century and, reinforced by Spanish models, continued to develop there. Architectural elements from the Renaissance were used throughout the period, but in a more dramatic manner and on a larger scale. Colonial baroque's somber beginning, or "pure," style (*purista*), which dates roughly from 1621, depends heavily on the Renaissance (whose precision and refinement it subtly changes). Toussaint calls the more amplified style that appeared around 1650 "rich baroque" (*barroco rico*) and the style that breached formal limits for ornamental richness in the last third of the seventeenth century "exuberant baroque." His categories are based upon the quantity of decoration, however, and not upon the appearance of certain designators such as column types.[34] By contrast, González Galván bases his categories mostly on column or design typology; thus they cannot be used in and of themselves for dating.[35]

Francisco de la Maza also thought it more appropriate to classify styles according to type. In 1662 construction began on the lateral façades of the Cathedral of Mexico using the twisted columns of the *salomónico* type (see figure 6.2h for a salomónico column). Based on Maza's system of classification, the purest *barroco salomónico* runs from that date to the earliest years of the eighteenth century.[36]

Barroco estípite was introduced to New Spain with the Spanish artist Jerónimo de Balbás, who worked in this style on the Altar de los Reyes in the Cathedral of Mexico from 1718 to 1737.[37] The style had its greatest impulse with the Spanish architect Lorenzo Rodríguez and his work on the metropolitan parish church in Mexico City between 1749 and 1768. Often called late baroque or ultrabaroque (*ultrabarroco, barroquismo*) and occasionally referred to as Churrigueresque, the period between 1730 and 1770 might be considered colonial baroque's most splendid moment in the sense of both maturity and richness.[38] Where, however, it becomes almost impossible to sort out their structural from their decorative elements, late baroque retablos and façades of northern New Spain are also commonly called *anástilo,* meaning without any particular style.

Developments within the baroque movement in architecture can readily be seen in the retablos and church façades. The framework of the retablo—an architectural altar screen designed to support the paintings and sculpture—began to evolve from the functional into the expressive. Ultimately, the retablo and, by extension, the church's frontispiece, or retablo façade, became sculptural masses that competed with the saints' images they were intended to support. This serves as a key distinction between early and later baroque.

Colonial baroque retains the basic cruciform plan of churches developed in Europe in the sixteenth century, with increasing ornateness and drama in decorative elements. While early baroque respects the building's structural integrity and architectural orders as well as the two-dimensionality of walls and ceiling, in later stages these elements, the sense of classical order, and even the principles of structure become gradually obscured and ultimately lost in a thicket of gold, spirals, and ornamentation.

Baroque painting was modeled after the imported oeuvre of Spanish and Flemish painters and their workshops—whether as originals, copies, or prints—with Francisco de Zurbarán and Peter Paul Rubens being the dominant influences during the second half of the seventeenth century. A disciple of Zurbarán, Sebastián López de Arteaga (1610–1656?) emigrated from Cádiz to New Spain in 1643. Through him, his disciples José Juárez (fl. 1635–1660)—whose family was to firmly embed the color, style, and mannered formulas of baroque in the art of New Spain—and Pedro Ramírez (fl. 1560–1578), and later through Baltasar de Echave y Rioja (1632–1682), tenebrism (dramatic light and shadow), startling textural effects, and the unidealized representations of Zurbarán were introduced into the painting of New Spain. The engravings and works of Rubens exercised an immediate influence on the art of New Spain, in particular through Spanish paintings whose realism and chiaroscuro took on Rubens's exuberance and rosy coloration.

The works of another Sevillan, master painter Bartolomé Esteban Murillo (1617–1682), can be genuinely appreciated for their gracefulness, elegance, and emotional sensitivity, as well as their composition, color, and draftsmanship. Murillo, widely copied and imitated on both sides of the Atlantic, was greatly admired during and after his lifetime. His influence on religious painting in Spain was enormous, although not necessarily positive. In the hands of artists not nearly as gifted as he in controlling the emotional tone of religious subject matter, Murillo's tenderness becomes sentimental, even cloying—what we today might find maudlin.

By the end of the seventeenth century, the golden age of baroque painting in New Spain had almost passed. The following generations, marked only by virtuosity of brushwork and sketchy fluidity, are best represented by two other families of painters: the Correas, six of them—the most prolific being Juan (fl. 1675–1739); and the de Villalpandos, Cristóbal (1649–1714) and his son Carlos (1680–?). Of these two families, Cristóbal de Villalpando attracts the most attention. A superb draftsman and masterful painter, he was the most elegant and grandiose painter Mexico ever produced. Many of his works are of heroic proportions, highly imaginative with brilliant colors, and surging with energy. It is not casually that he is referred to as the "Mexican Rubens."

Although there were other baroque artists in eighteenth-century New Spain, except for José de Ibarra (1688–1756) and Miguel Cabrera (1695–1768), they range from moderately interesting to tiresome and mediocre. Cabrera enjoyed enormous prestige, and his art was extremely influential. He and his workshop produced a tremendous number of paintings, to which must be added

2.15. Main façade, San Francisco de Asís, Chihuahua City, 1992. On July 31, 1811, the decapitated bodies of Father Hidalgo and two of his supporters were interred in the San Antonio chapel until after the War of Independence, when they were removed and reburied with highest honors in Mexico City.

hundreds of forgeries bearing his false signature (see also discussion of Cabrera under "Painters" in chapter 10).

Largely because of the centuries involved, baroque is the dominant style in northern New Spain's church art and architecture. Because architecture is less likely to be uprooted and replaced, it is our best, most continuous guide to the widest range of stylistic development. Examples of baroque in northern New Spain range from the somber—the façade of San Francisco de Asís in Chihuahua City (figure 2.15); to the moderate—the salomónico columns and fairly subdued treatment of the main façade of the Cathedral of Durango (figure 2.16); to the exuberant—the east and west frontispieces of the same structure (figure 2.17), with salomónico and *tritóstilo* columns combined, or the east and west frontispieces of the Cathedral of Chihuahua (see figure 2.12), with their segmented fluted columns and bifurcated motifs. The estípite style, a hallmark of the later baroque, appears first modestly in upper stories, such as on the east façade of the Cathedral of Durango (mentioned above), and then prominently, such as in the Retablo de Nuestra Señora de la Merced at San José de Parral (Chihuahua; figure 2.18). Columns compete for attention and finally lose ground to the niches and spaces between them in an inter-estípite style, such as in the altar of the Capilla de San Francisco de Asís de Sombrerete (Zacatecas; figure 2.19). There were, of course, architects and stonemasons who completely disregarded the prevailing stage of baroque and who tucked in columns and decoration of other stages wherever they saw fit.

Occasionally—and mostly in and on churches and retablos created by unsophisticated artists—stonemasons, plasterers, and other artisans simply got carried away. Inspired by the baroque spirit, on the one hand, and

a.

2.16. *Main façade, Catedral de Durango, 1982: a. overall, b. detail of frontispiece. The misplacement in the second story of the second column to the left (that is, the direction of the spiral), as well as the slight differences in the shorter column next to it, perhaps went unnoticed by the maestro de obra until it was too late to be rectified. Rather than detracting from the structure's appearance, these flaws somehow contribute an individual character.*

b.

2.17. East frontispiece, Catedral de Durango, 1982. Symbols associated with the Immaculate Conception are incorporated into the frieze in the entablature above the cornice of the first story on this frontispiece as well as the one on the west side of the cathedral.

by what is sometimes referred to as *horror vacui*—the fear of emptiness—on the other, they seemed intent on filling every square inch of the surface with figures and designs. The eye is bounced like a Ping-Pong ball from one point to another, and the effect can be overwhelming. The façade of San Sebastián in Concordia (Sinaloa) is a good example. Not only the columns but all other elements on the façade—windows, niches, frontispiece, and portal—are completely covered with designs. Even the surface between these elements is embellished with *angelitos* (cherubs), arabesques of leaves and flowers, and fields of patterns in panels (see figure 2.11).

2.18. Retablo de Nuestra Señora de la Merced, San José de Parral, Chihuahua, 1982. The shield of the Mercedarian Order and the chains in the second story proclaim the avocation of this recent replacement of the figure of the Virgin Mary and Christ Child. Ordinarily, she is immediately identifiable by her white garments and full-length scapular with the order's emblem upon it, and the fact that both she and the Christ Child proffer miniature scapulars to their devotees.

2.19. Main retablo, Capilla de San Francisco de Asís de Sombrerete, Zacatecas, 1983. The awkward embellishments around and above the niches mark the provincial quality of this inter-estípite retablo. In addition, molding is used to simulate columns as a cost-saving measure.

2.20. San José y San Miguel de Aguayo, San Antonio, Texas, 1990: a. main façade; b. sacristy rose window. The figures surrounding the doorway are replicas of the partially destroyed original statues. Notice also that the rising ground level of the church grounds had covered most of the base around the church until it was finally uncovered.

Rococo

Considered a logical progression of the baroque, rococo in New Spain dates roughly from 1750 to 1790. The French gave the movement its name (from French *rocaille*, rock work) and its greatest importance. Whereas the Gothic, Renaissance, and baroque movements persisted long enough to develop specific structural devices or significant changes in plan, the rococo mood, motifs, and color schemes appear more like grafts onto a former style than a style in themselves. And where its immediate predecessor, the baroque, suggests a masculine, virile mood, rococo represents the feminine. Charm and prettiness replace the splendid and robust.

Rococo is best described as decoration—a playful dissolution of all structural elements: worldly, lighthearted, frivolous, making lavish use of shell-like motifs and C-curves or S-curves. In place of structural members, it gives us purely ornamental niche pilasters and ornamented articulations; in place of substance, craftsmen's ingenuity. Like all other styles during the colonial era, the rococo was introduced to New Spain from Europe, and the works of engravers served to disperse its influence, including, in this case, engravings from central Europe.[39]

In northern New Spain, two good examples of rococo can be found on the main façade and the sacristy window of San José y San Miguel de Aguayo in San Antonio (Texas; figure 2.20a–b). Others can be seen in extraneous decorations on church walls, retablos (figure 2.21), frames, door panels, spandrels, and altar furniture, as well as in decorative color schemes, gold- and silverwork (*orfebrería*), and engravings. The lateness of the style vis-à-vis the building activities of missions or churches in the far northern reaches, its superficiality, the dramatic break provided by

2.21. Main retablo, Nuestra Señora de las Nieves, Palmillas, Tamaulipas, 1996. Although vigorously handled and well carved, the C- and S-curves, trademarks of the rococo, appear isolated and disconnected because of their placement, almost like patchwork. Thoughtful analysis of the raised carving throughout the retablo reveals very little success in integrating the shell-like motifs with each other or with any of the other designs. The current liberal use of a dark red paint for the background, instead of gold leaf over the entire surface, unfortunately exacerbates this shortfall.

neoclassicism, and the violent disruption—from 1810 to 1821—caused by the War of Independence were all probable reasons for rococo's scarcity in northern New Spain's architecture.

NEOCLASSICISM

Founded in Mexico City in 1785, the Academy of San Carlos was the leading exponent of neoclassicism, a style that discarded the excessive drama and floridness of the baroque in favor of the measured balance and refinement of the classical order. Many of the concepts of neoclassicism were inspired by the late-Renaissance architect Andrea Palladio (1508–1580), author of *The Four Books of Architecture*. Palladio had very likely studied the rediscovered and newly published writings of Vitruvius (Marcus Vitruvius Pollio, fl. 46–30 BC), which had become a vade

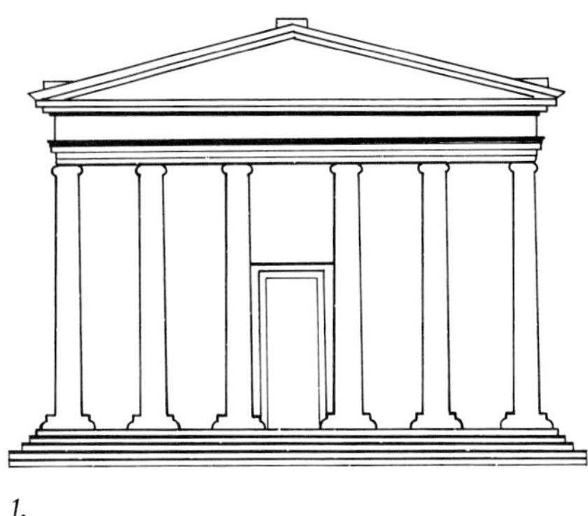

2.22. Neoclassicism: a. main façade, Misión Santa Bárbara, California, 1987; b. Eustyle temple of Vitruvius. The figures along the top of the pediment—representing Faith, Hope, and Charity—were badly damaged during the earthquake of 1925, and the current ones are replicas.

mecum for progressive architects during the fifteenth and sixteenth centuries in Italy and throughout Europe. Palladio was known for his elegant and intellectual approach to Renaissance ideas, especially harmonic proportions. His development of the colossal order, in which columns of all orders rise from the ground through several stories, can be seen in late-eighteenth and early-nineteenth-century examples in northern New Spain, such as on the late-baroque frontispiece of Nuestra Señora del Rosario (Sinaloa). Likewise, the façade of Santa Bárbara (California; built 1815–1820) displays these colossal orders, and much is made of its close resemblance to an illustration in the mission library's edition of Vitruvius (figure 2.22a–b).[40]

In comparison to their baroque counterparts, neoclassical art and architecture are rather severe. Decoration and ornamental embellishments are restrained, if not altogether absent. The concepts of this movement are linked to the belief that aesthetics, like society, are at their purest and best in their most basic and functional form; this theory encouraged the study and appreciation of the Greek orders.

The curriculum at the Academy of San Carlos included independent classes in drawing, painting, and sculpture. Plaster casts of Greco-Roman statuary were imported for the students to study and draw, with the result that figures in sculpture and paintings appear classical, complete with togas, period hairstyles—and even Grecian noses. The heavy emotional quality of the baroque, its dramatic use of gold leaf on polychrome religious figures, and its sense of the sudden and unexpected were swept away in favor of the cool refinement of classicism, although a cloying sentimentality persisted in figurative art.[41]

Tequitqui

In addition to styles brought from Europe, there were styles in Mexican art and architecture that expressed a distinctive New World quality. These are occasionally referred to as *tequitqui* or *mestizo*. A Nahuatl word, tequitqui means "one who pays tribute," as does mudéjar in Arabic, although mudéjar also applies to a specific vocabulary of designs, materials, and treatments. José Moreno Villa first used tequitqui in 1942 to describe a particular type of sixteenth-century sculpture characterized by its two-dimensionality (bas-relief silhouettes in surface carving that have almost a pressed-flat appearance) in which he perceived pre-Conquest concepts and

2.23. Detail of main frontispiece, La Purísima Concepción de Sombrerete, Zacatecas, 1983. The visual effectiveness of the protruding lion gargoyles was enhanced when the surrounding rubble walls were still covered with their homogenizing original plaster.

arrangements of figures and subjects.[42] In its strictest sense, tequitqui refers to ornamental sculpture of sixteenth-century New Spain produced by native sculptors employed or impressed into service by the early Christian friars or immigrant European builders. Partly because it has been established in the literature and partly because it expresses certain artistic canons present in immediate post-Conquest central New Spain, I feel tequitqui is a valid term, but suggest that it be confined to its strictest sense. Although there are no examples of tequitqui in this narrow sense in northern New Spain, there are many that can be classified as mestizo.[43]

MESTIZO

Implying a mixture in art and architecture of elements from the native population of New Spain and their conquerors, *mestizo* refers to the characteristically fresh treatment of Old World traditions and Christian iconography by native artisans and builders. A fusion of the indigenous (non-Indian as well as Indian) and the European in seventeenth- and eighteenth-century sculpture, painting, and architecture, it is not confined to New Spain, nor is it defined by particular materials or techniques. Mestizo is commonly used to describe a surviving and persistent native factor in Mexican art and architecture frequently referred to as "popular" or "folk"—a spirit, flavor, and a lively freshness in presenting themes and handling materials. Clear examples of mestizo in northern New Spain can be seen in the façades of La Purísima Concepción de Sombrerete (La Parroquia, Zacatecas; built ca. 1775; figure 2.23), and San Pedro y San Pablo de Tubutama (Sonora; built ca. 1785; figure 2.24).

2.24. Main frontispiece, San Pedro y San Pablo de Tubutama, Sonora, 1987: a. Whitewashed now, the radiant disks on either side of the sundial on the remate used to have remaining bits of color (courtesy of Arizona State Museum, Tucson); b. Late-nineteenth- or early-twentieth-century photo (cleaned and touched up). Some of the men are standing on the remains of an atrium cross, while the unusual main entrance on the side of the church's nave can be clearly seen in relationship to the dome over the transept crossing on the left. (Photo generously given to the author by Father Kieran McCarty; photographer unknown)

b.

2.25. Main frontispiece, Santo Domingo de Sombrerete, Zacatecas, 2001. The porous quality of the stone as well as the harsh climate caused significant damage to both the columns and figures. Many in this photo are replicas, replaced over a recent, lengthy restoration project. The walls were originally intended to be plastered to the carved stone frontispiece.

REGIONAL VARIATIONS

Arising as unique solutions to aesthetic problems in specific geographical areas, regional variations respond more to the constraints and challenges of the climate, materials, and culture of their respective areas than to a desire to emulate artistic monuments or fashionable forms. Three artistic variations in northern New Spain can be justifiably classified as regional: the sculptural tradition (*estilo Bajío*) of Querétaro, the popular religious art (*santo*) tradition of Nuevo México, and the Spanish mission architectural tradition of Alta California.[44] Despite identifiable differences within each one, taken together, the three form a distinguishable group.

Querétaro

At the entrance to the Bajío on the way from the rich mining areas of northern New Spain to the capital, Querétaro was blessed with fertile soil and a temperate climate. By 1680, it was the third most important city in New Spain, after the capital and Puebla. As early as 1531, a "maestro real de arquitectura de la ciudad de México" directed building projects from Querétaro. In the following three centuries, artistic production of the highest quality met the needs of large and prosperous convents (male and female), churches, and wealthy secular clients. The city's economic opportunities attracted artisans, some of whom remained and established studios.[45]

2.26. Retablo de Nuestra Señora de la Luz, from La Castrense military chapel, now in El Cristo Rey, Santa Fe, New Mexico. Traces of remaining paint indicate that a much brighter, and perhaps even gaudy, vision would have originally greeted the worshippers. (Courtesy of the Museum of New Mexico at the Palace of the Governors, Neg. #19656)

2.27. New Mexico retablo of Nuestra Señora del Rosario, Santa Fe. (Photo by A. Richardson; courtesy of the Martha Egan collection)

Querétaro's unique artistic contribution was sculpture, including not only religious statues but the sculpted decoration on niches, retablos, and façades. Typical of this sculptural tradition, the work of Querétaro-based sculptor Pedro de Rojas (1699–1772) is distinguished by its extravagant use of fantastic combinations of plant and animal forms. It may well have inspired the frontispiece of Santo Domingo de Sombrerete (Zacatecas; figure 2.25), the frontispieces in the missions of the Sierra Gorda (Querétaro), or even elements in the stone Retablo de Nuestra Señora de la Luz in the military chapel La Castrense in Santa Fe (New Mexico). Completed in 1761, the retablo was removed in 1859 and now resides in El Cristo Rey (also in Santa Fe; dedicated in 1940; figure 2.26).[46]

Nuevo México

The need to be self-sufficient imposed by isolation and limited economic resources served as a catalyst for developing a local religious art industry in the province of Nuevo México. After Independence, the territory was even more neglected and isolated. From the eighteenth century through the start of the twentieth, local artisans (*santeros*), most with no formal training, made religious images (santos) for both churches and individuals. With little or no understanding of anatomy or perspective and frequently receiving their inspiration from prints or engravings imported from Europe, the santeros used smoothed soft woods (pine and cottonwood) coated with locally prepared gesso and pigments to create their images on panels (retablos) or as sculpted figures (*bultos*). These images more than make up for what they lack in realism and polish with an emotional unity of line, form, and color that is direct, sympathetic, and approachable (figures 2.27 and 2.28).

2.28. New Mexico bulto of San Isidro el Labrador, private collection. The blunted, stylized features and softness of contours and details are fairly typical of New Mexican figures.

Alta California

The resemblance of the mission churches of Alta California to those of Mallorca and the southern coast of Spain is no coincidence, but rather the direct result of their having been inspired by Father Junípero Serra and his companions, natives of Mallorca. Indeed, the churches of Alta California feel "Mediterranean," with their lower elevations, raftered ceilings, tiled roofs, and (often) pierced bell walls (*espadañas*) rather than tiered bell towers (figure 2.29a–b). While all these architectural

2.29. Alta California missions showing typical features that distinguished them from missions in other provinces: a. San Gabriel Arcángel, San Gabriel (Newman Postcard Company, ca. 1910, private collection); b. Mission Santa Inés. (Santa Ynez, I. L. Eno postcard, ca. 1910, private collection)

2.30. Nuestra Señora de la Purísima Concepción de Acuña, San Antonio, Texas. (H. A. Moos postcard, ca. 1900, private collection)

choices admirably fitted the resources and physical environment of California, they strongly reflect the effects the Mallorcans best understood. Thus, the floor plans of most of the churches are simplified and their façades almost starkly plain.

Of the original structures, half were destroyed or severely damaged by earthquakes, and nearly all were restored, rebuilt, or replaced. Most of the extant churches—restored from the late eighteenth through the early nineteenth centuries—bear the clear imprint of neoclassicism: in decorative elements (plain pilasters, Doric-like columns, unbroken pediments), in the use of jasperizing (to produce a marble-like effect), in the design of retablos, and in the motifs and symbols of wall paintings.

It is interesting to note, however, that the five missionary churches Father Serra founded in the Sierra Gorda (Querétaro; ca. 1750–60) do not resemble those of Alta California, founded after his assignment there in 1769. Not surprisingly, they are more closely related, in plan and decoration style, to Nuestra Señora de la Purísima Concepción de Acuña in San Antonio (Texas; completed 1755; figure 2.30), San Xavier near Tucson (Arizona; completed 1797; see figure 2.1), and La Purísima Concepción in Caborca (Sonora; completed 1807; see figure 2.2)—the first built under the direction of Franciscans from the Colegio de Guadalupe in Zacatecas (Zacatecas); the last two, under the direction of Franciscans from the Colegio de Santa Cruz in Querétaro (Querétaro).[47]

PLANS

The early clerics, master masons, and architects of northern New Spain were not confronted with the problem of designing unique structures for novel situations. Products of fifteen hundred years of development, the religious structures from these individuals' backgrounds, vocations, and education served as their guides. Beyond this, the size and form of a church depended on its function (whether it was for diocesan or regular clergy and, if for regular, for which order), on the supporting population, and on the resources and materials available.

CHURCH BUILDINGS

Although neither the Catholic Church nor the various religious orders dictated the exact shape or size of a church building, there were certain absolute requirements. The structure had to be built as a church and never used for any other purpose. It had to be permanent and to have the following elements: a sanctuary area (in sight of, but separate from, the congregation) for an altar and celebrants, where services would be performed, a nave for the congregation, and a choir for the singers. If the church was a parochial church or was specially designated to provide baptisms (as were mission churches) then it would also have a baptismal font with suitable space around it, and a porch, portal, or some available space for use at the beginning of the baptismal rite.[1] Both the height of the altar and the material for its construction were prescribed. Whether mission or diocesan, the church had to be first consecrated (or sometimes merely blessed, as in the case of isolated mission churches, whose friars were empowered to do so) and had to contain at least one consecrated altar or, in most cases, one *ara* (see discussion of altar stone under "Sanctuary," "Main Altar," in chapter 7).

In addition to meeting many of the same structural requirements as diocesan churches, mission churches had a larger choir, where friars could recite their daily office, and a direct entrance from the convento to the church, usually via the cloister. The floor plan for almost all the religious structures in northern New Spain can be described as rectangular—occasionally with a rounded or polygonal modification in the apse, an extreme example of which is El Santo Ángel de la Guarda de Satevó near Batopilas (Chihuahua; built ca. 1750 by the Jesuits). Here the walls of the collateral (that is, side) chapels, and apse are curved; those of the sacristy (off the sanctuary) would, if joined, form a complete circle (figure 3.1). Nevertheless, even though the rear of the church presents a bombé, or polylobal, profile, its basic floor plan remains rectangular.[2]

Even churches with transepts at the crossing still are considered rectangular. A notable deviation from this plan is La Tercera Orden de Sombrerete (Zacatecas; built ca. 1770; figure 3.2), attached to the Franciscan convent there, whose exterior hides the octagon accommodating the nave and sanctuary. Collateral altars and the sacristy are sunken into the massive corners of the structure. The mortuary chapel of San Luis Rey de Francia in Oceanside (California; completed in 1815; figure 3.3) is laid out along similar lines.

Deviation from strictly right-angled corners may also be found in a number of churches in Mexico City. The earliest was San Miguel de Chapultepec in the barrio of Tacubaya (built 1554–1568; subsequently destroyed).[3] Others include El Pocito, the small polylobal chapel in La Villa (built 1777–1791; figure 3.4a–b), and Santa Brígida, an oval-nave church in the center of the city (dedicated in 1745; razed in 1933).[4]

The accompanying illustrations are included to give the clearest possible idea of the various plans discussed.[5] While variations are to be expected, I have attempted to select examples that most clearly demonstrate the factors involved. I have drawn examples both from the continental United States and from Mexico to heighten awareness of the historical and artistic positions occupied by these churches and of their interrelationships.[6] The boundary between the two countries should be viewed in this context as an artificial line; the structures found in the United States are not isolated examples but salient expressions of the Spanish philosophy toward colonization and pacification of new lands. They are also a viable artistic legacy.

Rectangular

[No Aisles] In its simplest expression, a rectangular church consists of a nave with no aisles and with the main altar and main entrance at opposite ends.[7] This structure can be elaborated on by including a separate room to the side of the entrance to the nave for the baptistery, and an additional room, the sacristy, to the side of the sanctuary (near the altar end) for the robing of clerics. This shape might be covered simply with beams and a flat roof, or with a more complex vaulting system. Doors and windows might be included along the nave's walls, with a window above the main entrance.

Rectangular, no-aisle churches were uncommon in Spain during New Spain's viceregal period. Consequently, their persistence in New Spain must be due to factors other than mere Spanish precedence. Limits imposed by poor engineering and building skills or the lack of sophisticated scaffolding would surely have influenced the floor plan and number of aisles, as would the desire among the early missionaries to construct buildings that reflected the Apostolic Church in its primitive simplicity. The archaic trapezoidal shape of the apse found in some structures, in addition to increasing the illusion of depth, helped concentrate the congregation's attention on the altar and the religious services, as did the usual device of raising the sanctuary area above the floor level of the nave. Practically and strategically speaking, a single open area also allowed the priest more easily to keep an eye on the worshippers, as well as instilling a unifying effect upon the congregation (figure 3.5).

[Multiple Aisles] Rectangular churches having one or more aisles on either side of the nave include the basilica and hall church.

Basilica. Basilicas were illuminated by clerestory windows; their ceilings were higher over the nave than over the aisles.[8] The basilica form was adopted from Roman architecture.[9] In its temporal use, the word "basilica" is a broad term for a hall. The first Christian basilicas were often sites of Roman law courts or places of public affairs converted to churches. Consequently, the basilica became a stylistic model for early Christian architecture. The building had a porchlike appurtenance called a "narthex," which served as a vestibule, aisles and galleries along its sides, and the apse at the opposite end. In the raised and rounded apse end, where the judge once presided surrounded by his assessors, the bishop now sat on his throne surrounded by his presbyters (for Christians, a symbol of Christ and his Twelve Apostles). The crowds of spectators who stood and watched the legal proceedings became the body of Christian worshippers, who had no active part to play in the liturgy. By the year 1000, the cruciform basilica had already assumed most of the forms and features we recognize as typical of the great age of medieval Christian building (figure 3.6).

Although not common in northern New Spain, and traditionally reserved for cathedrals, the basilica floor plan, roof, and window arrangement can be found in four former Jesuit mission churches: San José de Comondú (Baja California Sur), San Ignacio de Loyola de Humariza and El Nombre de Jesús de Carichic (both Chihuahua), and San Joaquín y Santa Ana de Nuri (Sonora). The current Cathedral of Durango (Durango; begun in 1645; main façade completed in 1721; eastern and western façades completed in 1763; figure 3.7) is a classic example of a basilica form built for cathedral functions, as is the much smaller and far more modest church planned by Bishop Reyes for his cathedral at Álamos (Sonora; begun in 1786; figure 3.8).[10] The Cathedral of Chihuahua, built 1725–1760 as a parochial church with cathedral ambitions, also has a basilica plan (figure 3.9). Churches such as San Joaquín y Santa Ana de Nuri or San José de Comondú, on the other hand, were built in the basilica form simply to create a larger space for the mission congregation, or because of a lack of sufficiently long beams or of the technical skills necessary to throw a vault across the aisles.

The term "cathedral" denotes the bishop's church and his "seat" (see **Cathedra** entry in chapter 11).[11] The great cathedral-building activities in Europe during the sixteenth and part of the seventeenth centuries—of which the cathedrals of Mexico City, Puebla, Morelia, Mérida, and Guadalajara were a part—is represented in northern New Spain by one example only, the Cathedral of Durango. The remaining structures in northern New Spain that are today designated as cathedrals were parish churches raised to the status of cathedrals. The Cathedrals of Chihuahua and Monterrey are two such examples.

Hall church. Hall churches had no clerestory windows; their ceilings were as high over the aisles as over the nave.

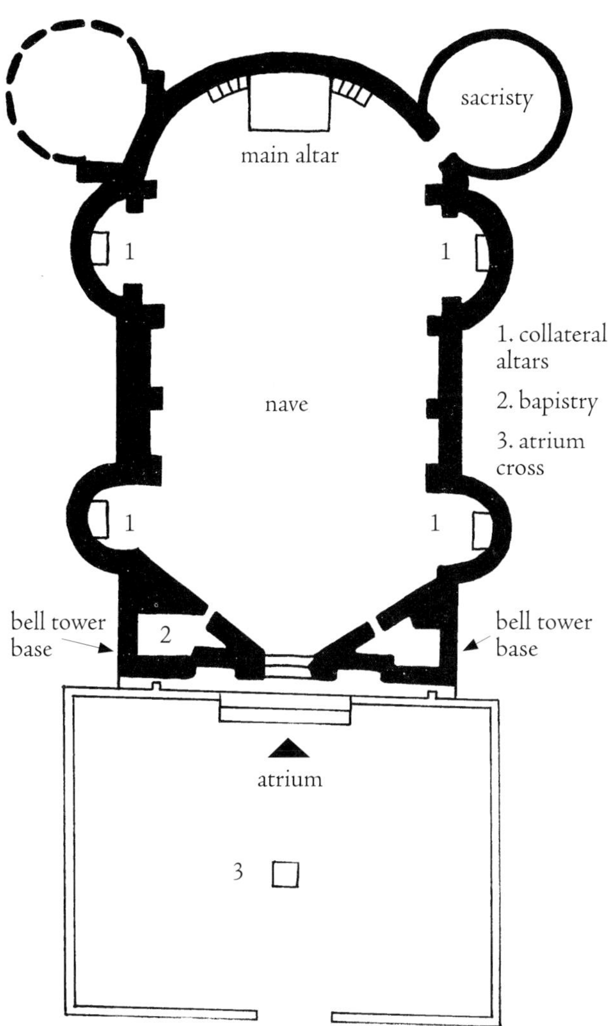

3.1. Plan, El Santo Ángel de la Guarda de Satevó, Batopilas, Chihuahua.

The hall church was a typical plan in sixteenth-century northern Europe (*Hallenkirche*) and Spain, predominantly among parish churches in the small towns of Old and New Castile. The eighteenth-century Santa María de Natívitas in Bachíniva (Chihuahua) may be the only extant example of a colonial hall church in northern New Spain (figure 3.10a–b).

Cross-Shaped

Cruciform churches have a nave with intersecting transepts, and may or may not also have multiple aisles. Predominant in eighteenth-century northern New Spain, the

3.2. Roof and outside nave wall, La Tercera Orden de Sombrerete, Zacatecas, 1983. The interior oval profile can be seen embedded within the rectangular exterior walls.

cruciform floor plan was so called because the junction of the transepts created a form identifiable as a Latin cross (figure 3.11). The use of the cross shape with symbolic intent dates back to Christian churches of the mid-fourth century.

Disguised Aisles

Churches having lateral chapels that constitute disguised aisles are said to have a "cryptocollateral" floor plan, whether rectangular or cross-shaped and with or without formal aisles along the nave. Begun in 1541, San Agustín in Mexico City was the first church built in New Spain with this plan, which Sartor traces to medieval, in particular to "Catalan Gothic," churches and to Renaissance churches in southeastern France.[12] The late medieval scheme of converting a church's outer aisles into chapels was successfully exploited by the Jesuits in Portugal throughout the sixteenth century.[13]

Three churches of northern New Spain also serve as examples of cryptocollateral plans: the Cathedral of Durango (see figure 3.7), rectangular with a nave and two formal aisles; San Luis Gonzaga de Bacadéhuachi (Sonora; completed ca. 1750; figure 3.12), a cruciform structure with a nave and two aisles running from its transept to an ambulatory behind the main altar; and La Parroquia de la Asunción de Parras (Coahuila; also called "Santa María de Parras"; begun in 1648; enlarged in 1681), a rectangular church with no formal aisles whose slender nave is almost overwhelmed by the depth and

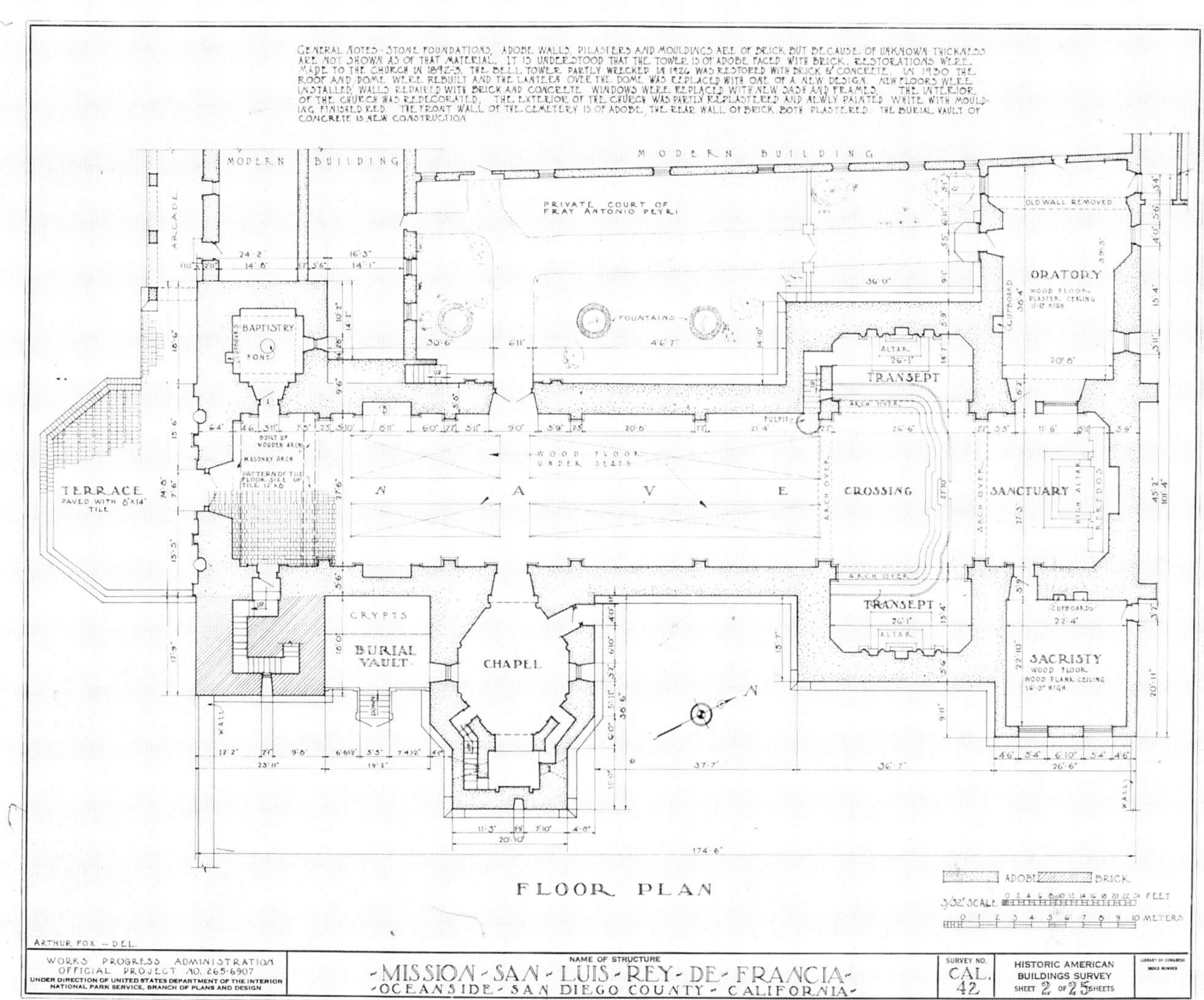

3.3. *Plan, San Luis Rey de Francia, Oceanside, California. (Courtesy of Historic American Building Survey)*

width of the collateral chapels (figure 3.13). The rarity of the cryptocollateral plan in northern New Spain is due partially to the scarcity of the style in central New Spain, and partially to the missionaries' preference for the rectangular, no-aisle form as mentioned previously. The prosperity of the mining community of Durango and the power of its bishopric must have encouraged the cathedral builders to imitate the basilica and chapel plans seen in several churches in Mexico City and Puebla. The church at Bacadéhuachi, however, is more enigmatic. Although the records tell of Franciscans being instructed to build a new church at the site of a ruined Jesuit church, there is a remarkable coincidence between this floor plan and that of European Jesuit churches.

Capillas, Camarines

Also considered part of the principal church building are lateral chapels (*capillas laterales*), along the interior sides of the nave and oriented perpendicular to it, and annex chapels (*capillas anexas*), outside the principal nave and oriented either perpendicular or parallel to it (see figures 3.11 and 3.13).[14] Annex chapels are often later additions and may represent a different style of construction. Priests and nuns were required to perform their private devotions out of sight of the laity occupying the nave of the church. The sanctuary, therefore, could not be used, thus requiring a separate chapel.[15] Both lateral and annex chapels can be found with all types of church plans.

a

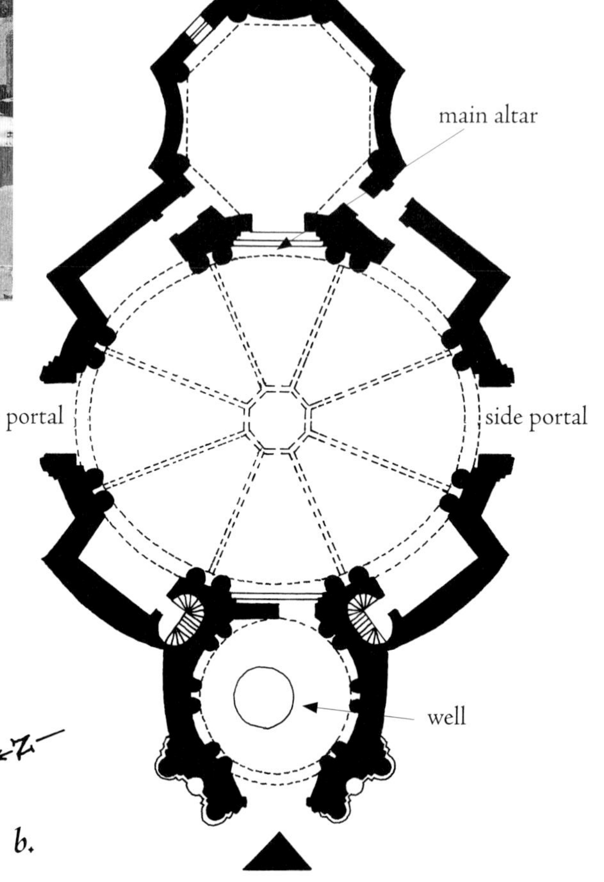

b.

3.4. El Pocito chapel, La Villa, Mexico City: a. exterior, ca. 1910 (Latapi and Bert postcard); b. plan.

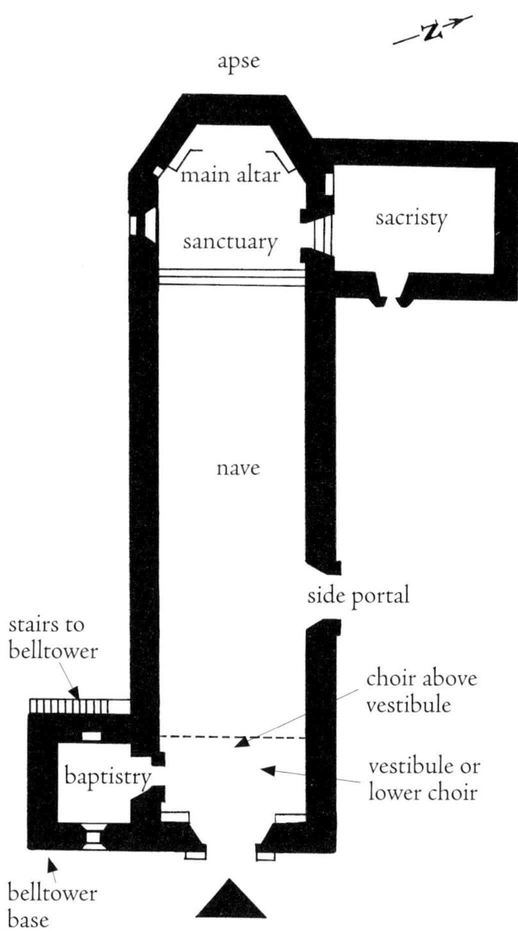

3.5. *Plan of a rectangular, no-aisle church with trapezoidal apse, Nuestra Señora de las Nieves, Palmillas, Tamaulipas.*

Occasionally, a small room referred to as a *camarín* was constructed to provide a dressing and storage space for an important cult figure. In Jesuit structures it was apparently popular to place it on the Gospel (left) side of the nave. There was usually a small retablo against one wall and the room was accessible from the nave. Used with frequency among the Jesuit Order for its special devotion to Our Lady of Loreto, camarines might also house some other image particularly revered by the community and other religious orders. *Cofradías* (religious brotherhoods) also adopted this practice; and in addition to the image they sponsored, clothing and jewelry donated by the image's devotees were stored or guarded there. Kubler considered the camarines as perhaps one of the most uniquely Hispanic features of baroque architecture. An example occurring in northern New Spain is San Miguel Arcángel de Oposura (now Moctezuma, Sonora; figure 3.14). Another might possibly have been the small room now used as a parish church office in San Ignacio de Loyola de Kadakaaman (Baja California Sur; figure 3.15). Other likely camarines are the odd protuberance behind the apse of San Luis Gonzaga in Bacadéhuachi (see figure 3.12) and the collateral chapel of Nuestra Señora de la Asunción de Arizpe (figure 3.16)—both former Jesuit missions in Sonora.

Orientation

Although the tradition established in the Middle Ages for church orientation stipulates that the main altar is to be in the eastern end of the building, with the main façade facing west, centuries later, necessity or expediency resulted in mixed compass orientations for churches in northern New Spain and throughout the New World.[16] Franciscans appear to have been the most conscientious observers of the original tradition, mostly during the sixteenth and early seventeenth centuries. After that time (the influential Jesuits discarded the east-west orientation following the Council of Trent), and particularly in northern New Spain, churches pointed in all directions.[17] From remaining evidence, when a mission church was built within an existing village, the size of the convento and church, as well as its orientation, accommodated the space available. In sites where space was not a constraint, the axial directions still appear arbitrary. Indeed, one eighteenth-century architect professed ignorance as to why churches should point east at all.[18] Kubler suggests the orientation of New Mexican churches might have been determined by the local timing of ceremonies. Early morning services seem to have been favored by the Pueblos in New Mexico; hence their structures often face east (with the main altar at the west end of the church).[19] Anyone who has watched the sun move along the walls of many of northern New Spain's colonial churches, picking out niches and illuminating altars, cannot help but wonder if perhaps the churches had been oriented to the path of the sun on patronal days.[20] For churches having a transverse clerestory window, the light on the altar and in the apse would have been most effective and most dramatic if the structure were also facing east (with the main altar in the west; see "Windows and Clerestories" under "Outer Body" in chapter 5).

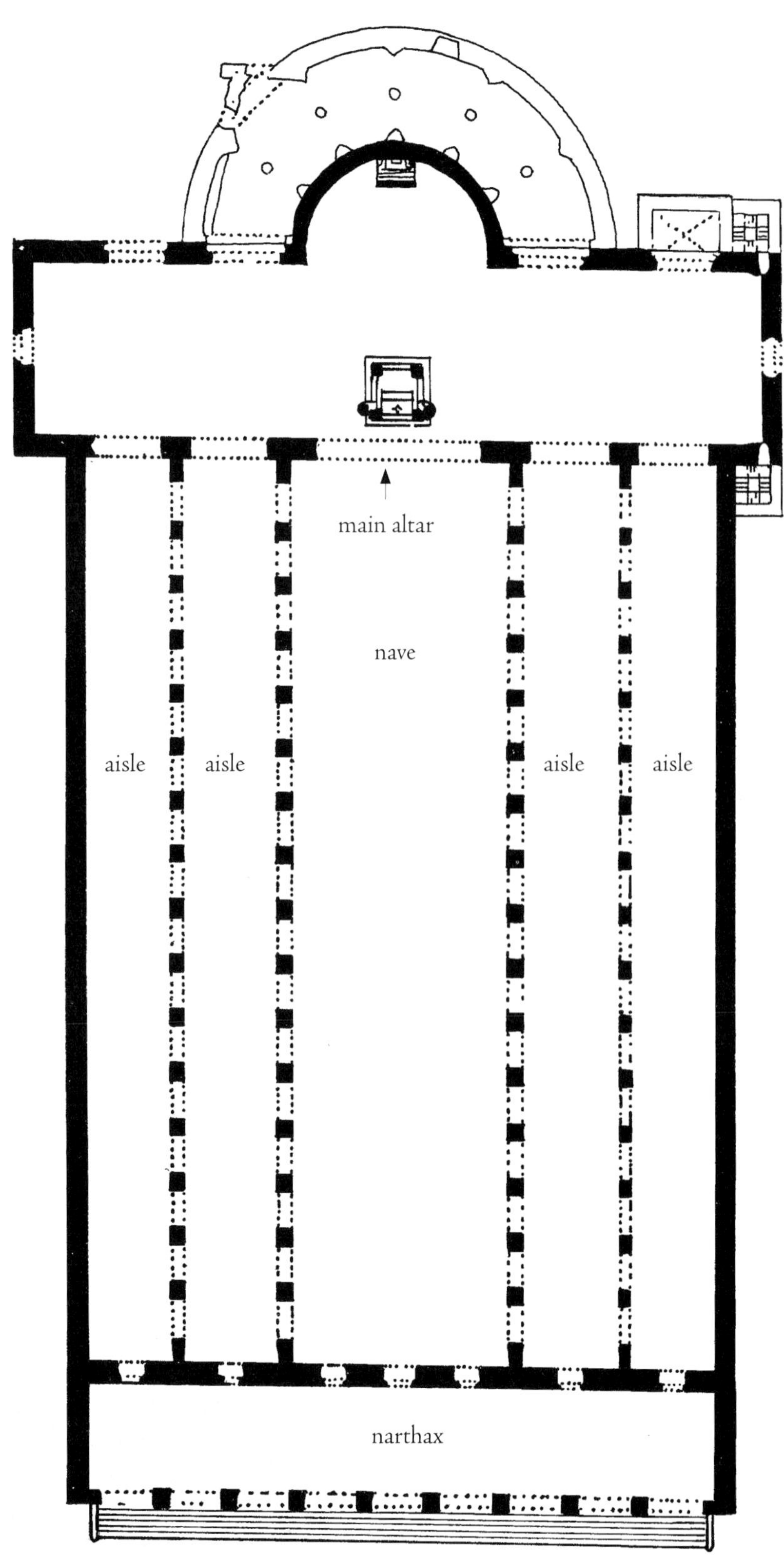

3.6. *Plan of a cruciform basilica, Saint John Lateran, Rome.*

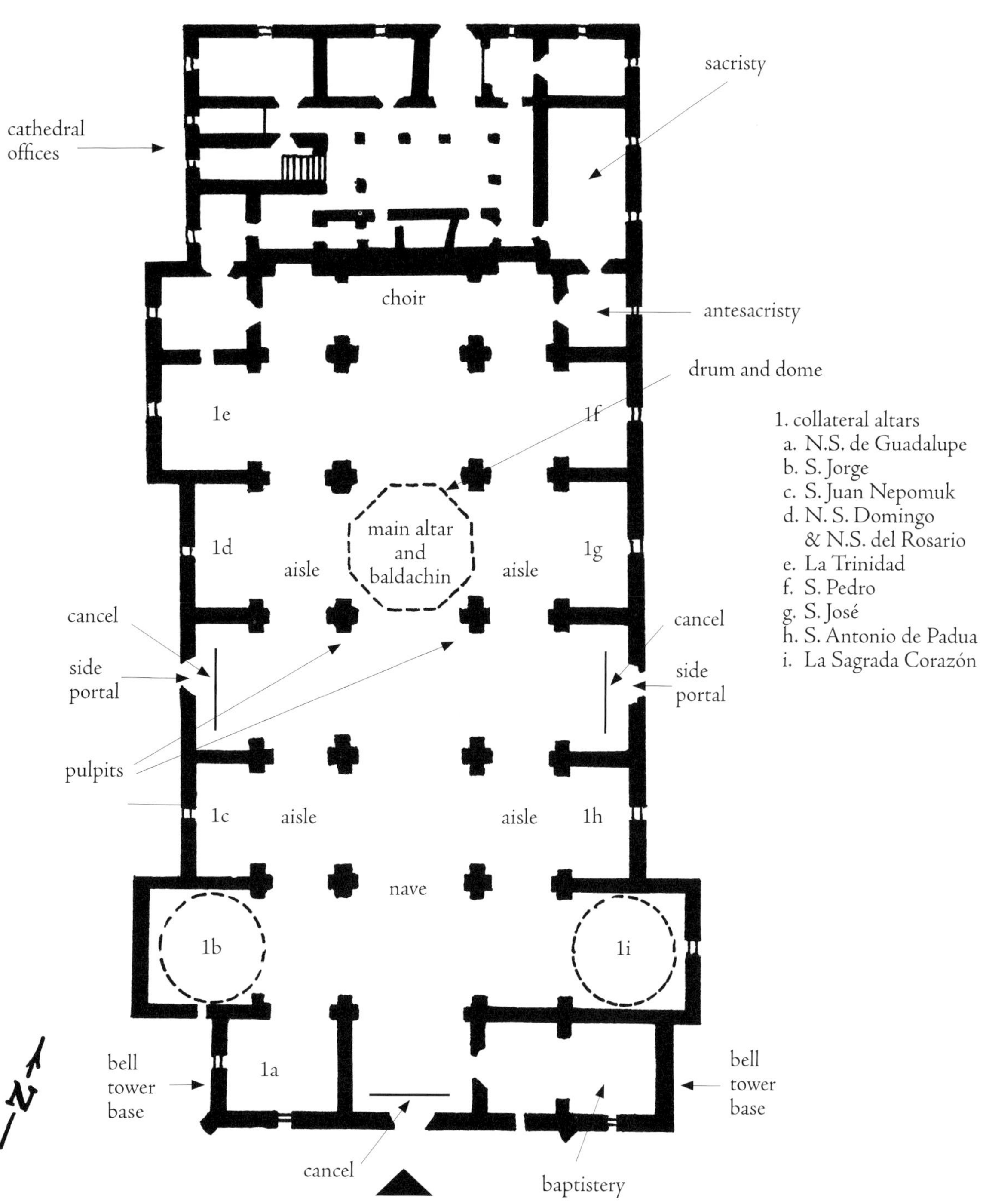

3.7. *Plan of a basilica, Catedral de Durango.*

3.8. *Interior of a basilica, Nuestra Señora de la Asunción del Real de los Álamos, Sonora, 1980.*

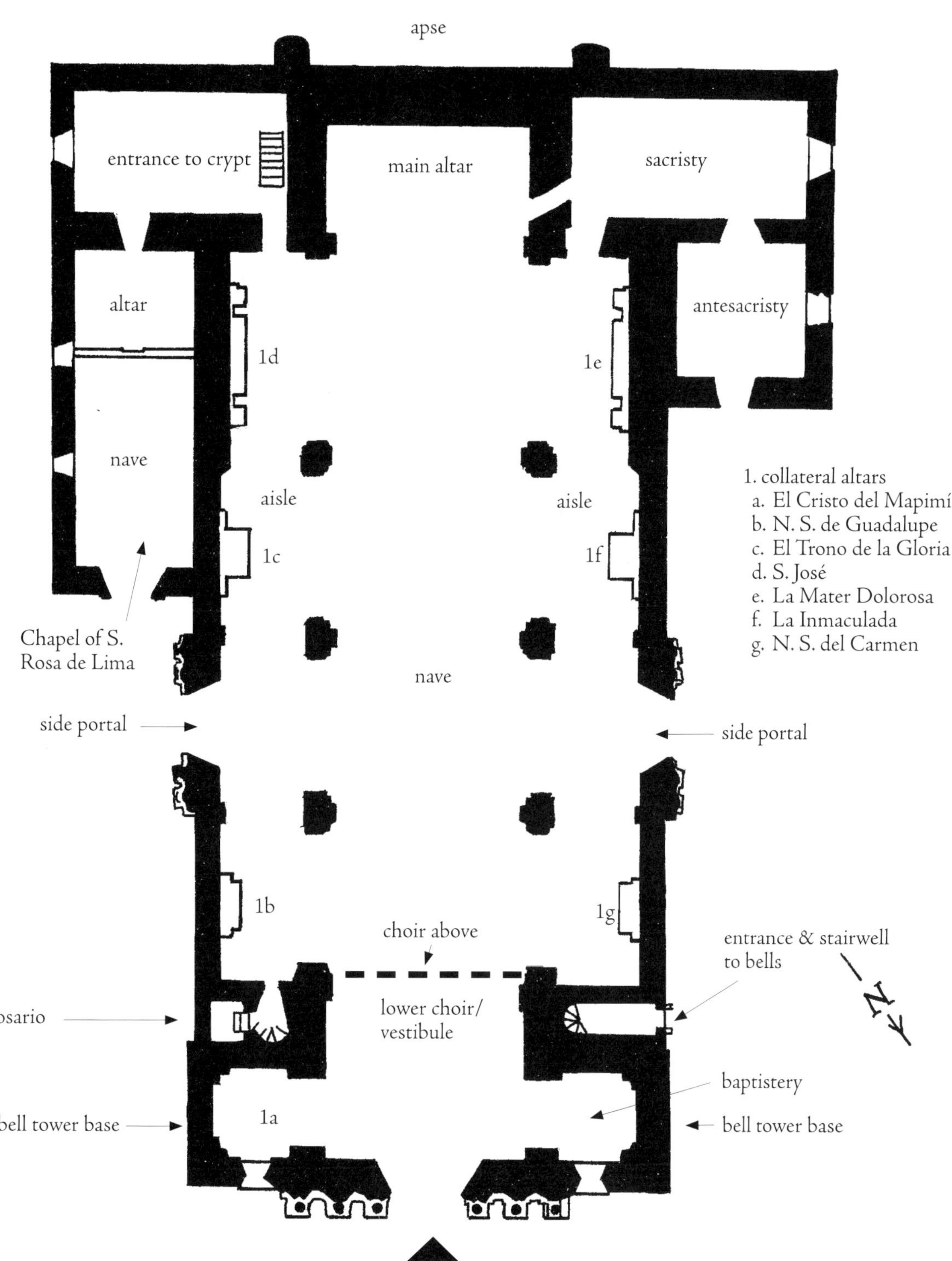

3.9. Plan of a basilica, Catedral de Chihuahua.

3.10. A hall church, Santa María de Natívitas, Bachíniva, Chihuahua: a. interior, looking from the altar toward the main door, 1992. Note that the ceilings of the nave and the aisles are at the same level; b. plan.

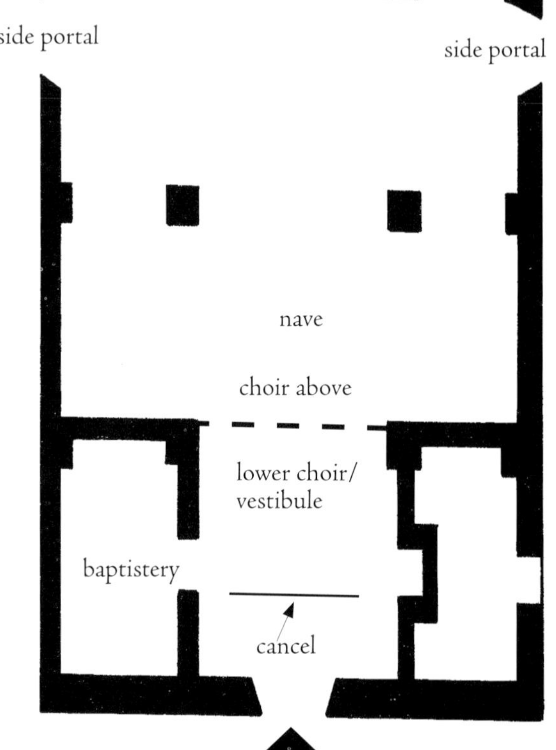

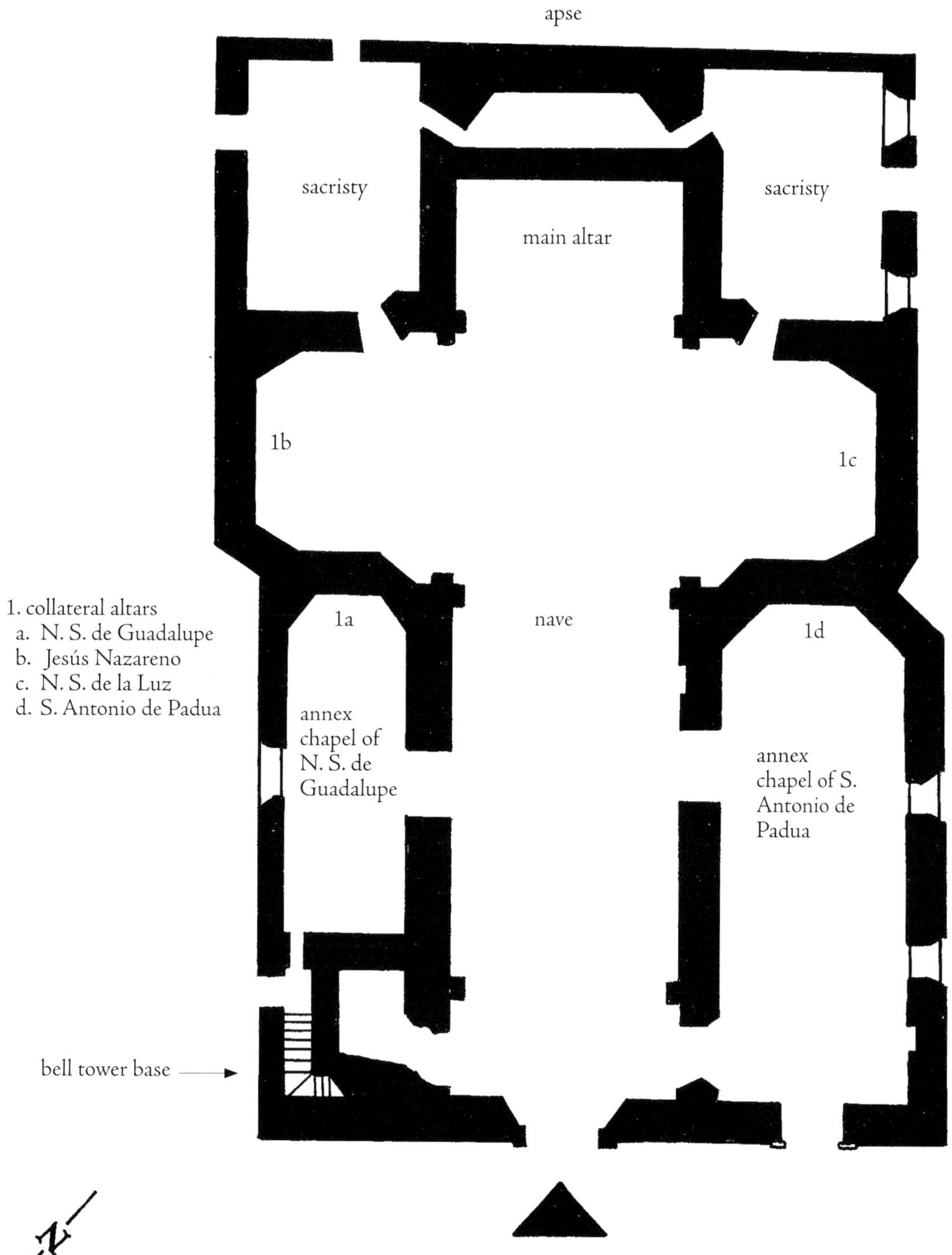

3.11. Plan of a cruciform church, San Francisco de Asís, Chihuahua City, Chihuahua.

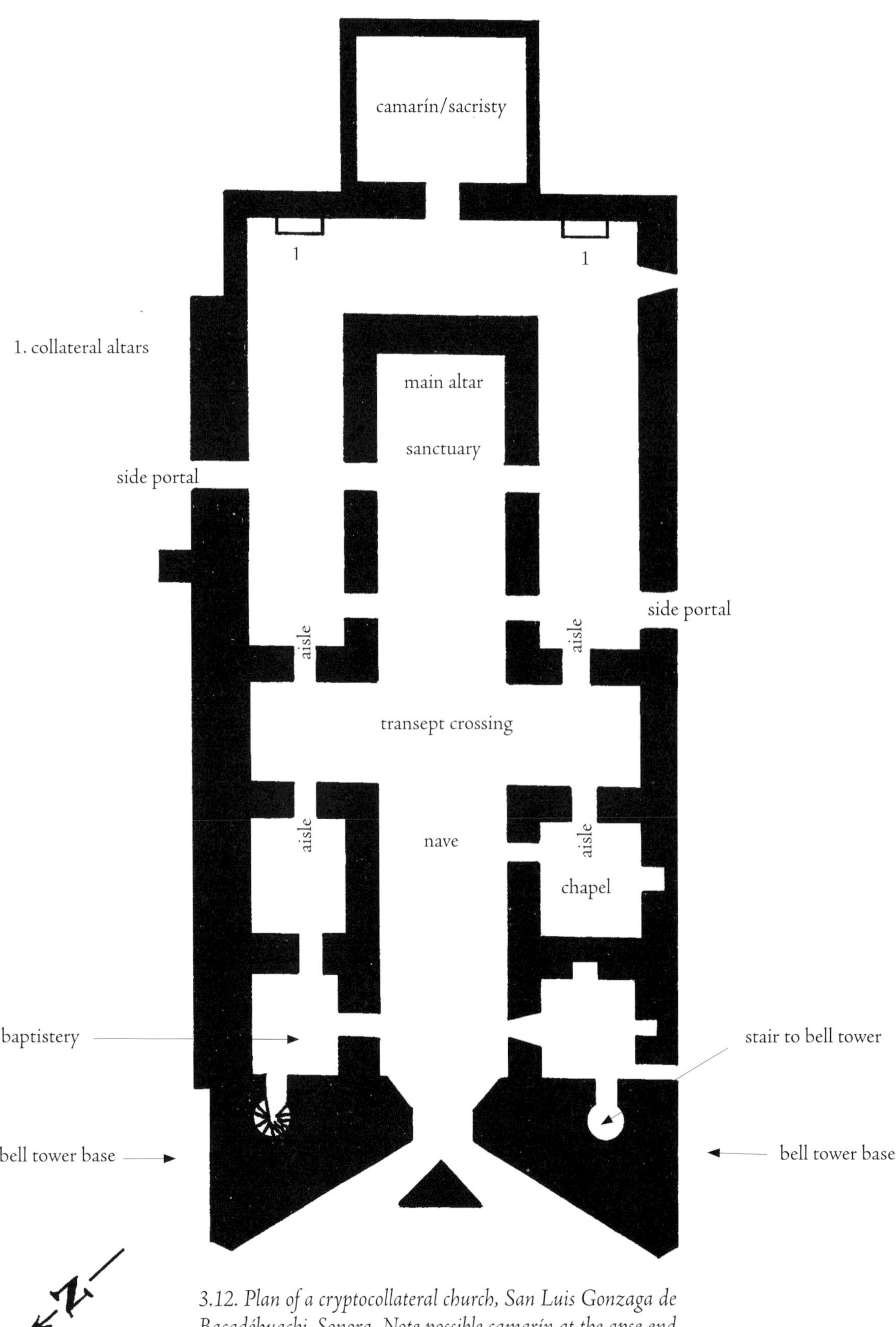

3.12. *Plan of a cryptocollateral church, San Luis Gonzaga de Bacadéhuachi, Sonora. Note possible camarín at the apse end.*

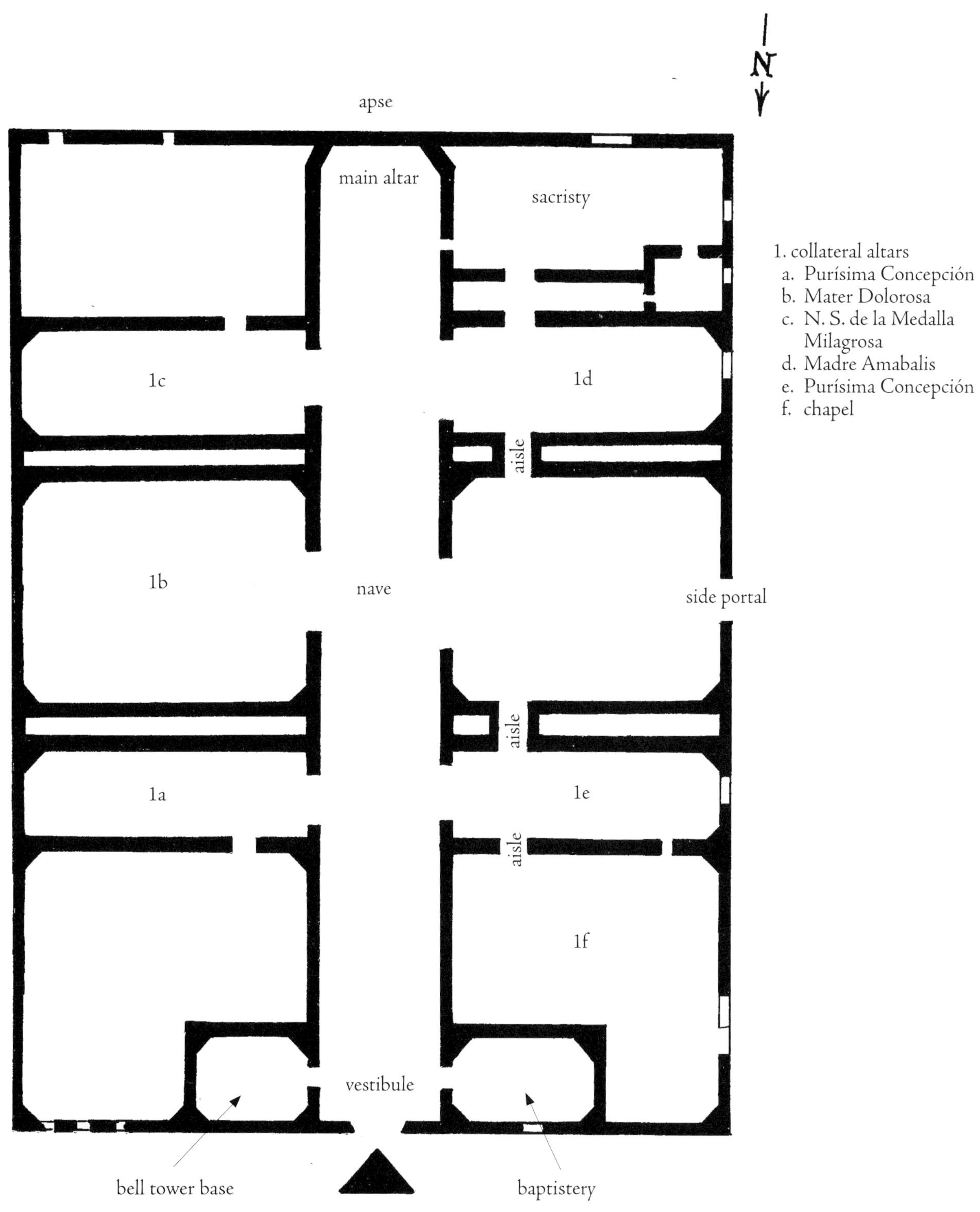

3.13. Plan of a cryptocollateral church, La Parroquia de la Asunción, Parras, Coahuila.

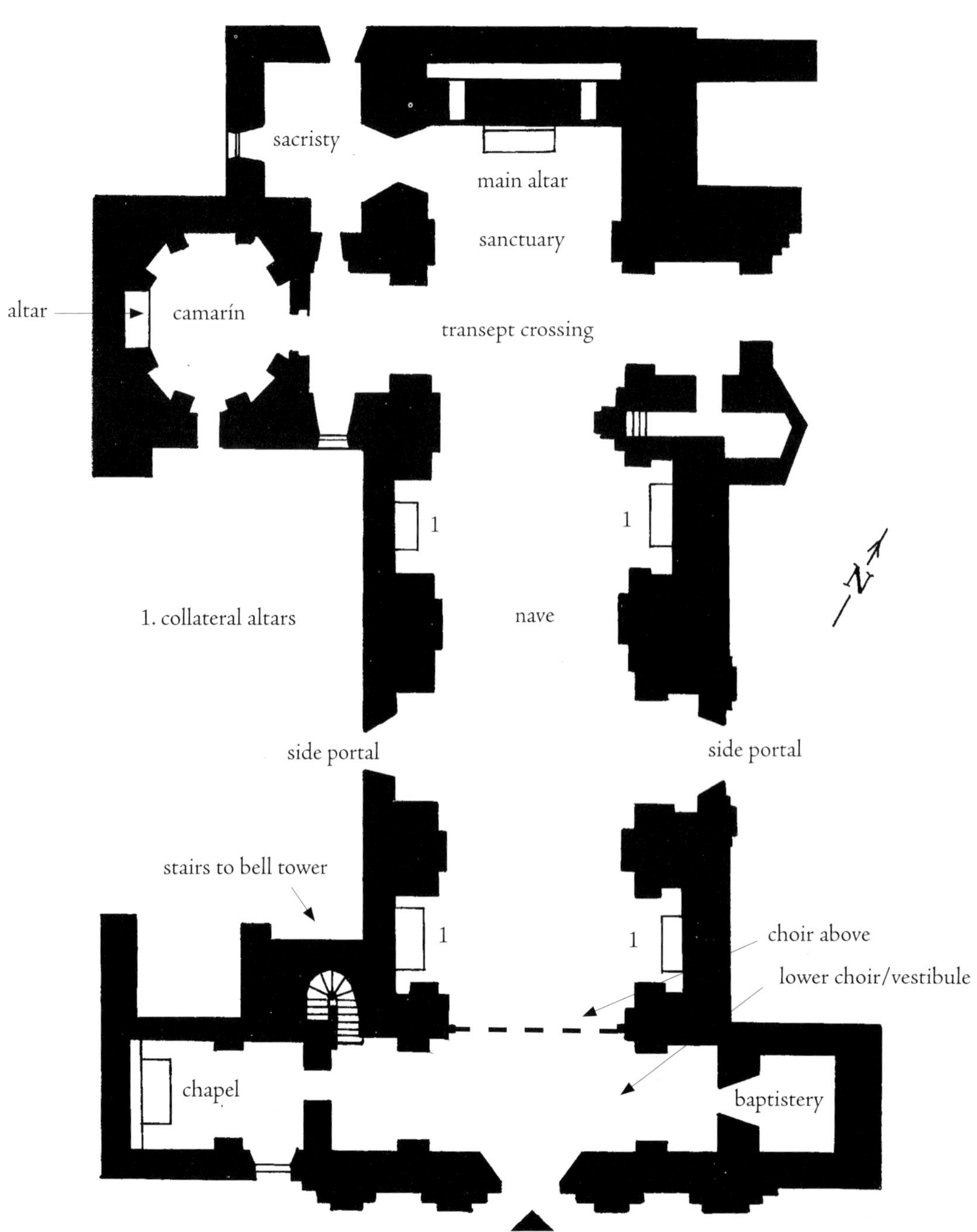

3.14. Plan of a cruciform church with camarín, San Miguel Arcángel de Oposura, Moctezuma, Sonora.

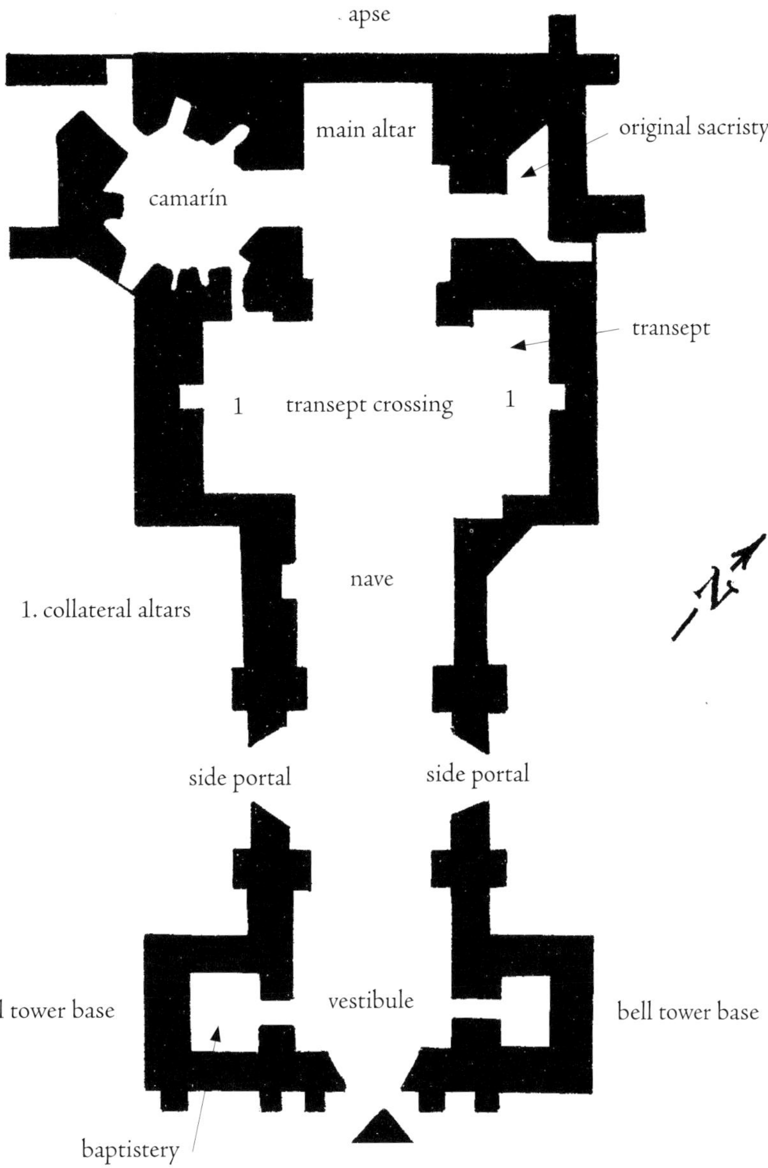

3.15. *Plan of a cruciform church with an apparent camarín, San Ignacio de Loyola de Kadakaaman, Baja California Sur. Destruction and subsequent remodeling of parts of the original church and its complex may have reduced the sacristy and altered the original function of the camarín.*

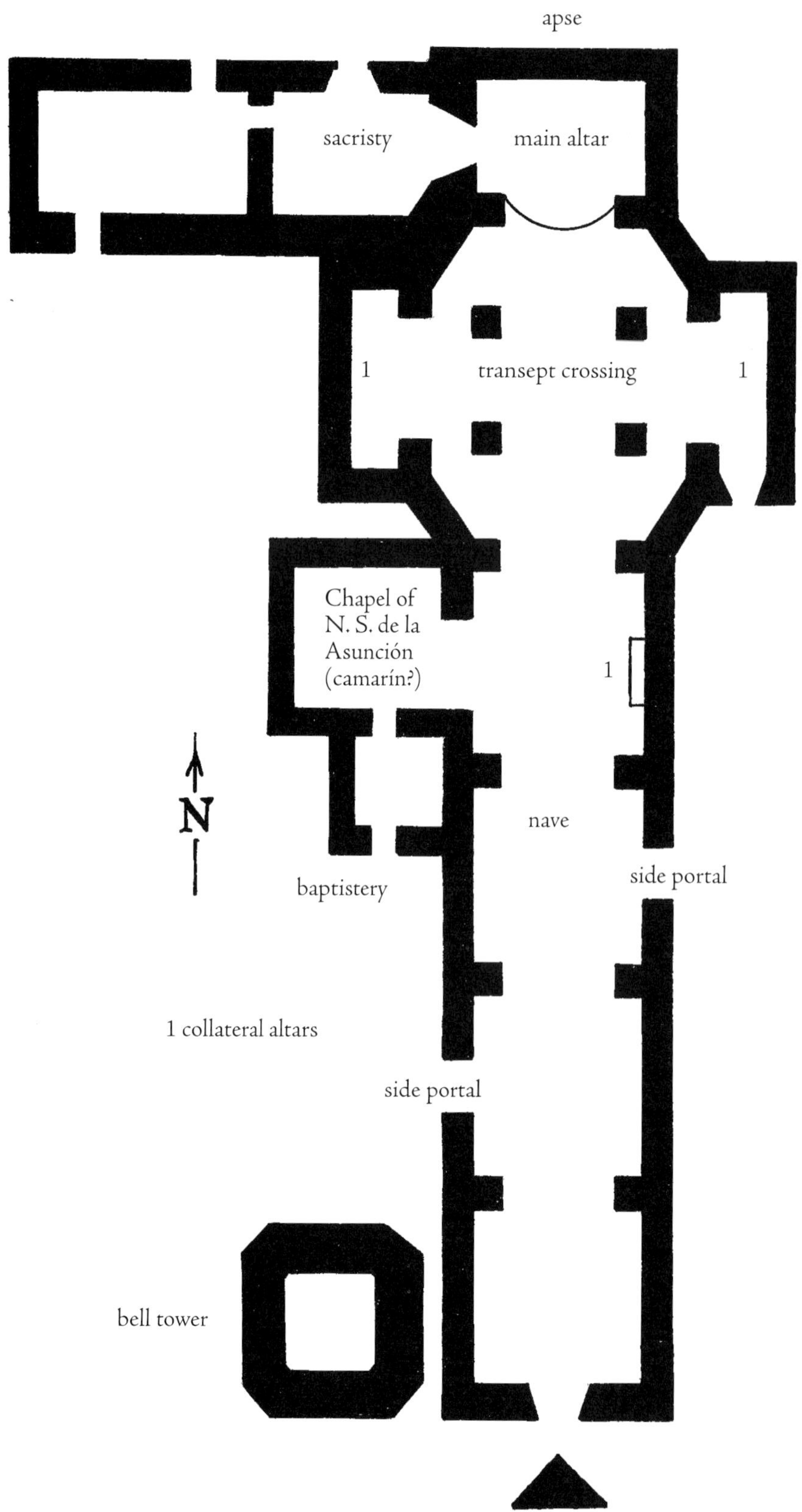

3.16. Plan of a cruciform church with camarín, Nuestra Señora de la Asunción de Arizpe, Sonora.

Church Complexes

Size, axis, material, and form of the church building might vary, but the plan for a church complex contained certain essentials from which there could be no deviation. The mission church complex comprised a church, *atrio* (walled courtyard), and burial ground, which was usually enclosed by a wall (*barda;* figure 3.17a–b).[21] To the side of the church, and connected to it by its own passage, was the *convento.*[22] This consisted of a series of rooms and spaces, arranged around a small enclosure, *claustro* (cloister), for the priests, and sometimes for the Indian retinue that served as cooks, gardeners, or porters. Included were storerooms, a *sala* "de profundis," a kitchen, a dining room (refectory), and occasionally a small office or library.[23] An entrance to the convento facing the same direction as the main church façade allowed direct access to the patio, to a small vestibule, or to a porch referred to as the *portería,* where business could be conducted or travelers might spend the night (if not accommodated in a spare room within the convento). There was usually also access to the quarters from the patio, or to the gardens, orchards, or attached corral from the cloister. Additional rooms within the complex might serve as classrooms. In some cases, quarters for the Indians were arranged around the mission building, with young unmarried women housed separately from the men. Depending on the need for defense, the outlying houses might be grouped along protecting walls. Mission industries might be incorporated within the convento or in the outlying buildings.

Apparently based on Spanish prototypes and the need of sixteenth-century friars to accommodate large Indian congregations during the early years of colonization in central and southern New Spain, four special elements of building and design were developed for the monastery or church complex. These were (1) the atrium (*atrio*), a large walled courtyard facing the main entrance; (2) an atrium cross (*cruz del atrio*), a large cross near the center of the atrio or on an axis with the entrances through the atrio walls; (3) the *capillas posas,* or *posas,* a set of small secondary chapels located in the corners of the courtyard; and (4) an open chapel (*capilla abierta* or *capilla de indios*) for the celebration of the Mass, constructed in the front wall of the monastery complex, to the side of the main entrance of the church and open on one side to permit the outdoor congregation to observe the liturgy.

Not all of these elements were part of the standard plan for mission complexes in northern New Spain. The large courtyard (atrio), developed to hold enormous crowds during the early years of conversion in central New Spain (and perhaps inspired by the courtyards of indigenous religious temples, or of the mosques of Moorish Andalucía), was a ubiquitous element in Spanish New World architecture, and northern New Spain was no exception.[24] In the study of northern New Spain's colonial churches, the atrio should be considered not only as a staging ground for some of the church's interior activities or as an enclosure for the church graveyard or for minor religious structures, but as an integral part of the church—an extension of its interior space along its principal axis. This spot, usually walled, was dominated by the church's façade and frontispiece and served as an open-air theater for religious plays, processions, and dances. Most atrios are still intact in northern New Spain, and in many cases still serve their original purpose.

Crosses were probably erected in the atrios in front of the mission or diocesan churches. Crosses (although not always entirely original) are in place today at the former Jesuit mission churches of El Nombre de Jesús de Carichic and Santa Rosa de Lima de Cusihuiriáchic (figure 3.18), both in Chihuahua, and at San Francisco de Vigge-Biaundó (Baja California Sur). Evidence of the existence of others and their widespread use can be seen in historic drawings, lithographs, and photographs (figure 3.19a).[25]

Another feature of many church complexes in northern New Spain was a sundial (*muestra de sol* or *relojito de sol*), most often mounted on the outer wall of the church building, occasionally on a flat stone embedded in the ground or atop a freestanding column. The simplest type, and one of the oldest methods for measuring time, was a scratch dial, which has only lines to mark the times for services, hours, or work periods. More elaborate sundials included numbers or other symbols. Each sundial was exactly oriented for its particular location: the gnomon, or style, had to be set on the noon line (representing the true north-south meridian) of the dial's horizontal face, the angle of the gnomon equaling the latitude of the site. Remains of sundials may be seen at the former mission churches of San Pedro y San Pablo de Tubutama (Sonora) and San Juan Bautista (California), at the parochial church of San José de Parral (Chihuahua), or near other religious

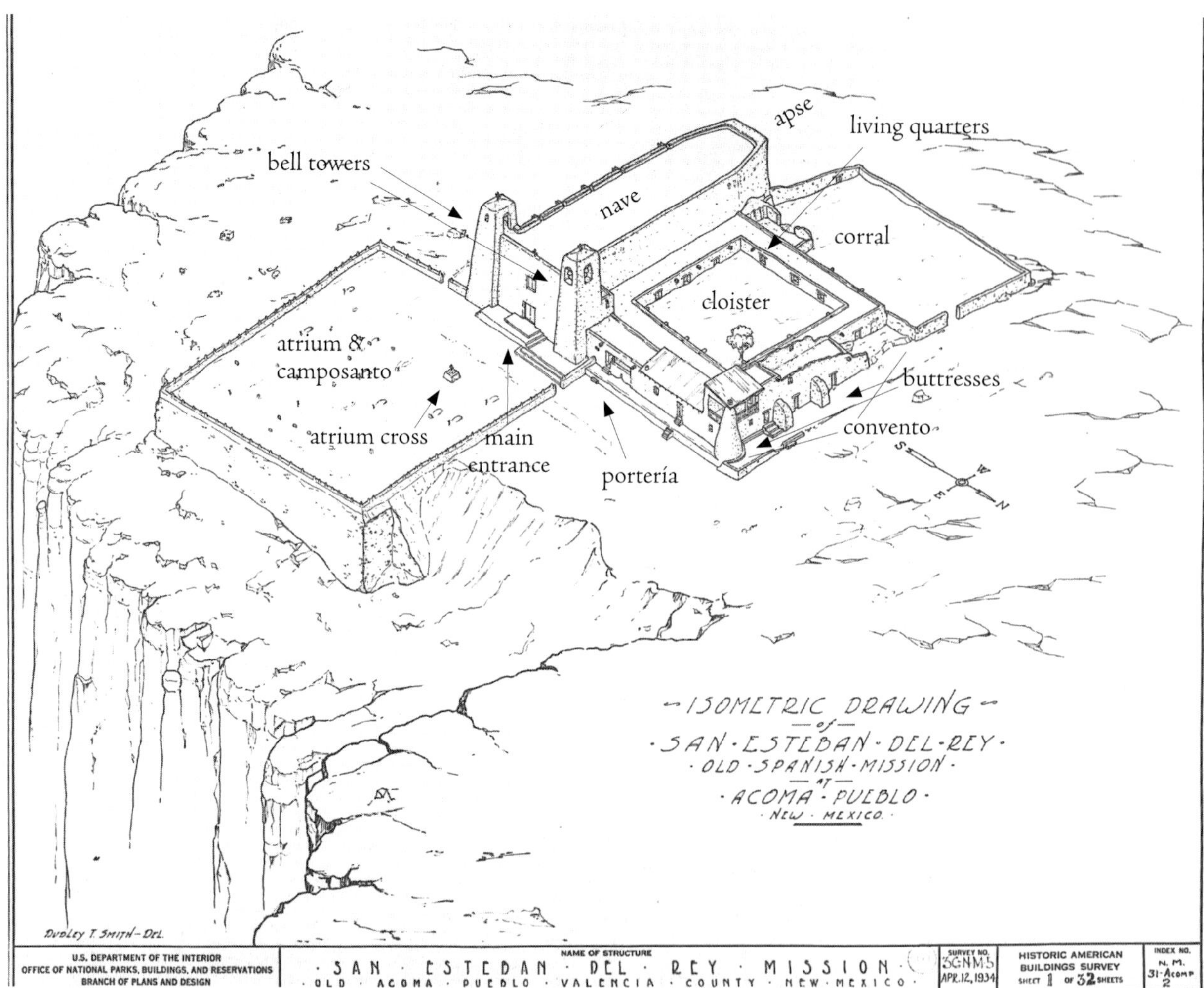

a. *3.17. Church complex, Mission San Esteban de Ácoma, New Mexico, 1934: a. overview; b. (facing page) plan. (Courtesy of Historic American Building Survey)*

structures, such as the Jesuit *colegio* (academy or college) in Durango (Durango).[26] The few remaining examples are simple affairs, sometimes nothing more than a rod set in an outer wall; most sundials have disappeared with the restorations or replasterings of the past three centuries.

The absence of any extant structure that could be classified as a capilla posa and of any specific references to them in colonial accounts strongly suggests that capillas posas were not used in northern New Spain, although open chapels may have been used to some degree.[27] Kubler describes certain components in a few New Mexican mission churches that may have served for the saying of Mass before crowds standing in the atrio, and Domínguez's description of the rooms attached to the portería at Nambé adds credence to this idea.[28] Ellis also suggests that the roofed balcony over the main entrance of the parochial church of Santa Fe (New Mexico)—now part of the Cathedral of Santa Fe—and overlooking the atrio and cemetery, still intact in 1817 but not mentioned in the Domínguez report of 1776, may have served as part of an open chapel.[29] Many New Mexican churches shared this feature (see figure 3.19a–b). The east façade of San Juan Capistrano in San Antonio (Texas; figure 3.20) may also have been modified to serve as an open chapel.[30] Unfortunately, no contemporaneous description of religious services supports these hypotheses.

Although McAndrew states that "neither European nor native tradition offered any suitable model for the forms of the open chapel," more recently Spanish historians have proposed Andalusian antecedents for both the

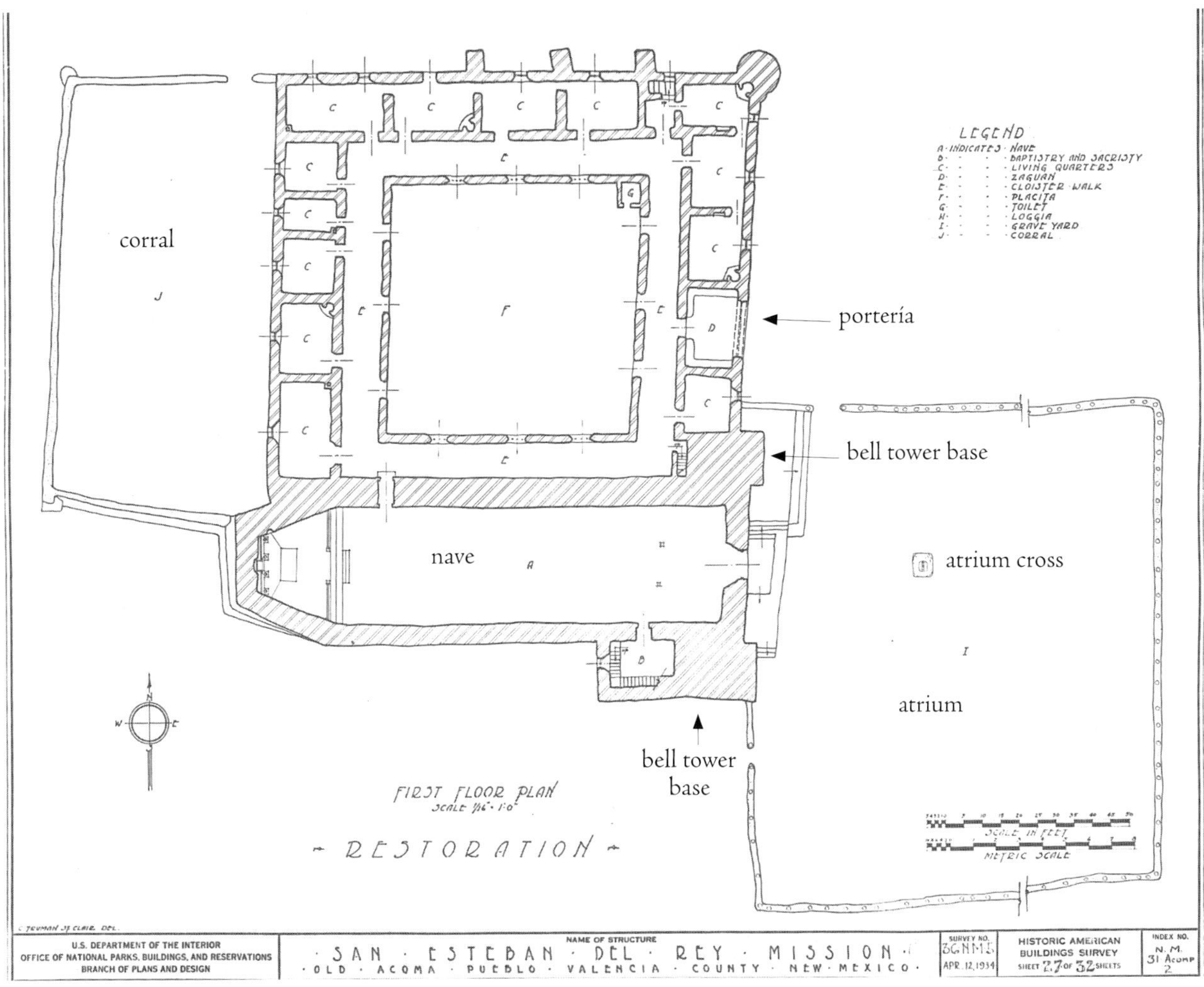

b.

open chapels (capillas abiertas) and the capillas posas, in particular, the Convento Casa Grande de San Francisco (Sevilla), where, interestingly enough, early Franciscan friars bound for the New World were housed and outfitted prior to embarking.[31] The presumption is thus that these friars would have had ample opportunity to experience the convenience of certain arrangements and later apply them in the New World. Whereas open chapels have been considered the most original liturgical contribution made by the Church in the New World, Morales sees the Andalusian antecedents of this feature in a side doorway (constructed in 1539) to the Plaza of San Francisco at the Convento Casa Grande de San Francisco, Sevilla, where an altar could have been erected and Mass said, and in a balcony of the early-sixteenth-century Franciscan convent of Valladolid, which overlooked the plaza and from which Mass was said on festival days.[32]

As possible Spanish antecedents for the capillas posas of New Spain's sixteenth-century convento churches, Castillo Utrilla has proposed the courtyard chapels of the Convento Casa Grande de San Francisco (demolished in the mid-nineteenth century)— apparently prominent features, although the exact locations of the two chapels that opened onto the atrio have not been determined.[33]

Nuns' Churches

Nuns' churches are immediately recognizable by the placement of the main portals. Because the women were cloistered and not to be seen by the public during services,

3.18. *Atrio cross, Santa Rosa de Lima de Cusihuiriáchic, Chihuahua, 1991.*

3.19. New Mexican churches, ca. 1920: a. San Buenaventura de Cochití (private collection); b. San Felipe Apóstol, San Felipe Pueblo. (Fred Harvey Company postcard, private collection)

3.20. East façade, San Juan Capistrano, San Antonio, Texas, 1990.

they occupied parts of the church behind obscuring and defending screens. Because all ceremonies in the church were open to the public, a compromise was reached to provide access to the public and seclusion for the nuns. To accommodate both, the church's central axis was turned parallel to the street and two portals placed next to each other within identical frontispieces on the outside of the nave's wall. The portal closer to the main altar served to admit the ordinary public, while the one closer to the rear of the church, where the nuns were allowed to peer through heavily grilled or screened openings, admitted the women's friends and families.

Most nuns' churches in viceregal Mexico were founded in the central part of the country, chiefly in Mexico City. From these, others were established in the cities of Puebla, Oaxaca, Guadalajara, Querétaro, Morelia, Atlixco, San Juan de los Lagos, Irapuato, and Aguascalientes, to name a few sites. Although there were eight different orders of nuns in New Spain and a number of subdivisions (some with a number of different convents), the Franciscans, Conceptionists, Dominicans, and Carmelites were the most assertive in founding convents outside Mexico City.

Despite efforts over almost two hundred years to officially establish convents for women in northern New Spain, and despite apparently genuine interest among most of the ecclesiastical community in the diocese, there was never royal support or consent. The reason always given was lack of financial support within the community. The only completed nuns' church in New Spain, Santa Ana in Durango city, was built around 1780 for Capuchin nuns. When funding for a convent at the same location failed to materialize, the church was eventually converted to parochial use (figure 3.21).

3.21. *East façade of a nuns' church, Santa Ana, Durango, Durango, 2000.*

As early as 1635, a nuns' church and convento was proposed for Durango, primarily for the education of daughters of the miners of Parral. A girls' school under religious direction was finally established in 1802, but it was not until 1853 that northern New Spain received its first convent, founded in Durango by the Barefoot Carmelites.[34] Under the direction of the dynamic and somewhat erratic archbishop of Linares, Andrés Ambrosio de Llanos y Valdés, a convent for Capuchin nuns was begun in Monterrey (Nuevo Léon) sometime after 1792, only to be abandoned before completion, along with other ambitious projects.[35]

Oratories

"Oratory" refers to a specific building or section of a building set aside for divine worship, intended primarily to serve a school, an individual, or a family, rather than the general public; for example, a small chapel in a private house or within a larger church. While "chapel" (capilla) can also refer to an oratory, it is used chiefly to designate either a partially enclosed portion of a church opposite the baptistery, such as the Capilla del Cristo de Mapimí (figure 3.22) or a small building with an altar to one side of the church, such as the Capilla de Santa Rosa de Lima, the small attached chapel to the left of the east entrance (figure 3.23), both in the Cathedral of Chihuahua (see also figure 3.9). Chapels were erected for masses or for devotions particular to a religious order or individual figure. "Oratory" and "chapel" describe the function of an area—whether attached or detached—rather than its structure or relative location.

3.22. La Capilla del Cristo de Mapimí, Catedral de Chihuahua, 1991. The small paintings of the Virgin Mary and Saint John the Evangelist in combination with the crucifix convert the entire retablo into a representation of the Crucifixion.

3.23. La Capilla de Santa Rosa de Lima (left), Catedral de Chihuahua, ca. 1940. (Photographer unknown)

3.24. Mortuary chapel (left), San Francisco Xavier del Bac, Tucson, Arizona, early twentieth century. Cast concrete balconies appear to have been recently installed upon preexisting wooden zapatas. (Postcard, private collection, photographer unknown)

Cemetery

A *camposanto* (literally "holy field") is a cemetery or burial ground outside the church proper and usually associated with every mission and diocesan church prior to the mid-nineteenth century (see figure 3.17a–b). Burials inside churches were reserved for congregants receiving special honor, as befitted their rank or participation in the church's affairs. The more expensive locations were close to the main altar, the cheaper ones under the choir loft. Burial locations outside were also strategic, the most desirable being those closest to the church.[36] After 1789, by the Spanish king's command, cemeteries were to be located outside the settlement because the practice of burying the dead in churches or nearby was believed to cause epidemics. However, burials in and near churches continued for years.[37] Mortuary chapels, where the body lay in state before burial, and *osarios* (charnel houses or putrefaction chambers), where the body was allowed to decompose so that the bones might later be buried in a much smaller area (thereby permitting the walled cemeteries to accommodate the remains of many), were features of some missions and churches. Surviving examples of mortuary chapels are at San Xavier near Tucson (Arizona; figure 3.24) and San Luis Rey in Oceanside (California; see figure 3.3). The silo-shaped or circular structure behind San José de Tumacácori (Arizona) may also have served as a charnel house (figure 3.25). The Cathedral of Chihuahua contains an architectural element behind the east tower between the exterior wall of the church and the staircase to the tower, referred to as the *pozo de ánimas* (well of souls), which likely served the same purpose. No longer in use, this narrow space which rises above the nave, ventilated by a series of small windows and surmounted by two pinnacles under which souls in Purgatory are seen in prayerful attitudes, was originally accessible by a staircase, which has been removed (figure 3.26).

No matter how many or how few of these features a church complex included, it is important to remember that, just as it had in Europe from the earliest era of Christianity, the church complex in New Spain did not function strictly as a religious center. Many times it accommodated temporal activities. Extra grain was stored and distributed there; festivities were held; dances, games, and sports took place in the atrio or churchyard; and because the church

3.25. Possible charnel house, San José de Tumacácori, Arizona, 2002.

was usually the best-constructed building (sometimes out of stone or brick) in a settlement or town, it served as a fortress and refuge from marauding Indians and bandits. These temporal functions played a definite role in the choice and arrangement of the materials that went into constructing the complex.

Church Sites

When a site was selected for a new settlement, the church would inevitably occupy the most strategic (and sometimes also most defensible) position for greatest emotional impact and accessibility.[38] The advantages of beginning in a new location are obvious from the standpoint of town planning and defense. A plaza was always included in the schema and, in theory at least, depending on the terrain, streets were laid out on a grid.[39] Homes and shops would ring the plaza, and the lives of most people would center around this neighborhood. Governmental buildings in one-plaza towns were regularly built off the same open space. Population and resources, as always, determined the size of these structures. The church was always situated with its principal façade facing the plaza, so that it could be seen from all sides and venerated.[40]

The placement of a church on the foundations of a deliberately destroyed native religious structure served both practical and profoundly psychological ends: it encouraged continuity of worship at the now-Christianized sacred site, and it supported the native converts in their new Faith by replacing the signs and symbols of paganism with those of Christianity. Superimposition, as practiced by the Catholic Church since the sixth century, consisted of placing a Christian object of ritualistic impor-

3.26. *Pozo de ánimas (upper right), east façade of the Catedral de Chihuahua, 2000.*

tance—an altar, a cross, or even an entire church—on the site of the destroyed corresponding pagan object it was intended to replace. This "tabula rasa" policy was stringently observed in New Spain, although there were few examples of large, permanent Indian settlements with ceremonial centers in northern New Spain when the Spanish arrived. Where they did occur, in northern New Mexico and Arizona, the seventeenth-century Christian churches were deliberately constructed over kivas of the Pueblo Indians.

CHAPTER 4

BUILDERS, MATERIALS, AND TECHNIQUES

All these [craftsmen] trust to their hands, and everyone is wise in his work. Without these cannot a city be inhabited.

—ECCLESIASTICUS 38:31–32

BUILDERS

It is only appropriate to focus our attention first of all on the men and women who designed, prepared the materials for, built, decorated, and furnished the churches of northern New Spain—or who supported those who did. The oft-repeated answer to "Who built the churches in northern New Spain?" is "The priests." This notion has been given credence by early mission documents.[1] Indeed, in isolated areas among nonsedentary natives, and especially in New Mexico from the early seventeenth to the early nineteenth centuries, the friar may have been the only individual who understood even the rudiments of constructing a permanent church. In Jesuit Baja California, missionary Miguel del Barco is credited with building, from 1744 to 1758, the magnificent stone church San Francisco de Vigge-Biaundó (see figure 2.9); and missionary Francisco Escalante, with building the stone church Santa Rosalía de Palermo de Mulegé (completed in 1766, see figure 6.24). Thus, by default in many cases, the priest became the "architect." Priests were certainly literate and educated, and if they had prepared for their assignment to an unsettled area, they may have even taken steps to accumulate knowledge concerning design, construction techniques, proportions, and materials, perhaps taking advantage of the widely available translations of Alberti and Vitruvius, as well as other architectural treatises (consider, too, the medieval tradition of monks as architects).[2]

What is more likely, however, is that only someone formally trained in architectural theory would have had the understanding of mathematics, geometry, and engineering necessary to design and build any but the most rudimentary of church structures. For the overwhelming majority of extant churches in northern New Spain, especially those with vaulted ceilings, the thickness of the bearing walls had to be carefully computed with respect to the span of volumes, wall height, nature of materials, windows, and door openings, and the load strength for rafters, arches, and beams carefully taken into account. Indeed, both documentary and archaeological evidence fully supports the conclusion that new, architecturally more sophisticated structures were built to replace the small, deteriorated, or impermanently constructed original buildings.[3]

Although little is known about the mostly anonymous individuals who designed and built the churches of northern New Spain, archival records give names of architects, master masons, carpenters, and other skilled craftsmen for monumental works in important urban centers, especially those associated with mineral wealth, such as Chihuahua or Durango.[4] Besides these, numerous scattered references support the thesis that sophisticated systems of architecture and material preparation were both sought and used in other parts of northern New Spain. Documents from the Pimería Alta speak also of the need for specific engineering skills relating to the design and construction of a church in southern Sonora, while census reports from farther north include "Spaniards" (probably imported craftsmen) at mission sites during times of construction.[5]

In 1757, it was noted that major works in Nuevo Santander had been undertaken by unnamed "albañiles" or "personas inteligentes"; the very next year, construction specialists were imported from Mexico City and Querétaro into that province to build Franciscan missions.[6] Franciscan inventories and histories of the San Antonio missions are peppered with references to master masons, professional craftsmen, and architects.[7] In Baja California, work on a Jesuit mission was stopped because of the lack of satisfactory skilled craftsmen, and later in Alta California, master stonemasons were imported from central New Spain in 1796 for the construction of the Franciscan missions.[8]

Important throughout northern New Spain were masons (*albañiles*) and master masons (*alarifes*). Besides knowing how to work with rocks, bricks, and mortar, master masons were also expected to be able to function as contractors or project managers (*maestros de obras*), architects, and construction supervisors; their training included principles of geometry and algebra as well as knowledge of materials and techniques. The alarife was expected to understand both masonry and architecture, whereas the albañil was not. To achieve the rank of alarife, an applicant was expected to be knowledgeable about all types of buildings and parts of buildings, their construction and theory, including various types of arches and rafters, and wall thickness and height in relationship to different types of materials and number of stories. When serving as contractor or project manager, the alarife was responsible for the concept of the building: its proportions, function, and materials. The terms albañil, *arquitecto, cantero* (stonecutter), and alarife were often used interchangeably until the middle of the eighteenth century, when they were formally defined: a cantero was understood to be in charge of stone working and an albañil of laying stones or bricks, whereas an alarife or arquitecto was understood to draw up plans and direct works.[9]

A crucial factor governing artisan behavior and economics in the major cities of central and southern New Spain were the guilds (*gremios*) and lay brotherhoods (cofradías).[10] A powerful institution in Spain and Portugal, the guild system was imported to their colonies in the Americas; within the first three decades after the Conquest of New Spain, carpenters, sculptors, painters, gilders, instrument makers, and silk makers had formed guilds. While there is no conclusive proof that painting, sculpture, silversmithing, the production of textiles, or the building of religious structures was under the formal control of the guilds outside important urban centers such as Mexico City, Guadalajara, Querétaro, Oaxaca, and Puebla, the artisanal tradition fostered by the guilds is clearly present in the apprenticeship training systems for various crafts in the smaller cities and settlements of northern New Spain. Moreover, many products and services provided to northern New Spain can be traced to cities where the guilds held sway and thus brought with them the guilds' clear influence by setting standards to emulate. Indeed, it is more than likely that some individuals working in northern New Spain received their training within the traditional guild framework, fulfilling the requirements of their ranks before moving up north. References to craftsmen as *maestros* or *oficiales* in the censuses and contracts of northern New Spain can safely be presumed to reflect the skills and training of these craftsmen and their having met the requirements to receive these titles, within or without the guild system.

In addition to their principal purpose (training members and protecting jobs), guilds also set and maintained the standards for recruitment, training, wages, and hours of apprentices and workers.[11] Their elected officers inspected shops to ensure compliance with guild standards and to mediate in case of disputes between members. An extremely conservative system, guilds became dedicated to preserving inherited ranks, techniques, and standards.

Early proscriptions against Indian participation in the painting and sculpting of religious imagery were rooted in the belief that they were likely to create something heretical. From the earliest years, however, Indians were employed as sculptors, painters, carpenters, and so on, and, in the seventeenth and eighteenth centuries, were gradually included in the rank of master. Blacks, mulattos, and slaves, also denied admittance to the master rank in the sixteenth and early seventeenth centuries, nevertheless functioned as skilled journeymen.

In the seventeenth and eighteenth centuries, there were some fifty active guilds in New Spain, the majority founded in the sixteenth century.[12] By the end of the eighteenth century, however, the guild system had deteriorated completely, partly because of corruption, partly because of the guilds' inability to adapt, but mostly because, with an expanded market and economy, they had simply outlived their usefulness. The system was finally abolished by the Convention of Cádiz in 1820.

Guilds had three established ranks: apprentices (*aprendizes*), journeymen (oficiales), and masters (maestros). Only masters could own shops and sell directly to the public. Only they could become members of a guild, vote, and approve additions to their ranks. Individuals could and did practice more than one specialty within their craft (usually related, like painting garments and painting flesh tones for polychrome statuary), but were required to undergo thorough training and subsequent examination in each specialty.

The apprentice lived in his master's household, where he learned the skills as well as the social and religious aspects of his craft. After training from two to six years, he became a journeyman, receiving a salary but remaining under the supervision of the master. A few wealthy masters effectively limited entry to the rank of master to members of their own families and close friends. Not having enough capital to become established as a master posed a serious obstacle: a journeyman had to pay for his examination by masters in the guild; on attaining the rank of master, he had to buy his tools and materials and to rent or buy his shop. Because masters were not allowed to work as journeymen, from the seventeenth century to the end of the viceregal era, the ratio of journeymen to masters was disproportionately high.[13]

The abundance of skilled laborers available among the indigenous populations of central New Spain was not even remotely present in northern New Spain. This dearth required enlisting individuals who had any technical skills, training those who did not, or importing into northern New Spain artisans for masonry, carpentry, blacksmithing, and decorating. Indeed, artisans imported to work on the mission churches of Alta California were expected, as part of their contracts, to pass on their skills and knowledge to native workmen.[14]

Although throughout New Spain women provided food and support services for their menfolk working as builders, in northern New Spain, their contribution went beyond this. Based on what we know about pre-Conquest and postcolonial New Mexico, as well as on certain references by friars and soldiers, women there most likely prepared adobe bricks, carried these to the walls of churches being built, and possibly even put the bricks into place; moreover, they engaged in the mud plastering or replastering of walls made from such bricks.[15] And in Alta California, women were known to haul sand and straw used in the manufacture of roofing tiles for the mission churches.[16] From pre-Conquest times, Indian women have been actively involved in ceramic and textile production, crafts in which they still excel and which they almost certainly pursued in northern New Spain.[17] In the absence of official recognition, the role of women in decorating and furnishing the religious structures of viceregal Mexico must be largely surmised, although nuns and genteel laywomen are known to have embroidered, fringed, or otherwise embellished ecclesiastical garments and altar cloths. Although, because of the attractive wages, the embroidery trade itself was the exclusive province of men and controlled by male guilds, women of modest means were allowed to dominate, at lower wages, cotton spinning, candy making, dressmaking, and silk thread making, trades at which they could support themselves without having to leave their homes.[18]

Materials

Documents describe Indians and Spaniards preparing shelters, sometimes little more than *enramadas*—crude thatched shelters without walls—for the newly arrived friars and their religious services. In the early years of northern New Spain's colonization, virtually every kind of material, shelter, or indigenous construction technique was used; even a house in one of the pueblos was pressed into service until a permanent church could be erected.[19]

Mud and Clay

Two of the simplest and most available building materials, mud and clay were used extensively throughout northern New Spain. They can be poured, puddled, patted, pounded, or molded into bricks or entire sections of wall. Hardened by firing, they lend themselves to more versatile and durable applications.

[Adobe Bricks] From the Arabic *at-tub* (sun-dried brick), adobe was introduced into Spain by the Moors. It is one of the world's oldest building materials, dating back to around 5,000 BC, when it was used in Crete. To make an adobe brick, a stiff, doughlike mixture of earth (with high clay content), water, and (where available) straw is firmly packed into a rectangular wooden mold. When the mud begins to pull away from its sides, the mold is removed and the block allowed to dry. If the humidity is low enough, the brick is turned on end after a few days to continue drying; after a week, it can be stacked for curing, a process that takes about a month. For ease in handling, adobe bricks are most often made near the building site, provided the soil type is suitable. While sizes vary, the bricks rarely exceed thirty-five pounds, about the heaviest weight a worker can handle unassisted.[20]

[Fired Bricks] Although they require more skill and resources to produce, fired bricks (*ladrillos*) are stronger than sun-dried bricks—and more resistant to erosion. Their smaller size and weight make them more versatile for horizontal, vertical, and especially curved fitting. Ladrillos were used not only for walls and floors but also on roofs between the beams, as in the first mission church of Santa Clara de Asís (dedicated in 1784 and replaced in 1818) and the mission church San Gabriel Arcángel (both California).

In brick making, the molded wet clay bricks, sometimes cut or specially shaped for decorative purposes

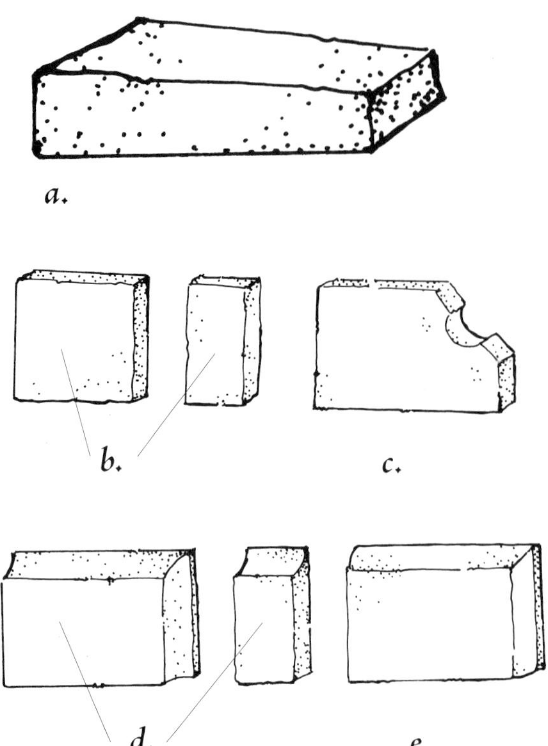

4.1. Molded bricks types used for the reconstruction of Mission La Purísima Concepción, Lompoc, California: a. "key" tile, b. full and half floor tiles, c. column tile, d. cove tiles, e. corner tile.

(figure 4.1), were allowed to dry in the sun, then fired near or at the construction site in a kiln not unlike those still used in rural areas of Mexico today (figure 4.2). The sun-dried bricks and fuel were arranged in layers to form a tower, with ample spaces left for draft, and covered with old bricks and earth. The fuel was then set on fire, the kiln allowed to burn itself out, and the bricks removed when cool. Depending on the skill of loading, the initial dryness of the bricks, and the consistency of heat, the bricks were more or less the same temper from center to sides of the brick tower, with those longest exposed to the heat being the hardest.

[Tiles] To make roofing tiles (*tejas de barro*), sometimes called gutter tiles because of their semicylindrical shape, stiff clay was rolled flat and pressed between two molds (*moldes de teja*) or paddled over a form before firing (figure 4.3).[21] Apart from the missions of Alta California, most of the churches of northern New Spain had untiled roofs; it would seem that the arid climate made tiles unnecessary.

4.2. *Brick kiln near Santa Ana, Sonora, 2001.*

They are found, however, set in mortar on the pitched roof of Nuestra Señora del Pilar y Santiago de Cocóspera (Sonora), and may once have graced a pitched roof on San Miguel Arcángel de Moctezuma (also Sonora), both built under Jesuit supervision.

Unglazed tiles (*pisos de barro*), made in molds and fired, were used as a flooring material, even though they wore down very quickly. The transept of the mission church San Juan Capistrano (California; finished in 1803), for example, was floored with diamond-shaped unglazed tiles.

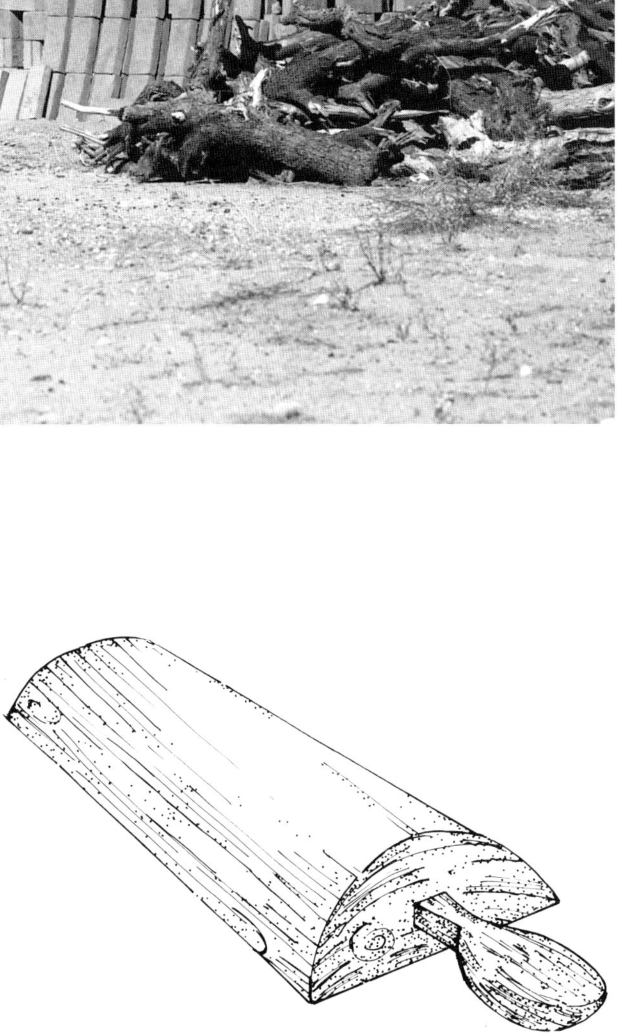

4.3. *"Burrito" roofing tile mold, La Purísima Concepción, Lompoc, California.*

Loza blanca (literally, white pottery) and *azulejos* (glazed tiles; from the Arabic *az-zulai* for faience ornamental tile), brought to Spain by its Moorish invaders and produced there as early as the twelfth century, were introduced into New Spain in the sixteenth century. Loza blanca pottery is often referred to as *talavera* or *majolica* (*maiolica*), from the areas in Spain where it was produced or distributed, Talavera de la Reina and Majorca. It is a distinctly Hispanic type of ceramic: a soft, compact clay is given a tin coating that, when fired, forms a dense, opaque white, hard glaze. Colors are usually applied over the tin coating before the final firing. Loza blanca was produced for a short time in Mexico City, with Puebla becoming the principal producer from the seventeenth century on. In surprising decorative touches, talavera plates and cups were embedded in the outside apse wall of San José de Copala (Sinaloa); and Chinese trade plates embedded in the outside walls of the bell tower of Nuestra Señora de la Asunción del Real de los Álamos (Sonora; figure 4.4a–b).[22]

Although azulejos were by no means common in northern New Spain, using a Moorish technique called *alicatado* (glazed tile veneer), artisans completely tiled the outside of the dome of Nuestra Señora del Rosario in Charcas (San Luis Potosí) with crowned monograms of Mary, also in tile, as accents; they spangled the outside dome of the Cathedral of Durango (Durango) with tiles, setting tile crosses within each segment as well as the entire baptistry dome. The tile dado tradition, which flourished throughout central New Spain, is reflected in the trompe l'oeil decorations of northern mission churches such as San Xavier del Bac in Tucson (Arizona; figure 4.5).[23] The dado on many nave (and other) walls was painted to about chest height in imitation of the azulejo dados found in Spain and central New Spain, which served to protect the walls from grime or damage. Such decoration, whether tiled or painted, also served to break up the wall space with a different color and texture, creating visual interest and a greater sense of space and depth.

Worked Wood

Wood was given the greatest variety of treatments and served more functions, including some ordinarily served by metal, than any other material used in northern New Spain. It was generally readily available, sometimes in abundance, easier to work than other, scarcer materials, and durable, thus can be seen at every site.

Used for its intrinsic beauty and strength, wood could be hewn, sawed, smoothed, gouged, chipped, carved, inlaid, bent, painted, and covered in gold or silver leaf. It could be finished to look like stone, metal, or leather. Wooden pintles could replace metal hinges; wooden pegs and tenons, nails. Carved, gessoed, and gilded, it resembled gold repoussé. Able to withstand significantly greater tensile stresses than masonry or concrete, and technically far easier to manipulate than either, wood was ideal for roofs. Cedar, cypress, cottonwood, aspen, pine, fir, mesquite, redwood, and oak (all native to northern New Spain), as well as ebony and mahogany (which had to be imported), were used for furniture, beams, palisades, floors, paneling, window and door frames, railings and glazing bars for glass, balustrades, doors and shutters, as well as in religious objects such as statues, paintings, candleholders, crosses, and missal stands. Because there were few sawmills from the sixteenth to eighteenth centuries, planks of wood had to be prepared by ax, adze, or hand-pulled saws, with the distinctive marks left on the planks from each of these tools. Wood exposed to the elements was painted, varnished, or otherwise sealed. (For a sample of tools commonly used by colonial carpenters and masons, see figure 4.6; for other uses of wood, see chapter 7: "Furnishings.")

Other Plant Materials

Used by indigenous peoples to build semipermanent dwellings or camp shelters, readily and often abundantly available timbers, palm trunks, poles, cactus ribs, stakes, branches, palm fronds, reeds, twigs, and grasses were also used by the early friars to construct the first, rudimentary church buildings in northern New Spain. These materials could be driven into the ground, woven, wedged, or tied together, plaited and daubed, stacked, or thatched to make palisades for protective enclosures and to form scaffolding and the walls, ceilings, and roofs of simple structures.

Rocks and Stones

In the absence of machines to lift and tempered tools to cut and shape stone, this most permanent of building materials in northern New Spain was used in sizes workers could manage on their own or with the help of draft animals—and harder varieties, in their natural shapes. The builders of early churches chose rocks and stones over adobe simply for practical reasons—that is, where a suitable supply was close at hand, and water and clay soil were scarce. With the arrival of more sophisticated tools and equipment—and the ability to

a.

b.

4.4. Pottery used as decoration: a. exterior apse wall, San José de Copala, Sinaloa, 2000; b. bell tower, Nuestra Señora de la Asunción del Real de los Álamos, Sonora, 1980.

4.5. Restored trompe l'oeil dado on nave, crossing, and transept walls, San Francisco Xavier del Bac, Tucson, Arizona, 2005. (Photo by Meredith L. Milstead)

cut, finish, dress, and install even massive pieces—aesthetics entered into the decision of whether and how to use rocks and stones.

Puebloan Indians of the Salinas district (New Mexico) built large, multistoried housing complexes out of ledge stone—sandstone or limestone in naturally occurring flat slabs. Lacking iron tools to cut or shape these slabs, the Indians used most pieces as they occurred, breaking larger pieces with stone tools or wedges to achieve manageable sizes. Seventeenth-century Spanish architects in the same area also built with ledge stone, adjusting the thickness of the church walls to accommodate their greater height (figure 4.7).

Volcanic or igneous rock (lava or basalt) was used, as naturally occurring boulders, for foundations and in random rubble walls; or, squared and dressed, for ashlar masonry. The foundation and walls of San José de Comondú (Baja California Sur), for example, are built entirely of *tezontle*, a strong, relatively light, porous volcanic rock.[24]

Alabaster (a translucent, pale to white, fine-grained gypsum or banded variety of calcite) was cut and polished to make baptismal fonts and pulpits, or to replace glass in church windows in northern New Spain. Most notably quarried in the district of Tecali (Puebla), alabaster is referred to in some Mexican documentary sources as *tecali* (from Aztec *tetl*, stone, and *calli*, house) and in others as *yeso*.[25]

Popularly called Mexican onyx (*ónix mexicano*) because of its superficial resemblance to real onyx (a variety of chalcedony), alabaster appears in the extant baptismal fonts of San Francisco de Vigge-Biaundó and San Ignacio de Kadakaaman and (as tecali) in the inventories of other mission churches of Baja California, where it most likely was quarried locally. It was used for pulpits of churches scattered throughout northern New Spain, such as those of Nuestra Señora de Guadalupe in Ojo de Agua and Nuestra Señora del Rosario in Charcas (both San Luis Potosí; figures 4.8 and 4.9); and as glazing (*transparencias*) in the churches of Baja California, where it conveniently occurred in pieces four to five feet long, a foot and a half wide, and three to four fingers thick.[26]

Minerals

Included here are all mineral building materials, from dense and opaque to lightweight and transparent, excepting only minerals used as rocks and stones or as pigments (see below).

[Lime and Gypsum] When properly mixed, lime plaster (*argamasa*), made from slaked lime, sand, and water, can be applied to stone, brick, adobe, lathing, or wood to create a nearly permanent surface, provided the support remains undisturbed and dry. Dating back to at least 3500 BC, it was used generously and skillfully by the Greeks and Romans for creating carved reliefs.[27] Both before and after the Reconquest, lime plastering was developed to an extraordinary degree throughout the Islamic world, including Moorish Andalucía, where it served as inspiration for New Spain's architects and artisans.

To prepare lime plaster, limestone, chalk, or seashells, usually placed on a grate in a kiln, were thoroughly burned over a wood fire, and their constituent calcium carbonate reduced to calcium oxide or quicklime. The quicklime was then slaked—soaked for several months in water—and dried. The resultant slaked lime (*cal apagada*) could be mixed with a small amount of water and sand to make plaster or mortar or mixed with considerably more water alone to make whitewash (*jalbegue*). Lime plaster can be extremely durable; it can be carved, molded, and burnished, and takes paint well, lending itself to elaborate treatments of walls, altars, ceilings, and façades. Lime mortar was manufactured and used throughout northern New Spain except in New Mexico from the seventeenth century on.[28]

Heated to drive off three-quarters of its water by dehydration, gypsum becomes plaster of paris (*yeso mate*), which hardens quickly when mixed with water. Unlike lime plaster, however, gypsum plaster does not resist erosion, and when used on exposed exteriors, it must be periodically restored. Gypsum plaster and whitewash were used in Nuevo México before 1680.

"Stucco" (*estuco*) today refers to a cement plaster applied to exteriors, although it once referred to a high-quality lime plaster used on interior walls. "Mortar" (*mezcla*) and "cement" (*cemento*), which can be specific mixtures of lime, sand, and water, more often appear in the records of northern New Spain as catchall terms for any substance used to bind stones or bricks together.[29] Where lime mortar was not available, mixtures of other materials such as mud, clay, and charcoal ash were used by the indigenous people and in early church construction.[30]

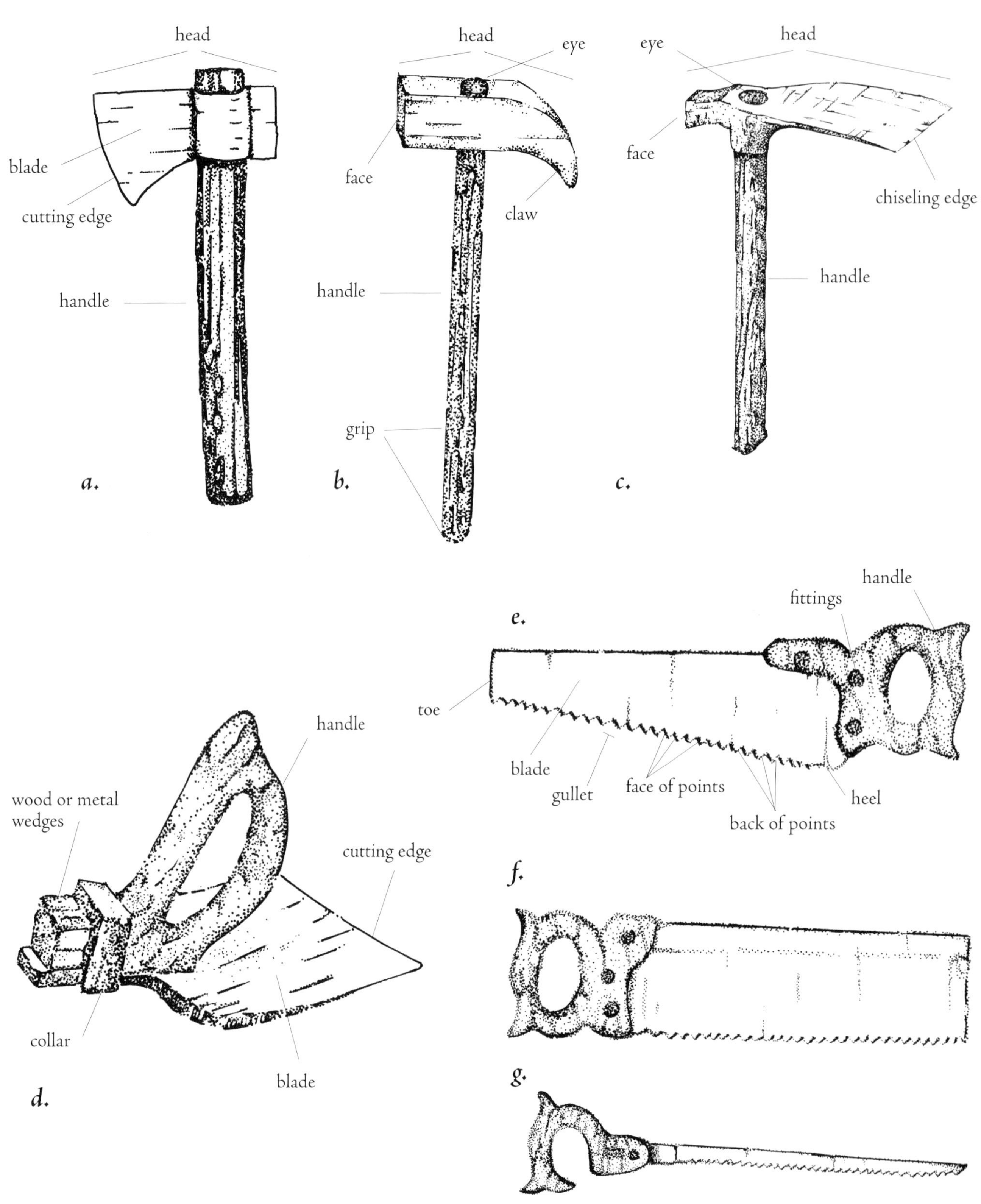

4.6. Carpentry and masonry tools: woodworking tools: a. hatchet, b. hammer, c. adze, d. hand adze e. saw, f. backsaw, g. compass saw

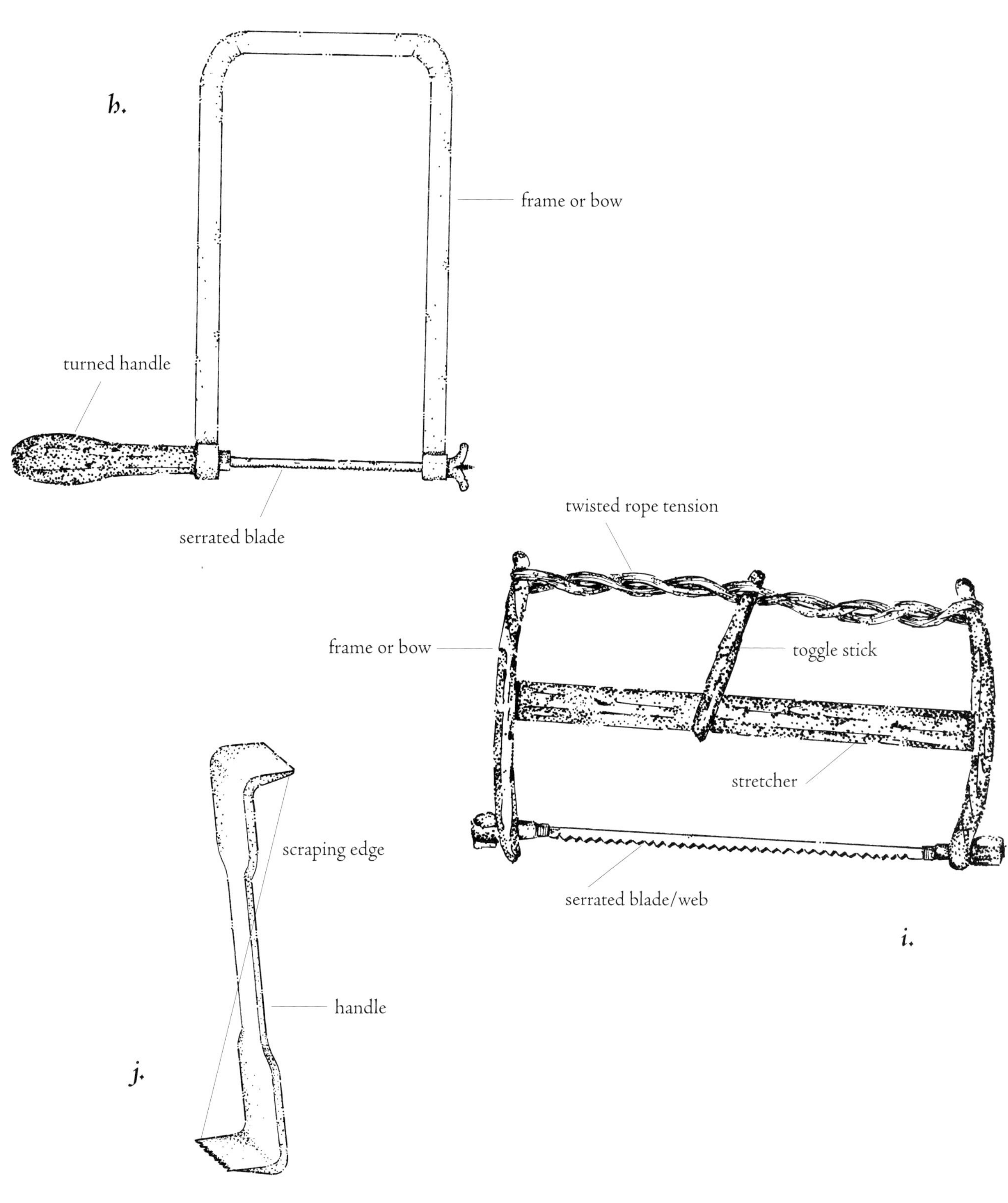

4.6 (continued). Carpentry and masonry tools: woodworking tools: h. scribing/coping saw, i. frame/bow saw, j. scraper

continued on next page

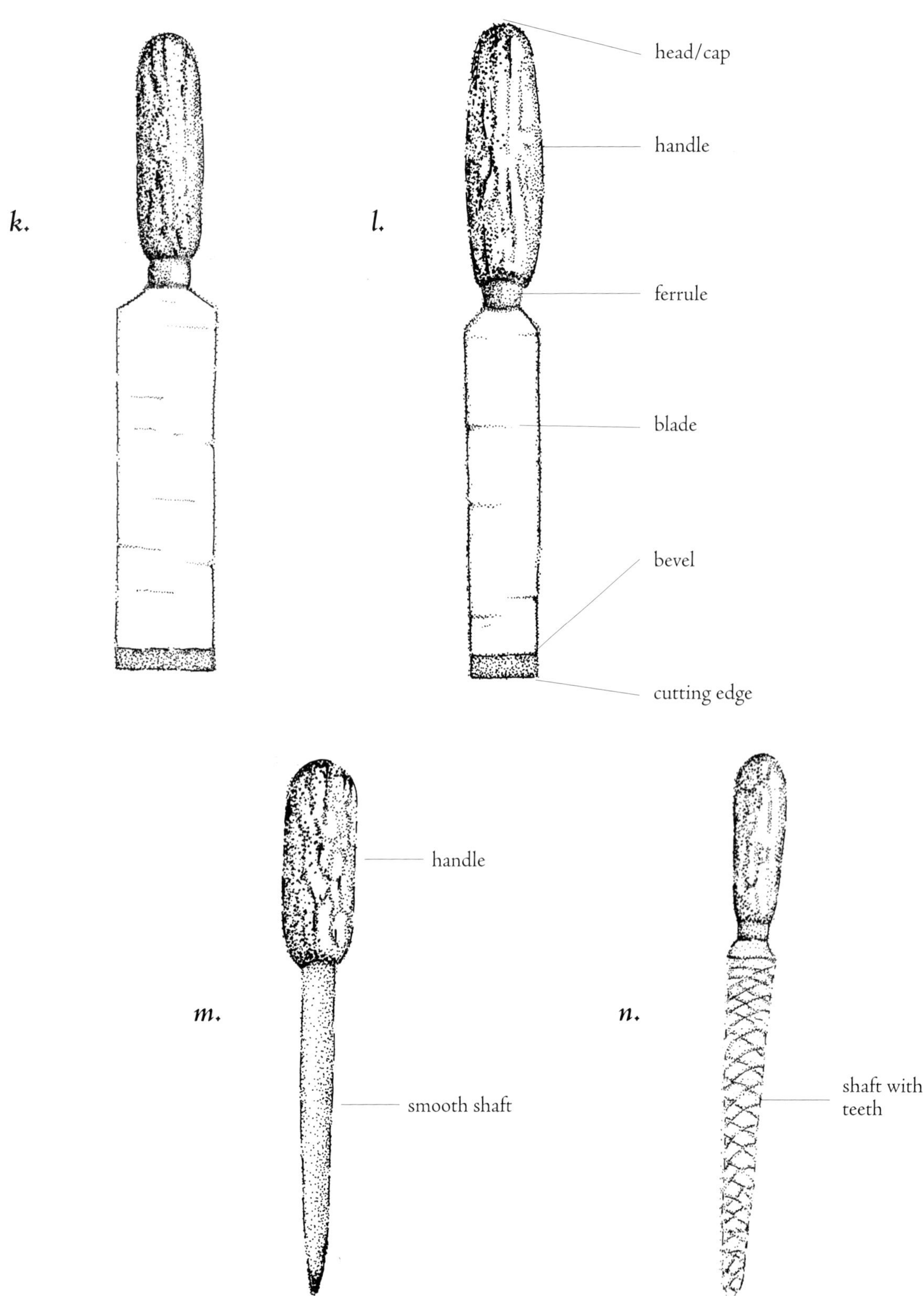

4.6 (continued). Carpentry and masonry tools: woodworking tools: k. wood chisel, l. gouge wood chisel, m. wood punch, n. rasp

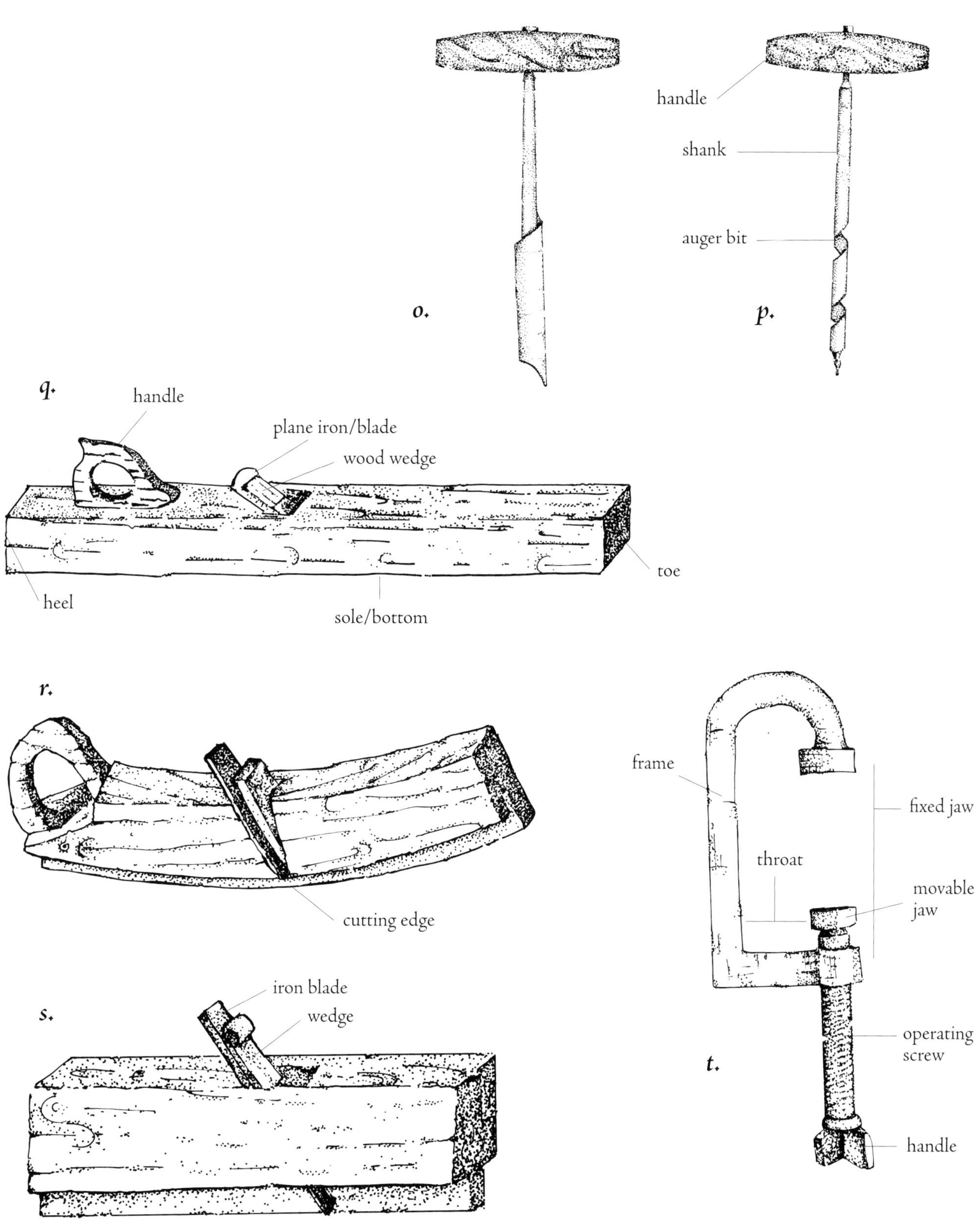

4.6 (continued). Carpentry and masonry tools: woodworking tools: o. auger, p. wood auger/gimlet, q. plane, r. curved molding plane, s. molding plane, t. clamp

continued on next page

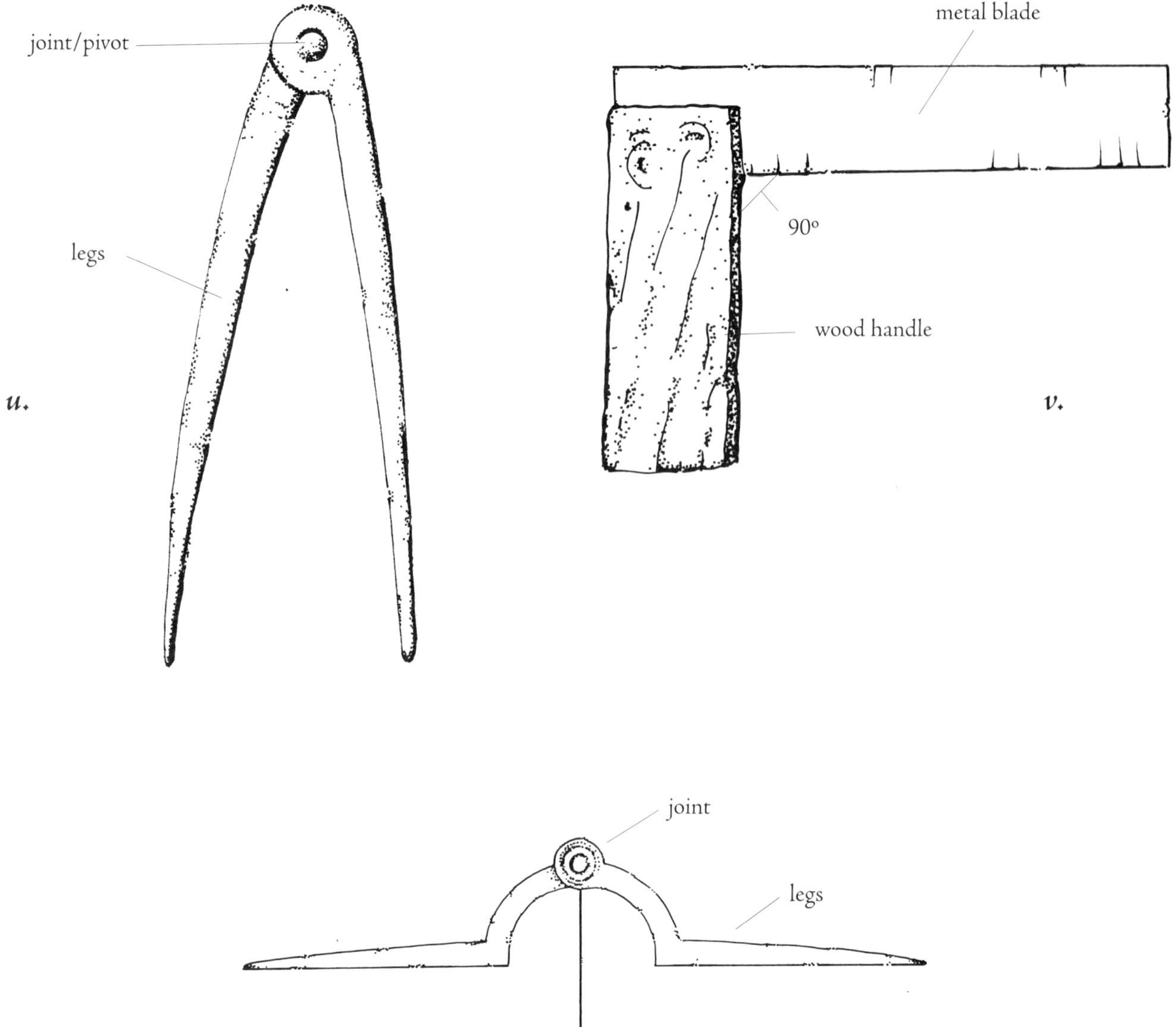

4.6. Tools for measuring: u. compass/divider, v. square, w. level

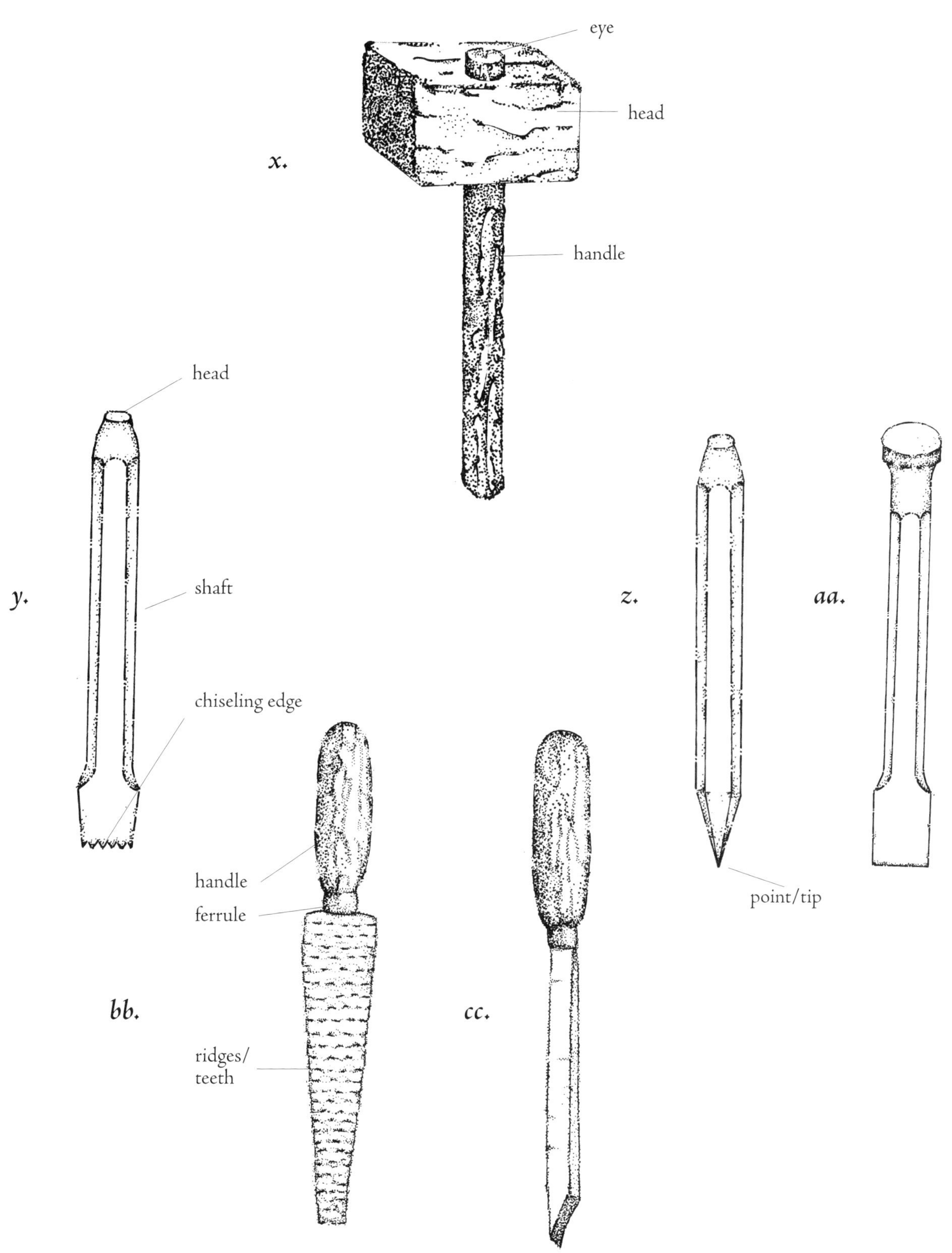

4.6 (continued). Stoneworking implements: x. mallet, y. toothed stone chisel, z. pointed stone chisel, aa. flat stone chisel, bb. file, cc. mortise chisel

continued on next page

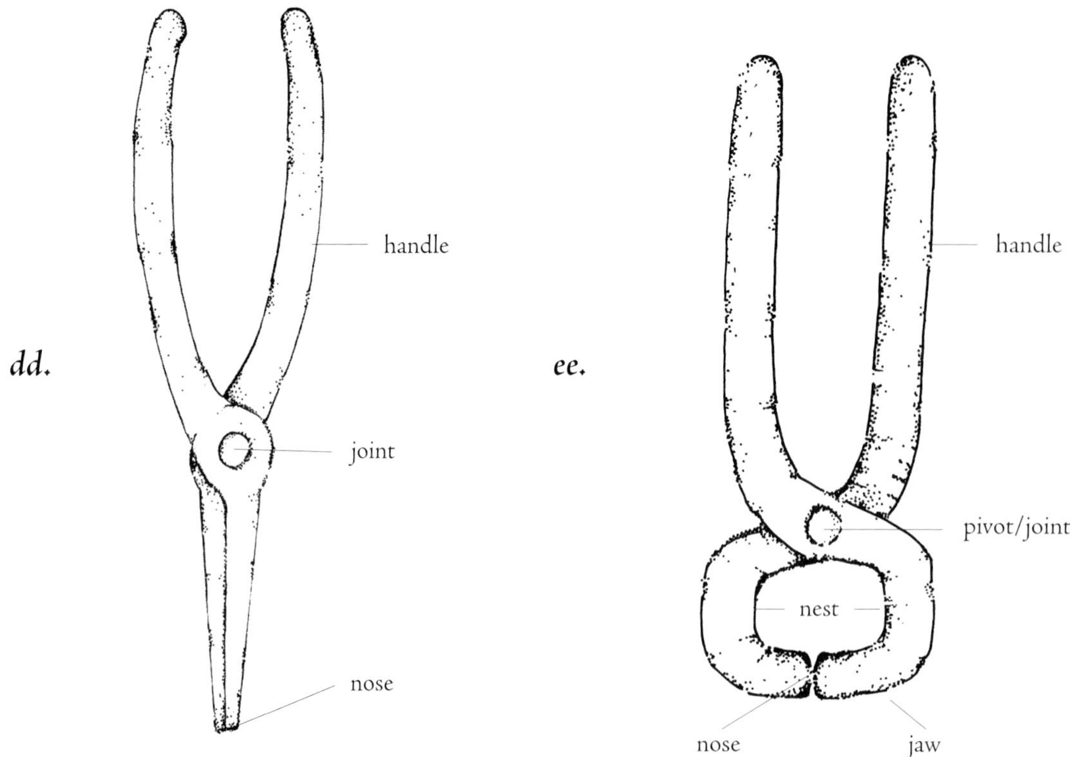

4.6. Miscellaneous tools: dd. pliers, ee. pincers/pliers.

4.7. Detail, San Gregorio de Abó ruin, Salinas National Monument, New Mexico, 2002. Various conservation efforts over the years have stabilized the walls with additional lime mortar between the pieces of rock.

4.8. Pulpit, Nuestra Señora de Guadalupe, Ojo de Agua, San Luis Potosí, 1984, Saint Matthew and Saint Mark, left and right, respectively.

4.9. Pulpit, Nuestra Señora del Rosario de Charcas, San Luis Potosí, 1984, Saint Luke and Saint Mark, left and right, respectively. The use of the rococo-style embellished C-curve helps date the pulpit to sometime in the mid to late eighteenth century.

[Iron] Although the Spaniards knew of many rich iron ore deposits in northern and central New Spain, these were not exploited; the mining of silver preempted all other mining activity. Indeed, the decision not to produce iron locally and the expense of importing iron and manufactured iron goods from Mexico City, Puebla, and San Miguel de Allende were to significantly hamper the agricultural and industrial development of northern New Spain.

A precious commodity throughout the northern frontier, iron appears in church inventories as nails and hardware for doors, balconies, railings, and so on; because of its high cost, other materials were substituted wherever possible. Wooden pegs replaced nails in roofs, doors, and furniture; furniture, doors, and shutters were joined and doweled together. Doors and windows swung on wooden pintles; rawhide or sisal was used for smaller hinges. The hand of local blacksmiths can be seen in the widely varying hardware on doors and methods of hinging, hanging, and fastening them. To provide an enriched surface, the heads of the nails were greatly enlarged, although ornamental nail heads (bosses) forged in geometric or botanical shapes, so common in churches throughout central and southern New Spain, were reserved for rare, extravagant displays in the north. Figure 4.10 shows a variety of hinges and other ironwork used on furniture, doors, windows, and shutters in northern New Spain.[31]

Other often fine examples of the blacksmith's art were the wrought iron crosses (most now replaced) atop many cupolas and pediments in northern New Spain, some quite elaborate and filigree-like, which may also have served as lightning rods (see figure 2.16a).[32] Not uncommonly, a weather vane in the shape of a rooster was incorporated into the cross, as at Nuestra Señora de los Dolores de Pedreceña (Durango) and at Santo Ángel de la Guarda de Satevó, Batopilas (Chihuahua, where the cross is rapidly deteriorating; see **Cock or rooster** entry in chapter 11).[33]

[Selenite and Mica] Found in the mountains of northern New Mexico in pieces as large as 10 × 18 inches, selenite (*espejuela;* a transparent crystalline form of gypsum) and mica served as glazing.[34] For the most part, however, oiled sheepskin parchment, waxed paper, or cloth was used until glass became available. Mica was also used for decorative purposes, embedded in the risers of the altar steps at San Bernardo de Awátovi (Arizona) and in the altars at Nuestra Señora de Navidad de Chilili and San Miguel Arcángel de Tajique (both New Mexico), all seventeenth-century mission churches and now ruins.[35]

Glass

Founded in 1542 in Puebla, by the eighteenth century, New Spain's glass industry produced not only window glass but vessels and decorative pieces deemed superior to any in Spain and comparable to the finest of Venice and France.[36] In the churches of northern New Spain, window glass provided light, especially in domes and along nave walls; it kept out dust, animals, and the elements; and it protected holy objects, paintings, and sculptures in their frames and niches (see "Glass and Mirrors" under "Retablos" in chapter 10). Most notably, Father Eusebio Francisco Kino's mission headquarters of Nuestra Señora de los Dolores de Cósari (Sonora), San Francisco de Vigge-Biaundó (Baja California Sur), San Xavier in Tucson (Arizona), and the Cathedral of Chihuahua (Chihuahua) all had glazed windows.[37]

Leather

Animal skins—cured, scraped thin, or left in their natural state—were used in a variety of ways in building the churches of northern New Spain. Large hides, sometimes stretched on a frame, served as doors or dividers between quarters and as shutters; slung between poles, they were used as handbarrows to haul building materials. Strips of rawhide were used to bind poles and tree limbs together in scaffolding and roofing, or were braided or twisted into ropes. Smaller pieces of heavy, cured leather were used as hinges, while paper-thin parchment sometimes served as a substitute for window glass.

Pigments

Color delights the eye and speaks to the heart. It sets off architectural elements, and makes painting and sculpture realistic. Certain colors have taken on special meanings since humans first learned how to make them from rocks and plants (see **Colors** entry in chapter 11).

In northern New Spain, designs and decorations were painted on façades and walls with pigments prepared from a variety of materials, usually on site.[38] Blacks were produced mostly from carbon, whether as charcoal or bone

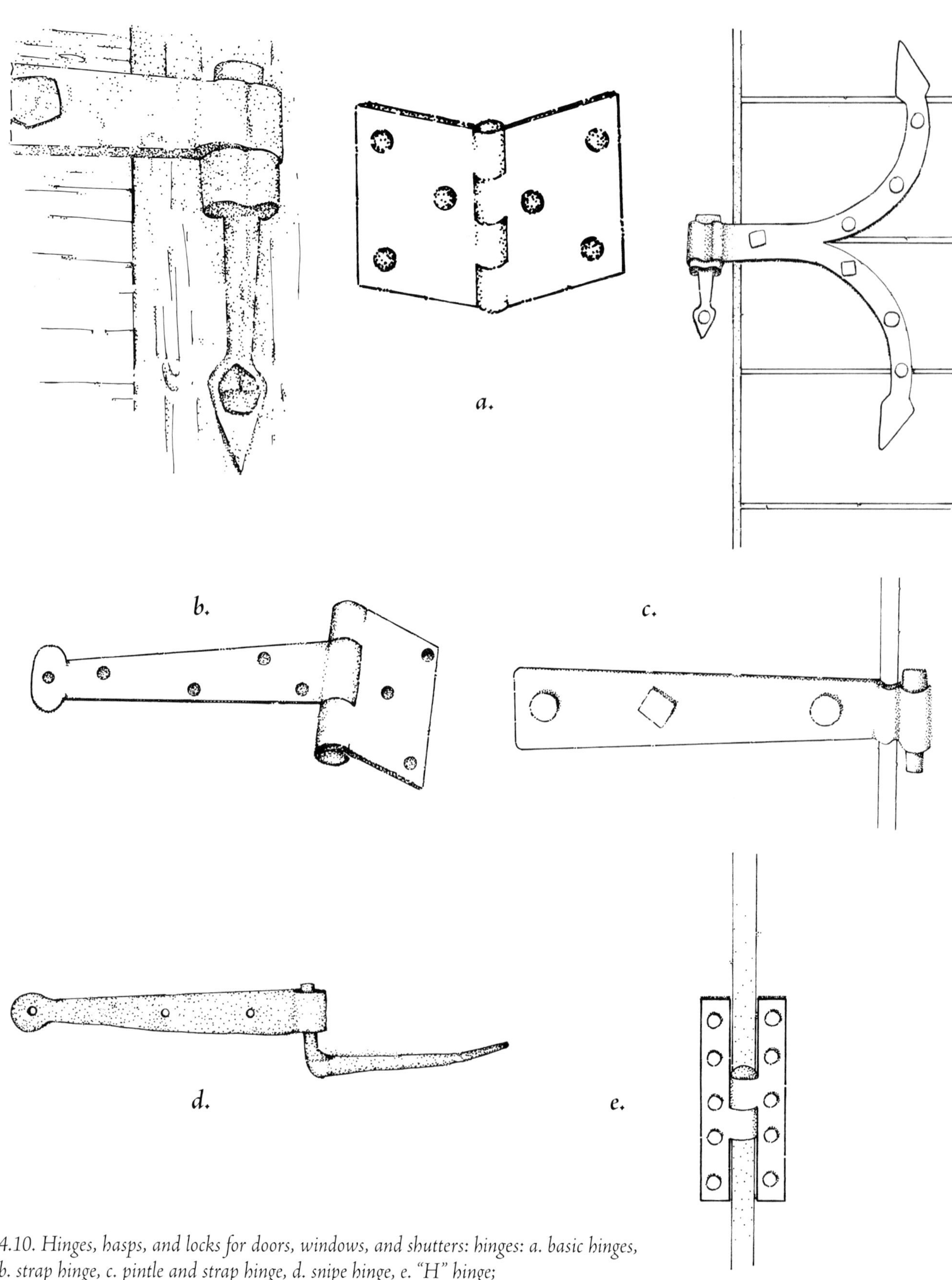

4.10. Hinges, hasps, and locks for doors, windows, and shutters: hinges: a. basic hinges, b. strap hinge, c. pintle and strap hinge, d. snipe hinge, e. "H" hinge;

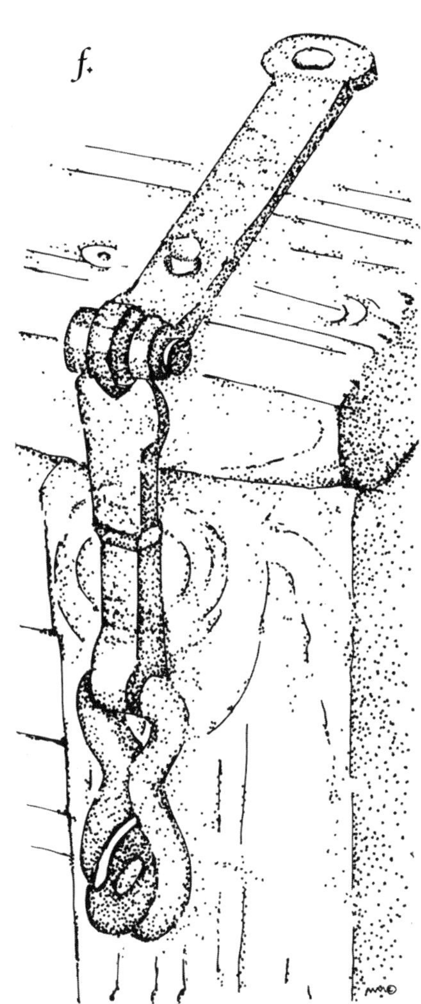

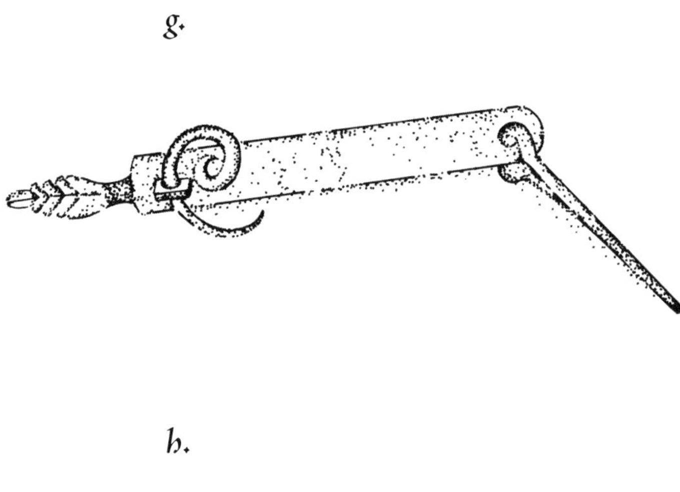

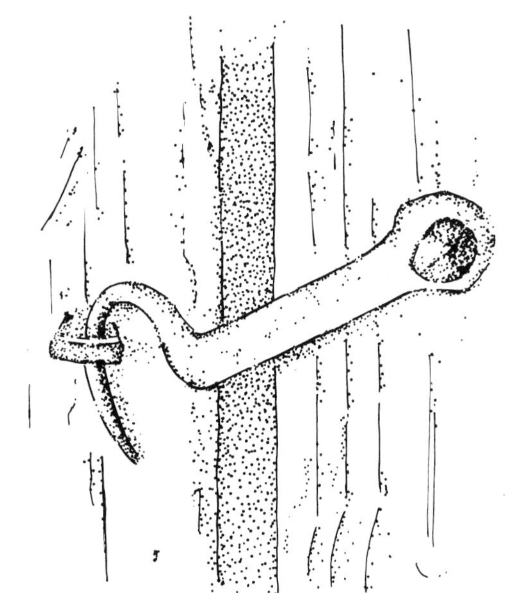

4.10 (continued). hasps: f. chest hasp with link closure, g. hasp and hook, h. hook and eye;

continued on next page

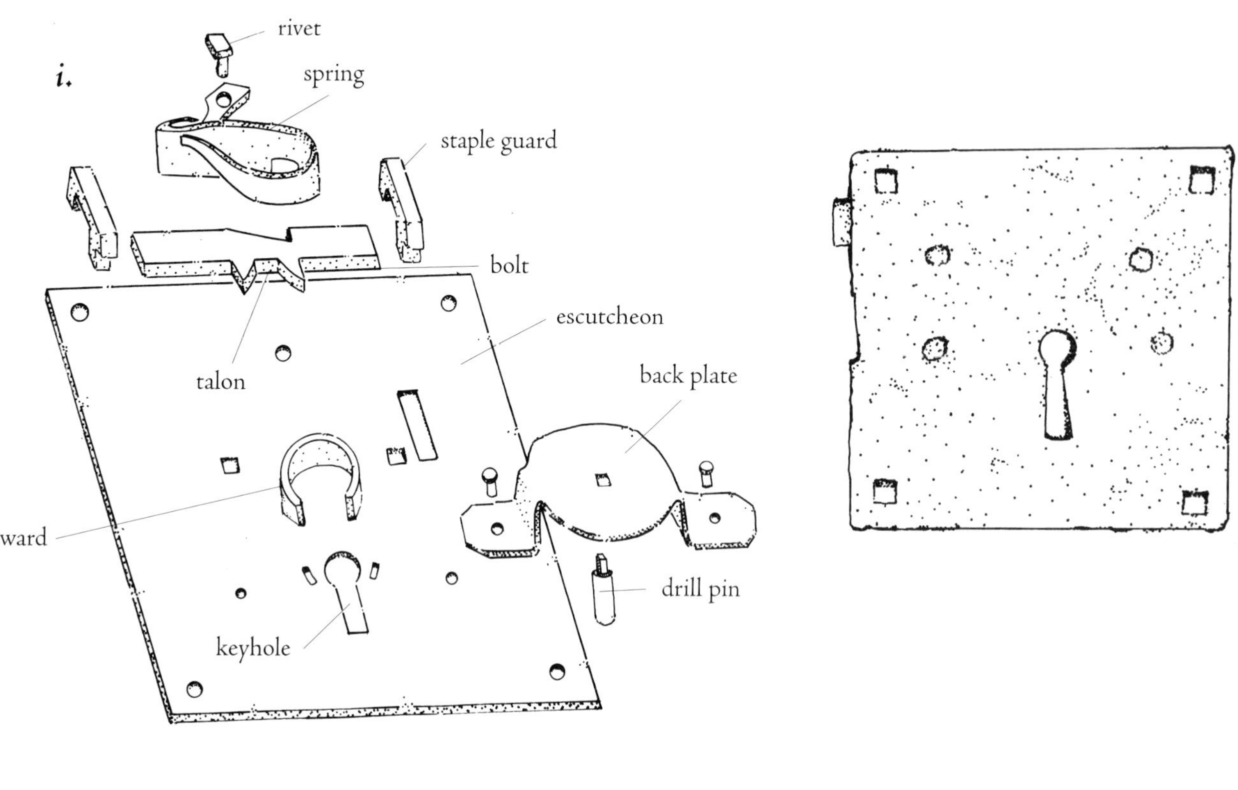

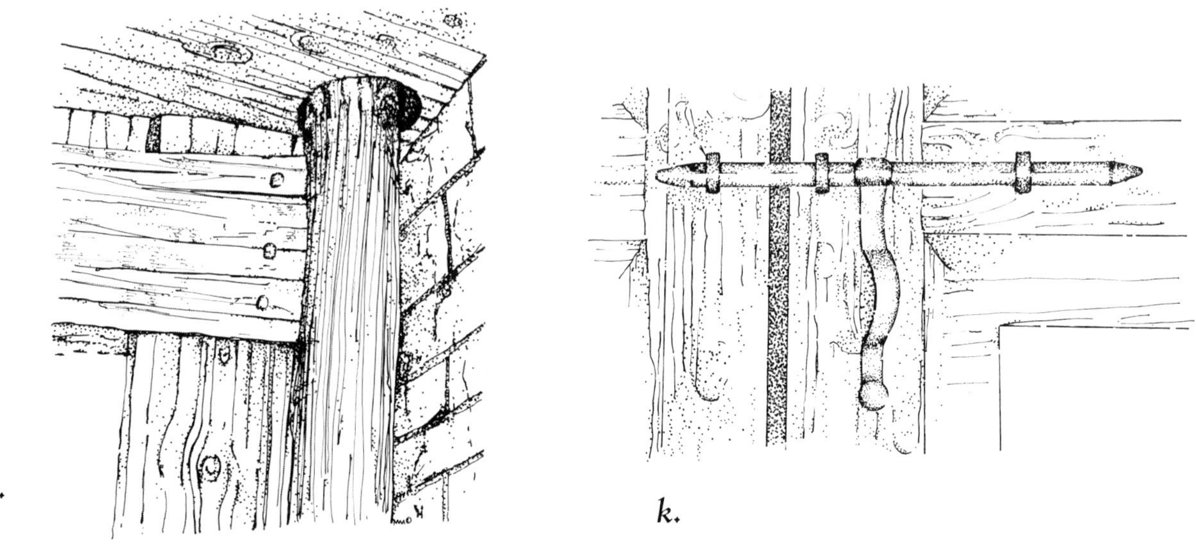

4.10. i. lock and lock plate, j. pintle and grunion, k. sliding bolt

black, and in California, also from an oxide of manganese.[39] To produce ochers, umbers, and siennas, special mineral-laden earths were purified, then roasted for deeper and redder colors. Other browns were made from iron and manganese minerals. Blues were produced from indigo (which produced a lovely, though light-sensitive, dye) and from colored clays, beidellite, and other copper minerals. Although both have been found in the decorations at San Xavier near Tucson (Arizona), Prussian blue (made from iron and the highly toxic gas cyanogen) and smalt (made from glass colored with cobalt oxide) would have required a sophisticated knowledge of chemistry and were therefore probably imported. Greens were produced from copper carbonate and from a native clay containing iron silicate; reds, from hematite, an oxide of iron found in clay, earth, or stone, and from cinnabar, an oxide of mercury. Yellows were made from ferrous minerals, such as the yellow varieties of goethite and limonite, or from arsenic trisulfide, whereas whites were made from plaster of paris, kaolin, and white earths. Combined to produce various colors, hues, and shades, most of these pigments were prepared and used by the indigenous peoples before the Conquest to decorate their bodies, ritual structures, and personal paraphernalia. (For additional information on painting materials and techniques, see "Paintings" in chapter 10.)

Binders and Sealers

To suspend the particles of a pigment and to bond them to one another and to the object being painted, a binder or medium was needed. Human and animal blood, the juice from the yucca plant and its fruit or from the prickly pear cactus (*tuna castilla*), chewed seeds, pine and mesquite resins, gums, and egg whites were all used as binders at one time or another by the native artisans of northern New Spain.[40] The Spaniards introduced still other binders, such as fig juice, and drying oils from seeds and nuts. They also added milk, blood, egg white, pitch, fig juice, or grain gluten to lime mortar stucco to retard drying and to make the stucco easier both to manipulate, especially in modeling, and to burnish.[41]

Mixed with fine earths or clays, domestic animal blood was used as a floor sealer in nineteenth-century structures in New Mexico. Gelatin or hide glue and pine pitch and sap were also used as sealers, as was petroleum tar (*brea*) on the tule roof of the old sacristy at San Luis Obispo.

TECHNIQUES

Native building methods and materials included wattle and daub, puddled adobe, adobe "bricks" shaped by hand, random or coursed rubble construction, rammed earth (*tapia*), palisades of poles or tree trunks, and plastering with adobe or gypsum. Both Indians and Spaniards used mud floors, adobe plastering with gypsum coatings, whitewashed interiors and beams, pitched roofs covered with tules, reeds, thatch, or fronds, multistoried buildings, and flat roofs covered with earth.

Techniques of cutting sod blocks,[42] molding adobe bricks, firing clay bricks, and making tiles; of stone cutting and monumental carving; of preparing and applying lime mortar and plaster; of carpentry joining; of refining and casting brass and bronze, as well as forging steel and smelting tin; and of making glass—all known and used in Europe since classical times—were introduced into northern New Spain by the Spaniards, as skills transmitted by Spanish craftsmen, as imported end products, or as industries later established there. The basic techniques of block laying, buttressing, and arch and dome construction are directly traceable to the Romans, while mudéjar styles of woodworking, plastering, brickwork, and metal work derive from the Moors. The natives provided the labor, either voluntarily or through impressed service.

Church construction progressed most rapidly at the apse and sanctuary end, where the most sacred object resided, then proceeded toward the façade, one bay at a time. Thus large structures under construction for decades bear witness to changes in styles from one end to the other, the oldest style being at the sanctuary end of the church.

Bell towers were usually the last building element to be completed. Many times a church begun with evangelistic fervor or at the start of an economic boom could not be finished before priorities or fortunes changed, leaving just one bell tower or just the tower bases complete. Later, less impressive towers in a different style might be erected on bases intended for much grander ones. Services could be held once the church and its parts had been blessed, even though the structure was sometimes far from complete.

While evidence suggests that most of the later, more complex churches of New Spain were drawn before they were built, renderings in any form resembling blueprints as we know them do not exist. Drawings of highly idealized façades, cross sections, or undimensioned sketches are occasionally found in domestic and foreign archives, apparently to give some idea of a proposed feature or building—or of a building's plan or relationship to other buildings.[43] Many of these are just sketches, however, and were never intended to transmit the architect's design to the workmen—that was the role of the architect, master mason, or maestro de obra. On the other hand, engravings of architectural details published in Spanish and Italian treatises on architecture played a vital role in disseminating style, proportions, and decorations for many of the churches of New Spain, including at least one example in northern New Spain, Mission Santa Bárbara (California; see figure 2.22a–b).[44]

Working from memory or perhaps a sketch, the builder in charge (friar or master mason) would set forth the overall measurements, sizes of rooms, orientation, floor plan, and façade design. Orienting by astronomical observations if a magnetic compass was not available, and beginning with some determined point as a corner, he would pace off the basic floor plan. With a measuring cord (*cordel*) and stakes, arcs could be swung and, using centuries-old proportional systems, widths and heights of naves, points of intersection of transverse aisles, the placement of windows and doors, and even the arches for these could be calculated and marked. A mason's level (*nivel de albañil*) and plumb line (*cuerdo de plombada*) helped true walls, doorways, and windows to the horizontal and vertical; right angles were made using a simple carpenter's square (*escuadra*).

Foundations

Most early builders understood the importance of a level and firm base whose width correlated with the proposed height of the walls: a good foundation would reduce the possibility of uneven settling. Although stone walls were sometimes begun at the bottoms of trenches, as a rule, separate foundations of river stones, basalt boulders, or cut blocks mortared together with lime or adobe were laid in the trench to ground level or above, and the walls—adobe, fired brick, or stone—built on top of these. For some adobe churches, walls were simply laid directly on the ground without any foundations. Many churches included a specific finished stone at one corner, appropriately called a cornerstone or foundation stone (*lápida*, literally, tablet or slab), which functioned not only to buttress the building but also as a smooth and prominent place on which to inscribe who built or dedicated the church and when. Cornerstones have a long architectural and symbolic tradition—especially within the Catholic Church—for these reasons, they are among the first stones laid and are especially blessed or acknowledged.[45]

Scaffolding

To build any wall higher than a worker could reach from ground level required some form of scaffolding (*andamio*). One common technique made use of putlogs (*almojayas*) inserted into the wall at right angles in a horizontal line at intervals of about four feet; these were braced both vertically and horizontally by poles (*almas*) or boards lashed together.[46] Ladders or ramps provided access to walkways holding laborers and building materials (figure 4.11). When a building was finished or a section completed, the putlogs were cut off or removed and the holes filled or plastered over, to be reused during repairs in some cases. Although they can be clearly seen on the exteriors of buildings that have lost their plaster (figure 4.12), or where the holes were filled or plastered over with a different material, because of the greater care given to finishing interiors, such holes are rarely visible on the inside walls.[47]

Centering and Shoring

A system of falsework dating back to Roman times, centering and shoring requires scaffold platforms, either supported from the ground or attached to the building itself. Centering is a temporary framework used to provide support and shape for curved surfaces; and shoring, heavy timber struts and grillage to support and brace both the platforms and the centering. Typically, a scaffold would span the distance between opposing walls at the haunches of a vault, arch, or dome, just above the impost level. Blocks for vaulting would be laid out on this scaffold; after the first layer had been put in place and mortared, another layer would be added on top of it, the first layer supporting the second and subsequent ones. Wooden centerings would be built to locate the keystone or to secure the blocks as they were put into place and mortared. Figure 4.13 illustrates the centering and shoring system used in 1980–1981 at Nuestra Señora de Guadalupe in Aguascalientes (Aguascalientes),

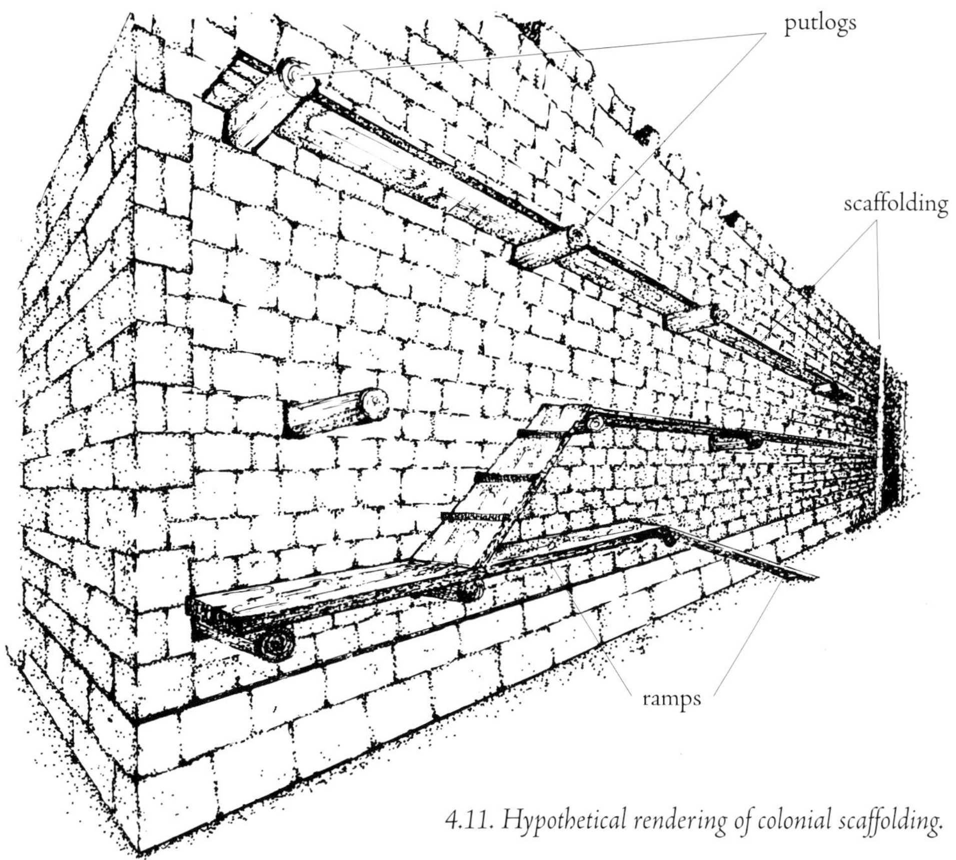

4.11. Hypothetical rendering of colonial scaffolding.

a neobaroque structure. Pieced together with scrap lumber, nails, and wire, this system held everything in place until the arch was completed and the mortar set; where lumber was lacking, adobe blocks could be used for shoring.[48] Centering and shoring systems were probably used during the building, plastering, and painting of domes throughout New Spain.

Mud, Sticks, Poles, and Timbers

In the rammed earth ruins of what is now Arizona and Chihuahua, Spaniards encountered an indigenous building method that must have reminded them of the tapia technique brought to their homeland by Moorish builders.[49] Another method once used in parts of northern New Spain was puddled adobe, whereby the natives made walls from mud without the use of molds. The mud was applied in fifteen- to twenty-inch layers, patted or paddled into shape, and left to dry before the next layer was laid. In a third method, described by Pedro de Castañeda, women built walls from balls of mud and ash they shaped with their hands and that were held in place with mortar of the same material.[50] Structures made using tapia, puddled adobe, or hand-shaped "bricks" took considerably longer to build than those made with molded adobe bricks, which quickly replaced all three methods among native builders.

Wattle and daub (*embarro*), in use among the Pueblo Indians before Spanish contact, was a simple, rapid, indigenous method for building a shelter. Builders first sank heavy corner forked posts (*horcones*)—and depending on the length of the wall, additional heavy posts as well—into the ground along the wall line. Leaving openings for windows and doorways, they then set about forming the wattles into walls. The thicker, more rigid stakes, reeds, or poles they placed vertically between the heavy posts along the wall line; the thinner, more flexible branches, twigs, and grasses they interwove horizontally among, or tied vertically to, the uprights, working from ground to roof. Next, they pressed, patted, smeared, and smoothed on the daub—a mixture of adobe and plant material (usually

4.12. Main façade, Nuestra Señora de Loreto (now destroyed), Chihuahua City, late nineteenth century. The absence of bell towers as well as missing plaster that would have obscured the putlog cavities signal an unfinished church structure; however, the religious statues in the niches and the cross over the door indicate probable utilization as a functioning church at one time. In this case, the expulsion of the Jesuits from Mexico in 1767 terminated construction activities here and the bricked-up windows and door were modifications for later uses, including a temporary prison for Father Hidalgo and a military garrison. (Photographer unknown)

4.13. Centering and shoring, Nuestra Señora de Guadalupe, Aguascalientes, Aguascalientes, 1980. Besides serving as supports for the various carved stone pieces of the arch, the wood members also provide scaffolding and ladders for the stonemasons. This neobaroque church was under construction for a large part of the twentieth century.

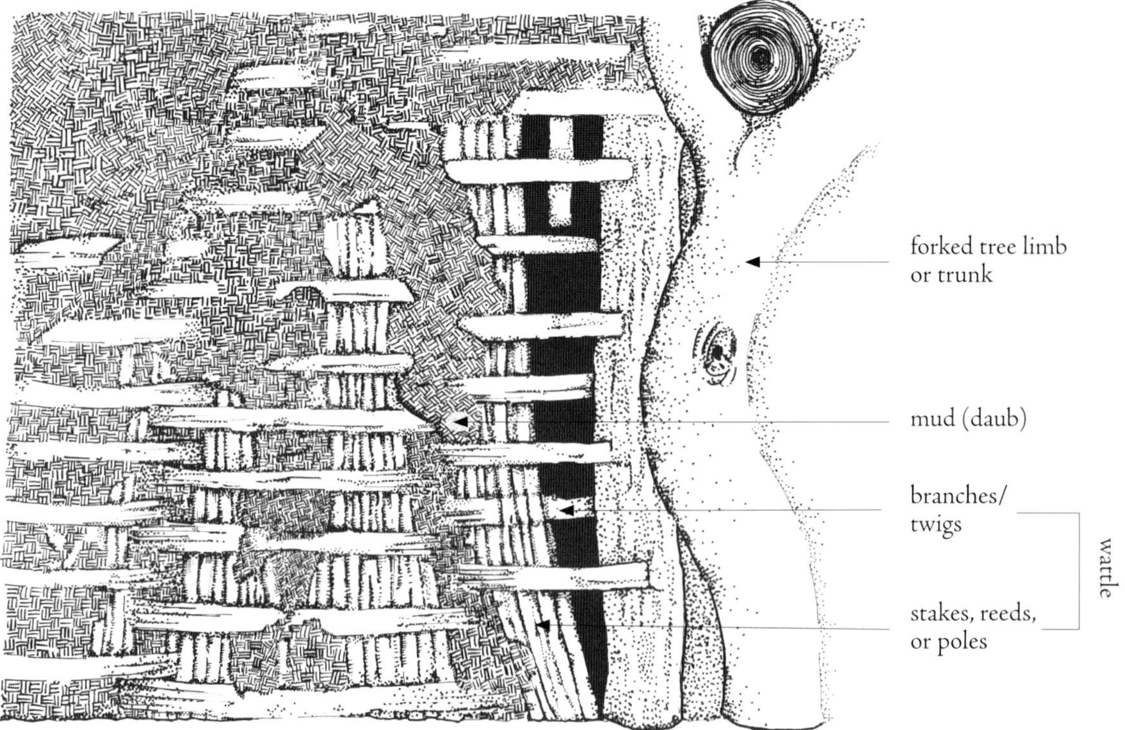

4.14. Wattle and daub.

straw)—and allowed it to dry (figure 4.14). Slaked lime in the daub ensured the strength of the walls for an impressively long time. Finally, they whitewashed or plastered the surface, and covered the completed walls with a roof, most often a thatch of grasses or palm fronds. Early settlers used wattle and daub to build houses and some of the first churches in northern New Spain.[51] When combined with large timbers, it lent itself to the construction of multistoried buildings, such as those found in England and Spain, although wattle and daub structures in northern New Spain probably did not exceed a single story.

Ideal for the hottest vegetated areas of northern New Spain, *bajareque* was essentially wattle without daub: horizontal and vertical elements were plaited, wedged, or tied together without plaster. In both wattle and daub and bajareque, the large vertical and uppermost horizontal wall braces served as supports for the roof.

Where timber was readily available, most notably in California, Colorado, and Texas, the Spaniards built their stockades or forts as palisades (*palizadas*) by placing timbers vertically on end and close together, a technique they most likely adopted from the indigenous mountain peoples of northern New Spain. Although there is no direct reference to palisade churches except in parts of Alta California,[52] these may well have been built in other wooded areas of northern New Spain—and even in Baja California—during the first years of colonization.

Stonework

With European technologies for quarrying, lifting, transporting, and dressing stone, the masons of northern New Spain could readily work and treat stone in a variety of ways, no matter its size, shape, or hardness. For ashlar (*sillar*) masonry, they cut and dressed stone into squared blocks with smooth faces; for coursed ashlar, they used blocks of the same size, laid in parallel, horizontal courses (figures 4.15 a, b); and for broken or random ashlar, blocks of different sizes (sometimes hammer-dressed—cut and roughly squared), fit together in uneven courses (figure 4.15c). To accentuate courses and joints, masons could also work stone blocks in relief using the *almohadillada* technique (from Arabic *al-mufadda*, pillow), with individual blocks having, as the name suggests, a pillow-like appearance.

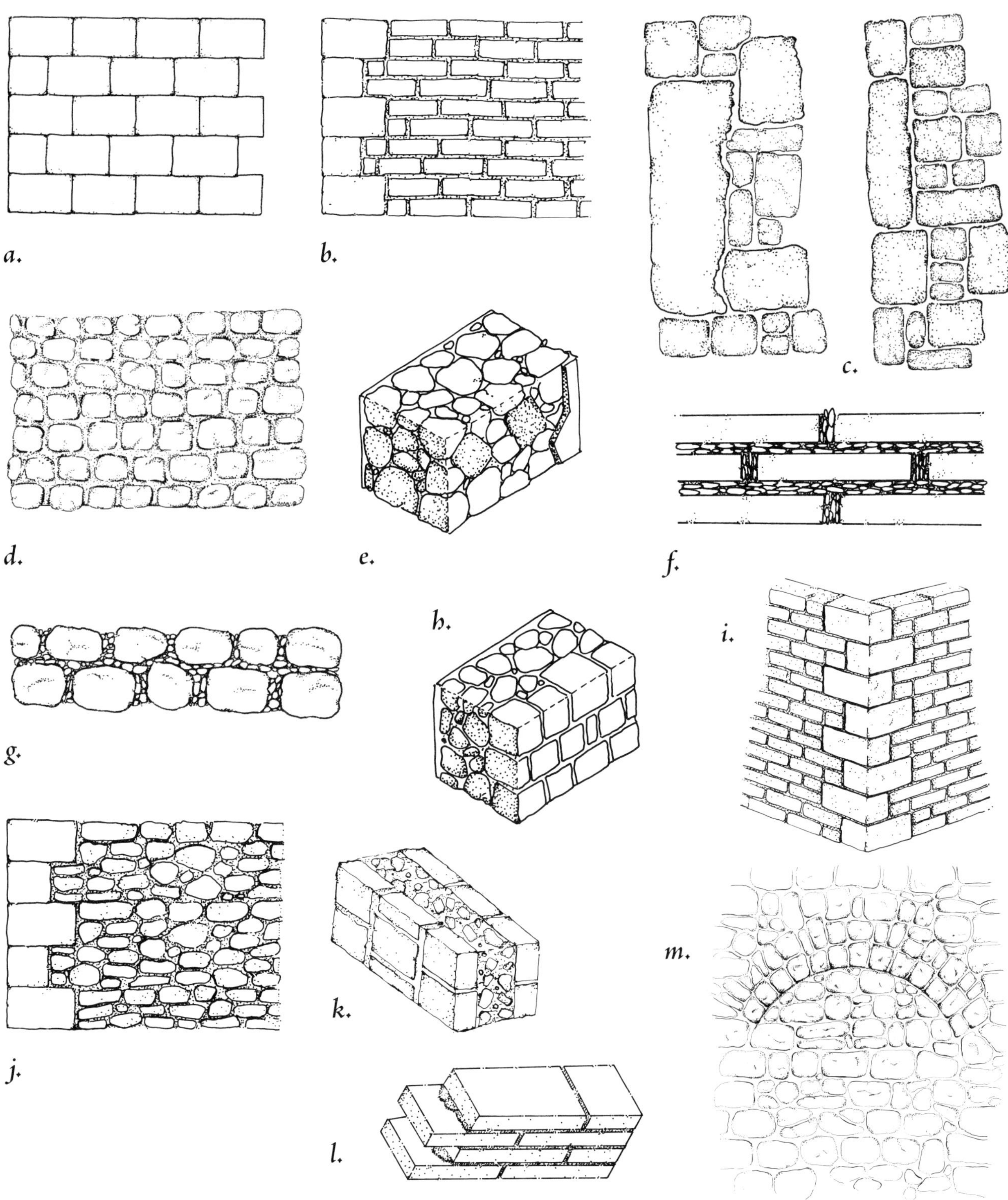

4.15. Stone masonry courses: a. ashlar, b. coursed ashlar, c. broken, or random, ashlar, d. coursed rubble masonry (mampostería), e. broken, or random, rubble with a partial plaster coating, f. ashlar mudéjar technique with rajuelas, g. coursed rubble mudéjar technique with rajuelas, h. coursed ashlar over rubble, i. coursed ashlar with quoins, j. random rubble with ashlar quoins, k. rubble-filled wall (piedra con mezcla), l. brickwork, m. blind relieving arch.

4.16. Rajuelas, San Antonio de Padua de Tula, Tamaulipas, 1996.

For rubble masonry (*mampostería,* from *mano* and *puesto,* hand put; sometimes also called *calicanto*), they made use of irregular, unworked stones; like ashlar, rubble masonry could be coursed or random (figures 4.15d, e). An adobe mortar, sometimes containing plant fibers (chiefly straw), was used among the Puebloan builders, who discovered that a wall had greater strength if the mortar was pressed in between the stones after the wall was laid up. Basalt, found in naturally small pieces or broken to manageable sizes, was a common rubble wall stone (and foundation stone), as were limestone and sandstone. Using a traditional mudéjar technique, masons would sometimes tap small slivers of stone (*rajuelas*) into the mortar joints of rubble masonry walls to fill and strengthen them as the mortar dried and hardened (figures 4.15f, g). Appreciating their (most likely unintended) decorative effect, restorers have in recent restorations left the rajuelas exposed to view (figure 4.16).

4.17. Entrance between La Tercera Orden de Sombrerete and La Capilla de San Francisco de Asís de Sombrerete, Zacatecas, 1983. Quoins are used here with coursed ashlar as well as random rubble. The change in building materials could very possibly signal a reduction in construction funds, and with adequate plaster covering both types of masonry construction, no difference would be detectable.

Partly for aesthetics and partly for stability, masons sometimes combined ashlar with rubble masonry (figure 4.15h, figure 4.17): ashlar quoins (dressed stones on the outside corners of buildings, figure 4.15i) were usually laid to establish level courses or to create an alternating large and small effect, here used to help buttress the wall and to create an interesting contrast in texture between the dressed quoins and the irregular rubble work; and rubble used for the remainder of the walls (figure 4.15j).

To raise massive walls without the expense or the skill needed to produce a large number of cut and dressed stone blocks or fired bricks, the masons of northern New Spain resorted to a building technique used extensively by the ancient Romans and throughout Spain by the Moors. They built two thinner, parallel walls a short distance apart—an outer and an inner retaining wall—and poured rubble with adobe or lime mortar (*piedra con mezcla*) between the two (figure 4.15k). The two walls were held together with pieces of wood or with headers (also called bond stones or bonders), a bonding course of stone or brick spanning the gap between them. The mission church San Xavier near Tucson (Arizona) as well as its sister church, La Purísima Concepción in Caborca (Sonora), are two of the many churches in northern New Spain constructed with rubble-filled walls, a technique that continues to be used in Mexico. Along interior walls, masons sometimes laid a continuous bench (*banqueta* or *banco*) of masonry, whether stone or brick; along the outside foot of the walls, they often laid a projecting base course called a water course, slightly sloped for weathering and generally ashlar even when the rest of the walls were rubble, to act as a raised foundation (see figure 7.14). To protect the building's corners from passing wagons, builders might place a projecting masonry element called a *guardacantón* (corner guard), usually a pilaster or column but sometimes simply a rounded mass, at each corner.

Brickwork

Molded adobe bricks enabled masons to raise higher walls, up to thirty-five feet high, and thus to span greater spaces, although, owing to adobe's low structural strength, these walls tended to be thick and massive. Churches of impressive size and stability were made from adobe bricks throughout northern New Spain.

Like fired bricks, adobe bricks might be laid on a foundation or directly on level ground in parallel, horizontal courses; they were held in place with mortar (usually adobe) between their horizontal and vertical faces (figure 4.151). And also like fired bricks, adobe bricks were staggered from course to course so that the center of any one brick was over or under the joint of two other bricks. Higher walls were made thicker at the base, tapering slightly toward the roof. Walls were also made thicker when needed to support heavy roofing timbers or to offset openings for windows or doors.[53]

To help prevent brickwork walls from bulging, builders stretched a rod, chain, or strap between opposite walls, secured at each end by an outside anchor or metal clasp, sometimes with a piece of wood serving as a washer. This measure was usually not taken until years after a structure was built, when the brickwork had settled and begun to deform; it can be seen in San Pedro y San Pablo in Tubutama and San Ignacio de Cabórica in Caborca (both Sonora), where the "washers" are clearly visible in the upper section of the main frontispiece or façade (see figures 2.24a and 5.15).

Lime mortar was used to hold fired (usually low-fired) bricks in place. Where the mortar was more resistant to erosion, a network of lime ledges between the bricks was created as the bricks washed away. Another case of differential erosion occurred when masons combined fired and adobe bricks, using fired bricks in the foundations of a building and to provide a protective facing or coping for walls, arches, columns, and façades made of adobe bricks. Because fired and adobe bricks react differently to temperature and moisture, the joints between the two tend to pull apart after a few years, cracking any plaster used to cover the seams. The exposed bricks then ultimately erode at different rates.

Plastering

The verb "to plaster" (*aplanar*) can mean to coat a surface with just about any material. In northern New Spain plastering was done chiefly with adobe, sometimes mixed with plant fiber or ash, or sometimes with lime or gypsum, most often mixed with sand, applied first by hand or paddle and later by trowel. For both practical and aesthetic reasons, it is likely that almost all of the completed churches in northern New Spain were originally plastered inside and out. By covering and smoothing over irregular surfaces, edges, and joints, plaster masked unevenness in construction materials and techniques and protected outside walls from erosion and frost.

Current practices in church restoration, which call for exposing the "honest quality" of wall construction and materials, most often defeat the original aesthetic intention of the builders and may even be deleterious to preservation. Stripping plaster from ashlar and rubble walls makes the contrast between the two much more pronounced than originally intended. While it might be interesting to see the differences in material or technique that mark the various stages in a building's construction, the builders intended these differences to be hidden under layers of plaster (see figures 2.23 and 4.17). And while the risk of damage to exposed exterior surfaces might be negligible for stone walls with mortar joints full to the surface, it is significant for fired brick walls, and unacceptably high for adobe walls.

4.18. Plasterer's grooves, San Luis Rey Mission, Oceanside, California, ca. 1900. Behind the Franciscan friar, missing plaster reveals grooves still retaining chunks of stones that functioned as keys. (From Library of Congress archives)

To ensure that the plaster (whether lime or adobe) would firmly attach itself to the wall, plasterers struck (scratched or cut grooves into) the adobe wall or plaster undercoat (figure 4.18) and dampened it to keep it from absorbing moisture from the plaster too quickly and cracking. They sometimes placed small wooden pegs or slender, sharp rocks into the walls, level with the walls' surface (*rejonear*), to provide "keys" around which plaster would more readily attach. To apply fresh plaster over older plaster, they first roughened the surface with a pick or hammer to provide holds for the new plaster, then thoroughly wetted the roughened surface, again to prevent it from absorbing moisture too quickly.

When lime plaster was applied in several coats, the first, a rough or scratch coat, consisted of lime, sand, and gravel as needed, and the subsequent, finer coats, con-

4.19. Main façade, Nuestra Señora de la Asunción de Opodepe, Sonora, 2001. Geometric figures and outlines of flowers, vases, and humans appear within each of the panels that help form the frontispiece.

sisted of lime with little or no sand. Sometimes the final coat was scored to create the illusion of ashlar masonry; sometimes rocks were pressed into the still-wet plaster to form patterns and designs (figure 4.19);[54] sometimes relief decorations were molded or carved into it, as were the bas-relief human figures and spiral designs on the main frontispiece of San Pedro y San Pablo de Tubutama (Sonora; see figure 2.24); and sometimes such effects were emphasized by painting the plaster in contrasting colors. For example, the bas-relief tassel and wheel motifs on the bell tower of Cinco Señores in Santander Jiménez (Tamaulipas) are painted burnt sienna, in sharp contrast to the yellow of the tower's walls, strongly suggesting an ajaraca effect (see figure 2.6).[55]

The hard, slick surface of lime plaster was of utmost importance in conducting water off and away from the roof and walls of church buildings as quickly and efficiently as possible. Traditionally, after an initial coat of plaster made with heavy gravel to fill spaces in the block work, the roofs, domes, and drainage channels were given a fine, burnished plaster coat. Including hematite or ocher in the plaster allowed the drainage channels on the sides of walls to be burnished more highly, making them still more impervious to water and, by reducing friction, helping to keep the water within the channels. The original red on the drainage channels at San Xavier near Tucson (Arizona)—regrettably since replaced by red paint in restorations—was most likely red ocher (*tipichil* or *almagra*), a material that, when stone-polished, took on a smooth, compacted, shiny finish. The drainage channels at the rear of San José de Tumacácori (Arizona), some thirty miles to the south, have been more fortunate, retaining their original yellow ocher surface, burnished as smooth as marble.

Even though a good deal more resistant than adobe, the coarse, low-fired bricks so widely used in northern New Spain were porous and therefore subject to spalling and erosion. For that reason, the exterior surface of walls made of these bricks was generally plastered with lime; for aesthetic reasons, the interior was also plastered. Adobe brick walls, on the other hand, were more effectively plastered with adobe, which was patted on and then smoothed, with plant fibers added for greater cohesion where humidity was a factor.

As tastes changed or a congregation became more sophisticated, earlier florid or didactic decorations, generally stained, peeling, or badly worn, were simply painted, whitewashed, or plastered over. Ironically, this helped to preserve some of them, as recent restoration projects on the missions of California and the Pimería Alta have shown.

Roofing

A thatch roof (*techo pajizo*) was one of the fastest and simplest to construct. Plant materials, such as palm fronds or long grasses, were tied in evenly spaced bundles to a pitched lattice of poles. Starting from the eaves and moving row by row up to the peak of the roof, the thatchers lashed their bundles to the horizontal supports, then lashed the two sides of thatching together over the ridgepole, sometimes placing a line of forked sticks along the pole to keep the sides from parting (figure 4.20).

Flat or terraced roofs (*techos de azotea*) were most common in the arid parts of northern New Spain (and are used to this day); when maintained, they served amply to protect buildings from the scant rain. To span the width of the structure, builders rested large beams (vigas), sometimes decorated with painting and carving, on corbels or on corbelled impost blocks (zapatas or canes) atop columns. Across the beams, either perpendicularly or diagonally in a herringbone pattern, they placed small pieces of adzehewn wood (*tableras*), peeled aspen, cottonwood, or other narrow, smooth limbs (*latillas* or *sabinos*), or sawn planks. They then laid tules, reeds, brush, or grass on top of these;

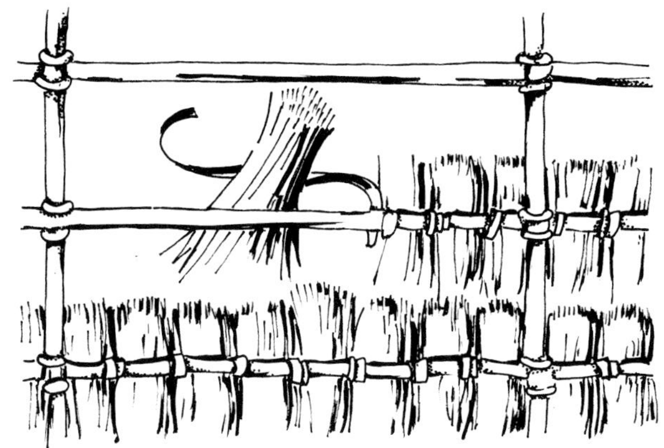

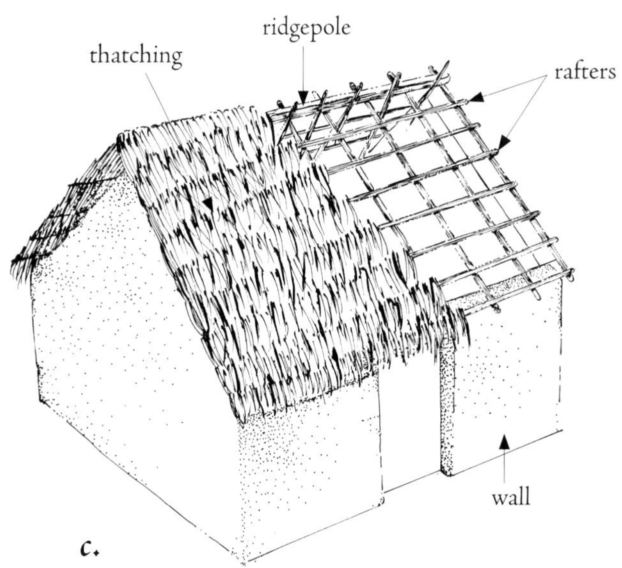

4.20. Roof thatching: a. using bundles of grass, b. using palm fronds, c. in place on a roof.

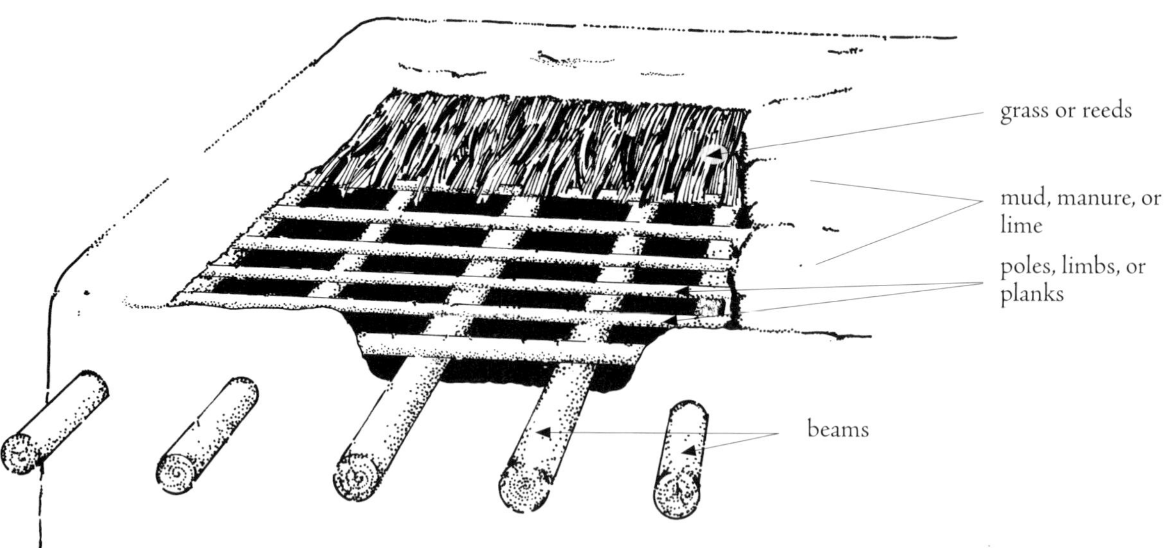

4.21. Cutaway drawing of a flat roof made from vigas, latillas, straw, and mud, with a plaster sealant.

4.22. Flat roof with drainage system, La Capilla de Nuestra Señora de Guadalupe de Sombrerete, Zacatecas, 1984. Notice the slope on both elevations of the roof, including the section over the nave. The transverse clerestory window is guarded by wooden bars in front of the glazed opening.

covered the entire roof with adobe or animal manure; and sealed this with a plaster of lime or with *possolan*. Care was taken to fit the ceiling elements together snugly so that the upper layers of adobe or manure did not sift through, and the roof inclined in one direction toward one or more drainage channels or spouts. Roofs throughout the U.S. Southwest and northern Mexico continue to be made in this manner (figures 4.21 and 4.22).

Drains (*canales, caños,* or *drenes de aguas pluviales*) were used to conduct water off roofs and away from buildings,

4.23. Choir loft showing post and lintel construction, Nuestra Señora de Guadalupe, Ciudad Juárez, Chihuahua, 1988.

sometimes across other roofs at lower levels and down the sides of buildings. Rainwater could also be drained away via enclosed drainpipes attached to the walls (*bajadas de agua adosadas*) and via troughs on roofs, behind parapet walls, or down the outside face of main walls (*bajadas de aguas integradas*). Drain spouts (canales) for all types of roofs were made from roofing tiles, from clay tubes thrown on a potter's wheel or molded in two pieces and then joined before firing, or from carved stone or wood.[56]

[Post and Beam Structures] The builders of northern New Spain used three structural systems for spanning spaces: (1) post and beam (or lintel), (2) vault or arch and pier, and (3) truss. The simplest of the three systems—post and beam (*pilares y jácenes*)—was preferred for seventeenth- and eighteenth-century Franciscan and Jesuit churches in Nuevo México and the Pimería Alta, respectively, as much for practical as for aesthetic reasons. Vertical supports (posts or walls) bore horizontal elements (beams or lintels), a system that could be applied not just to roofs but also to windows, doors, choir lofts, and porches (figure 4.23; see also figure 3.19a and b). To provide a large weight-bearing surface for the beams, bolsters (zapatas; also called impost blocks) were placed on top of the supporting posts or walls; the exposed sides of these blocks were most often decorated.

[Vault or Arch and Pier Structures] The vault or arch and pier (*bóveda*) system spans an open space, usually with masonry, by transmitting the bearing weight laterally and downward from piece to piece onto the vertical supports. Builders rested the ends of each arch on imposts, which were set atop the supports and whose edges usually projected out as molding. Not all arches

4.24. Ashlar window frame of the baptistery, San José de Copala, Sinaloa, 1979. The unusually elaborate treatment of the window reflects the importance of this baptistery.

were arched, however. Flat arches, so called because their intrados and extrados are flat, were used in many ashlar window frames in any number of masonry churches in northern New Spain (figure 4.24). Such arches differ from post and lintel construction in the number of their horizontal pieces and the way in which they transfer downward thrust. The keystone, or center brick, in a flat arch thrusts down vertically, while the other pieces, the voussoirs, whose sides slope away at an angle, thrust out laterally; the keystone and voussoirs were sometimes specially cut to form interlocking units.

Vaults or arches (see figures 6.17 and 6.18 and "Arches, Vaults, Half Domes" under "Architectural Details" in chapter 6) took a number of forms, depending on their location and the amount of bearing weight that could be supported by the mass of the walls, by piers, or by buttresses. To redirect or disperse downward thrust, masons placed blind relieving arches, generally flush with the surface of a wall and covered in plaster, over arches or lintels that could not sustain the weight above them (figure 4.25; see also 4.15m).

Colonial builders made use of three types of vaults: barrel, groin, and spherical. Developed even before Roman times, a barrel vault (*bóveda de cañon*) is simply a continuous arch in which wedge-shaped stones or ordinary bricks are fitted together to maximize stability by minimizing the

4.25. Blind relieving arch, Catedral de Durango, 1983. Thanks to the absence of the exterior plaster, colonial methods of strengthening large walls are clearly visible.

width of the mortar joints between the stones or bricks. Barrel vaults spanning large spaces required massive buttressing to accommodate the tremendous outward thrust on supporting walls and piers. To ensure that downward pressure was exerted evenly across the vertical supports, barrel vaults were built to a minimum height with no windows above the spring line, which resulted in a dark ceiling and a tunnel effect (figure 4.26).

A groin vault (*bóveda de arista;* figures 4.27 and 4.28) is formed by two barrel vaults intersecting at right angles; the line of intersection is called the groin (*aristón*). More complicated to construct than barrel vaulting, groin vaults are found in the more pretentious churches, such as the Cathedral of Durango. In some of the eighteenth-century Jesuit and Franciscan mission churches, such as San Ignacio de Kadakaaman (Baja California Sur) or San Pedro y San Pablo de Tubutama (Sonora), the groin vaults were decorative rather than structural. In the purely decorative vaults in the parochial church of San José de Parral (Chihuahua), for example, windows were placed along the walls above the impost or spring line, so that light playing across the groin lines—often accentuated by plaster relief or painted designs with a medallion, boss, or decoration in the center where the angles met—would produce interesting and delicate shadow effects (figure 4.29).

Spherical vaults are divided into domical, semidomical, and flattened domical types. A domical vault, or dome (also called a cupola when other than the main dome;

4.26. Barrel vault.

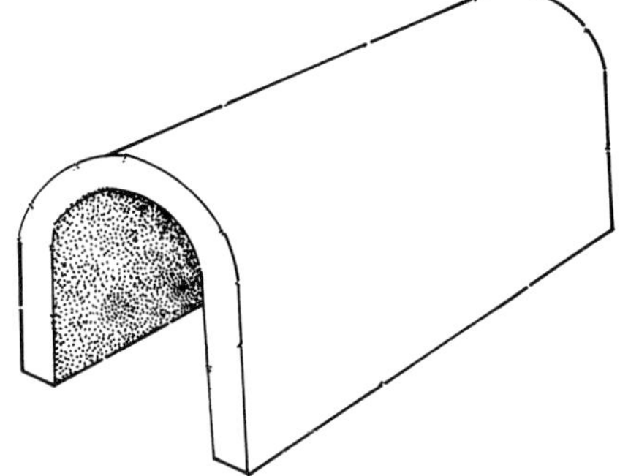

4.27. Groin vault.

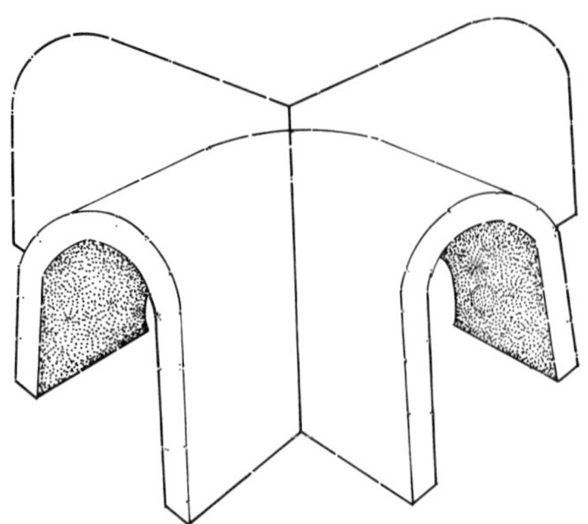

4.28. Groin vault roof with drainage system, San Mateo de Sombrerete, Zacatecas, 1983. After the dome was completed, cracking in the corners of the drum required the additional reinforcement of buttresses.

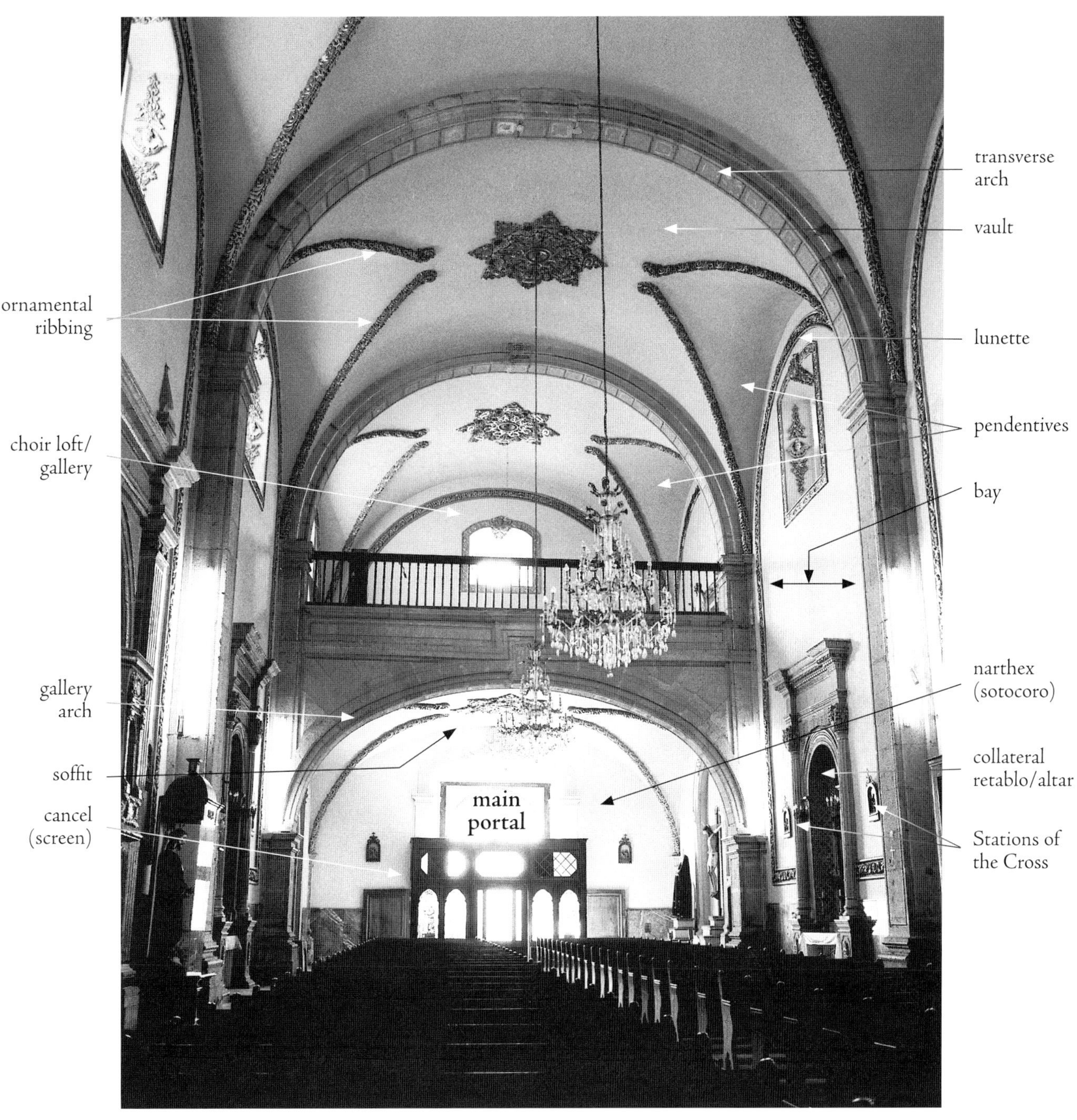

4.29. Interior, San José de Parral, Chihuahua, 1982, looking from the main altar down the nave toward the main portal.

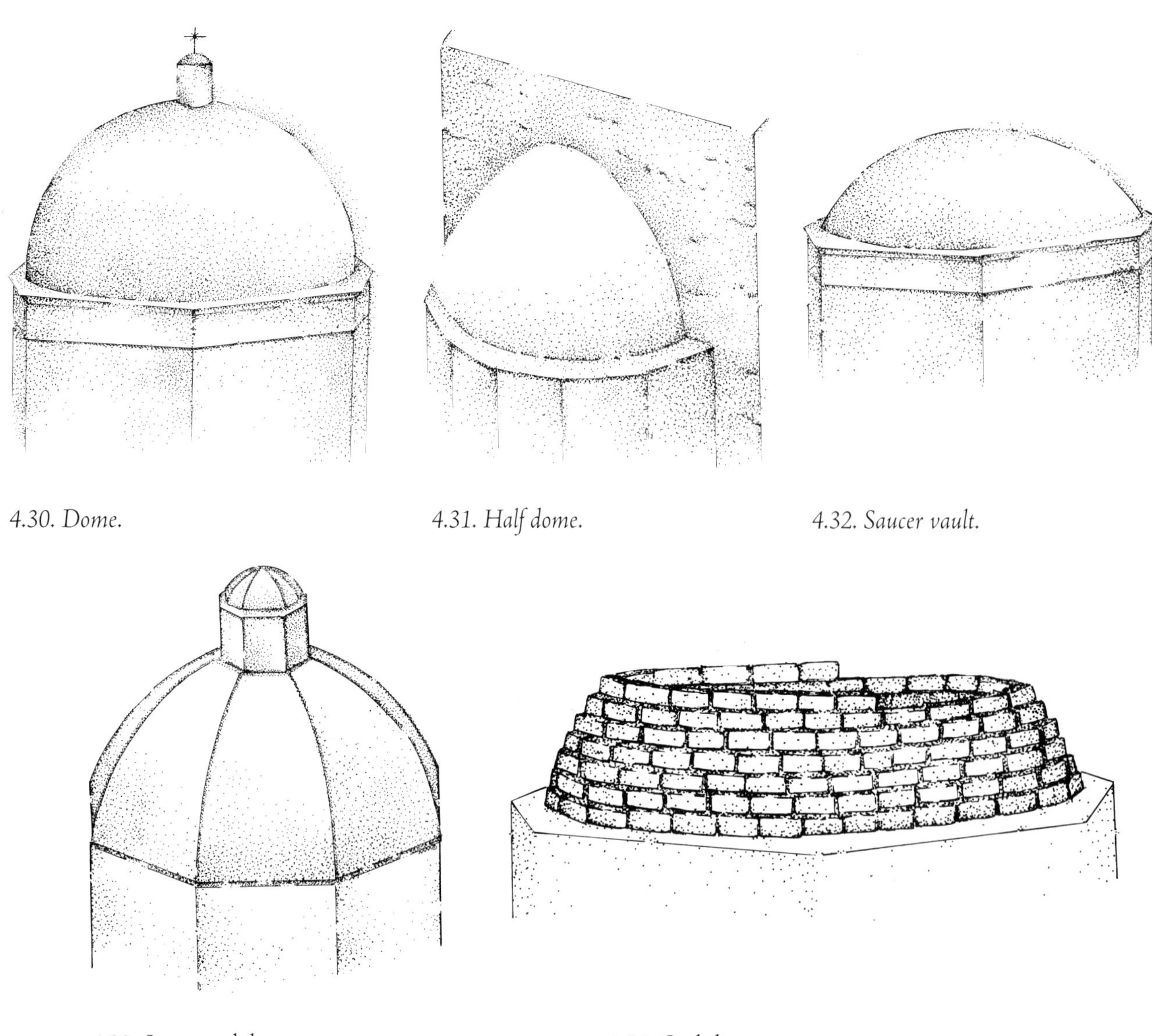

4.30. *Dome.*

4.31. *Half dome.*

4.32. *Saucer vault.*

4.33. *Segmented dome.*

4.34. *Corbeling.*

Spanish: *cúpula* or *naranja*), was mounted on a drum and used to cover a crossing (figure 4.30). A semidomical vault or half dome (*media naranja*) was used to cover a small chapel or apse (figure 4.31). Separate vaulting over a bay, crossing, or small room often took the form of a dome. A flattened domical vault, or flattened dome (*cúpula pateriforme* or *bóveda rebajada*), commonly called a saucer vault, was used to cover a bay in a nave or transept (figure 4.32). The higher and more dramatic segmented dome (*cúpula segmentada*), built by laying up tapered sections from a drum (figure 4.33), appeared atop metropolitan and other important churches such as the Cathedrals of Chihuahua and Durango (see figures 3.23 and 5.20).

To construct flattened domes without supports or centering, viceregal bricklayers and stonemasons used one of the oldest vaulting methods, corbeling (*ménsula*): they laid mortared bricks or stones in concentric rings, stepping inward with each successive course until the arc of the dome was completed (figure 4.34). They also followed the late Roman practice of applying cement over the brick skin of a vault or arch to create a permanent framework. This allowed them to construct and support domes with far less masonry. Indeed, prerestoration photographs of San José de Comondú (Baja California Sur) and La Purísima Concepción in Caborca (Sonora) show the relatively thin domes built using this technique suspended atop partially

4.35. La Purísima Concepción de Nuestra Señora de Caborca, Sonora, 1935. Sometime after the flood of 1914, the nave was bricked up just before the crossing, as shown here, and the church continued to be used until it was abandoned for another structure built much farther away from the river. Although the apse, crossing, and right transept of this structure were rebuilt, flooding in 1994 again severely damaged the rear of the building. (Photo by George Grant, from the George B. Eckhart missions collection. Courtesy of Arizona State Museum, University of Arizona)

destroyed walls, thanks in large part to the strength and cohesive qualities of the cement on the domes' inside and outside surfaces (figure 4.35).

To mount a circular, elliptical, or polygonal dome on top of a square or rectangular area, builders made use of either squinches (*trompas*), laying up masonry, tapered toward the center, across the corners of the area to be spanned to support the drum for the dome; or pendentives (*pechinas*), springing arcs from corner to corner and pier to pier along the sides of the area to be spanned to support a cornice and drum for the dome. Although pendentives required a great deal more engineering skill than squinches—builders had to construct concave spandrels (triangular sections) of vaulting between the square or rectangular area and the circular, elliptical, or polygonal dome—the result was a much loftier, airier superstructure (figure 4.36).

Because ribbed vaulting, a Gothic structural device used in central Mexico from the mid-sixteenth to the mid-seventeenth centuries, required a large and skilled labor force, and because most vaulted masonry churches in northern New Spain were built after this period, it is unlikely any example was produced. Instead the effect could be simulated, as at the mission church San Carlos Borromeo in Carmel (California; see figure 2.10 and also "Gothic" in chapter 2). There are, however, a number of examples where the angles formed by a groin vault on the interior, or by segments of a segmented dome (*cúpula gallonada*) on the exterior, have been decoratively accentuated; during the late nineteenth and early twentieth centuries,

4.36. Crossing of the Catedral de Chihuahua, illustrating a circular dome supported on pendentives, 2002. Besides the Fathers of the Church on the spandrels, Christian symbolism appears upon each arch keystone.

Gothic revival architecture prompted much remodeling in this style. An exaggerated example is the soffit (underside) of the choir loft of La Purísima Concepción in Sombrerete (Zacatecas), where plaster ribbing has been attached, complete with liernes and bosses (figure 4.37).[57]

Masonry supports abutting the façade and walls of churches, buttresses served both structural and aesthetic ends, allowing builders to construct thinner walls with greater space for windows.[58] Pillared buttresses (*estribos* or *contrafuertes*) were piers built into or against a wall from which vaulting or bracing for the roof could spring, while flying buttresses (*arbotantes* or *botareles*) carried the outward thrust of the bearing weight to freestanding piers or nearby walls by means of rampart arches (figure 4.38a).[59] Developed and exploited in Gothic architecture to achieve soaring heights and the largest possible space for windows with the least apparent support, flying buttresses were used rarely and modestly in northern New Spain, as, for example, at the parochial church in Álamos (Sonora; figure 4.38b) and the Cathedrals of Chihuahua (see figure 5.1) and Monterrey.[60] The volutes on the towers of San Xavier del Bac near Tucson (Arizona) and La Purisima Concepción de Nuestra Señora de Caborca, Sonora, though less massive and dramatic than masonry pillars and flying buttresses, serve admirably as both decoration and structural supports (see figure 2.1 and 2.2).

*[**Truss Structures**]* In areas of moderate to heavy precipitation, builders used the truss (*armadura*), a rigid framework of rafters, beams, and braces—and the third

4.37. Soffit of choir loft showing Gothic revival vaulting accents, La Purísima Concepción de Sombrerete, Zacatecas, 1983. The grunions that once supported the original doors can still be seen on either side of the main door (behind the cancel).

structural system for roofing—to construct pitched roofs of moisture-resistant materials. They built these roofs for all the missions of Alta California, a few in the Pimería Alta, and some among the Tarahumara.[61] Although the width of the area that could be spanned depended on the length of available beams, the king truss (figure 4.39a) could achieve a much greater height than the post and beam system (figure 4.39b). Less complicated than a dome or vault, a pitched roof nevertheless required an understanding of stresses, spans, and weights of materials. Moreover, whereas masonry and finishing coats of plaster provided adequate protection from the elements for vaulted or domed churches, the truss of a pitched roof needed to be covered and insulated. Depending on the availability of materials or their ease of manufacture, and especially on the climate, the planks or poles laid on top of the truss were covered with wood shingles (*tejamaniles*), attached by pegs or nails; with ceramic tiles (tejas), secured by pegs and mortar and laid in courses, their convex sides alternating up and down (figure 4.40a); or with thatch (*paja*). Another roofing solution using wood involved *canoas* (canoe-shaped timbers), an ingenious method using long, hollowed poles turned over and under each other not unlike semicircular ceramic roof tiles. and used in at least one Jesuit mission, San Francisco Javier de Tetaguíchic (now La Virgen de Guadalupe de Tetaguíchic), Chihuahua. The planks beneath the tiles

4.38. Buttresses: a. pillared buttresses, San José de Parral, Chihuahua, 1982; b. (facing page) flying buttresses, Nuestra Señora de la Asunción, Álamos, Sonora, 1981.

or shingles formed a ceiling, which could be painted or decorated.

Flooring

Builders used a variety of materials to make floors that were smooth, presentable, and easy to clean. Many of the simpler churches in northern New Spain had floors of packed earth. After removing any rocks and unevenness, by excavation if necessary, the builders brought the floor surface up to level, with layers of progressively finer material. The top layer was often sifted dirt, dampened and tamped down hard and smooth. Or they might add a red ocher material (tipichil, almagra) or animal blood to the top layer, then polish it to a dark red or red-brown, extremely smooth and dense surface. Thresholds or stoops were commonly huge slabs of local stone, shaped or unworked. Some sites used flagstones (*lagas*) for their floors; others, mortared stone or lime mortar alone; still others, low-fired tiles or wood planks. The floor (most likely the original) of La Santa Vera Cruz de Sombrerete (Zacatecas) consists of planks 2 × 5 feet in size surrounded by mitered framework—each plank inscribed with a separate number to mark a grave in the church (figure 4.41).[62]

The same church might have floors made from a number of different materials. In the Cathedral of Chihuahua, for example, the Capilla del Cristo de Mapimí once had a *piso de loza* (tile floor); the main body of the church, a *piso*

b.

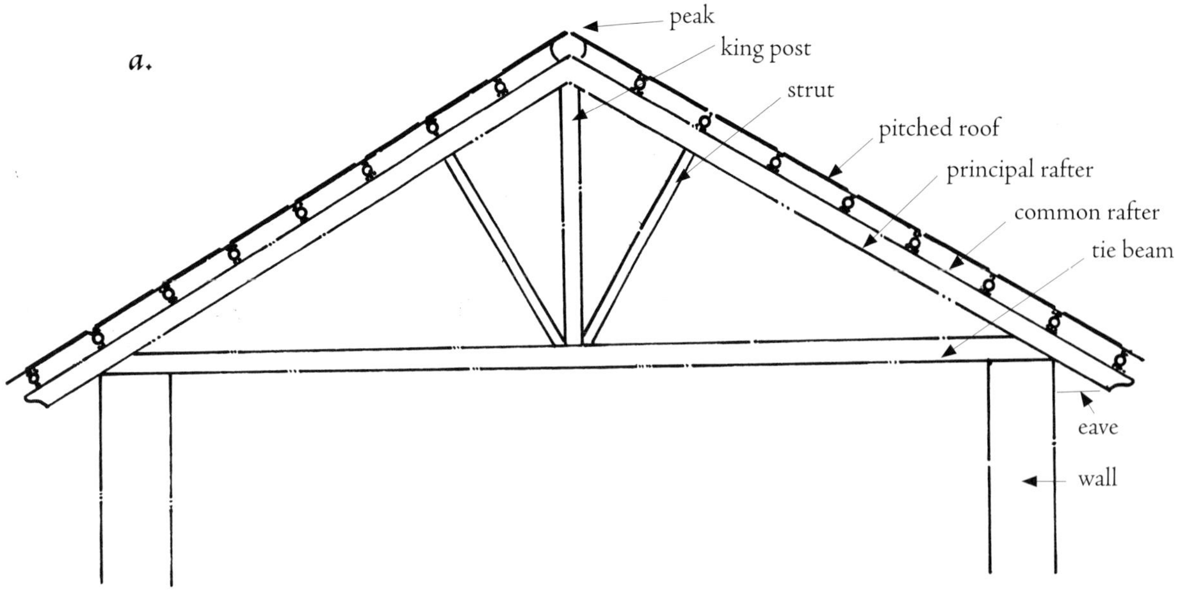

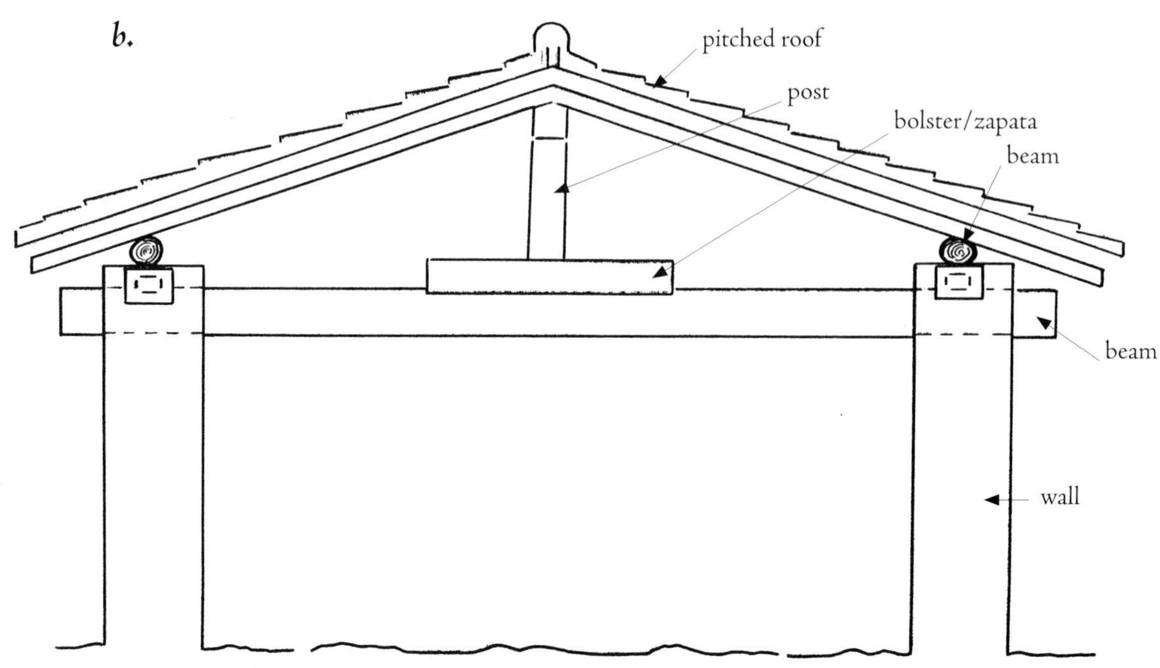

4.39. Pitched roofs: a. king post system; b. post and beam system.

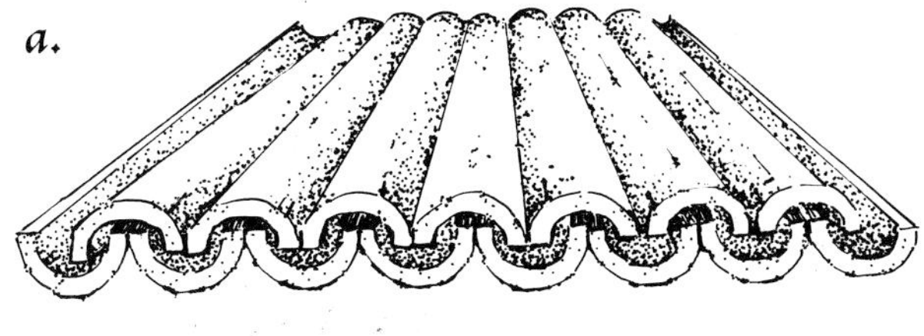

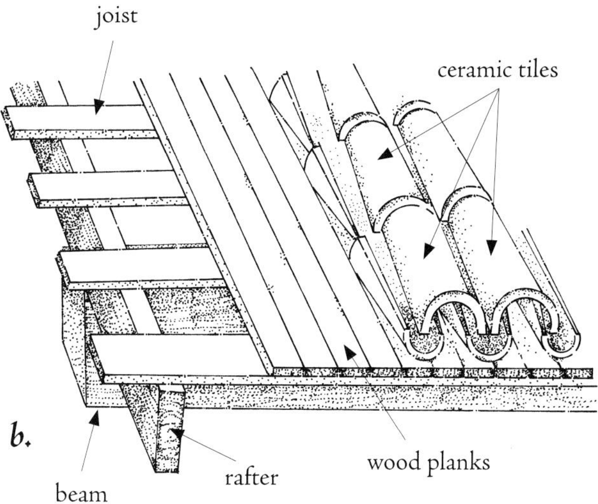

4.40. Roofing techniques used with a trussed roof: a. canoas, made using hollowed-out tree limbs or trunks, b. ceramic tile roof.

de tarima (wooden platform floor, possibly wood planks on joists); the baptistery, a *piso de mampostería* (floor of small, unworked stones and lime); and the sacristy, a *piso de cantería* (floor of cut or worked stone).[63] Unfortunately, almost all the original church floors in northern New Spain, whether dirt, stone, tile, or wood, have been replaced or covered over with modern cement or tile.

Stairs and Staircases

Stairs were constructed by several methods: (1) placing stones or bricks at staggered heights and then either leaving the material natural or plastering it over to make it blend in with surrounding materials; (2) by placing a piece of wood in front of each step and filling the space behind with rubble and mortar; or (3) by making stairs from solid, milled or hewn lumber that was pinned, doweled, or nailed together (figure 4.42). In bell towers too small to accommodate flights of stairs, a spiral staircase (*caracol*, snail; figure 4.43) provided access to the bells and roof . Wedges of stone or wood (usually mesquite) were cut for the steps. One end of each step could be tapered and a rounded protrusion drilled through, lined up, and secured to the steps above and below it, or fitted into the neighboring piece pintle style, with allowances made for the step that would nest against it. Alternatively, the stairwell shaft (*árbol*) could be notched horizontally at appropriate intervals and the steps fitted in. Either way, the sides of the stairwell were used to support the loose end of each step.

Decorative Work

Remnants of paint on carved stone figures on the façade of the Cathedral of Chihuahua; on figures, cornices, and the door frame of the side portal of Santa Eulalia de Mérida (Chihuahua); and on the stone retablo of La Castrense in Santa Fe (New Mexico); painted plaster on the stone arches of the Convento de San Francisco de Asís in Sombrerete (Zacatecas); on the volutes accompanying the beastly gargoyles along the roof's edge of San Juan de Dios (Durango, Durango; see figure 6.33); and on the painted plaster figures and façade of San Xavier near Tucson (Arizona) are just a few of many examples of the widespread custom of adding color to stone and plaster features—both inside and out. Notwithstanding the weathered, begrimed, or "renovated" appearance of many churches today, color was used to create realism and add richness to images on churches throughout northern New Spain, just as it had been on Greek, Roman, and Gothic statuary. Moreover, beams, corbels, tablas, and latillas—carved, painted, or arranged in patterns—provided additional spaces for decorative treatment, as did the risers of stairs, which could be covered with fired ceramic tile, painted, or even faced with pieces of mica, as at San Bernardo de Awátovi (Arizona).[64]

[Windows, Façades, and Exterior Walls] Because of the greater expense of building with stone and the paucity of qualified stonemasons on the frontier, finished stone was restricted, even in examples such as the Cathedral of Durango, to façades; pillars; an occasional retablo (see below); and cornice, door, and window trim.[65] Finely cut decorative stonework around windows and doors, or sometimes covering entire façades, was used

4.41. Interior of La Santa Vera Cruz de Sombrerete, Zacatecas, showing what is probably the original wooden floor, 1983. The small notch at the end of each plank facilitated raising it in order that a grave could be prepared in that section of the floor.

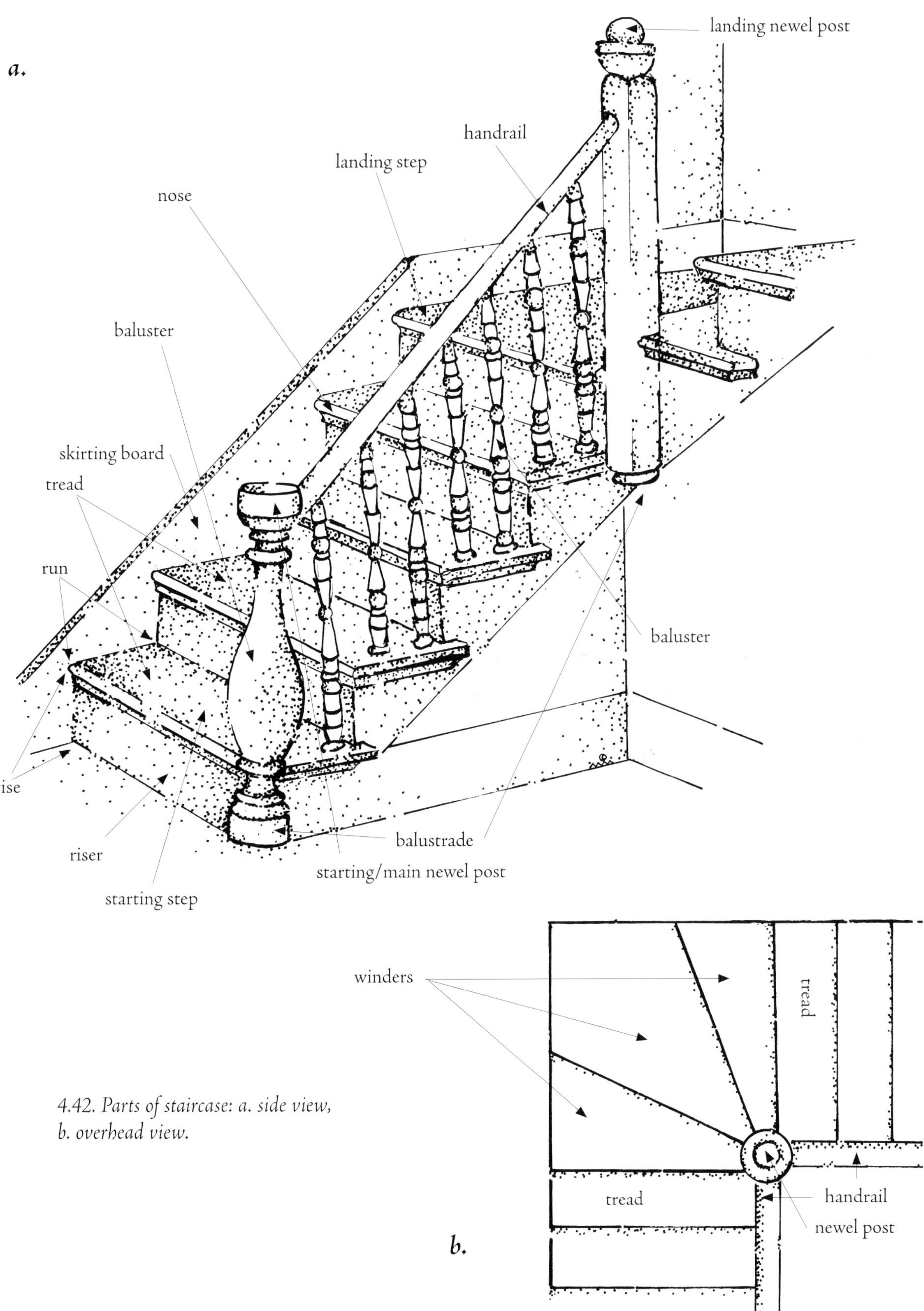

4.42. Parts of staircase: a. side view, b. overhead view.

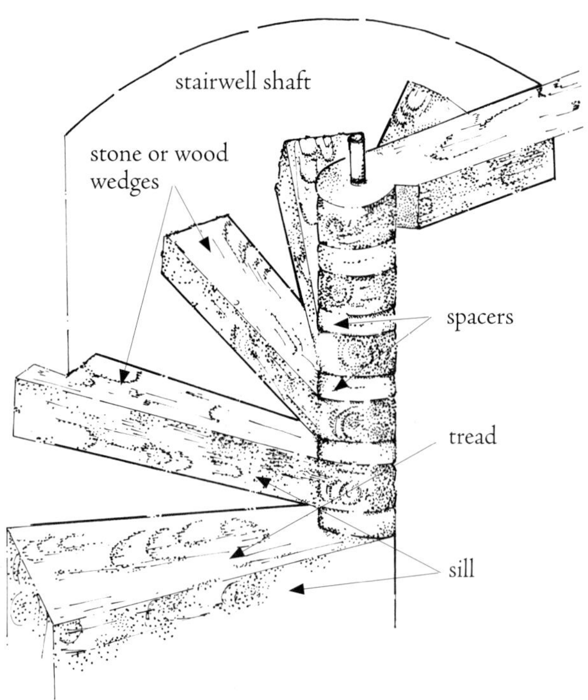

4.43. *Construction of a spiral staircase.*

to give a sense of sophistication and permanence to a façade or church made essentially of rubble stonework.

Limestone was carved while wet (usually at the quarry site to reduce weight and thus transportation costs), allowed to harden, and then polished, a centuries' old practice among stonemasons. Such a method can be seen in the elaborate carving around the main portal and sacristy window at the mission church San José y San Miguel in San Antonio (Texas); the deep undercuts and limpid decorative stonework have almost the feel of carved wood (see figure 2.20b). As a contrast, the stiffer, more straightforward stone carving on doorways, columns, and pilasters of the main frontispieces of the Cathedrals of Durango and Chihuahua has a drier and less spirited effect (figures 4.44 and 4.45).[66]

[Interior Walls] Lime plaster over adobe, fired brick, or stone—or adobe plaster over adobe—gave interior walls a pleasing aesthetic, helped preserve them, and provided a smooth surface upon which religious or simply decorative motifs could be painted. Most interior wall decorations took the form of painted embellishments and accents around windows, doors, and holy water fonts. More extensive decorations included painted dados, as at San Xavier near Tucson (Arizona, see figure 4.5); larger-than-life figures such as Death, the Devil, or the Virgin Mary, as at San Diego de Alcalá del Pitiquito (Sonora); architectural elements covering entire sections of wall, as on the inside of the drum at San Pedro y San Pablo in Tubutama (Sonora), on the apse wall behind the main altar of San José de Tumacácori (Arizona), and on the transept wall behind the collateral altar of La Purísima Concepción in Caborca (Sonora), the last two painted to resemble retablos; and trompe l'oeil decorations at San Miguel Arcángel de la Frontera near Paso Robles (California).

Scattered throughout northern New Spain's mission churches, most notably at San Xavier near Tucson (Arizona), were murals of narrative scenes. Artisans brushed onto dry white plastered walls either tempera (pigments suspended in water-based animal protein or plant resin binder) or, using the *fresco secco* technique, water-based paints mixed with lime water (see also "Painting on Walls" under "Paintings" in chapter 10).[67] Paints were applied to areas either (1) inscribed by a compass; (2) with the aid of pencil or charcoal sketches or stencils made from strips of leather, parchment, or paper (which allowed artisans to rapidly cover large areas with continuous or repeated designs); or (3) freehand to suggest a texture or a different building material (such as jasper or marble), to provide "fillers" for large areas of bare wall, or to enhance the overall effect of a painted scene.

[Ceilings] In their *artesones* and in their deeply carved corbels and beveled or scored beams imitating alfarje pieced woodwork effects, some church ceilings in northern New Spain clearly reflect mudéjar influences (see figure 2.5).[68] Decorative ceiling treatments that fitted pieces of wood together in coffers or elaborate geometric and lattice-like patterns, the artesonado and alfarje techniques were inherited by the Spaniards from the Moors, modified, and exported to the New World, where they were used extensively for both practical (shortages of large, clear pieces of wood) and aesthetic reasons. Besides the magnificent ceiling of Santa Rosalie de las Cuevas, two notable examples of artesonado ceilings in northern New Spain—in imminent danger of being lost through neglect or "barbaric renewal"—are the painted and coffered soffit of the choir loft at San Felipe y Santiago in Janos and the chapel ceiling at Santa Rosa de Lima in Cusihuiriáchic

4.44. Detail of carved east frontispiece, showing Saint Mark, Catedral de Durango, 1983.

4.45. Detail of carved main frontispiece, Catedral de Chihuahua, 1982.

4.46. Soffit of choir loft showing artesonado techniques, San Felipe y Santiago de Janos, Chihuahua, 1987. The numerous well-meant but ineffective restoration attempts on this structure have failed to preserve the painting on the soffit.

(all Chihuahua; figures 4.46, 4.47, and 6.10; see "Mudéjar" in chapter 2).

Unusual decorative ceiling treatments also included wattle and daub, locally referred to as *jacal*, applied to the balcony ceiling between the bell towers at San Francisco de Asís in Santa Fe (New Mexico).[69] Bentwood ribbing (perhaps the work of a boat builder?) was used for the camarín ceiling at San Miguel in Moctezuma (Sonora; figure 4.48). In other examples, the choir loft and dome ceilings of San Xavier near Tucson (Arizona) and the choir loft ceiling of its sister church, La Purísima Concepción in Caborca (Sonora), were all given a "pleated" plaster treatment.

[Doors] Wooden doors were given special and occasionally very elaborate treatment on the outside face (for symbolism in the treatment of doors, see **Doors, gates, and portals** entry in chapter 11). The outside paneling was beveled, carved, or both (the doors always swung inward for lighting as well as defense), whereas the inside pieces and framing were left unfinished, with the marks of the carpenter's adze often in evidence. The carved pan-

4.47. Artesonado chapel ceiling, Santa Rosa de Lima de Cusihuiriáchic, Chihuahua, 1991. The corrugated steel roofing may be seen in several sections where the wood panels have fallen and not been replaced.

els and pieces relate directly to the artesonado tradition of the mudéjar craftsmen and are common features in the churches of northern New Spain. Making doors and furniture from panels held in place by a framework saved both wood and weight. Where wood was more abundant, doors were sometimes made from thick planks secured with huge nails to a frame behind.

Although door leaves were usually rectangular, the paneling on the top section was often arranged in an arc to harmonize with the arch of the portal. Sixteenth-, seventeenth-, eighteenth-, and early-nineteenth-century portals, main and side, were usually of heroic proportions, designed to accommodate the passage of processional figures (*pasos*).[70] Because it was impractical to leave the entire door open simply to allow worshippers to enter or leave the church, doors were built within doors—wickets within leaves, both having hinges (see figures 2.16 and 5.4). And because churches were often plagued by mice, a small opening (*gatera*, cat's door) was made in the bottom of one of the doors to accommodate the resident cat. Gateras can be seen in the former mission churches of San Juan Bautista and San Fernando Rey de España (both California) and San Ignacio in Kadakaaman (Baja California Sur; figure 4.49).

4.48. Interior of the camarín at San Miguel Arcángel de Oposura, Moctezuma, Sonora, notable for its bentwood ceiling, 2002.

4.49. Sacristy door containing a gatero, San Ignacio de Loyola de Kadakaaman, Baja California Sur, 1987.

Chapter 5

The Church Building

There is no "typical" church building. Even churches sharing common materials, locations, builders, and funding will vary in their dimensions, floor plans, tower arrangements, and façade treatments, not to mention any number of architectural details. As with floor plans, however, the basic parts of the church building were prescribed by canon law. And because these parts were also subject to the prevailing architectural style of the time, there are dependable generalizations and descriptive terms to guide us in viewing or analyzing the interior or exterior of a particular church.

Outer Body

Although canon law makes no prescriptions as to the exterior of a church building, tradition dictates that the church be the tallest and most impressive structure in the community and that its outer adornment reflect the solemnity and, if possible, the majesty of its sacred purpose (figure 5.1).

Crosses

Numbering from one to twenty-four, small crosses can occasionally be seen painted or carved on the outer walls of the churches of northern New Spain. Called dedication crosses, these mark the places where the structure was blessed when it was formally dedicated; canon law prohibits their removal.[1] Crosses placed on other exterior walls of the church complex most often mark the Stations of the Cross (see under "Nave, Aisles, Transepts" later in the chapter). A freestanding cross may also be placed at the top of a church façade or frontispiece, especially where this constitutes the church's highest point (see also "**Cross** entry in chapter 11).

5.1. Catedral de Chihuahua, ca. 1880, with exterior features labeled. (Private collection, photographer unknown)

Façades, Frontispieces, Portals

A church may have side and rear façades in addition to its main, or principal, façade (*imafronte*). That the ornamented frontispieces throughout northern New Spain had much in common with the ubiquitous baroque retablos is no accident. Indeed, being directly inspired in their plans, architectural details, and decorative motifs by their churches' interior retablos, frontispieces may properly be referred to as *retablos exteriores*, a building concept imported from Spain (see "Retablos Exteriores: Cathedral of Chihuahua" under "Retablos" in chapter 10).[2] The assertiveness and didactic character of these frontispieces are direct emanations of counterreformational demands. The retablo arrangement of the frontispiece (*frontispicio*) provides an appropriate setting for outdoor religious ceremonies or processions and may offer a preview of the main altar's backdrop. Indeed, the terms used for the parts of the frontispiece and the retablo are virtually identical.

Because the architectural front of most churches contains the principal entrance, or portal (from Latin *porta*, large door), the greatest amount of exterior decoration is ordinarily concentrated there.[3] The main portal draws on the powerful symbolism of a gateway to a walled city, palace, or temple. It serves not only as the entrance to the City of God but—like the main portal to pagan temples before it—as a backdrop for religious ceremonies and pageants.

Depending on the church site and plan, and the ambition or inclination of the builders, the main frontispiece could take a variety of forms.[4] Humble as a church might be, builders gave special treatment, if only a niche over the door or an enlargement of door jambs, to this most important frontispiece, which marked the threshold between the exterior world and the sacred area within (figure 5.2). Accordingly, Charles Borromeo instructs that the frontispiece should be made majestic and be adorned with elements of sacred history (figure 5.3).[5]

In the large, well-developed churches of northern New Spain, the frontispiece commonly has nine sections, created by three horizontal registers, or stories (*cuerpos*), and three vertical bays (*calles* or *carreras*), with those at the sides usually narrower than the central bay, where the main portal is located. The vertical bays are separated by columns; the intercolumniations (*entrecalles*) between them contain niches for statues or spaces for other decorative treatments. In an ultrabaroque elaboration, these spaces boast estípites, intricately decorated columns or pilasters, most often with their own niches for statues. When developed to project above the roofline, the central bay's top section forms a pediment or gable (*frontón*), occasionally surmounted by religious statues, coats of arms, or simply finials (remates; see figures 2.16 and 5.3).

Following a tradition established in the Renaissance, different orders of columns were commonly used in the registers, with the heaviest and largest columns at the bottom and progressively lighter and smaller columns in each ascending story. The Cathedral of Saltillo (Coahuila; figure 5.4), for example, has four large salomónico columns in the first register, four estípite columns in the second, and two small salomónico columns in the third. Although the use of different kinds of columns in successive registers might occasionally reflect changing architectural styles over the prolonged period it took to complete most frontispieces, stability and aesthetics, as spelled out by Vitruvius, are the most likely reasons for placing more massive and ornate columns in the lowest, and progressively lighter and more delicate ones in each higher, register.[6] Even within the same register, the number, and occasionally also the style, of columns separating the bays may vary. These departures from architectural harmony and symmetry, however, most often add to the baroque qualities of richness, drama, and the unexpected.

The frontispieces in northern New Spain range from the simple and sparsely adorned on more humble or early-nineteenth-century mission churches, especially of Alta California, to the highly elaborate and impressive on the churches and cathedrals of wealthy mining or trading centers. For the latter, an abundance of decorative elements might flank the main portal: niches and bases holding statues of saints; monograms of the religious orders, Christ, and Mary; and other religious symbols carved in stone or plaster. Frontispieces usually contain a sculpture of the dedicatory figure, with secondary figures arranged in registers and bays in well-developed examples, following the same rules as retablos in the choice, precedence, and arrangement of the figures (see also "Retablos Exteriores: Cathedral of Chihuahua" and "Iconographic Balance" under "Retablos" in chapter 10 and introductory remarks in chapter 11).

Along with or instead of a cornerstone, a church might have a stone plaque (*lápida*), sometimes separate

5.2. Main façade, Santa María de las Cuevas, Chihuahua, 2003. Even in a simple church such as this, the frontispiece was a grand entrance into the City of God.

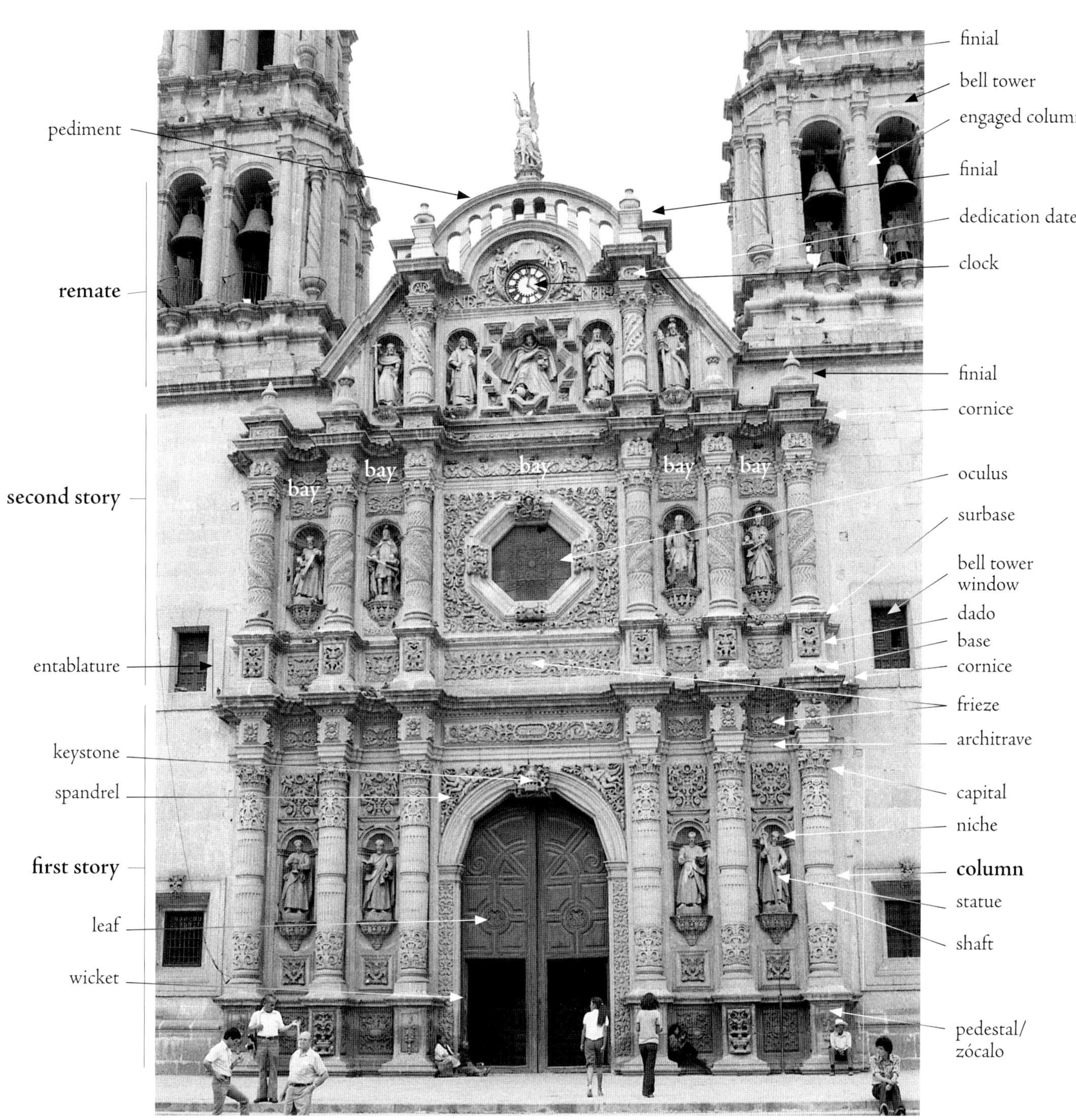

5.3. Main frontispiece, Catedral de Chihuahua, 1982. The uppermost central figure is St. Francis of Assisi; the Twelve Disciples fill the other niches.

5.4. Main frontispiece, Catedral de Saltillo, Coahuila, 1940. Although containing a veritable hodgepodge of sculptured architectural designs, the cathedral's facade nevertheless imparts an appropriate dignity partially because of the massiveness of the two outermost, rounded piers. (Private collection, photographer unknown)

from, but often incorporated into, the frontispiece. Like a cornerstone, the plaque would be inscribed with the date the church was dedicated or completed and with the names of those who supervised or funded its construction (see also "Foundations" under "Techniques" in chapter 4).

Based on the presence and arrangement of bell towers and certain other features, façades can be divided into three principal types. The simplest, or plain wall façade (figure 5.5), contained no bell towers, a door, and perhaps a window or two (especially when the church had a choir loft). Bells might be hung in a bell wall crowning the main façade (figure 5.6) or at the side of the church—either attached (see figure 2.29a–b) or freestanding. The simplicity of the plain wall façade could be deceptive, however, serving the symbolic or aesthetic purposes of churches that were far from humble or primitive.

In the second type, a single-tower façade, for reasons of economy or to serve the symbolism of a particular religious order, the façade was conceived and built to have one bell tower (figure 5.7). The Jesuit Order, for example, used this type of façade not only in northern but throughout central and southern New Spain, even for churches as large and impressive as San Francisco Javier de Tepotzotlán (México) and La Compañía in Guanajuato (Guanajuato).

In the flanking tower façade (see figures 2.1 and 2.16a)—the third principal type—bell towers were placed at the corners of the main façade and incorporated into the shape and form of the structure, without intruding into the nave. These massive towers served as buttressing; when hollow, as most were, they provided an extra room for worship or rites and a passage to the choir loft, roof, and bells (see figures 3.7, 3.9, 3.14, and 3.15).[7]

Decorative treatment was also given to the façades around the side portals, with the degree of elaborateness depending on the richness of the church's overall decoration. These might be similar to the façade around the main portal, but were almost always lesser in degree. An exception to this strong general rule, the side portal of San José de Parral (Chihuahua; see figure 2.14) received more attention than the main portal, most likely because it faces the principal plaza. Entrances to the sacristy and to chapels from the street or courtyards were also decorated (see also "Doors" under "Techniques" in chapter 4).

Atypical façades did occur, such as the hinged façade (where a significant part of the façade's sides are constructed forward at an angle to the center section) at San Luis Gonzaga de Bacadéhuachi (Sonora; figure 5.8); and façades embellished by porches or porticos in New Mexican churches (see figure 3.19a–b) and at San Francisco de Asís (Mission Dolores) in San Francisco, among other mission churches of Alta California. Other examples include main façades located to one side of the nave at Santa Ana in Durango (Durango; see "Nuns' Churches" under "Church Complexes" in chapter 3; see also figure 3.21) and at San Pedro y San Pablo de Tubutama (Sonora; see also figure 2.24b).

Besides the main portal, there might be side portals along the length of the nave, depending on the size of the church and location of adjoining buildings.[8] Even in large churches, there were usually no more than two other sets of exterior doors placed along the nave, one on either side facing each other somewhere after the baptistery and before the crossing or sanctuary. The side entrances gave access to the church from the convento or church grounds. If a convento was attached to a church (excepting in a nuns' church), its main entrance faced the same direction as the church's main façade. This doorway area, the portería, took the form of a recessed vestibule or porch and may have served as an open chapel in some of the New Mexican churches (see also discussion of open chapels in "Capillas, Camarines" under "Church Buildings" in chapter 3). If the church was coupled with another; for example, a parochial church joined to the side of a convent church or a cathedral (as at the Cathedral of Saltillo), there might be passages connecting the two in areas to which only the staff had access, but not through doors opening into the nave or aisles.

Exterior Balconies

Like their interior counterparts, these platforms, sometimes supported on corbels or ménsulas, projected from walls and were enclosed by a balustrade (top railing and balusters; see figure 2.16b). Although not required parts of the church exterior, balconies appeared in a few of the mission churches of northern New Spain, as well as in the Cathedral of Durango (Durango), where they were likely used by clergy to address congregants gathered in the atrio below (see figure 2.16b).

5.5. San Miguel Arcángel de la Frontera, near Paso Robles, California, ca. 1910. (Newman Postcard Company, private collection)

5.6. An example of a bell wall in a plain wall facade, San Antonio Paduano de Oquitoa, Sonora, 1978. Over the years, replastering and repairs to the raised band of cut bricks along the edge of the frontispiece have subtly changed its form, giving it a less dramatic and softer profile.

5.7. Flanking tower façade, San José de Parral, Chihuahua, 1982.

5.8. Hinged façade, San Luis Gonzaga de Bacadéhuachi, Sonora, 1965. The original massive, three-stage towers were nearly completely destroyed in an 1887 earthquake. Repairs produced these truncated and much less impressive versions. (By Pál Kelemen. Courtesy of Arizona State Museum, University of Arizona)

5.9. Nuestra Señora de la Asunción del Real de los Álamos, Sonora, 1980. Construction was halted when Bishop Reyes left his post abruptly, and the planned second bell tower was never built.

Towers

Many churches originally intended to have two matching towers, with the symbolism of *porta coeli* (gate to Heaven) clearly in mind, wound up having either one tower—as in the case of Nuestra Señora de la Asunción del Real de Álamos (Sonora; figure 5.9), originally planned by Bishop Reyes to be a cathedral with two flanking towers—or two that did not match. Sometimes, only the base of the second tower was completed; sometimes, a second tower—with different proportions or in a different style—was added many years after the rest of the church.

Two flanking towers create the illusion of lightness in their vertical thrust, all the more so from the mid-seventeenth through the eighteenth centuries, when they are combined with frontispieces that are higher than they are wide. The plain bases of the towers often serve as an effective foil to the elaborate decorative treatment given the frontispiece. Or the ornamentation of the frontispiece may spill over onto the bases, increasing the visual importance of the main portal and diminishing the imposing statement of the towers.

The belfry (from the Middle French *berfrei*, siege tower; in Spanish, *campanario*) was placed over a specially constructed base as part of, or attached to, the church building. Occasionally, churches would have separate bell towers, properly called campaniles (*campaniles*), sometimes freestanding, as at Nuestra Señora de Guadalupe in Ciudad Juárez (Chihuahua; figure 5.10) and Nuestra Señora de la Asunción de Arizpe (Sonora; figure 5.11), but more often butted up against the church wall, as at Nuestro Padre San Ignacio de Loyola de Onavas (Sonora; figure 5.12). Bell towers having more than one story, called staged bell towers, may be found in northern New Spain

THE PLAZA AND CHURCH OF EL PASO

5.10. Nuestra Señora de Guadalupe, Ciudad Juárez, Chihuahua, with a freestanding bell tower, ca. 1850. (Drawn by A. de Vandacourt and produced by Sabony, Major and Knapp, New York)

from the eighteenth century on. Such towers parallel frontispieces in their treatment, with the progression from relatively more massive to lighter effects accentuated by the use of different styles of columns in successive stages (see figure 2.16a).

In lieu of bell towers, the mission churches of Alta California commonly had a massive bell wall (also called a campanario) built to one side of the main portal. Bells were hung in the windows or open spaces of this wall and could be rung using ropes that extended to the ground or to a platform, as seen at Santa Inés (Santa Ynez) near Solvang (California; see figure 2.29b). They might also be hung in a less massive bell wall, called an *espadaña*, which could be a perforated parapet or extension of the main façade above the roofline, a device used throughout New Spain from the sixteenth into the nineteenth centuries, as at San Francisco de la Espada in San Antonio (Texas; figure 5.13).[9]

Where a bell tower or wall was in disrepair, not completed, or beyond a builder's capabilities, bells were hung between poles or on a frame in front and to one side of the church's entrance. This practice can be still seen at several sites in Chihuahua (figure 5.14) and Sonora.

Towers for access to the roof, such as the one on the west corner of the façade of Nuestro Padre San Ignacio de Loyola de Cabórica (Sonora; figure 5.15, left) and at the east corner of San Francisco Javier de Vigge-Biaundó (Baja California Sur; see figure 2.9, left) could also serve defensive purposes. Loopholes can be clearly seen in the bell tower of San José de Tumacácori (Arizona). The size, shape, and location of a small, protruding feature with one small window on the northeast, sanctuary end of the nave

5.11. Nuestra Señora de la Asunción de Arizpe, Sonora, 1999. The ambitiousness of this structure, like that of the one in Álamos, is a reminder of the important economic, clerical, and military significance these places once held.

5.12. Main façade, Nuestro Padre San Ignacio de Loyola de Onavas (rebuilt), Sonora, 2000.

5.13. San Francisco de la Espada, San Antonio, Texas, 1990, showing the espadaña. The unusual mixtilinear interior and exterior profiles of the arch is the result of erroneous arrangements of the voussoirs.

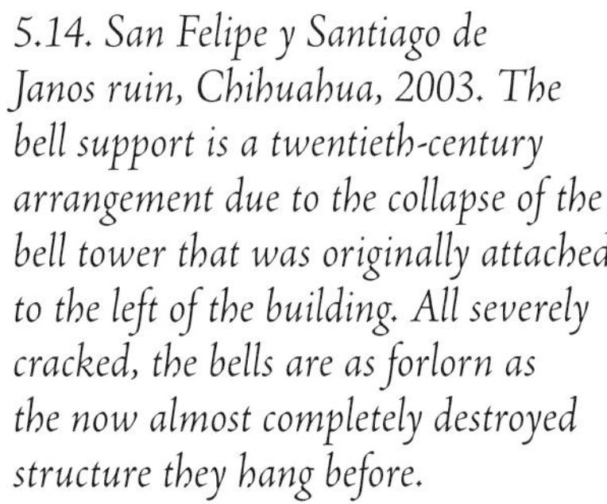

5.14. San Felipe y Santiago de Janos ruin, Chihuahua, 2003. The bell support is a twentieth-century arrangement due to the collapse of the bell tower that was originally attached to the left of the building. All severely cracked, the bells are as forlorn as the now almost completely destroyed structure they hang before.

5.15. Nuestro Padre San Ignacio de Loyola de Cabórica, Sonora, 2001. The tower for access to the roof is on the left. The strategic size of the windows throughout and their placement would have made this building eminently defendable.

of San Ignacio de Loyola de Kadakaaman (Baja California Sur; figure 5.16) strongly suggest a sentry post.

The nave of a church could be arranged so that it formed part of the defensive wall of a village (as suggested by the Laws of the Indies, ordinance 133). Two possible examples are San Pedro y San Pablo in Tubutama (Sonora)—the only church in northern New Spain other than the nuns' church Santa Ana in Durango (Durango) whose main portal is constructed on the side of the nave—and San Antonio de Padua in Casas Grandes Viejo (Chihuahua), both sites established among rebellious Indians.

Parapets and Crenellations

Although the archbishop of Sevilla had forbidden fortified churches and cemeteries in 1512, conditions were held to be different in New Spain. Following the medieval Andalusian tradition, influenced in turn by the Moors, fortified parapets appeared on sixteenth-century monastic churches in New Spain. The stepped crenellations seen in Nicholas Brown's circa 1870 photograph of the north chapel of the Cathedral of Santa Fe (figure 5.17) are strongly reminiscent of the twelfth-century battlements around the Patio de los Naranjos of the great mosque of Sevilla, later incorporated into the cathedral begun in the mid-fifteenth century. Although, after the reconquest of New Mexico, most eighteenth-century New Mexican churches were crenellated, remodeling, reroofing, or destruction of mission churches throughout northern New Spain has, in all instances, eliminated these crenellations.

A parapet wall around the nave, transepts, and apse served aesthetic, functional, and defensive purposes. A low wall could hide the roofline and create an even profile. It could shunt runoff water to a few points, helping to prevent erosion or excessive moisture at the foundation

5.16. Northeast corner of the sanctuary, San Ignacio de Loyola de Kadakaaman, Baja California Sur, 1987. The small tower-like structure resembles a sentry post, and damage to the plaster around the "porthole" is said to have been done by bullets during the early part of the twentieth century.

5.17. North chapel, Cathedral of Santa Fe, New Mexico, ca. 1870. Although hardly necessary for defense when the new cathedral (portal facing viewer) was built, crenellations were nevertheless placed on all the uppermost horizontal edges, most likely for a homogenous appearance. Subsequent building modifications have eliminated them all. (By Nicholas Brown, courtesy of the Museum of New Mexico at the Palace of the Governors, Neg. #55484)

line. Finally, it could protect the church's defenders as they repelled attackers.

Strictly decorative rather than defensive, the widely spaced projections along the roofline of the abandoned church San Lorenzo de Tabalá (Sinaloa; figure 5.18) are strongly reminiscent of Italian Renaissance and baroque architecture. These projections might more appropriately be called finials (remates) than crenellations, as might similar projections on San Xavier near Tucson (Arizona) and its companion church, La Purísima Concepción in Caborca (Sonora) (see figure 2.2). Although the gigantic, urnlike objects, appropriately called *macetones* (large flower pots) or *jarones* (large jugs), along the roofline of the naves of San Francisco Javier de Vigge-Biaundó (see figure 5.19) and Santa Rosalía de Mulegé (see figure 6.24) and atop the façade at San Ignacio de Kadakaaman (all Baja California Sur), create a massive, defensive effect, they, too, are strictly decorative and, like the finials of San Lorenzo de Tabalá, hark back to the Italian Renaissance (see also "Finials, Crowning Ornaments" under "Architectural Details" in chapter 6).

Domes

Well more than half the churches in northern New Spain were crowned with a dome (many had more than one). The most prominent feature of a domed church's profile after its bell tower, the main dome was usually placed over the crossing (occasionally over the apse or sanctuary) on an octagonal wall or a drum (*tambor*), often supported by four vaulted arches (*arcos torales*). Although most church domes in northern New Spain were smoothly plastered and unadorned, some were decorated with colored tile or with molded or sculptured accents along their segmented edges. A few, such as the main dome of Santiago Apóstol de Altamira (Tamaulipas) and the baptistery dome of the Cathedral of Durango (Durango; figure 5.20), had windows piercing the drum or vaulting, which served to lighten the dome's appearance and to illuminate the area or room it covered.[10]

The main dome—as well as lesser domes over bell towers, chapels, or sacristies—might be crowned by a

5.18. San Lorenzo de Tabalá (ruin), Sinaloa, 2000. The finials along the roof are purely decorative.

5.19. The roof of San Francisco Xavier de Vigge-Biaundó, Baja California Sur, looking toward the dome over the sanctuary, 1987.

5.20. The baptistery dome (left) of the Catedral de Durango has windows in both the drum and vaulting (1984).

lantern (*linternilla*), a slender vertical structure composed of a cluster of columns or series of windows, or simply a polygonal shape with openings.[11] The position and shape of the lantern created a dramatic and aesthetically pleasing effect. The lantern's windows or openings provided additional light to the area or room beneath the dome as well as to the underside of the dome itself. Access to the lantern and to the top of a domed tower was usually gained by iron hand- and footholds or by wooden ladder, though sometimes steps (*escalenitas;* figure 5.21) were molded onto the dome's surface.

Windows and Clerestories

Augustine held that Christ was literally, not just metaphorically, the Divine Light. Through God's light, all could be seen and understood as one. The mortals stumbling in their darkness had only to lift their eyes to the illuminated altars and upper reaches of a church, where celestial beings, salvation, redemption, and Heaven were suggested and often portrayed. Under Moorish, baroque, and counter-reformational influences, clerestories, windows, and other openings were placed so that light would pour through them to spotlight the main or collateral altars or special niches at certain times of the day.

Fenestration thus served symbolic, dramatic, and aesthetic as well as practical and strategic ends. Church windows were placed high above ground level to prevent profane outsiders from spying on sacred services;[12] to allow the lower walls to be covered by altars, niches, and decoration; and to be less distracting to the worshippers. They were commonly placed in the main façade, in a bell tower, or along the stairwell to illuminate inside rooms or passageways. In larger churches, windows above the side portals, usually incorporated in the portals' decorative schemes, helped light the center of the nave and the altars and aisles along the sides of the nave, as well as the underside of the main dome and the area around its drum.

Along the unsettled frontier, windows were kept small and few for defensive purposes. Where iron and craftsmen were available, first-story windows were sometimes covered by grilles (*rejas*), often fine examples of artistic blacksmithing. Where iron was scarce, grilles could be made from long, upright, wooden railings turned on a lathe.

As the retablos mayores grew larger beginning in fifteenth-century Spain, windows in the rear of the apse were eliminated. Because neither congregation nor celebrants would any longer be blinded by light coming in over the main altar, builders and decorators were free to develop striking ceiling treatments above the apse. Apsidal windows were retained, however, in churches where the choir was behind the main altar, which was moved forward into the crossing, as is the case at the Cathedral of Durango (Durango), where the windows were needed to illuminate the choir and its occupants.

Builders of seventeenth- and eighteenth-century rectangular (single-nave) and cruciform churches in New Mexico (and a surprising number elsewhere in northern and central New Spain) solved lighting problems with a transverse clerestory window. They raised the roof level before the sanctuary (rectangular plan) or at the front of the crossing (cruciform plan) and created a transverse opening across the nave to direct light onto the main altar or crossing. In some cases, they oriented the church itself to receive the best possible lighting. While the transverse clerestory is not unique to the New World, coming from Andalucía and originally North Africa,[13] its exact form appears to be distinctly New World and may have been limited to central and northern New Spain (see figures 2.4a–b and 4.22).

Roof type also helped determine the placement of side windows. With groin vaulting, windows could be placed above the impost level. Barrel vaulting usually necessitated placing them below the impost level, which created a darker ceiling as opposed to those lighted by the higher windows in groin-vaulted structures. With pitched or flat roofs, windows pierced the side walls between piers or buttresses about two-thirds of the distance up the wall. The need to avoid excessive light and to control temperature extremes could have been as much of a factor in determining the size of windows as bay widths, aesthetic considerations, and technical skills.

Not surprisingly, the most elaborate decoration was often given to windows in the frontispiece. Although, for the most part, they were harmoniously incorporated and contributed to the overall decorative effect, in a few cases, they were the focus of attention in the frontispiece or competed with the rest of it (figure 5.22).

5.21. Escalenitas in the dome of Mission Santa Bárbara, California, ca. 1920. (Private collection, photographer unknown)

Many church windows have the same shapes as arched door openings and therefore also the same type names (figures 5.23 and 5.24). By adjusting the framing or jambs of a window, builders could accentuate or alter its shape. Generally wider within than without through splaying (embrasure), which funneled as much light as possible through walls thicker below than above, many lower windows also varied significantly in shape from outside to in. With gored splays, the top of a square or rectangular window could become oval. The greater light let in by such windows also alluded to amplitude in the mystical sense.[14]

5.22. Detail of the main frontispiece, showing the oculus and, above and to the sides of it, two atlantes that may represent seraphim; Santo Domingo de Sombrerete, Zacatecas, 1982.

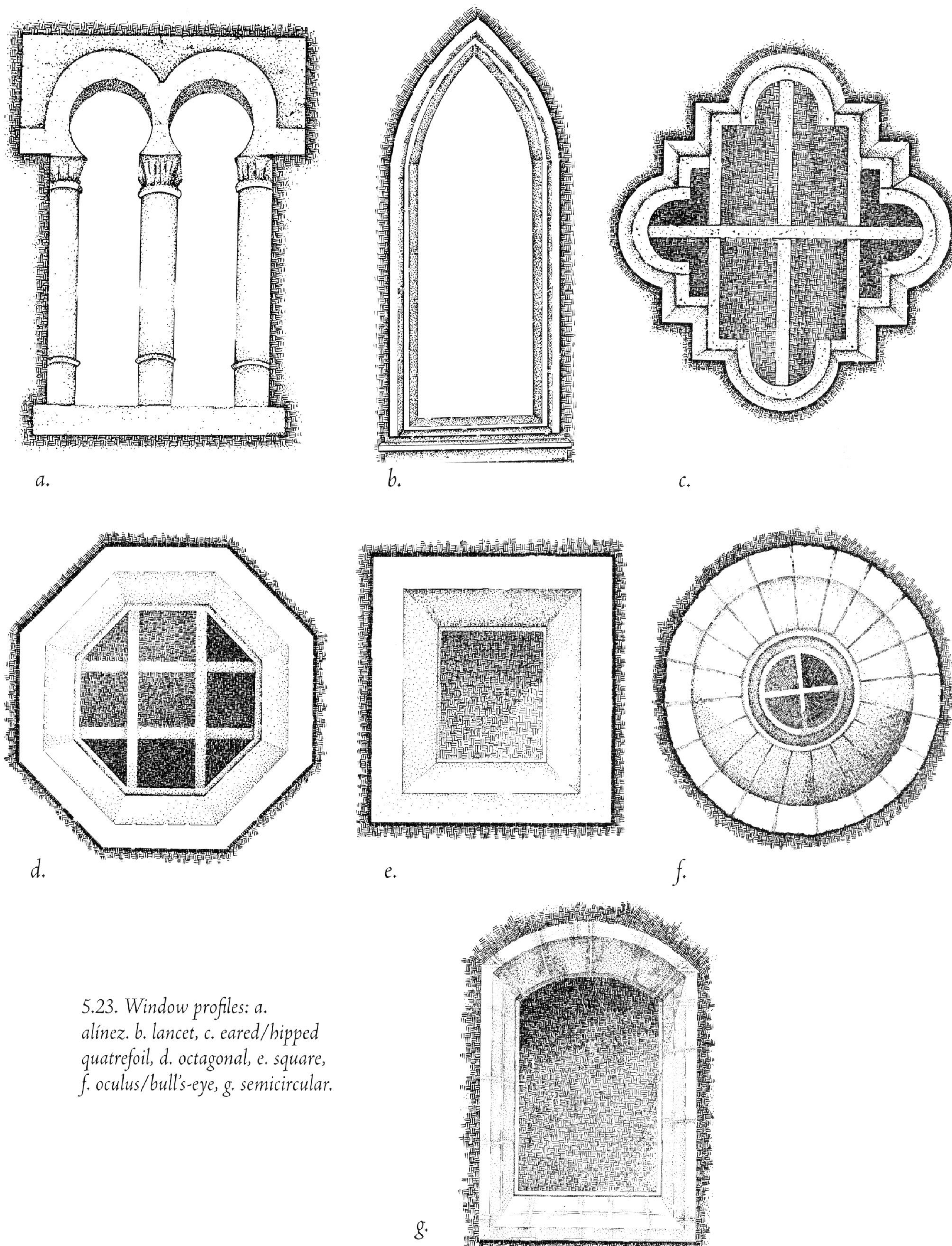

5.23. Window profiles: a. alínez. b. lancet, c. eared/hipped quatrefoil, d. octagonal, e. square, f. oculus/bull's-eye, g. semicircular.

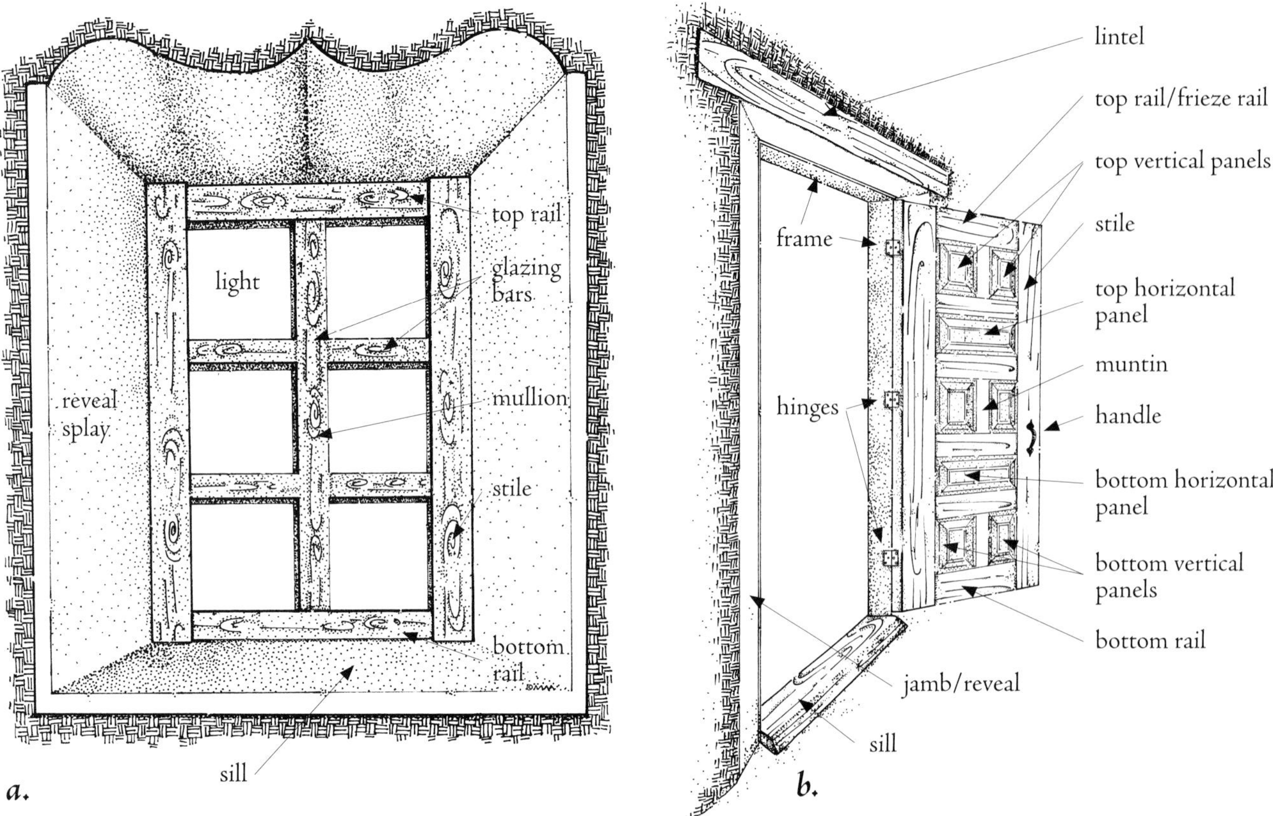

5.24. *Comparison of the parts of a window (a) and door (b). The window frame is mixtilinear in type.*

Splaying could also work the other way, however, forming windows wider on the outside than inside, as those in the first story of bell towers serving no defensive function.

Inner Body

In writings on religious symbolism since the Middle Ages, the principal parts of the church interior are referred to as parts of a body: the apse or sanctuary as the head, the transepts as arms, the nave as the body (effectively, the trunk or torso), and the main entrance as the foot.[15] Indeed, some have thought that the tilting of the axis of the apse and sanctuary from the central axis of the nave in some seventeenth-century New Mexican churches was meant to represent the sagging head of the crucified Christ. More likely, however, this effect, along with the gradual sloping downward of the apse ceiling and upward of the apse floor, was deliberately intended to focus attention on the main altar.[16]

According to canon law, a church had to have a sanctuary, sacristy, baptistery, and choir—the last three preferably as separate rooms, but all four at least as distinct areas. Although tradition held that baptistery and choir should be at the front of the church by the main portal, whereas sanctuary and sacristy should be at the rear with the main altar, their placement was not prescribed.

Vestibule, Choir, Baptistery

Levels above or below the ground floor were connected by steps or flights of steps (figure 5.25; see also "Stairs and Staircases" under "Techniques" in chapter 4). The area behind the main façade of most rectangular churches is divided by a mezzanine floor, which creates an upper choir (*coro*)—a gallery, loft, or tribune above for the choir and organ—and a lower choir (*sotocoro*) in the vestibule below. In the rectangular plan, access to the choir loft was by stairs, most often within a forward tower base, on the outside of the building, or within an attached convento. Rarely were there stairs directly from the lower to the upper choir, and then almost always in rudimentary churches such as Santa Rosa de Lima de Sombrerete (Zacatecas).

5.25. Interior staircase, Santa Rose de Lima, Sombrerete, Zacatecas, 1984. The steep incline was necessary in order to keep the staircase tucked under the very shallow choir loft.

Just inside the main entrance to the church and opposite each other were matching holy water stoups, generally embedded within a wall or pillars (less often, there was a single, larger, freestanding stoup).[17] Although canon law made no provisions regarding their placement, appearance, or composition, tradition dictated that they be conveniently available to congregants entering the church, that they be seemly, and that they be made of durable material.[18] Stoups in Sonora were often made of copper; those in Baja California, of alabaster; elsewhere in northern New Spain, of limestone or smooth-as-marble lime plaster.[19] Two of the most dramatic holy water stoups are to be found in La Purísima Concepción in Caborca (Sonora; figure 5.26; on the symbolism of the skull, see also **Skull** entry in chapter 11).

The lower choir could be used as a staging area for processions; in the absence of a formal baptistery, as a baptismal area; and for placement of a wooden screen (*cancel*; see under "Vestibule" in chapter 7). Because the lower choir is located in the vestibule, modern seating usually begins immediately beyond it. The upper choir, a part of the church from which the congregation was excluded during services, where priests, choir members, and musicians perform their tasks, is peculiar to Spanish religious

5.26. Holy water stoup, La Purísima Concepción de Nuestra Señora de Caborca, Sonora, 1982. Unfortunately, heavy layers of plaster over the years have blunted some of the details as well as obliterating the painted accents.

architecture; its importance developed during the late Gothic period. The soffit of the upper choir, or choir loft, is frequently decorated with carving, painting, or plaster relief (see figures 2.5, 4.29, 4.37, and 4.46). Although most often above the vestibule, in certain large cathedrals, such as the Cathedral of Durango (Durango), the choir is situated at the other end of the church, immediately behind the pulpit and main altar, where it may be set apart from the nave by railings, partitions, and a raised floor level (*bema;* originally, a feature of Roman basilicas).

On the ground floor of churches having towers, usually in the tower base on the left side as one faces the main altar (although occasionally on the right), there was often a baptistery, a small room containing a baptismal font and specially reserved for baptisms. Its location reflects the medieval concept of the church embodying the history of the world as the builders or churchmen understood it.[20] The forward position of the baptistery signifies that one enters the Church by Baptism. In the seventeenth-century Franciscan mission churches of San Bernardo de Awátovi

(Arizona) and San Gregorio de Abó (New Mexico), the baptistery is detached from the nave. In churches having no separate room for baptisms, the baptismal font is placed in the vestibule, as mentioned above, or along the side of the nave, well before the sanctuary.[21] Tradition and the symbolic act of baptism by submersion (signifying burial, followed by resurrection with Christ) dictated that the floor of the baptistery (or of the immediate area around the baptismal font) be lower by one step than the main floor of the church, although changes in floor levels during remodeling make it difficult to determine whether this was strictly observed in northern New Spain.[22]

On the opposite side of the vestibule, across from the baptistery and in the base of a matching tower if the church had two towers, a small room sometimes served as a chapel or storage space. Access to the towers and upper choir could be through this room, the baptistery, or both.

Nave, Aisles, Transepts

The central part of the church—its main body and a symbol of the Church Militant—the nave (from Latin *navis*, ship) is reserved for the congregation.[23] It may be flanked by aisles, which run its entire length (see figures 3.7 and 3.9). Although separated by an arcade of pillars and arches along that length, the aisles are nevertheless sometimes considered part of the nave.[24] Nave and aisles can be divided by bays: principal divisions marked by piers, windows, sections of vaulting, or roof levels, rather than by walls.

The inside walls of the nave or outer aisles (or, less often, the outside walls of a cemetery, cloister, or church) are divided equally and according to canon law into fourteen blessed spaces referred to as the Stations of the Cross (*Vía Crucis*). These may begin on either the Epistle or the Gospel side of the church. Each may contain a painting, print or engraving, plaque, or bas-relief sculpture representing its particular station, or simply a cross and number (see also "Stations of the Cross" in chapter 12).

Transepts, armlike extensions at right angles to the naves in cruciform churches, intersect immediately in front of the sanctuary. Referred to as the crossing, this area may be crowned with a dome on a drum, in turn supported by pendentives or squinches.

Apse, Sanctuary, Sacristy

The end of the church where the main altar is located is called the apse (from Latin *apis*, vault)—a symbol of the Church Triumphant. Originally, "apse" referred to the vaulted, semicircular or polygonal eastern end of the basilica or cathedral, where the bishop's chair was situated. Later, however, the apse became the rectangular, polygonal, rhomboidal, or semicircular termination of the nave opposite the main entrance. In rare instances, access from the apse to chapels or the main altar could be gained by an ambulatory (*ambulatorio*), an aisle along the inside wall of the apse.

In the strictest sense, the sanctuary (*santuario*) is the space between the communion rail (*comulgatorio*) and the main altar, an extension of the nave that includes the principal, or high, altar area (*capilla mayor*).[25] Here the ceiling is usually more elaborate than elsewhere in the church, and the floor level raised, to give the congregation a better view and to symbolize the exalted nature of the Mass, a standard device since perhaps the fourth century. Traditionally, the number of steps from the nave floor to the raised altar platform is odd, the practical effect of which is to have the priest arrive at the altar on the same foot with which he began to climb.[26]

Symbolizing the closeness of the faithful to Christ through the rite of Communion as well as the separation of things celestial from things terrestrial, the communion rail divides nave from sanctuary and congregation from celebrants, and is generally placed at the edge of the raised altar platform, with a triumphal arch overhead to set it apart. Also called a threshold arch and sometimes bearing only its own weight, the triumphal arch appears first in Byzantine architecture, tracing its origins to the Roman triumphal arch and, before that, to the sacred gateway of Mesopotamian temples. For early churchmen, this arch symbolized Christian triumph and the entrance to glory through death and resurrection (see figures 6.19 and 6.31; see also discussion of *retablos arcos triunfales* under "Retablos," "Form," in chapter 10).

The sacristy (*sacristía*) is a room (in most mission churches smaller than the sanctuary area) in which the clergy put on their vestments and prepare for services. It is almost always attached to the apse end of the church and connected to the sanctuary even in the simplest rectangular church. Within the sacristy, the sacred vessels and vestments for the Mass were stored away in a special closet (*armario*), area, or chest. Larger churches might have sacristy anterooms (*antesacristías*), a room or series of rooms, one leading into the other, between the sacristy and the outside entrance, as at Nuestra Señora de la Asunción in Álamos (Sonora), Bishop Reyes's proposed cathedral, and the Cathedral of Chihuahua (Chihuahua; see figure 3.9).[27] Although most often a single room, separate from the nave and built to one side of the church, the sacristy can also be an area behind the altar created by the retablo or by an extension of the nave, as in San Luis Obispo and several other Alta California mission churches.[28] Most sacristies have two doors, one leading directly from the sanctuary and the other to the outside or the convento. Where the diocese or see was especially rich, there might also be a treasure room (*sala de tesoros*) adjoining or opposite the sacristy to hold ornaments and church accessories made of precious metals.

Tribunes

Tribunes are balconies, *miradors* (lookouts, viewing points), or even windows—with or without lattice screening—that allow priests on the second floor to keep tabs on the congregation and allow infirm churchmen to attend services without having to leave the level of their rooms.[29] Remnants of tribunes can be seen in the ruined mission churches of San Gregorio de Abó and Nuestra Señora de los Ángeles de Porciúncula in Pecos (both New Mexico); this element is also present in the former mission church of San José y San Miguel in San Antonio (Texas).

Crypt

A cellar of a church used for burials and enclosed by foundation walls, the crypt (from the Greek *krupto*, to bury), or osario, was sometimes built partly aboveground, creating a higher floor level, as in the Cathedrals of Durango and Chihuahua. Most crypts in northern New Spain, however, were little more than an exhumed part of the floor, which was then filled in and covered over, with a stone plaque or other commemorative device to mark each burial site. Indeed, the floor of Santa Vera Cruz in Sombrerete (Zacatecas; see figure 4.41) consists of a series of wooden planks, miraculously preserved from "renovation," which are numbered to designate specific gravesites. In this and other such cases, several bodies might be buried at a single site, the burial area eventually becoming a mishmash of bone particles. (See also "Flooring" under "Techniques" in chapter 4.)

CHAPTER 6

DETAILS AND MOTIFS

Through their location, arrangement, and relative size, architectural and decorative elements served to express a wide variety of styles, variations on styles, and special treatments in the churches of northern New Spain. But it fell to the smallest recognizable parts of those elements to bring that expression into focus. Here I consider architectural details and decorative motifs (which could be religious or secular, but not profane—at least not in the eyes of the clerics guiding the project), both inside and outside the church building. I deal separately, however, with details and motifs of retablos and with religious imagery (to include paintings) in chapter 10: "Religious Images and Retablos."

As in previous chapters, Arabic and Spanish terms are cited with parenthetic English translations or simply by themselves where there is no widely accepted English equivalent or where the English equivalent is cumbersome. Key terms and other terms whose exact meaning may differ from English to Spanish or vice versa appear in English with parenthetic Spanish translations. Some etymology is provided as a heuristic or mnemonic device.

ARCHITECTURAL DETAILS

Columns

Generally circular in section, freestanding, and designed with prescribed proportions and parts, columns are vertical elements used for support, decoration, or both. Besides supporting arches, roofs, and ceilings, they were used freely in northern New Spain to decorate flanking door openings, niches, and windows in the frontispiece and side portals. They also contributed importantly to retablo assemblages and can be found in miniature as candelabrum and monstrance bases.

Engaged, applied, or attached columns or semicolumns are attached to, partially buried in, or recessed into a wall, with the name used depend-

6.1. An example of recessed columns, San Antonio de Padua de Tula, Tamaulipas, 1996.

ing on the amount of profile showing or the relationship between the element and the wall. An engaged or attached column or pier is created "in the round," with a freestanding shaft but with the pedestal and entablature incorporated into the backing wall. "Applied" and "recessed" are technically distinct terms, distinguished by the amount of column showing and the crispness of the delineating line. The visual effect is much the same, however—a partially revealed column emerging from the wall (figure 6.1). Most columns on portals or towers in northern New Spain were engaged. Some were nonsupporting, structurally nonfunctional, and placed as decorative framework for statues on frontispieces, imitating the gridwork of earlier retablos (see figures 5.3 and 5.4).

Depending on the shapes of their parts, columns may be categorized into architectural orders. The Greeks made use of three orders: Doric, Ionic, and Corinthian. The Romans used these three with slight differences and added the Tuscan and composite, to form what are referred to as the five classical orders. Vitruvius described the design, proportions, and use of the first four orders; in 1540, Serlio established the exact proportions and decorative elements of all five orders for Renaissance and succeeding architects.[1] The columns of all classical orders except Tuscan were fluted, with the number of flutings fixed at twenty (separated by a sharp edge, or arris) for Doric columns and at twenty-four (separated by a small fillet) for Ionic, Corinthian, and composite columns. Although architects have often modified the proportions of the orders and combined orders to meet various stylistic needs, each classical order can be broken down into three compound parts, and each part, into three divisions (figure 6.2a–e). These may be placed under a general category of purista, where the shafts of Greco-Roman origin are used in all their purest form and composition.

Most of the original architectural and decorative elements of the churches in northern New Spain during the colonial era can be loosely called "baroque," as defined in chapter 2. Because it is so firmly rooted in the Renaissance and in mannerism, most of the familiar characteristics of those two styles are recognizable in the baroque—amplified, animated, and combined in exciting and sometimes startling new ways. Although the five classical orders seldom appear in their purest forms, certain column types having classical proportions appear in whole or part during the early baroque and then again during the neoclassical period.

Four specific column types seen regularly throughout northern New Spain are salomónico, tritóstilo, estípite, and candelabrum (figure 6.2f–i). Transplanted from Europe, these column types responded to the individualism of New Spain by assuming distinctive and often unique forms. Hallmarks of different stages of the baroque and sometimes indicators of construction dates, the first three types can be found in great abundance, whereas the fourth, candelabrum, which leapfrogs a few centuries between the late Renaissance and mannerism and appears redesigned in combination with other late baroque elements, is less abundant.[2] Dating must be done cautiously, however: some types appeared simultaneously, and provincial conservatism often fostered resistance to others.

[Salomónico] So called because of its presumed use in Solomon's temple, a column of the salomónico type has a twisted shaft with a Corinthian-like capital; it is either spiral, as if the shaft itself had been twisted, or cylindrical, with helical carving in the form of grapevines or festoons of other plant shapes along its entire length. Twisted columns held great appeal for the baroque architect, not only because they heightened the contrast between light and shadow, but also because they seemed to defy natural laws governing columnar strengths and bearing weights. The salomónico column type appeared in central New Spain in 1646, was fashionable in the large cities there until about 1730, then extended into northern New Spain, where it lasted through the middle part of the eighteenth century and where columns were usually paired, with spirals going in opposite directions (see figure 6.3; also see figure 2.16b).[3] A variant of the salomónico column type, with fluting or grooving twisted in whole or part, the *entorchado* column type appears in Sevilla in the last half of the sixteenth century and continues into the first two or three decades of the seventeenth century. This style was used in northern New Spain about the same time as salomónico columns, most notably on the second story of the frontispiece of the Cathedral of Chihuahua (figure 6.4).

[Tritóstilo] Roughly translated as "column of thirds," tritóstilo is characterized by a three-part shaft whose bottom third is separated from its upper two-thirds by a cincture—a rounded, beltlike molding—and given a different, usually more elaborate treatment. This might include bifurcated designs, meandering foliage, or geometrical patterns, in addition to fluting, to which the generally much plainer upper part of the shaft served as foil. Occasionally, the order of elaboration might be reversed, with the bottom part remaining relatively staid and the top given a salomónico treatment. The tritóstilo shaft could also be banded into equal thirds, with each part given different treatments. There are many handsome examples of tritóstilo columns in northern New Spain, which span roughly the same period as the salomónico. The upper story of the main frontispiece of the Cathedral of Chihuahua contains two such columns, which appear to be supporting the date of completion of the cathedral (figure 6.5).

[Estípite] Characterized by stacked geometrical parts, the largest and most recognizable being an inverted pyra-

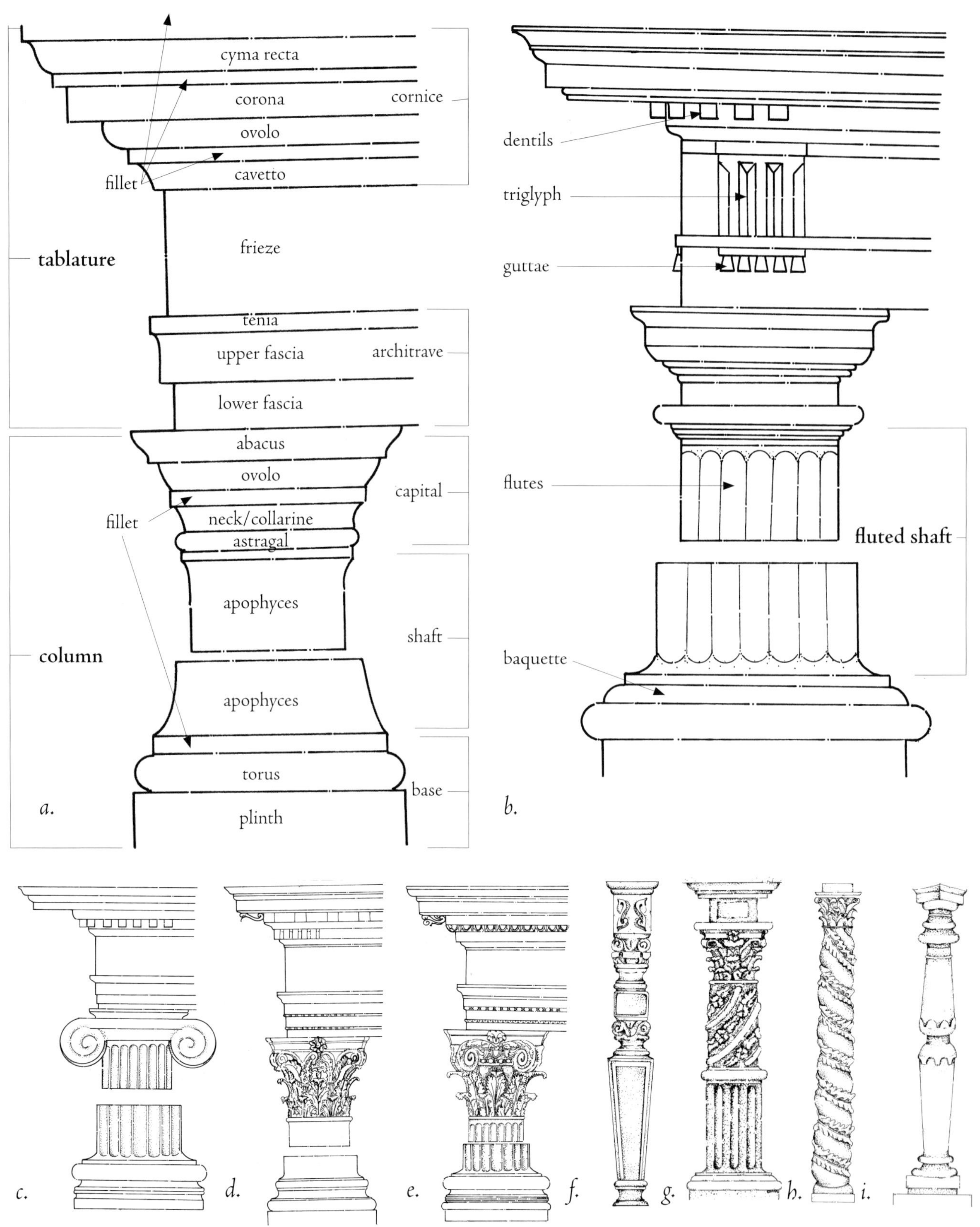

6.2. Columns: a. parts of a classical column, b. Doric column with parts, c. Ionic column, d. Corinthian column, e. composite column; **northern New Spain column types:** *f. estípite, g. tritóstilo, h. salomónico, i. candelabrum.*

6.3. *Detail of main frontispiece showing salomónico columns, Santo Domingo de Sombrerete, Zacatecas, 2001.*

6.4. *Detail of main frontispiece showing entorchado columns, Catedral de Chihuahua, 1996.*

mid, estípite (from Latin *stipes*, gen. *stipitis*, tree trunk) is one of the most visually exciting column types found in New Spain, including northern New Spain, and is most generally associated with the late baroque (or ultrabaroque) style sometimes referred to as Churrigueresque (see "Baroque" in chapter 2). Part of the late northern mannerist vocabulary introduced into Spain through Wendel Dietterlin's illustrated treatise on architecture (first published in Nuremberg in 1593), the estípite reached its most fantastic development during the eighteenth century in Spain and New Spain.[4] This column type dominated the architecture of New Spain from about 1730 until 1790 and persisted in some parts of northern New Spain into the first decade of the nineteenth century. Although estípite columns are generously distributed throughout almost all of northern New Spain, where they represent either the predominant or exclusive type of columns or pilasters flanking portals or in retablos, they are dramatically absent in the mission churches of Alta California.

Used either as an engaged column or a pilaster, an estípite generally has a Corinthian-like capital. Squared or rounded blocks, sometimes covered with medallions or floral treatments and often separated by flattened "cushion" pieces, are stacked for the upper one-half to three-quarters of the shaft's length, which is always supported by an elongated pyramidal shape (an inverted obelisk). In the most extreme examples, the blocks, cushions, and the obelisk are all covered with garlands of plant shapes or with swags draped along the edges, some blocks being reduced to confections (figure 6.6). The estípite can be traced back

6.5. *Detail of main frontispiece showing tritóstilo columns, Catedral de Chihuahua, 1996.*

to ancient Crete; based on the herm (from Hermes, messenger of the gods and protector of merchants, travelers, and thieves), a column or pilaster in the shape of a bust of Hermes atop a tapering shaft used in Greek and Roman architecture, the estípite sports a capital and a stack of blocks in place of the god's head and chest.

[Candelabrum] Also called a "profile" or "segmented" column, candelabrum takes its form from a popular late Renaissance or mannerist column type and traces its origins to Andalucía and to Sevilla in particular. The shaft is generally pinched in the middle and is divided into alternately swelling and contracting plain or fluted sections, decorated with foliage or strapwork. Although rare in other parts of New Spain, candelabrum columns appear on many towers or façades in northern New Spain, most often those built in the second half of the eighteenth century. Found as columns on the main frontispiece of the Cathedral of Chihuahua (see figure 5.3) and on the corners of the bell tower of San Sebastián in Concordia (Sinaloa; figure 6.7), and as pilasters on the bell tower of La Purísima Concepción in Álamos (Sonora; figure 6.8), to name just three examples, candelabrum columns might almost be considered a regional characteristic of late-eighteenth-century northern New Spain.

[Other Column Types]

Mosaico. In the *mosaico* column type, the shaft is interlaced with a network of straps in whose openings other decorations may be placed, creating a mosaic arrangement. Mosaico columns were occasionally used in northern New Spain during the mid-eighteenth century (figure 6.9).

Revestido or retallado. Particularly popular in Sevilla from about 1540, columns of the *revestido,* or *retallado* (clothed or dressed), type were used there in various forms through almost the middle of the seventeenth century,

6.6. Estípite columns, retablo de Nuestra Señora de Guadalupe, San José de Parral, Chihuahua, 2001.

6.7. Detail of bell tower featuring candelabrum columns, San Sebastián, Concordia, Sinaloa, 1979.

6.8. Detail of bell tower with candelabrum columns, Nuestra Señora de la Asunción del Real de los Álamos, Sonora, 1980.

6.9. Mosaico columns in a detail of the main frontispiece, San Sebastián, Concordia, Sinaloa, 1979. Note also the seraphim-like creatures adorning the arch imposts.

6.10. Main retablo, San Ignacio de Loyola de Parras, Coahuila, 2001. Notable features are the revestido (retallado) columns and the arabesques topping the retablo.

when they first appeared on frontispieces and retablos in northern New Spain. Here their shafts were usually covered with stylized plant ornamentation. They can be seen in the main retablo of San Ignacio de Loyola de Parras (Coahuila; figure 6.10).

Estriado. Also from the mid-seventeenth century, columns of the *estriado* type—which are fluted or grooved the entire length of their shafts—sometimes served as the top two-thirds of tritóstilo columns.

Almohado. In the rarer, more somber *almohado* (literally, pillow) column type, flattened, sometimes bevel-edged elements are stacked on top of each other. Two Chihuahuan examples, of varying complexity, are found in the main portals of San José de Parral (built 1673–1686; see

6.11. Almohado columns on the main façade, El Nombre de Jesús, Carichic, Chihuahua, 2001.

figure 5.7) and El Nombre de Jesús de Carichic (built ca. 1695; figure 6.11).

At the foot of a wall, the bases of columns of all types often rested on rectangular blocks or plinths called socles (*zocles*), as did piers and the bases of pedestals. Socles could have their own cornices, bases, or both; in northern New Spain, they were usually decorated in bas-relief with bifurcated, geometric, or plant designs, the level of their decoration generally paralleling that of the frontispiece.

Piers, Pillars

Differing from columns in their shape and sometimes also in their function, piers are typically masonry elements that serve as main supports for principal arches and occur elsewhere in the church building.[5] They may be rectangular or circular in section, freestanding or embedded, single or clustered. To lend a certain lightness to their otherwise massive appearance, piers were chamfered, as are those in the Cathedral of Durango (figure 6.12), or clustered, as are those in Santa María de Natívitas in Bachíniva (Chihuahua; see figure 3.10a). Freestanding piers were used in churches with multiple aisles to allow free passage between nave and aisles, to provide relatively unobstructed views of the main altar and services, and to support the roof over both nave and aisles; in cruciform churches with multiple aisles, they were also placed at the corners of the crossing to support the church's main dome. Brick or rubble piers, and sometimes even stone piers, were plastered and most often left unadorned, although occasionally mortar lines were inscribed or painted on them to simulate stone masonry. Capitals, if present, usually reflected the dominant architectural style of the church interior.

Although "pillar" is sometimes used interchangeably with "column," strictly speaking, it refers to *any* upright columnar support. Pillars need not belong to any particular order or combination of orders; neither their form nor their proportions are prescribed. Generally having a base and a cornice, pillars may be square or octagonal as well as circular in section.

Pilasters

A flattened protrusion that juts from a wall a third, fourth, fifth, or sixth of its width, a pilaster (from Latin *pila*, column) is a form of pier; it might take the form of an engaged pier or wall-pier shaft used to mark bays as an extension to the vaulting arches above; of an engaged column along the vertical side of a portal beneath the arch, and usually flanked by the frontispiece's columns; or of plaster or masonry decoratively applied to walls to suggest a pier or column. Pilasters "support" pediments or replace columns on frontispieces or in retablos. Column types apply to pilasters as well.

In addition to the very popular estípite pilaster, two other pilaster types were commonly used in northern New Spain. Fluted pilasters appear in New Spain in the early part of the seventeenth century and persist in northern New Spain throughout the eighteenth century (figure 6.13). Paneled (*de aplicaciones*) pilasters, whose panels may be plain or serve as formats for painted, engraved,

6.12. Interior of the Catedral de Durango, view of the nave, east aisle, and main altar with examples of piers, 1982.

or applied ornamentation, appear throughout New Spain from the mid-seventeenth through the eighteenth centuries (figure 6.14). Recessed slightly and surrounded by molding, the panels are commonly decorated with plant motifs rising from vases or urns, with festoons of fruit or flowers, or with overall patterns of strapwork, vines, figures, and *pinjantes* (pendants; see "Decorative Motifs"). Pilasters consisting of a series of smaller panels or horizontal divisions are sometimes called segmented. Because of the flatness of the pilaster, the capital, when present, is translated from round to flat.

Niches, Niche-Pilasters

A recessed area in an interior or exterior wall, altar, or retablo, a niche (from Latin *nidus*, nest; in Spanish, *nicho*) is designed to hold a piece of sculpture, specifically a religious figure (at least in New Spain). The niche is many times apse-shaped, covered by a half dome, and commonly embellished with decorative treatment around the opening and goring on the upper inside surface. Among the most bizarre examples of niches are those in a collateral altar of the former hacienda church Nuestra Señora de los Remedios southwest of Chihuahua City. Here bloated infant herms face away from each other on either side of two niches flanking a recessed crucifix (figure 6.15).

In frontispieces constructed as retablos exteriores or on ornate side portals, niches are placed between pairs of engaged columns in side bays, on all stories, and in the projecting top of the center bay. Some authors also consider *hornacinas* (from Vulgar Latin *fornicina*, diminu-

6.13. Interior of the Catedral de Chihuahua, showing fluted pilasters and the carved limestone retablo, ca. 1880. (By Ben Wittick; courtesy of the Museum of New Mexico at the Palace of the Governors, Neg. #15658)

6.14. Paneled pilaster on a pier supporting the choir loft, San Pedro de Aconchi, Sonora, 1977.

6.15. Crucifix retablo of Jesús Cristo containing two unusual niches flanking the crucifix, former hacienda church of Nuestra Señora de los Remedios, southwest of Chihuahua City, Chihuahua, 2001.

tive of *fornix*, arch or vault), wall spaces hollowed out for statues, to be synonymous with "niches" (see figures 2.12 and 6.5).[6] From about 1765 until the end of the baroque era in central New Spain, portal and retablo decorations developed to such a state that the estípite columns, sometimes combined with other column types, began to lose their significance in comparison with the areas developed between the columns. These spaces were usually occupied by niches, or at least pedestals upon which religious figures were supposed to stand. In the case of portal decorations, a hollowed-out place—sometimes nothing more than a shell motif or a gored undersurface shallowly scraped or molded into the wall—was created to provide some protection for the figure and to add to its aesthetic feeling. In the last stages of the baroque, the desire for increased ornamental excitement overwhelmed the columnar arrangements. Now the center part became as decorated as the columns, and occasionally more so, creating another pseudo-structural column between the flanking pair of columns and competing for visual attention. In these frenetic last stages, the religious figure was almost lost in the assemblage, the plane of the wall dissolved, and the function of the supporting members negated; cornices and horizontal elements may be lacking or greatly subdued.

Extant niche-pilasters (also called inter-estípites) are scarce in northern New Spain; of the many factors possibly contributing to this, two stand out: (1) the lateness of their appearance in relationship to the settlement of the north and its building programs; (2) the widespread removal of the "outmoded" baroque retablos and their replacement with neoclassical counterparts. Niche-pilasters can still be seen on either side of the main portal of San José y San Miguel in San Antonio (Texas; see figure 2.20a), as well as the retablo at Nuestra Señora de las Nieves in Palmillas (Tamaulipas; see figure 2.21). Although the sculptures are replaced by paintings in the retablos of San Ignacio de Kadakaaman (Baja California Sur; figure 6.16), the spaces and the decorative impact remain the same.

Arches, Vaults, Half Domes

Not only the arches themselves but also their imposts might be decorated, as are those for the arch in the main portal at San Sebastián in Concordia (Sinaloa), adorned by small, feather-winged creatures (if seraphim, then definitely whimsical; see figure 6.9). Whether they form parts of doors, windows, niches, or arcades, arches are distinguished by the outline of their exterior curve (extrado) and their interior curve (intrado, soffit, or archivolt; figures 6.17 and 6.18).

The treatment of stone arches ranged from a rounded to a squared profile with exposed surfaces that might be fluted, carved, painted, and stenciled in a variety of patterns, or simply left plain. Brick arches—and often even stone ones—were plastered and then painted to simulate cut and finished stone. The triumphal arch and the arch over the baptistery door of Santa María de las Cuevas (Chihuahua) were painted to simulate not only separate stones but arch segments jasperized in bright reds, blues, yellows, and purples (figure 6.19).

Apart from their important structural function, keystones (*claves* or *dovelas*) also served as focal points on arches. Keystones over portals were commonly carved and painted with religious symbols or images (the Sacrament, Christ, Mary, saints, angels). These symbols or images could appear in thematic arrays, as they do over the portals and crowning the arches along the nave of the Cathedral of Chihuahua (figure 6.20). Like the arches themselves, keystones in the more elaborately decorated churches may be carved and painted on all three exposed surfaces.

Two architectural details used to decorate the ribs or intersections of ribs of the vaulted churches of northern New Spain figured prominently in Gothic, Renaissance, baroque, and neoclassical churches of both the Old and the New World: the crocket (from French *crochet*, diminutive of *croc*, hook; in Spanish, *fronda*), a projecting, hooklike decorative ornament most often assuming a plant shape and, in Gothic churches, appearing along the edges of spires, ribs, gables, and pinnacles; and the boss (from French *bosse*, lump, knob; in Spanish, *capa* or *roseton*), a plaster ornament placed at the intersection of vault ribs. Whereas bosses can be seen in vaulted churches throughout northern New Spain, crockets appear only rarely. They adorn the outer ribs of the segmented domes in both the Cathedral of Saltillo (Coahuila; figure 6.21) and the Church of San Francisco de Asís in Chihuahua city (Chihuahua).

Half-moon areas of a wall or vaulted ceiling created by an arch, vault, or intersection of vaults, were called lunettes (*lunetas*), as were half-moon windows or paintings. Although such areas were not specifically intended

6.16. Main retablo in which the original niche positions have been filled by paintings, San Ignacio de Loyola de Kadakaaman, Baja California Sur, 1987.

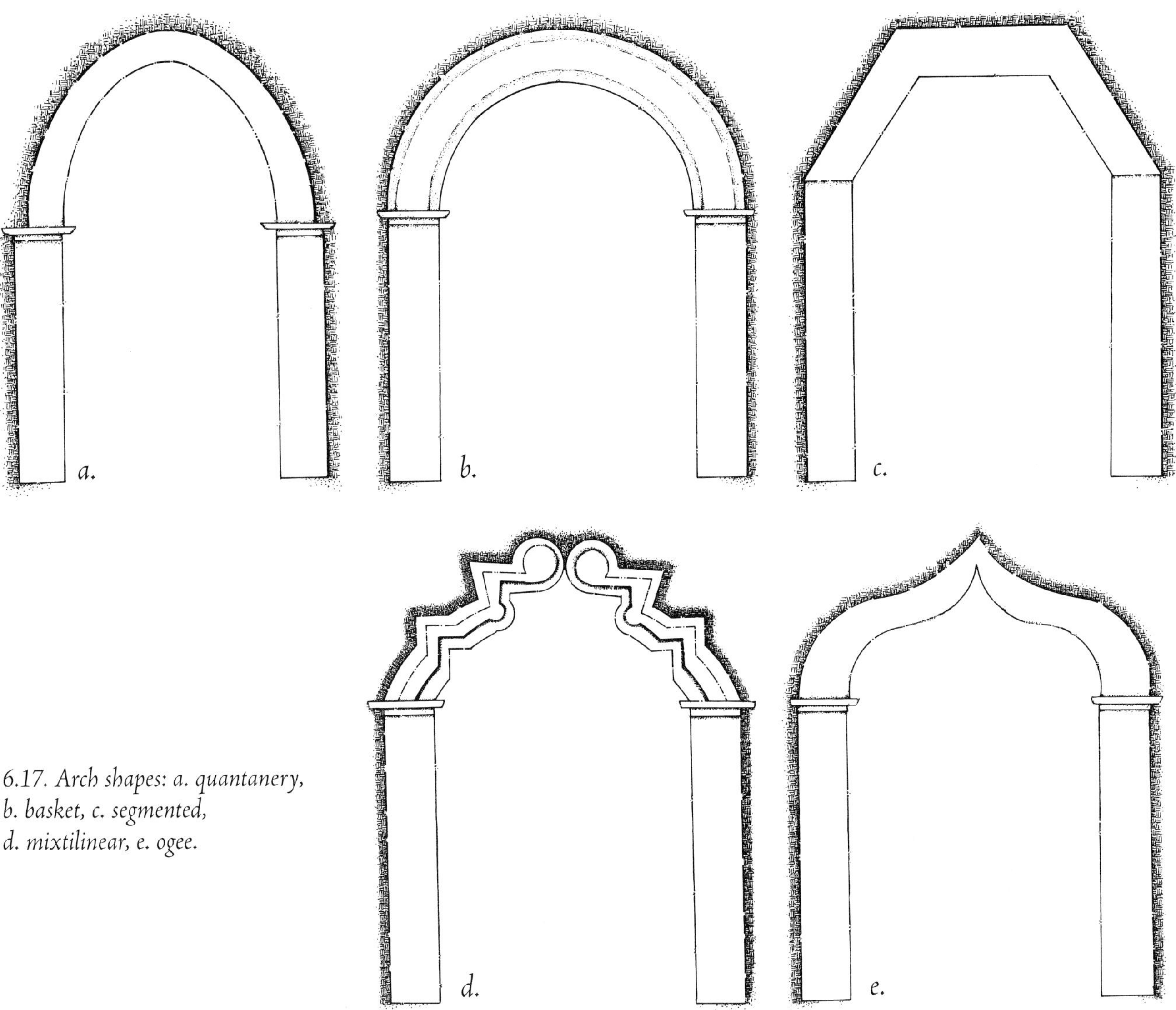

6.17. Arch shapes: a. quantanery, b. basket, c. segmented, d. mixtilinear, e. ogee.

for decoration, and most often were left unadorned, in the more elaborately decorated churches, lunettes could be decoratively outlined and could contain fields of geometric or floral designs or even complete religious paintings (see figure 4.29). Goring refers to three-dimensional grooved, lobed, scooped, or half-moon shapes whose troughs radiate away from a common center. Dating back to the Romans, goring was used by Moorish and Byzantine builders to adorn domes and half domes—and niches, doors, and windows, both inside and out. In the form of a grooved half dome or projecting device shaped like a scallop, cockleshell, or wave in stone, plaster, or wood, it appears as the crowning decorative accent for niches, doorways, or retablos, most spectacularly above the main portal of the Cathedral of Saltillo (Coahuila; figure 6.22; see also figure 5.6 and **Scallop shell** entry in chapter 11).

Pediments

A pediment (frontón) is a crowning, centrally positioned triangular element found on a façade in classically based architecture, on a gable—and, since the Renaissance, over doors, niches, or windows surrounded by cornices. Pediments appear on baroque church façades (and almost all neoclassical façades and retablos) in northern New Spain.[7] In keeping with the baroque, the top of the pediment may be curved, curled, or broken, as it is on the façade of San

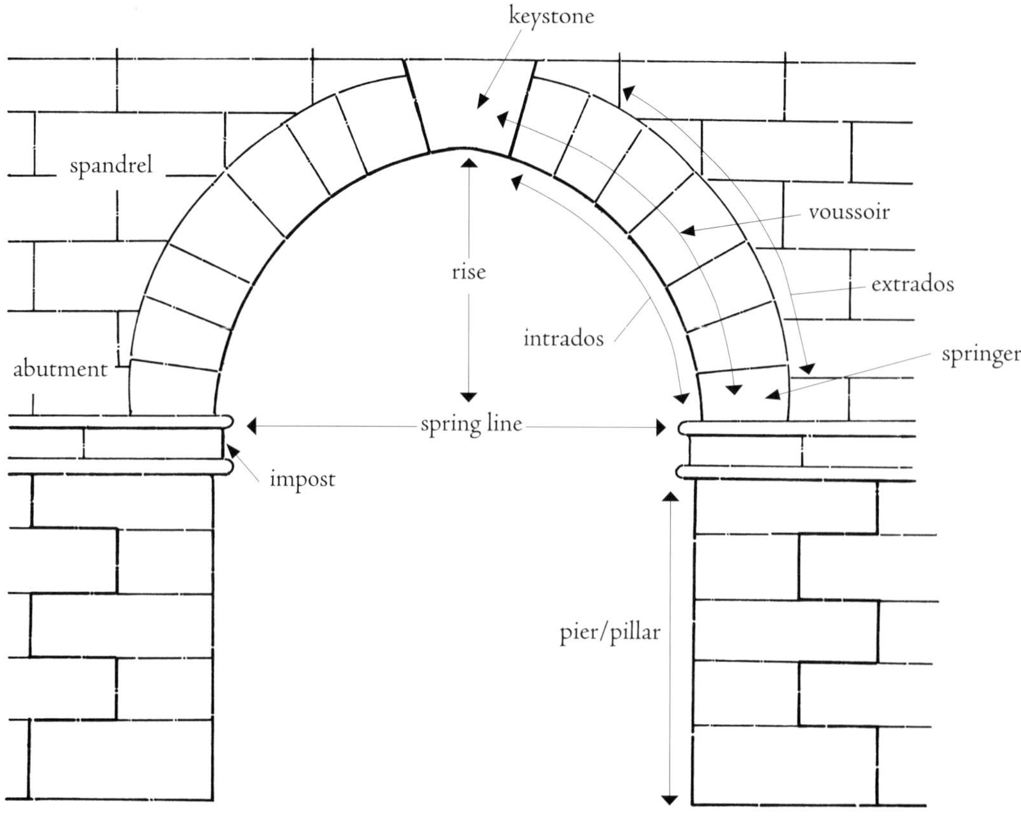

6.18. Parts of an arch.

Carlos Borromeo (Tamaulipas); the bottom may also be broken (see figure 6.23 for pediment types). Unlike a triangular finial (see below), a pediment spans the full width of whatever it crowns. The space enclosed within the pediment's triangle, the tympanum, lends itself to adornment with sculpture, bas-relief, or lettering. On the apex of a pediment and seen in northern New Spain as a direct result of neoclassical influences, acroteria (singular, acroterion) were either pedestals for statues or ornaments, such as the three for the virtues atop the façade pediment of Mission Santa Bárbara in California, or the statues or ornaments themselves (see figure 2.22a).

Finials, Crowning Ornaments

Vertical, (usually) tapering elements, finials (remates) were used to cap or terminate buttresses, gables, canopies, columns, pediments, walls, roofs, and retablos. Projecting from parapets or cornices, from the corners of church buildings or bell towers, or from the tops of retablos, finials (most often as groups of figures, vases, or other sculptural ornaments) were used to suggest battlements in much the same way as crenellation. One particularly dramatic use of finials appears along the roofline of the Cathedral of Durango, where a celestial army of twenty-nine stone angels, bearing symbols of the Immaculate Conception, keeps guard over the faithful (see figure 5.20).

Not all finials were freestanding, and some even took the form of pilasters. They could be tapered or rounded and could assume all manner of shapes, sometimes providing the only relief to an otherwise somber façade or roofline, as do the half dozen large "pots" that march across the warehouse-like roofline of Santa Rosalía de Mulegé (Baja California Sur; figure 6.24).

Crowning ornaments in the shape of crosses were placed directly above the main portal of a church, on its highest points, and on its principal dome. Other crowning ornament shapes included roosters, suns and moons, and the monograms of Christ or the Virgin Mary. These could be fixed or could rotate to serve as weather vanes, sometimes with the cardinal directions indicated. Among the extant weather vanes and elaborate fixed crosses are

6.19. Triumphal arch, Santa María de las Cuevas, Chihuahua, 2000.

6.20. Detail of keystone portraying Nuestra Señora de la Regla, east portal, Catedral de Chihuahua, 1962.

6.21. Dome of the Catedral de Saltillo, Coahuila, 1981. Some of the crockets have been broken off, ostensibly by lightning.

6.22. Main portal of the Catedral de Saltillo, Coahuila, 1966. The papal insignia on the keystone signified a bishop's jurisdiction over this diocese.

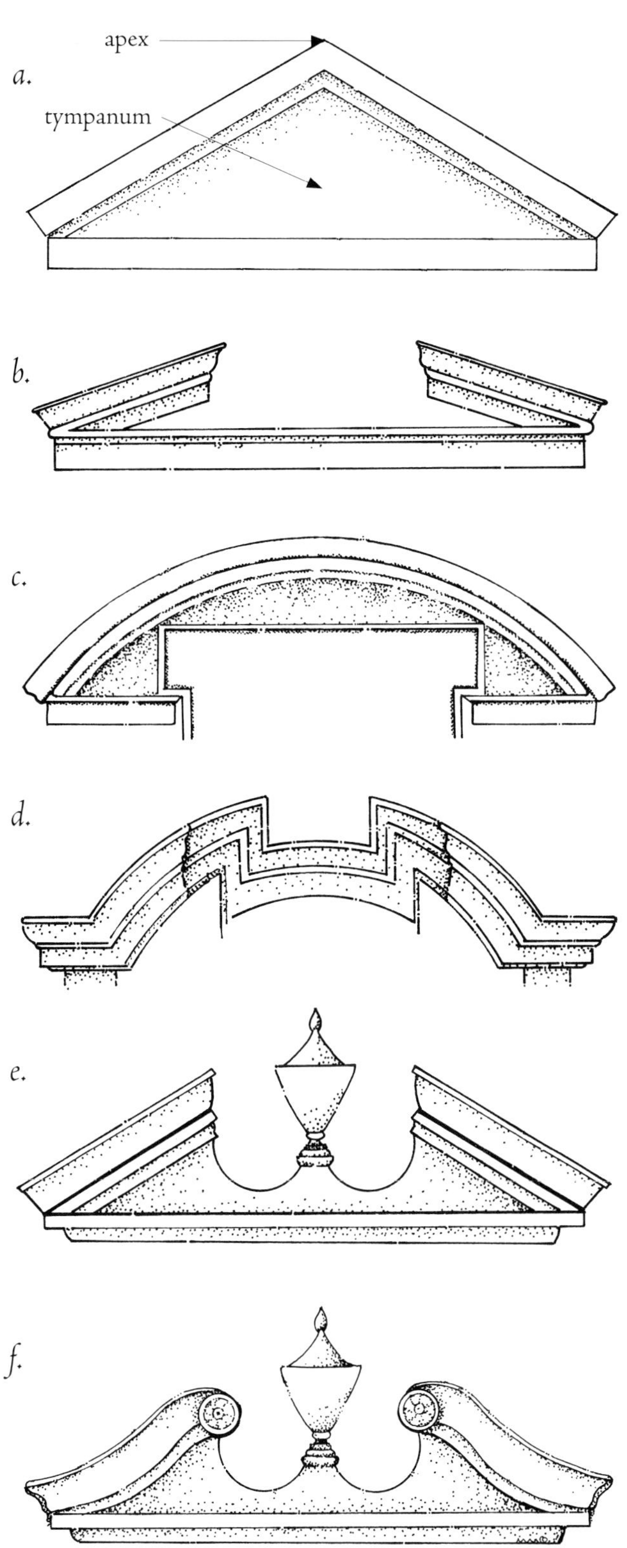

6.23. Pediments: a. triangular, b. broken, c. curved with broken bottom, d. mixtilinear, e. broken with central finial urn, f. broken scrolled with central finial urn.

6.24. Santa Rosalía de Palermo de Mulegé, Baja California Sur, 1987, with a prominent row of finials along the roofline.

fine examples of colonial blacksmithing (see figure 3.23; see also **Cock or rooster** entry in chapter 11).

Outside Walls

Many exterior walls may once have borne special sculpted or molded religious images, but as a result of political upheavals, anticlerical feelings during the early twentieth century, and insensitive building restorations, all but a few examples have been obliterated. A photograph taken in the late nineteenth century (see figure 5.1) clearly shows the (now obliterated) fourteen Stations of the Cross in bas-relief along the lower outside wall on either side of the frontispiece of the Cathedral of Chihuahua. *Estampas* were other religious images in bas-relief, usually portraying the chalice and Host. Carved from stone, estampas were incorporated into the outside apse wall at or above eye level, and placed to indicate where in the church interior the Host was reserved. (Devout Catholics to this day remove their hats, cross themselves, or both, when passing them.) Although they may once have graced many churches in northern New Spain, I know of only four extant estampas there, three in the state of Chihuahua. One, a small stone plaque with a chalice, is on the parochial church of San Francisco Javier de Satevó (figure 6.25); a second, shuttered and locked, is on the

6.25. Exterior of the apse, San Francisco Javier de Satevó, Chihuahua, 1990. The plaque (estampa) marks the location of the Host in the church.

Cathedral of Chihuahua; and a third, elaborated into a street chapel complete with a tile plaque of the Virgin of Guadalupe, is on San José de Parral (figure 6.26).[8] The fourth estampa, in the form of a raised cross (with fourteen niches for stone carvings of the Stations of the Cross, seven on either side of the church along the outer wall), can be seen on Nuestra Señora de Guadalupe in Ojo de Agua (San Luis Potosí).

Windows

Double-arched and divided in the center by a column (*mainel, meneau*), pendant, knob, or other feature, biforate windows or openings (commonly but incorrectly referred to as *ajimece* in Spanish) reflect the mudéjar, Gothic, and Renaissance influences on church architecture in Spain and New Spain. Two good examples can be seen

6.26. Apse exterior, San José de Parral, Chihuahua, 1996. The tile plaque is a recent addition that helps transform the original estampa into a street chapel.

in Sombrerete (Zacatecas): one on the frontispiece of Nuestra Señora de la Soledad (figure 6.27) and another in the bell tower of the Capilla de Nuestra Señora de Guadalupe (figure 6.28), the first quite likely influencing the second.

First appearing in Gothic churches but continuing through the Renaissance and the baroque in New Spain, oculi, or bull's-eyes, were round or octagonal windows whose shape might be refined in a variety of ways (see figure 5.3). A quatrefoil oculus (*oculo cuadrafoliado*) had four lobes; an eared, or hipped, quatrefoil oculus (*oculo estrellado*—starred oculus) had angular hips or ears protruding at the cusps in its frame or molding (figure 6.29); both types can occasionally be found throughout northern New Spain (see also figure 5.22).

Corbels and Ménsulas

Projecting blocks of stone or wood, carved or molded and, in northern New Spain, often decorated with painted geometric designs, corbels (from Middle French *corbel*, diminutive of *corp*; from Latin *corvus*, raven) were used to support beams, arches, balconies, retablos, or single statues along interior walls.[9] The hundreds of corbels that march along the sides of high, long ceilings in many early mission churches of northern New Spain, such as in San Pedro de Aconchi (Sonora; figure 6.30), give these ceilings a sturdy, if somewhat toothy, appearance. Most often left unadorned, the exposed surfaces of corbels may be carved, painted, or both; the profiles, while usually square, can be curved (sometimes in volutes) or undercut. Indeed, so

6.27. Detail of biforate window in the main frontispiece, Nuestra Señora de Soledad de Sombrerete, Zacatecas, 1983. The deterioration of the stone is due to frost wedging—a condition occurring when moisture trapped within the stone freezes and expands, causing it to crack, peel, and spall. This is a fairly common phenomenon in the local, porous limestone.

6.28. A good example of biforate openings in the bell tower of La Capilla de Nuestra Señora de Guadalupe de Sombrerete, Zacatecas, 1983.

6.29. San Carlos Borromeo de Carmelo de Monterey, Carmel, California, ca. 1910. Note the hipped quatrefoil oculus above the main portal. Nowadays landscaping and surrounding modern urbanization make this structure almost unrecognizable. (Vroman postcard, private collection)

deeply undercut are the corbels of El Nombre de Jesús in Nombre de Dios (Durango) that birds nest in them.

Although typically uniformly decorated where they support beamed ceilings in northern New Spain, corbels in the most significant parts of church, say, those flanking the sanctuary, were sometimes given special decorative treatment, as are those carved into figures in San Ignacio de Loyola de Parras (commonly referred to as "El Colegio"; Coahuila; figure 6.31).

A *ménsula* (little table) is an element similar in function to a corbel, but larger and usually more decorative or with a more dramatic profile. Placed into the walls, these cantilever projections are reserved for specific areas requiring greater strength, such as the choir loft or a transverse clerestory window (see figure 4.41; see also figure 4.34 for a different use of the same principle).

Moldings

Shaped profiles applied or formed in a continuous line to delineate or emphasize the difference between planes or areas, to create decorative bands of light and shade, or to outline window or door frames, moldings are among the earliest forms of architectural decoration. Moldings, whose surfaces can be and most often are decorated, appear on virtually all architectural elements, as well as on lamps, chalices, and furniture throughout northern New Spain, with certain shapes reserved for bases or supports (figure 6.32).[10] Church builders there made generous use of carved floral and geometric designs on flat moldings outlining arches and window frames and on continuous moldings along entablatures.

One type of mudéjar molding, typically made of wood and used along walls inside a number of churches in northern New Spain to bolster the corbels and the courses of adobe brick at these critical stress points, is *arrocabe* (bed molding). A stunning, elaborately carved, and multilevel example surrounds the entire nave of Nuestra Señora de Guadalupe in Ciudad Juárez (Chihuahua) (see figure 4.23). In fired brick churches, arrocabe molding is purely decorative, whether molded from plaster or formed from the projecting edges of the bricks.

6.30. *Interior, San Pedro de Aconchi, Sonora, 1977.*

6.31. Detail of triumphal arch showing an elaborately carved corbel, San Ignacio de Loyola de Parras, Coahuila, 2001.

Drain Spouts

A common solution for throwing rainwater a half meter or more from the sides of a church building, drain spouts were often carved from stone, sometimes in the form of gargoyles (from Old French *gargouille*, throat; perhaps from the gurgling of the rainwater), such as the human-breasted lioness spouts along the edge of the roof of San Juan de Dios in Durango (Durango; figure 6.33), or the (standard) lion spouts on the façade of La Purísima Concepción in Sombrerete (Zacatecas; see figure 2.23, left). Some were molded from clay (see also "Roofing" under "Techniques" in chapter 4); others were formed from sheets of tinplate or lead (*chiflón de plomo*) rolled into a pipe shape and decorated on the end with cutout and soldered pieces. Wooden drain spouts took the form of troughs, typically unadorned, made from three planks or carved from a single section of log or beam.

Decorative Motifs

Decorative motifs may take any number of shapes across a variety of categories.[11] Some are based on geometric patterns, while others are derived from natural, figural, or plant forms. Discussed in this section are decorative motifs seen throughout northern New Spain in their pure form, modified, or in combination with other motifs. They

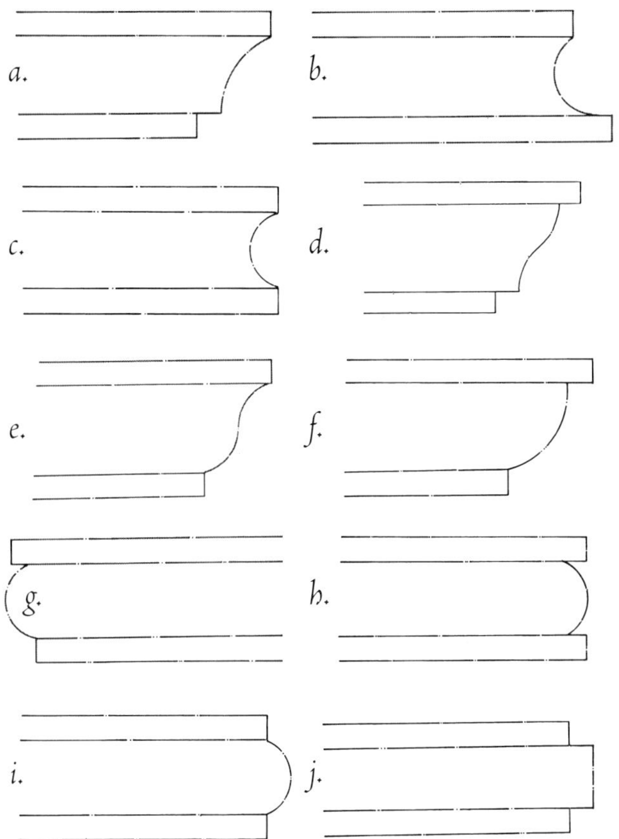

6.32. Molding profiles: a. cavetto, b. scotia, c. gouge, d. cyma ogee reverse, e. ogee cyma recta, f. ovulo, g. torus, h. flush bead, i. astragal or bead, j. fillet or band.

6.33. Gargoyle on drain spout, San Juan de Dios, Durango, Durango, 1996.

appear principally on dados, walls, cornices, columns, and friezes, but also on other elements of the church building, sometimes combined in a molding; they may be painted, carved in relief, or incised. Some fall into a number of categories or into no particular category at all, inviting viewers to come up with their own terms for them.[12]

Human and Animal Shapes

Christian builders and decorators have been free since the mid-ninth century to use both human and animal motifs to represent religious tales and Christian dogma. Although such motifs in the churches of New Spain were often carryovers from the Romans or Moors, most were "sanitized" and given Christian meaning.

The human face provided constant inspiration. Faces of cherubs (*angelitos*) are liberally used to fill in smaller decorative spaces: carved in wood on pulpits and retablos; painted on decorated ceilings; and sculpted in stone on spandrels (the roughly triangular spaces between the extrado of an arch and the cornice above it), baptismal fonts, keystones, niches, and capitals. The face of Christ on the napkin of Veronica also serves as a separate and complete design element on keystones or retablos. Sculptured faces used as decoration are referred to as masks or mascarons (*mascarones*).

Grotesques (*grotescos*), as the name suggests, are ugly and bizarre images; they are based on the male face, with expressions ranging from droll to fiendish. Examples of grotesques occur between the columns on the first story of the side portals of the Cathedral of Chihuahua (figure 6.34) and on the keystone of and beneath the front window of the bell tower of San José de Copala (Sinaloa; figure 6.35).

Angelitos, entire juvenile figures of indeterminate gender, are commonly found as a "supporting" motif beneath ledges or at junctions between arches and walls and attached to retablos. They are also seen playing musical instruments, holding signal attributes of religious personages in paintings or sculptures, or clustered around the base of certain images of the Virgin Mary. The face or half figure of Christ, Mary, God the Father, and the saints can be used decoratively as well as symbolically. Thus, the half figure of God the Father has been sculpted with his hands in gestures of benediction inside and at the top of the niches of the Four Evangelists, two of whom appear on the east and the other two on the west side portals of the Cathedral of Durango (see figure 12.14). The half figures of various sainted religious women and men adorn the dome's interior and side transept altars of San Xavier in Tucson (Arizona) (see figure 10.1).

Herms, atlantes, and caryatids are stylized human forms morphed into columns or pillars. Caryatids are sculpted female figures used as columnar supports, whereas atlantes are their male counterparts (herms may be either male or female; see discussion of the classic herm in "Columns," "Estípite," under "Architectural Details" in chapter 6). Although rare in northern New Spain, and generally used as architectural accents to suggest the Renaissance, they sometimes appear in strange and singular ways. For example, two bearded creatures with wings covering bodies that taper to a single clawed foot grasping a ball stand guard in the upper story of the façade of Santo Domingo in Sombrerete (Zacatecas; see figure 5.22). These figures may have been intended to represent seraphim, the highest order of angels, who have three pairs of wings and use one pair to cover their bodies. Other figures with human heads whose bodies appear to be wrapped like mummies (possibly the result of some restoration attempt) can be seen across the first story of the façade of El Señor de la Misericordia in Linares (Nuevo León). All of these examples represent a definite, whimsical mestizo treatment of classical motifs.

Parts of the body used as motifs include the eye, representing God the Father, frequently placed at the top of neoclassical retablos, replacing the baroque equivalent of a bearded patriarch bestowing blessings; and the crossed arms of Christ and of Saint Francis of Assisi, often placed inside a shield on façades and retablos, symbolizing the Franciscan Order. (For symbols of the other orders and for religious symbolism as a whole, see chapter 9: "Religious Hierarchy and Orders, Ecclesiastical Vestments" and chapter 11: "Symbols and Attributes," respectively.)

Skeletons and bones serve both decorative and didactic functions. Three skulls and crossbones arc over the outside doorway of the cemetery at Mission Santa Bárbara (California). The same motif is placed in the rear of the church over the dual holy water basins at La Purísima Concepción in Caborca (Sonora; see figure 5.26). At the neighboring mission church of San Diego de Alcalá in Pitiquito (also Sonora), larger-than-life painted figures of the skeleton of Death (figure 6.36) and the Devil face each other on opposing piers across an aisle.

6.34. A grotesque on the east frontispiece, an example of a bifurcated design, Catedral de Chihuahua, 2000.

6.35. Grotesques (above and below the window) on the bell tower, San José de Copala, Sinaloa, 2001.

6.36. *Pier in San Diego de Alcalá del Pitiquito, Sonora, 1982, on which Death is painted, facing the Devil on the opposite pier.*

6.37. Detail of the sanctuary cornice showing a rare, purely decorative use of animal motifs, San Francisco Xavier del Bac, near Tucson, Arizona, 2003.

An animal shape that from earliest times held great significance to Spanish Christians of both the Old and the New World—and which can therefore be seen carved and molded on altars, walls, and cornices throughout New Spain—is the scallop shell. This motif, closely linked to goring, was used in extraordinary ways during the Churrigueresque (ultrabaroque) era of architecture (see also **Scallop shell** entry in chapter 11).

Almost always intended to serve a symbolic function (hence treated separately in chapter 11), animal motifs were very seldom used for purely (or even primarily) decorative purposes in the churches of New Spain. A rare exception to this rule is San Xavier in Tucson (Arizona), home to a veritable bestiary of decorative animals: painted quails scatter throughout the jasperized inside surface of the drum of the main dome; a cat and a rat glare at each other from under the volutes on either side of the upper story of the main façade; and a snake pursues a rabbit along a cornice in the sanctuary (figure 6.37)—to name a few animal motifs whose meaning, as they are arranged and portrayed, does not fall within the norms of Christian symbolism. The otherwise surprising dearth of indigenous human and animal motifs in the church painting and sculpture of northern New Spain is very likely the result of the tabula rasa policy practiced by the missionaries and of heavy-handed neoclassical restoration on the part of their successors.

Plant Shapes

Of all decorative motifs in the churches of northern New Spain, plant shapes are by far the most frequent. Singly or in clusters, flowers abound on columns (particularly on salomónico and estípite columns and Corinthian or composite capitals). Olive and grape leaves, palm fronds, ears of corn and heads of wheat, grapes, pomegranates, pineapples, roses and lilies, and ivy and grapevines twine and dangle on, around, or from columns, frontispieces, and retablos. To builders caught up in the spirit of the baroque, spandrels in particular cried out for some special touch, most often plant motifs such as the bold, protruding pineapple-like elements on the main frontispiece of San Sebastián in Concordia (Sinaloa; see figure 6.9).[13] These elements are fully at home with the diagonally placed baskets of flowers on the cornice of the main portal and

6.38. South transept, San Pedro y San Pablo de Tubutama, Sonora, 1957. Palmettes are molded on the piers in the far left and right of the photo. Symbols of the Passion are molded onto the face of the retablo between the columns: left to right: pliers, crown of thorns, nails, and scourge. (By James Officer. Courtesy of Arizona State Museum, University of Arizona)

with the profusion of flowers carved on the upper story of the façade.

A stylized palm leaf used widely and persistently in Moorish arts and crafts, the palmette is related to goring and the scallop shell motif. What appear to be palmettes in northern New Spain may in some cases be the result of ineptness on the part of craftsmen trying to achieve a scallop shape, such as on the piers in the transept of San Pedro y San Pablo in Tubutama (Sonora; figure 6.38). Even where plant shapes were used primarily as pleasing decorative motifs, however, their Christian symbolism would certainly also have been considered (see chapter 11 for what they symbolize).

Grotesques, masks, and plant or animal shapes often serve as the pivotal points from which bifurcated designs (designs whose principal motifs are divided into two mirror-image halves) begin. Such designs are usually aligned on a vertical axis. Revived in the Renaissance, bifurcated designs can be seen in many mid- to late-baroque churches of northern New Spain, such as between the columns of the side portals of the Cathedral of Chihuahua (see figure 6.34).

Geometric Shapes and Patterns

By using the simplest of arcs or intersecting lines to delineate an area and then dividing that area into as many spaces as desired, one could create an endless variety of undulating bands, twists and cables, zigzags, diaper patterns, and radiating designs. The baroque cast of mind took liberties with the geometric details of classical architecture, rearranging them and using them in original ways not intended by classical architects, most often to achieve purely decorative effects. Thus, the church decorators of northern New Spain graced the (classically unadorned) lower edges of cornice moldings and the bases of columns

6.39. Examples of compass flowers on the main portal of Nuestro Padre San Ignacio de Loyola de Cabórica, Sonora, 2001.

and piers with rows of dentils and guttae (singular, gutta), small square and rectangular shapes originally confined to architraves by the classical Greeks and Romans.

Three of the most notable geometric design schemes used widely throughout northern New Spain are diapers, arabesques, and compass flowers. Diapers array geometric motifs within repeating designs, mostly in rectangular or diagonal grids, often along walls or dados as tilework or as painting that imitates tilework (see figure 4.5). Arabesques, first developed by the Arabs, as the name suggests, are intricate, usually fine-lined schemes, originally of stylized plants but later of intertwining scrolls, human or animal shapes, and swags, combined with plant motifs, often on panels or pilasters in Renaissance and baroque architecture. Defying boundaries, arabesques create the effect of looseness. They appear on the north wall of the east transept of San Xavier (Arizona), on the ceiling of Santa María de las Cuevas (Chihuahua), and above and around the top story of the main retablo of San Ignacio de Parras (Coahuila; see figure 6.10). Compass flowers (six- or twelve-petaled flowers inscribed within compass-drawn circles) decorate painted, carved, or inscribed doors, furniture, walls, and woodwork throughout northern New Spain. They serve, for example, as the predominant design scheme on the lintel of the main portal at San Ignacio de Loyola de Cabórica (Sonora; figure 6.39).

Where its didactic purpose was paramount, ornamentation was often isolated on devices resembling heraldic shields such as cartouches (plane or convex) or escutcheons (figure 6.40), or was placed on scrolls (see below). From simple ovals to more elaborate profiles, with or without armorial bearing, escutcheons were carved over doorways and on keystones and spandrels. They were used to present secular or religious coats of arms, anagrams, and initials of religious personages (or were included in paintings bearing the subjects' coats of arms). "Escutcheon"

6.40. An escutcheon on the exterior of Santa Ana in Durango city, Durango, 1996.

also refers to the metal plate from which a handle is suspended or to the lock plate on chests, doors, and drawers (for other geometric motifs, see figure 6.41).

Popularly explained as taking their form from cut paper ornaments used for decoration during fiestas, *guardamalletas* (lambrequins or valances), pinjantes (pendants or fringes), *faldoncitos* (little skirts or flaps of fabric), and *guanteletes* (gauntlets or wrist-length dress gloves—pendant-like ornaments with scalloped or other geometrically shaped edges) appeared in New Spain in the seventeenth century and were much used through the eighteenth. Their flat, fringed outline was carved on frontispieces and side portals under niches, on column bases, and on niche-pilasters, as well as molded, painted, or carved on retablos or other interior architectural elements (see figures 2.20a–b, 6.13, and 6.41gg).[14]

6.41. Geometric ornamental motifs: shapes: a. round or spherical, b. oval, c. orb, d. square, e. square with chamfered corners, f. square with rounded corners, g. drum, h. convex

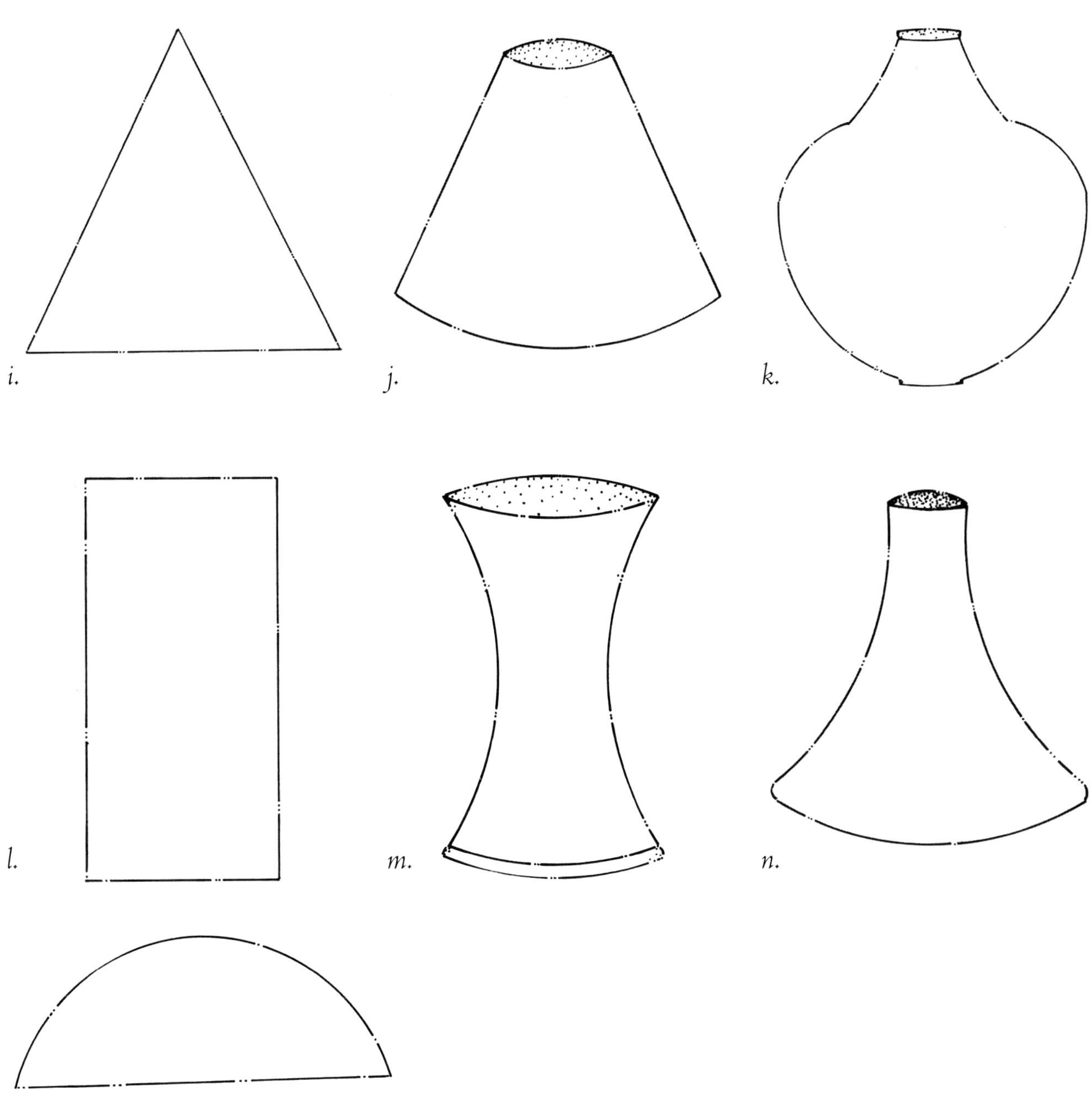

6.41. (continued). Shapes: i. triangle, j. truncated cone, k. bulbous, l. rectangle, m. concave, n. flare, o. hemisphere

continued on next page

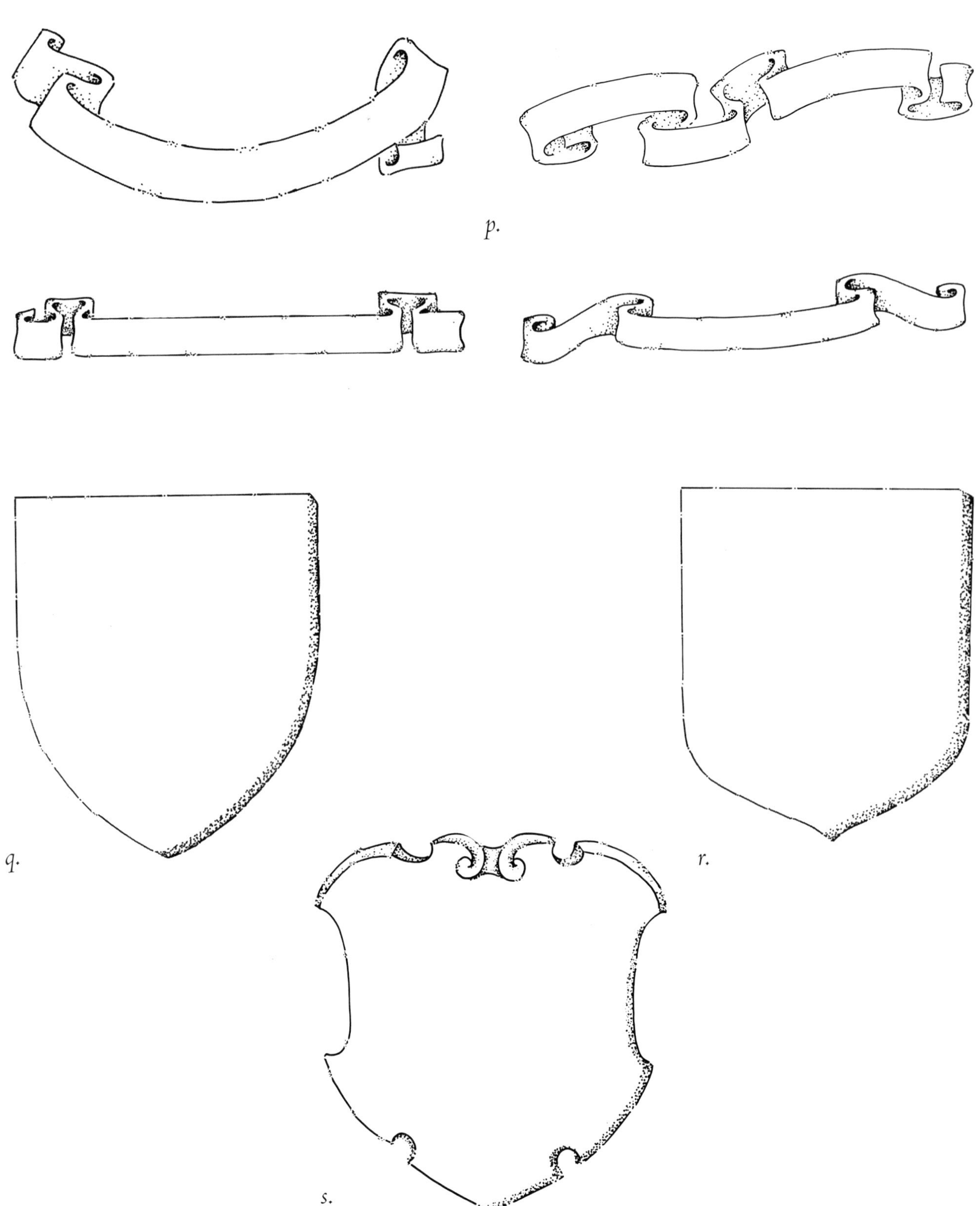

6.41. Geometric ornamental motifs: banners and shields: p. banners, q. simple shield, r. semi-ornate shield, s. ornate shield

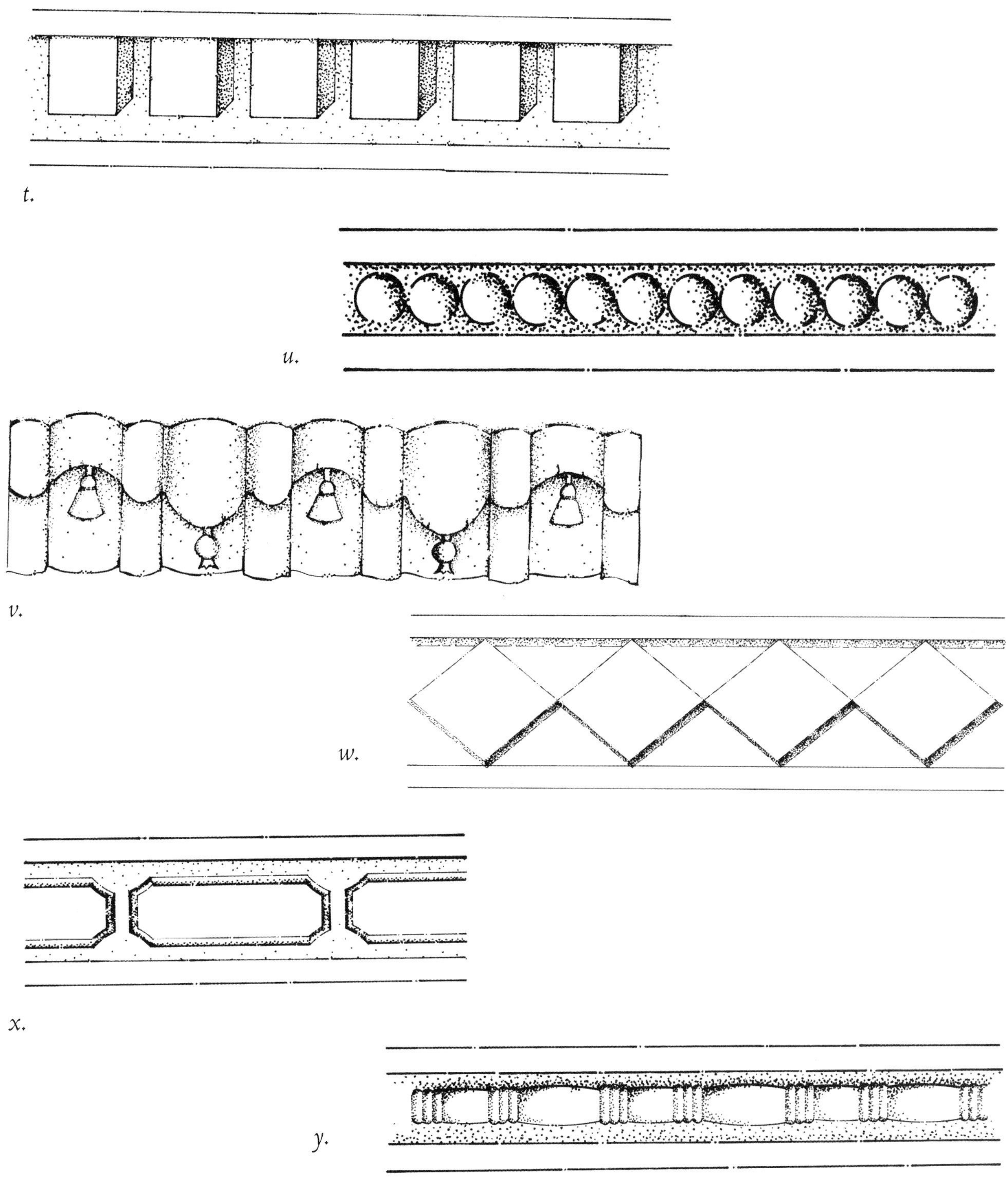

6.41. (continued). Border motifs: t. dentil, u. pearls or beads, v. tassel and bell or pomegranate, w. lozenge, x. cartouche, y. bead and reel

continued on next page

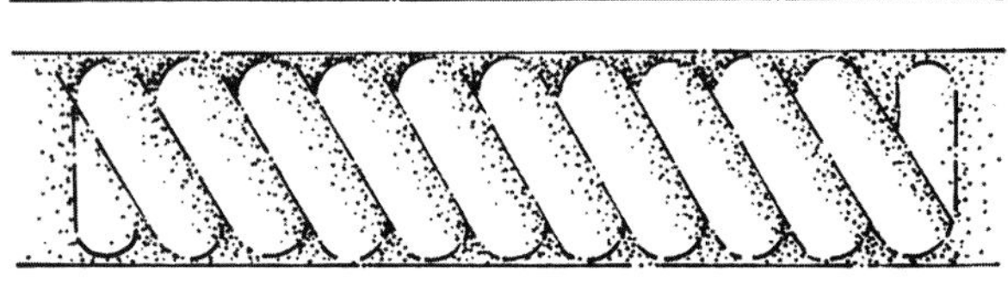

z.

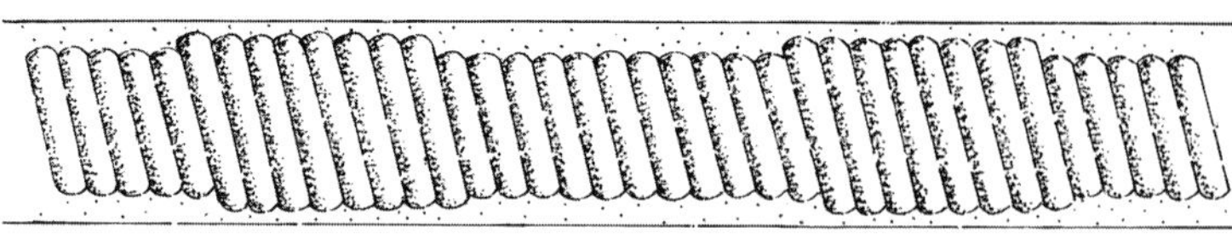

aa.

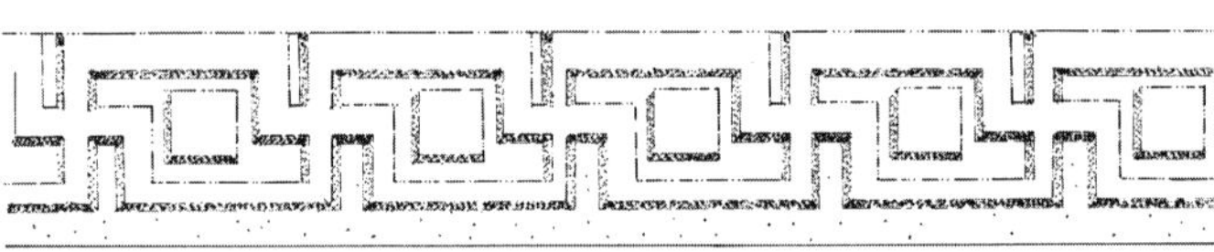

bb.

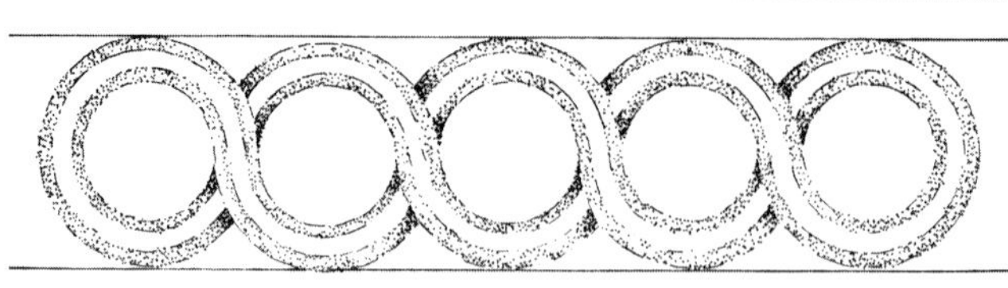

cc.

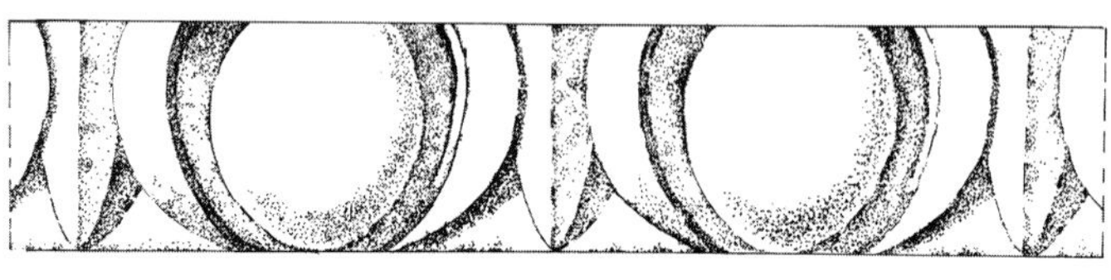

dd.

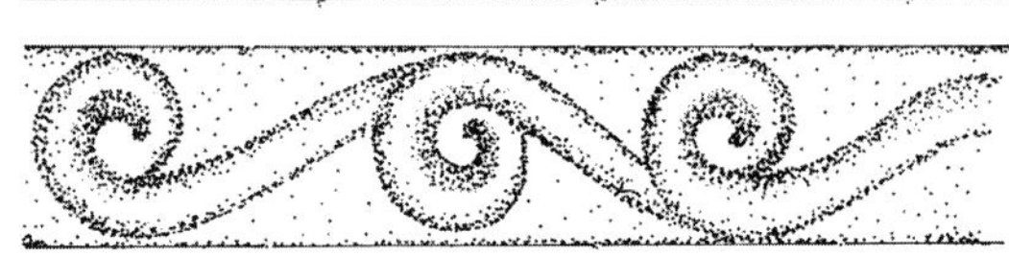

ee.

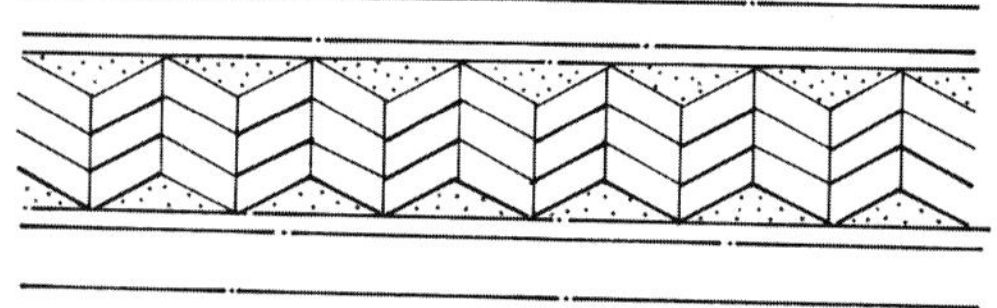

ff.

6.41. *(continued). Border motifs: z. cable, aa. cable, bb. fret, cc. guilloche, dd. egg and dart, ee. wave scroll, ff. chevron*

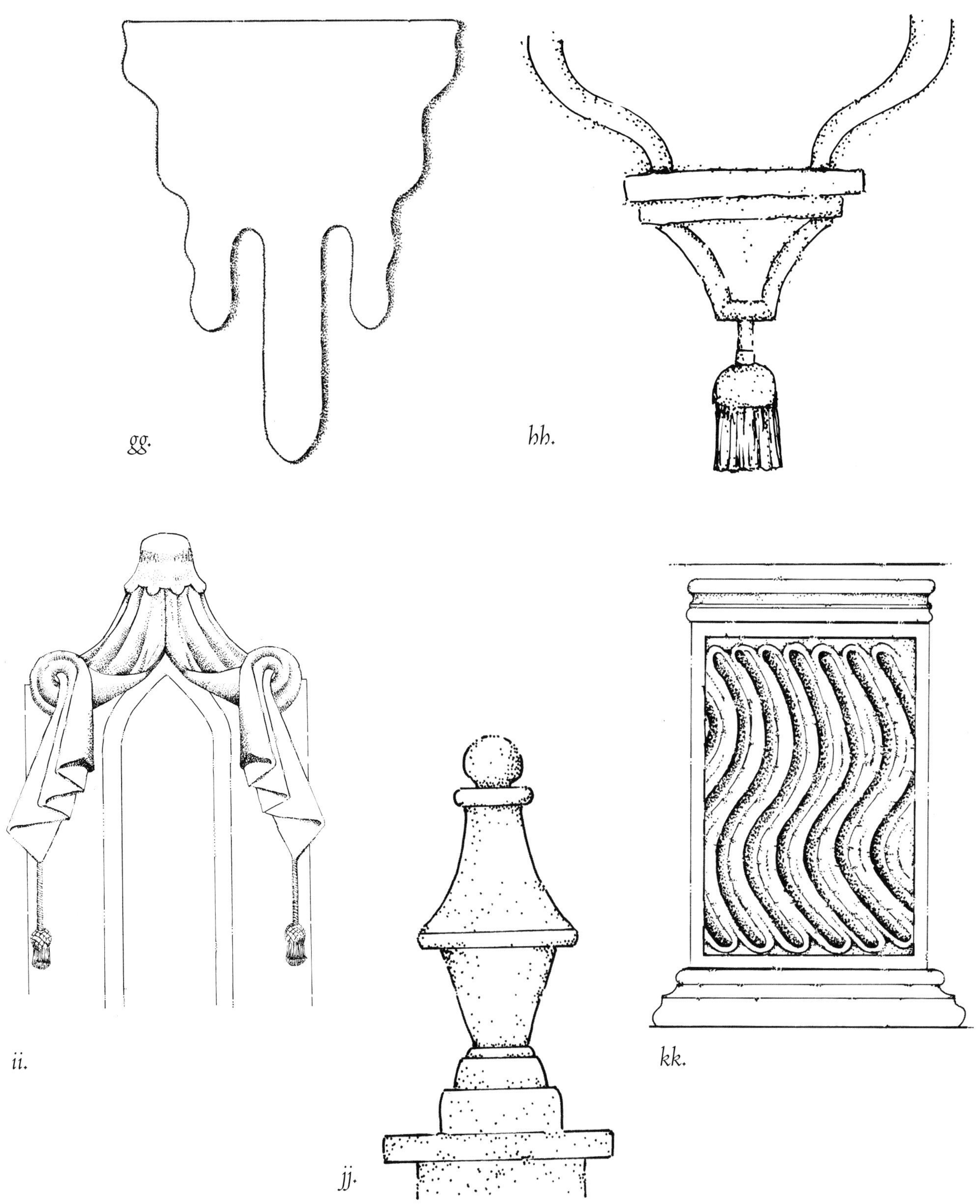

6.41. Ornamental motifs: gg. guantelet, hh. tassel, ii. drapery, jj. pedestal and ball finial, kk. fluting

continued on next page

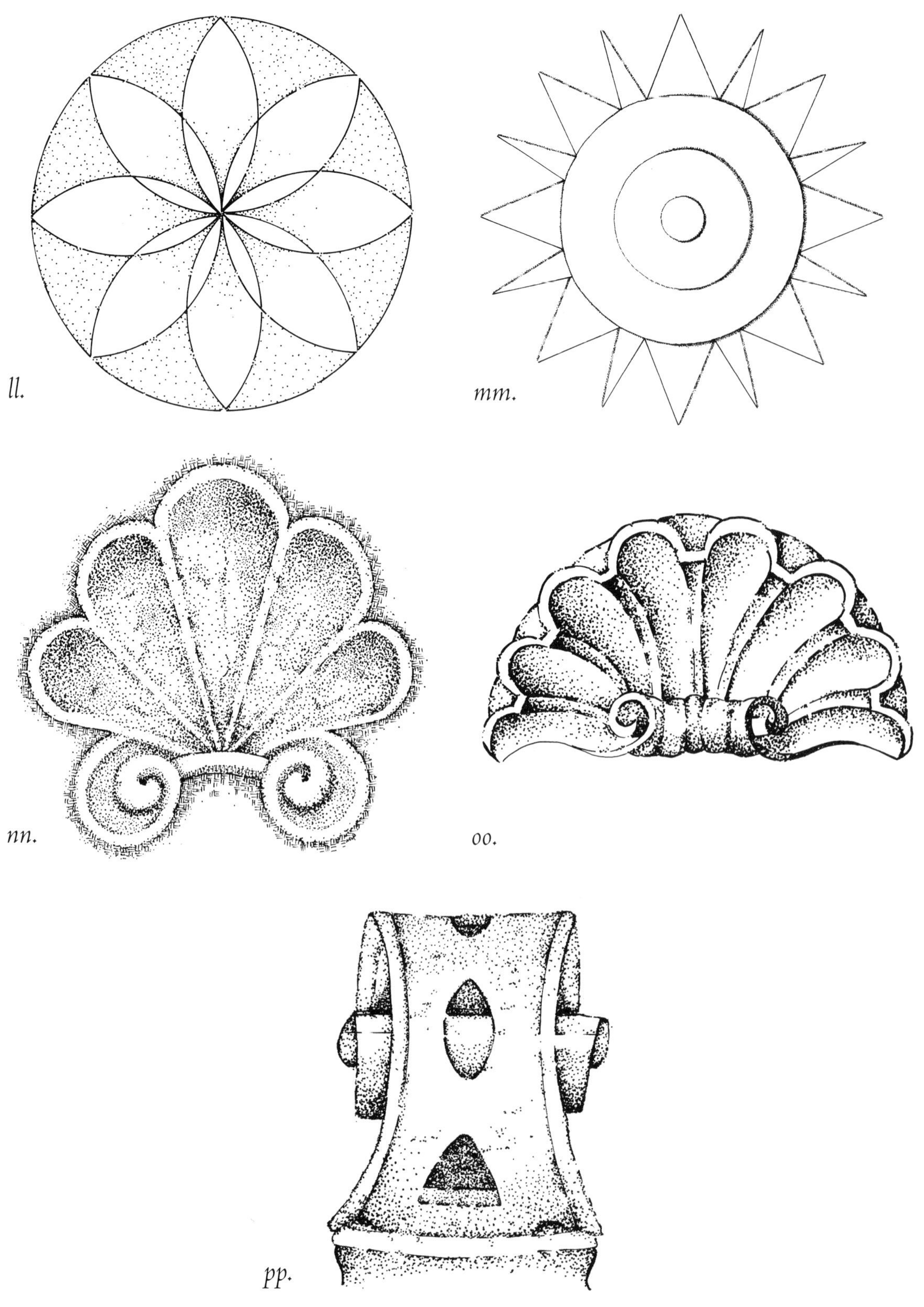

6.41. (continued). Ornamental motifs: ll. compass flower, mm. sun or radiant, nn. palmette, oo. cockle shell, pp. strap

6.41. (continued). Ornamental motifs: qq. scroll, rr. grotesque, ss. puttis or cherubs, tt. bifurcated leaves

continued on next page

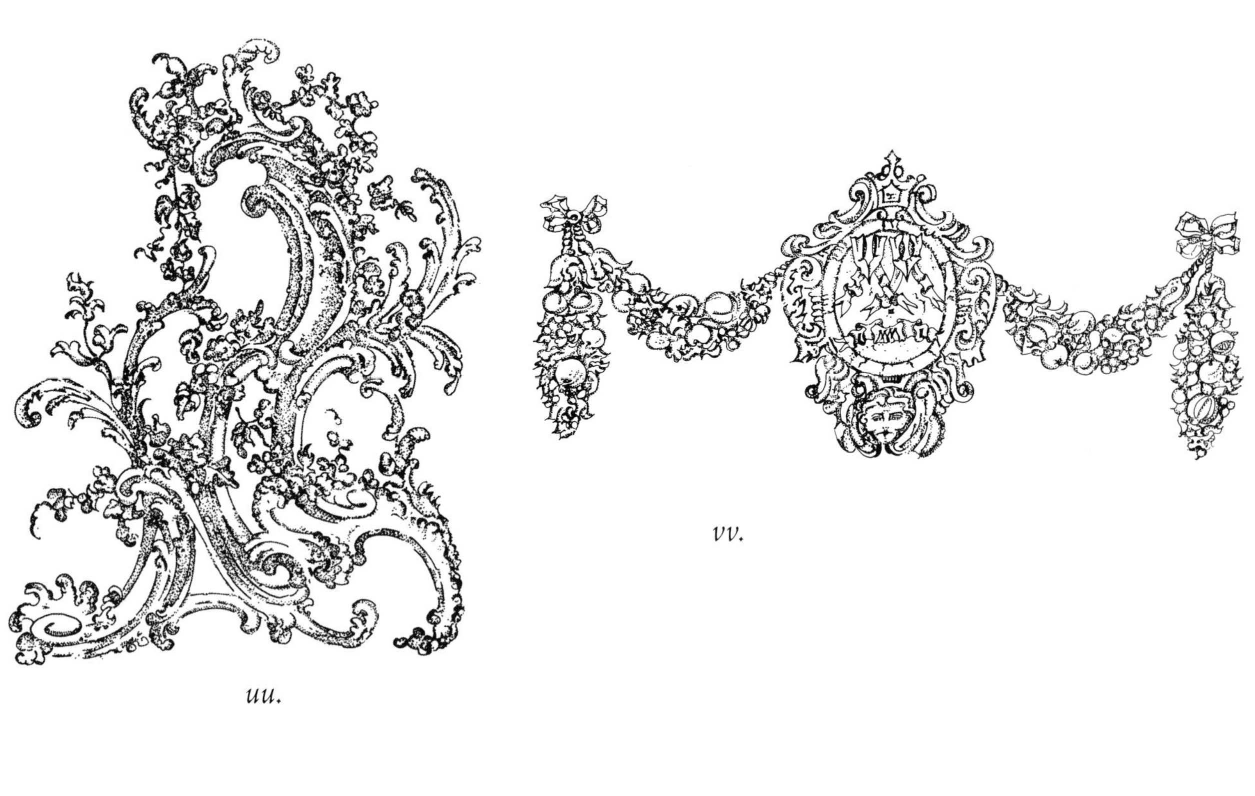

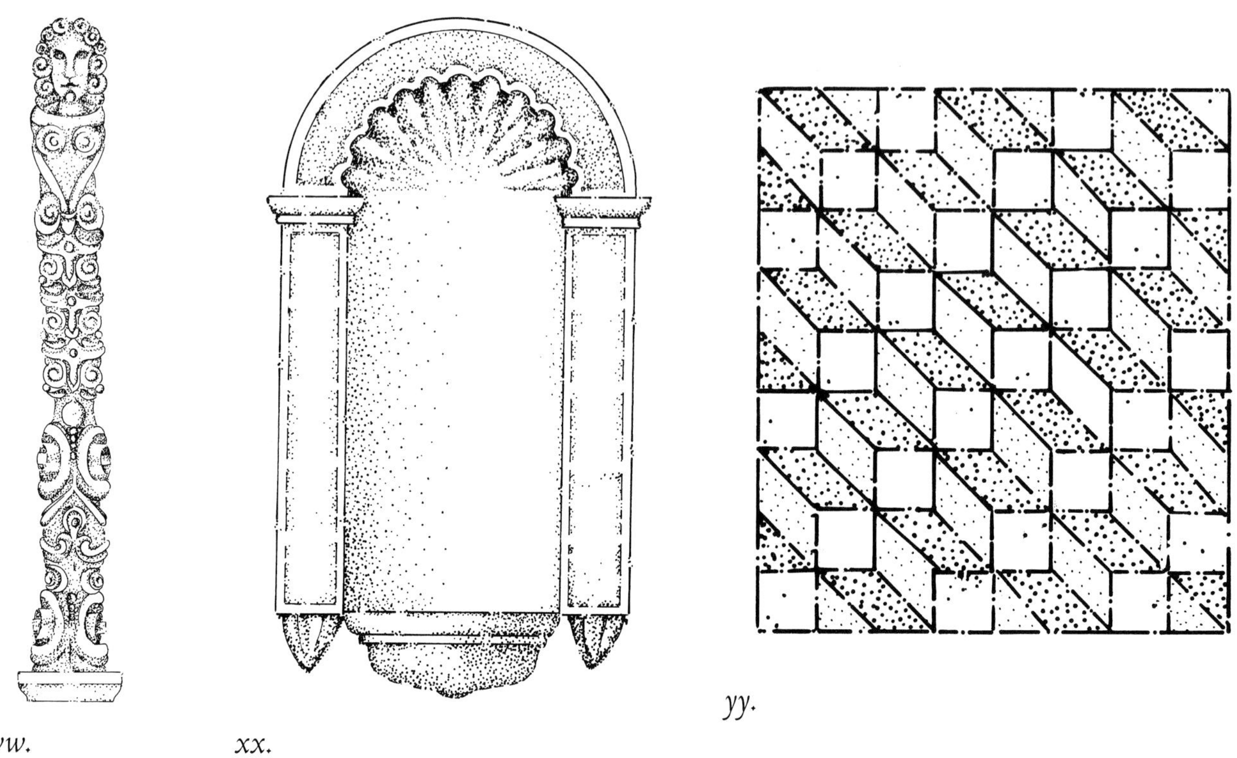

6.41. (continued). Ornamental motifs: uu. rococo "C" scroll or rocaille, vv. swag, ww. headed pilaster, xx. niche, yy. diaper.

6.42. *Interior, San Miguel Arcángel de la Frontera, near Paso Robles, California, ca. 1910. The mural on the left illustrates trompe l'oeil painting. (Newman Postcard Company, private collection)*

Scrolls, Banners, Festoons, Ribbons, Strapwork, and Cables

Ornaments in the form of partly rolled paper, with undulating bands of spirals that flow in and out of their neighbors, scrolls appear as the volutes of Ionic and Corinthian capitals, whereas banners appear as flags or pendants. Particularly common in eighteenth-century painting and sculpture, banners (*banderolas*) serve chiefly to present figures' names or distinctive attributes and to symbolize the Church Militant (those holding them are thus warriors of Christ). Whether hanging vertically or flying horizontally, they are often square or rectangular with triangular notches in the free ends and crosses atop the poles. Silver banners are commonly borne by sculpted figures.

Both scrolls and banners may be used to bear other specific information, as on the triumphal arch of Santa María de las Cuevas (Chihuahua), where horn-playing angels are unfurling a banner with "Beatam me dicent omnes generationes" (Let all generations call me blessed) upon it (see figure 6.19), or on the frontispiece of San Sebastián in Concordia (Sinaloa), where angels are bearing scrolls with "Ave" and "Maria" (see figure 6.9, center top).

Intricate networks of interlaced lines and scrolls carved or molded in very low profile, strapworks look like two-dimensional cutout patterns. In northern New Spain, they are applied over columns, most notably mosaico columns, but may also appear on pilasters and panels (see "Mosaico" under "Columns" above).

Trompe l'Oeil

A French term meaning literally "fool the eye," trompe l'oeil describes painting done to create the illusion of reality. Painted simulations of interior architectural elements such as engaged columns, cornices, and moldings were popular in baroque architecture. Several examples in northern New Spain, although not sophisticated, suggest that trompe l'oeil was known and used by frontier decorators well into the neoclassical era. The interior murals of San Miguel Arcángel (California; built 1818; figure 6.42) were painted using trompe l'oeil, as were a door facing an actual door and jasperized treatments on columns and pediments on the collateral altars in San Xavier del Bac (finished 1797; Arizona) and, to a much more limited degree, the area around the main retablo of San José de Tumacácori simulating a shadow (built ca. 1820; Arizona).

CHAPTER 7

FURNISHINGS

And whatever more shall be needful for the house of thy God, which thou shalt have occasion to bestow, bestow it out of the king's treasure house.

—EZRA 7:20

Most viceregal documents detailing ecclesiastical furnishings, and sometimes also their makers, costs, and donors, pertain to large metropolitan churches in central and southern New Spain.[1] Even for the inventories that contain extensive lists of church furnishings in northern New Spain, exact and detailed explanations are not the general rule. Further complicating matters, many furnishings left behind in the Jesuits' mission churches upon their expulsion in 1767 were distributed among other churches.[2]

The priest in charge of each church was responsible for providing accurate inventories of the buildings, furnishings, and accoutrements when he turned his church over to the priest who replaced him. This and the following two chapters are based in large part upon inventories made between 1665 and 1820, and on records made by other clerics, by church and civil authorities, or by their delegates at about the same time (see "Church Inventories Cited" in "Sources").[3] However much these inventories might vary in extent and accuracy, their format remained essentially the same. After a brief description of the church, most inventories would begin with the silver, starting with the chalice and monstrance because of the great significance of the Eucharist and silver's intrinsic value. Articles on the main altar were described before those on the collateral altars, which, in turn, were described before articles in the baptistery and sacristy. Ecclesiastical garments and linens appeared as the last of the church appurtenances, but before the priest's household effects and church tools.[4] The complete, detailed inventory of San Miguel Arcángel de los Ures (Sonora), made around 1796, gives us a good idea of a well-furnished mission.[5] Here we find exact information not only on the placement of objects, but also on their color, quality, and composition, as well as the identity of religious images, particularly sculptures (on the difficulty of identifying these, see also "Sculptures" in chapter 10).[6]

In this chapter, we shall concentrate on church furnishings *other than* liturgical articles (which are discussed separately in chapter 8: "Liturgical Linens and Objects") and furnishings used to adorn church walls within and without (discussed separately in chapter 10: "Religious Images and Retablos"). Down the centuries, merchants and traders have always managed to provide an astonishing quantity and variety of goods to the most isolated of areas—where there was a need (and money to finance it), somehow they found a way. Northern New Spain was no exception. Goods ranging from bells, metal hardware, and tools to musical instruments and books,[7] from olive oil, wax, and wine to vestments, religious images, and altar furnishings came not only from central and southern New Spain, but also from lands across the globe. Paintings and sculptures were imported from Spain from the earliest days of missionary activity; ivory, ceramics, and wooden articles, from the Orient starting in the seventeenth century;[8] religious prints, from Flanders, Spain, and Italy; and silk, calico, and other fabrics, from China, France, Spain, England, Holland, and the Near East. Nor were bulky items excepted. Entire retablos were broken down, packed in boxes, and shipped to missions in the farthest reaches of northern New Spain, to be reassembled at their destinations.[9] The forged iron railings for the pulpit in the Cathedral of Durango were imported from Sevilla sometime before 1721; bells for the Alta California missions, from Peru, Alaska, and the east coast of the United States in the early nineteenth century.

The Spanish Royal Treasury provided each missionary priest, in addition to an annual stipend, an initial "start-up" grant for clothing, tools, and furnishings for himself, the church, and his charges.[10] Diocesan churches also relied on tithing, donations from parishioners, and revenues from their properties to purchase their furnishings. Some missionaries made it a point to procure especially fine pieces. In particular, some Jesuit mission inventories list an abundance of statues, paintings, silver lamps and liturgical objects, and ecclesiastical vestments described as of the highest quality.[11] To instill pride among the congregation and to encourage reverence for the "temple of God," great care was taken in the selection and maintenance of furnishings. Indeed, some friars felt that rich furnishings and decorations and impressive architecture would help create the splendor, drama, pomp, and mystery needed to draw new converts to the Faith and away from their former pagan beliefs and practices.

Although art, architectural drawings, single prints, and style books, as well as artists and architects themselves, were exported to Spain's colonies, "to firmly establish that other Spain by repeating its own formulas and taste," hundreds of paintings as well as silver liturgical objects produced in the New World were shipped back to Spain among the goods of returning Spaniards, many to be given to a church, convento, or religious organization (many levels of colonial society—nobles, high-ranking civil officials, clerics, wealthy miners, and merchants—participated in Spain's gift economy).[12] Pieces most in demand in Spain reflected exotic aspects of life in the New World, such as screens with wilderness landscapes and paintings of indigenous peoples or people of mixed blood (*castas*), or objects made from or with feathers, cane (*caña*), tortoiseshell, and mother-of-pearl. Numerous paintings of Our Lady of Guadalupe—some by important New Spain artists such as Cristóbal de Villalpando, Juan Correa, Rodriguez Juárez, Miguel Cabrera, and José de Paez, but most by anonymous artists—were shipped back with returning Spaniards. Religious images and liturgical objects, particularly articles made of silver (or sometimes gold), were given to Spaniards' former parish churches in Spain.[13] While devotion was the ostensible motive for the gifts, public recognition of their social success in the New World was certainly also in the minds of the donors. Although the greatest number of silver articles found are portable altar furnishings such as those used in the celebration of the Eucharist (monstrances, chalices, trays, etc.), entire altar frontals of silver, commissioned from important artists in New Spain, were also exported to Spain.

The following information about furnishings is based on inspections of scores of churches throughout northern New Spain, on historical descriptions and inventories, and on examination of hundreds of objects or their photographs. Furnishings will be discussed by location within or without the church, starting outside at the belfry, then proceeding from front to rear (vestibule to sacristy). Certain furnishings typically found in several parts of the church will be discussed at their first or most prominent instance (or both) and their presence elsewhere simply noted. Where articles of a particular kind were documented in northern New Spain sources but were neither available nor described, I have made my best educated guess as to their form, function, appearance, and composition, relying on inventories and other archival materials that describe similar articles from comparable Spanish colonial churches outside northern New Spain, and on canon law in effect during the colonial era. Where examples of ecclesiastical silver or jewelry were unavailable in church collections, I have examined those in private or museum collections. I made heroic efforts to trace pieces to their original sites and to ensure that information about them was relevant to the period and area.

Belfry

Although bells were very likely invented during the Bronze Age, when they were first used by Catholic churches remains unclear. Some have ascribed their introduction to Paulinus, bishop of Nola in Campania (ca. 400); others, to Pope Sabinianus, Saint Gregory's successor (ca. 600); they were in general use by the eighth century. Bell making did not, however, become a science (campanology) until the fifteenth century, in the Netherlands, when the developing science of harmonics provided the impetus for tuning bells to desired pitches. Before that time, bells had been used only for signaling deaths, church services, or emergencies.

The sizes of bells varied with their functions. Known chiefly by their Latin names, bells ranged from the relatively small *tintinnabulum*, used in the refectory, dormitory, or sanctuary, to the often much larger *campana*, hung in the campanile or belfry and rung for the Angelus and to gather the congregation, and the *signum* (signal bell), hung in any number of places outside the church. Handbells ranged from the tinkling *nola* (after Nola, Campania, where it is supposed to have originated), used in the church choir, to the often silver and more melodious *campanita* or *campanilla* (Sanctus, or Communion, bell; described under "Altars and Sanctuary," "Mass" in chapter 8) used in the celebration of the Mass, to the shrill-pitched *squilla* (in Spanish, *esquila*), used in the monastery refectory (for an esquila of another type and function, see below).[14] The three kinds of bells most often listed in mission inventories of northern New Spain were the large bells that hung in the belfry, in a bell wall, or on a frame outside the church; the handbells used during Mass to direct the congregation's attention to the most solemn parts; and the small wheel-mounted bells (*ruedas de campanillas, rodettas,*

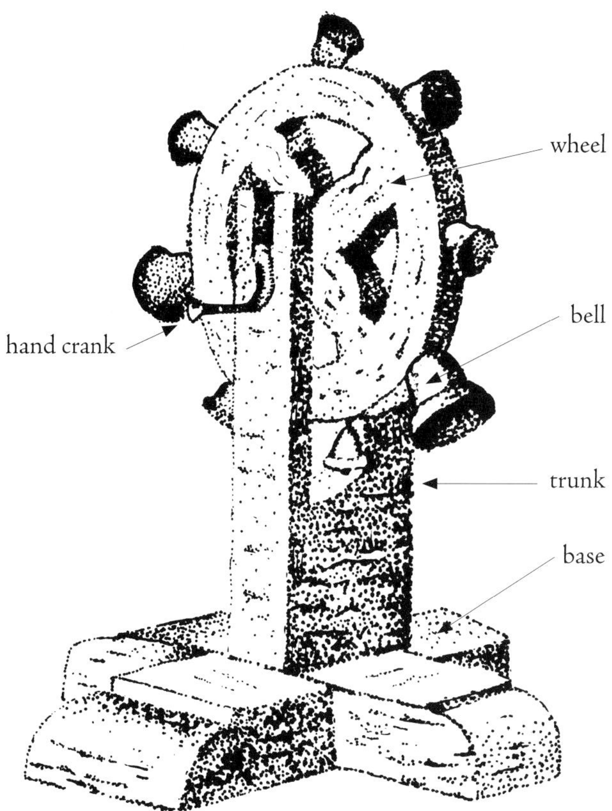

7.1. Wheel-mounted bells (actual size about 30 inches).

campanas de la Gloria; sometimes also called *tintinnabula*; figure 7.1) used during certain religious services. Mission inventories also referred to bells in general as *timbres* (although *timbres* today designates bells equipped with a spring mechanism for sounding).

Because no bells of any sort could be rung after the intoning of the Gloria during Mass on Holy Thursday until Easter Vigil on Holy Saturday, other noisemaking devices made of wood were pressed into service.[15] Of these, cog rattles (*matracas;* figure 7.2) and clappers (*pregores;* figure 7.3) are used in northern Mexico to this day.

Some church bells were gifts of the king and sent from Spain. Others were made in New Spain, cast either on-site or at a foundry elsewhere.[16] Still others, such as those at the Alta California missions, were imported from Chile, Peru, Massachusetts, and Russian Alaska in the late eighteenth and early nineteenth centuries.

Bells played an important role in the daily life of the communities of northern New Spain. Principally used to summon the congregation to services, they were also used to warn of danger or to mark a time of rejoicing, as well as to regulate the daily routine of the missions.[17] In some

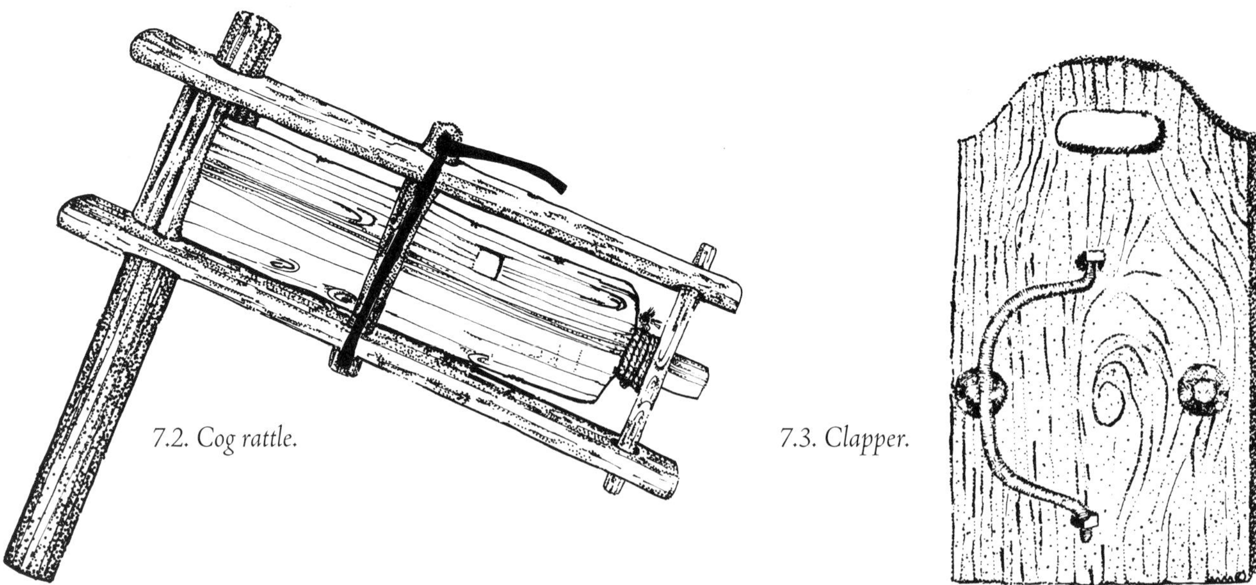

7.2. Cog rattle.

7.3. Clapper.

places, bells were tolled when a person was dying or had just died, the number of strokes indicating male, female, child, or member of the clergy.[18]

Before being hung, bells were solemnly "baptized" by a bishop or by a priest who had a bishop's permission ("faculties") to withdraw them from profane use and consecrate them to God and his service. Psalms were recited and the bells were first sprinkled with holy water and then anointed with chrism and the oil for the sick. They were also given names, and their namers called godparents.[19]

The hanging bells in the belfries of northern New Spain were either stationary or swinging. The first had headstocks consisting of four or more ears or shanks, to be tied or chained to a beam or other horizontal support in the belfry. The clapper was then struck against the side of the bell. Swinging bells, also called esquilas, had flat headstocks, to be attached to wooden yokes by a system of bolts. Tall, massive, sometimes carved affairs, the yokes acted as counterbalances, turning on bearings and gudgeons, or in grooves in a metal-sleeved frame or the sides of the belfry. Bells and yokes were designed to turn over completely.[20] The bell would ring twice as it rolled over and the clapper struck its opposite sides, in a rhythm distinctly different from that of chimed bells, i.e., stationary bells struck by clappers. In a practice called clocking, bell ringers throughout much of northern New Spain used the clapper to strike the bell on one side only, setting up uneven patterns of vibration that often caused their bells to split.[21]

Yoked (or swinging; figure 7.4) and eared (or stationary; figure 7.5) bells were used in belfries throughout northern New Spain (for comparison, figure 7.6 shows a modern system of hanging and ringing a bell).

The ratio of the bell's diameter to its sound bow and weight determines its tone and note. The proportions of a bell and the angle of its sides and sound bow can produce sounds ranging from staccato to resonant. (Unduly long bells do not project over long distances.) The form of the curves and details of the shape are important factors in bell casting and were arrived at by experience.[22] Although I could not locate any contemporary descriptions of bell casting techniques in northern New Spain, it is likely these differed little from techniques in use in Spain and elsewhere in Europe at that time.[23]

Because of its resonance, bronze—an alloy of copper and (usually 13–25 percent) tin—is the ideal metal for bells.[24] After being cast, bells could be tuned (by carefully trimming away metal within or without), and those in metropolitan and wealthier provincial churches often were. Most bells cast and used in northern New Spain, however, were crude affairs, neither tuned nor polished, with no attempt made even to remove the casting slubs or sprues. Although a large, three-tiered bell tower could accommodate as many as twelve bells, today even the largest bell towers rarely house more than eight.[25] When the physical property of a church was destroyed during armed conflicts, bronze bells were not excepted. Some may have been melted down and recast into cannons.[26]

7.4. Yoked (swinging) bell, Nuestra Señora de Guadalupe, Ojo de Agua, San Luis Potosí, 1984.

7.5. Eared (stationary) bells, Nuestra Señora de Balbanera de la Aduana, Sonora, 1982.

Vestibule

Immediately inside the main doors was an area beneath the upper choir called the vestibule, or lower choir (sotocoro), that could serve as the staging area for some religious observances. In the vestibule were holy water fonts, or stoups (see "Vestibule, Choir, Baptistery" under "Inner Body" in chapter 5), and entrances to the baptistery, bell towers, or both. A cancel, a great wooden screen, was installed separating the vestibule from the nave, to provide privacy for church activities when the outside doors were open and to act as a baffle against wind and drafts. (Canceles were often also placed inside the side doors of large churches.) Placed far enough back to allow the wicket doors of the church to swing inward, the cancel also had doors through its sides to allow worshippers to enter the nave. Some canceles, such as the massive reconstructed examples at all three entrances of the Cathedral of Durango (figure 7.7), have larger central doors, most likely to facilitate processions. Large churches, whether parochial or cathedral, would use this device; smaller churches had little use for it.

Baptistery

Because it contains blessed water and is the scene of Christian regeneration, the baptismal font (from Latin *fons*, fountain; in Spanish, *pila*) is the second most important place in the church after the main altar. Constructed as a basin on a pedestal, the font was placed in the baptistery, a room or space reserved for the sacrament of Baptism. Although the shape was not rigidly prescribed, basin and pedestal were traditionally octagonal (as a reminder of the eight people saved in Noah's ark), with the pedestal, or the baptistery floor itself, sunk one step below the floor of the nave in accordance with Church tradition (see "Vestibule, Choir, Baptistery" under "Inner Body" in chapter 5).

The font's basin was divided into two parts—one to contain the baptismal water and a smaller part to catch the used water.[27] The font was to be made of nonporous

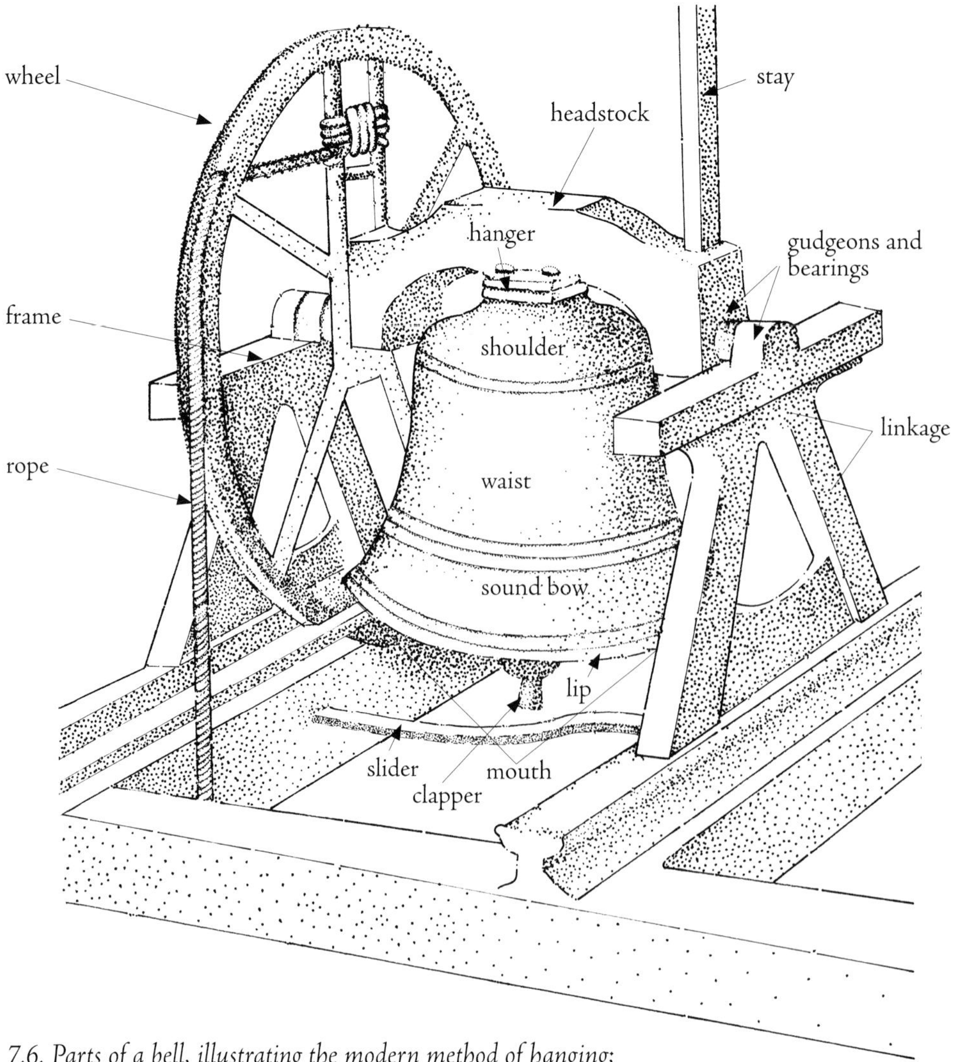

7.6. Parts of a bell, illustrating the modern method of hanging; the colonial method was simpler but used the same principle.

material, preferably stone, because Moses smote the rock to bring forth saving water in the wilderness (Numbers 20:11) and that rock was held to symbolize Christ (1 Corinthians 10:4), and to be covered so as to protect the blessed water (holy water with blessed salt and a few drops of Oil of Catechumens and Holy Chrism).[28] In many baptismal fonts of the Pimería Alta, the basin was made of copper with a hinged copper lid (other basins and covers were made of tin, *laton*) and mounted on a pedestal of lime plaster and brick or carved stone, perhaps because no stone suitable for the basin was available. The copper lids were sometimes decorated with religious monograms in repoussé (figure 7.8). Whatever it was made of, the font's cover was often secured with a hasp and lock to prevent contamination, superstitious use, and ignorant or careless handling of the blessed water.[29] Although the marble or composite stone baptismal fonts seen today in many colonial churches are mostly postcolonial replacements, the alabaster fonts (*pilas de tecali*) at the former mission churches of Baja California and Tamaulipas may well be original. Mission inventories also include other objects used for baptismal fonts, such as metal and ceramic bowls from China.

The holy oils in their silver vessels, the blessed salt, a silver baptismal shell, a book containing the rite of Baptism, vestments for the ceremony (stole and surplice, baptismal robe, and *capillo*—a cap placed on the baby's head in the ceremony), candles, and linens were all stored

7.7. Cancel (reconstructed), Catedral de Durango, 1996.

7.8. Baptismal font, San Francisco Xavier del Bac, Tucson, Arizona, ca. 1940. (Courtesy of Historic American Building Survey)

in a cupboard or ambry or, at the very least, on a special table in the baptistery. In churches where space was at a premium, religious sculptures used only on special occasions, altar ornaments, and even church furniture no longer in use could be stored in the baptistery, which usually had its own door and some means of securing it.

Upper Choir

In most churches, a choir loft was constructed over the main entrance for the organ and for singers and other musicians. This architectural solution improved church acoustics and allowed music to filter down from an unseen and lofty position, thus adding to the mystery of the religious services. The choir galleries in the Cathedrals of Durango and Mexico City are split, with each side intended to house a separate organ.[30] The two organs (and the choirs they accompanied) in these basilica-shaped cathedrals were used to bounce the strophe and antistrophe of church music antiphonically back and forth from one side of the cathedral to the other, as done in the basilica-shaped churches of Europe.

From the earliest days of the Conquest, music served as the missions' single greatest attraction for the native Americans, a fact not overlooked by the missionaries, who used it effectively as a conversion and educational tool (figure 7.9a). Indeed, so exuberant was the Indians' enthusiasm for music that, in 1556, the first Church Council to be held in New Spain felt compelled to limit the number of singers and to prohibit the playing of any instrument except the organ in churches.[31] As these restrictions were forgotten, ignored, or relaxed, music for instruments other than the organ was gradually allowed back into the churches, although it did not become prominent until the eighteenth century.

The importance of music in the religious rites, and the deep enjoyment it provided, gave rise to a diversity of instruments, the need for skilled musicians, and a well-developed repertory for the Mass as well for Passion plays and ceremonial dances. Music played throughout New Spain included masses, psalms, oratorios, antiphons, litanies, lamentations, Salve Reginas, Eucharist hymns (*alabados*), and hymns of praise (*alabanzas*). Furthermore, Indians, mestizos, Spaniards, and *criollos* alike—many of whom became instrument makers, teachers, or both—produced a wealth of colonial compositions. Although most of the specific information regarding colonial music, types of instruments, and their makers concerns central New Spain, frequent citations suggest that similar music, instruments, and instruction were present throughout northern New Spain as well.[32]

In Nuevo México, San Felipe Pueblo may have had an organ as early as 1609. By 1641, there also may have been organs in the other New Mexican missions.[33] Organs were also installed in the Jesuit churches of the Pimería Alta and Baja California and among the Tarahumara and in diocesan churches of central northern New Spain. Furnishings and supplies prescribed for the founding of New Mexican mission churches included a set of clarions (*clarines;* treble-pitched trumpets; later, simply any solo trumpets), bassoons, trumpets, and a book of chants for every five priests.[34]

From the early seventeenth century until the conversion of mission to diocesan churches in the early nineteenth century, church records make frequent mention of mission choirs and orchestras. Schools were established at both Franciscan and Jesuit missions where singing and the playing of instruments were taught as central to the overall goals of the Alta California mission system; at least one mission used music to teach the catechism; the Indians there were taught to sing hymns in four-part harmony, in unison, and to musical accompaniment.[35]

I compiled the following list and descriptions of instruments from sixteenth-century clergymen's lists of instruments played or taught; from seventeenth-, eighteenth-, and nineteenth-century accounts of instruments in use in northern New Spain's missions during both religious and secular celebrations; and from instrument lists found in the guild ordinances of Mexico City.[36]

Although organs were present in pre-Christian Greece, it was several centuries before the organ assumed the form we recognize today, namely, a keyboard instrument with pipes arranged in scalelike rows. Organs were being made in Spain by the fifth century, but only in the fourteenth through sixteenth centuries did their range and tone color develop significantly and their use expand throughout Europe. During the High Renaissance, interest in polyphonic music led to the enlargement of register stops for church organs. Seventeenth-century technical innovations greatly increased their range of musical capabilities. The Dutch, French, and German organs in particular developed wide ranges of tone color. The Spanish organs, and

7.9. Main retablo, San Francisco Xavier del Bac, Tucson, Arizona: a. detail of angels playing instruments, 1980 (by author); b. entire retablo, 2005. The angels shown in the detail are above the capital on estípites on either side of the titular figure. (Photo by Meredith L. Milstead)

a.

b.

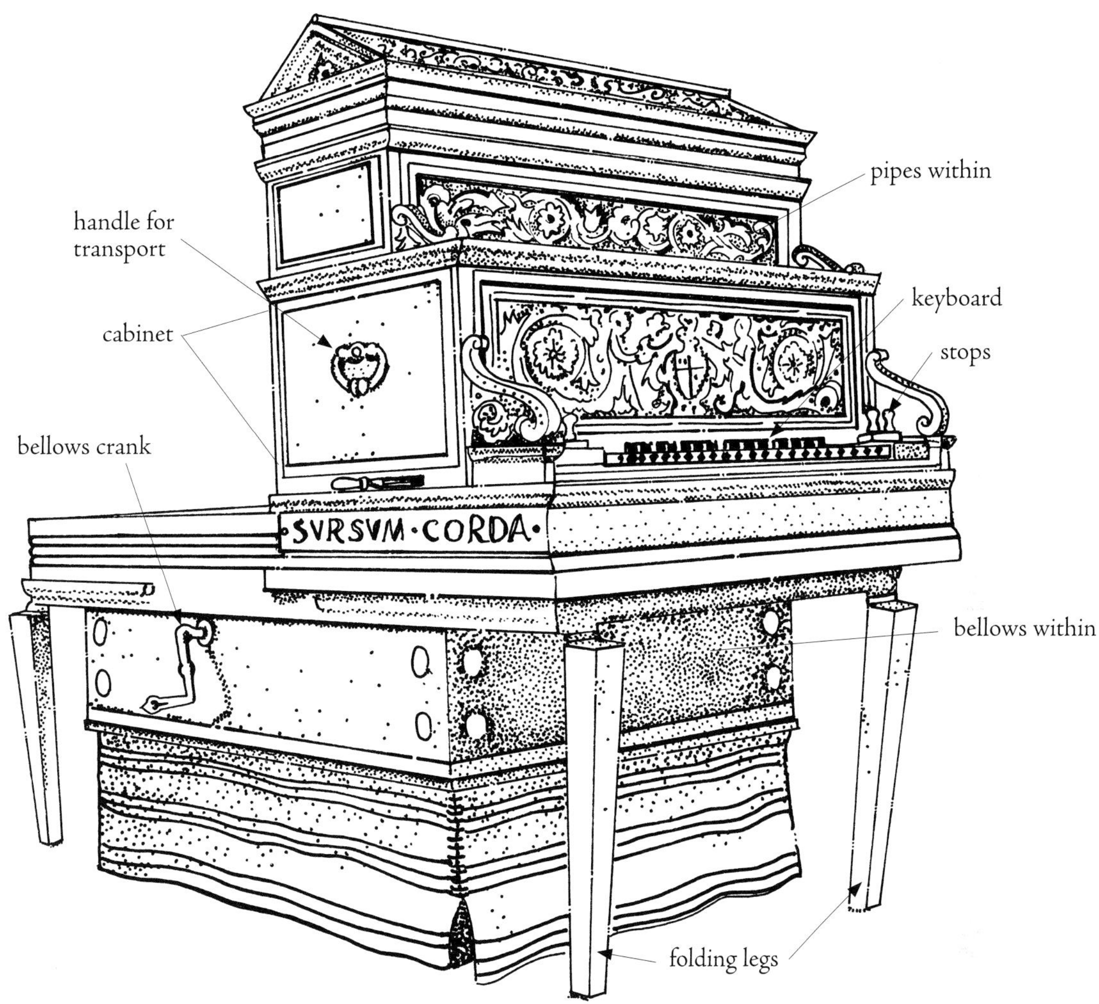

7.10. Positive organ of eighteenth-century type.

therefore also those of New Spain, were most heavily influenced by the Dutch.

Organs began to be built in New Spain as early as the late sixteenth century, when Juan de Torquemada reported that they were in almost all of the conventos and churches administered by religious orders, and that, under Spanish direction, the Indians both made and played them.[37] Over the next two centuries, the portative organ (a small, weak-toned instrument played with one hand and pumped with the other) appeared mostly in art and questionably in practice, whereas the positive organ (a medium-sized, full-toned, stopped instrument played with both hands and usually requiring a second person to pump the bellows) was used in churches throughout northern New Spain. Figure 7.10 is based on an eighteenth-century positive organ at Santo Domingo in Zacatecas (Zacatecas) and a replica of one at La Colegiata in Osuna, Spain.

Although seventeenth-century mission inventories in Nuevo México mention neither the size nor the type of organs listed; proceeding on the basis of period, logistics, and cost, we can deduce that these were most likely positive organs, cabinet-shaped instruments ranging in size from small and relatively portable—as wide as a standard desk—to large and massive, with elaborately carved and painted doors and sides. Spiess described the typical Spanish organ of the sixteenth and seventeenth centuries as "a one-keyboard instrument without pedals, the keyboard having a compass of from bass C to A-2, i.e., the A above middle C. The pipes were usually enclosed in a cabinet, the doors of which were open during playing of the instrument, the cabinet acting as an aid in projecting the sound. Ordinarily there were a limited number of stops, or sets of pipes."[38] Horizontal pipes called trumpets *en chemade* were a feature peculiar to great Spanish organs after 1620, of which a few extant examples remain in Mexico (although unfortunately none in northern New Spain). The immense size of these pipes and the fanciful decoration around them (including angels and sometimes even mermaids) gave such organs an otherworldly appearance.

In a class by itself, and falling somewhere between true organs and music boxes, was the barrel organ (*organillo*), whose barrel, a cylinder dotted with steel nails and staples, was "programmed" for a variety of tunes. The nails and staples raised balanced keys connected to the valves of the pipes, which admitted the stream of air from the wind chest. No skill or mastery of music was necessary for its operation. In the late eighteenth century, the friar of Mission San Carlos Borromeo received a barrel organ as a gift from a British navigator, and several others are recorded as being in use in Alta California missions in the years following. The repertories for such organs included popular music, which was performed along with sacred music by the Indian congregants there.[39]

Woodwinds were represented in New Spain by flutes (end-blown and transverse), recorders, clarinets, *chalumeaux* (similar to clarinets), shawms, *dulzainas* (a type of shawm, the precursor to the oboe), oboes, bassoons and double bassoons, *fagottos* and dulcians (primitive bassoons), and krumhorns. The brass instruments of New Spain included serpents, sackbuts (early trombones), cornua, and trumpets, straight or bent. Stringed instruments were represented throughout New Spain by violins, violas, cellos, bass viols, rebecs, citterns, lutes, lyres, guitars, *vihuelas*, violas da gamba, *violas da braccia*, zithers, *bandurrias*, psalteries, and harps.[40] Listed among percussion instruments in the church inventories of New Spain were snare drums, bass drums, and tympani, tambourines, bells, cymbals, *teponaztlis* (split wooden drums used by the natives in central New Spain), and triangles. A harpsichord is included in the musical instruments inventoried in 1773 at Nuestra Señora de Loreto de Concho (Baja California Sur), although its source is not known; Estrada also reports that in Durango in the eighteenth century there was an instrument maker of pianos and clavichords.[41]

Other furnishings associated with the upper choir are music stands or choristers' desks (*facistoles* or *facistoles de coro*), used to support music books in which the notes and words were often greatly enlarged, enabling them to be read at a distance. A music stand commonly took the form of a pedestal with a four-sided platform top sloping slightly inward (figure 7.11). The platform was made wide enough to accommodate lamps, or candleholders were directly incorporated into the stand. The few remaining examples are sometimes quite lavishly decorated. Some of the choir books they held, with parchment leaves, colored notes, and gilded decoration were highly prized not only for their content, but for their artistic value as well.

Finally, the upper choir was furnished with choir stalls (*sillería del coro*) and chairs, often elaborately adorned, to seat the choristers. Although few original stalls remain, two fine but diverse examples are the chair backs painted on the upper choir walls of San Xavier del Bac near Tucson (Arizona; figure 7.12) and the ones with medium-relief figures of saints, archangels, and God, polychromed and gilded, in the Cathedral of Durango (figure 7.13).[42]

Nave and Transepts

During the viceregal era, arrangements for seating were minimal. Those attending services either stood or knelt at appropriate times; women occasionally sat on the floor or on cushions. Although chairs were sometimes provided for the infirm; a few benches (*bancos* or *escaños*) might be pushed against the walls in rural areas; and bench-tables, molded low shelves, might be incorporated into the walls, seating arrangements in the nave were minimal (figure 7.14). Benches with kneelers (*bancos con reclinatorio*) did not appear until the mid-nineteenth century. Indeed, well into the twentieth century, congregants in rural New Mexico stood or knelt on the floor, with men and women separated from each other (figure 7.15).

Confessional

After the adoption of the Rituale Romanum in 1614 and until Vatican II, confessionals were of three basic types: (1) a closetlike room or rooms, either freestanding or built into the nave wall, containing two or three sections; (2) a more open, boxlike affair; or (3) a chair with a combination kneeler and screen. The penitent and the priest confessor were separated by a curtain or covered grille (*tabella*) at face level, not only to assure anonymity

7.11. Music stand, Catedral de Durango, 1983.

7.12. Choir seating, San Francisco Xavier del Bac, Tucson, Arizona, 1980, a rare original example.

7.13. Choir seating, Catedral de Durango, 1983. The backs of the choir seats portray the Trinity; the Virgin Mary and Joseph; significant Dominican, Franciscan, and Jesuit saints and founders of orders; John the Baptist; archangels; and King Louis of France.

7.14. La Purísima Concepción de Nuestra Señora de Caborca, Sonora, 1977, showing the nave, main portal, and benches along the walls.

7.15. Interior, San José de la Gracia, Las Trampas, New Mexico, 1940, where congregants still had no benches and were separated by sex in the colonial manner. (Courtesy of the Library of Congress)

but, in the case of female penitents, to protect the priest from temptation.[43] Those confessing knelt as a sign of penitence. In New Spain, however, it was neither unusual nor forbidden for boys and men to confess to their priest face-to-face, kneeling at the priest's feet rather than at his side hidden behind the confessional screen. Indeed, to this day, a face-to-face confession is thought to be a sign of humility and courage.[44]

The confessional incorporated into the wall of the nave has no European antecedents; a particularly spectacular example of such a confessional in northern New Spain is in San Diego de Alcalá in Pitiquito (Sonora; figure 7.16). Depending on the number of priests available to hear confessions, churches often had more than one confessional. Confessionals ranged from the relatively simple in poorer mission churches, such as the reconstructed example from La Purísima Concepción in Lompoc (California; figure 7.17), to the ultrabaroque in wealthy metropolitan churches, such as the original example from the Cathedral of Durango (figure 7.18).

7.16. *Confessional built into the nave, San Diego de Alcalá del Pitiquito, Sonora, 2001.*

Pulpit

Medieval friars are credited with integrating the pulpit into church architecture. According to Durandus, the pulpit (from Latin *pulpitum*, stage, platform) signified an "imitation of our Lord, who went up into a mountain that he might preach the Gospel."[45] It could be a raised platform enclosed by a low wall, a rostrum (*caja de púlpito*), or simply a railing from which the preacher delivered his sermons (figure 7.19). The pulpit had to be forward of the main altar, although it could be on either side of the church. In churches having two pulpits (most had only one), the sermon was traditionally given and the Gospel sung from the pulpit on the Gospel (left, or ambo) side; the Epistle was sung from the pulpit on the Epistle side, which was often less elaborate.

Raised platform pulpits were mounted by stairs from the nave or occasionally directly from an opening in the nave wall from the sacristy or a transept area. Because of the importance of this furnishing, the pulpit was usually finely carved, painted, or paneled; and although many were hexagonal and made from wood, pulpits were also made in other shapes and from stone or brick and lime plaster. The images or attributes of the Four Evangelists might be included on their sides (see figures 4.8 and 4.9); sometimes an eagle was incorporated into a device for holding the Gospels, as on the pulpit at San Juan Bautista (California; figure 7.20).

Above the preacher as he stood in the pulpit was a tester or sounding board (*tornavoz*, literally, voice turner), which reflected his voice and served as a focal point of attention. In the center on the soffit or underside, the tester

7.17. Confessional (replica), La Purísima Concepción, Lompoc, California, 1987.

7.18. Ultrabaroque confessional, Catedral de Durango, 2001.

was decorated with religious symbols, often a dove—signifying the Holy Ghost or divine inspiration—in sculpted or painted form. At Santa Rosa de Lima in Cusihuiriáchic (Chihuahua), the tester was fashioned to function much as the body of a stringed instrument, complete with S-holes in the soundboard and heads of cherubs painted around the edge.

Placed at equal intervals along the walls of the nave or outer aisles of the church (occasionally on cloister or cemetery walls or exterior nave walls) were fourteen small crosses (sometimes accompanied by paintings, engravings, prints, plaques, or bas-relief sculptures illustrating scenes from Jesus' Passion), referred to as the Stations of the Cross (Vía Crucis; see also "Nave, Aisles, Transepts" in chapter 5 and "Stations of the Cross" in chapter 12 for their placement and iconography, respectively).

Along the nave and transepts, as well as in the crossing and sanctuary, hung chandeliers. Mounted from the ceiling by rope and chain, these could be lowered to light and replace or refuel candles or lamps. Two types appear in illustrations of colonial church interiors and some still remain in northern New Spain: the *araña* (spider; figure 7.21), having four horizontal arms of worked wood in the form of a cross, with platforms on the terminal ends to support candles or lamps; and the *corona* (crown; figure 7.22), having one or a series of concentric iron or tin-plated rings that increase in size in descending order, attached

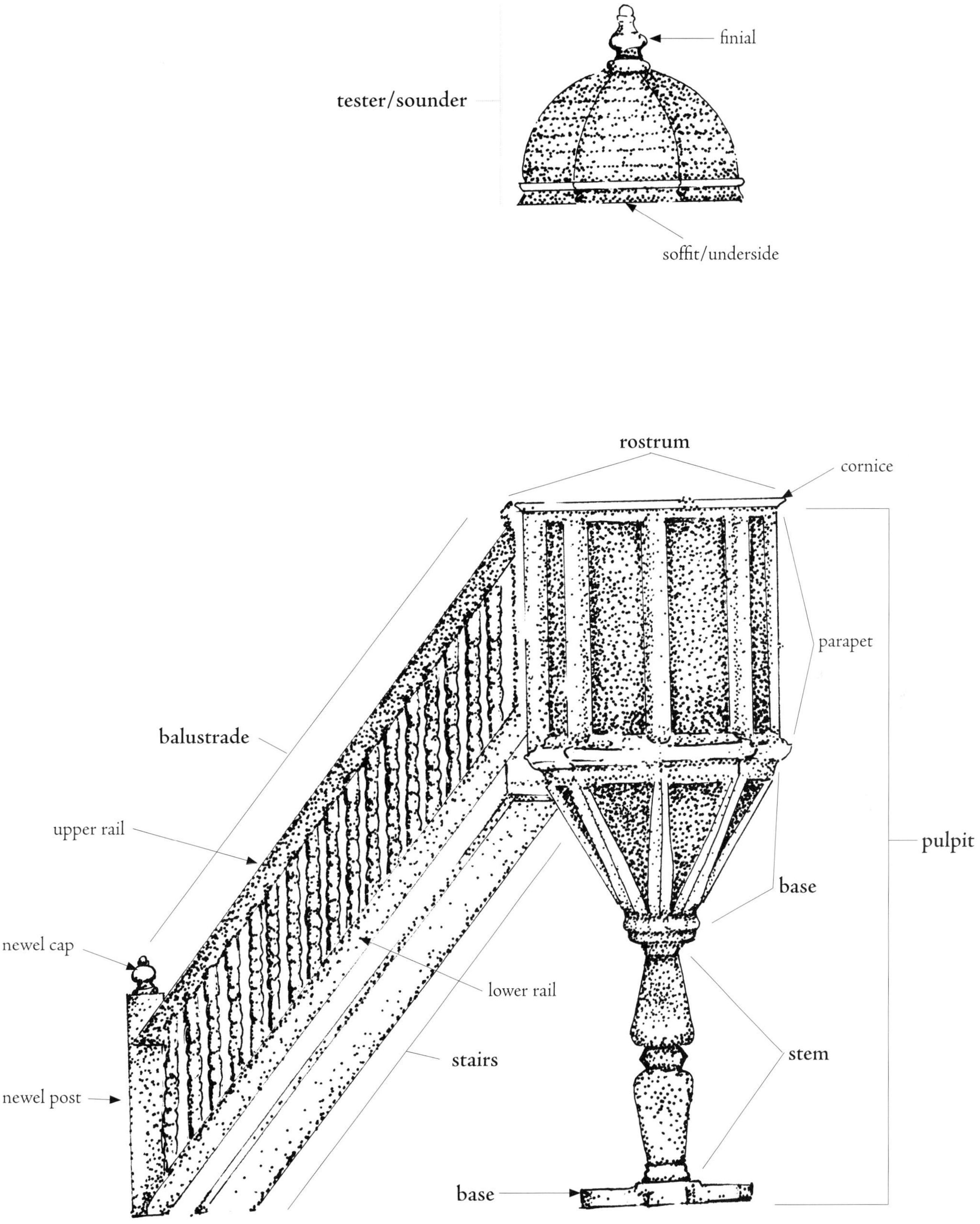

7.19. Parts of a pulpit.

7.20. Pulpit, San Juan Bautista, San Juan, California, 1987.

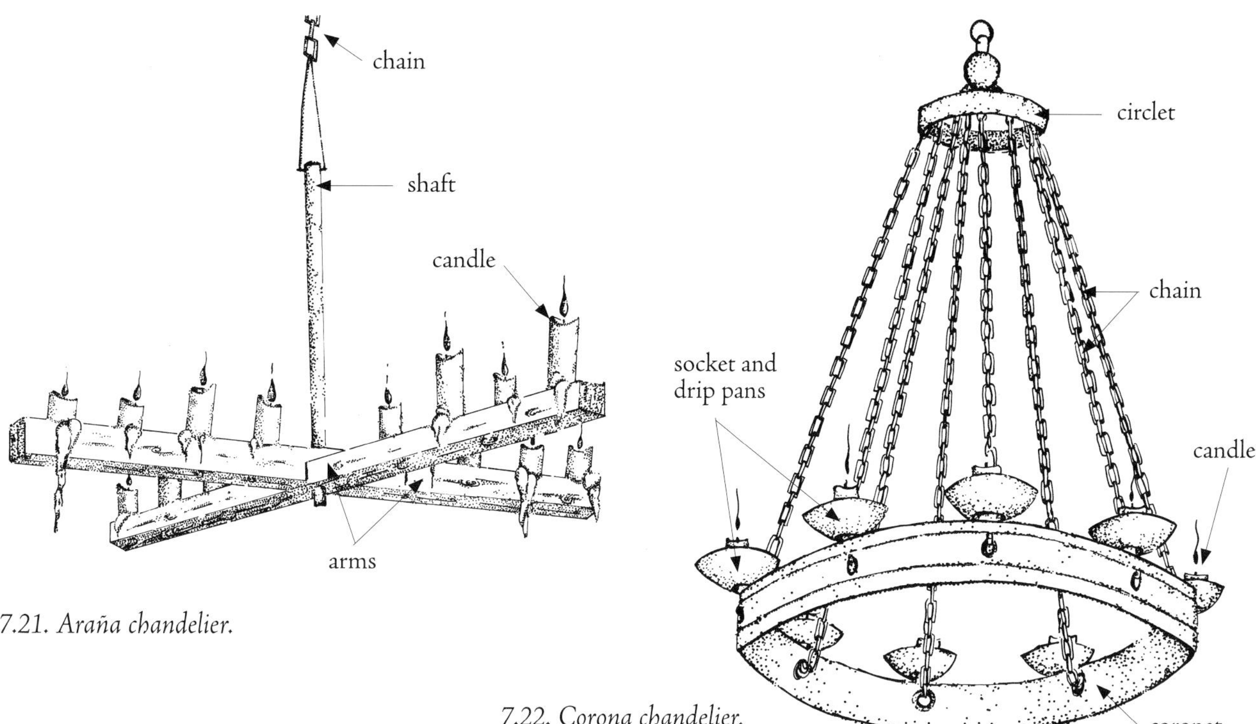

7.21. *Araña chandelier.*

7.22. *Corona chandelier.*

to each other by chains or straps, with places or sockets for candles or lamps in each ring. Although the corona is said to have descended from the fifth-century tradition of pious monarchs dedicating their crowns to their parish church, where they were hung on gold chains above or near the main altar, its more likely antecedent may be the ring lamp used to illuminate mosques, a huge affair dating from the early Ottoman Empire and in use to this day. A symbol of the Resurrection, chandeliers were reserved for use in churches on special occasions.

Collateral Altars

Built along the nave or transept walls of larger churches were collateral, or side, altars, some with their own (collateral) retablos, smaller or less elaborate than that for the main altar, and niches holding religious images. Occasionally, collateral altars and their retablos were of different dates and styles. Dating back to the ninth century, such altars were designed for private devotions to particular saints and sponsored by individual patrons, guilds, or religious organizations, who paid for their construction and maintenance. From the late sixteenth century through the seventeenth century, single-nave churches with single altars prevailed: the number of priests in northern New Spain was limited, and there were few cofradías that could afford to provide proper maintenance and financial support for collateral altars. From the eighteenth century on, however, with the region's increasing population and prosperity, almost all churches in northern New Spain could respond to the counterreformational veneration of saints by providing separate altars or chapels dedicated to them. Although never as large nor as iconographically important as the main altar, collateral altars nevertheless began to compete with it in brilliance and elaborateness. Moreover, because only one priest could perform Mass at a given altar and time, to serve ever larger congregations, collateral altars were needed to allow more than one priest to say Mass at the same time.

Dedicated to a sacred personage or theme, collateral altars, like every fixed altar, had titles. Unlike the main altar, however, they were to be raised only one step above the nave, creating a footpace, or predella (from Italian, little stool; see also "predella" under "Retablos" in chapter 10). In churches of modest means, a collateral altar might be as simple as a waist-high plastered adobe or fired brick altar table (*mensa*), or a ledge supporting images, vases, or candlesticks, with the image of the sacred personage to whom the altar was dedicated placed over the altar in a niche or hung on a wall behind and above the altar in a central position (see figure 9.8). However, no shrine for any religious image—painting or sculpture—would be considered a proper altar unless it contained an altar stone (ara) and had room for the essential objects for saying Mass (crucifix, candles, chalice, etc.). Like main altars, collateral altars were not intended to serve as shrines or as ledges for religious imagery but were locations where priests would say Mass.

In most of the larger churches of northern New Spain, sometimes along the nave or walls, sometimes in a separate, adjoining chapel, there was a collateral altar dedicated to Mary, referred to as the Lady Altar, or Lady Chapel. Although current canon law prescribes the Gospel (left) side of the church for this altar, it appears in northern New Spain on the Epistle side as well. Even if the whole church, and consequently the main altar, is dedicated to Mary, there may still be a Lady Altar as well.

At the far end of the nave, in front of the sanctuary and under the dome, if one was present, some mission churches had a catafalque, or sepulcher monument (*catafalco, monumento, pira,* or *túmulo*), a stage or platform on which to place a coffin for funeral services or a frame covered with black cloth simulating a casket for memorial services (which represented the deceased when a requiem Mass was said on the third, seventh, and thirtieth day after, as well as on the anniversary of, the deceased's death). A common type of catafalque used into the twentieth century was a bier or coffin (*féretro*) draped with a black velvet cloth, elevated by scaffolding and surrounded by candles. The cloth might be embroidered with crosses or skulls and crossbones. A European tradition dating from the late Middle Ages, the catafalque reached its most fantastic expression during the baroque and into the mid-nineteenth century.[46] To honor important persons after their death, multistoried catafalques, supported by columns, cornices, and friezes, surrounded by and fairly bristling with hundreds of tall candles, and displaying sculptures, paintings, verses, and epitaphs that extolled the virtues of the deceased, converted the church nave into a "fortress of sorrow" (*castrum doloris*). Full-blown, well-developed examples appeared mostly in the large, metropolitan churches of central New Spain. In the case of a monarch or members of his immediate family, they served not only to commemorate the deceased but also to assure subjects that the monarchy would continue in an orderly fashion. While only a few written descriptions, drawings, or engravings of catafalques of such monumental dimensions erected for deceased royalty and important members of the Church and State are still in existence, it is safe to assume that the biers (*andas para los difuntos;* figure 7.23) and the tables (*mesas*) used to support coffins referred to in the mission records of northern New Spain were much simpler affairs and involved only local funerary honors. Although a handful of much smaller viceregal catafalques can be seen in museums or tucked away in church storerooms, none are from northern New Spain.[47]

The balustrade separating the nave (or crossing in cruciform churches) from the sanctuary also divided the clergy and celebrants of the religious ceremonies from the congregation. In use since the earliest Christian architecture, it was called the Communion railing (comulgatorio) for the obvious reason that Communion was given to congregants here.

Railings or grilles, many demonstrating genuine artistry, were often used to divide, separate, enclose, or secure other parts of the church or convento, such as collateral altars, the baptistery, choir loft, or stairs from one area to another. Incorporated among their bars and supporting vertical pieces can be found monograms, coats of arms, and other decorative touches.

Although mostly of wrought or cast iron in central and southern New Spain, balustrades (*barandas, barandillas, barandados;* figure 7.24) in northern New Spain were almost always made of wood. They were commonly turned on lathes, carved, or sawn from boards to create decorative profiles and are generally gessoed and painted.[48] In cathedral interiors, such railings, in this context called *crujías,* were used to create a passage through the center of the nave from the lower choir to the main altar, which facilitated the flow of people during Communion. Those in use in the Cathedral of Durango were imported from Spain in the early eighteenth century.

Sanctuary

Furnishings in the sanctuary area included a few chairs (*sillones fraileros;* figure 7.25) and benches (bancos) for the clerics, kneelers (reclinatorios), the seat for the bishop (*sitiale;* slightly higher than the rest of the seating if the church was his cathedral), choir stalls if the choir was

7.23. *Funeral bier, San José de la Gracia, Las Trampas, New Mexico, 1940. (Courtesy of the Library of Congress)*

behind the main altar, and a credence—a small table at the Epistle (right) side of the altar to hold the cruets, basin, towel, chalice, paten, and so on until needed.[49]

The same materials, techniques, and tools (see figure 4.6) used for general carpentry in church construction were used to fashion and join all types of church furniture.[50] Most chairs, benches, and tables in northern New Spain were made from local woods with mortise-and-tenon construction. Although leather was sometimes used to reinforce joints or for the sitter's comfort, most of the furniture found in the sanctuary of a typical church in northern New Spain was heavy and simply constructed, with gouge-and-chip decoration or perhaps deeper carving on the legs, aprons, and chair backs, which sometimes bore religious symbols or the heraldic devices of religious orders. Marquetry—pieces of wood or ivory, fitted and

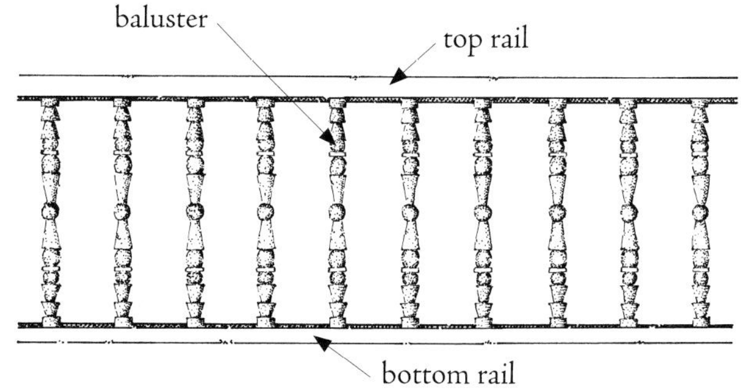

7.24. *Parts of a balustrade*

glued together and inlaid into a common background—was used in desks or surfaces not subject to a great deal of wear. While they could range from quite simple to fairly sophisticated in construction and decoration, almost all of the Spanish-style benches and chairs were straight-

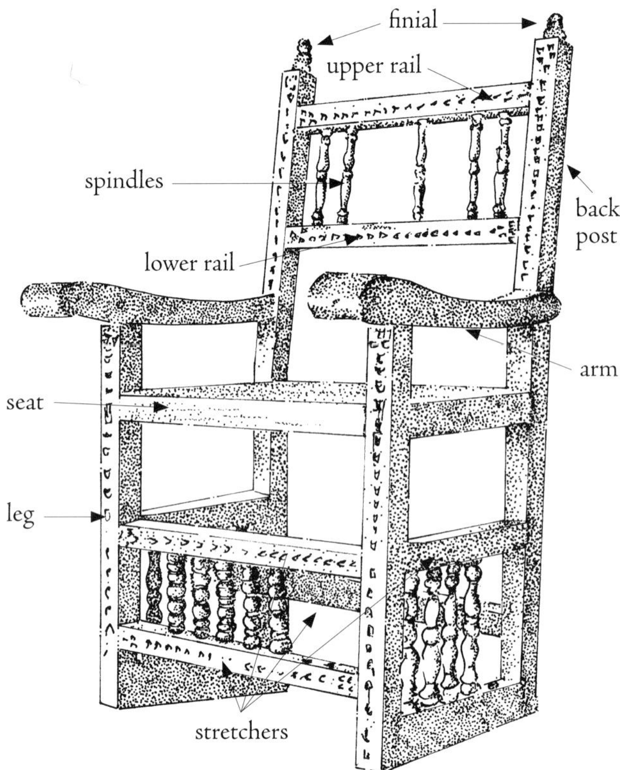

7.25. Sanctuary chair (sillon frailero), drawn from the one at San Francisco Xavier del Bac, near Tucson, Arizona.

backed; built on or close to right angles and on a scale to signify the importance of the sitter; and ornamented with varying amounts of bone, marble, shell, and tortoiseshell, silver, and iron (iron locks, hasps, hinges, bolts, and nails frequently doubled as decorative elements). The seats and backs of the chairs were sometimes covered with leather, plain or embossed. When nails were used to hold the leather against the frame, they were placed so their oversized heads (*tachuelas*) provided decorative interest. In the sanctuary of churches that could afford such luxuries, chairs were padded and covered with tooled and polychromed leather or with fringed velvet, secured by gilt-head nails, offering comfort and a display of wealth and creating a rich, decorative effect.[51]

Church furniture also typically included benches (bancos; figure 7.26) and tables (mesas; figure 7.27). French influences appear from the time of the Bourbon kings (beginning with Felipe V in 1700), while Moorish influences, reflected in the mudéjar style and artesonado manner of woodworking, have persisted from the sixteenth century to this day. From China and Japan came lacquered furniture inlaid with tortoiseshell or seashell, while from the Philippines (as well as central New Spain) came painted, leather-covered cedar trunks and imitations of English Chippendale.[52] During the eighteenth and early nineteenth centuries increased trade with the Orient and with European countries other than Spain was reflected both in styles of church art and in imported church furnishings.

Included in almost every church inventory is at least one rug. Church tradition placed one before each altar to adorn and add solemnity to the area and to define its boundaries. Depending on a church's finances, rugs ranged from those categorized by early churchmen as "Oriental" or "Turkish" to those woven locally. Carpets were also imported to New Spain from Spain, whose production was deeply influenced by the Moors.[53]

Occasionally in the churches of northern New Spain, hooks may still be seen in place on either side of the sanctuary, about halfway up the wall. These were intended to hold the Lenten cloth (in Latin, *velum quadragesimale*), a purple covering used to cloak sacred images behind the main altar from Passion Sunday (two weeks before Easter Sunday) until the Gloria at the Holy Saturday Mass, when it would be pulled aside or dropped, a tradition since medieval times. Durandus explains why images in a church were covered or removed during Lent: "because after [Passion Sunday] . . . the Divinity of Christ was hidden and concealed in Him" (see also **Curtain** entry in chapter 11).[54]

Prominently displayed above the main altar (or collateral altars) was a lamp or a candle enclosed in a glass case, called the sanctuary lamp or tabernacle lamp (*lámpara del santísimo*, lamp of the Most Holy Sacrament). A sanctuary lamp has been required since the sixteenth century to alert the faithful that the Blessed Sacrament was reserved in the tabernacle. The lamp is also perceived as a "guard of honor" before Christ night and day: "The lamp in the church is Christ," Durandus tells us, "as He saith, 'I am the light of the world.'"[55] It was required to burn olive oil, if available, a symbol of peace, mildness, purity, and strength (see "Retablos, the Eucharist, and the Counter-Reformation" under "Retablos" in chapter 10).[56] In northern New Spain, the sanctuary lamp was made from brass, silver-plated brass, or silver; usually ornamented to attract attention to its significance, it was hung or placed near every altar in which the Blessed Sacrament was reserved.

7.26. *Typical example of a church bench.*

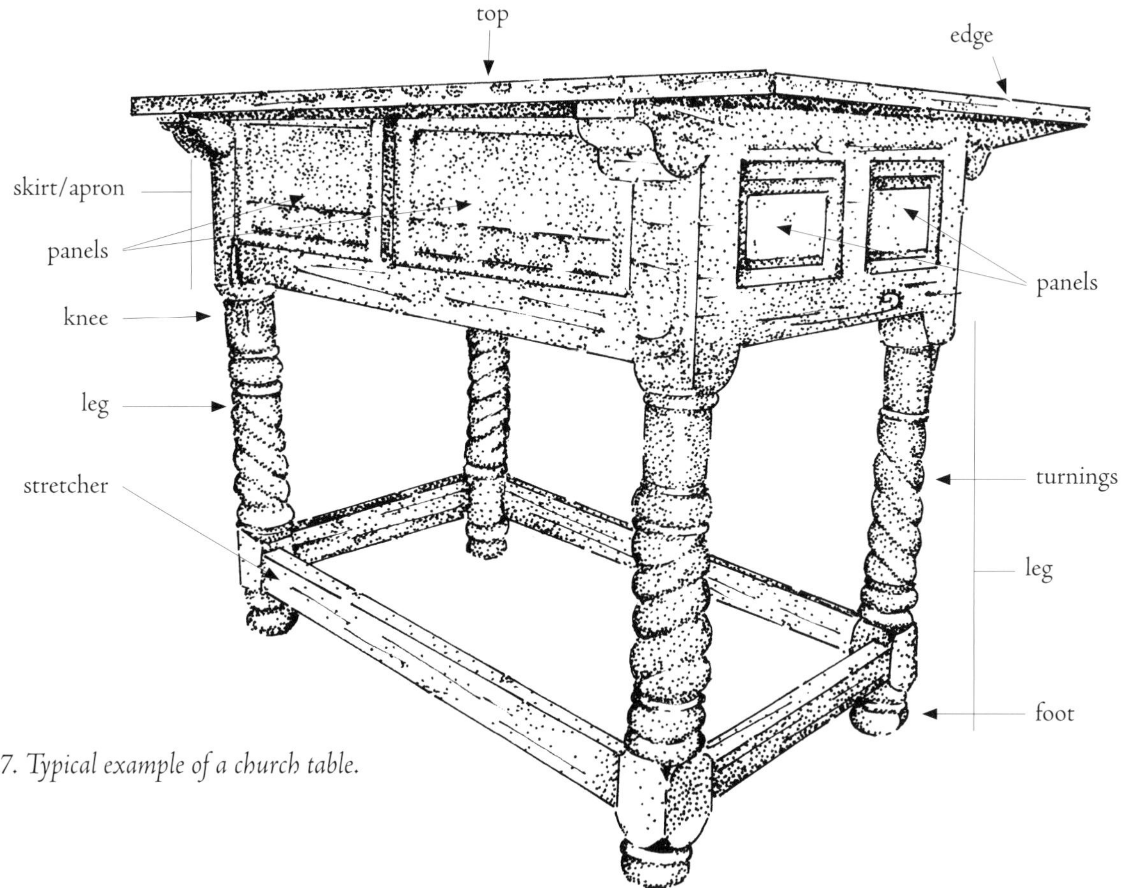

7.27. *Typical example of a church table.*

Brackets or sconces for lamps and candles to illuminate the sanctuary and the collateral altars remain on older retablos or on apse walls and on nave and transept walls. The light from these candles or lamps enabled the priest celebrant and other ministers to read from prayer cards, the missal, or other ceremonial books, and the congregation to follow and participate in the service.[57]

Main Altar

The focal point of the entire church, where the principal liturgical rite, Mass, was celebrated, the main altar (*altar mayor;* from Latin *altare,* in turn from *altus,* high) was raised above the level of the nave by three or more steps (including the footpace, or predella, on which the priest stands during most of the Mass).[58] Almost always centered on the main altar, joined to it, and built into the gradine (ledge) or retablo was the tabernacle, where the Blessed Sacrament was reserved for adoration and for Communion, whether within or without the Mass, as for the sick or the dying (*viaticum*). Like the Hebrew altar, the Catholic altar was a place of sacrifice. Indeed, "The Holy Sacrifice of the Mass" was thought of as a mystical reenactment of Christ's sacrifice on the "altar" of Calvary. The altar, often referred to in Latin as *mensa* (table), harked back to the table shared by Christ and his Twelve Apostles during the Last Supper. By association, the retablo is occasionally included in colonial references to the altar.

In viceregal New Spain, as in Mexico today, the Catholic Mass was to be offered on a stone altar, or at least an altar stone (ara) consecrated by a bishop or a priest designated by him, containing holy relics (in a special cavity called the sepulcher, Spanish *sepulcro*) and inscribed with five Greek crosses, one on each corner and one in the center, representing Christ's five wounds.[59] The altar could be either fixed (made of permanent, immovable stone) or, where such was not available, portable, consisting of a small, flat altar stone (ara), large enough to accommodate the Host and the greater part of the chalice, slightly raised so that the priest could feel its limits through the altar cloths in order to rest the chalice on it, and placed into a recess in the center of an altar table (mensa).[60] Although the consecration of an altar remains one of the most solemn rites of the Catholic Church, this can be performed separately from the dedication of the church building itself.

An altar was supposed to have a canopy—of a blue fabric "decently painted" or of a very precious piece of silk or velvet in the form of an arch—which would cover the whole altar and especially the celebrating priest. This appears to have been a device of some antiquity: an ornamental baldachin supported by pillars at its four corners, capped with silver bowls, and referred to as a "ciborium" is included in a fourth-century description of the main altar of Hagia Sofia.[61]

Baroque retablo design began crowding out the altar canopy, and even by the late sixteenth century it was on its way out. Nevertheless, there are multiple references to cloth altar canopies (*pabellones*) in the church inventories of northern New Spain. Other solutions to providing an altar canopy included adding a carved plaster scallop at San Xavier del Bac near Tucson (Arizona; see figure 7.9b) and painting the sanctuary ceiling at San José de la Laguna (New Mexico; figure 7.28) and at Mission Santa Clara (California; destroyed in the fire of 1928 but replicated in a reconstruction).

An awning, canopy, or covering supported by columns or poles over a throne, altar, sacred image, or tomb and made from cloth, stone, metal, or wood, is called a baldachin (*baldachino, baldaquín, dosel, palio, pabellón de trono o altar,* or sometimes *ciprés*). This term also refers to a portable awning or canopy supported at its four corners (or along its sides if the space to be covered is large) and used to cover dignitaries, sacred relics or images, and especially the Blessed Sacrament when carried in religious processions—the poles supporting it being either carried by individuals or attached to a litter. Listed in many mission inventories, baldachins were made chiefly of luxurious fabrics, such as satin or velvet, and were most likely suspended from the roof or back wall above an altar.

In New Spain and later Mexico, "baldachin" encompassed both cloth and stone or metal canopies covering the main altar. It also referred to the multistaged constructions (also called *manifestadores*) incorporated into the retablo mayor or erected in front of it and serving to present or display the consecrated Host in an ostensorium as well as to cover and support the titular figure of the church. One of the most celebrated baldachinos was a fantastic-appearing tower, replete with elaborate columns called "cypresses" (cipreses, for their resemblance to the straight, slender, tapering conifer) designed by Jerónimo de Balbás in 1718 for the high altar of the Cathedral of Mexico

7.28. Sanctuary of San José de la Laguna, Laguna Pueblo, New Mexico, 1945(?). The ceiling painting is an evolution of the altar canopy. (Photo by Laura Gilpin; courtesy of the Amon Carter Museum)

City to cover a gold and enamel image of the Virgin of the Assumption more than a yard high made in 1610 by the silversmith Luis de Vargas.[62]

Extant later baldachinos—including late-nineteenth-century neoclassical examples, most notably those at the Cathedral of Durango (figure 7.29) and the parochial church San Juan Bautista de Analco (figure 7.30), also in Durango city—can give us at least a general idea of how baldachins were used during the viceregal era (see also **Baldachin** entry in chapter 11).

The altar table was not to be used as a shelf, though altar cards and the missal with its stand could rest there. Builders often constructed a gradine, or ledge, beside the altar to provide a surface for candlesticks, a crucifix, reliquaries, vases for flowers, and embossed or decorated silver, tin-plated, or brass freestanding ornaments (*ramilletes*) resembling a vase with flowers. After the Mass, altar cards, missals, missal stands, and other objects used for the service were removed.

Sacristy

In this area, reserved for the vesting of the clergy, chests of drawers, lidded chests, and cupboards—a few extant examples of which can be seen throughout northern New Spain—were used to keep vestments, sacred vessels, books,

7.29. Baldachin, Catedral de Durango, 2001.

7.30. Baldachin, with titular figure San Juan Bautista de Analco, Durango city, Durango, 1983.

7.31. Vestment chests of drawers in the sacristy, Catedral de Durango, 1983.

other equipment necessary for conducting services, and other valuable items such as musical instruments. The chests of drawers (*cajoneras* or *vestuarios*)—some fairly crude and probably made by local carpenters—are often deeply carved or paneled and have forged iron handles and pulls (figure 7.31). Vestments and altar linens were laid flat inside the drawers. The lidded chests have forged iron hinges, hasps, escutcheons, locks, and handles and were intended to secure items in cases where there were no cupboards with locks. Painted and lacquered wooden boxes from Michoacán as well as the cedar-lined, decorated, and brass-trimmed leather chests from the Philippines were also used.[63] Large freestanding sacristy wardrobes (*armarios monumentales de sacristía*) were designed to accommodate copes (*copas pluviales*), vestments associated with wealthier parishes, and were thus not likely to be found in missions or small parish churches.

Sacristy furnishings often included a mirror to assist the priest in his vesting and paintings on themes intended to provide points for meditation while he dressed (sacraments, saints, or aspects of Christ's or Mary's life), as well as a crucifix, vessels allowing the celebrant to wash his hands, a vesting table if the top of the chest of drawers was not suitable, a book stand, candlesticks, lamps, and if there was enough space perhaps a chair or bench. Against and into one wall of the sacristy, a piscina (figure 7.32), a special sink with a drain, provided the means to dispose of blessed liquids, which could not mix with common liquids. Old vestments, altar cloths, and any consecrated wooden or cloth objects were disposed of by burning and

7.32. Piscina, San Francisco Xavier del Bac, near Tucson, Arizona. (Courtesy of Historic American Building Survey)

the ashes buried.[64] In large churches, a special washstand called the *lavamanos,* a much larger and more elaborate affair, served much the same purpose: a washing place for priests' hands as well as vessels. From the late eighteenth century on, sacristies might also have wall clocks to help the priest begin services on time.

Sacramental wafers were prepared using an iron, griddle-like device called a wafer maker (*hostiario*), which consisted of hinged, flat disks with handles to permit opening and closing, and which, when not in use, was most likely kept in the sacristy. One or more religious symbols, such as Christ crucified, were recessed into one face, in order to create designs on the flat, thin, crisp pieces of unleavened bread. The disks were heated such that the thinned batter, when placed between them and pressed firmly, quickly cooked. "Hostiario" also referred to the vessel for holding the wafers; such a vessel could be made of wood because, until the wafer was consecrated, it was simply bread.[65]

Kept in the sacristy as well were several other odds and ends. Often mentioned in mission church inventories were the thirteen small coins (*arras;* originally, one gold and twelve silver coins), which represented Christ and his Twelve Apostles, given by husbands to wives and symbolizing remuneration for her dowry or reward for her personal qualities, an archaic relic of the Mozarabic Rite.[66] Three small flasks with stoppers (*botellas para los óleos sagrados*) were used to keep the Holy Chrism, Oil of Catechumens, and Oil of the Sick consecrated by the bishop on Holy Thursday.[67] These in turn were stored in a chrismatory (from Medieval English, *crisme,* anointing; in Spanish, *crismera*), a box or container made from wood, silver, or tinplate. Also stored in the sacristy were small banners (banderolas or estandartes) bearing the painted images of Christ or the saints or the insignia of a religious order, sometimes embossed in repoussé silver. Both basic types were essentially rectangular, with sides parallel and either erect or undulating; most, probably for

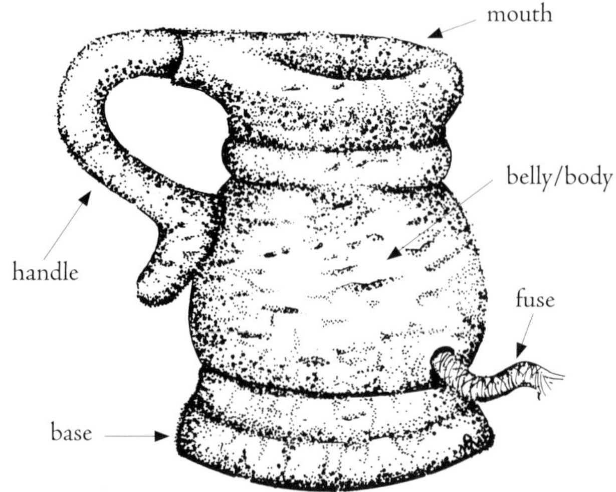

7.33. Salute cannons, used throughout Latin America as noisemakers during festivals.

aesthetic reasons, had a triangularly notched outline on the unattached edge. One type was attached to a vertical staff and the other to a horizontal one, in turn attached to a vertical staff or pole, usually surmounted by a cross, sometimes made of velvet with gold braid trim.

Finally, tucked away in sacristy closets or drawers were useful utensils such as mortars and pestles or small hammers, used to crush the incense for the censers, candlewick trimmers (*tenacillas* or *despabiladeras*), and small chisels (*punteros*) to remove hardened candle wax.[68] (Candlewick trimmers were scissorlike instruments, often made of silver and elaborately engraved, with a small cup attached to the back of one blade to catch the wick trimmings). Also stored there were miniature iron or bronze cannons (*mortidas, morteretes, cámaras de bronce para fuegos,* or *cañones del fuego*) for noisemaking during festivals, the latter used throughout Latin America, although rarely found in northern New Spain today (figure 7.33). Small wheel-mounted bells, cog rattles, and clappers not kept in the choir loft were also stored in the sacristy (see figures 7.1, 7.2, and 7.3).

Chapter 8

Liturgical Linens and Objects

And another angel came and stood at the altar, having a golden censer; and there was given unto him much incense, that he should offer it with the prayers of all saints upon the golden altar which was before the throne.

—Revelation 8:3

The linens and objects described in this chapter are often listed in mission or church inventories as *alhajas* (from Arabic *al-haya*, necessary object or utensil), a term applied to silver, gilded silver, or gold articles (*orfebrería*) used in offering the Mass, as well as to furniture, vestments, and fine fabrics (see also chapter 7: "Furnishings" and chapter 9: "Religious Hierarchy and Orders, Ecclesiastical Vestments").

Linens

A collective term for the cerecloth, altar cloths, altar frontal, chalice veil, pall, burse, and purificator, "linens" (generally referred to as *cotensio* or *cotense*, literally, coarse linen) also included gremial and humeral veils (described in chapter 9) as well as processional canopies and casket or catafalque covers (see below). Although linen was the most desirable fabric, cotton was also used.[1] Linens such as chalice veils and burses accompanying the chasuble and matching it in color and decoration were called accessories (*avios*).

Altar

A waxed linen cloth placed directly upon the altar stone and beneath the altar cloths, the cerecloth, or chrismale (*guardapolvo, encerado,* or *hule*), served to protect the altar cloths from the oiliness of the altar stone anointed with chrism, although it might also prevent spilled consecrated wine from being lost or touching the altar. The three altar cloths themselves (*manteles de altar* or sometimes *palias*) were thought to represent an apostolic tradition, symbolizing as they did the grave linens of Christ. Their principal function was to catch any fragments of consecrated bread and to absorb any spilled consecrated wine (Christ's body and blood). These three blessed white linen cloths covered the altar during Mass, the two undercloths (which might consist of a single cloth folded in two) covering the entire surface of the altar, and the upper and finer cloth reaching almost to the ground on the right and left sides of the altar.[2] Violet veils (*velos*) were also used to cover altar fronts, altarpieces, and statues during the last two weeks of Lent.

Covering the side of the altar facing the congregation and sometimes extending to the floor was the altar frontal, or antependium (*frontal*), usually a decorated piece of cloth but sometimes precious metal. Indeed, certain church inventories of northern New Spain refer to frontals made entirely of silver. They might be fashioned from materials other than cloth or precious metal, or even painted directly on the front of the altar.[3] Frontals could cover all sides of an altar—or none at all should the side facing the congregation be specially decorated. (Black frontals and vestments were forbidden when the Blessed Sacrament was kept in the tabernacle, purple being used instead for a Requiem Mass.) Throughout northern New Spain, inventories listed altar frontals together with chasubles and other colored vestments, underlining the rule that the frontal and vestments were to be of the same color to signify liturgical seasons, specific feast days, and other Church ceremonies.

When not in use, the altar cloths were to be protected with a pink or red wool (or sometimes silk) vesperal cover (*badana encarnada*). If modern translations are accurate, this was in fulfillment of the Lord's instruction to Moses on Mount Sinai for the tabernacle: "And thou shalt make a covering for the tent of rams' skins dyed red" (Exodus 26:14). The vesperal covers described in the mission inventories of northern New Spain would be removed, folded, and stored away before services so that the altar could be dressed.[4]

During Mass, the Sacred Host, chalice, and ciborium were placed upon a corporal (from Latin *corpus*, body; in Spanish, *corporal*), a square piece of white linen folded into nine equal sections, usually undecorated, although sometimes red was allowed on the borders. The monstrance was also placed on a corporal. When not in use, the corporal was stored in a burse (from Late Latin *bursa*, hide or leather, bag or purse; in Spanish, *bolsa*, *bolsa de corporales*, or *cubierta para cáliz*), a pouch approximately twelve inches square. Dating from at least the mid-seventeenth century, the burse was made from silk, stiffened with cardboard, and was also used to transport the corporal to and from the altar.

The chalice veil (*velo para cáliz*) served chiefly to cover the chalice and its paten until the Offertory of the Mass, when the chalice was unveiled (figure 8.1). The chalice veil and burse matched the vestments in color, varying with the feast day or Church season, and were usually part of a set that included the chasuble, stole, and maniple. To protect its contents from contamination, the chalice was covered after the consecration by a pall (from Latin *pallium*, covering; in Spanish, *palia*) or by a chalice cover (*hijuela*), a piece of stiffened cloth (*paño de cáliz*), usually plain linen, although the chalice could have an ornamented cover attached to it. According to Saint Charles Borromeo, the palia was to be made of silk and decorated with gold and silk threads, and indeed was sometimes made of precious metal.[5] In colonial prints and paintings, the chalice cover is shown to be decorated with embroidery on its top side.

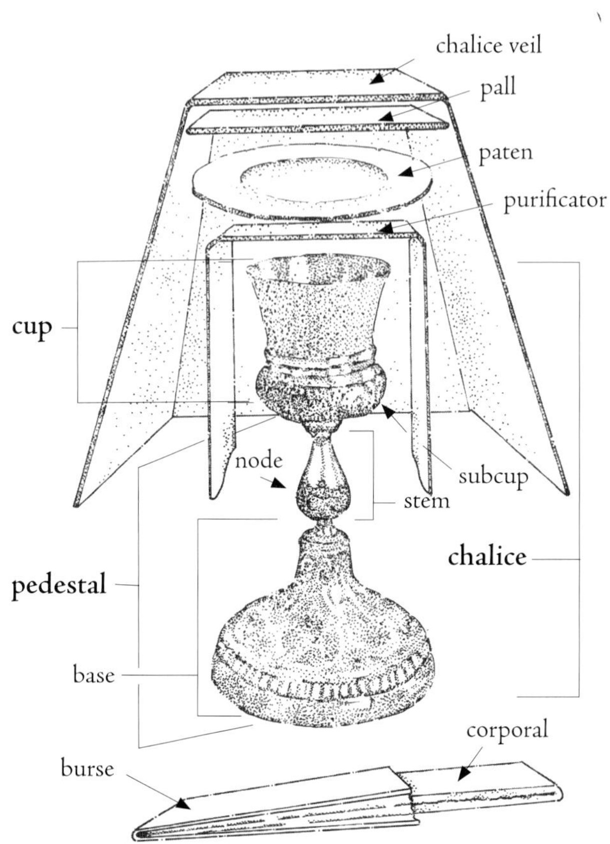

8.1. Tulip-style chalice and chalice covers. The chalice was placed on the corporal, which was folded into nine sections. The burse is the bag in which it was stored when not in use.

After receiving Communion from the chalice, the celebrant would dry his lips with a purificator (*purificador*), a folded linen napkin, which he would also use to dry the chalice and ciborium after the prescribed ablution of these vessels. Linen finger towels (sometimes referred to as "Lavabo towels"; in Spanish, *cornus altares*) were placed on the credence table or on a corner of the altar. These were used to dry the celebrant's hands after the Lavabo, the ritual washing, at the Offertory.

Processional

Usually highly decorated, made of a luxurious fabric such as silk or satin, and supported by four or more poles, a portable, ceremonial canopy (*palio* or *palio procesional*) was carried in processions to protect the Blessed Sacrament, the images or relics of saints, and civil or ecclesiastical dignitaries entering a cathedral. Accordingly, ancient Church tradition established the order of those carrying the canopy and which position each would take.

An honorific device originating in the non-Christian Near East, a ceremonial parasol or portable baldachin, either rigid or collapsible, called an umbrella (*umbela* or *sombrilla*), came into Christian ceremonial use around the twelfth century. The umbrella, also made from a luxurious fabric, served chiefly to protect the Blessed Sacrament when the priest went to administer the viaticum to the sick, although it was also used to protect religious dignitaries and even religious statues on certain occasions.

Funerary and Other Liturgical Linens

Coverings (palias, *colchas, cortinas*) for the casket or the catafalque during a Requiem Mass were almost always black, although they could be made of various fabrics (from cotton to velvet) and could be richly ornamented, with borders and symbols sewn in silver thread.

Also included among liturgical linens were yokes or cords used by the bride and groom during wedding ceremonies; hoods (*bonetas*) for the infant and towels for infant and priest alike during Baptism; and protective coverings for baptismal fonts, ciboria, and ostensoria (monstrances), as well as ornamented sleeves for cross staffs (*mangas de cruz*) and covers of various colors for the reclining figures of Christ and the saints.

Objects

Even though they had a practical purpose, liturgical objects could be and often were made of precious materials and elaborately embellished. Indeed, some were considered important art objects. Although many have been lost to theft or economic exigency, some colonial pieces are still in use or locked away in church treasuries. The richness and artistry of these objects served to honor Christ, the craftsmen's skills, and the donors' generosity, as well as to reflect the prosperity of the church community (figure 8.2).[6]

Altars and Sanctuary

In addition to the altar linens already discussed, the high (main) altar and collateral altars each had an altar cross (*crucifijo de altar*), a crucifix placed in the middle of the altar in plain view of priest and congregation alike, recalling Mount Calvary, which the altar was said to represent. While celebrating Mass, the priest would often raise his eyes or bow to this crucifix.[7] In northern New Spain, the Christ figures of these crucifixes could be carved from ivory, cast from silver or bronze, carved from wood and gilded and painted, or molded from plaster—or even from corn and orchid paste—and painted. Placed over or on altars, in chapels and shrines, or on church and sacristy walls, some eighteenth-century examples portray Christ's wounds and agony in ways that seem distressingly graphic to modern eyes.[8] (See also **Crucifix** entry in chapter 11.)

The main altar was to be covered by some type of canopy or awning, commonly called a baldachin (discussed under "Sanctuary," "Main Altar" in chapter 7, as well as **Baldachin** entry in chapter 11). Sacred relics, vases of flowers, and holy pictures, the retablo, and other furnishings in the sanctuary were desirable but not essential to the performance of services.

Mass

Lighted liturgical candles were intended to symbolize Christ, joy, and honor, and were required to be on the altar during the Mass. Their blessing, quality and color (they had to contain a high percentage of pure beeswax and to be white, except for those used in Requiem Masses, which could be yellow—the color of unbleached candle wax), size, and number were prescribed by canon law. The

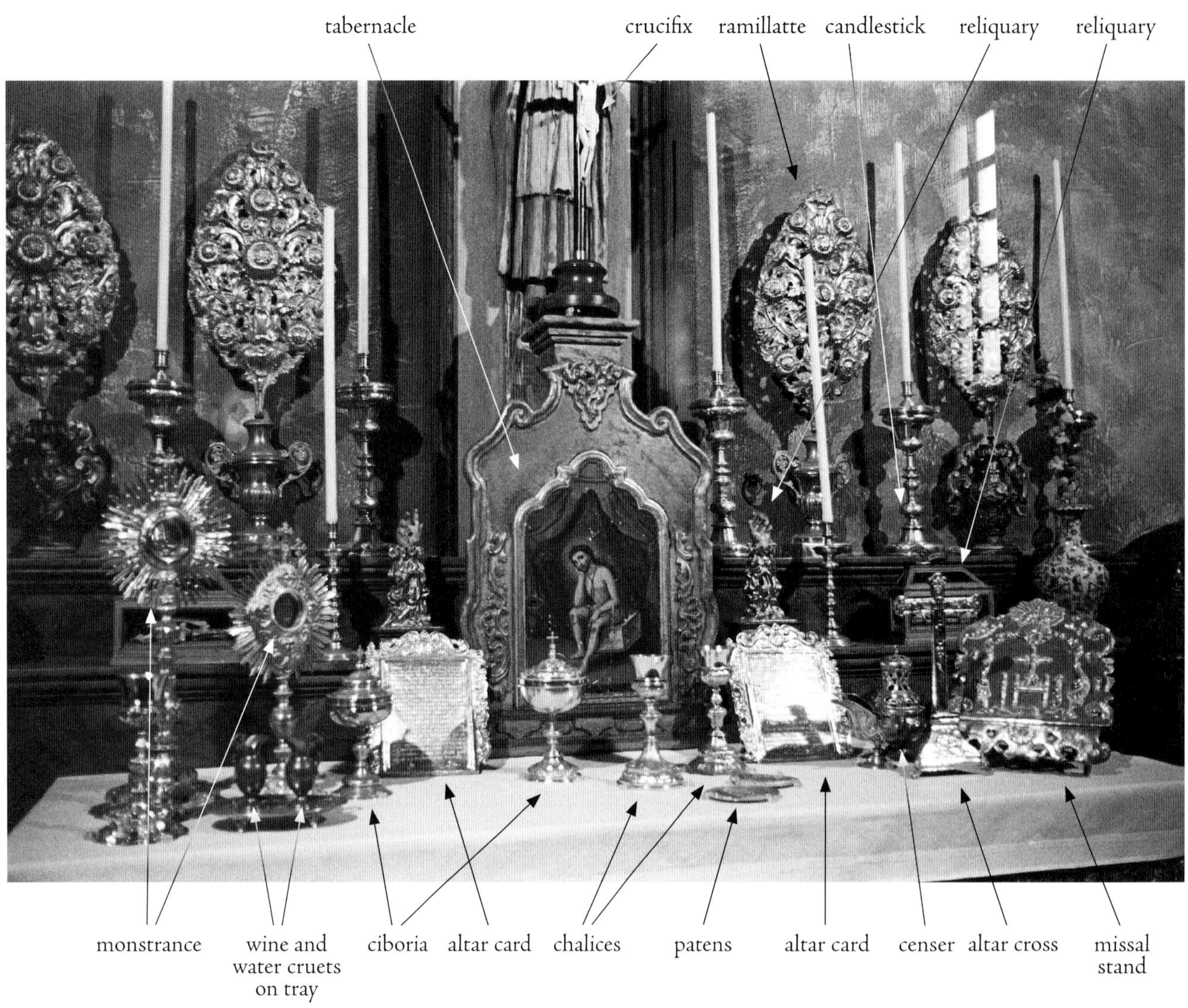

8.2. Silver altar objects, San Carlos Borromeo de Carmelo de Monterey, Carmel, California, 1987.

main altar was to have up to twelve or more candlesticks: six large candlesticks for High Mass; two candlesticks for Low Mass; four for a bishop's Mass when offered privately and seven when celebrated pontifically in the bishop's own diocese (see ***Bugia*** entry in chapter 11); and at least twelve when the Holy Sacrifice of the Mass was offered during exposition of the Blessed Sacrament. In northern New Spain, the liturgical requirements that there be six candles on the main altar and two on collateral altars were met by having a separate holder for each candle, rather than using candelabra (see figure 10.15; see also **Candle** in chapter 11).

Church inventories record both the number of candlesticks (*candeleros*) present and the material from which they were made, whether carved and gilded wood, bronze, brass, iron, plain or gilded, worked or unworked silver. Candleholders ranged in height from a few inches (*blandoncillos, paletillas,* and *palmatorias*) for tapers, to more than five feet (*blandones* or *hacheros*) for the large candles having multiple wicks. Their size depended largely on whether they were to be used on an altar or were to stand on the floor. On Holy Saturday, a special, large candle stand was placed on the Gospel (left) side of the church to hold the paschal candle, made of beeswax and large enough to burn during services for the entire forty days from Easter to Ascension. Of the few extant viceregal paschal candle stands, some are as tall as a man and as large around see also **Candlesticks** entry in chapter 11).

In New Spain, the candelabrum (plural, candelabra; in Spanish, *candelabro, portacirio,* and sometimes simply candelero) was used in the homes of the wealthy, as illustrated by colonial paintings and engravings of fashionable interiors, but far less often in churches.[9] Two candelabra called *centilleros,* having five or more sockets (*luces, arandelas*) each on the same level and in a row rather than on separate arms, were placed alongside the monstrance for the exposition of the Blessed Sacrament. Another called the *tenebrario,* triangular in shape, mounted on a tall pedestal, and bearing fifteen candles, was customarily used during Passion Week in cathedrals, colegio churches, and monasteries for Tenebrae, a service dramatically symbolizing Christ's Passion and death and practiced since the eighth century. Seven unbleached candles were placed along each of the tenebrario's sloping sides and one at its pinnacle. These candles were extinguished one by one after each of fifteen Psalms were read from the breviary, until the sanctuary or chapel was left in darkness. A particularly fine tenebrario made from wood inlaid with mother-of-pearl can be seen in the Cathedral of Durango (figure 8.3). Neither the tenebrario nor the paschal candle stand were used for any purpose other than that described here (see also **Candle** entry in chapter 11).[10]

8.3. Tenebrario, Catedral de Durango, 1996.

Before celebrating the Mass, the celebrant priest ritually washed his hands at the sacristy lavabo. A bishop's hands were washed in the sanctuary using a pitcher and basin (*aguamanil* or *jarro y lavabo, palangana,* or *fuente;* commonly made of silver; see also **Pitcher and basin** in chapter 11). After the recitation of the Creed at the beginning of the Offertory of the Mass, a collection plate (*petitorio*), made of any of a variety of materials (from straw or wood to tinplate, brass, or even silver), was passed to collect offerings from the congregation.

Cruets (in Latin, *urceali;* in Spanish, *vinajeras*), twin containers for the wine and water used at Mass, were usually placed on a small tray (*charolilla, bandeja,* or *salvilla*), which often had special indentations for them on its ends and for an altar bell in its center. The use of cruets, which were said to symbolize Christ's pierced side, dates from the thirteenth century; in northern New Spain, they were made from a variety of materials: gold-plated silver, silver, glass, and tinplate. To avoid confusion as to their contents, opaque or metal vessels were marked with a "V" and an "A" (signifying *vino* and *agua,* respectively).

Central for celebrating the Eucharist, the chalice (from Latin *calix,* cup, cuplike structure of sepals of a flower or bud; in Spanish, *cáliz*), a cup without handles on a pedestal and base, held the consecrated wine and water, which with the consecrated bread, was essential to the offering of the Mass. The priest celebrant was the first to receive Communion from the chalice. As one of the most important sacred vessels, it had to be consecrated by a bishop or by a priest with a bishop's permission. The earliest chalices were made of glass, rock crystal, metals (precious and otherwise), marble, wood, earthenware, porcelain, and ivory. In the third century, the use of glass and crystal was expressly forbidden; gradually, materials other than nonferrous metals were eliminated because of their tendency to rust, leak, or break. Although the shape and adornment of the chalice varied through the centuries, the Church required that it be made of an unbreakable material (that is, metal). Whichever metal was used for the rest of the chalice, the interior (cup) at the very least had to made of gold or gilt silver—as did the upper surface

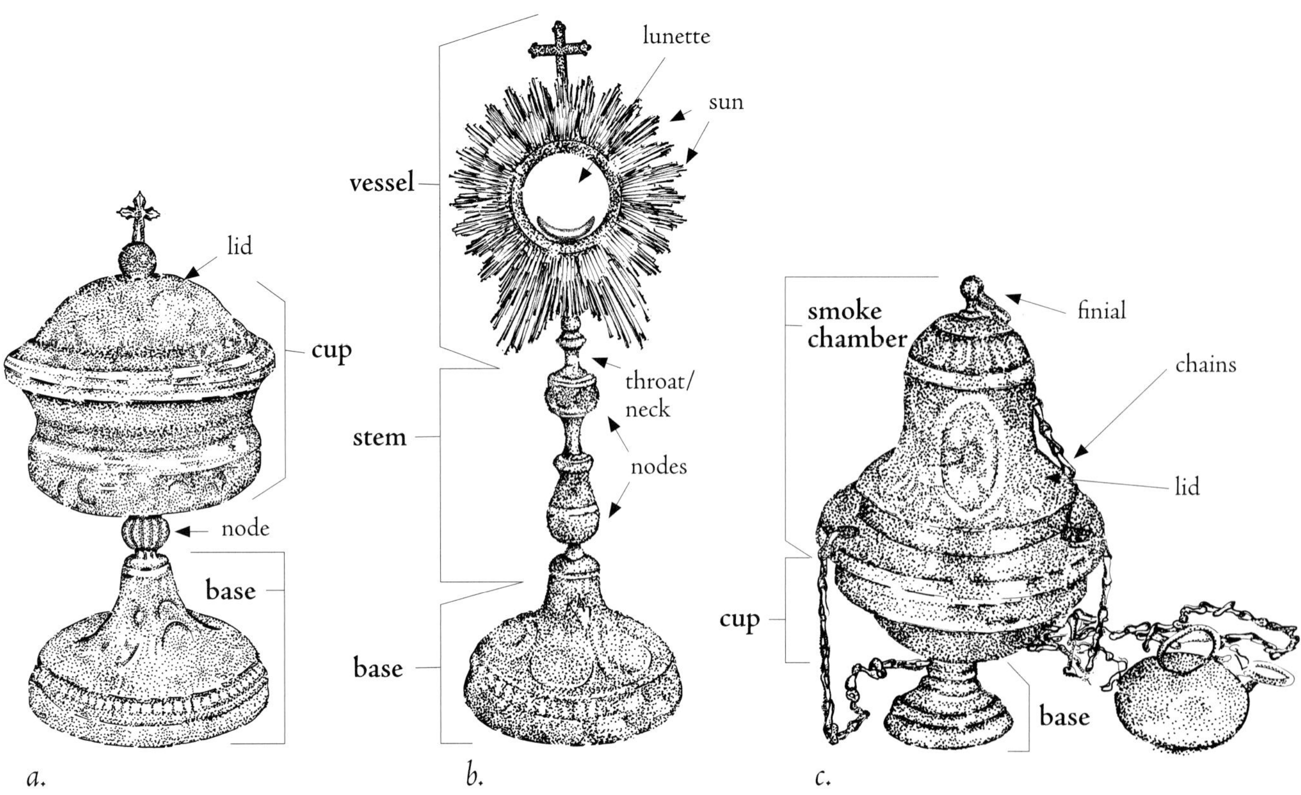

8.4. Selected altar objects: a. ciborium, b. monstrance, or ostensorium; c. censer, or thurible.

of the paten used in conjunction with the chalice.[11] The chalice had to have four distinct parts: cup, node (*nudo;* a globular thickening of the stem, sometimes embedded with precious stones, to hold the chalice securely), stem, and base (see figure 8.1). Because it was believed to contain Christ's blood and to represent his sacrifice, the chalice was most often richly adorned; indeed, it was likely to be the most precious liturgical object in the church. A chalice usually bore a small cross or crucifix on its base, which helped distinguish it from an uncovered ciborium.

A shallow plate with a convex center, the paten (from Latin *patina,* flat dish; in Spanish, *patena*) held the Sacred Host during parts of the Mass; a similar plate (communion plate) was placed under the chin of each person receiving Communion to catch any fragments of the Host that should fall.[12] Because of its contact with the Host and the chalice, the paten had to be consecrated by a bishop or a priest designated by a bishop. It was sometimes made entirely of gold; at the very least, its concave surface had to be made of gold or gilt silver.

The ciborium (Latin, cup; from Egyptian, husk of a bean; in Spanish, *copón*), which evolved from the pyx (see below), was a lidded metal vessel resembling a covered chalice, used to reserve, transport, and distribute Communion to the faithful. It could also take the form of a small tower-shaped casket or a Eucharistic dove, suspended over the altar. The ciborium had to be blessed by a priest and was kept in the locked tabernacle when it contained consecrated Communion wafers; its use in the Christian Church dates from at least the fourth century (see figure 8.4a).

The missal (meaning "of the Mass"; from the Latin *missale;* in Spanish, *misal*), sometimes referred to as the "Mass book," contained all the readings, prayers, and chants (with musical notations) required for the celebration of the Mass throughout the liturgical year. These included much of the New Testament as well as important Old Testament readings. In addition, the missal contained a calendar of feast days, papal decrees and instructions on celebrating the Mass, blessings connected with the Mass (holy water, candles, marriages, etc.), and supplements on special Masses for specific countries, religious orders, or dioceses.[13] To assist the celebrant's memory at places in the Mass where it was inconvenient to consult the missal, altar cards (*sacras* or *palabreros*), also called canon, or secret, cards (referring to prayers secreted from the missal), were set upright on the altar, against the tabernacle or gradine.[14] Printed, lettered, painted, or pasted sheets or boards, they were often elaborately framed, their frames most often carved from wood and gilded, although sometimes made of silver or tortoiseshell (*caray*). Other religious books in use in northern New Spain were breviaries (*breviarios*), daily readings from four-volume compendiums of psalms, prayers, and hymns; readings from the New and Old Testaments and from the Fathers of the Church commenting on the Bible readings; and the *Rituale Romanum*, containing numerous sacramental rites and blessings. A parish or mission library might also have books of sermons, as well as works on philosophy, theology, Church history, and the lives of the saints.[15] Because significant segments of the New and Old Testaments were contained in the missal and breviary, Bibles might not have been present in every parish or mission.

A lectern (from Latin *lector*, reader) or missal stand (both called *atril* in Spanish) was used to support books used during Mass and other religious services. A lectern could take the form of a chest-high pedestal or be constructed as part of a pulpit; a missal stand was small enough to be placed on the altar. Although sometimes made of elaborately worked silver, lecterns in northern New Spain were most often carved from wood, painted and gilded.[16] Three lecterns with eagle motifs may still be seen on-site: two bearing wrought iron double-headed eagles, attached to either end of the Communion rail in the Cathedral of Durango, and the third bearing the eagle of John the Evangelist on the pulpit of Mission San Juan Bautista in San Juan (California; see figure 7.20; see also **Eagle** entry in chapter 11).

To call attention to the more solemn parts of the Mass, as at the close of the Preface, when the priest intoned, "Sanctus, Sanctus, Sanctus, Deus Sabaoth," and several times during the consecration rite of the Mass, a small handbell (*campanita, campanilla*) called a Sanctus, or Communion, bell, was rung. It was often set on a tray (*bandeja, salvilla*) in a specially recessed area between the water and wine cruets, placed at one side of the altar or on the credence table. Like the tray itself, the bell could be made of silver, whereas the cruets were generally made of glass. Communion bells appear in colonial church inventories throughout northern New Spain (see also "Belfry" in chapter 7 and **Bells** entry in chapter 11).

The pax (Latin, peace; in Spanish, *paz* or *portapaz*), sometimes called an osculatory, was a small tablet or disk of ivory, metal, or other material bearing a holy image. It was presented for the faithful to kiss at High Mass after the Agnus Dei was concluded, when the kiss of peace or ceremonial reverence was traditionally exchanged by clergy and congregation. The pax could have a handle or be mounted on a pedestal; or it could be replaced by another liturgical object—cross, reliquary, Gospel book, or paten. Although a few colonial examples still exist, as a liturgical object, the pax is no longer used.

Processional or Display

The monstrance (from Medieval Latin *monstrare*, to show; in Spanish, *custodia, custodia de mano*, or *viril*), or ostensorium (*ostensorio*), was an elaborate vessel used to display the Blessed Sacrament or to carry it in procession. The monstrance had to have three parts: vessel, stem, and base. Although its decoration followed the artistic canons of the time, a common design, devised in the Middle Ages, consisted of a chamber of two pieces of glass crystal in which a consecrated Host was held by a lunette (*lúnula*), a crescent-shaped device so that the Host might be seen and revered (see figure 8.4b).

Seated, stationary monstrances (*custodias asientas*) were immense, heavy objects kept within the church for display of the Host, whereas processional monstrances (*custodias procesionales*) were smaller and portable versions used for Eucharistic Benedictions and in processions.[17] The monstrance in the form of a sun (*viril con rayas*), which became popular during the sixteenth century throughout Europe, was the most common in northern New Spain. To carry Holy Communion to the sick (though not necessarily dying), priests used a small box or cup, usually of silver, called a pyx (Latin, box; in Spanish *píxide*).[18] Usually small, round, and plain, the pyx could be made of gold, silver (plain or gilded), or other metal, but its interior had to be of gold or gilt silver.

Processional crosses (*cruces procesionales*), emblems of ecclesiastical authority, were usually elaborate and finely made, although I have seen nineteenth-century examples made from tinplate. Mounted on a staff tall enough to dominate the procession, the crucifix of the processional cross was almost always turned so that Christ's image faced forward.[19] The upper section could be removed from the staff and be placed in a holder on the altar. Perhaps the earliest use of the crucified figure of Christ, the processional cross has been in use since the fifth century (see also **Cross** entry in chapter 11). Like the cross, processional candlesticks (*ciriales*) were also set on staffs and designed to be separated and slipped into stationary supports after the procession.

In its strictest sense, "reliquary" (from Latin *reliquiae*, remains; in Spanish, *relicario*) referred to any type of vessel in which sacred relics (the body or part of the body of a saint, clothing, or anything intimately connected with the saint) were kept sealed. Veneration of these relics was permitted by the Church in honor of persons who were considered special "temples of the Holy Ghost." The size and shape of the container depended on the relic enclosed. Small boxes or caskets were sometimes modeled after the original shape of the relics they enclosed—an arm, head, cross, and so on. The most common, though, was a round case mounted on a pedestal and resembling a small monstrance. Because of the reverence paid to these remains, the reliquary was often richly decorated and made from precious metals, although unfortunately many of these have disappeared. A common method used throughout New Spain for storing relics for viewing was to seal them into a *retablo relicario*. ("Reliquary" also refers to a type of religious medallion; see discussion under "Sculptures," "Wax," in chapter 10.)

Other Liturgical Objects

At the beginning of the principal Mass on Sundays, the congregation was sprinkled with holy water. The use of holy water was a reminder of Baptism, the purifying sacrament of Christian initiation, and was meant to evoke the Flood, Moses' crossing of the Red Sea, Christ's baptism, and the water that came from Christ's side at the Crucifixion. Holy water was also sprinkled in the blessing of graves, religious objects, or persons. The holy water sprinkler, called an "aspergillum" (from Latin *aspergere*, to sprinkle; in Spanish, *aspersorio* or *hisopo*), was traditionally a sprig of hyssop or palm, which was replaced by a brush on a short rod during the fourteenth and fifteenth centuries, and eventually became a perforated metal ball (with a sponge enclosed) attached to a short handle.[20] A bowl, bucket, or similar vessel called the "aspersorium" (*acetre*) carried the holy water into which the aspergillum was dipped. The sprinkler and vessel, though often made of silver, beautifully chased and engraved, were occasionally made of tin or even of wood.

To pour baptismal water, the priest used a baptismal shell (*concha para bautizar* or *taza*), a shallow dish, typically scallop-shaped and made of silver, although several church inventories in northern New Spain list an actual seashell ("un concha del mar").[21] A cross might appear on the reverse, as might a small handle or protuberance for easier handling. Although there is no biblical basis for the portrayal, Saint John was traditionally shown baptizing Christ with a seashell (see also **Scallop shell** entry in chapter 11).

Incense was burned in a censer, or thurible (*incensario* or *turíbulo*), a cuplike container having a small footed base and covered with a perforated lid. It was hung on three chains to facilitate swinging by hand; a fourth chain pierced the lid so that it could be lifted in order to place the incense on a piece of burning charcoal or to remove ash (see figure 8.4c). Designed to be carried and swung in processions and during the Benediction at High Mass, the censer was also used and even required at many other ceremonies and blessings. An incense boat (*naveta*) and spoon (*cuchara*) were often listed in conjunction with the censer.[22] Censer, incense boat, and spoon alike were often made of silver, sometimes gilded, although censers could also be made of bronze or brass (see also **Incense** entry in chapter 11).

Traditionally, the church considered long hair a vanity; cutting one's hair short signified humility, penance, and renunciation of the world. Liturgical scissors (*tijeras litúrgicas*), used for tonsuring, were richly decorated because of their ritual significance. They were most likely stored in the sacristies of cathedrals and larger churches.

CHAPTER 9

RELIGIOUS HIERARCHY AND ORDERS, ECCLESIASTICAL VESTMENTS

Let no one take pride in his rank,
for faith and charity are everything.

—SAINT IGNATIUS OF ANTIOCH

Roman Catholic clerics could be distinguished according to their level in the Church hierarchy or their membership in a religious order by specific articles of clothing, colors, and accoutrements, as could the liturgical roles these clerics played (figure 9.1).[1] The hierarchy of the Church consisted of the four minor orders (porter, reader, exorcist, and acolyte), received by those studying for the priesthood, and the three major orders (subdeacon, deacon, and priest—the last including bishop, archbishop, patriarch, and pope).

HIERARCHY

Following, from lowest to highest, are the most important positions in the Church hierarchy, together with some of their most recognizable badges of office.[2]

Acolyte

Belonging to the highest of the minor orders, an acolyte (from Greek *akolouthos*, attendant or follower) was in charge of lighting and carrying candles and mixing the wine and water for Mass.[3] He wore an alb and sometimes a surplice, but not the maniple, amice, stole, or other vestments worn by priests.

Subdeacon

Belonging to the lowest of the major orders, a subdeacon sang the Epistle, carried the chalice to the altar, and gave the Kiss of Peace to the choir at a Solemn Mass. The earliest written mention of the title appears in a letter from Pope Cornelius in 251. A subdeacon could be distinguished from a deacon by his less ornate formal tunic, although deacon and subdeacon often wore identical vestments.

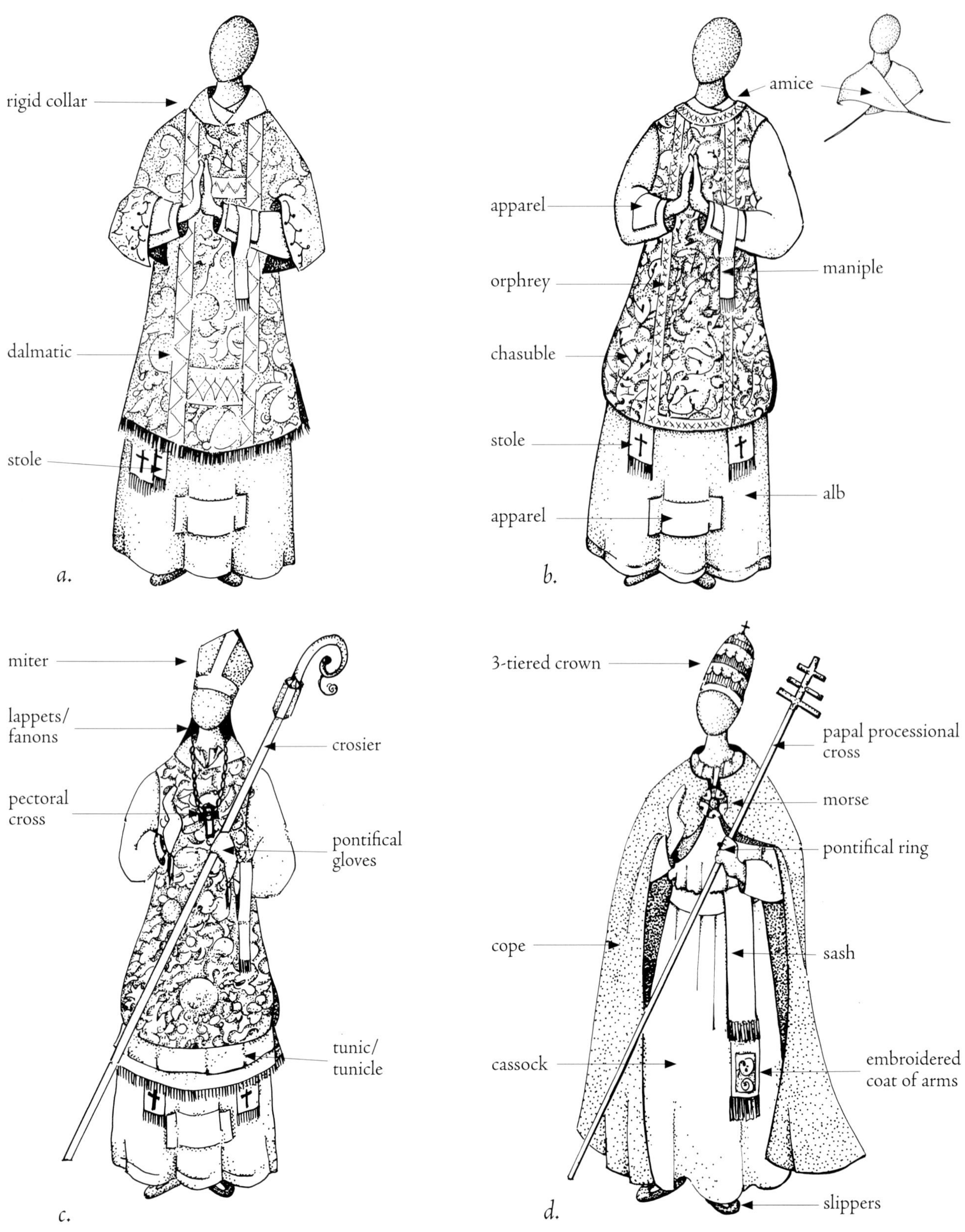

9.1. Vestments of a. deacon, b. priest (the inset shows the amice without the overlying layers of vestment), c. bishop, and d. pope. Note that each higher ecclesiastical rank added a layer of robes on top of the preceding rank's vestments. For clarity, each element is labeled in only one illustration.

Deacon

As a member of the clergy ranking just below a priest, a deacon assisted a priest or bishop during Mass. The title (from Greek *diakonos,* servant or waiting man) dates from the first century. A deacon's everyday garb was similar to that of a priest, although during religious services, he could be distinguished from a priest by his dalmatic and stole.

Priest

Although the title (from Greek *presbuteros,* honored older man) originally referred not only to a Christian minister but to any Christian elder, by the beginning of the third century, it had adopted its modern, more limited sense.[4] An ordained priest was a priest of the second order who, through his ordination, was empowered to administer the sacraments of Holy Communion (Mass), Baptism, Extreme Unction, Penance (Confession), Confirmation (with delegation), and Matrimony. A priest's everyday garb was a cassock, a fitted, black, ankle-length gown with long sleeves.

Abbot and Abbess

The title (from Late Latin *abbas,* abbot; originally, from Aramaic *abba,* father) dates from the fourth century and designates the head of an ecclesiastical community, originally an elderly monk. By the sixth century, with the ascendance of monasticism, it was used exclusively as the title of the superior of an abbey of monks. In 1063, the first mitered abbot was invested by Pope Alexander II, the miter (headgear) signifying that abbots were equal in rank to bishops and that their abbeys were therefore not under any bishop's jurisdiction. In full vestments, an abbot was indistinguishable from a bishop; his everyday garb was the habit (*hábito, vestido*) of his order, always accompanied by a crosier (from Medieval Latin *crocia,* crook), a common name for the pastoral staff (*báculo pastoral*).[5] Usually simpler than a bishop's, the abbot's crosier had a crook that curved inward, signifying that his governance was purely domestic and restricted to his abbey. Made of either wood or metal and about six feet long, the crosier, a symbol of pastoral authority and jurisdiction, represented both the shepherd's care for his flock and the priest's rod of correction. When walking in the presence of a bishop, an abbot covered his staff with a pendant veil, a white silk or linen scarf with gold fringes and tassels, attached at the top of the staff before the crook (see also **Crosier** entry in chapter 11).

The superior of an abbey of nuns dressed in the habit of her order and might hold a crosier. The crosier and pendant veil attachment were common attributes of Saint Gertrude the Great, by misplaced association with the abbess Saint Gertrude of Nivelles.

Bishop

Ideally chosen by the clergy and parishioners of his diocese, according to the reforms of Pope Gregory VII (1073–1085), a bishop was a priest of the first order who could administer all the sacraments, ordain priests, and consecrate other bishops. Monasteries not under the direction of abbots were subject to the jurisdiction of bishops, who governed their respective dioceses. The title (from Greek *episkopos,* one who watches over) first appears in the second century in Saint Ignatius of Antioch's admonition for obedience to bishops, who were considered the successors of the Apostles.[6]

A bishop could be distinguished at all times by his pectoral cross and episcopal ring and when pontificating (presiding) or attending pontifical Mass by his miter and his crosier, whose crook curved outward, signifying that his rule extended over an entire diocese. Ceremonial vestments proper to a bishop, called "pontificals" (*pontificales*), included buskins, sandals, gloves, tunic and dalmatic (made of lightweight linen, both were worn under the chasuble symbolizing the fullness of priesthood), as well as gremial veil (see following) and morse.

Archbishop

In use by the end of the second century, the designation was a permanent title by the fourth. Chosen by his peers to be the chairman of their councils or bishop of several dioceses, an archbishop was empowered to ordain bishops. He could be distinguished from a bishop by the pallium of white wool (a long scarf ending in pendants) and by the cross or crucifix surmounting his pastoral staff.

Cardinal

A deacon, priest, or bishop chosen to assist the pope in administering the Church, a cardinal belonged to a group called the Sacred College, from which the pope himself was elected. The title (from Latin *cardo,* hinge, hence someone of primary importance) has been in general use since the ninth century. A cardinal could usually be distinguished by his characteristic red robe (since 1294) and sometimes also by his broad-brimmed, flat-crowned hat with tassels (instituted by Pope Paul II between 1464 and 1471). While New Spain neither had nor was visited by cardinals, Saints Bonaventure and Jerome appear as cardinals in a number of Spanish colonial paintings.

Patriarch

A bishop of the highest rank below the pope in jurisdictional affairs over certain places, such as Jerusalem, the patriarch was not subject to any ecclesiastical authority but that of the pope and his appointed legates. A patriarch could be distinguished from an archbishop by the cross with two transverse bars surmounting his pastoral staff.

Pope

The title (from Late Latin *papa;* Greek *papas,* papa, title of bishops) appears in the fifth century with the supremacy of the Bishop of Rome over other bishops, although papal supremacy was not universally accepted until two centuries later. The pope signs his utterances "Papa," as well as "Servus Servorum Dei" (Servant of the Servants of God). In ceremonial or sacramental garb, he can be distinguished by his three-tiered crown or tiara and by the cross with three transverse bars surmounting his pastoral staff. His robes are white.

CLERGY

"Clergyman" or "cleric" (from Greek *cleros,* lot, as in casting lots) refers to a man "drawn" to perform a sacred function. Clerics who belonged to a diocese rather than withdrawing from the world, were under the jurisdiction of a local bishop, pursued work that was largely parochial, and lived among their parishioners belonged to the diocesan clergy. They took no vows except for the requirement for celibacy. Priests and religious men who had taken solemn vows, and who might include brothers and other professed members of particular religious orders or congregations living in religious communities according to certain sacred rules, belonged to the regular (*regula,* rule) clergy. These individuals could be identified by their habits: full-length, loose, long-sleeved, hooded (except for Jesuit regulars) garments with a belt or cord that varied in color or in some of their parts from order to order.[7]

As an outward symbol of Christ's crown of thorns, both diocesan and regular male clergy had the crowns of their heads tonsured upon taking simple or Holy Orders. The tonsure (from Medieval Latin *tonsura,* shearing) varied in extent between types of clergy and among different orders: from a small area (diocesan clergy) to all or nearly all of the crown (regular clergy), with a wider fringe of hair (corona) among Franciscans, Cistercians, Carthusians, and certain Benedictines, and a narrower one among Dominicans, who shaved the whole crown above the top of the ears.[8]

I have devoted less attention to the diocesan than to the regular clergy for the simple reason that the overwhelming majority of churches in northern New Spain throughout the colonial era were missions, served by regulars. Diocesan clergy were certainly also present there, however. They accompanied exploratory expeditions to Baja California in 1632 and 1633.[9] They assumed priestly duties, often alongside the friars, after the latter had Christianized an area and a permanent settlement had been established. Indeed, in the cities or permanent settlements that had significant Spanish and mestizo as well as Indian populations, it was not unusual for the Indians to attend a mission church with regular clergy, while their Spanish and mestizo coreligionists attended a diocesan church with diocesan clergy.

Not all of the following religious orders for men and women were physically present in northern New Spain. They are included nevertheless to help readers identify the particular orders of clerics they encounter in painted, sculpted, and engraved portrayals.

Friars

Members of mendicant orders, friars (from Latin *fratres,* brothers) were forbidden to possess property, not only personally but in common. Subject to the central, highly organized authority of their orders, they worked in the active ministry at large, having their headquarters at a friary.[10] The four original mendicant orders were the Augustinians, Carmelites, Dominicans, and Franciscans; later mendicant orders included the Hospitaliers, Mercedarians, Minims, Servites, and Trinitarians.

Monks and Nuns

Members of religious communities of men, monks lived apart from the world under the vows of obedience, chastity, and poverty. Benedictines, Carthusians, and Trappists were monks in this strict sense, although the term was sometimes loosely extended to Augustinians, Franciscans, Dominicans, and others who worked outside their monasteries teaching, preaching, and ministering to the sick.

Women in religious orders were divided into nuns strictly so called (*moniales;* in Spanish, *monjas*), who belonged to an organization taking solemn vows, and sisters (*sorores*), who took simple vows. In New Spain, both nuns and sisters were cloistered throughout the colonial era, with varying degrees of personal freedom according to the rules of their particular orders. Most of the female orders were inspired by male religious communities; the rules, habits, and often also names of their respective orders were patterned on those of their male counterparts.[11] Not all men's orders (for example, neither the Jesuits nor the Hospitaliers) had a corresponding women's order.

Prelates

Ecclesiastical authorities who exercised jurisdiction by their office, prelates (from Latin *praelatus,* one set aside) included vicars, prefects apostolic, abbots, and bishops.[12]

Orders

The following is a brief outline of ten religious orders whose members are represented in the paintings, sculptures, and engravings of northern New Spain. Although the Jesuits, Franciscans, and Dominicans were the three orders most actively involved in missionary work in northern New Spain, other orders were present in other capacities. Line drawings are included to clarify points about the habits of particular religious orders. The orders are discussed alphabetically by popular name, with the popular name in Spanish given in parentheses, and with the official title of the order and its initials or abbreviation as it appears after the names of its members given in the text.

Augustinians (Agustinos)

Founded in 1256 and based on the rule of Saint Augustine, the Order of Hermits of Saint Augustine (OSA), was the third mendicant order in New Spain, where they landed in 1533 and were assigned two *provincias.* Augustinian friars wore a black hooded robe, a leather strap belt, and sandals. Augustinian nuns (*agustinas*) wore a black tunic or robe, veil, and mantle (when outside or traveling), with a white wimple providing a dramatic contrast; their habit was belted and they wore shoes. In colonial paintings, both friars and nuns were commonly portrayed in full-length cloaks, which they donned on taking their final vows to symbolize their renunciation of the desires of the flesh and their withdrawal from the secular world (figure 9.2).

The friars' missionary efforts, which began in 1533, were first confined to southern New Spain and shortly after that to Veracruz and to the west and north. They were in Hidalgo by 1534; in 1602, they established a provincia in Michoacán. Augustinians are recorded as having arrived in Sombrerete (Zacatecas) in 1613 (where they would, by the eighteenth century, erect a small but nicely proportioned convento and church) and as having sent friars to minister to Indians later placed under the charge of the Franciscans.[13] They were present in the city of Durango in 1623, where they remained until at least 1742, with a hospital, a small chapel, and a convento.[14]

Benedictines (Benedictinos)

The founding of the Order of Saint Benedict, OSB, in 529 marked the beginning of Western monasticism. Organized in close communities of men guided by an abbot and adhering to the rule of a common life of prayer, contemplation, and manual labor, the order emphasized education, liturgy, and the arts. Benedictines, known also as "Black Monks," wore a black habit with a small cape, leather belt, and shoes rather than sandals. Arriving in Mexico City in 1602, the order was never firmly established in New Spain.

Capuchins (Capuchinos)

The Order of Friars Minor, Capuchin (OFM Cap) was one of the three independent branches of the Franciscan Order, begun in 1525 as a reform movement under the leadership of Matteo da Bascio. A Capuchin wore a coarse brown habit tied with a cord, a distinctive hood (*capuche,* from which it is said the order was named, '*scappuchini* being colloquial Italian for "hermits"), and sandals. Although the men's order was not present in Mexico until

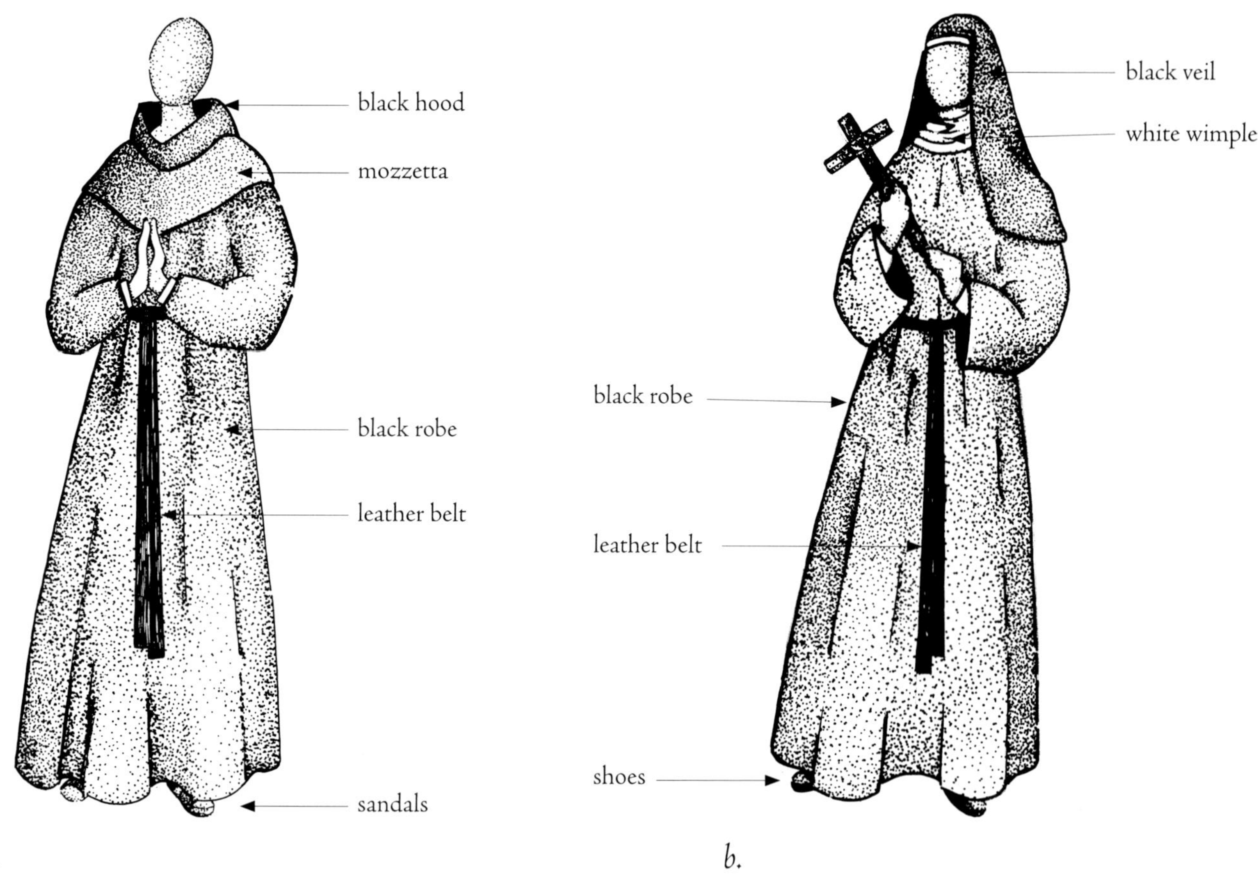

9.2. Habits of an Augustinian friar and nun.

1907, the women's order, a branch of the Poor Clares whose members are called "Capuchinesses" (*capuchinas*), arrived in New Spain in the latter half of the seventeenth century, founding convents in Mexico City (1665), Puebla (1704), and Guadalajara (1761) and establishing schools throughout central New Spain. Their efforts to establish convents in Durango and Monterrey, though noted in the records, were unsuccessful. The nuns' habit, belted with the knotted Franciscan cord from which a rosary hung, reflected their extreme austerity and absolute poverty. The robe and scapular were usually the same color of brown, with a black veil and white wimple—all made from the roughest cloth to mortify the flesh. Patches were commonly seen on their sleeves, and they wore coarse sandals.

Carmelites (Carmelitas)

The Order of the Brothers of the Most Blessed Virgin Mary of Mount Carmel (O Carm) was said to have been founded in 1155. The Carmelites, which included the Barefoot Carmelites (OCD; who in fact wore sandals), were also known as "White Friars" from their white mantles; they claimed direct descent from hermits living on Mount Carmel in the Holy Land since Old Testament times and counted the prophet Elijah as a founder. Carmelite friars were active in New Spain by 1586, arriving with the intention of carrying on missionary activities in Nuevo México, California, and the Philippines; some of their members accompanied Viscaíno in his sailing exploration along the California coast in 1602.[15] For various reasons, however, some political, their activities were restricted to the central part of New Spain, where they established conventos and built churches. They founded their first colegio and their first hospital in Mexico City in 1601 and 1615, respectively. Until Independence in 1821, they had a number of conventos in New Spain, but none in northern New Spain.

A Carmelite wore a white mantle over a brown robe, scapular, hood, and belt, and shoes or sandals. He might also wear the distinctive badge of the Carmelites on his

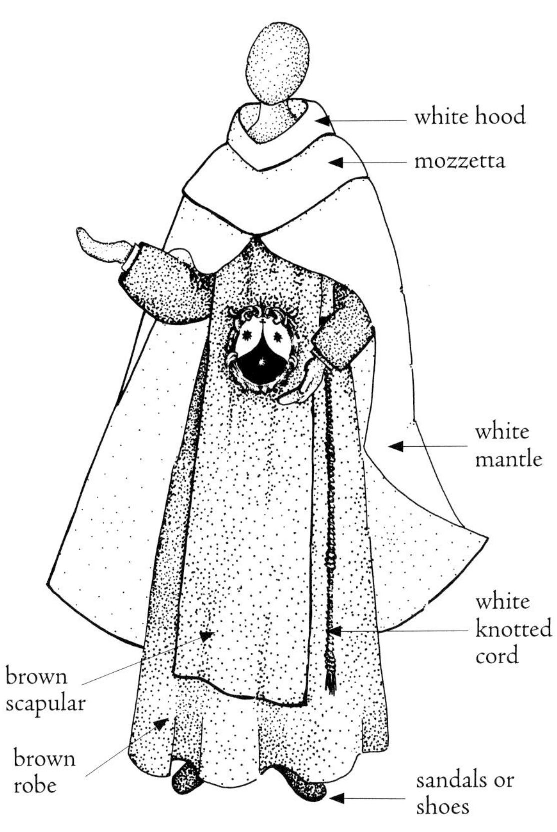

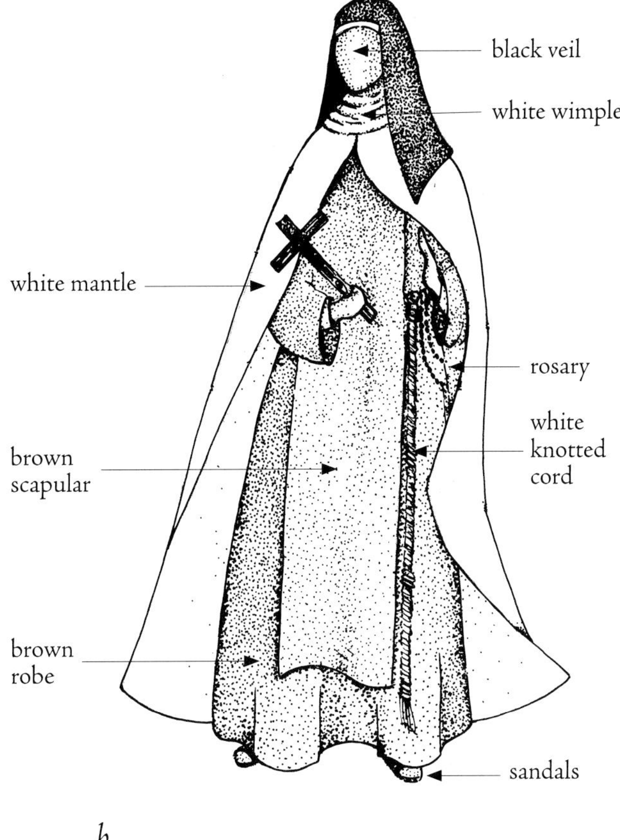

9.3. Habits of a Carmelite friar and nun.

scapular. A Carmelite nun (also *carmelita*) wore a plain, brown robe and scapular without insignia, girded by the knotted Franciscan cord from which a rosary hung, a white wimple, and a short black veil (novices' veils were white), with a white mantle, fastened at the neck and almost completely covering the robe. Instead of shoes, they wore straw or fiber sandals (figure 9.3, see also **Heraldry** entry in chapter 11).

Carthusians (Cartujos)

The Order of Carthusians (O Carth), considered the most austere of the Benedictine orders, was founded by Saint Bruno in 1084 as a reformed order. Carthusians wore a robe, belt, and scapular with hood joined at the sides by bands—all white.

Cistercians (Cistercienses)

Founded at Citeaux by Saints Robert of Molesme, Alberic, and Stephen Harding in 1098, the Cistercian Order of the Common Observance (SO Cist) was a reformed order and one of the most popular branches of the Benedictine Order. Known also as "White Monks" or "Trappists," the Cistercian wore a generous white (unbleached wool) habit with wide sleeves, knee-length black scapular with attached hood, black belt, and shoes.

Dominicans (Dominicos)

The Order of Preachers (OP), another mendicant order, was established by Saint Dominic of Guzmán in 1215 for the salvation of souls by means of preaching (see figure 12.21). The second group of friars to be established in New Spain, the Dominicans, also known as "Black Friars," arrived in 1526. Although the growth of its jurisdiction was slow, the order eventually had four provincias. A Dominican friar wore a white robe and scapular; a black mozzetta, hood, cape, and belt; and shoes.[16] A Dominican nun (*dominica*) wore a white, large-sleeved robe, with large rosary (and sometimes religious medallions) hanging

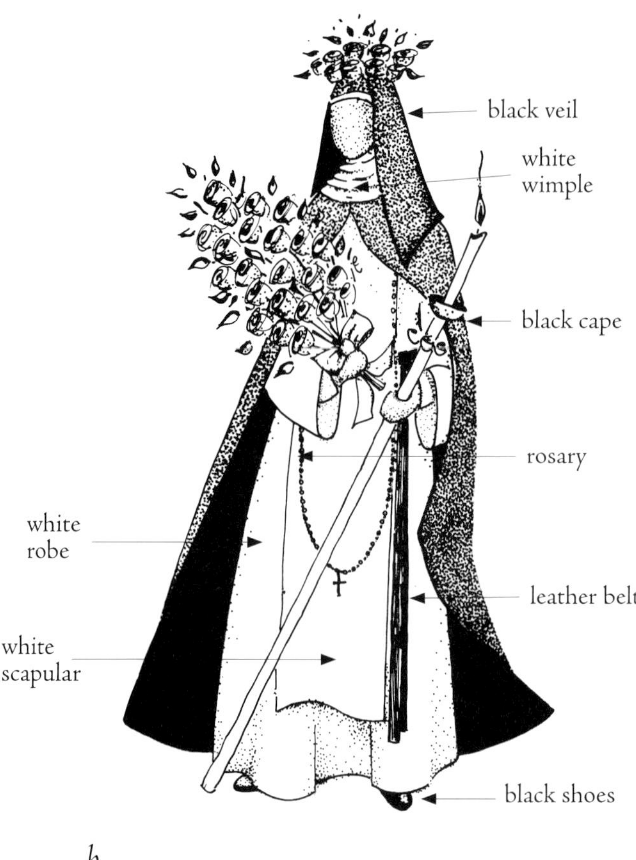

9.4. Habits of a Dominican friar and nun.

almost to the knees, and white wimple; the cloak and veil were black (novices' veils were white), in keeping with the heraldic colors of their order (figure 9.4).

Especially active in southern New Spain from the mid-sixteenth century on, the Dominican friars were involved in the Bajío; by the mid-eighteenth century, they had traveled as far north as Sombrerete, Zacatecas. Later, after the Jesuit expulsion in 1767, they were engaged in missionary activity in Baja California, taking over some of the sites formerly served by the Jesuits and establishing others.

Franciscans (Franciscanos)

The Order of Friars Minor (OFM) was founded in 1209 by Saint Francis of Assisi as a mendicant order with strict vows of poverty (see figure 12.22). Arriving in 1524, the Franciscans were the first order to be established in New Spain, where they had five provincias and founded seven missionary colegios. Franciscans were the second most active missionaries after the Jesuits. When the latter were expelled from New Spain in 1767, Franciscans were assigned to many of the former Jesuit missions, and they continued establishing their own missions there up to the first two decades of the nineteenth century.

As intended by Saint Francis, the first Franciscans wore a simple woolen habit and sandals: a robe that formed a cross when the arms were extended and was similar to that worn by the Umbrian peasant of the time.[17] The robe was later tied with the order's distinctive knotted cord (see **Cord or rope** entry in chapter 11) and a short cape and hood added (figure 9.5). Drawing on Saint Francis's rule, Saint Bonaventure (1217–1274) determined that the robe should be of undyed natural black and white wool blended to create a gray (the prescribed color from 1260 until 1897—and that worn by the Franciscans of Alta California), with a small round hood to distinguish the friars from peasants. Notwithstanding Bonaventure's determination and a later papal decree, however, friars from the Colegio de Santa Cruz in Querétaro and oth-

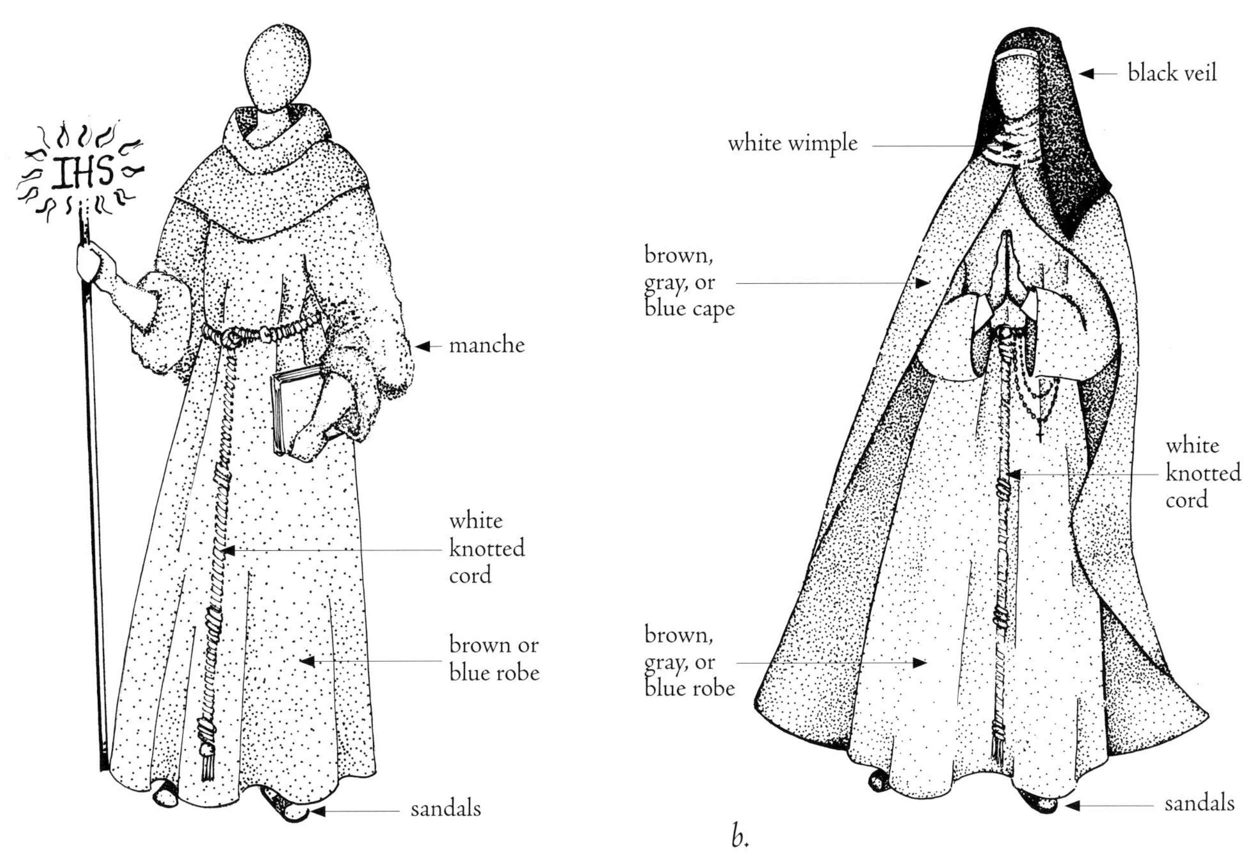

9.5. Habits of a Franciscan friar and nun. The nun's habit is specific to the Poor Clares, the branch corresponding to the Friars Minor; each branch had a somewhat different habit. (By Meredith L. Milstead)

ers in Mexico City wore what would later become the classic brown habit of the Franciscans, while friars of the Colegio de Guadalupe in Zacatecas (and many others) wore blue.[18]

Because the Franciscans' vow of poverty meant their habits could have no pockets, sometime during the Middle Ages the sleeves of their robes were modified to accommodate a prayer book, a modification called a manche (from French, sleeve, esp. a hanging sleeve) clearly apparent in eighteenth-century Spanish colonial prints, paintings, and sculptures. Both Franciscan and Jesuit missionaries were often portrayed in broad-brimmed hats (whether made of straw or felt is unclear) to protect their eyes and faces from the sun.

Of the three distinct and independent branches within this order—Friars Minor, Conventuals, and Capuchins—the Friars Minor figured most importantly in the history of northern New Spain. Their order of nuns, the Poor Clares (*clarisas*), was founded in 1212 by Saint Francis and Saint Clare; they wore gray, brown, or blue robes belted with the knotted Franciscan cord, and cloaks of the same color, with white wimples and black veils (novices' veils were white). Each branch of the Franciscan nuns had a distinctive habit (see "Capuchins [Capuchinos]" earlier).

Hospitaliers (Juaninos)

Founded in Granada in 1540 for the care of the sick, the Order of the Brothers Hospitaliers of Saint John of God (OH) arrived in New Spain in 1603 and proceeded to found hospitals throughout the country. They were active in northern New Spain by 1610 in the city of Durango, where they were given the Hospital of Santa Veracruz, established the Convento de San Cosme y San Damián in 1631 and a school in 1719, and dedicated the Church of San Juan de Dios there in 1739.[19]

Like the Augustinians, the Hospitaliers wore black robes, belts, scapulars, and round hoods. Hospitaliers were skilled in surgery and nursing, extending their care to crippled children, the elderly, and people with epilepsy, leprosy, and mental deficiencies. In 1681, the Juanino friar José Guijosa accompanied Jesuit missionary Eusebio Francisco Kino and another Jesuit to Baja California on an expedition to form a permanent settlement at the port of La Paz (Baja California Sur).[20] In 1688, they were given charge of a hospital for miners in Parral (Chihuahua).[21] Their mission churches in Parral and Durango were converted to diocesan churches and are still in use.

Jesuits (Jesuitas)

The Society of Jesus (SJ) was founded by Saint Ignatius of Loyola in 1538. Jesuits were active in New Spain from 1572 as educators and missionaries. Until their expulsion in 1767, they were the most active order in New Spain, deeply involved in educational activities and missionary efforts in northern New Spain, where they distinguished themselves especially in the modern states of Baja California Norte and Sur, Chihuahua, Durango, Sinaloa, and Sonora from the end of the sixteenth century into the eighteenth century. At the time of their expulsion, they had established 25 secular secondary schools (colegios), 11 seminaries, and 125 missions.[22]

A Jesuit wore an ankle-length black cassock with thirty-three buttons and long, narrow sleeves, similar to the habit of the secular clergy, and shoes (figure 9.6). The number of buttons is said to reflect the years of Christ's life. Historians explain the absence of a women's congregation as largely due to the misogyny of the founding Jesuits, particularly Ignatius, who equated women with the Devil.[23]

Mercedarians (Mercedarios)

The Glorious, Royal, and Military Order of Our Lady of Mercy (ODM) was, according to tradition, founded by Saint Peter Nolasco in 1225 for the ransoming of captives from the Moors. Although Mercedarians accompanied Hernán Cortés to New Spain in 1519, the order was not officially established there until 1595. They established conventos and schools throughout southern and central New Spain.

A Mercedarian wore an all-white robe, belt, scapular and hood, with a white cloak for outdoors, and either shoes or sandals. He might also wear the distinctive badge of the Mercedarians on his scapular (see **Heraldry** entry in chapter 11).

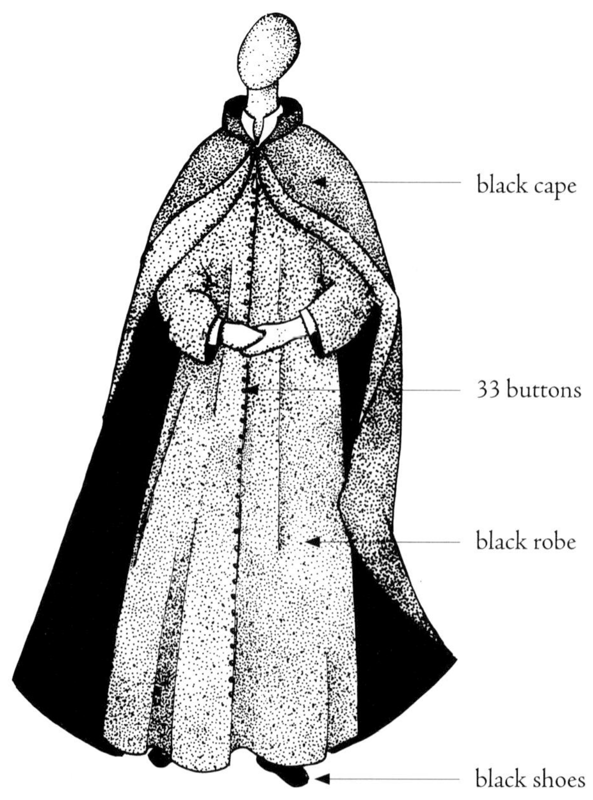

9.6. Habit of a Jesuit priest.

Minims (Minimos)

The Order of the Minim Hermits of Saint Francis of Paola (OM), founded in 1436 as a mendicant order, took its name from the Latin *minimus* (least), which the order adopted to show its abasement beneath the Franciscan Friars Minor. Based on the rule of Saint Francis of Assisi, it required a fourth vow—perpetual abstinence from meat. Minims distinguished themselves as preachers and teachers. Although Fray Bernardo Boyl, the first Spanish Minim, accompanied Christopher Columbus as apostolic vicar to America on Columbus's second voyage in 1493, Minims played only a very limited role in New Spain and were virtually absent from northern New Spain. A Minim friar wore a wide-sleeved, woolen robe (usually shown as brown) tied with a cord, a cape and hood, and sandals. Spanish colonial images of their founding saint include a scapular.

VESTMENTS

When celebrating Mass, the subdeacon, deacon, and priest wore an amice, alb, cincture, and maniple. The subdeacon also wore a tunic; the deacon, a dalmatic and stole; and the priest, a chasuble and stole. In addition to these items, bishops and certain other members of the hierarchy wore a rochet under the alb, a miter, pontifical gloves and ring, a pectoral cross, stockings, and buskins.[24]

In this section I discuss the different vestments, habits, and accompanying articles associated with rank or occasion. These evolved slowly from the everyday attire of polite society of Imperial Rome, ceremonial robes of Jewish priests, and medieval clothing. In the Middle Ages, the forms and parts of the garments were modified and enlarged, and they were provided with symbolic significance. Their forms and colors began to be regulated with the reform of the Church in the twelfth century; Mass books approved by Pope Saint Pius V in 1570 included the vestment colors prescribed by the Council of Trent.

Sources for my descriptions of the vestments include official Church directives and more than three hundred inventories of churches and chapels in northern, central, and southern New Spain. Some generalizations can be made about clerical vestments based upon these inventories. In New Spain, all priests wore the appropriate vestments over their habits or cassocks when officiating at services. Although, not surprisingly, the number and quality of vestments in prosperous parishes far exceeded those in poorer communities or missions, even in the humblest mission, great importance was placed on appropriate garments and accoutrements for religious services.[25] Vestments are frequently found under the heading "alhajas" (see introduction to chapter 8).

The use and material of vestments in northern New Spain, as elsewhere in the Catholic world, was determined by Church tradition and religious symbolism.[26] I have included etymologies, where helpful, and the Spanish names for most items. Also included are garments and accessories worn by prelates elsewhere in New Spain, as illustrated in viceregal paintings and engravings, and presumably worn by their counterparts in northern New Spain, or at least by prelates visiting there.

Everyday Garments

The ecclesiastical uniform of all clerics save members of religious orders having distinctive habits, the cassock (*sotana*) was a close-fitting, full-length robe secured down the front with small buttons or lapped over and to the side with a sash. Its color varied according to the rank of the wearer. A collar (*cuello*), to keep the cassock clean around the neck, appeared during the sixteenth century, derived from secular rather than ecclesiastical attire. Usually white, the collar at first was turned down over the cassock; lace or exaggerated needlework was expressly forbidden (a prohibition often ignored if colonial portraits are to be trusted).

Liturgical Garments

The first sacred vestment that celebrants of the Mass and their immediate attendants put on was the amice (from Medieval Latin *amictus*, cloak; in Spanish, *amito*), a rectangular piece of white linen about sixteen inches long and thirty-six inches wide. Placed first on the head before being lowered to the shoulders, the amice was worn over the cassock or habit and under the alb by subdeacon, deacon, and priest; it covered the neck and shoulders and was tied in place around the waist with ribbons or strings attached for that purpose. Sometimes a collar of stiffened embroidered silk about twenty inches long and eight inches high was attached to its upper edge, creating an appareled, or ornamented, stiff collar above the other vestments. Of the different types of amices, the California mission inventories specify only the *amito clásico*. The amice may have derived from a scarf worn to protect the throat from the cold or the rich vestments from stains, or it may once have been used to cover the head (before the biretta was introduced) en route to and from the altar (the hood on monks' and friars' robes perhaps also deriving from this). The amice was referred to as the "helmet of salvation" (against the malignant enemy) in the prayer the priest said when putting it on, and also as the "discipline of the tongue," an allusion to the cloth covering Christ's face during his scourging by the soldiers. Often ornamented and bearing a small cross, the amice signified the protection of divine grace, Christ's yoke, and a pure heart.

The alb (from Latin *alba*, fem. of *albus*, white; in Spanish, *alba*) was a floor-length, white robe full and wide enough to permit genuflection and equipped with generous, narrow-cuffed sleeves. It may have derived from the chiton, a typical men's garment worn in Greece during the last six centuries before Christ. In the Middle Ages, the alb was frequently made of silk and richly ornamented with silver and gold. From the eleventh to seventeenth centuries, it was common to attach an apparel (discussed later) to the front, back, and each side of the alb. After the seventeenth century, the hems and cuffs were adorned with lace. California missions inventoried two distinct types, *alba clásica,* the more elaborate alb used for solemn ceremonies during feast days (*días clásicos*), and *alba ordinaria,* the plain, "everyday" alb.[27] Subdeacon, deacon, and priest wore an alb, putting it on after the amice and under other vestments. It symbolized purity of heart, chastity, and innocence of life, and alluded to the simple garment that clothed Christ during his trial by Herod and his court.

A distinctive vestment of prelates deriving from the alb, the rochet (from Old French *rochet,* diminutive of *roc,* mantle; in Spanish, *roquete*) was a white, form-fitting, narrow-sleeved, knee-length garment with white linen on the upper part and lace on the bottom. Its present-day form dates from the seventeenth century.

Attached to the top of the amice and to the front, bottom, and sleeves of the dalmatic were small rectangular panels of embroidery (*bordados*) called apparels (from Latin *apparare,* to clothe; in Spanish, *paratura*), or ornaments (*ornamentos*), often elaborated with religious scenes.[28] Dating back to the Middle Ages, apparels appear in colonial paintings, on sculptures of officiating priests, or in museums or churches as collected objects apart from their original garments.[29] Designed to be removed when the garments were washed or replaced, these richly embroidered pieces, among the few cloth items to survive from northern New Spain, give us at least an idea of the workmanship and history of Spanish colonial religious attire. Originally intended to protect the alb at points of wear (edges of sleeves, above the hem of the garment—front and back—and sometimes near the neck opening), they were later relocated and used for purely decorative purposes. They appear in the eleventh century attached to the plain alb (*alba pura*). Apparels may have derived from the *segmentae,* circular or rectangular embroidered pieces sewn onto or worked into the linen tunics of Imperial Rome's fashionably dressed.[30] From their location on the amice and dalmatic, apparels came to symbolize Christ's bondage and stigmata (as such, they were also called *plagae* or *plagulae,* literally, blows or little blows). In New Spain, apparels on the sleeves of dalmatics were called *bocamangas* and the large apparel on the front, a *faldón.* They fell into disuse around the mid-nineteenth century.

A full-length cape, sometimes elaborately and richly decorated, open in the front, and usually worn with the stole over the alb, amice, or surplice (but never over the chasuble), the cope (from Late Latin *cappa,* cape, hooded cloak; in Spanish, *capa,* or sometimes *capa pluvial*) derived from the hooded cape used by early pilgrims as an outdoor garment to protect the wearer from the rain. Not in universal use until the eleventh century, the cope was well established as a liturgical garment by the thirteenth. When laid flat it formed a perfect half circle; a vestigial, sometimes elaborately decorated, hood was attached in back below the collar. The cope was held together at the breast by a large simple clasp or sometimes by a large, jeweled, and richly worked brooch or two-part clasp called a morse (*formal*), or fibula. The morse developed from a square or rectangular piece of cloth, growing progressively more embellished with gemstones, pearls, and embroidery as time passed and becoming, for bishops, an often intricate piece of jewelry made of gold and precious stones. The cope was also worn by those assisting the celebrant at solemn Masses or Benedictions and for solemn divine offices, as well as in processions.

During Mass, when administering a sacrament, when preaching, for obsequies, and for other rites, the deacon, priest, or bishop wore around his neck a stole (from Latin *stola,* dress or gown; in Spanish, *estola*), a narrow, decorated, and usually fringed piece of silk about eight feet long, about four inches wide at the center, and six inches wide at the ends.[31] The deacon wore it diagonally over the left shoulder with ends joined under the right arm; the priest wore it crossed at the girdle if over an alb, otherwise hanging loosely; the bishop always wore it uncrossed. Its ends showed beneath the chasuble or dalmatic. The pope might wear the stole as a sign of his universal jurisdiction. Its colors matched the chasuble and maniple, and it might bear three crosses—one in the center and one on each end. The stole was a sign of power and dignity and a symbol of immortality from its resemblance to Christ's yoke. In New Spain, a very large stole used in Lenten Masses was called an *estolón.* The stole worn by ecclesiastical dignitaries of cathedral and collegiate churches during solemn functions was referred to as a *capa de coro.*

A cincture or cingulum (from Latin *cingere,* to gird; in Spanish *cíngulo*), also called a girdle or cord (*ceñidor* or *cordón*), was a rope of linen, wool, hemp, or silk, colored or natural, used to confine the alb at the waist, to hold the stole against the body, and, more generally, to serve as a belt. Representing the bonds of Christ, the cincture symbolized self-restraint and sacerdotal purity and was worn by subdeacon, deacon, and priest (see also "Franciscans [Franciscanos]" earlier and **Cord or rope** entry in chapter 11). A sash or belt (*faja*)—a wide band of silk moiré finished with tassels—was worn around the waist by subdeacons and priests serving as ecclesiastical dignitaries during ceremonies. Its color varied according to the rank of its wearer.

Deriving its name from the sheaves gathered in Psalms 126:6, the maniple (from Latin *manipulus,* handful, sheaf of wheat; in Spanish, *manípulo*) was a decorated band of silk about thirty inches long, three inches wide in the center, and five inches wide at the ends, secured (sometimes with a pin) so that it hung in equal lengths. It was worn over the left forearm by the celebrant of the Mass, the deacon, and the subdeacon, garbed with the vestments proper to each. Its color and material matching those of the chasuble, stole, dalmatic, and tunic, it was sometimes decorated with three crosses, one in the center and two on the ends. Symbolically the napkin used to wipe away tears shed for sins, it may have evolved from a kind of handkerchief used to wipe the celebrant's hands and face during the Mass. The maniple symbolized the fruits of good works.

Originally introduced to keep clerics' hands warm, pontifical gloves (*guantes pontificales*) assumed a more sacred character in the ninth century, when French bishops classified them as liturgical garments and prescribed a prayer for putting them on. Their use became customary in Rome by the tenth century. In the thirteenth century, the color of the episcopal gloves was white with ornamented backs; during the Middle Ages, the gloves were often richly embroidered with gems. By the sixteenth century, the colors of the pontifical gloves corresponded with the liturgical colors, namely, red, white, green, and violet. The gloves were made of silk, usually with large cuffs that covered the lower part of the sleeves of the alb, and ornamentation that varied according to the dignity of the wearer. A bishop wore them only for pontifical Masses but never at requiem Masses nor on Good Friday.

Made of silk and embroidered with gold, worn over ordinary stockings, and reaching to the knees, buskins (*cáligas*), or liturgical stockings, date from the end of the seventh century.[32] They were reserved for the pope until the ninth century, when they became the exclusive property of bishops and other prelates. They should be the same color as the vestments, although black is forbidden because they are not worn on Good Friday or for requiem Masses.

Said to represent the purple robe Pilate had placed on Christ when he was mocked as King of the Jews, the chasuble (from Late Latin *casubla,* hooded garment, great coat; in Spanish, *casulla* or *planeta*) was the principal vestment worn by the priest at Mass, and the last to be put on.[33] Because it covered the other vestments, it symbolized Christian charity and protection. The chasuble used in New Spain (and in Mexico and other Latin American countries to this day) had a distinctive, fiddle-back shape (opened out and laid flat, it resembled a fiddle—a form in use at least by the thirteen century). It was made of silk or satin heavily embroidered with sacred symbols and sometimes richly brocaded, or of velvet or tapestry; lined with cotton, linen, silk, or wool in contrasting colors; and trimmed with decorative bands of gold or silver metallic braid, called orphrey (discussed later). The sides were open, allowing the alb and arms to be exposed; the neckline was rounded in the rear but slightly deepened in the front; and the front panel was slightly shorter than the one in the back. Some church inventories list chasubles of five distinct colors—white, red, green, purple, and black—the different colors corresponding to different religious feasts or ecclesiastical seasons.

Instead of the chasuble, the subdeacon wore the tunic (*túnica*), and the deacon wore the dalmatic (*dalmática*); these matched the color of the chasuble worn by the celebrant and were often of a set with it, of the same material, lining, and embroidery. During penitential seasons, subdeacon and deacon might wear a substitute for the tunic and dalmatic, a dark, plain chasuble whose front was somewhat shortened by folding it up from the bottom, called *planeta plicata.* In New Spain, the dalmatic (originally worn by the inhabitants of Dalmatia, as its name suggests) was often portrayed as a scapular-like cloak, worn over the alb and cut diagonally from top to bottom to give it a slight flair, with square lappets on each side of the shoulders, secured below the arms with small ribbon ties sewn onto its edges and sides. It was derived from a white tunic worn by the ancient Romans and by emperors and kings in the Middle Ages. With the increasing sumptuousness of fabrics and embroidery in the sixteenth century, open-sided dalmatics replaced sleeved ones for greater ease of movement. The rigid collar (*alzacuello* or *collarino*) seen in viceregal paintings and sculptures harked back to the ancient friar's hood. Of plain, embroidered, or brocaded materials, the dalmatic was at least knee-length and ornamented, with two narrow vertical strips from shoulder to hem joined at the bottom by a horizontal band; it matched the chasuble in color, material, lining, and embroidery. A shorter, lighter version of the dalmatic (*dalmática menor* or *línea*), made from lightweight silk, was worn by bishops, abbots, and cardinals under their chasubles during pontifical Masses. In the deacon's vestments, the dalmatic symbolized gladness, salvation, and righteousness. Originally and distinctively, it was worn by popes, then by archbishops, and finally by deacons during Mass or in processions. Saints Lawrence, Leonard, and Stephen were usually portrayed in dalmatics.

The surplice (from Medieval Latin *superpellicium*, overcoat of skins; a fur winter overgarment worn by clergy in northern Europe over their robes of office during the Middle Ages; in Spanish, *sobrepelliz* or *cota*) was a loose hip- or knee-length white linen shirt, with sleeves extending to the elbows or longer; its sleeves and hem were often trimmed with lace. It was worn over a priest's cassock or habit in a choir or for processions and when performing any blessing or sacrament for which an alb was not prescribed. It might also be worn by acolytes and choirboys. From the sixteenth century on, the surplice grew more elaborate, evolving from a plain linen garment, to one trimmed in lace, to one made almost entirely of lace.

A circular band of woolen cloth worn about the shoulders with a pendant strip front and back, and embroidered with six black crosses, the pallium (palio) symbolized the pastoral office and the lost sheep sought by Christ and brought back across his shoulders. As such, it was worn by (metropolitan) archbishops, in recognition of their being leaders of the Church and shepherds of their flocks, and by the pope, signifying his universal, supreme pastoral authority and the fullness of his episcopal power. The pallium's Y shape was a reminder of the Crucifixion.

A precious metal braid or embroidered band applied to dalmatics, chasubles, and copes, the orphrey (*cenefa, franja de oro*) served as decorative edging and as a device to cover seams. On chasubles, it might take the form of a cross or pillar or be Y-shaped. (The center vertical strip was called *pilar* or *columna*, pillar or column.) On dalmatics, the orphrey created the column shape, front and back, with sometimes a horizontal connecting piece between the two vertical bands. Introduced in the ninth century, orphreys were simply conventional ornamentation and not essential to the garments' appearance.

Because of the preciousness of these liturgical vestments and the resultant great care they received, examples from throughout the colonial era have survived in good condition; they can be found in a number of church museums in what was formerly northern New Spain.[34] These can be approximately dated from the types of fabric and braid used, and the techniques of decoration.

[Liturgical Veils] A long, rectangular shawl, usually fringed and ornamented, the humeral veil (*almaisal* or *almaizal*; from Latin *humerus*, shoulder) was worn about the shoulders of a priest or subdeacon carrying or holding sacred vessels, especially those which held the Blessed Sacrament; it covered his arms and hands and, when required by rite, the vessels themselves. The gremial veil (from Latin *gremium*, lap; in Spanish, *gremial*) was a square piece of cloth, plain or ornamented, placed on a bishop's lap to protect the chasuble during certain ceremonies such as the blessing of the candles and the branches.

[Overgarments] Deriving from a garment that laborers wore over their clothes to protect them from soiling, the scapular (from Medieval Latin *scapula*, shoulder; in Spanish, *escapulario*) was rectangular, usually shoulder-wide and ankle-length. Passed over the head so that one piece hung in front and the other in back, it was always worn over the robe of a religious habit; it could be hooded and belted. A symbol of the yoke of Christ, the scapular served as a short work cloak for the Benedictines and was used by several other religious orders as a distinctive part of their habits, sometimes differing in color from other parts (see also **Scapular** entry in chapter 11.)[35]

The *cappa magna* (Latin, great mantle; in Spanish, *capa magna*) dated from about the fifteenth century. A generous mantle that covered the entire body, was open over the chest, and had both a hood and a long train (*cola* or *cauda*), it was worn by high-ranking prelates (bishops, patriarchs, and cardinals) and by the pope on special occasions and required a train bearer. The colors of the cape varied with the rank of the individual wearing it and with the occasion.

Another long, ample robe with wide sleeves, and having the same color as their particular habit, the cowl (*cogulla*) was commonly confused with the hood by the same name. It was worn by some religious orders, notably Benedictines and Cistercians, in choir.

A short, hooded cape, reaching to the elbows or the belt, possibly an abbreviated form of the cappa magna, the mozzetta (from Italian *mozzo,* Latin *mutilus,* mutilated, curtailed; in Spanish, *muceta, esclavina,* or sometimes, *manteleta*) was of medieval origin. In the fourteenth century, it came to signify the privilege or jurisdiction of the wearer. It was worn over the rochet by bishops, abbots, cardinals, and the pope (whose mozzetta was formerly trimmed in ermine). Although considered a nonliturgical garment, the mozzetta took its color from the liturgical season and the wearer's rank. It might be either completely closed or closed by buttons down the center.

Over the rochet and under the mozzetta, prelates might wear a short cloak to the knees with open areas for the arms called a mantalet (manteleta). Its color was determined by the rank or religious order of the wearer. Although there are occasional references to a "muceta" in the mission inventories of northern New Spain, the recorder (usually the resident priest) was very likely referring to some other garment, for example, the *valona,* a very short cape opening in the front and covering only the shoulders, used by clerics as part of their everyday attire, whose color corresponded to their rank. The cape used by pilgrims, on which they attached their badges of pilgrimage, and shown in portrayals of sacred pilgrims such as Saint Roch and the Child of Atocha, was called an *esclavina.*

[Undergarments] The principal and undermost garment of all religious habits for men and most women, and probably of medieval origin, the tunic (*túnica*) was a loose ankle-length usually narrow-sleeved gown worn by members of religious orders.[36] This tunic is not to be confused with the liturgical vestment worn by subdeacons or that worn by abbots, bishops, and cardinals under the dalmatic during pontifical Mass.

Prelates and other members of clergy wore ordinary stockings (*medias*), which varied in color from black for ordinary clergy to purple for bishops, red for cardinals, and white for the pope. Prelates of religious orders wore stockings of the same color as their habit. Over these stockings, when celebrating or attending Mass (except a requiem Mass or on Good Friday), bishops and prelates wore buskins.

Head Coverings

Figure 9.7 illustrates typical head coverings for priests, bishops, Doctors of the Church, and popes. In use since the sixteenth century, the skullcap (*solideo*) originally served to cover the clerical tonsure but later came to signify ecclesiastical dignity. It might be worn by all clerics, its color depending on the rank of the wearer and the liturgical season. Those worn by bishops were called *zuchettos* (Italian diminutive of *zucce,* gourd or pate). A small, square, ridged cap, the biretta (*birrete* or sometimes *bonete*) was worn by priests and prelates; a biretta with a tassel signifies a Doctor of the Church (figure 9.7a). It also varied in color with rank from black for priests to purple for bishops, red for cardinals, and white for the pope. Originally a soft skullcap, the biretta later added ridges to facilitate handling. It frequently appears in Spanish colonial art and as a decorative device on church buildings, its top sometimes graced by multicolored tufts or pompons (figure 9.8). Saints Ignatius of Loyola, Francis Xavier, John Nepomuk, and Teresa of Ávila were usually portrayed wearing birettas; in the case of Teresa, it was honorific.

In addition to the biretta, the easily recognized pontifical hat (*sombrero, capelo*) appears on portal decorations, over ecclesiastical coats of arms (figure 9.9, see also figures 6.40 and 9.7b), as incidental ornamentation on buildings or walls, and in colonial sculptures and paintings. Broad-brimmed with a low crown, the pontifical hat was derived from a pilgrim's hat; its brim was pierced by two cords from which hung a series of tassels. Although all priests were entitled to wear a pontifical hat, the number of the tassels and the color of the hat would vary according to the rank of the wearer.[37]

Ceremonial headdress of bishops, archbishops, and the pope—and originally of Jewish high priests—the miter (*mitra;* from Greek and Latin, turban or headband) consisted of two flat, stiffened peaked pieces of material sewn halfway up the sides, with fanons attached in the back (see figure 9.7c). The miter began as a very low and cone-shaped hat and did not develop its characteristic center separation, with two rounded points, or horns,

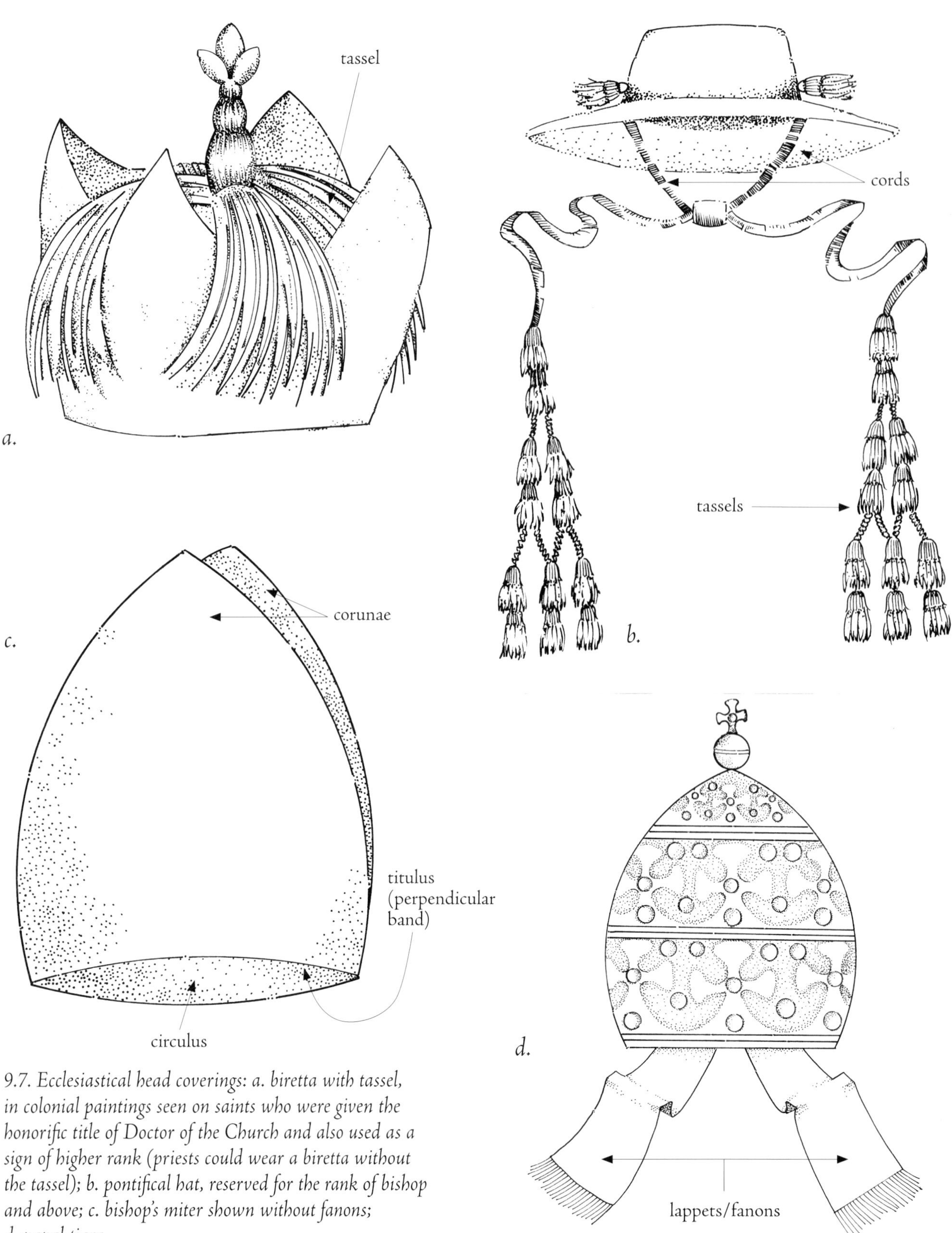

9.7. Ecclesiastical head coverings: a. biretta with tassel, in colonial paintings seen on saints who were given the honorific title of Doctor of the Church and also used as a sign of higher rank (priests could wear a biretta without the tassel); b. pontifical hat, reserved for the rank of bishop and above; c. bishop's miter shown without fanons; d. papal tiara.

9.8. Collateral retablo of San Juan Nepomuceno, Nuestro Padre San Ignacio de Loyola de Cabórica, Sonora, 1978. A decorative biretta caps the retablo.

9.9. Remate, east frontispiece, Catedral de Durango, 1982.

called cornuae, said to symbolize the cloven tongues of fire that descended upon the Apostles during Pentecost (Acts 2:1–2), until the twelfth century. The position of the horns was changed from left and right (one over each ear) to front and back in the thirteenth century; the miter attained its full height in the seventeenth.

A general symbol of authority used in the consecration of a bishop to signify the helmet of salvation and the symbol par excellence of episcopal dignity, the miter came in three types: *simplex*—plain white silk damask or linen; *aurifrigiata*—gold or silver on white silk and studded with tiny pearls; and *pretiosa*—jeweled or decorated with gold and silver plate ornaments. When used alone or in combination with a crosier, it symbolized episcopal jurisdiction and sacred rank. It also appears as an attribute of Saint Bernardine of Siena, symbols of the three bishoprics he refused. Although the two peaks of the miter were also said to allude to the two rays of light coming from Moses' forehead at the time he received the Ten Commandments, according to Pope Innocent III (pope 1198–1216), they represented the Old and New Testaments. In portraits of bishops in New Spain, the miters appear to be extraordinarily elongated. An early colonial example, presumably a pretiosa, is preserved at the Hispanic Society, New York City. It is adorned with bits of colored feathers, recalling the feather work of the pre-Columbian Indians.

Hanging down from the back of the miter were fanons (fanones), *infulae* (*ínfulas*), or lappets, two ribbons or fringed strips of fabric, sometimes ornamented. Although the fanons might once have tied the miter in place, they came to serve no practical purpose, instead symbolizing the spirit and letter of the Old and New Testaments. When the miter was shown alone or as an attribute, they might not be included.

The pope wore the papal crown or tiara (*tiara*), usually shown with three divisions or tiers—said variously to symbolize imperial, royal, and sacerdotal power; the Church Militant, Penitent, and Triumphal; and the Trinity—only at his coronation and on other nonliturgical occasions (see figure 9.7d). When exercising liturgical functions as Bishop of Rome he, like all other bishops, wore a miter. The tiers were added by different popes at different times, the third by either Benedict XI or Clement VI in the early fourteenth century. Like "miter," "tiara" refers to a headdress of Oriental origin. Silver and occasionally gold tiaras are frequently listed in inventories of Jesuit missions, associated with the image of Our Lady of Loreto, a Marian figure whose attributes include a papal tiara; they also appear in paintings and sculptures portraying God the Father in the "Throne of Glory" theme (see also "Mary" and discussion of God the Father in chapter 12).

The hood (*cogulla, capuz, capillo, capucha de fraile*) was either a flat vestigial collar attached to a cope or a part of a monk's or friar's habit used as a head covering. The nonfunctional hood on the liturgical cope, by regulation to be worn only for certain ceremonies and processions, became an accessory that increased in dimension and ornateness. In northern New Spain, the hood had ties to attach it to the cape and occasionally had a large tassel at the bottom.

A covering over the head and shoulders of nuns, the veil (*velo*) was derived from the medieval dress for a married woman, nuns being deemed brides of Christ. Another medieval covering taken from secular dress, a wimple (*toca*) was a hoodlike affair that nuns wore over the head, framing the face, and covering the hair and neck, but always under the veil. The colors of the veil and wimple were determined by the wearer's religious order. Mary is sometimes portrayed in a wimple in colonial paintings and sculpture in northern New Spain and elsewhere.

Pectoral Crosses

A sign of dignity worn by bishops, abbots, and some abbesses, the pectoral cross (*pectoral*), as its name suggests, was worn upon the chest; it was acknowledged in the fourteenth century as a distinguishing episcopal ornament.[38] Bishops wore it exposed at all times. The pectoral cross was of two types—ordinary and pontifical. Both were Latin crosses. The ordinary was made of gold or filled gold, without precious stones and suspended from the neck by a gold chain. This could be worn over the cassock. The pontifical cross was made of gold and might be studded with precious stones (depending on the rank and privilege of the wearer) or hollowed to contain relics of the saints, and was suspended from the neck by a cord colored to match the dignity of the wearer's dress. These are usually seen in portraits of prelates.[39]

Pontifical Rings

Although, strictly speaking, worn only by popes, the pontifical ring (*sortija* or *anillo*), which symbolized the spiritual marriage of the wearer to the Church, was also part of the insignia of abbots, some abbesses, bishops, and cardinals.[40] Pontifical rings were worn on the third finger of the right hand; those having precious stones were reserved for different ecclesiastical ranks and ceremonies. Bishops wore them as far back as the seventh century, the ring being conferred on him at the same time as his staff.

Chapter 10

Religious Images and Retablos

Almost from the beginning, Christianity developed and used religious images. That the Church first tolerated, then censured and rejected, then finally accepted and even endorsed these images had little effect on the central role they would play in the minds and hearts of believers across the centuries. There could be no greater tribute to this role, from both aesthetic and psychological perspectives, than the often magnificent altar screens (retablos) that displayed the images, sometimes powerfully and dramatically, but always tellingly, behind and above the altars of the churches of northern New Spain.[1]

Religious Images

Popularly called *santos* in New Spain, religious images (*imágenes religiosas*), whether painted, sculpted, or printed, were originally intended to instruct. As Durandus teaches, "Pictures and ornaments in churches are the lessons and the Scriptures of the laity."[2] From the earliest years of Christianity through today, these images have served to convey precepts of moral behavior, religious and political dogma, and the hierarchy of religious personages, as well as to show honor and veneration toward Christ and the saints. Later, some of the images would also function as aids to worship. Although conscious of the popular tendency not only to believe that the physical images themselves, rather than the saints they portrayed, were interceding with God, but also to imbue these images with all manner of magical powers, the Catholic Church nevertheless encouraged devotion to religious images as a means of strengthening the ties of the faithful to the Church's beliefs and of turning converts away from their former pagan beliefs.

That the catacombs were adorned with paintings of Christ, the saints, scenes from the Bible, and allegorical groups should help dispel the idea that the first Christians were opposed to religious images or that they considered them idolatrous. With Constantine's official tolerance of the Faith in the fourth century, Christian decorative art and iconography emerged into the light of day. Images created for the veneration of specific religious personages were condemned by the Church hierarchy almost from the very beginning, yet under the guise of education, tradition, and history, such images began to appear in churches at least as early as the fourth century in the form of pictures of bishops, kings, and saints, living and dead.[3] Beginning with the mandatory presence of a cross in churches in the fifth and sixth centuries (an altar cross or crucifix would not become mandatory until the beginning of the thirteenth century) and the appearance of a silver dove (representing the Holy Spirit) over the altars by at least the early sixth century, the organized Church came to accept religious images, notwithstanding periods of iconoclasm.[4]

Even though there was no comprehensive or explicit Church policy on the arrangement of images, from as early as the seventh century, painted figures were regularly included on interior walls, on façades, and in altar areas. Moreover, the earliest examples of Christian decoration bear witness to the deliberate placement of significant images in specific locations, as well as to a careful balancing of thematic elements. As the official proscription against religious images was relaxed and the cults and reverence toward the Church's heroes increased, a system of categorizing and arranging figures and symbols gradually evolved. That this system was still in effect throughout the colonial era is testified to by myriad examples in the churches and retablos of New Spain. The output of painted and sculpted religious images, whether as singular objects or as parts of other decoration, was enormous. It drew not only on the religious fervor of the colonial era but also on the wealth and success of the religious orders, parish churches, haciendas, and mines, with conventos apparently serving as the biggest customers.[5] Images of Christ (perhaps nothing more than a simple crucifix) were always present, often with images of Christ's earthly parents, Mary and Joseph, in diocesan and regular churches throughout New Spain. Furthermore, scenes from the lives of the founders of particular orders or depicting more esoteric Christian themes typically appeared within conventos, their cloisters, and their chapels.

As noted in chapter 2, certain subject matter, mannerisms, and techniques popular during particular periods allow us to establish approximate dates and sometimes origins for otherwise unidentified religious images. European trends during the viceregal period were transmitted both directly and indirectly through immigrant artists, their work, and imported two- and three-dimensional representations from Spain, chiefly at first from Sevilla, to New Spain.

The few extant documents on retablos in northern New Spain (among what must have been hundreds) tell us much about their material, size, and cost, as well as their placement and the arrangement of the images they contained. Paralleling the instructions in these documents, other iconographic elements in the churches of northern New Spain were carefully arrayed in the symmetric construction or placement of niches, images, altars, and even chapels.

San Xavier del Bac

One fine example of such careful arrangement is this extraordinary mission church just outside Tucson (Arizona), whose original decoration is remarkably intact. Built in an isolated and economically insignificant part of northern New Spain as a Franciscan mission, San Xavier bears clear witness to a carefully planned balance of iconographic and thematic elements in its extensively painted walls and niches full of statues of saints.[6]

Images of the four Doctors of the Church, Saints Ambrose, Jerome, Gregory, and Augustine—ubiquitous throughout New Spain at the crossing of the transept and nave—are painted on the squinches of the crossing at San Xavier. The close relationship between the Franciscan and Dominican Orders, expressed in many other churches of New Spain by the inclusion of images, symbols, or motifs of both orders, is played out in this mission church in several two- and three-dimensional forms. On the choir loft's west wall, Saint Dominic receives the rosary from the Virgin; the ships in the background signify the naval victory at Lepanto, a victory inspired by Our Lady of the Rosary. Opposite, on the choir loft's east wall, is a mural of Saint Francis of Assisi receiving the stigmata. Below, in the lower registers on the south walls of the east and west transept, respectively, are murals of Our Lady of the Rosary and Our Lady of the Pillar of Zaragoza. An image of Saint Dominic is located prominently in the west transept, while that of another Dominican saint, Vincent

Ferrer, appears on one of the squinches of the sacristy, whose saucer dome ceiling is graced by the black-and-white medallion of the Dominican Order.

On the east and west sides of the drum, Saint Rose of Lima is opposite Saint Rosalie of Palermo—neither formally a member of a religious order (Rose was a Dominican tertiary and Rosalie an anchoress) but both known for their rigorous penitence and both associated with roses (see also "Rose of Lima [Rosa de Lima]" and Rosalie of Palermo [Rosalía de Palermo]" in chapter 12). The north and south figures in the drum are Mary as the Divine Shepherdess, special symbol of the missionary effort, and a figure that may be Fray Margil de Jesús, founder of the Franciscan missionary college of Santa Cruz, Querétaro (Querétaro). Much of the drum's decoration has been destroyed by moisture; one can barely discern the images of the eight Franciscan saints that ring it. Facing north, we can see in counterclockwise order (1) Francis of Assisi, founder of the Friars Minor, located closest to the sanctuary and above the image of the Divine Shepherdess; (2) Bonaventure; (3) James of Álcala; (4) John of Capistrano; (5) an obliterated figure, possibly Anthony of Padua; (6) Colette of Corbie; (7) Bernardine of Siena; and (8) on Francis's left hand, Clare of Assisi. Above and between them are what remains of eight angels holding a scepter, a palm, or a crown, symbols of sainthood. Above these, in even more deteriorated condition, are parts of eight medallions, two having crossed pastoral staffs. All the saints and angels have been painted in separate medallions, ornamented with leaves. The pastoral staffs, also in medallion form, are connected to each other and the center rosette by a series of knotted Franciscan cords. A cross, possibly a crucifix, is in the center of the dome, the head of the cross pointing toward the apse.

Further balancing of thematic elements occurs above the paintings in the upper registers. On the southern wall of the east transept (dedicated to the Sorrowful Mother), the child Mary is being shown the prophecies by her mother, Anne, while her father, Joachim, looks on. In the west transept (dedicated to Jesus the Nazarene), Mary and the infant Jesus are painted in the upper register. The niches in the bottom registers of the north walls of the transepts contain the parents of Jesus: Joseph in the west transept and Mary in the advocation of the Immaculate Conception in the east transept.[7] Mary's importance is further stressed through the large statue of her as the Immaculate Conception, located in the center of the retablo above the titular figure of Saint Francis Xavier and below God the Father. Murals in the upper register of the sides of the walls of the sanctuary depict the first and second of the Joyful Mysteries of Mary: the Annunciation on the Gospel (left) side and the Visitation on the Epistle (right) side (see also "Mary" in chapter 12). These are balanced below by scenes of the Nativity (the third Joyful Mystery, also called the Adoration of the Shepherds) and the Adoration of the Magi.[8] With the Gospel side taking precedence over the Epistle, beginning at the top (on the left, facing the retablo), the sanctuary can be read chronologically: first, the Annunciation, where Mary is informed she is to be the mother of Christ (Luke 1:28–31); on the opposite side, Mary is shown arriving at Elizabeth's (Luke 1:43); below and on the left is the Nativity, or Adoration of the Shepherds (Luke 2:7–17); and, facing this, the Adoration of the Magi (Matthew 2:1–12). This order appears to affect the placement of the murals along the sides of the nave: the Last Supper of Christ and his Twelve Apostles (Mark 14:12–26) on the left, and the Pentecost (Acts 2:1–4) on the right. (The significance of images of the Apostles is briefly discussed in chapter 12.)

Eight women saints significant to the Franciscan Order appear in the sculpture modeled in eared quatrefoil medallions in the uppermost registers of the two transept altars—four on each side (figure 10.1). Occupying prominent positions in the center of the east and west transepts, respectively, are Clare of Assisi, cofounder with Francis of the Franciscan Order for Women (the Poor Clares), and Teresa of Ávila, reformer of the Carmelite Order. Clare is flanked by Queens Elizabeth of Portugal (left) and Elizabeth of Hungary (right); Teresa, by two Benedictine nuns, identified as Gertrude the Great (left) and Scholastica (right). Immediately off the nave on the north walls are two Poor Clares, identified as Agnes of Prague (east transept) and Colette of Corbie (west transept).

Returning to the medallion images of the four nun saints—Teresa of Ávila, Gertrude the Great, Scholastica, and Colette of Corbie—their hands and faces have been painted a rich, dark brown (a color called in Spanish *quemado*; literally, burnt; figure 10.2), as have those of the cherubs supporting them and of Saint Rosalie of Palermo on the west side of the drum. After careful examination of this last image and analysis of a paint sample taken from it, Christopher Stavroudis and I concluded in 1980 that

10.1. Detail of the east transept showing female saints: left to right, top to bottom: Agnes of Rome, Cecilia of Rome, Agatha of Catania, Sicily, Lucy of Syracuse; San Francisco Xavier del Bac, Tucson, Arizona, 2005. (Photo by Meredith L. Milstead)

the darker flesh tone was not the result of overpainting accidentally turned dark, as some scholars have proposed, but was painted deliberately. Indeed, I am convinced this was so for all these images and that the clergy overseeing the project tolerated the darker skin color in acknowledgment of the Native Americans they served.[9]

Francisco Pacheco, the Counter-Reformation, and Spanish Colonial Art

Of particular interest to the student of Spanish colonial art is *Arte de la pintura,* written over a forty-year period by the Sevillan artist Francisco Pacheco (1565–1654), inspector of art for the Inquisition of Sevilla, and published in its final form in 1649. Besides formulas for different processes and guidelines for iconography, his treatise includes the ideals for painting and the rulings on church art set forth by the Council of Trent in 1563, which Pacheco and other Spanish artists attempted to follow—and which, for the first time, made it mandatory that clergy direct all church decoration. Painting was to serve Catholicism not only in the glorification of God and his servants but also in the creation of works that would move, correct, and sustain individuals to that end. Arguing that artists should strive for theological and iconographical correctness in their representations by consulting learned theological advisors, that their principal goal was to achieve a state of grace through the study and practice of their art, and that "Christian images are directed not only toward God, but also toward ourselves and our fellow man," Pacheco cited Petrarch: "A well-painted picture gives us a pleasure that raises us to the realm of celestial love by leading us to its divine origin."[10]

a.

10.2. Detail of the west transept, San Francisco Xavier del Bac, Tucson, Arizona, 2005: a. Overall, b. medallion sculpture of Santa Gertrudis the Great. The dark skin tone on the nun saints was an apparent acknowledgment of the native congregants. (Photo by Meredith L. Milstead)

b.

Edicts, directed principally at engravings, were enacted throughout the Counter-Reformation, indeed, throughout most of the colonial period, censuring "erroneous" images or articles used in religious worship. Paintings, books, reliquaries, religious medals, rosaries, and vestments also came under the scrutiny of the Inquisition. Items considered heretical, pseudo-religious, obscene, or seditious and representations of uncanonized saints were subject to censure.[11]

Nevertheless, the state left the training and regulating of painters and sculptors of both religious and secular art largely to the guilds (and, informally, to those trained by the guilds) until late in the eighteenth century. Indeed, the Academy of San Carlos in Mexico City, the first formal fine arts academy under royal patronage in New Spain, was not founded until 1785.[12] Using plaster casts of Greek and Roman works, its imported Spanish instructors so successfully infused European academic—neoclassical—canons into their student painters and sculptors that the academy's stifling influence on the painting and sculpture of New Spain and Mexico lasted into the first decade of the twentieth century. Although one can certainly criticize the academy's insensitivity to the Mexican spirit, here at least painting and sculpture were taught as separate subjects instead of as adjuncts to retablo and church decoration.[13]

Painters

The guild ordinances of 1557 created a hierarchy of painters—apprentices (aprendizes), journeymen (oficiales), and masters (maestros)—and established examination fees, as well as fines for those who violated the terms of the ordinances. Revised in 1686, these ordinances stipulated that apprentices had to be Spanish; modified in 1704, they permitted Indian painters to sell their works provided they had passed the master examination, becoming *maestros examinados*.[14]

For that examination, a candidate maestro had to produce a work that demonstrated his knowledge of anatomy, the proportions of humans and animals, and perspective, as well as his ability to achieve specific effects of light and shadow, of fabrics, and of flesh with paints and glazes, on the one hand; and to depict different facial types and expressions, human and animal figures in various positions, architecture, landscapes, flowers, fruits, and foliage, on the other. Moreover, he had to do so in as permanent a fashion as possible, so as not to cheat his customers. Although the ordinances make no mention of them, a maestro had to know other secrets of the trade as well, chief among which were how to apply sizing and priming to linen, how to prepare metal and wooden supports, how to grind and make pigments, and how to prepare paints and varnishes—skills he acquired in fulfilling the duties of his apprenticeship.

Because of the enormous amount of decoration required by the burgeoning construction of churches and conventos during much of the colonial era, most paintings tended to be group efforts of workshops. A master painter would train and keep assistants who would follow his instructions and many times do the bulk of the painting from his sketch or cartoon. The maestro might step in at the end and place a few finishing touches to the piece, tying it all together, adjusting lines or color tones, and even perhaps signing his name. Generally, however, signatures are to be found on works created as individual pieces or on the most important painting in a retablo rather than on minor works in a series used to fill spaces in a retablo or on a wall. Signatures are now missing on many paintings in northern New Spain because of subsequent cropping, deterioration of paint and canvas, or overpainting in restorations, or because the artist may have signed only one in a series of paintings. Whatever the reason, the absence of a signature often makes it impossible to match a painting with the correct painter's name in the multitude of names known to us from contracts, guild records, or other legal documents.

Paintings signed by or attributed to competent and significant artists in Mexico City were spread throughout northern New Spain, not only in large metropolitan churches but in small villages and missions as well. Some of these works are still extant. Sebastián Salcedo, whose paintings dated "1779" are included in a collateral altar of La Enseñanza, Mexico City, is represented in northern New Spain by a painting of Our Lady of Guadalupe bearing the same date at the church of the same name in Santa Fe (New Mexico). A painting of the Immaculate Conception behind the altar in the *sala capitular* of the Cathedral of Durango is certainly the work of Miguel Cabrera (1695–1768), an extremely popular and important eighteenth-century Mexico City painter, as is another canvas representing the titular figure in the Santuario de

Guadalupe in Chihuahua City. A signed painting of Saint Rosalie in the Cathedral of Santa Fe may well be Cabrera's; numerous other paintings in the churches of the city of San Luis Potosí are attributed to him.[15] Also at the Santuario de Guadalupe in Chihuahua City are four large paintings by José de Paez (born 1720 and active in Mexico City from about 1755 to 1790). Paez painted the canvases for the retablo mayor of San Francisco de Asís, also in Chihuahua City; some six individual paintings from that now-disassembled retablo are in the choir and sacristy.

A painting of Our Lady of Sorrows by another Mexico City painter, Juan Correa (active 1675–1714), accompanied Father Eusebio Francisco Kino, Jesuit missionary to the Pimería Alta in the late seventeenth and early eighteenth centuries, to Mission Dolores in Sonora.[16] On the sacristy wall of the Cathedral of Durango are four large but not particularly good paintings dated "1686" and attributed to Correa, but more likely done in his workshop, as probably were parts of the now-disassembled main retablo dedicated to the life of Christ. Also attributed to Correa are (at least) four paintings in the Santuario de Guadalupe in Chihuahua City and nine in Nuestra Señora de Guadalupe de Cuzárare (formerly, Los Cincos Señores de Cuzárare; Chihuahua).[17] A much-restored painting of the Assumption of the Virgin signed "Juan Correa," which according to Domínguez, was given to the Indians of the Pecos mission by the king of Spain, is now in the parish church of the village of Pecos (New Mexico).[18] The enormous number of works attributed to Correa can be partly explained by his large workshop and by his widespread popularity, which spawned many imitators, if not outright forgers. Indeed, works and pieces bearing his signature can be found throughout Mexico, Guatemala, and Spain (especially in Andalucía). An excellent painting of the Baptism of Christ in the baptistery of Santa María de Charcas (San Luis Potosí), signed "Juan Correa" and dated "1690," is definitely his.

Clearly departing from the European convention of blond hair, blue eyes, and fair skin, some of the images of the infant Jesus and cherubs (angelitos) painted by Correa—and by a number of other seventeenth- and eighteenth-century artists in New Spain—are clearly dark-haired, dark-eyed, and dark-skinned. In noting these departures, Elisa Vargas Lugo proposes that their work was influenced by the racial mixtures around them and, further, that Correa, himself a mulatto, was expressing the spiritual equality of *gente de quemado* (dark-skinned people of mixed blood) with their fair-skinned, "pure-blooded" European counterparts.[19]

The work of a lesser Mexico City painter, Fray Juan de Herrera (1729–1780), hangs in one of the chapels of San Miguel Arcángel in Moctezuma (Sonora). Works by Ramón de Torres (active from 1777), also from Mexico City, are displayed in the Cathedral of Chihuahua; his signed painting of Saint Ignatius of Loyola, property of the Museum of International Folk Art in Santa Fe (New Mexico), is presumed to have belonged originally to a New Mexican church. There are certainly still other paintings by these and lesser-known but competent artists awaiting identification tucked away in other churches of northern New Spain.

Paintings

Until the nineteenth century, subject matter, materials, and techniques were closely watched by the Church, which was concerned with correct representation of religious figures and themes, and by the guilds, concerned with monitoring craftsmanship, materials, and price. Guilds not only established guidelines for skills, training, and hierarchy of craftsmanship, but also acted to exclude certain racial types from their upper ranks, particularly in the sixteenth century (see also discussion of guilds under "Builders" in chapter 4).

The paintings produced by colonial artists in traditional workshops were artistically and technically competent. Yet, at the same time, most lacked creativity and individuality, seldom going beyond the academic, predictable, and ecclesiastically correct.[20] In contrast, paintings by native artists or nonacademics, however unpolished and technically maladroit, stood out for their vitality and novelty (especially in solving problems of perspective), and often for their distinctive character, robustness, and charm.

Although, reflecting the power of the baroque, most viceregal paintings are highly charged with emotion, the cloying sentimentality and saccharine sweetness present in many reflect efforts to copy certain highly popular Spanish artists, in particular, Bartolomé Esteban Murillo (1584–1640), whose oeuvre was characterized by elegance, grace, and gentle sensitivity. Neoclassicism would preserve much of the sentimentality of Murillo's less gifted imitators, but replace the exuberance and virility of the baroque with the cool refinement and proportion of the rediscovered classical artistic and architectural ideals (see also chapter 2).

Pigments and Paints

By finely grinding and washing native or imported colored minerals or by using organic substances, in their natural state or prepared by chemical methods, the artists of northern New Spain (or their apprentices) produced the pigments needed for their paints. These pigments were then suspended in some medium: in the case of oil paint, in a drying oil, preferably linseed but also any of several less expensive oils produced from pressing or heating certain seeds, such as salvia, sunflower, or hemp; in the case of tempera paint, in milk and egg white.[21] (See also "Pigments" and "Binders and Sealers" under "Materials" in chapter 4.) Diluted with solvents, the paints were then brushed onto the prepared panel or surface.

Painting on Walls

In this most straightforward approach, images were painted directly onto plaster walls. Exterior as well as interior surfaces were decorated—façades and crossings, with trompe l'oeil columns, cornices, and moldings; dados, with painted tilework patterns; ceilings and inside walls, with portraits or scenes from the lives of saints and with all manner of geometric, plant, and figural motifs. Every opportunity was taken to embellish church walls within and without for the greater glory of God and his servants as well as to inspire and instruct the believers. Religious paintings, some celebrating the founders of orders or of particular conventos, others conveying more esoteric religious messages, also lined the cloister walls of the wealthier conventos.

In the sixteenth century, using the fresco secco technique, which might more accurately be called "painting with lime," artisans mixed their water-based paints with lime water before applying them to a smoothed, dried, and burnished plaster wall, upon which they had carefully sketched, traced, or stenciled a design. As with the original fresco (*buon fresco*) technique, fresco secco produced a delicate and transparent effect.[22]

In the seventeenth and eighteenth centuries, interior walls were more often painted with tempera paint, whose pigments were suspended in a water-based binder of animal protein, usually egg white and milk, although oil paint was also used on rare occasions.[23] Both kinds of paint gave artists a wide palette of opaque colors, from subtle to bold, that could be brushed on in layers without mixing with the colors beneath; they were often applied in areas inscribed by a compass, over pencil or charcoal sketches, or with stencils, most likely made from strips of leather, parchment, or paper, which enabled painters to rapidly cover large areas with a continuous or repetitive design. Freehand painting was used to suggest a texture or a different building material (such as jasper or marble), to cover up a bare wall, or to enhance the overall effect of other artwork.

The medieval device of the dossal (*dosel*), a richly worked hanging placed behind the altar or on a sanctuary wall, may have survived in the form of painted decoration on church walls, in particular, on the polygonal apses of New Mexican mission churches such as San José de la Laguna (before its whitewashing in 1968; see figure 7.28).[24]

Painting on Wood

Where canvas, tinplate, or copper sheets were unavailable, wood was used.[25] Images of saints, popularly called santos or retablos (see figure 2.27), were painted on pine or cottonwood panels (tablas) throughout New Mexico, mostly during the nineteenth century.

In other parts of New Spain, artists preferred cedar or walnut (mahogany, if available). Selecting wood with the fewest knotholes and imperfections, artisans shaped it into panels of the desired size, carefully smoothing the panels' outer surface, as well as their edges if they were to be joined together. Larger knotholes and resinous areas were burned or cut away and replaced with cylinders of the same wood; smaller knotholes or seams were covered with strips of linen; the cylinders and strips were then glued securely in place. For larger works, panels were joined together with glue, metal clamps, or dovetail mortising, reinforced from behind with heavy glue and often with a layer of canvas, leather, or maguey fibers, sometimes with crosspieces. The panels were then sealed with garlic juice or hide glue and given several coats of hot gesso (a gypsum and glue mixture), the second and each successive coat being applied before the previous coat had completely dried, until the surface was even; this was smoothed to a marblelike finish. Designs or figures were either drawn and painted or painted directly on the panels with oil or tempera paint.[26]

Painting on Fabric or Hide

Among the extant religious paintings in northern New Spain (excluding the New Mexico santo or retablo tradition), the most significant from an artistic standpoint are those of oil paint on fabric. The earliest references to paintings on fabric are in accounts of missionaries who carried with them scrolls (referred to as *sargas*) bearing representations of the mysteries of the Catholic Faith, to be used in converting and instructing the Indians.[27] Such paintings could be transported rolled on a dowel or small pole and kept secure within a tubelike case. Large paintings could be created in workshops, rolled and transported for installation, then restretched at their final destination. Indeed, the lightness and flexibility of the support figured significantly in the importation of fabric paintings into northern New Spain.

Examples of colonial oil paintings (*lienzos de pincel*, or *imágenes de pincel*) on fabric, in many cases on heavy linen canvas or jute fabric, can still be found in almost every church in northern New Spain—or in its inventory. Produced under a Spanish monopoly, linen canvas was costly and thus had to be economized.[28] When the width of the work exceeded the width of a bolt of canvas, pieces were sewn together and the seams covered over with gesso and sometimes also with strips of paper, although even smaller canvases might be stitched together in what appear to be attempts to use every available piece of the valuable material. Stretcher bars (*bastidores*) were joined into a frame using mortise-and-tenon joints or pegs, with crosspieces added for strength and to prevent warping, even for quite small paintings. The edges of the canvas were attached (with no margin because of the expense), usually with glue, to the stretcher bars, and held in place with small pegs or nails while the glue dried. The canvas was then sized—infused with hot hide glue—to seal, stiffen, and draw it drum taut; primed, usually with a thin coat of gesso, to smooth out surface irregularities and seal it even further; and given a coat of dark red-brown toning (iron oxide and ocher mixed in hide glue with a little gesso).[29] The artist would sketch his design onto the prepared canvas with charcoal either in sticks or as ink. Upon completion, the oil painting was allowed to dry before being given a final, protective coat of varnish made from plant resins, usually dammar but occasionally amber, ground and dissolved in turpentine or wine.[30] For transport over considerable distances, paintings could be removed from their stretcher bars, rolled up, and restretched on new stretcher bars at their final destinations.

Religious paintings on animal hides appear uniquely in the churches of New Mexico, dating from the mid-seventeenth century.[31] How many there were originally is not known. Domínguez mentioned almost ninety such works in his 1776 report, yet two centuries later, Boyd could account for only fifty-seven.[32] Buffalo, deer, and elk hides were tanned, and polychrome paintings of religious subjects painted upon them with water-based or, rarely, oil-based paints (figure 10.3). Although their provenance is unknown, these paintings are thought to be the work of the friars of Nuevo México or of neophytes under their direction, or perhaps to have been imported into the region from missions farther south.[33] While the artists may have had some direction, the paintings clearly lack perspective, proportion, and understanding of the principles of draftsmanship; reminiscent of the Renaissance in their decorative touches, they may well have been inspired by the imported engravings (estampas) of the sixteenth century.

Painting on Copper

Sheets of copper, pounded by hand to a thickness of about two millimeters, provided an excellent support for oil paints. The weight and rigidity of the sheets made them difficult to handle and transport, however, with the result that paintings on copper were rarely larger than 2 × 4 feet—and most no larger than 18 × 24 inches. Owing to their considerable expense, copper sheets were reserved for works executed with great care and technical skill. Such paintings, though rare in northern New Spain and generally antedating the nineteenth century, could be found in wealthier churches and conventos. The slightly undulating surface of the finely pounded copper, combined with its imperviousness, created a smooth, molded surface to the painting, conspicuously different from the textured surface of oil paint on fabric or wood.[34]

10.3. Painting on hide, Nuestra Señora de Guadalupe, New Mexico. (Courtesy of New Mexico State Museum, Santa Fe)

Prints

From the very beginning of the Conquest and colonization of New Spain throughout the nineteenth century, inspiration for decorations as well as religious paintings can be traced to imported European etchings and engravings, and later to lithographs—known generally as estampas or láminas.[35] Whether sold separately as inexpensive illustrations and distributed among converts and the devoted alike or used as illustrations for missals, Bibles, or religious tracts, they were widely disseminated to all areas of New Spain. Their influence can be clearly seen when they are compared with colonial paintings; the use of specific engravings is well documented in the Indian Juan Gerson's painting of the sotocoro of Tecamachalco (México) in 1562.[36] That estampas are found in many mission inventories reflects the widespread need for inexpensive, easy-to-transport religious images (see figure 12.19).[37] They are largely responsible for the rapid assimilation and copying by the artists of northern New Spain of styles and formulas—not only from Spanish but also from Italian, German, and Flemish artists. From the end of the eighteenth century, the even cheaper process of lithography replaced the engravings and etchings and served to introduce neoclassicism and new cults. The highly impermanent character of paper, however, has left few prints extant from the many that once existed in northern New Spain.

Sculptors

Whereas painters often signed their work, both for the prestige and as a guarantee of quality and religious orthodoxy, only in extremely rare instances were sculptures signed. This was so, not because sculptors were more modest or less responsible than painters, but because, far more than paintings, sculptures demanded an amalgamation of various skills and the collaboration of many artisans; and because, again far more than paintings, sculptures were perceived as parts of a retablo or altar assemblage, rather than as artworks in their own right. In communities large enough to support them, there were sculptors' workshops where the sculptures destined to fill the retablos of local churches and conventos, private chapels, or other localities were carved, assembled, gilded, and decorated.

Just like painters, sculptors were subject to their own set of guild ordinances, which set clear standards of performance. These standards applied not only to sculptors of figures but also to sculptors of architectural details and ornamentation, who had to know how to correctly reproduce the five classic orders. To become a maestro sculptor, a candidate had to demonstrate his knowledge of geometry, anatomy, human proportions, and drawing, as well as his mastery of sculpture, by sculpting both clothed and nude figures. In order to paint or guild figures, sculptors also had to be examined and approved for those occupations; those practicing without approval were subject to heavy fines. The friars' fear that religious ignorance might result in the incorporation of heretical images and symbols into religious art caused them to pay special attention to the work of native Indian painters and sculptors.

Sculptures

A great many colonial sculptures intended for use in church interiors were made from wood using techniques developed to a very high degree in Europe centuries before the Conquest.[38] These carvings in relief or in the round were meant to be painted, gilded, or both. For this reason, they are sometimes identified under the generic term "polychrome" (multicolored).[39] I discuss such sculptures and others intended for placement within and without the church building according to their constituent materials, construction, or purpose.

Wood

The principal woods used by guild workshops to produce almost all the religious sculptures in northern New Spain (outside New Mexico) were *ayacahuite* pine (*Pinus ayacahuite*), black poplar, cedar, chestnut, linden, mahogany, oak, pear, walnut, and yew.[40] Selected for their hardness, strength, grain, ease of sculpting and sanding, and resistance to splintering—and harvested only at particular times of the year to minimize the amount of sap present—these varieties were native to or imported into the guild regions of Mexico City, Querétaro, Puebla, and Guadalajara.

Apart from images for dressing (described later), figures sculpted from wood (bultos) can be grouped into two large categories: hollow, plank construction and solid wood body.[41]

Hollow, plank construction (*embón*). For hollow plank construction, the artisan created a rectangular box—sized to the dimensions of the figure required—from a number of wood planks fitted, glued, and doweled together.[42] Generally speaking, this technique was used for figures taller than one hundred centimeters (forty inches). Because weight was a consideration in larger statues, the planks enclosed an empty space if the back was to be decorated, or the back was deliberately left open if the statue was to be butted up against a niche. Cypress was the wood most commonly used. To combat its tendency, especially when not properly seasoned, to crack at joints and along the grain from alternately absorbing moisture (expanding) and drying out (contracting), planks were thinly sawn and planed from pieces chosen for their clearness (lack of knots) and smoothness of grain.

This basic box shape was used for the figure from the shoulders down, shaping the box into the desired figure. Arms, hands, and the head were either carved separately then attached with dowels and glue, or roughly shaped and attached, then finished with the rest of the figure. In many pieces, the base support and the feet were carved from the solid bottom of the box. Base, feet, body, and garments were treated as one piece in the original box assembly and were separated only by gouging away the excess wood. If the sculptor carved too deeply and cut through the sides, the flaws were covered with strips of canvas glued in place. If the figure was to have glass eyes, the sculptor sawed off the face, made cavities from behind for the eyes, secured glass eyeballs in place, and glued the face back on before attaching the head to the body with dowels. The quality of the wood was carefully considered; knots were sometimes removed and the holes covered with cloth patches and glue to prevent resin from leaking through and spoiling the finish. Strips of cloth were glued over all seams and wood joints to strengthen and conceal them. The figure was then given several coats of gesso in varying grades, from coarsest to finest. After sanding to achieve a marblelike finish, the decorating began. Figure 10.4 depicts an ideal reconstruction of this type of figure, many real-life examples of which exist in northern New Spain to this day.

Solid wood body (figuras de palo). Figures generally under one hundred centimeters (forty inches) in height were small enough to be carved from either a single piece of wood or from pieces glued and doweled solidly together, perhaps laminated for strength and to reduce the likelihood of splitting, twisting, and cracking. Arms, hands, and head were added to the body and decorated as they were for the hollow, plank construction.

[Cane, Corn Cane and Paste] Cane figures (*figuras de caña*) include corn cane and paste figures made by the Tarascans of Michoacán (*figuras de caña de maíz* or *figuras de pasta de Michoacán* or *tarascas*). These extremely lightweight images were created with certain pastes over supports of cane or corn cane fibers or pieces of wood and paper. They could be either stationary in their pose and decoration or hinged and dressed in cloth garments.

An excellent example of coopting indigenous techniques and materials to Christian needs is the process of creating molded and painted figures from plant materials, which was used in central and western Mexico in pre-Columbian times—notably in the areas of the Valley of Mexico, Tlaxcala, and Michoacán.[43] Originally employed in the making of idols, after the Conquest, the process was quickly recruited for producing Christian images, and this technique endured through much of the viceregal period.[44] Sizes of cane figures were distinguished in the late sixteenth century: small sizes were referred to as "domestics" (*domésticas*), probably implying a size for individuals' homes or chapels; life-size figures, as *estatura perfecta*.[45]

Figures were fashioned using a water-soluble glue (variously called *tzauhtli, tatzingue, tzatzingui, tatzingueni,* or *tzingui*) made from a particular orchid (*Sobralia citrina*) and a paste made from the pulp of the heart of a cornstalk.[46] Pieces of lightweight wood (*colorín* or *tzompantli*); bundles of corn stems; maguey stalks; rolled tubes of *papel amate* (a clothlike fiber made from wild figs); and even pages from discarded documents, manuscripts, and choir books provided a skeletal support. The paste was molded onto the framework to shape the body, face, hands, and feet of the figure. The various layers of paste, pith, paper, wood, and the like were bound together with the orchid-bulb glue, which, though not as strong as animal or hide glues, lost less volume upon drying and prevented cracking or separation between the different veneers. The surface of the figures was treated in the same way as traditional *maque* lacquerware of Michoacán. Salvia oil (*chía*), sifted dolomite (*tepúshuta*), and *aje* (an oily, yellowish substance from the scale insect *Coccus axin*), and the appropriate pigments were carefully mixed together.[47]

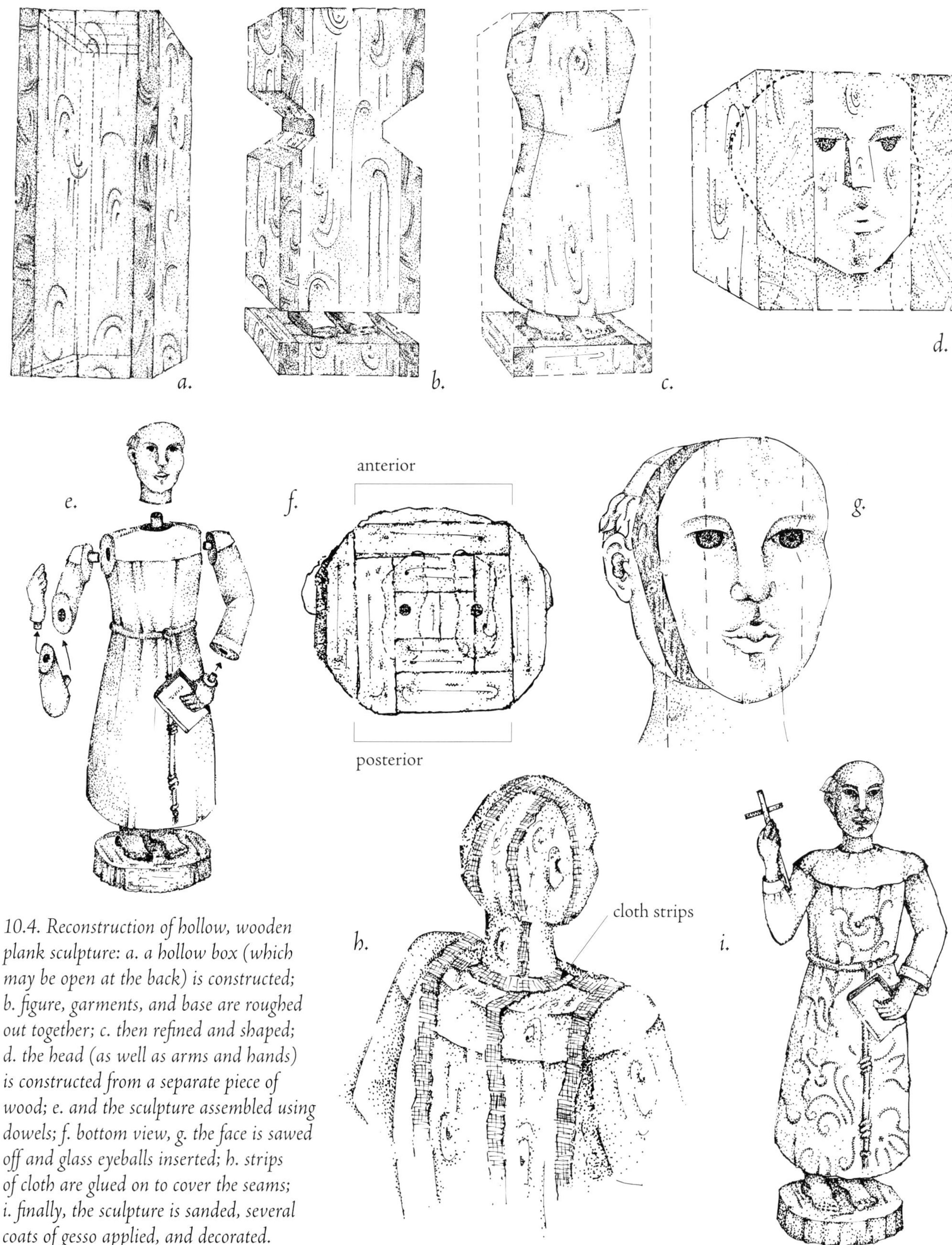

10.4. Reconstruction of hollow, wooden plank sculpture: a. a hollow box (which may be open at the back) is constructed; b. figure, garments, and base are roughed out together; c. then refined and shaped; d. the head (as well as arms and hands) is constructed from a separate piece of wood; e. and the sculpture assembled using dowels; f. bottom view, g. the face is sawed off and glass eyeballs inserted; h. strips of cloth are glued on to cover the seams; i. finally, the sculpture is sanded, several coats of gesso applied, and decorated.

10.5. Image for dressing, La Virgin María, private collection: a. undressed; b. dressed (dressed by Meredith L. Milstead).

The lacquer mixture was smoothed on in thin coats with the palm of the hand.[48] The figures were dressed either in real cloth garments or in garments molded from the same paste. The ease of transporting and producing such lightweight figures made them practical and affordable; indeed, based on church inventories, they were distributed throughout northern New Spain and are found scattered there in churches and private collections to this day. (A small caña corpus currently in the archives of the Diocese of Tucson, Arizona, is said to have originally belonged to the Convento de San Agustín at the foot of Sentinel Peak, also in Tucson.)

[Images for Dressing] A sculpture genre that flourished during the nineteenth century, though there are examples from previous centuries, images for dressing (*imágenes de vestir*; figure 10.5a–b), which could be made from either wood or cane, can be divided into two types: hinged and framework or candlestick.

Hinged figures (figuras de gozne). Most simply described as mannequins, hinged figures came in all sizes and in a variety of different forms. Their articulated joints (shoulders and elbows at the least) allowed them to assume different poses or postures and facilitated changing their clothes. Made to be covered entirely with garments created specifically for them, the figures' torsos and limbs were carved smoothly, with the barest hint of body contours, while great detail was given to the exposed hands, face, and feet. Reverence dictated that the body be painted down to the ankles and wrists and up around the shoulders (giving an unclothed statue the appearance of someone in long johns). Light blue was the most popular color, but occasionally brown was used. Wooden joints or leather hinges were fitted at the arm and shoulder and occasionally at the wrist, hand, hip, and knee for figures of Christ intended to be posed in different ways to illustrate scenes from the Passion (figure 10.6). These figures could be positioned at columns, shown embracing Mary in a dramatization of the last meeting between mother and son prior to his Crucifixion—a scene referred to as "the encounter" (*el encuentro*); attached to crosses; or placed in sepulchers. Depending on the incident of the Passion to be portrayed, Jesus might be clothed in an actual purple robe (most often velvet trimmed in gold braid) and white tunic, a loincloth, or a shroud.

Framework, or candlestick, figures (bastidores or candeleros). The face and hands of framework, or candlestick, figures, and generally also the torso and arms, were carved or molded in the round, painted, and attached to a truncated, cone-shaped support made of ribs or slats nailed or doweled to a platform. The conelike framework could be left open or covered with glue-soaked cloth attached at critical points and occasionally painted and decorated. Both sections, the support as well as the usually plain upper half (torso), were concealed by the figure's garments. This method of construction could eliminate considerable weight for those life-size figures specifically intended as processional figures. Furthermore, the desire for dramatic realism could be achieved most easily by dressing the figure realistically; and if the figure were intended to be clothed anyway, there would be no reason to carve and paint it entirely, complete with garments, when only the hands and head were to be seen. Even though they would be completely clothed, the upper torso and arms to the wrist were nevertheless painted to simulate clothing. The technique for carving, the inclusion of glass eyes, and the application of flesh-colored paints were the same in these as in other images for dressing.

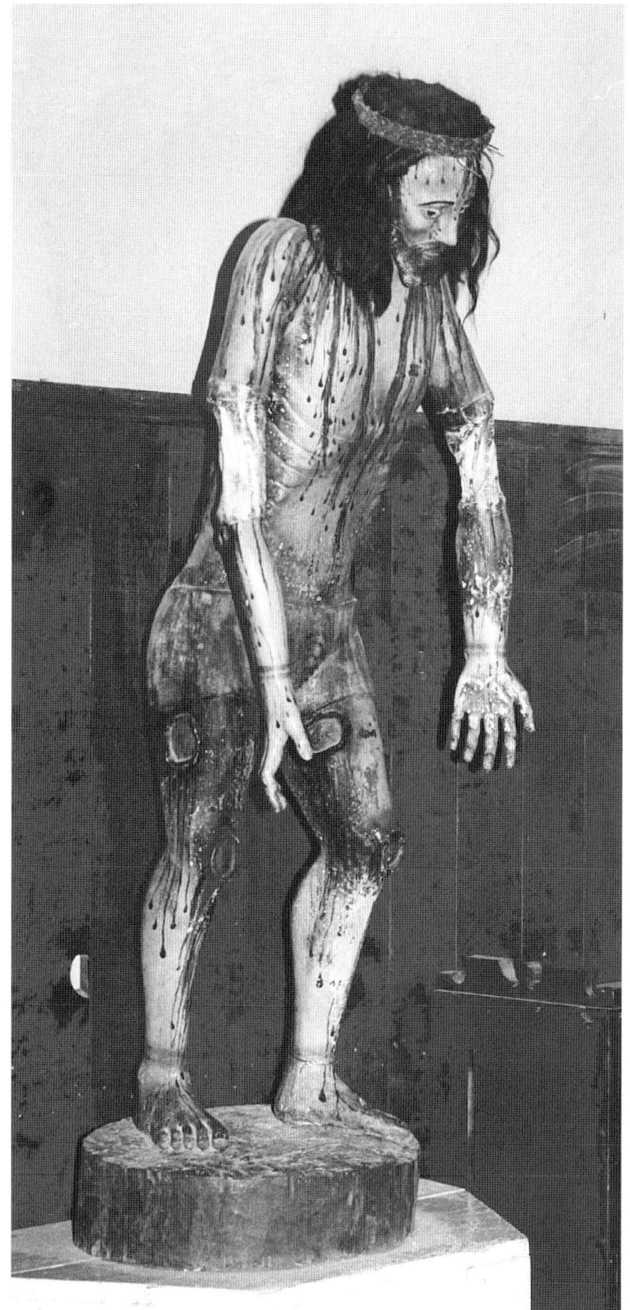

10.6. Hinged figure of Christ, Santa María de Natívitas, Bachíniva, Chihuahua, 1992.

A frequent subject of images for dressing was the Sorrowful Mother (La Mater Dolorosa; figure 10.7). After being carried in processions during Holy Week, her image was then placed on an altar or space dedicated to her, such as one associated with the Crucifixion, for the rest of the year. But Mary was not the only subject created, nor were all the images life-size. Other cult images also commonly had changes of wardrobes, whose extent and richness depended on the devotion and wealth of cult followers, who might be either individual parishioners or religious orders. Indeed, clothing for religious images is commonly listed in church inventories throughout northern New Spain, where it was considered part of a church's accountable property.

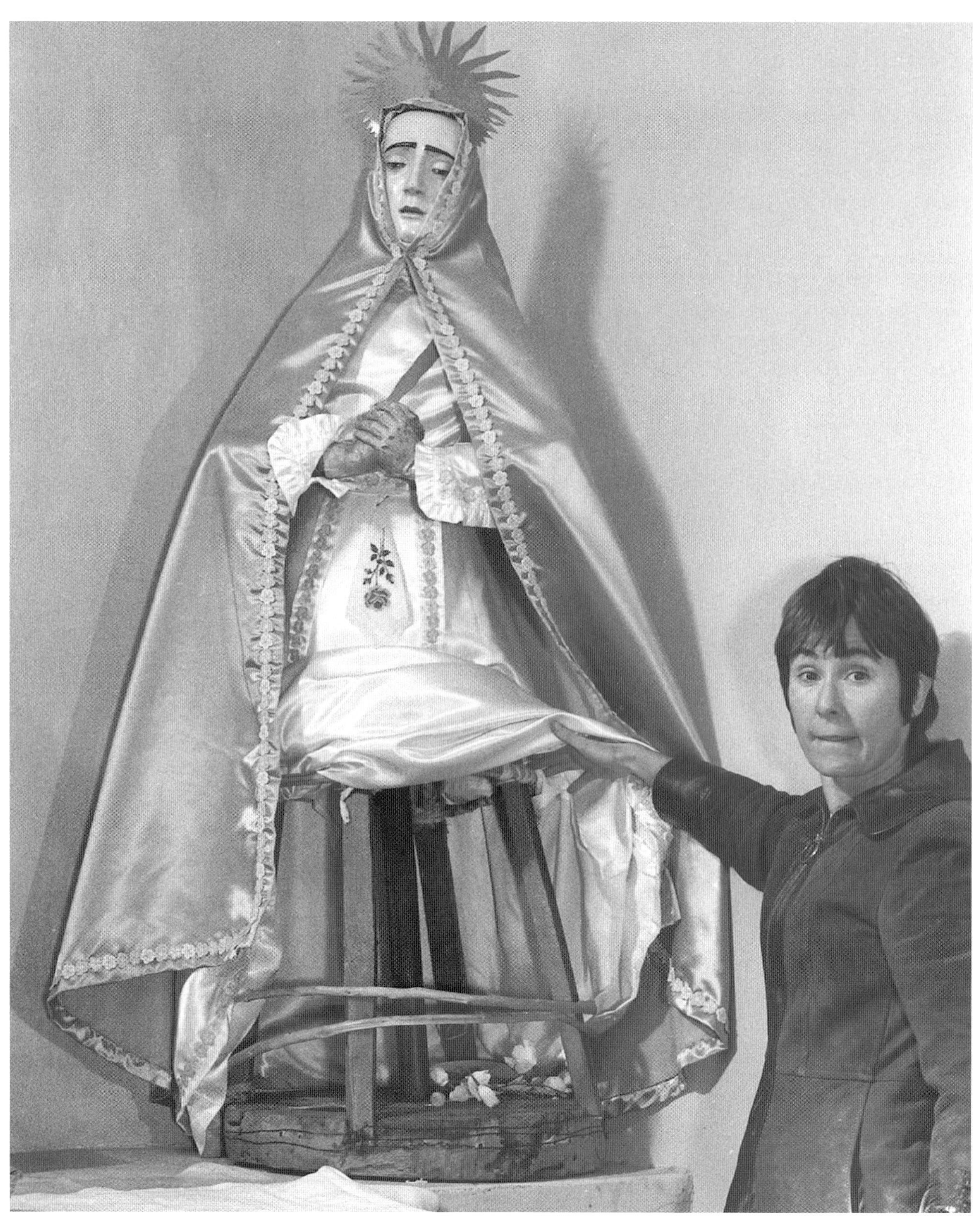

10.7. Candlestick figure, La Mater Dolorosa, San Pedro y San Pablo, Tubutama, Sonora, 1975. The author is holding up the image's skirt to show the figure's construction.

Although the tradition in Spain of offering embroidered clothes to the Virgin dates back to the thirteenth century, in the sixteenth and seventeenth centuries, Spanish bishops officially censured the dressing of religious images; in 1585, the third Provincial Council of New Spain sternly ordered that images' garments be made an integral part of the figures.[49]

In Spain sculpted figures of a particular holy personage occasionally became regarded as someone else—even someone of the opposite sex. Although reattribution could occur innocently through loss of a figure's original attributes or with the development of beliefs or confusion on the part of the public concerning the image and its identification, occasionally a figure's identity was changed deliberately. In some instances, body parts were exchanged or the figure redressed because of some specific local need. This was considered neither a perversion nor an abuse but rather a matter of practicality.[50] While not common, there are a few such examples of such "cross-dressed" saints (*santos travestidos*) in northern New Spain. For example, the sepulchered figure revered as San Francisco Xavier at San Xavier del Bac near Tucson (Arizona) is in reality an articulated figure of Christ, most likely the sepulchered Christ mentioned in accounts of figures left at this church for safekeeping by the natives of Mission San José de Tumacácori (Arizona) when the latter mission, some thirty miles south of San Xavier, was abandoned in 1828.[51]

[Images with Glued Cloths] Another technique used to create realistic garments for a sculpted religious image, introduced in the second half of the eighteenth century, was glued cloths (*telas encoladas* or *telas escayolas*). A figure was carved with a minimum of garment detail, then cloth cut to fit it, a garment constructed, and then sometimes the figure actually sewn into the garment. Attached to the figure with nails or pegs, the cloth was dipped in gesso and draped or pushed into shapes as it dried, with gathers and folds skillfully manipulated to suggest the volume of the figure and to create the illusion of real garments ruffled by a breeze. Additional coats of gesso were applied to help hide the seams and secure the cloth firmly to the wood body. Once covered with gesso and smoothed, the cloth garment was painted and decorated like any other type of sculpted figure. Images with glued cloths are found throughout northern New Spain in varying sizes and degrees of elaboration. Some smaller images have almost all their garments carved from wood, with cloth attached as a mantle or cape only; others have only the barest body form shaped from wood and are garbed entirely with gesso-stiffened cloth. Ambitious examples are life-size angels that appear on either side of the sanctuary at San Xavier del Bac in Tucson (Arizona). Sleeved tunics, completely sewn and fitted, with sleeves pushed up over the elbows, were placed on these images, then coated with layers of gesso. Waists were created by cinching a sisal cord around the images' middles (the cord appears to have served also as a hanging device while the images were drying and being painted). To suggest that the angels were in flight, their skirts were pulled back into ruffles, exposing their knees and legs to simulate the effects of wind upon cloth. Various colors were used to create a floral pattern, and gilt paint applied along the garments' edges to create a rich trim (figure 10.8). The fire-damaged figure of Saint Cajetan now in the museum of San José de Tumacácori affords us a clearly exposed view of the technique (figure 10.9).

[Processional Figures] In addition to sculptures made specifically for inclusion within a retablo or within their own niches along the walls of the church, groups of sculpted figures, polychrome and life-size and representing Jesus, Mary, and various saints in scenes from the Passion, were mounted on portable platforms to be carried through the streets during Holy Week by a number of men, either in their hands and arms or on their backs and shoulders. Single, especially significant sculpted figures were similarly treated on their feast days. The appearance of these processional figures (pasos) in New Spain was strongly curtailed from the start of the nineteenth century; little remains in modern Mexico of the baroque tenor, spectacle, and emotion that once surrounded these figures during Holy Week and on feast days—and that still do in contemporary Spain, especially Sevilla.

Lime Plaster

Figures could be carved or molded from lime plaster thickly applied to walls and other architectural elements, or they could be cast into shapes and attached to surfaces or supports. Although good-quality lime plaster skillfully worked lends itself to minute and intricate surface detail, generally speaking, plaster carving in northern New Spain was rather heavy-handed. There were, of course, excep-

10.8. Image with glued cloths, one of several angels in the sanctuary of San Francisco Xavier del Bac, Tucson, Arizona, 2001. (Photo by Meredith L. Milstead)

tions. Some excellent examples of the plasterer's craft may be seen in the retablos and the angels and other religious images about the collateral altars of San Xavier del Bac near Tucson (Arizona). The use of molded plaster figures large enough for inclusion in retablos did not become widespread until the mid-nineteenth century, but these have now replaced the traditionally sculpted wood figures in most new or refurbished churches and altars. Lime plaster was also used to create religious images for exterior display. Not surprisingly, most have been badly eroded. Judging from sections that were at least somewhat protected, however, the handling is vigorous, though not particularly refined.

Limestone

Found mostly on church exteriors throughout northern New Spain, with a few exceptions such as the retablos from La Castrense in Santa Fe (New Mexico; see figure 2.26) and in the Cathedral of Chihuahua (Chihuahua; see figure 6.13), limestone sculptures survive in anywhere from excellent to lamentable condition, depending on the hardness of the stone and the efforts made to protect it from the elements. On some façades where a soft variety of stone was used, erosion has caused profound damage to individual statues as well as to entire frontispieces (see figure 6.27), making assessment of the sculptors' skill all but impossible. During the neoclassic era, the coolness and propriety of limestone and lime plaster made them preferred replacement materials for the wooden, gilded baroque retablo. In many limestone sculptures, however, the original crispness of detail has been obscured by repeated applications of whitewash, plaster, and paint on both figures and framing elements.

Alabaster

Fairly easy to carve, alabaster has an appealingly smooth, satiny finish and a translucent glow. Most pieces have a soft, rounded quality directly related to the structure of the material and the difficulty or impossibility of achieving a sharp, hard edge. Although extant examples in northern New Spain are few, the high technical quality of the work attests to the experience and skill of the sculptors, about whom unfortunately little is directly known.

Besides the baptismal fonts of Baja California, two fine examples of alabaster sculptures in northern New

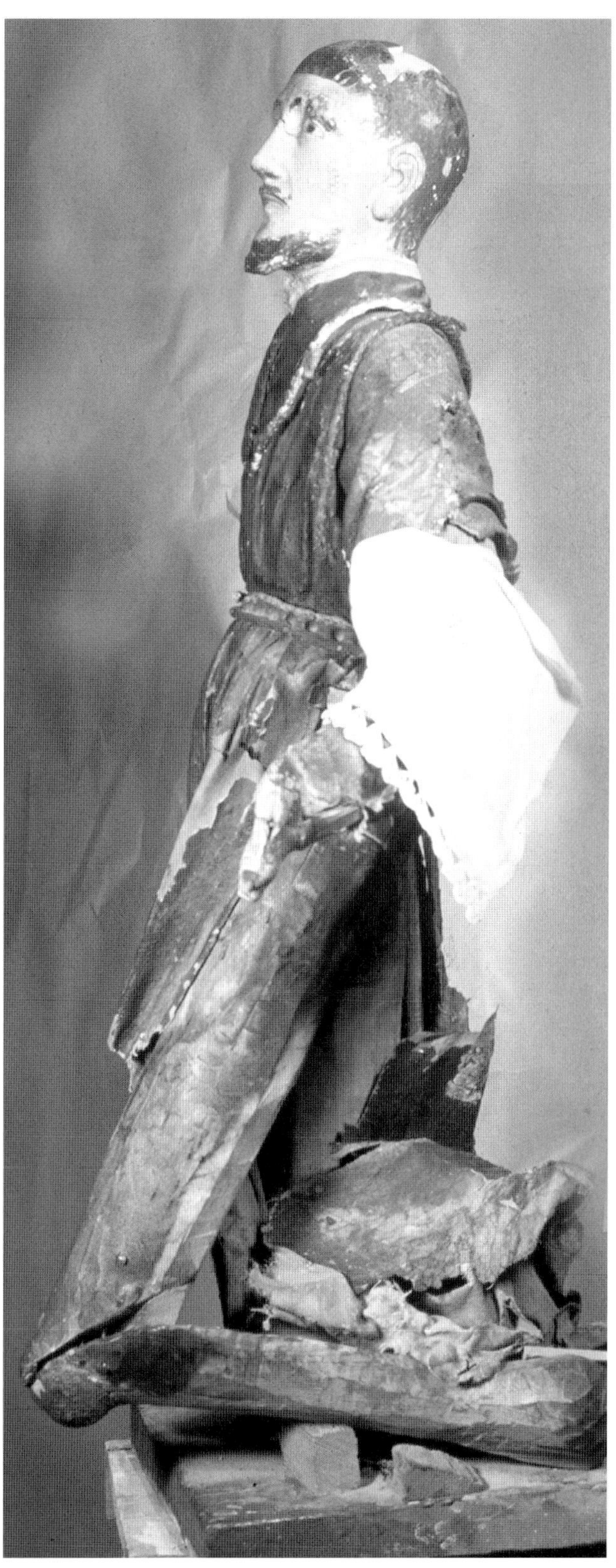

10.9. San Cayetano, prior to conservation, an image with glued cloths in the museum of San José de Tumacácori, Arizona, 1975.

Spain are the pulpits of Nuestra Señora de Guadalupe in Ojo de Agua and Nuestra Señora del Rosario in Charcas (both in the state of San Luis Potosí; see figures 4.8 and 4.9). Most likely done by different sculptors (the quality of the work at Charcas is finer, the proportions of the figures and ornamental designs more sophisticated, and the figures polychrome with touches of gilt), both pulpits depict the Four Evangelists. It is also possible that, hidden beneath layers of paint or whitewash, are still other alabaster relief carvings on frontals, retablo predellas, and baptismal fonts elsewhere in northern New Spain.

Ivory

Numerous ivory figures of saints, Christ, and Mary—or ivory heads and hands to be attached to wooden bodies—were imported into New Spain from the Philippines; these are listed in mission inventories throughout northern New Spain.[52] Trade in ivory figures and parts of figures flourished from the sixteenth to the mid-nineteenth centuries. Dutch and Portuguese traders brought uncarved ivory from East Africa, Mozambique, and India to the Spanish and Portuguese colonies of Manila and Goa, respectively, where it was used for creating exquisitely carved religious figurines, some of which made their way to New Spain. Ivory pieces may also have been produced in New Spain by Oriental immigrants, as they almost certainly were by non-Orientals there.[53]

Christian images sculpted from ivory by sixteenth-century Chinese artisans exhibit not only Oriental facial features but anatomical conventions derived from the Buddhist art of India.[54] It is therefore not surprising to see ivory images of the Christ child with chubby thighs and knees, a sagging belly, and a neck ringed with folds of fat. Similarly, those of the Virgin and Saint Joseph share the thick-lidded, half-closed eyes; fleshy, elongated earlobes; tapering hands and feet; and rings of fat about the neck of Buddha images. Paint and gold leaf were used to enhance details; many of the larger images of Christ crucified reflect the natural bend of the elephant's tusk in the slowly curving body.

Metals

Because of their weight and in some cases cost, metals were reserved for miniature figures (see also chapter 8 for further discussion of the use of precious metals). These ranged from crudely cast specimens of iron and brass to exquisitely refined pieces in gold and silver. Small brass and lead figures of Christ crucified, symbols of the Passion, bas-relief figures of La Mater Dolorosa, the I N R I (see also "Letters and Monograms" in chapter 11), and decorative finials were shipped to churches throughout northern New Spain where, on arrival, they were mounted on wooden crosses (figure 10.10).[55]

10.10. Missionary crosses, private collection. The metal figures were cast separately and shipped to churches, where they were mounted on crosses.

Wax

Natural, colored, or bleached beeswax was molded or cast into religious figures in New Spain. Figures were molded or cast on a wire framework from colored waxes stiffened with agents such as whiting to retard sagging or distortion. They were later carefully dressed with cloth garments or covered with colored and gilded wax molded, carved, and inscribed to suggest clothing. Because wax is sensitive to heat and its unprotected surfaces susceptible to damage, few wax sculptures survive in northern New Spain. Nevertheless, the ease of molding multiple images from this inexpensive material, which can be treated to simulate rich and precious effects, suggests that a large body of wax figures about which we are unaware probably once existed. The pieces that do survive are impressive in

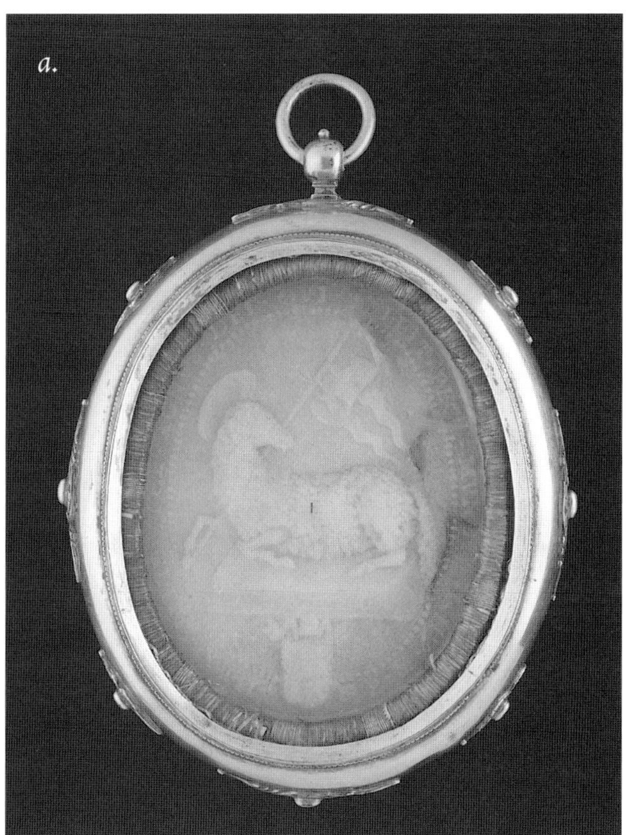

10.11. Agnus Dei medallion, private collection: a. front and b. back. (Photo by J. Anthony Richardson)

their variety, the quality of their workmanship, and the unusual and pleasing effect of the material. Of particular interest are the still-extant figures, heads, and busts of religious characters made from wax that adorned niches and shelves of churches or shrines, as well as the figures of the Holy Family, angels, and a variety of animals that filled colonial and nineteenth-century *nacimientos.* The translucent and sometimes tinted wax is attractive and can generate a startlingly lifelike impression of flesh.[56]

Another category of wax objects are round or oval Agnus Dei medallions, ranging from one to six inches in diameter and bearing a raised effigy of Mary, a saint, or a pope on one side and a lamb with a flag or banner representing Christ as the Lamb of God on the other. Sometimes framed or encased in silver reliquary cases, Agnus Dei medallions may date from the early fourth century; by at least the ninth century, they were certainly being made as they are now, from the remnants of the paschal candle of the preceding year.[57] The material, form, and accompanying blessings of these medallions all have symbolic significance. The white wax represents the purity of Christ's conception; the cross associated with the lamb, his sacrifice. Thus, just as the blood of the paschal lamb of old protected households against avenging angels, so these consecrated medallions protect their wearers or possessors against the power of evil. They are solemnly blessed by the pope only on the Wednesday of Holy Week in the first and every seventh year of his pontificate. The prayers of blessing invoke divine protection against the dangers of plague, flood, fire, storm, and childbirth. Miraculous effects have been traditionally associated with these blessed objects, which occasionally are listed in church inventories of northern New Spain, very possibly a gift or token of devotion from some member of the congregation (figure 10.11).

Sculpture Decorators

As previously noted, traditionally four different kinds of craftsmen may have worked together to produce a

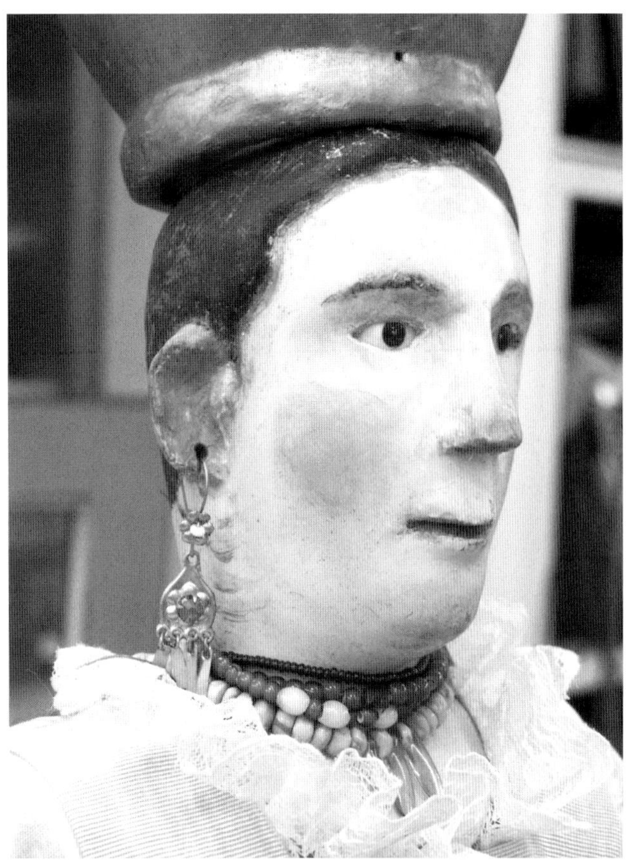

10.12. Detail of La Virgen María, private collection. (Photo by Meredith Milstead)

religious figure carved in the round (*bulto redondo*), or a gilded bas-relief figure (*santo dorado*). They were the sculptor (*entallador* or *escultor*); the painters—the one who painted garments (*imagenero*, which sometimes also refers to the sculptor as well) and the one who painted hands and face (*encarnador*)—and the gilder (*dorador*), who applied gold or silver leaf. In provincial areas, however, all steps of production may have been done by the same individual.

Decorative Techniques

In his *Arte de la pintura*, Francisco Pacheco describes the techniques involved in applying *encarnación* (flesh tones) to, gilding and painting, and otherwise decorating polychrome figures.[58] It is my opinion as an art historian and conservator of polychrome figures who has closely examined hundreds of polychrome images from throughout Mexico, Spain, Central and South America, and the Philippines, that most of the Old World techniques Pacheco describes were also observed by traditional sculpture decorators in the New World.

[Encarnación] Because the idea was to create a figure that would be as lifelike as possible, startlingly so in some instances, artisans paid great attention to simulating natural flesh tones. Meticulously blending and applying oil paint for lips, hair, and modulations of the flesh was a specialty among the decorators of religious sculptures. This technique was called encarnación and its masters, encarnadores.

Other techniques and devices reinforced the realism of encarnación. Occasionally, figures of Christ and Mary were created with smooth skulls (usually smaller than skulls would ordinarily be so that the heads when wigged would appear normal size); their scalps were delineated by dark paint so that human-hair wigs could be applied, especially on images for dressing (imágenes de vestir; figure 10.12). Other modifications on the heads include holes in Mary's earlobes for earrings and holes in the heads for supporting halos or, in the case of some figures of Christ, *las tres potencias* (see also **Tres potencias** entry in chapter 11).

To heighten the sense of realism, fringes of hair were glued to the figures' eyelids, creating lashes, and chips of bone or sometimes even real teeth were inserted into figures' mouths. Pieces of bone were incorporated in figures of Christ to simulate the exposed bones of his tortured body; hinged images for dressing were provided with a molded or carved and painted loincloth and with blood and wounds graphically portrayed in gesso and paint (see figure 10.6). And drop-shaped crystal beads or pearls were imbedded into the cheeks of La Mater Dolorosa to simulate tears.

[Gilding and Painting] A technique of gilding and painting the portion of the figure that represents the clothing, *estofado* (literally, quilting) was used on both wood figures and decorative woodwork. After the figures had been carved, coated with layers of gesso, and smoothed, the encarnación was applied and a layer of bole brushed onto the areas that would represent clothing. This extremely fine clay, usually red if gold leaf was to be used or gray or yellow if silver leaf, was mixed with glue to provide a base and enriched tone. The leaf was then applied with the aid of a wide, thin brush, which attracted and held the leafing until it was brought barely into contact with the

10.13. La Inmaculada, illustrating the estofado technique, private collection.

slightly damp bole. Once transferred to the surface, the leaf was gently tamped, allowed to dry and set, and then burnished. Some larger figures, constructed for retablos and intended to be viewed only from the front, were given the bole and leaf treatment on the facing side only. Most smaller pieces, including those intended for private altars, were decorated on all sides. A number of different burins, gouges, and punches were used to emphasize floral or geometric designs by punching or pressing gently around the edge of the pattern. Sometimes, using a technique known by the Italian term *sgraffito,* decorators would scratch through the overlying layer of paint to reveal the gold or silver leaf underneath. Leaving the design open, paints (oil- and water-based) were applied to the rest of the garment area over the remaining leaf, different colors for various layers of clothing as appropriate. With additional little touches of color for accents, the total estofado effect was one of sumptuousness (figure 10.13).

Like so much of viceregal art, estofado pieces were produced not by a master artist working alone, but by a team of artists, each having a particular specialty. The gilder (dorador) applied and burnished the gold that the estofador would then paint over and scratch through to create an imaginary cloth suggesting brocade or cloth shot through with gold or silver—always keeping in mind not just the color scheme of the retablo, but which colors were predetermined by religious dogma, the religious orders, and the status of the figure represented.

These gilded statues and the retablos that supported them acquired metaphysical significance with their richness and their capture and transfer of light. They embodied the ideal of counterreformational art: to transport the viewer by faith and belief, rather than by reason. That the images of saints from religious orders based on austerity and poverty were clothed in garments that seemed made from the richest of gold brocade was deemed not incongruous, but altogether acceptable and appropriate. In a society that measured wealth in priceless fabrics and social standing by the type and quality of a person's clothing, the opulent raiment bestowed on these images made abundantly clear to viewers the significance of God's chosen and the Church's triumphant message.[59]

The estofado tradition, abandoned early in Spain, persisted in New Spain, where regional sensibilities asserted themselves and conservative attitudes maintained the status quo into the beginning of neoclassicism. In *estofado a la chinesca* (Chinese-type estofado), silver leaf was used instead of gold, but a gold effect was created by brushing a coat of yellow lacquer over the silver. Designs were then added in various colors. Used as early as the sixteenth century on Spanish sculpture, this technique may have been inspired by the translucent effect achieved by Oriental lacquerware. From the mid-seventeenth century on, estofado was increasingly replaced by polychrome (*policromía*), in which the figures' garments were painted directly onto the gesso and gold leaf applied only to highlight designs.

10.14. Image for dressing, La Mater Dolorosa, signified by a silver dagger, San Diego de Alcalá del Pitiquito, Sonora, 2001.

Ornaments

Figures of Christ, Mary, Joseph, and some other saints were frequently given halos and crowns of silver, occasionally of gold, and Mary was given jewelry (*aderezos*).[60] These crowns and jewels, ranging from crudely shaped and incised examples to skillfully made ornate pieces that included precious and semiprecious stones, were made to accommodate figures of all sizes. Mary and Joseph are crowned to indicate their majesty and membership in the celestial hierarchy (the crowns technically should not be present in scenes depicting their mortal lives), while crowns on saints indicate their royal blood, as they do on the sainted Kings Ferdinand of Spain and Louis of France, and the Silesian duchess Saint Hedwig. In addition to halos, crowns, scepters, and rosaries, other objects of silver and gold include daggers in Mary's heart in her role as La Mater Dolorosa (figure 10.14) or the half moon beneath her feet in her role as the Immaculate Conception, Christ's crown of thorns or the tres potencias, silver sandals on El Niño figures, and Joseph's blossoming staff.

Jewelry was usually reserved for Mary, as tokens of devotion and to honor her role as Queen of Heaven. The personal jewelry of wealthy women was often donated or promised to Mary, although unfortunately few examples of the colonial jewelry that once adorned Marian figures remain. Descriptions in church inventories, portraits of colonial women, and colonial paintings of important religious images tell us much about the type and form of ornamental jewelry that may once have adorned religious sculptures in northern New Spain, as well as the effect it created.[61] From these sources and from the few remaining pieces, we know that such jewelry contained rubies, amethysts, pearls, emeralds, jet, coral, and diamonds set in cast or filigree gold and silver. Pearls were either set singly, sewn to the garment, or strung for necklaces or in ropes for swag effects over clothing.[62] Glass, silver, gold, and brass beads (with brass and silver often being gilded) appeared in necklaces and bracelets, from which hung "colored stones," very likely of glass.

Sumptuary laws to limit or control the amount of jewelry colonial women could wear were circumvented by the creation of ornamental jewelry as devotional items. A specific category meeting both descriptions, reliquaries (relicarios) are mentioned in church inventories scattered throughout northern New Spain in conjunction with the ornamental jewelry of the dressed images of the Virgin Mary, particularly those of Our Lady of the Rosary.[63] Most likely gifts from devout members of the community, these relicarios were primarily round or oval miniature religious paintings on copper, shell, and parchment, encased in silver (or sometimes gold), often with a glass cover for display and protection—not unlike a watch case or locket. Although they were worn mostly by women, other small medallions of any number of different shapes and materials that displayed or encased relics or items with religious themes might be also considered reliquaries and worn by either sex. Such medallions ranged from the size of a woman's little fingernail to three inches or more across (see also chapter 8 for the other type of relicarios).[64]

Votive Offerings

Items somehow appropriate to mention at this point are votive offerings—tokens of gratitude for divine intervention in moments of dire need. Throughout northern New Spain, though not nearly as often as in central New Spain, religious images venerated for their miraculous abilities were given votive offerings. These came largely in two popular types: the *milagros* (literally, miracles)—small replicas of limbs, organs, entire human forms, animals, or other representations, cast, cut out, or otherwise formed from metal or wax; and ex-votos—small paintings on canvas, tinplate, or wood panels.[65] Although archival evidence is scant, based on Spanish precedents, chances are good that a tradition of milagros existed in northern New Spain in colonial times.

Retablos

Behind most colonial altars was an altar screen, the retablo—generally an architectural creation of wood, stone, or brick and lime plaster that supported and framed religious images (painted, sculpted, or both). Sometimes, however, the retablo appeared as a canvas backdrop (or simply a wall) painted to simulate an actual retablo, suggesting that, where funds were limited, it was the idea and not the actuality that mattered. Its close association with the altar is such that in inventories "altar" often includes or is used interchangeably with "retablo." For the sake of precision and euphony, I have used the Spanish term throughout the text.[66]

Retablos evolved in Spain during the fourteenth century and were built there and in New Spain into the nineteenth century.[67] Depending on the space and finances available, they ranged from unpretentious, one-niche affairs for a single, central image surrounded on the sides and top by a few other images or architectural ornaments to enormous, elaborate multiniche assemblages as tall as the ceiling that held numerous images in the theme of the altar and enrich the entire altar area. No matter what its size or form, however, the retablo was designed to serve as a backdrop for the religious drama.[68]

In the absence of documentation, we can approximately date a retablo from the style of its columns, decorative devices, paintings, or sculptures, and from the overall effect of its elements. For example, in late-baroque retablos (mid- to late eighteenth century), the ornamental enrichments, paintings, sculptures, and architectural members often seem to merge painting and sculpture into one large confection (see also "Baroque" in chapter 2; "Columns" under "Architectural Details" in chapter 6; and "Sculptures" above).

With the advent of neoclassicism at the end of the eighteenth and beginning of the nineteenth centuries, however, all but a handful of gilded baroque retablos would pass into oblivion: some would be covered over; others, simply destroyed or dismantled, their components shipped off to poorer churches.[69] Where once reigned the baroque, with its theatrical swirls of golden columns, its intense contrasts of light and shade, and its unexpected, almost dizzying juxtaposition of angles and axes, now ruled the neoclassical, with its unbroken horizontal and vertical lines, its cool, unpainted gray stone or jasperized wood, its spare, classical columns, pediments, and niches, and its subdued statuary.[70]

Retablos Exteriores: Cathedral of Chihuahua

During the Counter-Reformation and the beginning of the seventeenth century, the affirmation of certain Catholic tenets placed much greater emphasis on religious processions and on the role of certain saints, causing religious figures and symbols to spill out of the interior of church buildings. As statues of religious personages such as Christ, Mary, the angels, and the saints were placed in niches in the main and side frontispieces, or atop their pediments or gables, these came to be regarded as retablos exteriores and were treated accordingly (see figures 2.12 and 2.17).

To resist the elements, the figures in retablos exteriores were generally carved from stone. Although there are some examples of figures made from carved lime plaster over a fired-brick core, they have weathered badly. Some or even all the niches in many façades (both main and side) now lack figures, whether because they were intended to remain empty or because their statues have been destroyed (by vandalism, war, insurrection, the elements, or a combination of these) and have never been replaced.

Bargellini's description shows us how the sculptural programs for the inside and the outside of the Cathedral of Chihuahua form a coordinated whole, with certain saints' images repeated along the main axis of the church, and with iconographic elements related to the cathedral, its community, and its cofradías elaborated on main and side portals.

Thus the portals contain the Apostles, Doctors of the Church, founders of the Dominican, Franciscan, Jesuit, and Oratorian Orders, angels, prophets, and saints in a systematic scheme. Inside, there are altars to Saint Joseph and the Christ of Mapimí, especially revered by local mining communities. The Virgin of Regla and Saint Benedict can be linked to specific important Chihuahuan personalities, Saint Rose of Lima, on the portal of the Capilla del Rosario, appears to have arrived with her devotees from Cusihuiriáchic (Chihuahua), another mining community, where she is the patron saint. Cofradías account for still others, such as the figure of Our Lady of Sorrows, given her own altar near the crossing.[71]

Structural Elements

Figure 10.15 illustrates the various parts making up a typical retablo.

[Base] Sometimes called the *banco* or *apostolado*, the base of the typical retablo was a predella (from Italian *predella*, kneeling stool) that contained images of religious personages who were the foundations of belief: martyrs, Apostles (hence the term apostolado), or founders of religious orders. Supporting this predella and as high as the top of the altar was the gradine (*sotobanco*, under or lower shelf), often made of masonry.

[Body] Above the base, in the body (cuerpo) of the retablo, were the columns, pilasters, and entablatures that supported the niches (*nichos* or *cajas;* sometimes also called *artesones, hornacinas, quadros,* or *marcos*),[72] statues, and paintings—and that created vertical and horizontal divisions. The framework (*armadura*) of the retablo consisted of the structural members behind the paintings and sculptures (never intended to be seen and therefore not decorated) and the forward-facing ornamental and architectural elements and supports, which were gessoed, gilded, and painted. The vertical divisions between pairs of columns built to contain religious paintings or sculptures were called "bays" (*calles* or *carreras*); those between

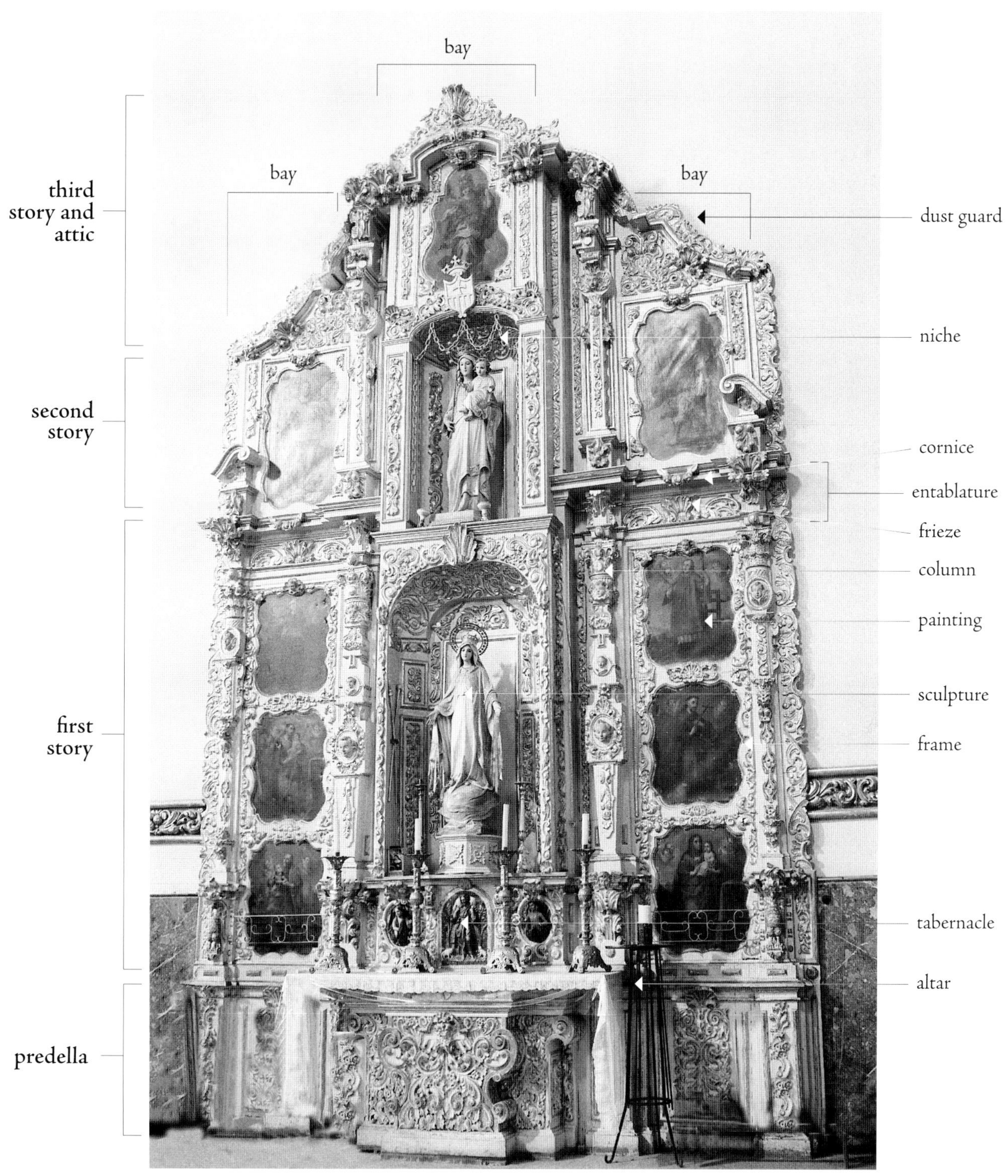

10.15. Parts of a retablo: collateral retablo of Nuestra Señora de la Merced, San Jose de Parral, Chihuahua, 1979.

columns, "intercolumnizations" (entrecalles), while the horizontal divisions were called stories or registers (niveles or cuerpos). Ordinarily, a rectangular niche was described as squared (*cuadrados*) or rounded (*redondos*), depending on the shape of its top edge. The top and bottom of the retablo were referred to, respectively, as the ceiling and floor (*cielo* and *suelo*); the main panel or surface was described by Palomero Páramo as "frontada," meaning "facing forward."[73] As a general rule, freestanding sculptures appeared later than paintings on wood or canvas in retablos, very likely in response to the desire for more realistic and lifelike images so prevalent in the Spanish baroque. At the end of New Spain's most dramatic baroque era (ca. 1740–1785), the spaces for sculpture (intercolumnizations) were the areas of concentrated decoration, which tended to overwhelm and dissolve the bays and stories, creating a wall of undulating, almost pulsating, gilded and polychromed sculpture and sculpture niches.

The most significant images were placed in the central bay of the retablo, which was usually wider than the bays on either side. Depending on its form, the topmost section of this bay was called the gable or attic (*gablete* or *ático;* but also *frontón, remate, sobrecuerpo, coronamiento, cabeza, cabecera,* or *typanium*).[74] It was most often devoted to an image or symbol of God or the Trinity, with God the Father symbolized as the uppermost vertex of a triangle. To help keep dust from settling on its figures and paintings, a device called a *guardapolvo* (literally, dust guard), and ranging from a simple molding to a canopy-like projection, was incorporated into the top edge of the retablo (figure 10.16; see also figure 2.18).

The various orders of columns reflect whatever style was popular or in fashion, and many retablos contain a variety of different orders of columns: to lighten the overall effect, the heaviest and largest columns were placed at the bottom, with progressively lighter and smaller columns in each ascending story, a device used since the Renaissance (see also "Columns" under "Architectural Details" in chapter 6).

Details and Motifs

In the later stages of the colonial baroque era, as both interior and exterior retablos grew ever more complex and ornate, those inside took the lead in their refinements and elaborations. The richly decorated column types of the mid-seventeenth century, such as the revestido columns that dominate the upper two stories of the retablo of San Ignacio in Parras (Coahuila; see figure 6.10; see also "Columns" under "Architectural Details" in chapter 6), were succeeded by the more elaborate and fanciful columnar elements of the eighteenth-century estípite style, such as those in the Retablo de Nuestra Señora de la Merced at San José de Parral (Chihuahua; see figure 2.18). Female herms flank the image of Saint James the Greater (Santiago Matamoros) in the stone retablo carved for La Castrense, now in Cristo Rey, Santa Fe (New Mexico). The four three-headed figures in the first story of that retablo have capitals of carved plant motifs, making them resemble canephorae (sing., canephora; in Spanish, *canéforas*), columnar female figures whose heads are crowned with baskets of flowers (although, true to the estípite style, each of the La Castrense figures is supported by an inverted pyramid, rather than by feet; see figure 2.26; see also "Human and Animal Shapes" under "Decorative Motifs" in chapter 6).

Common "supporting" retablo motifs included grotesques (grotescos) and cherubs (angelitos), both wonderfully exemplified in the retablo for the Mater Dolorosa altar at Santo Tomás de Villanueva de Tojorare (Chihuahua) along the south wall of the church. Here polychromed grotescos can be seen spewing flames from beneath the pedestals of statues of Saints John the Evangelist and Mary Magdalen, while still others, on the retablo's pilasters, dribble foliage from their mouths. Here, too, four beefy little seminude angelitos strain from a kneeling position to support the estípite columns of the retablo (figure 10.17a–c). Sculpted miniature angelitos also serve as corbels under columns or niches in the Nuestra Señora de la Luz retablo at San Francisco de Asís in Chihuahua City (figure 10.18) and in retablos at other churches throughout northern New Spain.

Palomero Páramo and Spanish Colonial Retablos

In his well-organized work on Sevillan Renaissance retablos, Palomero Páramo uses a system of thinly sliced classifications according to plan, function, iconography and iconographic cycles, and methods or materials of construction.[75] Because of the appropriateness of his terms to retablos in New Spain generally and to those in northern New Spain specifically, and because I prefer Palomero

10.16. Main retablo, El Templo de los Cinco Señores, Santander Jiménez, Tamaulipas, 1996.

a.

10.17. Collateral retablo of La Mater Dolorosa, Santo Tomás de Villanueva de Tojorare, Chihuahua, 2001: a. overall, the three figures are John the Evangelist, Mary as Our Lady of Sorrows, and Mary Magdalen; b. detail of grotesco; c. detail of angelito.

c.

b.

10.18. *Collateral retablo of Nuestra Señora de la Luz, San Francisco de Asís, Chihuahua City, Chihuahua, 2001.*

Páramo's treatment of retablo structure to that of other authors, I have adopted much of his schema and many of his terms, with occasional adjustments.[76] The following classifications of northern New Spain retablos are based on Palomero Páramo's categorizations as well as other descriptors used in inventories or standard sources discussing Mexican retablos. Thus retablos can be classified according to basic technique of images, placement, plan, form, function, theme, or any combination of these.

[Basic Technique] Retablos comprising painted images were often called *retablos de pincel* (literally, retablos of the brush), those comprising sculpted images, *retablos de talla, de tallado,* or *de perspectivo* (cut, carved, or three-dimensional retablos), and those comprising both, *retablos mixtos* (literally, mixed or combination retablos).

[Placement] Depending on their position within a church, retablos were categorized as principal, or main (mayores), or as collateral, or side (colaterales). This is a fundamental distinction. Each church had only one retablo mayor, placed behind the main altar within the sanctuary, an area located in the apse or at the termination of the nave. Retablos mayores, where space and funds permitted, were usually created in three stories, with a gable or attic and from three to seven bays. The theme of the retablo

mayor reflected its importance as the principal retablo and sometimes magnified the significance of the church's titular figure. For example, in a church dedicated to Saint Dominic, the retablo mayor might contain scenes relating to the life of this founder of the Dominican Order and include as well images of other saints who complement Saint Dominic and his order. Likewise, in a Franciscan church, the retablo mayor might feature images of the Immaculate Conception or scenes from the life of Mary and her parents alluding to the Immaculate Conception, the Franciscans being prime promoters of this doctrine.

The retablos colaterales were built to be placed in the transepts, in separate chapels, and along the walls of the nave.[77] Though they might be as large as two stories and three bays, they were not to exceed the size of the retablo mayor. Their themes typically related to specific cults or functions, particular advocations of donors, or the patron saint of a cofradía.

[Plan] Retablos built parallel to the wall were called lineal (*lineales*), whereas those whose sides were swung forward as if on hinges with angles close to 45 degrees were called octagonal (*octagonales* or *ochovados*). The overwhelming majority of retablos in both New Spain and northern New Spain are lineal. Although the polygonal apses of sixteenth-, seventeenth-, and eighteenth-century churches make the octagonal plan a reasonable choice, few such retablos remain, and those are only from the eighteenth century. Whitewash may have covered many retablos painted on the walls of polygonal churches (therefore also classified as octagonal), and specific archival descriptions of original retablos are scant, making it impossible to accurately estimate their number. A handful of mid-eighteenth-century octagonal retablos can be seen in northern New Spain; notably, the retablo mayor of the polygonal apse church of Guadalupe in Sombrerete (Zacatecas; figure 10.19), the retablo mayor and retablos colaterales of San Xavier del Bac, Tucson (Arizona), and the retablo mayor of Nuestra Señora de las Nieves in Palmillas (Tamaulipas; see figure 2.21).

[Form] Three of the five architectural forms commonly assumed by retablos in Renaissance Spain made their way to northern New Spain. Crucifix retablos (*retablos crucifijos*) were built to hold an image of the Crucifixion in a central cruciform recess, flanked (beneath its arms) by representations of Mary and Saint John the Evangelist. Retablos in the form of triumphal arches (*retablos arcos triunfales*) were crowned by monumental, round-arch gables, whose shape and symbolism were inspired by the Roman commemorative monuments to victory. And tabernacle retablos (*retablos tabernáculos*) were shallow structures designed to focus attention entirely on a single, central niche holding the dedicatory image.

Retablos crucifijos appear twice in the Cathedral of Chihuahua: in the polychrome and gilded wood retablo (completed 1762) of the Capilla del Cristo de Mapimí (see figure 3.22) and in the stone retablo (built 1801–1813) of the Mater Dolorosa altar (figure 10.20), as well as in several other churches in Chihuahua. In the Pimería Alta, the polychrome and gilded fired brick and lime plaster retablo in the eastern transept of San Xavier del Bac, Tucson (Arizona)—coincidentally also a Mater Dolorosa altar—can be properly classified as a retablo crucifijo (figure 10.21). A much simpler but nevertheless dramatic example is the retablo of the altar on the south wall of the former hacienda church of Nuestra Señora de los Remedios (Chihuahua; see figure 6.15).

Retablos arcos triunfales, which because of their rounded profile on the top and their position at the end of the apse served only as retablos mayores, appear in a number of churches of northern New Spain. In the former Jesuit mission church of Nuestra Señora de Loreto (Baja California Sur), paintings are arranged in a segmented arc on the top section, which is flush against the ceiling and walls and surrounded by a wooden and stone framework. The retablos mayores of other Jesuit churches nearby, San Francisco Javier de Vigge-Biaundó and San Ignacio de Kadakaaman (figure 6.6), have different arrangements in their molding and framework, but their profiles and placements still qualify them as retablos arcos triunfales. Other examples of retablos arcos triunfales include the former Jesuit retablo mayor now in place in San Francisco de Asis, Chihuahua, and the retablos mayores of Nuestra Señora del Rosario, Rosario (Sinaloa; figure 10.23). Victory symbolism notwithstanding, this particular form of retablo appears to have been chosen for aesthetic rather than doctrinal reasons.

Typically made of lime plaster over fired brick and intended to hold only one image, retablos tabernáculos abound in mission churches throughout the Pimería Alta and Chihuahua, most likely for reasons of economy and to serve late-eighteenth- and early- nineteenth-century

10.19. Octagonal main retablo, La Capilla de Nuestra Señora de Guadalupe de Sombrerete, Zacatecas, 1984.

10.20. Crucifix collateral retablo of La Mater Dolorosa, Catedral de Chihuahua, Chihuahua, 1992.

10.21. Crucifix collateral retablo of La Mater Dolorosa, San Xavier del Bac near Tucson, Arizona, 2004. (Photo by Meredith L. Milstead)

neoclassical tastes. Three notable examples are the retablos along the nave walls of San Ignacio de Cabórica (one of which is illustrated in figure 9.8) and along the wall of the north transept of the nearly ruined La Purísima Concepción in Caborca (figure 10.25; both in Sonora).[78]

[Function] Sacramental retablos (*retablos sacramentales*) occupied the head of a collateral chapel (capilla), were reserved for the Blessed Sacrament, and functioned as permanent guardians of the elements of the Communion. Reliquary retablos (*retablos relicarios*) were constructed to display the relics that motivated their construction,[79] whereas sepulchral retablos (*retablos sepulcros*) fused retablos with funerary monuments.

[Retablos, the Eucharist, and the Counter-Reformation] Centrally located on the principal altar and permanently attached there, the tabernacle (from Latin *tabernaculum*, tent, from *taberna*, hut; in Spanish, *tabernáculo*, but also called *sagrario*, from Latin *sacratus*, sacred, consecrated) was simply a cupboard with a lock for reserving the consecrated bread of the Eucharist (the Sacred Host). It was generally incorporated into the gessoed and painted wood of many baroque altars. In compliance with Church law,

10.22. Triumphal arch (former) main retablo, San Francisco de Asis, Chihuahua, Chihuahua, 2006.

10.23. Triumphal arch main retablo, Nuestra Señora del Rosario, Sinaloa, 2000.

10.24. Triumphal arch main retablo, Santa Rosa de Lima de Cusihuiriáchic, Chihuahua, 1993.

10.25. Tabernacle collateral retablo of Jesús Nazareno, north transept, La Purísima Concepción de Nuestra Señora de Caborca, Sonora, 1982.

10.26. Detail of the tabernacle showing Christ as the Good Shepherd, retablo de Nuestra Señora de la Merced, San José de Parral, Chihuahua, 2004.

the interiors of many tabernacles in northern New Spain were painted and gilded or lined with fabric. A curtain could also be hung across the tabernacle's opening behind the small door.[80] The side of the closed door facing the congregation often bore a representation of the Agnus Dei (Lamb of God), Christ as the Good Shepherd, the suffering face of Christ, or other image symbolizing the Blessed Sacrament or Christ as the sacrificial offering (figure 10.26). Although there might be more than one tabernacle in a church depending on the number of chapels where Mass was held, only one might be used for reserving the consecrated Host at any given time.

Spurred by the Counter-Reformation, the emerging Eucharistic cult gave rise to the Forty-Hour Devotion (approved by Pope Paul IV in 1560) as well as to the development of benedictions, processions, and other observances expounding this doctrine. The exposure of the Blessed Sacrament during the Forty-Hour Devotion and other activities centering around the Eucharist, in turn, led to creation of a special vertical case (*expositorio* or *manifestador*), built into or added onto the retablo, in which the consecrated Host in its monstrance could be displayed and adored. Usually semicircular in cross section and made of precious metals with a richly decorated interior and a door that would slide along its side, the expositorio or manifestador functioned somewhat like the tabernacle, which had lost some of its visual prominence due to the overpowering decorative development of the retablo during the baroque. In New Spain, it was sometimes incorporated into an isolated, tall, tapering construction associated with the main altar, called a cypress (ciprés) for its resemblance to the slender conifer (see also **Cypress tree** entry in chapter 11).[81]

[Theme] *Retablos cristíferos* and *retablos marianos* were specifically dedicated to Christ and Mary. The first cycle for Christ was that of his birth, infancy, and public life, with appropriate scenes of the Epiphany, the flight into

Egypt, his Circumcision, his Presentation at the Temple, the earthly and heavenly Trinities, Jesus among the Doctors, his Baptism, and his presence in the house of Lazarus. The second was the cycle of the Passion, which included the Last Supper, Christ's washing the feet of his Apostles, his praying in the Garden of Gethsemane, his betrayal by Judas, the mockery by the crowd, his flagellation, his crowning with thorns, his being presented to the people ("Ecce Homo"), various scenes on the road to Calvary, waiting to be crucified, the crucified figure, Descent from the Cross, Mary receiving his dead body, and the interment. The third and last cycle, that of the Ascension, depicted Christ's Resurrection, his appearance to Mary Magdalen, his descent into Limbo, his Transfiguration, and finally his Ascension itself.

The first Marian cycle concerned her birth and infancy and consisted of her nativity, scenes with Saint Anne and Saint Joachim, and Mary's Presentation in the Temple. The second cycle, that of Redemption, depicted the Annunciation, Mary's espousal, her visit to Elizabeth, the Pentecost, and her death. The final cycle depicted her Ascension, her coronation by the Trinity, and Mary in her role as the Immaculate Conception (La Inmaculada).

Rosary retablos (*retablos rosarios*) were designed to display, in reliefs or paintings, the fifteen Joyful, Sorrowful, and Glorious Mysteries of the rosary, key events from the iconography of both Christ and Mary, in order that the faithful could contemplate each scene while reciting the rosary. One such retablo is that of Nuestra Señora de Guadalupe de San José in Parral (Chihuahua), which contains scenes from the Passion of Christ in the small ovals along the sides (see figure 6.6).

Hagiographic retablos (*retablos hagiográficos*) contained images and scenes from the lives of the Apostles, Evangelists, saints, and beatified individuals central to a religious order or important to a church community; examples are the retablo mayor of San Ignacio de Loyola (see figure 6.10) and the Retablo de los Siete Príncipes at the Santuario de Guadalupe, both in Parras (Coahuila; figure 10.27).

[Iconographic Balance] The figural arrangement of the typical retablo (whether interior or exterior) can be plotted with almost geometric certainty. Confusing as it may first appear, underlying it all are doctrinal and iconographic schemata—patterns of purposefully created balance and tension based on certain traditions. Just as the main altar takes precedence over the collateral altars, each figure or scene within its respective retablo is selected for its significance within the theme of the particular retablo and has a distinct and unique place in a niche, bay, or story. The chronological and symbolic hierarchy of the religious figures or themes—based on Church traditions, local cults, and cofradías—determines the vertical and horizontal placement of images. Iconographic symmetry was often achieved by placing representations of the same class and rank on opposing sides within the retablo. The order was usually from bottom to top in ascending importance, with the Gospel (left) side taking preference over the Epistle (right) side.[82] The placement of religious figures within certain classes of saints, such as Apostles, founders of religious orders, or saints noted for their piety, was determined by their status, subject always to the preferences of a particular church or order. Even before, but especially after 1563, when the twenty-fifth Council of Trent ruled that the clergy must direct the decoration of a church to ensure ecclesiastically correct and orthodox subject matter, clerics would oversee the details of the rendering of figures or scenes (see also introductory remarks in chapter 11 on symbolic placement and association of religious figures).

Images of the most important saints were arranged closest to that of the titular saint—the one to whom the altar was dedicated. The retablo mayor was always dedicated to the titular saint of the church, who was located prominently in its center, and if the retablo was large enough, usually in the first level above the predella in a section referred to as the *cuerpo de Gloria*. The next level, again depending on the size or theme of the retablo, usually contained an image of Mary or Christ, while the gable (gablete or ático) could include images of Mary, Christ, or angels but was in many cases reserved for images or symbols of God the Father, represented as a bearded patriarch in an attitude of benediction or symbolized as the uppermost vertex of the triangle of the Trinity (see also "God" in chapter 12). Departures from traditional figural arrangements were made to accommodate the style or form of a retablo or the needs of a particular time—or out of ignorance on the part of builder, restorer, or renovator. Thus, the titular saint's image might be placed in the second story rather than in the first (see figure 6.16).

10.27. Hagiographic collateral retablo of Los Siete Príncipes, El Santuario de Nuestra Señora de Guadalupe de Parras, Coahuila, 2006.

Creators, Builders, and Decorators

In some instances, retablos were made locally by resident craftsmen, as in some eighteenth- and nineteenth-century New Mexican and Californian churches.[83] In others, craftsmen were imported, and not uncommonly, retablos were ordered to be delivered in crates for assembly on site.[84]

Although, from guild requirements, church contracts,[85] memorias, and other archival documents elsewhere in New Spain, we know how tasks were divided and which materials were used in the construction of retablos, and sometimes even the names of artists who worked on them, we know very little about who created the various elements of the retablos or the specifics of how these elements were planned, prepared, and assembled. Indeed, for northern New Spain, apart from the church records of the Cathedrals of Chihuahua and Durango,[86] and apart from an infrequent reference to a source, an occasional request for some specific religious sculpture or painting, or an isolated notation of the number of crates required to ship the elements of a retablo, scholars have uncovered little detailed information about retablos.

Based on what we do know from elsewhere in New Spain and from colonial Spain itself, however, it is likely that teams of specialized artists and artisans worked separately to create the images and to build, paint, gild, and assemble the elements of the retablos. Nevertheless, from their coherent appearance and from consistencies in iconographic themes, stylistic devices, and sizes and proportions of their elements, it is just as likely that retablos were built and decorated under the careful supervision of a master planner.

Woodworkers who specialized in the art of building retablos (*ensambladores;* literally, "joiners"), and who, at least in Sevilla, differed from carpenters (*carpinteros*) in being able to read, understand, and interpret architectural designs,[87] were employed to translate these into the various structural elements of the wooden retablos. Carvers (entalladores; sometimes translated as "sculptors") would carve columns, capitals, niches, bases, and ornaments of the framework. Sculptors (escultores), expected to know thematic requirements for the various religious figures as well as the technical process, carved the figures (imágenes de talla). The painters (pintores) and gilders (doradores) would cover the joints, smooth the wood with gesso and bole, and apply paint and silver and gold leaf on both the framework and the sculptures themselves (see also "Decorative Techniques" under "Sculpture Decorators" above). For a retablo containing religious paintings (retablo de pincel), the individual pieces were painted by the pintores (who sometimes included both those who painted pictures and those who painted sculptures) to fit the sizes specified in the retablo plan. The ensambladores were then called in to join the pieces of the giant puzzle together by pin, peg, nail, and glue. As noted under "Builders" in chapter 4, however, the guilds and the division of labor within and between them played a much less important role on the northern frontier, especially at mission sites, than they did in the large cities of central New Spain.[88] Indeed, crossing guild lines, the craftsmen of northern New Spain were very likely certified in, and called upon to perform at the same time, a number of different specialties.

Although the principles governing iconography, size, and arrangement of religious images appear to have been the same for retablos made from stone or brick and lime plaster as for those made from wood, the skills needed were different. Masons (albañiles) replaced woodworkers (ensambladores); stone sculptors (escultores) replaced wood sculptors (entalladores). As with wood, during the baroque, the natural appearance of the stone was not considered appropriate for sculptures, furnishings, and most architectural features. Consequently, limestone and alabaster sculptures were polychromed and gilded. During the neoclassical era, however, based on mistaken beliefs about classical architecture, columns and pediments of retablos were most often left unpainted (see also "Columns" and "Pediments" under "Architectural Details" in chapter 6).

[Size, Distance, and Detail] The size of the retablos mayores and the distance from which they were to be viewed could affect how they were sculpted and painted. According to the canons of the baroque, church art should invite, indeed impel, viewers to participate in the emotion created by its images and scenes and to directly absorb their counterreformational message, which emphasized veneration of the saints, rather than to linger on the details of a particular image or scene. As a consequence, most huge baroque retablos, meant to be viewed from afar, do not stand close inspection. Their craftsmanship is often less than meticulous and their details less than fine; they contain few individual masterpieces. They were created not

as collections of elements complete and finished in their own right, but as unified, magnificent, even awe-inspiring assemblages. The reverse is often true of smaller, less elaborate retablos intended to be placed within small chapels or used for personal devotion. Because their smaller size and more intimate setting favored closer, more critical viewing, they were rendered with attention to even the most minute details.

[Made to Order] That a careful balance of the iconographic elements in each retablo was intended and understood can be clearly seen in certain church contracts, construction accounts, and inventories, for example, the contract for two retablos to be made in Mexico City for La Purísima Concepción de Sombrerete (Zacatecas) in 1685.[89] The contract stipulated that the main retablo was to be a retablo mariana (though it would contain representations of four of the Mysteries of the Rosary). On its first story the statues of Saint Peter and Saint Paul (considered cofounders of the Catholic Church) were to flank the tabernacle; and the images of Saint Anthony (probably of Padua) and Saint Francis (probably of Assisi)—both Franciscan saints—were to be placed on its second story. To their sides, there were to be paintings of the Annunciation (when Christ was conceived) and the Visitation (when Mary visited her kinswoman Elizabeth and the Christ child leapt in Mary's womb)—the first two Joyful Mysteries of the Rosary. Also on the second story of the retablo, an image of Our Lady of the Immaculate Conception was to be centered in a niche with her parents, Joachim and Anne, on either side. Above them, on the third story, the contract called for a painting on canvas of the Assumption of the Virgin (the Fourth Glorious Mystery), with images of San Andrew and Saint Catherine of Alexandra (both martyrs) on either side. Above all this, in the pediment, was to be a shield-shaped support with the Eternal Father crowning the Virgin Mary (the Fifth Glorious Mystery). At the base of the retablo, in the predella, were to be four paintings on canvas: Saint Joseph and Saint Dominic flanked by "the two Saint Roses" (probably Rose of Lima, a Dominican tertiary, and Rose of Viterbo, a Franciscan nun).

From the greater incidence of Franciscan saints than of Dominicans (three versus two) and their positions (Francis and Anthony are closer to the titular figure of the church—Our Lady of the Immaculate Conception—than are the Dominicans in the base of the retablo), we can safely conclude that the Franciscans were in ascendancy at the time of the contract. This is further supported by the principal and emphatically articulated theme of the retablo, the Immaculate Conception (here in association with two of the Joyful Mysteries), perhaps the most significant doctrinal cause espoused by the Franciscans.

The contract went on to describe a second and collateral retablo, a retablo cristífero, which was to be smaller and less ambitious, with images of the Veil of Veronica and of the Four Evangelists in the predella, and with a niche for a now-obscure cult figure, Our Lady of the Wall (Nuestra Señora de la Pared), flanked by oil paintings on canvas of Christ's Agony in the Garden of Gethsemane and of his scourging (the first and second of the Sorrowful Mysteries) on the first story. The second story was to have a painting of the Crucifix, flanked by (most likely painted) images of Jesus the Nazarene and "Ecce Homo." The retablo was to be crowned, in its pediment, by the Spanish coat of arms. The principal theme of this retablo was the Passion of Jesus, with representations of his emotional and physical suffering, public humiliation, the path to Calvary, and his instrument of death supported by images of the Four Evangelists. Although both retablos were completed and delivered to the Sombrerete church, only the retablo cristífero remains (much altered and with images quite different from those called for in the contract), to the left of the entrance (figure 10.28).[90]

Stone Retablos: La Castrense

Partly because of their susceptibility to fire, Carlos III decreed in 1788 that retablos must no longer be made of wood but instead of marble or some other fine-grained stone. This decree, the inherent qualities of stone, and the neoclassical retreat from elaborate altar screens filled with a multitude of figures sounded the death knell for gilded wooden retablos.

Northern New Spain is home to four of eight extant colonial stone retablos in Mexico. The stone retablo mayor of the Cathedral of Chihuahua, finished in 1792, was modified almost beyond recognition in the 1930–40 restoration of the main altar (figure 10.29); two other stone retablos in this cathedral, including the retablo marco of La Mater Dolorosa, are in a better state of preservation.[91] By far the best preserved of the four, however, is the stone

10.28. Collateral retablo cristífero, La Purísima Concepción de Sombrerete, Zacatecas, 2001.

10.29. Main retablo, Catedral de Chihuahua, 1991.

retablo from La Castrense, the Spanish military chapel in Santa Fe (New Mexico). Completed in 1761, removed from its original site in 1859, and stored for eighty years, this retablo was reassembled in 1939 (see figure 2.26) as the main altar of Cristo Rey, a church in the "Santa Fe style," complete with a transverse clerestory window designed by John Gaw Meem.

The retablo's dedication to Our Lady of Light and the choice and arrangement of saints it represents clearly indicate its donors' affection for the Jesuits. The retablo consists of two stories, a gable, and three bays. In the first story, the center panel contains the titular figure of the chapel, Our Lady of Light, whose painted image was brought to New Spain in 1707 by a Jesuit and placed in the Jesuit church (now the Cathedral) at León (León) in 1732, and whose cult was actively promoted by the Jesuit Order. Above her is Saint James the Greater (Santiago Matamoros), patron saint of Spain and soldiers. On the same story, in the Gospel side bay (preferential or left, facing the altar), is a panel with the image of Saint Ignatius, founder of the Society of Jesus and, opposite him, is Saint Joseph. Another figure important to the Jesuits, Saint John Nepomuk, patron saint of Bohemia and protector of the Jesuit Order, appears in the upper story on the Epistle (right) side. In the lower story, also on Epistle side, is the only Franciscan saint, Saint Francis Solano. In the gable is Our Lady of Balvanera, an image that most likely had special significance to the governor and his wife, perhaps the patron saint of their parish church or province in Spain, while—surmounting all—is God the Father.[92]

Made with Less

In a few of the poorer and more isolated churches, retablos were simulated by painting architectural members, religious images, and decorative elements directly on the apse, transept, or nave walls; indeed, some may still be seen in mission churches such as San José de Tumacácori (Arizona).[93]

In the same vein, a number of retablos in northern New Spain were built with a minimum of pieces—with shallow scrollwork and flat ornamentation tacked onto a flat board backing—instead of a multitude of layers of moldings, panels, niches, and deeply carved ornamentation. Strips of wood molding or tubes decorated with molding were used to create the effect of three-dimensional columns and hand-carved surfaces. Far less time and material, thus far less money, were needed to construct and assemble such retablos than those with deeply sculpted decoration. Two such examples can be found in San José de Copala (Sinaloa; figure 10.30) and in San Francisco de Asís, Sombrerete (Zacatecas; see figure 2.19). My 1982 photograph of the then disintegrating (but now restored) retablo of La Santa Vera Cruz in Sombrerete (Zacatecas; figure 10.31) gives a good front view of the complex construction of a typical wooden retablo.

Three-dimensional elements such as niches, ledges (especially sotobancos on the apse wall), or lime plaster reliefs carved into or built against a wall might be used to support paintings and sculptures in much the same way as retablos did. Architectural elements, decorative ornaments, and parts of sculptures, or even entire

10.30. Main retablo, San José de Copala, Sinaloa, 1979.

10.31. Detail of the main retablo, La Santa Vera Cruz de Sombrerete, Zacatecas, 1982. Since this photo, the retablo has been restored.

sculptures, could be formed with molds (*moldes* or *matrices*) from lime plaster—as were the reliefs on the estípite columns in the retablo mayor of San Xavier del Bac (Arizona; see figure 7.9a). Pieces identical in size and shape could be produced almost effortlessly with wooden or clay molds made rapidly on site and discarded after use.

Beautifully economical, a *retablo lienzo* (or retablo pintado) reproduced an entire retablo, complete with religious sculptures or paintings and architectural elements, on a large piece of joined canvas—like a stage backdrop. Works of this kind, most probably invented in Spain, would have been painted in artists' studios, rolled for ease of transport, and then simply hung from upper wall moldings or ceiling beams behind the altar. Because far fewer materials, far less of the artists' time—and none of the assemblers'—were used to make them, retablos lienzos cost a great deal less than actual retablos. If finances and circumstances later permitted, the various images could be cut out and placed in a retablo framework. Retablos lienzos in the strictest sense can be found at Nuestra Señora de Guadalupe in Santa Fe (New Mexico; signed and dated "José de Alcíbar, 1783"; figure 10.32), at San Juan Nepomuceno in Saltillo (Coahuila; signed and dated "Antonio Sanchez, 1775"), and at San José de Parral (Chihuahua; signed and dated "Antonio de Torres, 1719"). A notable fragment of a late-eighteenth-century retablo lienzo can be seen at La Capilla de San Francisco de Asís in Sombrerete (Zacatecas).[94] A variation with brackets through the canvas retablo to support statues occurs in Alta California at Mission Santa Bárbara (late eighteenth or early nineteenth century).

10.32. Retablo lienzo, San Juan Nepomuceno, Saltillo, Coahuila, 2002.

Glass and Mirrors

A retablo or a religious painting or sculpture associated with an altar may be protected by a glass-paneled display case (*vitrina;* also called *fanal* or *nicho armario*). Such cases permit the images to be seen and venerated, but protect them from the touches, kisses, and candles of devotees. Smaller paintings, prints, and sculptures intended for private devotion, as well as relicarios (see above under "Ornaments"), were also most often covered with glass. Often listed in inventories in association with a retablo, mirrors could either incorporated into the design of the retablo or later attached to it in various locations. As reflectors for lamps and candles, they helped illuminate the retablo and created a shimmering and otherworldly appearance that must have been impressive to the congregation.

Donors

Individuals and their families or associations, whether religious or commercial, often donated entire retablos or individual objects for inclusion within a retablo—such as a painting or sculpture of, or jewelry and clothing for, a particular saint. Sometimes the donor's name appears on a painting—most often prominently, painted across the side, well into the action of the scene.[95] Other times, donors' names and their gifts appear only in inventories, wills, or other church documents. The appearance of donor figures within a painting or as sculptures to be included in a retablo harks back to an old Church tradition and may have been common throughout northern New Spain (see also **Donors** entry in chapter 11).

Mounting

The backside of a retablo is especially revealing. Horizontal and vertical pieces, hand-adzed and never intended to be seen by the public, created a skeleton of support; many smaller pieces were carefully fitted together, probably to combat settling and shrinkage or perhaps because material in larger pieces was too expensive or simply not available. Brackets and supports were inserted into the retablo's substructure as well as into the wall to aid in its mounting.[96] Principal joints and sometimes the entire wooden surface were covered with strips of cloth and, in some early instances, with a stringy, fibrous paste.[97] Columns, niches, and decorative framing were then attached to the substructure. The entire outer face of the retablo was given several coats of gesso and bole, covered in gold or silver leaf, and burnished before the paintings and sculptures were finally secured in their appropriate places.

CHAPTER 11

SYMBOLS AND ATTRIBUTES

Take care, above all, not to reveal the secrets of the holy mysteries.

—DIONYSIUS THE AREOPAGITE

Faced with the problem of teaching doctrine to illiterates, the Catholic Church almost from its inception made use of easily understood symbols, perhaps humankind's earliest method for expressing and conveying beliefs. Because it "implies something more than its obvious and immediate meaning" and "appears only when there is a need to express what thought cannot think or what is only divined or felt," a symbol leads the viewer beyond the physical to something that cannot be seen or touched but must be felt or believed.[1]

Some of the earliest symbols and iconographic formulas, including poses and gestures, can be traced to earlier pre-Christian religions and cultures. For example, Christ the Good Shepherd takes its inspiration from the Greek Orpheus, Boukolos, the Herdsman (prophet, teacher, and martyr), or Hermes Kriophorus, the ram bearer; and Mary seated and holding the infant Jesus, derives from Isis, the Great Mother of the Egyptians, holding her son, Osiris.[2] The Tree of the World (or Center of the World) was incorporated into the Christian symbol of the cross, with Christ described as "the tree of life planted on Calvary, the tree on which the King of ages wrought our salvation," a symbol harking back to Nebuchadnezzar's dream in Daniel 4:7–15.[3] The ascension of important spiritual figures and the placement of offerings intended for heavenly divinities are profoundly and almost universally associated with symbols of the "center," the axis connecting the three cosmic realms of Earth, Hell, and Heaven, through which priests or the anointed are allowed to pass.

Christianity adopted and adapted rituals and myths, most likely originating in Mesopotamian cosmologies, from its closest antecedent, Judaism. Later, with Rome's primacy over Byzantium, it assimilated elements of Greco-Roman religious rituals, their goddesses, gods, and other myths.[4] Superimposing Christian symbols over these and other pre-Christian rituals and universal myths, appropriately modified through new interpretations and coupled with symbols already deeply rooted in the psyche, served as a powerful means to propagate the Faith.

Basic to the human mind and fundamental to the thought process, visual symbols have the power of communicating sentiment, ideals, and ideas, especially those lying outside the realm of logic or language. The Middle Ages gave rise to some of the richest and most convoluted visual symbolism ever invented. "To the medieval mind symbolism explained the observed facts of nature in terms of the Christian and eternal facts of life," and visual symbols were associated with practically every aspect and object of Christian belief in the Church's attempts to teach the precepts of the Faith.[5]

Symbols permeated every part of the Catholic religion. Some captured certain striking characteristics of saints or significant moments in their lives—in particular, their spiritual experiences—or key features of Church dogma. Through their symbolism, colors, numbers, shapes, articles of clothing, animals, minerals, and plants provided meanings on many levels, from the obvious to the esoteric, and for everyone from the simplest believers to the illuminati. Operating in the minutest details, in the entire church edifice or anywhere else, symbols afforded churchgoers a whole range of understanding. The nave was used to illustrate narrative cycles; the saints in their doctrinal hierarchy were illustrated, arranged, and placed according to the symbolic significance of each part of the church.

Pseudo Dionysius the Areopagite taught that "the symbolic reading of the world was the path of ascension by which humans might comprehend the way in which the lower, material world reflected the celestial world of true essences."[6] The world was seen as the veiled language of the creative principle. Humans, in an attempt to control or at least make sense of their surroundings, now interpreted elements of their lives and environment through the doctrine of the Church. Some of the richness of medieval thought as expressed in Catholic iconography, church furnishings, and the symbolic arrangement of architectural elements of the church building persisted into colonial times and spread throughout New Spain.

Durandus's twofold meaning of "church"—temporal and spiritual—in which he assigns symbolism to even the physical mortar and stones of a structure, was not a revolutionary concept, but rather a combination of preexisting ideas and beliefs. For example, mortar is made from lime (fervent charity) joined to sand (undertakings for the temporal welfare of our brethren) and mixed with water (spirit). Furthermore, the walls' stones are polished and squared (holy and pure) with Christ Jesus as the cornerstone and "All are bound together by one spirit of charity, as though fastened with cement; and those living stones are knit together in the bond of peace."[7] The sanctity and symbolism of building a church can be seen in the blessings bestowed on contemporary sites and foundations during construction.

All traditional cultures have used symbolism to relate the structure of their temples to the structure of the world. Proportions based on the square are rooted in earlier beliefs about the basic shape of the world. As a vestige of sun worship, temples served as solar calendars; the face and front of the universal temple was oriented toward the east, where the sun and all the planets and stars rose. Placing churches in the center of cities or towns—the "Center of the World"—follows in the symbolic tradition of ancient cultures in both the Old and the New World,[8] as does placing images of significant religious figures on either side of the portals: animals or guardian spirits protected the gates of pre-Christian temples, guarded those within, and were a deterrent to enemies.

"Reading" the church was "reading" Christ Jesus; the walls, altars, and retablos were the unlettered believers' Bible.[9] Christ, the Church, and the earth were viewed as equivalent by metaphor or metonym. Pope Boniface VIII, in his *Unam Sanctam*, calls the Church "the spouse and body of Christ," "the seamless garment." The shape of the cruciform church and, in some places, the slightly tilted apse popularly reinforced the idea of the church building as symbolizing Christ's body. In response to the decrees of the Council of Trent, the principal church in any city was to be cross-shaped and, because it symbolized Christ's body, its proportions should be those of a perfect human body.[10] The orientation of the church's central axis; the enactment of sacraments in specified locations within the church; the painting of ceilings blue with golden stars; the placing of a cross on the highest point of the church; the decoration of church interiors according to biblical or doctrinal themes; the placement of the altar and the arrangement of images of religious figures behind, above, and around it; the larger arrangement of religious images inside and outside the church; the preference of the Gospel over the Epistle side; the juxtaposition of Old with New Testament mysteries—in all these and indeed hundreds of other instances, aspects of Christianity were consciously and intentionally related in ways that would be immediately understood by—and remain with—the congregation.

Decorating the interior of many churches in northern New Spain are painted or sculpted images of the Four Doctors of the Church. Images of these four "pillars of the Church"—literally and figuratively sustaining the Church by their doctrine—appear on the four principal pillars under the dome. (See also introductory remarks under "Inner Body" in chapter 5 on symbolism of parts of the church building.) The progression from the baptistery (or baptismal area) area to the main altar or apse of a church represents the ascent of the spirit from birth to salvation. Coming from the material waters of the baptistery and passing by the Stations of the Cross along the walls of the nave to the crossing and the pillars, representing the foundations and Fathers of the Church, to the sanctuary, where the joining of humanity with the divine is enacted in the miracle of transubstantiation, with the bread and wine becoming the body and blood of Christ, the believer is thoroughly surrounded by and immersed in the symbolism of Church doctrine and Christian belief.

It is highly likely that every church in northern New Spain was decorated according to a doctrinally acceptable symbolic program. Although this is difficult to see in many churches owing to the loss or alteration of altars, portals, retablos, and decoration, it is readily apparent in structures whose decorative elements are mostly intact, such as the mission church of San Xavier near Tucson (Arizona) and the Cathedral of Chihuahua (Chihuahua).[11]

An ancient name for the Lord's Supper, Holy Communion, or the Mass, the Eucharist (from Greek *eucharistos*, grateful, from *charis*, favor, grace) assumed special symbolic significance and importance in the sixteenth century, especially in Spanish art, architecture, and orfebrería. Because the paten, chalice, ciborium, pyx, and monstrance came in direct contact with the Sacred Host, they were considered worthy of receiving highly elaborate designs and ornamentation. As a result, great care was given to their embellishment, with precious metals, enameling, and precious and semiprecious stones being used in their fabrication. Their symbolic importance (and perhaps also their monetary value) may explain why they are most generally the first items referred to in church inventories.

Baroque architecture and the dramatic use of light to emphasize the ritual at the main altar, capillas dedicated specifically to the Eucharist, the decoration of the tabernacles, and the retablos themselves were responses to the official adoption of the Eucharist as the central dogma of the Church in 1563.[12] "Eucharistic saints," those especially noted for defending, revering, or being associated with the Eucharist, are easily identified by their attributes—the monstrance, chalice, or lamb. (See "Anthony of Padua," "Barbara," "Catherine of Alexandria," "Dominic of Guzmán," "Francis Borgia," "Gregory the Great," "Ignatius of Loyola," "John the Baptist," "John the Evangelist," and "Thomas Aquinas" in chapter 12.) Some of the other themes of the Eucharist are the Last Supper, the Good Shepherd, the Mystic Lamb on a book of seven seals, the blood of Christ Jesus caught in a fountain or chalice, and the multiplication of the loaves and fishes.

Marian devotions based on doctrines such as that of the Immaculate Conception further enriched the Church's symbolism.[13] (For particular symbols, see **Mary** below; for specific advocations, see "Mary" in chapter 12.)

A symbol or attribute that might have had a specific meaning for a particular group at a particular time may later have taken on different or more general meanings. Where not otherwise noted, the meanings set forth here are based on currently accepted interpretations of Christian symbols (prior to Vatican II), traditional Hispanic beliefs, and inferences drawn from sources on northern New Spain relevant to the period under discussion.

Just how much influence native beliefs had on the decorative symbolism of northern New Spain is an open question. Highly stylized geometric motifs, plants, animals, and human figures in the mission churches of the Pimería Alta, Nuevo México, and Alta California are very likely the work of native artists, to whom native plants, animals, and traditional geometric forms were both more familiar and more comprehensible. Where these native symbols and their meanings coincided with their Christian counterparts, and this was known to the supervising friars, the use of these symbols was permitted within acceptable limits. The early friars were careful, however, to guard against any trace of pre-Christian or dissident beliefs in the decoration of sacred structures.

In addition to *symbol*, other terms may be used to impart narrower or more specific meanings. An *anagram* is a word or term created by transposing the letters of another word or term. An *allegory* is a symbolic depiction, usually of an abstract idea such as Fortune, State, Church, or Faith. An *attribute* is a distinctive mark or symbol used to identify and explain a saint. Attributes may be personal or general and may be incorporated into monograms and coats of arms, or simply used as decorative motifs. An *emblem*, in the strictest sense, is a pictorial device such as a banner, badge, seal, or other object that represents or suggests a religious or political group. An *insignia* is a badge or emblem of rank, used as a mark of office, honor, or membership. A *monogram* is a character created by intertwining two or more letters into one, especially the initials of a name.

Symbols associated with different parts of a church, its decoration, furnishings, and ecclesiastical vestments and accoutrements, mentioned briefly in preceding chapters, are discussed in greater detail here. Those associated with the various saints are further discussed in chapter 12: "Sacred Iconography." (For economy, cross-references to those saints give only their English names, even though both English and Spanish appear in the corresponding headings in chapter 12.)

Adder—see **Serpent** below.

Agnus Dei—see **Sheep** below.

Altar—general symbol for sacrifice, the altar also signifies the presence of Christ, the throne of God, and the Eucharist. (See also "Main Altar" under "Sanctuary" in chapter 7; "Altar" under "Linens" in chapter 8; and **Mary** below.)

Altar cross—symbol for Christ in his role as the world's savior.

Anchor—ancient Christian symbol for the true Faith and the hope of resurrection of the flesh (Hebrews 6:19), the anchor is also the symbol for salvation and steadfastness. It is the personal attribute of Saints Rose of Lima and Clement and also appears with a cross and a heart, emblems of faith and charity (figure 11.1).

Angels: Derived from a Greek translation of the original Hebrew *mal'akh*, which originally meant "shadow side of God" but later came to mean "messenger," the word "angel" refers to a winged bearer of tidings, a messenger of God.[14] By the fifth century, angels were divided into three orders, a hierarchy given credence in the following century by writings falsely attributed to Dionysius the Areopagite (who purportedly was told the hierarchy by the spirit of Saint Paul). Each of the orders was divided into three choirs, making a total of nine choirs of angels. In the highest order, "Seraphim," red-colored, bodiless angels with six wings and flaming candles, symbolize divine love; "Cherubim," angels dressed in blue or gold and carrying books, symbolize divine intelligence; and "Thrones," dressed in green judicial robes, symbolize divine justice. In the second highest order, "Powers," dressed in full armor and carrying flaming swords, wage war with evil demons and symbolize God's ultimate triumph over Satan and evil; "Dominions," crowned and carrying scepters and orbs, symbolize divine authority; and "Virtues," carrying trumpets, censers, white lilies of purity, or red roses representing Christ's Passion, symbolize prayer. In the third and highest order, "Principalities," who protect religion and dispense the fates of nations, symbolize God's direct involvement in the affairs of humankind; "Archangels," Heaven's warriors, symbolize the seven heavens, of which they are the princes; and "Angels," guardians of the innocent and God's messengers, symbolize God's presence.[15] This categorization was accepted by the Church as a factual view of the divine classification, and for centuries earthly orders were modeled on it, although the distinctions between the choirs are not readily apparent in the religious art of northern New Spain.

Angels commonly appear in painting and sculpture as cherubs—naked children with wings, symbols of innocence and heavenly endorsement—playing musical instruments, supporting the crown of the Virgin, presenting symbols of martyrdom, pulling back draperies, or holding attributes (see figure 7.9b; left and right middle, atop arches of center bay). In portrayals of Christ's Crucifixion, angels who hold the cross, a palm, the crown of thorns, or other symbols of the Passion are popularly called *pasionarios*;[16] those carrying censers, *turiferarios* (censer-bearing angels). Angels' heads and wings are frequently placed in spandrels, around the Virgin Mary, or under her feet, separating her from the realm of the earthly (see also "Archangels" in chapter 12 and "Virtues" below).

Animals—see specific kinds. According to Borromeo, no effigy of any beast of burden, dog, fish, or other living beast except as an expression of holy history was to be used in church adornment.[17]

Apostles—see specific Apostles under "Twelve Apostles" and "Other Saints" in chapter 12.

11.1. Anchor motif symbolizing the True Faith, spandrel of choir loft, Catedral de Chihuahua, 2001.

Apple—ambivalent symbol for lust and salvation; the forbidden fruit associated with Adam and Eve, the Fall, sin, and discord. When it appears in the hand of the Virgin holding the infant Jesus, the apple identifies Mary as the New Eve and Christ as the New Adam, and serves as the symbol of salvation and redemption from sin.[18] A pear may appear in its place; indeed, it may be impossible to distinguish which fruit is being held (see also "The Immaculate Conception" in chapter 12).

Ark—symbol for salvation, the flood, and Noah. (See also **Boat** under **Mary** below.)

"Arma Christi"—see **Instruments of Christ's Passion** below.

Armor—typifying soldiers and warriors, it is worn by Saints Michael, Martin of Tours, James the Greater (Santiago), Ferdinand of Spain, and Louis of France. Although also worn by the persecutors of Christ during his torture and Crucifixion, armor is a general symbol for resistance to evil—thus appearing as a girdle of Truth, a breastplate of Righteousness, a shield of Faith, a helmet of Salvation, and a sword of the Spirit (Ephesians 6:11–18)—and serves as a metaphor for the Christian Faith.

Arrow—symbol of martyrdom, as in the case of Saint Sebastian, and, when piercing the heart, of intense religious experience, as in the case of Saints Teresa of Ávila and Augustine. The arrow also signifies plague (Psalms 91:5–6), against which Sebastian was considered a protector.

Ass—see **Donkey or ass** below.

Aureola—Latin for "golden," the aureola or aureole (*resplendor* or *ráfage*) is light encircling and emanating from the head or entire body, a symbol of sacredness and holiness, seen in representations of God, Christ, the Virgin Mary, angels, and saints. When around the head alone, the aureola is generally called a halo or nimbus; when around the body, a glory or *mandorla*.

First used to represent members of the Trinity and angels only, the aureola was gradually extended to represent other holy figures honored by the Church. By the end of the sixteenth century, halos or nimbuses appeared in paintings as shimmering hazes with radiating rays or as plain rings, and on sculptures as highly worked flat plates of silver or gold sometimes with precious or semiprecious stones attached. Many sculpted images of La Mater Dolorosa have semicircular halos, while those of Christ have halos formed from three flames, called tres potencias (see also **Mandorla** and **Tres potencias** below).

Ax—symbol of martyrdom associated with Saint Matthias and sometimes Saint Jude (see also "Matthias" in chapter 12).

Bag—coin bag or purse is an attribute of two of Jesus' original Twelve Apostles, Saint Matthew and Judas Iscariot, and of Saint John of God, where it appears as a large bag (filled with food for the poor; see also "Matthew," "John of God," and note 46 in chapter 12).

Balance—see **Scales** below.

Baldachin—derives its name from Italian for Baghdad, source of the best silk brocades and precious fabrics used over sovereigns' thrones. Originally a Hellenistic device symbolizing the manifestation of a ruler's divine nature by a celestial covering—Heaven's tent, a cosmic world shelter—it was later used to cover altars. By implication, persons or objects portrayed beneath a baldachin are held to have spiritual significance (see also chapter 8).

Banner—device symbolizing victory commonly seen in Catholic painting and sculpture by the fourteenth century. Banners were also used to present a name or emblem of a sacred figure, or a slogan of Church doctrine, such as "Ecce Agnus Dei" (Behold the Lamb of God) on a banner held by John the Baptist, or of a religious order, such as "Ad majorem Dei gloriam" (To the Greater Glory of God) or its initials, A. M. D. G., on a banner or book held by Ignatius of Loyola and signifying the Jesuit Order (see figure 6.10, center middle).[19] Archangel Michael and most military saints are shown with banners, including Saints James the Greater (Santiago) and Louis of France. An emblem of the Church Militant, the banner marks the person holding it as a warrior of Christ. Christ himself holds a banner as a token of his Resurrection during his descent into Limbo. Banners may be vertical or horizontal, square or rectangular with a triangular notch missing from their free end.

Baptism—from the Greek for "to dip" or "to dip under," this first of the seven sacraments of the Church is itself an emblem of divine initiation into the family of the redeemed. A likeness of Saint John the Baptist, a lamb, a dove, or a scallop shell may represent this sacrament (see also **Book** below for all the sacraments).

Beehive—symbolizes the Christian community and eloquence of speech (honeyed words), sometimes serving as an attribute of Saint Ambrose.

Bells—call and encourage the faithful, rout evil spirits, and quell storms. According to Durandus, the sounding of a bell is the word of God, its hollow is the mouth of the preacher, its clapper his tongue.[20] Harking back to the fringes of the priestly robes of Aaron (Exodus 28:34 and 39:26), bells alternating with pomegranates are used as a decorative motif along the nave of San Xavier near Tucson (Arizona). (See also "Belfry" in chapter 7.)

Birds—traditional Christian symbol for winged souls (see specific kinds).

Biretta—see **Hat** below.

Blood—stands for sacrifice, atonement, and redemption. In depictions of Christ, blood and wine are interchangeable symbols that also symbolize the Eucharist. In depictions of martyrs, blood symbolizes the sacrifice of life for beliefs.

Boat—see under **Mary** and also **Ship** below.

Book—signifies the Bible or simply learning when held by saints, such as Thomas Aquinas and Catherine of Alexandria and by the Four Doctors of the Church; authorship or the founding of a religious order when held by saints such as Augustine and Ignatius of Loyola; the ministry when held by Saint Francis Xavier; a Gospel when held by any of the Four Evangelists; and missionary work when held by the Apostles. A book with seven seals is associated with Christ the lamb (Revelation 5:8). A book also represents the seven sacraments: Baptism, Confirmation, Holy Communion, Penance or Confession, Matrimony, Holy Orders, and Extreme Unction. A sealed book containing the names of the faithful (Psalms 139:16) may also identify the Virgin Mary.

Box or jar of ointment—which may resemble a pyx, is an attribute of Saint Mary Magdalen and a symbol of Christ's burial.

Bread—Eucharistic symbol, the body of Christ (Luke 22:19), God's providence, the word of God. Because it also signifies charity, a personal attribute of Saints Didacus of Alcalá (Diego de Alcalá) and Philip the Apostle; a dog with a loaf of bread in its mouth is an attribute of Saint Roch (see also "Didacus of Alcalá," "Philip," and "Roch" in chapter 12).

Bugia—small candlestick with saucer base and handle, used by a bishop to light the missal during a bishop's Mass.[21]

Building—see **Model of a building** or **Tower** below.

Bull—see **Ox or bull** below.

Candelabrum—symbol of salvation and spiritual light. A three-branch candelabrum represents the Trinity, a five-branched, the five wounds, and a seven-branched, the seven sacraments or seven gifts of the Holy Spirit. (See also **Candle, Candlesticks** below; "Altars and Sanctuary" under "Objects" in chapter 8.)

Candle—lighted, it represents Jesus: the wick hidden in wax is symbolic of the image of his soul, the flame his divinity, and its odor the fullness of Christ's perfection. White candles symbolize Jesus' humility, joy, and gladness, whereas yellow (unbleached beeswax) candles signify mourning and penance and are used during funerals and masses for the dead. A processional candle is a symbol of dignity. Mary may appear holding a candle, popularly perceived as a sign of her purification after childbirth. Three candles represent the Trinity, six the Church's constant prayers during Mass, seven the number of sacraments, and twelve the exposition of the Sacred Host. Eucharistic candles connote the coming of Christ, and the paschal candle, the Resurrection. A lighted candle in the hand of Saint Joseph denotes the light given to the world by the birth of Jesus.[22] Set in a tenebrario (a special triangle-shaped, fifteen-armed candelabrum on a tall pedestal) during Passion Week, the fourteen candles on the sloping sides symbolize the eleven faithful Apostles, the Virgin Mary, and the two women who were with her at the Crucifixion; the single candle at the top represents Christ. At the end of each psalm during the Tenebrae service (which takes its name from the Latin for shadows, darkness, gloom—symbolically suggesting the setting of the Sun of Justice, Jesus), part of Holy Thursday's, Good Friday's, and the Easter Vigil's nocturnal services, a candle is extinguished signifying the abandonment or flight of the Twelve Apostles and women.[23] After the Benedictus, the sole remaining candle at the top is briefly placed on the altar then hidden behind it, symbolizing the placing of Christ in his tomb—but it is not extinguished since death had no dominion over him; the Miserere is then sung in darkness (see figure 8.3). The use of candles for votive purposes may well be associated with offering up a burnt sacrifice, the candle consuming itself symbolizing the sacrifice and the smell of burning wax, prayer. Popularly used throughout the Catholic world, votive candles are offered with requests for divine favors and are placed near the image, symbol, or relic of the holy personage whose favor is being sought (see also **Candlesticks** below).

Candlesticks—two candlesticks symbolize the twofold nature of Christ, while six stand for the six days of Creation and the six hours spent by Christ on the Cross. Candlesticks before shrines and images signify veneration; elevated candlesticks at the sides of the altar symbolize the Lord's Supper; and the paschal candlestick on the Gospel (left) side of the altar from Holy Saturday until Ascension Day symbolizes the forty days Christ was on earth after his Resurrection (see also chapter 8).

Carpenter's square—attribute of Saints Joseph, Jude, and Thomas, who were carpenters by trade.

Castle—see **Tower** under **Mary** below.

Cathedra (Latin, chair)—bishop's throne and, by extension, episcopal authority, whence, because his cathedral houses his throne, comes the word "cathedral" for a diocesan bishop's church.

Cedar tree—steadfastness in the Faith and long life (see also under **Mary** below).

Censer—vessel for burning incense (see **Incense** below).

Chains or fetters—symbols of imprisonment associated with Saint Leonard, and Christ during the flagellation.[24] (See also **Instruments of Christ's Passion** below and "Jesus" in chapter 12.)

Chalice—general symbol of the Eucharist, the cup of salvation. When covered with a veil, it symbolizes the Last Supper. With a snake or dragon (poison), an attribute of Saint John the Evangelist. Saint Barbara may hold a chalice with a wafer in place of a monstrance (see also **Monstrance** below).

Child—when held in the arms of the Virgin or other saints, represents the infant Jesus. Saints Anthony of Padua, Joseph, Catherine of Siena, and Rose of Lima are frequently shown holding him. A small girl held by an elderly, bearded man is the Virgin carried by her father, Saint Joachim. A child or children accompanied by an angel appear in the theme of "The Guardian Angel." Two kneeling youths on either side of Saint Rita of Cascia are her sons (see also "Anthony of Padua," "Catherine of Siena," "Joseph," "Joachim," "Rita of Cascia," "Rose of Lima").

Chi-Rho—see under **Letters and monograms** below.

Church—from the Greek for "assembly" or "gathering," signifies both a religious structure and the Christian community. Seen as a model in the hands of a bishop, a male saint, or other religious personage, it signifies a particular church or the patron or founder of same; in the hands of the Fathers of the Church and Saints Gregory the Great and Jerome, it signifies the Church itself (see also specific parts of a church).

The "Church Suffering" refers to the souls of believers in Purgatory, who may be helped by the prayers of the living and the saints in Heaven; the "Church Militant," to all living members of the Church on earth who "wage the war of Faith" against "the world, the flesh and the devil," and who can help one another and be helped by the intercession of the saints and angels in Heaven and of the souls in Purgatory; and the "Church Triumphant," to dead believers who have fought the fight, triumphed, and now reside in Heaven (see also "Gregory the Great" and "Jerome" in chapter 12).

City—see Psalms 87:3.

Cloak—popular representation for the Carmelite Order. When spread by the Virgin over individuals kneeling by her side and at her feet, a cloak represents her protection and patronage for some particular group, usually a religious order. When being divided by a sword, it is an attribute of Saint Martin of Tours, who shared his cloak with a pauper later revealed to be Christ (see also "Martin, Bishop of Tours" in chapter 12).

Club—instrument of martyrdom of Saint James the Less and perhaps also Saint Jude (see also "James the Less" in chapter 12).

Coat of arms—see **Heraldry** below.

Cock or rooster—ancient pagan symbol of vigilance, the male chicken continued in this guise throughout Christian art and architecture, placed on church steeples and bell towers to guard the church and countryside against demons. Because the rooster crows at the break of day, it became a symbol of the preacher, who, by dispelling the darkness of the world and encouraging the steadfast to live by the light of the Lord, rouses Christians from their slumber—both physically and metaphysically. Only after the eleventh century did it become associated with Saint Peter; by the mid-thirteenth century, it was incorporated into weather vanes. (See also under **Instruments of Christ's Passion** below; "Peter" in chapter 12.)

Coins—see **Bag** above and **Bag of coins** under **Instruments of Christ's Passion** below.

Colors: The same color may represent different or even opposite qualities in different contexts. The five liturgical colors prescribed by the Church are black, white, red, green, and purple. The colors gold, blue (other than cerulean or sky blue), brown, pink, and yellow, though not liturgical, are also sanctioned for ecclesiastical decoration or garments. Cerulean blue, though permitted in decoration, is forbidden for vestments. Pink, the color of happiness and certain seasonal flowers, is used only on Guadete and Letare Sundays in mid-Advent and mid-Lent.[25]

Black—symbolizing death, mourning, and penance, is the color used during masses for the dead and on Good Friday. When combined with white, as in the habit of the Dominican Order, it symbolizes humility, penance, and purity of life.

Blue—representing Heaven, truth, hope, and spiritual love, is always associated with the Virgin in her role as Queen of Heaven.

Brown—color of humility and renunciation of this world; used by some religious groups such as the Franciscans, who adopted the color for their habit in 1897 in compliance with a decree of Pope Leo XIII (see also "Franciscans" in chapter 9).

Gold—symbolizes celestial light, beauty, perfection, incorruptibility, spiritual virtues, and eternity. A color for festivals such as Christmas, Easter, and Ascension, it may be substituted for other colored vestments except black.

Green—color of fresh growth and vegetation denoting victory and hope, spring triumphing over winter, life over death, and immortality. Its liturgical use occurs generally after Epiphany until Septuagesima Sunday (the third Sunday before Ash Wednesday) and after Trinity Sunday until the eve of Advent. It is commonly seen on tunics and mantles of Saints Joseph and Joachim (see also "Joachim" and "Joseph" in chapter 12).

Purple or violet—colors of royalty, justice, and the priesthood, but also of humility, suffering, sorrow, and penance. Jesus the Nazarene on his way to Golgotha is frequently robed in this color, so are the Virgin as Mater Dolorosa, and Saint Mary Magdalen. It is the color for Lent, vigils, Advent, and all days that bear the character of penance (see also "Mary Magdalen" and "Our Lady of Sorrows" in chapter 12).

Red—associated with emotions, royalty, divine love, faith, charity, and the Holy Spirit. Cardinals inherited this color of sovereign power from the Romans, and it is the distinguishing color of their dress (as soldiers of the pope). Because it is also emblematic of blood and fire, red is traditionally also the color of martyrs and of liturgical vestments used on their feasts and those of the Apostles and Evangelists, as well as on the Pentecost. The Virgin is frequently dressed in red robes, symbolizing her loyalty and love. Saint Mary Magdalen's hair and robe are also red (see also "Mary Magdalen" in chapter 12).

White—symbolizes chastity, innocence, purity, light, joy, and holiness. In scenes of the Annunciation, Mary is always clothed in white; the robe and sometimes mantle of the Immaculate Conception are depicted in this color. White is the liturgical color for Christmas, Easter, and Ascension, and for feasts of the Lord, the Virgin Mary, the angels, and those saints who were not martyrs. According to legend, the white habit of the Dominicans, to be covered with the black cape of penance, was assigned to them by the Virgin (see also "Dominicans" in chapter 9).

Yellow—represents the sun and, therefore, divinity. It is commonly used for Saint Joseph's clothing, where it symbolizes Joseph's trustworthiness, divine ordination, and sacred vocation as Mary's husband and Jesus' earthly father. The color of "the robe of glory," yellow was used for feasts of confessors. Dull yellow, symbolizing deceit and treachery, is used to depict Judas Iscariot (see also "Joseph" in chapter 12).

Column or pillar—symbol of steadfastness, strength, spiritual fortitude, and God, a column can also recall torture and death. According to *Meditations on the Life of Christ,* Mary rested against a column during the delivery of Jesus.[26] A pillar supporting a woman and child or held by the Virgin Mary identifies her as Our Lady of the Pillar of Zaragoza (Saragossa; see also "Mary" in chapter 12). The Pillars of Hercules figure prominently on Spain's coat of arms (see also **Heraldry** below).

Cord or rope—knotted, signifies the Franciscan Order, alluding to the rope that bound Christ to the column. Franciscans used cords or ropes as belt for their robes. The knots symbolize poverty, chastity, and obedience (see also "Franciscans" in chapter 9).

Crane—symbolizes watchfulness and loyalty. According to legend, all cranes form a protective ring around their leader at night. The one chosen as sentry stands on one leg and holds a stone in the other so that if the sentry crane should doze off, the stone will fall to the ground and startle it awake.

Crescent—although generally signifying Muslims or Moors, it may simply suggest eastern origins, as in the case of Saint Helen. Appearing with the Virgin, a crescent distinguishes her as the Queen of Heaven (see also **Moon** below and under **Mary**). A crescent in a circle symbolizes the Kingdom of Heaven and (along with a sun symbol) may be found on the breastplate of the Archangel Michael (see also "Mary" and under "Archangels," "Michael" in chapter 12).

Crosier—pastoral staff symbolizing the authority of abbots and abbesses, bishops and archbishops. Originally a straight pole (referring to the staff used by Apostles and pilgrims) in the seventh century, it assumed the shape of a shepherd's crook (referring to the pastoral role of clergy and Christ alike) in the eleventh century, later becoming highly ornamented. The staff's pointed bottom end represents a goad for the spiritually lazy; its straightness, righteous rule; and its crook, or head (separated from the staff by a knob), the pulling of souls toward God.[27] Attribute of Saints Ambrose, Augustine, Gertrude the Great, Gregory, and Teresa of Ávila (see also "Ambrose," "Augustine," "Gertrude the Great," "Gregory," and "Teresa of Ávila" in chapter 12).

Cross: The simple narratives of the Evangelists do not tell us exactly how Christ was crucified. Tradition, efforts on the parts of scholars, and visionary evidence given by saints such as Teresa of Ávila have provided the Christian Church and its art with the form of its most recognizable symbol.

Eusebius's *Life of Constantine* relates a popular tale of the Vision of the Flaming Cross, which appeared in the noonday sky with the legend "by this sign conquer" (see also **I H S** under **Letters and monograms** below) leading Constantine to convert to Christianity and to triumph over Maxentius at the famous Battle of the Milvian Bridge. (Conversion notwithstanding, Constantine would not actually be baptized until he lay on his deathbed.) According to the same tale, through a series of miraculous experiences, Constantine's mother, Saint Helen, discovered the location of the Cross Jesus was crucified on, and from that moment on, the cross was accepted as a designator of the Faith. The cross was popularly traced back to the tree of knowledge in the Garden of Eden, and down through King David and the Queen of Sheba to Calvary. Some of these tales built upon the "tree of life" themes in use centuries before the beginning of the Christian era. The early friars in New Spain naively saw the cross motifs in native American decoration as evidence of the pre-Conquest presence of the cross.

The symbol assumed a multitude of different forms (by some accounts, more than four hundred), based on interpretations of its role and specific doctrinal points (figure 11.2).[28] According to one interpretation, the cross represents the intersection of the eternal and infinite (the vertical element) with the earthly and finite (the horizontal element). Crosses are used in and on the church building, as well as on furniture, vestments, and other ecclesiastical accoutrements both as design elements and as marks of special significance for particular areas and objects.

Occasionally, a cross will be attached to the top of the crown worn by an image of Christ, Mary, or Joseph (alluding to their place as sovereigns in the Catholic religion) or to the top of a spire of a church (alluding to the triumph of the Gospel throughout the earth). When the infant Jesus holds a cross, it is a prophecy of his destiny. A cross is a general attribute associated with a number of saints such as Andrew and John the Baptist (on which see chapter 12). To symbolize the Resurrection, the cross in Christian cemeteries must be without Christ's body.

Calvary, or graded, cross—Latin cross on a three-step pedestal, said to represent the three theological virtues extolled by Saint Paul: faith, hope, and charity (1 Corinthians 13:13), as well as Mount Calvary, where Christ is supposed to have been crucified. Similar, pre-Christian stepped crosses were dedicated to the god Hermes in his mysterious aspect as the *logos* of Father Zeus.

Crucifix—originally, "the Crucified One" (from Latin *crux fixus,* fixed to the cross), cross with the figure of Christ upon it; central image of Christian worship in the

11.2. Crosses: a. Calvary, or graded; b. crucifix; c. fleurette; d. Jerusalem; e. Latin; f. papal; g. patriarchal; h. Saint Andrew's.

Western Church since the Middle Ages; found in every santuario in northern New Spain. Although the cross itself had been introduced as a Christian emblem after Constantine's triumph in 340, and although the second Council of Tours had decreed in 567 that elements of the Eucharist had to be kept under the figure of the cross upon the altar, use of the crucifix was not sanctioned until 705, by Pope John VII, and its placement on the altar was not required until the fourteenth century. Crucifixion scenes may include other figures such as the three Marys and John the Evangelist. Angels with chalices catching Christ's blood allude to the doctrine of the Real Presence. A crucifix and skull are symbols of penitence and attributes of Saints Mary Magdalen, Francis of Assisi, and Rosalie of Palermo. The crucifix alone in the hands of others signifies contemplation of Jesus' sacrifice and suffering and serves as an attribute of Saints Catherine of Siena, Rita of Cascia, and Aloysius Gonzaga (see also "Mary Magdalen," "Aloysius Gonzaga," "Catherine of Siena," "Francis of Assisi," "Rita of Cascia," and "Rosalie of Palermo" in chapter 12).

Fleurette cross—whose ends are modified to suggest a lily (fleur-de-lis), can be seen on the coat of arms of the Dominican Order as well as on badges of the military order of Saint James the Greater (Santiago; see also **Heraldry** below).

Jerusalem cross—five crosses combined in one, a cross potent between four crosslets. The prime crusader's symbol, later used by the crusader kings of Jerusalem and in the earliest coat of arms of the Franciscan Order (see also **Heraldry** below).

Latin cross (*crux immissa*)—one of the simplest crosses, with the vertical element longer than the horizontal. A Latin cross on top of an orb or globe, banded or plain, is a symbol of the triumph of Christianity throughout the world and is referred to, variously, as a victory cross, triumphant cross, or conquest cross.

Papal cross—attribute of popes or papal saints, for whom it is reserved. Although the three arms of this cross are often said to represent the Trinity, some have associated them with the pagan idea of a ladder to Heaven, a trip up and down this ladder being considered "essential for every spiritual leader with pretensions to firsthand authority."[29]

Patriarchal cross—said to have originated from the profile created by the Latin cross and the addition of the I N R I plaque, it has been associated with cardinals and archbishops since the fourteenth century.

Saint Andrew's cross or saltire (*crux decussata*)—the Apostle Andrew supposedly was crucified on a cross of this shape because to die exactly like Christ was for him too great an honor.

Crown—in northern New Spain, only three types of crowns are commonly seen in association with religious imagery: imperial crowns—associated with Spain, the Virgin Mary, Saint Joseph, and a few saints of regal status; diadems—around the heads of archangels; and celestial crowns—as wreaths worn or being given to martyred saints and popes (the papal crown is three-tiered).

A general symbol of royalty, victory and dominion, and the virtues, when set aside by a saint, a crown indicates that the rewards and pleasures of earth were rejected for those of Heaven. An angel holding a crown represents the virtues. A ring of plaited or twisted thorns, the symbolic crown of thorns associated with Christ and his Passion, may appear on the heads of Saints Catherine of Siena and of Rose of Lima (where roses are more evident than thorns). (See also **Thorn** and **Wreath** below; "Mary" in chapter 12; and chapter 9)

Crucifixion—see **Crucifix** under **Cross** above.

Cup—see **Chalice** above.

Curtain—used from early Christian times to symbolize dignity, revelation, and the possibility of knowing the spiritual truth behind all things. Appearing first as ceremonial concealment for late antique and Byzantine rulers, the curtain motif was later used with seated religious figures, notably the Evangelists, who were enthroned between open curtains. With the increased veneration of the Virgin, the curtain (as described by Ambrose in one of his letters) became part of Marian iconography[30] and was blended with the baldachin or a canopy of draperies, a decorative device that continued into the baroque in religious works (see figure 7.9b). The use of a curtain to conceal the main altar for the period from Passion Sunday (two weeks before Easter Sunday) until the Gloria at the Holy Saturday Mass is part of the religious drama of Holy Week and is still practiced in some of the churches in northern New Spain.[31]

Cypress tree—traditionally a mortuary emblem supposed to have the power of preserving the body from corruption and therefore planted in cemeteries, it is also associated with the Virgin (see also "Mary" in chapter 12).

Dagger—see **Knife** and **Sword** below.

Devils and demons—may represent Satan or sin and temptation in general. In two- or three-dimensional representations, they vary from symbolic animals such as snakes, scorpions, or lizards to horrific man-beast combinations—fiends with claws and pointed tails (see also **Dragon** below).

Dice—see under **Instruments of Christ's Passion** below.

Directions and sides—of the cardinal directions, west is associated with dying (from *occidit*—that which kills, the Abbess Herrade tells us); north with cold, night, darkness, the realm of Lucifer and powers of evil; east, a direction toward which worship and prayer are oriented (as in most religions), with hope, life, and rebirth; and south with warmth, sunshine, paradise, charity, and divine love. The practice of orienting the church building toward the east was not as common in northern New Spain during colonial times as it had been in Europe in preceding centuries (see also "Orientation" under "Church Buildings" in chapter 3).[32]

Of the two sides of the body (when facing forward), right is the side of honor: the good thief at the scene of the Crucifixion is on Christ's right, whereas the unrepentant thief is on his left, the sinister or evil side.

The Tridentine Council in 1445 prescribed certain sides of the sanctuary for the reading of the Gospel and the Epistles. The Gospel side of the church was on the left as one faced toward the altar, and the Epistle side was on the right. Because the Gospels contain the words of Christ, reading them took precedence over reading the Epistles, which are the testimonies and writings of the Apostles. This prescription is now obsolete, with both the Gospels and the Epistles being read from the same location.

Dog—traditional symbol of fidelity, orthodoxy, and watchfulness. A black-and-white dog is an attribute of Saint Dominic; a dog holding a loaf of bread in its mouth, an attribute of Saint Roch (see also "Dominic of Guzmán" and "Roch" in chapter 12).

Dome—considered a heavenly form from antiquity (*skene-orbis, ciborioum,* and globe combined into a single celestial and cosmic symbol). During the pagan Roman Empire, the hemispherical masonry dome, a Constantinian architectural convention, became the symbol of imperial immortality and was used by Christian kings in throne rooms and reception vestibules.[33] Reinforced in the West through the concepts of cosmic egg, divine helmet, and pine cone, the dome held a peculiar appeal to the early Christians in their cult of the dead, veneration for martyrs, and their yearning for some tangible image of a heavenly *domus.*[34]

Donkey or ass—the Bible presents this humblest beast of burden as the mount of princes.[35] The donkey carried Mary to Jerusalem, was present at the Nativity, was ridden by Mary and the infant Jesus in their flight to Egypt, and bore Christ in his triumphant entry into Jerusalem. It was as reward for this last service that Christ is said, in Spanish, French, and Italian legend, to have bestowed the dark dorsal cross that can be seen on some gray donkeys.[36] Donkeys or asses also appear in paintings of the miracles of Saint Anthony of Padua. According to one oft-told tale, when a donkey or other beast of burden bearing a religious statue refused to budge from an area near a church, it was divine will that the statue remain at that church—such, for example, was the case with a statue of the Virgin Mary and a figure of Christ at the mission church of San Elizario (Texas). (See also "Anthony of Padua" in chapter 12.)

Donors—figures in painting or sculpture representing individuals responsible for funding a religious order, a building of that order, a chapel or other church building, an altar or its decoration, or even the painting in which they appear. In what may be a unique sculpted example in northern New Spain, two figures—now decapitated—kneel on either side of the outer entrance to the sacristy of San Sebastián in Concordia (Sinaloa; figure 11.3).[37] The 1820 inventory of the presidio chapel at Tucson (Arizona) lists "a large image of Our Lady of Guadalupe with its gilt frame and various personages painted at her feet in devout postures," suggesting there once was another donor painting. Only the description of the painting remains.

Doors, gates, and portals—symbolize entrances to the hidden or sacred space behind them. Christ's words to

11.3. Headless donor figures at the sacristy entrance, San Sebastián, Concordia, Sinaloa, 1979.

Saint John, "I am the door; by me if any man enter in, he shall be saved" (John 10:9), begin the long symbolic tradition of a church's portal serving as the gateway to salvation and thus being an appropriate area for imagery having to do with salvation. Especially impressive are the doors to the main and side portals of most cathedrals in northern New Spain (see figures 2.12 and 2.17; see also **Gate** under **Mary** below; and "Façades, Frontispieces, Portals" in chapter 5).

Dove—an ancient symbol of great importance, generally representing peace, love, and tenderness. For Christians, following Saint John's description of the Baptism of Christ (John 1:32), the dove represents the Holy Spirit, the third person of the Trinity, often shown radiating the light of blessedness (see also discussion of "Throne of Grace" under "Trinity" in chapter 12). As a symbol also of meekness, modesty, humility, and purity (especially applied to the Annunciation), it is often included with the Virgin. Two doves are offered by Mary's parents, Joachim and Anne, at her Presentation in the Temple. As a symbol of the human soul, a dove may be portrayed leaving the body at the time of death. In Genesis, the return of a dove with an olive sprig to Noah's ark signaled the end of the flood. As a symbol of divine inspiration, a dove perches on the shoulders of and speaks to Saints Gregory the Great, Thomas Aquinas, and Teresa of Ávila. A sculptured or painted dove was often placed in the center of the pulpit's sounder to represent the divine word. With a palm branch in its beak, the dove is a symbol of victory over death; with an olive branch, of peace (see also "Gregory the Great," "Thomas Aquinas," and "Teresa of Ávila" in chapter 12).

Dragon—symbol of the Devil, equated with the snake and expressing evil. Archangel Michael battles one (sometimes shown with seven heads, as described by Saint John in Revelation 12:3; another dragon with seven heads, ten horns, a body like a leopard and feet like a bear appears in Revelation 13:1–2). The legendary Saint George is shown mounted on a horse as he slays a dragon (see also **Serpent,** both as a separate entry and under **Mary** below; "George" in chapter 12.)

Eagle—symbol for Saint John the Evangelist, resurrection, the Christian spirit, ascension, inspiration, and preaching, the eagle may be incorporated into lecterns.[38] An eagle with wings spread is a traditional design for reading stands or ambos. Among almost all pre-Christian cultures, the eagle signified divinity; Christianity absorbed this symbol, applying it both to God the Father and to Christ. An ancient tradition (attested to in Psalms 103:5) tells how the eagle, when it becomes old, flies close to the sun and then plunges into a fountain, regaining its youth. A symbol for Baptism, it also refers to the person baptized whose life is renewed by that sacrament. The double-headed eagle represents the Habsburg dynasty of Spain and the Holy Roman Empire; it has been obliterated from virtually all church buildings in northern New Spain (and throughout Mexico, for that matter), with the notable exception of Nuestra Señora del Rosario (Sinaloa), where double-headed eagles support niches on the second story on either side of the main frontispiece (figure 11.4; see also discussion of lectern under "Objects," "Mass," in chapter 8 and "John the Evangelist" in chapter 12).

Ermine—because of its white fur, the ermine symbolizes chastity, purity, and royalty. Commonly seen as decorative trim on the robe of Saint Joachim (Mary's father) and on the cape of Saint John of Nepomuk, where it implies nobility in the Church (see also "Joachim" and "John of Nepomuk" in chapter 12).

Evangelists—the Four Pillars of the Faith as the authors of the four Gospels, the Four Evangelists are objects of immense veneration in the Christian Church. Matthew and John, whose attributes are an angel and an eagle, were among the Twelve Apostles who personally knew Jesus. Mark and Luke, whose attributes are a lion and an ox, did not know Christ and composed their gospels in the middle part of the first century (see also "Matthew," "Mark," "Luke," and "John" in chapter 12).

Ewer and pitcher—see **Pitcher and basin** below.

Eye—represents the ever-present, all-seeing, all-knowing God; in a triangle, it represents the Trinity; when the triangle is surrounded by a circle and the eye radiates rays of light, the infinite holiness of the Triune God. Moving from the baroque to the neoclassical, the all-seeing eye within a triangle may replace the figure of God the Father at the top of a retablo. Eyes on a dish are the principal attribute of Saint Lucy (see also "Lucy" in chapter 12).

11.4. Double-headed eagle motif, a symbol of the Habsburgs, on the main frontispiece, Nuestra Señora del Rosario, Sinaloa, 2000.

Feather—signifies faith and contemplation; as a quill pen, the word of God (see also **Pen** below).

Fire—see **Flames** below.

Fish—with the widespread appearance of the acronym spelling the Greek word for fish from the initials of the Greek words for "Jesus Christ, Son of God the Savior," the fish became one of the earliest Christian symbols. Having water as their natural element, fish came to symbolize fertility, wisdom, purity, and resurrection (the baptismal font is called a piscina—literally, fishpond). Indeed, because some Christian theologians believed fish were not subject to God's curse in the flood, through Baptism, Christians and fish became symbolically one. Associated with this symbolic connection were the Church as a boat, the Cross as its mast, the Apostles as fishers of men, and Christianity as the net. An attribute of Saint Peter, a fisherman by trade (to whom Jesus said: "From henceforth, thou shalt catch men" in Luke 5:10) and of Archangel Raphael, who assisted Tobias in procuring the fish with healing gall for the young man's father's eyes (Tobit 6:1–5). Fish are sometimes seen in paintings of Saint Anthony of Padua because, according to legend, they would put their heads above the water to hear him preach (see also "Raphael" under "Archangels" in chapter 12).

Flames—may represent Hell, instruments of torture or martyrdom, or religious fervor. They may also be seen coming from the heart of Jesus or of many saints. Saint Dominic's dog holds a flaming torch. In scenes of the Pentecost, flames are shown over the heads of the Twelve Apostles and Mary. Flames also erupt from the mouths of grotescos beneath the pedestals of the statues of Saints John the Evangelist and Mary Magdalen in the retablo of the Mater Dolorosa altar in Santo Tomás de Villanueva (Chihuahua; see figure 10.17b; see also **Heart** below; "Dominic of Guzmán" and "Most Holy Mother of Light" in chapter 12).

Fleur-de-lis—emblem of France since King Hugh Capet. Although often a symbol of the Trinity and an emblem of the Virgin elsewhere, in northern New Spain it is more commonly associated with the Spanish coat of arms from the time of the first Bourbon king (1700). A fleurette cross (see figure 11.2c), whose ends are lily-shaped, is peculiar to the military order of Saint James the Greater (Santiago) and the Dominican Order (see also **Cross** above and **Heraldry** below).

Flowers—symbolize grace, beauty, and virtue (see also specific kinds).[39] Since the Middle Ages, along with other plants and trees, flowers have represented the odor of sanctity (Mary, as the conqueror of sin, smells ambrosial) and the vision of Heaven as a pastoral paradise. To these symbolic ends, and for other emblematic and decorative purposes, they were used throughout northern New Spain.

Fortress—see **Tower**.

Fountain—symbol of living water, paradise, and eternal life (see also under **Mary** below).

Fruit—may be a symbol of fertility and plenty (see also specific kinds).

Garden—see **Mary** below.

Gate—see **Doors, gates, and portals** above and **Mary** below.

Geometric shapes: The symbolism of geometric shapes owes a great deal to Plato's ideas about unity—the relationship of the whole to its parts—and about the universal harmony of rhyme and its geometric origins (see also "Geometric Shapes and Patterns" under "Decorative Motifs" in chapter 6).[40]

Circle—conforming with the Renaissance worldview, the circle was considered one of the perfect shapes, symbolizing eternity, balance, perfection, and Heaven.

Cross—Christ, the Church.

Eared quatrefoil—Gothic form merging circle and square, possibly to symbolize the union of Heaven and earth, the eared quatrefoil was a popular window shape throughout New Spain (see also figure 5.23c).

Square—opposed to the circle, a square represents earth, the four directions, order, and solidity. A square crowned by a semicircle (cupola profile) symbolizes the union of earth and sky.

Trefoil—three joined semicircles in the shape of a cloverleaf, a trefoil signifies the Trinity.

Triangle (equilateral)—symbolizes the Trinity.

Gestures—positions of eyes, hands, arms, feet, and even entire bodies assumed great importance in Christian art from the twelfth century on. Positions of the hands and eyes indicate particular roles saints might play at different times in their lives. For example, eyes rolled up with the whites exposed indicate ecstasy or direct communication with God—or, with hands on the chest, martyrdom. Eyes looking upward with the hands on the chest signify satisfaction. The right hand laid on the right side of the face signifies grief. Palms together signify prayer; hands open and cupped upward with arms extended, trust. The right hand of God, with which he created and judged, is a sign of energy and power. An elevated right hand with first and middle fingers raised and with ring and little fingers folded to the palm and covered by the thumb is a gesture of benediction; the nearly identical gesture, only with ring and little fingers not covered by the thumb, is called the "speaking hand" or "hand of Logos." The gesture of crossing oneself dates back to earliest Christianity: in honor of the Trinity, the forehead, heart, and left then right shoulder are touched with the right hand.

Kneeling expresses humility; and prostration, complete subservience to the will of God, as when a priest-to-be prostrates himself during ordination, expressing his complete willingness to be molded like clay in the hands of God.

Globe—symbolizes sovereignty and power. Mary stands on a globe representing the earth in portrayals of the Immaculate Conception (see also **Orb** below).

Gourd—signifies pilgrims, who used gourds (most often attached to poles or staffs) to carry water, and pilgrimages generally. Saint James the Greater (Santiago) may be shown with a gourd when clothed as a pilgrim, as may Archangel Raphael when journeying with Tobias (see also "James the Greater," and "Raphael" under "Archangels" in chapter 12).

Grapes—one of the earliest Christian symbols, synonymous with wine or the blood of Christ within the Eucharist. Popular decorative motif on salomónico columns (see "Columns" under "Architectural Details" in chapter 6).

Guardian angel—see under "Archangels" in chapter 12.

Hammer—see under **Instruments of Christ's Passion** below.

Hat—according to type, color, or both, signifies the rank or vocation of its wearer. Saints Francis Xavier, Ignatius of Loyola, John of Nepomuk, and Teresa of Ávila are often shown wearing a biretta, a square, ridged cap with a tassel on top; a cardinal's hat is usually either worn by or hanging nearby Saint Jerome. (See also "Head Coverings" under "Vestments" in chapter 9; "Francis Xavier," "Ignatius of Loyola," "Jerome," "John of Nepomuk," and "Teresa of Ávila" in chapter 12.)

Heart—signifies religious fervor, charity, and divine love; attribute of Saints Augustine, Catherine of Siena (possibly with accompanying cross), Francis Xavier, Gertrude the Great, Ignatius of Loyola (when the heart is crowned with thorns), and Teresa of Ávila. The Sacred Heart of Jesus is shown encircled by a crown of thorns, surrounded by flames, and sometimes pierced with three nails (figure 11.5). A heart pierced by a single arrow symbolizes contriteness; one pierced by seven daggers or arrows, the sorrows of Mary.

The earliest devotion of the Sacred Heart of Jesus can be traced to the eleventh-century Cistercian nun Saint Lutgarde d'Aywières, in whose visions Jesus embraced her and showed her his wounds. Similar visions by Saints Catherine of Siena and Marguerite-Marie Alacoque in the fourteenth and seventeenth centuries, respectively, helped establish the devotion, popular since the late 1600s, which has been expanded to include imagery and veneration for the Sacred Heart of Mary (see also "Sacred Heart of Jesus," "Most Holy Mother of Light," "Sacred Heart of Mary," "Augustine," "Catherine of Siena," "Francis Xavier," "Gertrude the Great," "Ignatius of Loyola," and "Teresa of Ávila" in chapter 12).

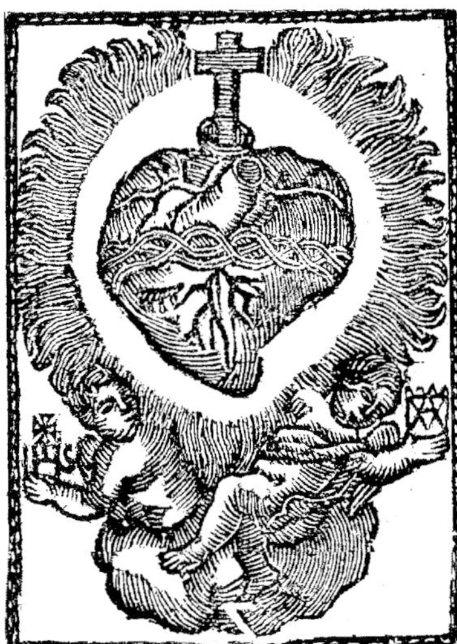

11.5. Sacred Heart of Jesus, eighteenth-century woodblock, private collection.

Heraldry: Originally a means of identifying groups in combat (dating back to Old Testament times) and developed to a high art in Europe as a means of distinguishing prominent families, heraldic insignia, shields, and ornaments were also used to distinguish religious orders and civil groups, as well as military orders and state officials throughout Mexico's colonial history.

On a shield in diagonally opposed quarters, the Spanish coat of arms contains a lion rampant and a castle (a large tower surmounted by three small towers), the symbols of León and Castilla, the two kingdoms that carried the main burden of the Reconquest. As other kingdoms and provinces became part of what is now Spain and as foreign royalty succeeded to the Spanish throne, their symbols were added to the coat of arms: vertical red and yellow stripes for Aragón; vertical gold chains against a red background for Navarra; the pomegranate for Granada; the double-headed eagle of the Holy Roman Empire for Charles I; the lily of France (fleur-de-lis) for Philip V, duke of Anjou and the first Bourbon king of Spain. Surrounded

a.

b.

11.6. Spanish coat of arms, main frontispiece, San Ignacio de Loyola de Kadakaaman, Baja California Sur, 1987: a. shield; b. Pillars of Hercules.

by a banner bearing the words "plus ultra" (more beyond), the two silver Pillars of Hercules are capped—one with the royal crown of Calpe (now Gibraltar) and the other with the imperial diadem of Abyla (now Mount Hacho).[41] In certain representations of the Spanish coat of arms, a double-linked chain of flints and steels, the emblem of the Order of the Golden Fleece, devoted to the protection of the Church, can be seen around the entire shield, together with a depiction of a sheep representing the Golden Fleece. Although its last Old World chapter was dissolved in the sixteenth century, the order exists in Mexico to this day, and the chain and sheep may be seen in portraits of members of the order as well as around images of the Virgin as patroness of that order. Completing the coat of arms, a crown appears placed above the shield.

After Independence, the Spanish coat of arms was chiseled off virtually all churches in Mexico. The barest outline can still be seen over the door of the former cathedral of Bishop Reyes, now the parochial church of Nuestra Señora de la Asunción in Álamos (Sonora); the remnants of the Spanish crown can be detected above the arms of the Republic of Mexico on the pediment of the Cathedral of Durango (Durango); on the main frontispiece of San Ignacio de Kadakaaman (Baja California Sur), the shield appears on one side of the main portal and the Pillars of Hercules on the other—both components ignored because of the church's remoteness and insignificance (figure 11.6a–b; see also 2.16b and 5.9).

The Mexican emblem, in which an eagle holds a writhing snake in its beak while standing atop a cactus on a rock in the center of a lake was the Aztec symbol for their capital, Tenochitlán. Although this ancient symbol was co-opted in 1523 by the Spanish conquerors as the coat of arms for Mexico City, and for all of New Spain in certain contexts, it did not become Mexico's official coat of arms until Independence in 1821. Its appearance on any church in northern New Spain therefore represents a postcolonial addition (figure 11.7).

11.7. Mexican coat of arms surmounted by the emblem of the Hospitaliers over the sacristy entrance, San Juan de Dios, Durango city, 1983.

11.8. Augustinian emblem

11.9. Carmelite emblem.

11.10. Dominican emblem.

The coats of arms or emblems of the various religious orders were placed over the portals of their churches and other buildings in New Spain. Cardinals and bishops were entitled to coats of arms, which might also appear on churches and palaces (see figure 9.9). An oval was the nearly universal shape for an ecclesiastical coat of arms, most likely to avoid the military associations of a shield. The following are coats of arms or emblems associated with religious orders or figures in the churches or religious art of northern New Spain.

Augustinians: Their emblem consists of a heart pierced by an arrow or arrows—usually three—representing God's intense love, which Saint Augustine felt in his conversion. The three arrows allude to the Trinity (figure 11.8).

Carmelites: Dating back to the fourteenth century, their emblem shows a stylized Mount Carmel in Israel with a cross on top and three stars (figure 11.9).

Dominicans: Their emblem is a cross whose arms terminate in stylized fleurs-de-lis. The arms and flowers are usually black and white, the colors of the order's habit (figure 11.10). Occasionally a rosary surrounds the cross; a dog with a torch in its mouth may also be included. An arm in armor, symbol of the Inquisition (an institution under Dominican control), shown with a patriarchal cross, which rests on an orb is another Dominican emblem.

Franciscans: The order's first emblem depicted the five wounds of Christ—*cinco llagas* or *armas celestiales* (five wounds or celestial arms)—and the stigmata of Saint

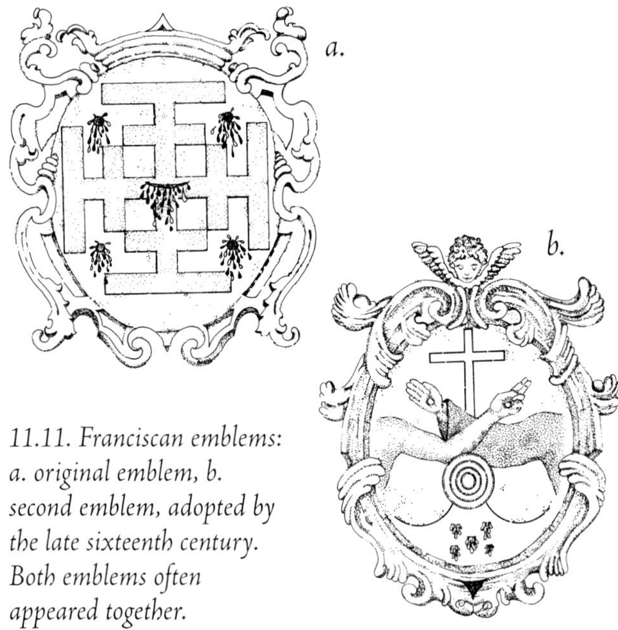

11.11. Franciscan emblems: a. original emblem, b. second emblem, adopted by the late sixteenth century. Both emblems often appeared together.

Francis. By the late sixteenth century, a second emblem was adopted: the crossed and nail-marked hands of Christ and Saint Francis superimposed on a Latin cross, with Saint Francis's hands identified by his tunic sleeve. By papal authority, a third emblem, containing the Jerusalem cross (see under **Cross** above), recognizes the order's role as guardian of the holy places of Jerusalem. The first two are often seen together (figure 11.11a–b); the third appears far less frequently.

Hospitaliers of Saint John of God: The order's emblem is a pomegranate, Saint John of God's personal attribute, crowned by a cross (figure 11.12; see also figure 11.7, and "John of God" in chapter 12).

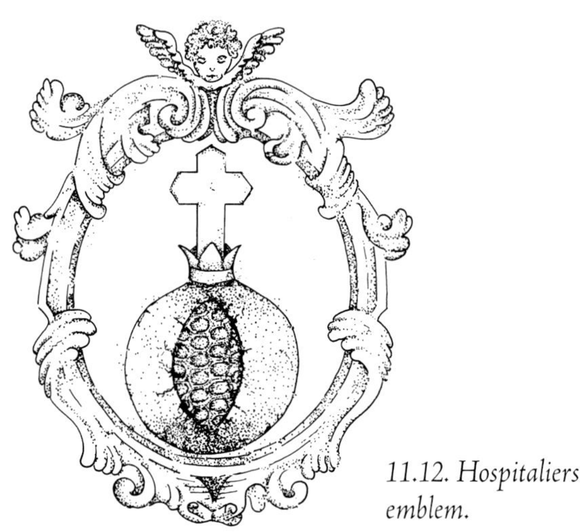

11.12. Hospitaliers emblem.

Jesuits: Originally used by Saint Bernadine of Siena and adopted by the order in the sixteenth century, the Jesuits' emblem is the Holy Name of Jesus and the letters "I H S," with a cross atop the transverse bar of the "H" (at whose base there may also be three nails; figure 11.13; see also **I H S** below). After the order was expelled from New Spain in 1767, many of the Jesuit emblems were obliterated.

11.13. Jesuit emblem.

Mercedarians: The order's emblem (figure 11.14) shows a cross in the upper part, with four red and white bars from the arms of Catalonia beneath, and a crown representing the royal patent granted by King James of Aragón, a cofounder of the order. Fetters may sometimes be seen in the lower part in recognition of the order's original mission: to ransom and recover captives of the Moors.

11.14. Mercedarian emblem.

11.15. Diocesan clergy emblem, woodblock, private collection.

Diocesan clergy: In their emblem, seen frequently in parish churches and cathedrals, the papal tiara or miter and the crossed keys of Saint Peter proclaim the diocesan clergy's direct allegiance to the pope (figure 11.15; see also keystone in figure 6.22).

Horn—specifically a trumpet, in the hands of an angel, signifies divine inspiration and particularly the message of the Last Judgment. It is also a frequent element in paintings of Saint Jerome: "Seeing the great scholar, orthodox doctor, penitent, and saint shattered by the trumpet's blast reminds good Catholics to take nothing for granted, to live today as though they will die tomorrow. It teaches bad Catholics fear, repentance, and mending of life. It promises heretics and schismatics eternal punishment."[42]

Horse—attribute of soldiers. Saints George, Martin of Tours, and James the Greater (Santiago) are usually shown on a horse, typically white, symbolizing purity. Pre-Christian symbolism of the horse as the soul (Greeks) or as bestowing intelligence (Egyptians) apparently did not transfer to Christian iconography.[43] Rather, horses appear as actual (nonsymbolic) mounts for soldiers, for example, in scenes from the lives of Saints George and Martin of Tours and during the conversion of Saul (see also "George," "James the Greater," and "Martin, Bishop of Tours" in chapter 12).

House—Our Lady of Loreto can be distinguished in that she is seated on a house borne by angels or is holding a model of a house in her hands (see also **Model of a building** and **Mary** below; "Mary" in chapter 12.)

I H S—see under **Letters and monograms** below.

Incense—Genesis states that God enjoyed the "sweet odor" of Noah's burnt offerings. Catholics have long held that the aromatic smoke of burning incense symbolizes prayers ascending to Heaven; it is used during church services to inspire believers to holiness through prayer and good works.

Initials—see **Letters and monograms** below.

Inkwell—see **Pen** below.

Instruments of Christ's Passion—Considered symbols of the Eucharist and powerful weapons against sin, the "weapons of Christ" ("arma Christi") were the instruments of Jesus' betrayal, arrest, denial, torture and Crucifixion. Painted or sculpted, they appeared either separately or in scenes of the Passion.

Awl—used to start the nail holes in the Cross.

Bag of coins—Judas's betrayal money.

Boxes of spices—three, for embalming.

Cloth—slender, long piece used to lower the body from the Cross, shroud in which Christ was buried (*sudarium*), and Mary's head cloth, with which she wrapped her son's loins. The first is often shown draped across the arms of the cross; the second and third, though traditional elements of Crucifixion scenes elsewhere, may not be present in northern New Spain (see also **Veil** below).

Cock or **rooster**—bird that crowed after Peter's denial.

Cross—principal symbol of Christ's sacrifice.

Crown of thorns—placed on Christ's head when he was mocked as King of the Jews.

Dice—used to cast lots for Christ's seamless garment.

Ear—cut from the high priest's servant by Simon Peter at Christ's arrest.

Hammer—used to drive the nails into Christ's hands and feet on the Cross.

Hand—that struck Christ during his mocking.

Head—of the betrayer Judas, who later hanged himself.

I N R I—see under **Letters and monograms** below.

Knife—circumcision knife, representing the first shedding of Christ's blood.

Ladder—used by followers to remove the body from the Cross.

Lance—that pierced Christ's side.

Lantern—carried by soldiers to find Christ in the Garden of Gethsemane.

Nails—that attached Christ's hands and feet to the Cross.

Pillar—against which he was bound and flagellated.

Pincers—used to pull the nails from the hands and feet of Jesus on the Cross (see also **Pliers** below).

Pitcher and basin—used when Pilate washed his hands after Christ's trial by the Roman authorities, sometimes interpreted as the pitcher and basin used by Jesus to wash his Apostles' feet.

Reed—mock scepter given Christ by his tormenters when he was presented to the Jerusalem crowds as King of the Jews, and thus included in "Ecce Homo" (Behold the Man) representations of him. Also identifies "El Señor de la Caña" (Lord of the Reed), an image of an exhausted and scourged Christ seated holding a reed.

Rope—used to bind Jesus.

Scourge—whip with which Christ was flagellated.

Skull and bones—indicates Golgotha, "the place of skulls." Because tradition places Christ's Cross on top of Adam's resting place, it may also refer to Adam's skull.

Sponge on a reed—held vinegar offered to Christ on the Cross to quench his thirst.

Towel—used to dry the Apostles' feet after Jesus had washed them.

Veil—towel or napkin with Christ's image, commonly called the "Veil of Veronica."

Ivy—traditional Christian symbol for everlasting life and the spiritual fertility of Jesus Christ, ivy may be incorporated into stylized running designs, in swags, or around columns.

Jar—see **Box or jar of ointment** above and **Vase** below.

Jeweled chain or collar—unique attribute of Saint Cajetan (see also Order of the Golden Fleece under **Heraldry** above).

J N R J or J N R T—see **I N R I** under **Letters and monograms** below.

Keys—signify ownership and authority, new life (an opened door), and a house. Attribute of Saint Peter. Jesus' own words: "And I will give unto thee the keys of the kingdom of heaven" (Matthew 16:19) establish Peter as guardian of the gates of Heaven. Crossed silver and gold keys tied with red ribbon are the symbol of the papacy and indicate successors to Saint Peter. Keys to Heaven and of secret keeping may also be given to martyrs, such as Saint John of Nepomuk (see also **Diocesan Clergy** under **Heraldry** above; "John of Nepomuk" and "Peter" in chapter 12).

Knife—instrument of martyrdom or torture. Saint Bartholomew was flayed alive with one (see also **Sword** below; "Bartholomew" in chapter 12).

Knot—see **Cord or rope** above.

Ladder—Judeo-Christian symbol of the link between Heaven and earth, and of the possibility of ascending into Heaven; used in spiritual metaphors: seven-rung ladder of virtue; martyrdom as ladder to Heaven (see also under **Instruments of Christ's Passion** above and **Mary** below).

Lamb—early and most frequent symbol for Jesus Christ, Lamb of God (Agnus Dei), commonly portrayed as "Cordero Mística" (the Mystic Lamb) on tabernacle doors and as standing or lying on a book (Bible) with seven seals (see also **Book** above). A lamb symbolizes the Nativity, Christ's purity and meekness, and his sacrifice and redemption of man, as announced by John the Baptist (John 1:29), hence also the Eucharist. When reclining, a lamb signifies suffering; when standing and holding a banner, victory over death. An attribute of John the Baptist and also of Saint Agnes, punning on the Latin *agnus*. Sheep refer to Jesus as the Good Shepherd and humankind as his flock (see also **Sheep** and **Shepherd** below; "Agnes" and "John the Baptist" in chapter 12).

Lamp—general image of incarnation (see also **Sanctuary lamp** below).

Lance—attribute of Saints Matthew and Philip of Jesus, who were both martyred with lances, perhaps also Jude (see also under **Instruments of Christ's Passion** above; and "Jude," and "Matthew" in chapter 12).

Lantern—see under **Instruments of Christ's Passion** above.

Laurels—see **Wreath** below.

Letters and monograms—The first letters of words in key Church slogans or in phrases used to describe Jesus came themselves to symbolize the Church or Jesus. Along with monograms (interlaced initials of a name—most often Mary's) and names spelled out in capital letters, these were commonly used in northern New Spain in decorations, on plaques, and as labels over doorways and on altars.

Chi-Rho—according to Eusebius's history of the life of Constantine, on the eve of the battle of Pons Mulvius on the Tiber River in 312—traditionally regarded as the turning point of the acceptance of Christianity within the Roman Empire—the Roman emperor saw in a dream a cross in the sky and heard a voice saying "in hoc signo vinces" (by this sign shall you conquer). Substituting the Chi-Rho (the Christogram, or monogram of XP) for the Roman standard, he won the ensuing battle. The two Greek letters XP are the first two letters of the Greek word for Christ: ΧΡΙΣΤΟΣ.

I H C—see **I H S** below.

I H S—from the Greek letters ΙΗΣ signifying ΙΗΣους (Iesus or Jesus), the capital eta, H, being mistaken for capital H, the abbreviation "Ihs" was often expanded as "Ihsesus." The letters were taken to signify "Iesus Hominem Salvator" (Jesus, the Savior of Men) by Saint Bernardine of Siena in 1424; and by others to signify "In hac salus" (In it [the cross] is safety, or salvation); "Iesus habemus socium" (We have Jesus for our companion); and "In hoc signo [vinces]" (In this sign [thou shalt conquer]). The letters form part of the emblem of the Franciscan Saint Bernadine of Siena and the Jesuit Order (see also **Heraldry** above).

I N R I—first initials of Iesus Nazarenus Rex Iudaeorum (Jesus the Nazarene, King of the Jews), an inscription written by Pilate and attached to the Cross on which Christ was crucified. The Scriptures say that it was written in Hebrew, Latin, and Greek, but only the initials of the Latin inscription commonly appear. Occasionally "J N R T" may be seen, standing for "Jesús Nazareno Rey [de] Todo" (Jesus the Nazarene King [over] All), and a New Mexican crucifix by José Aragón bears the initials "J N R J," standing for "Jesús Nazareno Rey de los Judíos" (Jesus the Nazarene King of the Jews).

J O S E—Joseph.

M A R I A or just **M A**—Mary.

Lightning—symbolizes destruction and God's vengeance. It is associated with Saint Barbara because her father was struck dead by lightning on his return home from her execution, which he had ordered (see also "Barbara" in chapter 12).

Lily—symbolizing purity, innocence, and virginity, as well as royalty, the lily appears in early Christian emblems for both the Virgin Mary and Jesus. Standing in a vase, it represents the Annunciation; accordingly, Archangel Gabriel may be portrayed as holding a lily. Since the thirteenth century, it has been a general attribute of chaste or virginal saints, such as Anthony of Padua, Catherine of Siena, Dominic of Guzmán, and Joseph. (See also **Fleur-de-lis** above and under **Mary** below; "Anthony of Padua," "Catherine of Siena," "Dominic of Guzmán," "Gabriel" under "Archangels," and "Joseph" in chapter 12.)

Lion—characterized as having strength, courage, fortitude, virtue, and sagacity, the lion became a symbol for Jesus. Mystic writers saw Christ's potent speech in the lion's roar, based on Old Testament prophetical texts such as Hosea 11:10 and Joel 3:16. Believed to sleep with their eyes open, lions symbolized vigilance and spiritual watchfulness, appearing as guardians and sentinels. Because lion cubs were thought to be born dead but brought back to life by their father after three days, the lion also symbolized the Resurrection. As the emblem of the Kingdom of León, two lions appear on the Spanish coat of arms. A lion is also an attribute for Saints Mark and Jerome (see also **Heraldry** above; "Mark" and "Jerome" in chapter 12).

Mandorla—Italian for "almond," an almond-shaped radiance (*visica piscis* or *aureola de cuerpo*) enclosing the entire body. It is commonly seen around the Virgin of Guadalupe, but rarely associated with other figures of the Virgin (see also **Aureola** above). A pre-Christian symbol of the female, the almond, as a sweet fruit surrounded by a tough shell, was held to signify the spiritual and hidden reality of the Incarnation of Christ. The staff of Aaron (Numbers 17:1–8) is described as a blooming almond stalk—a symbol of divine approval (see "Our Lady of Guadalupe" in chapter 12).

Mantle—essential attribute of sovereign power, worn by gods and humans. Elijah bestows his mantle on his successor and disciple, Elishah (1 Kings 19:19). In the Christian era, the mantle becomes a symbol of protection; the Virgin Mary (in her particular role as protectress or the Virgin of Misericord—of all mercy) is shown wearing a mantle over her spreading arms, under which are gathered individuals seeking her sponsorship or care, such as the Mercedarian and Carmelite Orders. Attribute of Saint Martin of Tours, who is always shown dividing his cloak with a beggar (see also "Martin, Bishop of Tours" in chapter 12).

Mary: Beginning as early as the twelfth century, the virginal purity of Mary and her position as Queen of Heaven were much developed and refined in the symbolism of the Church. In the late fifteenth century, the theme of "Tota Pulchra" emerged in Spain and later spread throughout New Spain. This distinct compositional treatment of the Immaculate Conception took as its central inspiration "Tota Pulchra es, amica mea, et macula non est in te" (Thou are all fair, my love, there is no spot in thee), a verse of the Song of Solomon (4:7) specifically associated with Mary. The Virgin is shown standing alone in a prayerful attitude surrounded by symbols from the Old Testament (and Apocrypha) affirming her preordained role as the Virgin Mother of God, as well as her beauty, purity, and majesty. (Much of the symbolism in Marian litanies is derived from these oft-cited Old Testament verses.) Above her may be present God the Father holding a scroll or uttering the "Tota Pulchra" verse; a dove, symbolizing the Holy Spirit; or the words of the verse alone. Scriptural or doctrinal sources of the symbols are cited (including the Litany of Loreto), as are key Latin phrases, which may appear by themselves in portrayals of the Immaculate Conception.

The following symbols are taken from paintings of the Immaculate Conception in the churches of northern New Spain and from painted and sculptured decorations on their façades, altars, ceilings, and walls. A number of these symbols can be seen beneath the cornice of the first level on the side portals of the Cathedral of Durango.

Altar = Ark of the Covenant (Foederis Arca; Litany of Loreto).

Boat = Noah's ark ("arca Diluvii")—Mary was regarded both as the ship of salvation and as a symbol of fertility.

Cedar tree—Exalted Cedar (Cedrus Exaltata), reflected in the prophecies of Ezekiel (17:3) and mentioned in Ecclesiasticus (24:13).

City of God—see Psalms 87:3.

Cypress tree—see Ecclesiasticus 24:13.

Dragon—see **Serpent**.

Fortress—see **Tower**.

Fountain—Fountain of the Gardens (Fons Ortorum; Song of Solomon 4:15).

Garden—Enclosed Garden (Hortus Conclusus; Song of Solomon 4:12).

Gate—Heaven's Gate (Janua Coeli) from Jacob's dream in Genesis 28:17, usually presented as a closed door or gate to a fortress. (The sanctuary screen in early Christian churches was also called "Janua Coeli.") God's pronouncement on the east gate of the temple in Ezekiel's vision: "This gate shall be shut, it shall not be opened, and no man shall enter in by it: because the Lord, the God of Israel, hath entered in by it, therefore it shall be shut" (Ezekiel 44:2) was taken to prophesy the coming of Christ, the gate symbolizing Mary's virginity.

House—House of Gold (Domus Aurea) or House of God (Domus Dei).

Ladder or stairs to Heaven—Jacob's Ladder (Genesis 28:12) and perhaps Saint John Climacus's (d. 649) "Ladder to Paradise," the title of his discourse on the attainment of moral perfection. Mary was held to be the ladder that Christ used to descend to earth and by which man can ascend to Heaven.

Lily—Lily among Thorns (Song of Solomon 2:1–2).

Mirror—Spotless Mirror (Wisdom of Solomon 7:26) and a mirror of justice (Litany of Loreto).

Moon—"fair as the moon" ("pulchra ut luna"; Song of Solomon 6:10). Usually the moon is accompanied by the sun, placed near and on either side of Mary's head.

Olive tree—Beautiful Olive (Oliva Speciosa; Ecclesiasticus 24:14). Ancient symbol of peace.

Palm tree—Exalted Palm (Palma Exaltata; Ecclesiasticus 24:14).

Rose—Rose without Thorns (without sin). A popular invocation of the Virgin, although not as important as the lily until the thirteenth or fourteenth century.

Perhaps in reference to Saint Ambrose's legend of roses growing without thorns until the Fall, in which Mary, as the new Eve, reverses Genesis 3:17–18 and thereby restores nature to its condition before the Fall. The rose of Sharon (Song of Solomon 1:1), roses at Jericho (Ecclesiasticus 24:14), and the rose as symbol of the Kingdom of Righteousness (Isaiah 35:1) are also other possible sources (see also "Our Lady of the Rosary" in chapter 12).

Serpent—trampled under Mary's feet, distinguishes Mary as the Woman of the Apocalypse in Revelation 12:1. In the seventeenth century, the dragon in John's text (Revelation 12:3) became a serpent to accord with Mary's role as the New Eve, a serpent, moreover, that she crushed underfoot, symbolizing her victory over sin.[44] (See also **Dragon** above and **Serpent** below.)

Star—Star of the Sea (Stella Maris), from a medieval liturgical hymn; perhaps originally derived from the "bright morning star" (Revelation 22:16) or Stella Matutina (Morning Star; Litany of Loreto). Also as Star of Jacob (Numbers 24:17). From the late seventeenth century, Spanish painters, inspired by Revelation 12:1, portrayed Mary with a cluster of twelve stars around her head, thought by some to symbolize the twelve tribes of Israel; thereafter, a twelve-star crown or halo became integral to the iconography of the Immaculate Conception.

Sun—"bright as the sun" ("electa ut sol"; Song of Solomon 6:10); also refers to Mary as the Woman of the Apocalypse (Revelation 12:1). Accompanied by the moon, the sun is one of her most commonly included symbols.

Temple—Temple of the Holy Spirit (Templum Spiritus Sanctus; 1 Corinthians 3:16).

Throne—possibly, the Throne of Solomon or Throne of Wisdom (see Revelation 12:5).

Tower—Tower of David with Bastions (Turris Davis cum Propugnaculis; Song of Solomon 4:4).

Tree—Blossoming Rod of Jesse ("Virga Jesse floruit"; Ezekiel 7:10; see also Isaiah 7:14 and 11:1), often called and portrayed as the "Tree of Jesse." The Latin words *virga*, meaning "rod," and *virgo*, meaning "virgin," were connected in medieval religious writings and the development of the imagery of the Tree of Jesse to explain that, just as the rod flourished without seed, so the Virgin conceived without man. A blooming tree is associated with the blossoming rod of Saint Joseph (see also **Rod or staff** and **Tree** below; "Joseph" in chapter 12).

Vase—Vessel of Spirit, Vessel of Honor, Vessel of Notable Devotion (Vas Spirituale, Vas Honorabile, Vas Insigne Devotionis; Litany of Loreto; see also **Vase** below).

Well—Well of Living Waters (Puteus Aquarum Viventium; Song of Solomon 4:15).

Mermaid—early Christian symbol for falsehood, desire, pleasure, vice, and temptation. Two of the rare examples of the mermaid motif in northern New Spain can be seen on the main frontispiece of the Cathedral of Monterrey (Nuevo León) and along the frieze of San Sebastián in Concordia (Sinaloa): the first most likely serving as a whimsical decorative accent, the second possibly reflecting pre-Christian Mexican myth (figures 11.16 and 11.17).

Mirror—represents the soul or mind, truth, and wisdom (see under **Mary** above).

Miter—ecclesiastical headdress of bishops, abbots, and popes. When seen at the feet of a friar, it indicates rejection of the honor of a bishopric, the number of miters representing the number of offers rejected. Thus, three and one are shown at the feet of Saints Bernadine of Siena and John of Capistrano, respectively (see also chapter 10; and "Bernadine of Siena" and "John of Capistrano" in chapter 12).

Model of a building—in the hand of a religious figure indicates patronage or protection of a building or city—or contribution to the Faith—by that person. Saint Augustine, as one of the Four Doctors of the Church, may hold one. Saint Barbara may hold a model of a tower and Our Lady of Loreto may hold a model of her house (see also **House**, **Temple**, and **Tower** under **Mary** above; "Augustine," "Barbara," and "Mary" in chapter 12).

Money—see **Bag** and **Bag of coins** under **Instruments of Christ's Passion** above.

Monstrance—symbol of the Eucharist. Saint Barbara may hold a monstrance, referring to her devotion to the Eucharist and to her last wish that all who honored her martyrdom receive the last Sacrament of Extreme Unction as an ultimate grace (see also "Barbara" in chapter 12).

11.16. *Mermaid motif, main frontispiece, Catedral de Monterrey, Nuevo León, 1996.*

11.17. *Mermaid and scallop shell motif on aisle cornice, San Sebastián, Concordia, Sinaloa, 2000.*

Moon—ancient pre-Christian symbol of feminine powers and mother goddesses; the Christians later incorporated the moon into symbolic portrayals of the Immaculate Conception. The moon may also appear in scenes of the Crucifixion (see also **Crescent; Moon** under **Mary,** both above; **Sun** below.)

Moors—symbolize infidels and Christian struggles against the Islamic world. Moors are frequently seen being trampled by Saint James the Greater (Santiago). (See also **Crescent** above and **Turks** below; "Saint James the Greater" in chapter 12.)

Musical instruments—general symbol denoting love, celestial harmony, and adoration. Angelitos may be seen playing instruments in honor of the Virgin, as on the retablo of San Xavier del Bac near Tucson (Arizona; see figure 7.9a). An organ is the attribute of Saint Cecilia, the supposed inventor of the instrument (see also "Cecilia" in chapter 12).

Nails—see under **Instruments of Christ's Passion** above.

Numbers: Symbols of quantities and ideas, numbers date back to pre-Christian times. Although the qualitative significance of numbers so crucial to Christian symbolism in the Middle Ages greatly diminished after the Renaissance, certain numbers have retained their symbolic value.

One—indivisible, stands for God the Father, the beginning, prime mover.

Two—duality of the divine and human nature of Christ, number of every creature saved in the Ark, thieves on the cross, angels at Christ's tomb.

Three—number of the Trinity, parts of humans (body, soul, spirit), Magi, denials by Peter, crosses on Calvary, Marys, Christian virtues (faith, hope, and charity.)

Four—number of cardinal points on the compass, Evangelists, Gospels, major prophets, Fathers of the Church, cardinal virtues (prudence, fortitude, temperance, and justice), and rivers of paradise.

Five—number of Christ and the Four Evangelists and of the senses; number of Christ's wounds and the stigmata of Saints Francis of Assisi, Francis Solano, Francis Xavier, and Catherine of Siena.

Six—number of days of Creation, attributes of the Deity, hours Christ remained on the Cross.

Seven—number of days in the week, sacraments, joys and sorrows of Mary, the last words of Christ, Christian virtues, deadly sins, gifts of the Holy Spirit, and archangels.[45] Magic number in both the Old and the New Testament, a general symbol of completeness, a perfect and sacred number.

Eight—number of beatitudes and fruits of the Holy Ghost, canonical hours, days after his birth Christ was circumcised, and days after his entry into Jerusalem Christ rose from the grave. As seven plus one, eight is a symbol for renewal or rebirth; traditionally, baptismal fonts were octagonal.

Nine—number of the choirs of angels, spheres, and rings around Hell.

Ten—number of perfection and symbol of order: the sum of the divine three (the Trinity) and the human seven (three of the spirit and four of the body); number of Commandments, as well as of lamps, virgins, and talents in Christ's parables.

Twelve—number of original Apostles, sons of Jacob, stones of the altar, gates of Jerusalem, days of Christmas, and tribes of Israel.

Thirteen—number of the Twelve Apostles plus Christ. That the thirteenth of this group was the betrayer (Judas) may have helped create the mystique of "unlucky number 13."

Fourteen—number of Holy Helpers (see "Fourteen Holy Helpers" in chapter 12).

Twenty-four—four and twenty elders.

Forty—number of days and nights of the flood, years the Israelites wandered in the wilderness, days Christ fasted and was tempted, days Christ remained on earth after his Resurrection.

Oak—Greco-Roman symbol of wisdom, faith, and strength, the oak assumed the same significance as a Christian symbol for Jesus or Mary (see also "Mary" and "Our Lady of the Oak" in chapter 12).

Olive tree—see under **Mary** above.

Orb—globe or ball, often crowned with a cross, held by God the Father, Christ, or kings, signifying sovereignty. An imperial Roman symbol of perfection and of the divine wisdom governing Rome and the world, an orb was placed on top of medieval and Renaissance domes and cupolas.

An orb in the hands of the Christ Child carried by the giant Christopher signifies the first three days of Creation: the division of light from darkness, Heaven from the firmament, and water from dry land.

Ox or bull—general symbol of strength and patience; in its sacrificial aspect, associated with the Nativity and with Saint Luke. Drawing on Ezekiel's and Saint John's visions, early Christian symbolists used the ox, on the one hand, and man, the lion, and the eagle, on the other, as hieroglyphs for Christ. The ox or bull is an ancient, universal, pre-Christian symbol of fertility and strength throughout Europe, Africa, and the Near East, hence an appropriate symbol for Christ, who until the fourteenth century, was held to represent (among other things) the fertilizing power that perpetuates life on earth. Oxen being driven by an angel are also depicted with representations of Saint Isidore the Farm Worker (see also "Isidore the Farm Worker" and "Luke" in chapter 12).

Palm—symbol of the tree of life, immortality, victory (borrowed from the Romans, signifying the same), and paradise. In one account of the flight to Egypt, Mary asks for dates from a palm, but they are too high for Joseph to reach. The infant Jesus bids the palm bend down, which it does. The palm frond carried by Jesus in his triumphant entry into Jerusalem on Palm Sunday prefigures his Resurrection. Palm branches signify glory and triumph over death, hence they are carried by or presented to many martyrs (see also **Mary** above).

Passion, symbols of—see **Instruments of Christ's Passion** above.

Pelican—symbol of the Eucharist, the redemption of blood sacrifice, and charity. In one common tale, the female pelican kills her young, only to have them revived three days later by her returning mate, who tears flesh from his breast and allows his blood to pour over them. The killing of the young is overshadowed by the mate's sacrifice; indeed, the pelican was thought to feed its progeny with its own blood until it died.[46] In a symbolic parallel, Christ suffers the Passion to redeem humankind—giving his blood for his brood. Biblical texts often quoted in support of this parallel are Isaiah 1:2 and Psalms 102:6; Saint Thomas Aquinas calls Jesus "Pius Pelicanus" (the Pious Pelican). The pelicans of northern New Spain seldom appear singly and sometimes serve as decorative corbels, especially on retablos. They often resemble swans, or even eagles, more than actual pelicans (figure 11.18).

Pen—often accompanied by an inkwell, a quill pen symbolizes authorship. General attribute of scholars, the Evangelists, and the Doctors of the Church (see also **Feather** above).

Piers—four principal supporting members at a church's crossing, commonly decorated (on their pendentives or squinches) with painted or sculpted images of the four Evangelists (Matthew, Mark, Luke, and John) or the Four Doctors, or Fathers, of the Church (Saints Ambrose, Augustine, Gregory the Great, and Jerome)—the pillars of the Christian and Catholic beliefs (see also specific saints in chapter 12).

Pillar—see **Column or pillar** above

Pitcher and basin—symbolize spiritual or ritual purity. Used by celebrants to purify themselves through ritual washing of the hands before they perform the Mass. Present in scenes of the Annunciation, the basin and ewer are a sign of Mary's perpetual virginity (see also under **Instruments of Christ's Passion** above).

Plants—decorative plant motifs in northern New Spain were most often selected for their symbolic significance and ornamental value rather than as reflections of local flora. For several reasons—the ineptness of decorators, the deterioration of the element or surface on which they appear, or both—such motifs may be difficult if not impossible to recognize. Identification must then depend on knowledge of the context. For example, a round object held by a nude female is most likely the apple of knowledge held by Eve. (See also specific plants.)

Pliers—instruments of torture; an attribute of Saint Apollonia (see also "Apollonia of Alexandria" in chapter 12 and **Pincers** under **Instruments of Christ's Passion** above).

Pomegranate—from Old French *pome grenate* (apple with many seeds), an ancient pre-Christian symbol of fertility, adopted by the Christians as a symbol for spiritual fecundity, eternal life, and charity. The fruit's tightly packed seeds were thought to represent the cohesive community of the faithful. In the Bible, the pomegranate stands for the oneness of the universe. An opened fruit represents the Resurrection and the opened tomb, the color of the seeds

11.18. Pelican motif, retablo of Nuestra Señora de la Merced, San José, Parral, Chihuahua, 2001.

recalling the blood of Christ; the spiky end, his crown. Pomegranates alternating with bells decorate the fringes of priests' robes in Old Testament scenes (see Exodus 28:34 and 39:26). Personal attribute of Saint John of God, the pomegranate is incorporated into the Mexican coat of arms above the sacristy door of the order's church, San Juan de Dios, in Durango (Durango; see figure 11.7; see also **Hospitaliers of Saint John of God** under **Heraldry** above; "John of God" in chapter 12).

Purse—see **Bag,** and **Bag of coins** under **Instruments of Christ's Passion** above.

Raven—first bird mentioned in the Bible; sent forth by Noah, it did not return to the ark, but was thought to remain away to feed on carrion. Because of this, the raven became a symbol of pagans—or sinning Christians—turning away from Christ's truth. Ravens are also credited, however, with feeding holy hermits in the desert and with serving as divine protectors and messengers.

Reed—the sponge soaked with vinegar offered to Christ on the Cross to quench his thirst was held by a reed. With a cross surmounting it, the reed is an attribute of Saint John the Baptist (see also under **Instruments of Christ's Passion** above and "John the Baptist" in chapter 12).

Rivers—four rivers of paradise (Pison, Gihon, Tigris, and Euphrates), frequently included in early illustrations of the Creation and the Garden of Eden may also represent the Four Evangelists and Gospels. The wavy pattern on the chapel doors of La Purísima Concepción near Lompoc (California; figure 11.19), reproduced from the main portal doors of Mission Santa Bárbara and popularly referred to as the "river of life," may well have been inspired by Garden of Eden iconography (see also **Water** below).

Robe—see **Cloth** under **Instruments of Christ's Passion** above.

Rod or staff—symbol of dignity and masculine power; attribute of Saint Joseph. According to legend, when a dove alighted on the rod of Joseph, it was a sign from God that he had been selected to be the husband of Mary.[47] Also an attribute of hermits and pilgrims, such as Archangel Raphael and Saint James the Greater (Santiago). A little hook is sometimes included on the end to hold a gourd or wallet. (see also **Crosier** above; "James the Greater," "Joseph," and "Raphael" under "Archangels" in chapter 12).

Rooster—see **Cock or rooster** and under **Instruments of Christ's Passion,** both above.

Rope—see **Cord or rope,** and also **Rope** under **Instruments of Christ's Passion,** above.

Rosary—first used by the Benedictines to help remember the number of prayers recited; named after the mystic rose garden of the Virgin. The pre-Christian pagans of Arabia and Egypt, and later Muslims, also used prayer beads. An attribute of Saint Dominic, who promoted the devotion in its present form, and of the Virgin of the Rosary (see also "Dominic of Guzmán" and "Mary" in chapter 12).

Rose—sacred to Venus and common symbol of the Virgin Mary. In garlands, roses refer to the rosary. Saints Rose of Lima and Rosalie of Palermo, as well as some other virgin martyrs, wear crowns of roses. White roses symbolize purity; red, suffering. Attribute of the Franciscan Saint Didacus of Alcalá (Diego de Alcalá), who is shown carrying a basket of roses (see also **Mary** above and **Wreath** below; "Didacus of Alcalá," "Mary," "Rosalie of Palermo," and "Rose of Lima" in chapter 12).

Rule—see **Carpenter's square** above.

Sacraments—see **Book** above.

Sanctuary lamp—symbolizing the Holy Spirit, a lighted sanctuary lamp (usually suspended) indicates the presence of the reserved Host.

Saw—the instrument of martyrdom of Saint Simon the Zealot and sometimes Saint Jude (see also "Simon" in chapter 12).

Scales—symbolizing the weighing of the good and the bad in souls appearing before God's judgment seat. As lord of souls and conductor and guardian of the spirits of the dead, Archangel Michael is frequently shown with scales, sometimes with figures included in their pans (see also "Michael" under "Archangels" in chapter 12).

Scallop shell—symbol of pilgrims and pilgrimages, as well as of baptism, rebirth, and regeneration. Signifying poverty and renunciation of worldly goods, scallop shells were used by pilgrims as vessels for food and drink. Attribute of Saint James the Greater (Santiago; and, by association, of the Compostela pilgrimage) and Archangel Raphael, who often wear this symbol on their capes or hats. Adapted perhaps from an earlier Hellenistic form, the scallop shell in the Moorish culture was perceived as

11.19. "River of life" motif, chapel door, La Purísima Concepción, Lompoc, California, 1987.

"the ear of the heart, which absorbs the dewdrop of the divine word," an appropriate metaphor for the earliest prayer niches (where the word of God is spoken) in Syria and Egypt.[48] In what may be a uniquely aesthetic rather than religious application of the motif in northern New Spain, scallop shells alternate with mermaids along the aisle cornice of San Sebastián in Concordia (Sinaloa; see figure 11.17; see also "Human and Animal Shapes" under "Decorative Motifs" in chapter 6; and "James the Greater," and "Raphael" under "Archangels" in chapter 12).

Scapular—consisting of two small rectangular pieces of cloth held together by two strings worn over the shoulders, attribute of the Sabbatine Privilege associated with Our Lady of Mount Carmel. The two most common scapulars seen in the art of New Spain are associated with Our Lady of Mount Carmel (Carmelites), and with Our Lady of Mercy (Mercedarians).[49] (See also "Carmelites" under "Orders" in chapter 9; "Our Lady of Mount Carmel" and "Our Lady of Mercy" in chapter 12.)

Scepter—symbol of reigning power or of dominion, commonly placed in the hand of the Virgin. God the Father may hold one, as may Christ, kings, and angels (see also **Reed** under **Instruments of Christ's Passion** above.)

Scourge—symbol of torture or chastisement; attribute of Saints Jerome, Rita, and also Ambrose, who may hold a scourge, which represents his driving the Arian heretics out of Italy (see also under **Instruments of Christ's Passion** above; "Ambrose," "Jerome," and Rita" in chapter 12).

Serpent—for its biblical role in the Fall of Adam (and humankind), the serpent is an enemy of God and, according to Augustine, a symbol of Satan. For Christians, the serpent represents "the seducer, the tempter, the deceiver, and the very incarnation of the Spirit of Evil"[50] and thus appears with a number of saints, such as John the Evangelist, Paul, and Philip. Because the snake sheds its skin and appears to be reborn, non-Christians have long associated the serpent with another symbol of rebirth and thus immortality, the moon, which is "reborn" each month. In Christian belief, humankind lost eternal life through the serpent, who professed to know the secret of immortality. God's curse on the serpent in the Garden of Eden (Genesis 3:14) is traditionally interpreted as the first promise of the Redeemer. Coiled around the world with an apple in its mouth, the serpent represents sin, which Mary as the Immaculate Conception and the Woman of the Apocalypse conquers (see also under **Mary, Dragon**, and Mexican coat of arms under **Heraldry** above; "Mary" in chapter 12).

Sheep—symbolize Christ's flock, humankind. The ram, which symbolized human survival in pre-Christian religions, became, as the sheep, an early Christian symbol for the survival of the soul (see also **Lamb** above).

Shell—see **Scallop shell** above.

Shepherd—Christ as the Good Shepherd (see figure 10.26) has its roots in Greco-Roman art. Early Christian artists adapted representations of Orpheus Boukolos (the herdsman) and Hermes Kriophoros (ram bearer). The metaphor of a teacher or leader being a shepherd who shows his flock or congregation the right way, and who guides their souls to Heaven was popularly accepted by the earliest Christians; the shepherd was a favorite symbol in the sepulchral art of the catacombs.

Christ as the Good Shepherd has a female counterpart in Mary, Divine Shepherdess of Souls (María Divina Pastora de las Almas), whose devotion arose in southern Spain in the first quarter of the eighteenth century. As "Good Shepherds," Jesus and Mary share the same attributes: sheep (often, for Mary, with roses in their mouths), a shepherd's staff, and a broad-brimmed hat (see also "The Divine Shepherdess" in chapter 12).

Ship—as the ark, one of the earliest symbols of the Church, appearing in the catacombs and representing safety from temptation, death, and destruction. The Church as a ship for the safe passage of the souls of the faithful to salvation is reinforced by the Apostles as "fishers of men," the Cross as mast, the Christian virtue of steadfastness as anchor, and by portrayals of Saint Peter and Christ as helmsmen (see also **Boat** under **Mary** above and **Water** below).

Skeleton—general symbol for death and the corruptibility of the body. At the mission church of San Diego de Alcalá in Pitiquito (Sonora), Death appears as a ten-foot-tall skeleton painted on one side of a pier (see figure 6.36; see also **Skull** below) with the Devil, equally large, painted on the other.

Skull—reminder of death and the transitory state of earthly life, commonly also symbolizing contemplation, inner vision, and penance. Attribute of hermits and penitential saints such as Catherine of Siena, Francis of Assisi, Francis Borgia (for whom the skull is shown to have a crown or to rest on a book), Jerome, Mary Magdalen, Rita, and Rosalie of Palermo. Beneath the figure of the crucified Jesus, the skull with crossbones recalls the legend that the Cross was made from the tree of life in the Garden of Eden and placed over Adam's grave atop Golgotha ("the place of skulls"). Three skulls and crossbones appear over the outside doorway from the cemetery at Mission Santa Bárbara in Santa Barbara (California; figure 11.20; see also **Skull and bones** under **Instruments of Christ's Passion** above; "Catherine of Siena," "Francis of Assisi," "Francis Borgia," "Jerome," "Mary Magdalen," "Rita of Cascia," and "Rosalie of Palermo" in chapter 12).

Souls—may be symbolically represented in a variety of ways: as birds, as human figures with wings, ascending from the mouths or bodies of the dead or dying, or—in scenes of Hell or Purgatory—submerged in flames (see also "Matthew" in chapter 12).

Spear—see **Lance** under **Instruments of Christ's Passion** above.

Sponge—see **Sponge on a reed** under **Instruments of Christ's Passion** above.

11.20. Skull and crossbones motif over the cemetery doorway, Mission Santa Bárbara, California, 1987.

Staff—see **Rod or staff** above.

Stake—general symbol of martyrdom, such as that of Saint Sebastian (See also **Column or pillar** and **Instruments of Christ's Passion** above; "Sebastian" in chapter 12).

Star—symbol of divine light and guidance. The Star of the Nativity guided the Magi to Bethlehem. Emblematic of Mary as Queen of Heaven. Saint Dominic may be identified by a star on his forehead (see also **Mary** above and **Sun** below; "Dominic of Guzmán" in chapter 12).

Steps—represent, in Christian and non-Christian traditions throughout the world, ascent and descent between hierarchical realms (see also **Ladder** under **Mary** above).

Stigmata—wounds that miraculously appear on the body of a human in the same places as those on the body of the crucified Christ symbolize saintly devotion. Prominent attributes of Saint Catherine of Siena (where they appear only on her hands) and Saint Francis of Assisi. Sometimes depicted as five wounds on a shield, the first emblem of Franciscan Order (see also **Franciscans** under **Heraldry** above; "Catherine of Siena" and "Francis of Assisi" in chapter 12).

Stones—symbolize martyrdom, as in the case of Saint Stephen, or mortification of the flesh, as in the case of Saint Jerome (see also "Stephen" in chapter 12).

Sun—symbol of God the Father (Malachi 4:2). Its prominence and life-giving force have made the sun emblematic of Christ and the celebration of Easter since early Christianity. Its light and heat also symbolize glory, spirituality, and divine justice, as well as truth and spiritual illumination. A darkened sun may appear with the moon in scenes of the Crucifixion, reflecting the darkness that fell over the land for three hours in Matthew, Mark, and Luke's accounts. The sun symbol may also appear on the chests of Saints Nicholas of Tolentino and Thomas Aquinas (see also **Sun** under **Mary** above; "Nicholas of Tolentino," and "Thomas Aquinas" in chapter 12).

Sword—general attribute of martyrs killed with the sword, held tip down in the case of Saints Agnes, Barbara, Catherine of Alexandria, and Paul. In the hands of warriors such as Archangel Michael (where it is often flaming) and Saint James the Greater (Santiago), the sword symbolizes power, authority, and justice. In the hand of Christ, it is the symbol of the Final Judgment. One or seven swords or daggers can be seen piercing the heart of Mary. (See also "Our Lady of Sorrows," "Agnes," "Barbara," "Catherine of Alexandria," and "Paul" in chapter 12.)

Temple—see under **Mary** above.

Thistle—symbol of penance.

Thorn—symbolizes sorrow, tribulation, and Christ's Passion. When combined with roses, thorns represent suffering and joy. A thorn in the forehead of an Augustinian nun identifies Saint Rita of Cascia. (See also **Crown** and **Crown of thorns** under **Instruments of Christ's Passion** above; "Saint Rita of Cascia in chapter 12.)

Throne—when occupied, general symbol of sovereignty.

Tiara—triple-tiered crown worn by popes on their coronation and symbol of papal supremacy and papal saints. It is worn by God the Father in the "Throne of Grace" theme; it may also be worn by Our Lady of Loreto, used to distinguish Saint Gregory the Great from the other Fathers of the Church, and incorporated in papal designs with crossed keys. (See also **Keys, Diocesan Clergy** under **Heraldry** and **Miter** above; discussion of tiara under "Vestments," "Head Coverings," in chapter 9; "Gregory the Great" in chapter 12.)

Tower—symbol of strength, impregnability, inaccessibility, and virginity. When shown with three windows or in three stages, a tower is the personal attribute of Saint Barbara (see also under **Mary** and **Model of a building** above; "Towers" under "Outer Body" in chapter 5).

Tree—symbol of knowledge, divine wisdom, and eternal life. Associated with Adam and Eve in the Garden of Eden and also with the Virgin. In the Tree of Jesse, a decorative motif visually explaining Jesus' lineage in the House of David (foretold in Isaiah 11:1–3), Jesse is shown at the root of the tree, with the trunk emerging from him and with the branches bearing his descendants down to Christ. In later depictions, David, identified by his crown and harp, replaces Jesse at the base of the tree, the figures of intervening descendants are removed, and those of Joseph, Mary, Jesus, Anne, and Joachim placed at the top of the tree (see also specific kinds of trees and under **Mary** above; "Anne" and "Joachim" in chapter 12).

Tres potencias—three distinct flames or areas of light emanating from the head of Christ that symbolize the three powers or faculties of the soul: memory, under-

11.21. Tres potencies emanating from Jesús Nazareno, San Pedro de Aconchi, Sonora, 1979.

standing, and will. Exclusive to Jesus, they may be seen in representations of him at any stage of his life. Developing perhaps from a cruciform halo (a Greek cross enclosed in a circle), the symbol was given special significance by the Spanish mystics.[51] On sculpted images, the tres potencias are often elaborately worked in silver or gilded silver and placed on top and on either side of Christ's head (figure 11.21; see also **Aureola** above).

Trinity—God the Father, Son, and Holy Ghost represents the heavenly Trinity; Jesus, Mary, and Saint Joseph, the earthly Trinity (see also **Dove,** and **Triangle** under **Geometric Shapes** above; "Trinity" in chapter 12).

Turks—attribute of the Franciscan Saint John of Capistrano, around whose feet they appear as turbaned heads (see also **Crescent** and **Moors** above; "John of Capistrano" in chapter 12).

Vase—traditional symbol of the feminine receptive principle and fertility. Associated with the Virgin (see also under **Mary** above). A draped or empty vase on a tomb represents death or a soul departed from the body.

Veil—symbolizes mystery, renunciation of the world, and modesty. The Veil of Veronica is an image of Christ's bloodied face appearing on a napkin, cloth, or veil (see also "Veronica" in chapter 12).

Vestments—see chapter 9.

Vine—common symbol of Jesus as taken from his parable in John 12:1–17. In many churches of northern New Spain, a grapevine may be seen twining around columns or as a running design along walls in cornices and friezes. As the Eucharistic Man of Sorrows, Christ is seen with grapevines emerging from his wounded side (see also **Grapes** above).

Virtues—Of the seven Christian virtues (faith, hope, charity, justice, prudence, fortitude, and temperance), only faith, hope, and charity were represented in northern New Spain: Faith as a woman with a cross and chalice; Hope as a woman with an anchor; and Charity as a woman with a heart. Most notable were the three figures placed atop the pediment at Mission Santa Bárbara (see figure 2.22a), replaced after a 1925 earthquake, and the figures of Hope and Faith in the spandrels of the sotocoro of the Cathedral of Chihuahua (see figure 11.1). The cluster of three heads atop the estípites in the stone retablo from La Castrense (now in El Cristo Rey) in Santa Fe (New Mexico) may well be those of Faith, Hope, and Charity.

Wafer—usually as a disk over the mouth of a chalice, symbol of the Eucharist (see also **Wheat** below).

Water—symbolizes death (the flood, the closing over of the Red Sea), on the one hand, and rebirth and regeneration (baptism), on the other. The ritual use and sacredness of water figure into baptism, the anointing or sanctifying of persons and things, and the ritual baths in spring or early summer to ensure fertility and health.[52] (See also **Mary** and **Rivers** above and **Well** below.)

Well—emblem of salvation and purification (see also under **Mary** above).

Wheat—represents the bread of the Eucharist, the body of Christ. Symbol of the Resurrection (John 12:24; 1 Corinthians 15:35–36, 42) and, when combined with a vine, of the Eucharist. Wheat may also appear with a skull or other reminder of death and the vanity of life.[53]

Wheel—broken and with spikes, is the personal attribute of Saint Catherine of Alexandria (see also "Catherine of Alexandria" in chapter 12).

Whip—see **Scourge** above.

Wings—on angels and archangels symbolize divine messengers. Attribute of Saint Thomas Aquinas when represented as the Angelic Doctor. Mary as the Woman of the Apocalypse may be shown with wings (see also **Angels** above; "Archangels" and "Thomas Aquinas" in chapter 12).

Woman—with cross and chalice symbolizes Faith; with an anchor, Hope; with a heart, Charity; and with an open book in hand, the Church (see also **Virtues** above and figure 11.1).

Wounds—symbol of Christ's Passion and of martyrdom; whether received by Christ or by martyrs, wounds are often graphically depicted (see also **Heraldry, Stigmata,** and **Thorn** above).

Wreath—symbolizing glory, honor, victory, and the promise of resurrection, the wreath may be composed of laurels or roses. It may be worn by or offered to Saints Catherine of Alexandria, John of Nepomuk, Rosalie of Palermo, and Rose of Lima, among others (see also "Catherine of Alexandria," "John of Nepomuk," "Rosalie of Palermo," and "Rose of Lima" in chapter 12).

CHAPTER 12

SACRED ICONOGRAPHY

Catalogued in this chapter are the symbolic portrayals of sacred figures, focusing on their distinctive attributes, as they appear in paintings, murals, engravings and etchings, and sculptures throughout northern New Spain. The visual metaphors of this sacred iconography developed over many centuries from the Gospels, from visions or revelations, and from apocryphal texts and popular legends. Certain symbols and attributes treated separately in chapter 11 reappear in this chapter, along with explanatory or hagiographic material, under particular sacred figures (God, the archangels, Jesus, Mary, the individual saints) and their manifestations (singly or in groups)—this to help readers in identifying or confirming the identity of these figures as they are portrayed and to deepen their understanding of the figures' symbolic significance. Because chapters 11 and 12 complement each other, readers are strongly encouraged to consult them in tandem, reviewing the meaning of symbols and attributes (chapter 11) and placing those symbols and attributes in particular iconographic contexts (chapter 12).

GOD

The Bible expressly forbids making any image of God, the Eternal Father (Dios, Padre Eterno).[1] Because of this prohibition, certain symbols were created from the very beginning of Christianity to indicate the Godhead, one of which was the equilateral triangle, which later stood for the Trinity (see below). The tetragrammaton, Y H W H (sometimes J H V H)—a transliteration of the four letters of the Hebrew name for God, rendered as "Yahweh" or "Jehovah" in English—was placed in the center of the triangle. To this, eighteenth-century neoclassicism added the all-seeing eye of God, most prominently seen at the top of retablos. The presence of God the Father and God the Holy Spirit was also indicated by an equilateral triangle and dove in scenes of the Baptism of Christ and the Annunciation.

Daniel's vision (Daniel 7:9) created an iconographic standard that came into use by at least the twelfth century, when the Church first tolerated representational images of God: an elderly, white-haired and -bearded, light-skinned Caucasian man—referred to as "God the Father." The prime mover and omnipotent, omnipresent deity, God raises his right hand in benediction and holds in his left hand an orb or globe, signifying his sovereignty over the world; he appears either as a sculpted bust or in a painting at the top of retablos (see figures 2.26 and 7.9b), in scenes where Mary is being crowned as Queen of Heaven, and in representations of the Trinity.

Trinity (La Trinidad)

God the Father, God the Son, and God the Holy Spirit, occasionally depicted as identical, are more often distinguished by specific attributes. Whereas the Church has never directed how the Trinity was to be depicted, for centuries it tolerated the portrayal of three identical images because of the vision of Abraham at Mambre (Genesis 18:1–3). Although this medieval Byzantine manner of expressing the unity of the three was condemned by Pope Benedict XIV in 1747, it nevertheless persisted in New Spain and later Mexico, appearing frequently on nineteenth-century folk retablos (or láminas) and in New Mexican religious imagery inspired by the imported European "chromos" (chromolithographs)—the form in which popular representations of the Trinity are available in Mexico to this day (figure 12.1).[2]

Tradition depicts God the Father as a bearded patriarch, enthroned, crowned (sometimes with a triple crown not unlike the papal tiara), with a globe in one hand and a scepter in the other. God the Son is depicted as the Lamb of God, a young bearded man with long hair holding a cross or a lamb. God the Holy Spirit may be depicted as a dove, the form he assumed at Christ's Baptism. In the Trinity theme "Throne of Grace," God the Father is depicted as a pontifically crowned older man, seated and holding in front of him his crucified son, while a white dove hovers between or above them. The Throne of Grace may be seen throughout northern New Spain in paintings, engravings, and sculptures (figure 12.2).

Archangels

These angels carry out the will of God and act as emissaries between Heaven and earth. Although the title Archangel may apply to any angel ranked above the choir of Angels, Christian tradition names just seven; of these, only Gabriel, Michael, and Raphael are portrayed with any consistency in northern New Spain. A rare exception is the Retablo de los Siete Príncipes at the Santuario de Guadalupe in Parras (Coahuila; probably imported from Zaragoza, Spain), which features all seven archangels, with Saint Michael in the most prominent and central position above the painting of Our Lady of the Pillar of Zaragoza (see figure 10.27). Michael and Gabriel appear in the Old Testament (Daniel) and Raphael in the Apocrypha (Tobit). The final "el" in their names is Hebrew for a divine being or something belonging to God.[3] Lucifer before his fall was also regarded as an archangel.

Shown as imposing masculine winged figures, identifiable by their clothing and attributes, and given the title of Saint, archangels have since the fourteenth century been portrayed as soldiers in armor, resembling Roman legionnaires, a convention encouraged by the Counter-Reformation and the concept of the Church Militant. Their helmets are sometimes replaced with diadems, which may also support plumes.

Guardian angels, who appear in the Old Testament and the Apocrypha as protectors of Moses, Lot, and Tobias, look after individual humans; they are invoked by mothers as protectors of their infant children and are sometimes included among the archangels. In portrayals of the Feast of the Guardian Angel (instituted by Pope Leo X at the beginning of the sixteenth century but not raised to an obligatory observance until the papacies of Pope Clement X and Pope Leo XIII),[4] the angel is shown guiding one or two children, reminiscent of portrayals of Tobias and Archangel Raphael (see also **Angels** in chapter 11).

Gabriel

This archangel, whose name means "God is my strength," signifies announcement. Most commonly shown with Mary at the Annunciation, generally dressed in white with a lily (symbolizing Mary's virginity), Gabriel bore the heavenly message that she would conceive and bear Jesus. Also associated with the Nativity, Gabriel was

12.1. "The Holy Trinity," Cathedral of Durango, 2006.

12.2. Throne of Grace sculpture in a collateral altar, Catedral de Chihuahua, 1992.

regarded as the angel of mercy, chief of guardian angels, angel of the north wind, guardian of all humanity, angel of revelation and vengeance, and patron saint of people who are crippled, maimed, blind, or paralyzed.

Michael

The most popular archangel in northern New Spain, whose name means "Who is as God," Michael signifies victory. He is always portrayed as resplendently clad in armor, wearing a breastplate (sometimes adorned with a sun or moon), helmet, boots or sandals with greaves (leg protectors), and a short tunic, the quintessential symbol of the Church Militant. His attributes are a flaming sword and scales. Typically, Michael is shown either weighing the souls of humans before God's judgment seat or casting out Lucifer, represented as the Devil or a serpent being trampled underfoot. Depicted alone, protecting Mary as the Woman of the Apocalypse, or grouped with other saints, Michael was regarded as the angel of repentance, mercy, and righteousness, angel of the east wind, protector against plagues, and defender of the Church. During colonial times, he was considered the patron of Christianity in New Spain.

Raphael

The second most popular archangel in northern New Spain, whose name means "God has healed," Raphael signifies healing. Usually shown dressed in a traveler's cloak with a staff and water gourd, and easily identified by his attribute (a fish), Raphael may appear alone or in the company of the young Tobias, whom he led on a hazardous quest for the gall of a fish to cure the blindness of Tobias's father (Tobit 6:1–5). Raphael was regarded as the angel of the west wind; patron saint of travelers and pilgrims; and protector of youth, innocence, and the old; he was invoked for protection against illnesses of the eye, tumors in the groin or genitals, and malaria and other fevers (figure 12.3).

HOLY FAMILY

Jesus, Mary, and Joseph are shown seated or standing, with Jesus at any stage of his young life up to the age of about twelve. The correspondence between the Holy Family (La Sagrada Familia) and "the blessed Trinity is

12.3. Archangel Raphael, a detail of the main retablo, San José de Copala, Sinaloa, 2000.

more than simply numerical," Chorpenning reminds us, citing hymns, devotional literature, and sermons that were widely disseminated among the faithful in sixteenth-century Spain.[5] Indeed, when God the Father (represented from the chest up, his head surrounded by an equilateral triangle or halo) is included in scenes of the Holy Family, hovering between Mary and Joseph above the infant Jesus, with God the Holy Spirit (represented as a dove) between God the Father and God the Son, the conjoined earthly and heavenly Trinity "not only draws out the profound theological significance of the life of the Holy Family, but also highlights Joseph's privileges."[6]

12.4. *Jesus with Joseph, keystone of the main frontispiece of San Francisco Javier de Batuc, reassembled at Pitic, Sonora. 1979.*

Five Holy Personages (Cinco Señores)

The infant Jesus, Mary, Joseph, and Mary's parents (Anne and Joachim) are all included in one setting. Whether they are in a line—the four adults strolling along with Jesus in the center—or in a cluster, attention is always focused on the infant Jesus.

Flight into Egypt (La Huida a Egipto)

A theme developed from Matthew 2:13–15, in which the Holy Family fled from Bethlehem at the urging of an angel to avoid the wrath of Herod, was a familiar subject as early as the eleventh century and was incorporated into a number of legends, not always shared throughout the early Christian world: the destruction of idols in a town through which they passed, demons exorcised by the infant Christ, a field of wheat that matured and was harvested ahead of schedule, and Jesus' commanding a date palm to lower its head so that Mary could pick its fruit. A palm also miraculously provided shade for Mary as well as shielded the Holy Family from Herod's soldiers. Other stories tell of how thieves were deflected from their intent to rob and harm the three travelers, and how the thief Dismas, who saved them from his companions, was the "good," or "repentant, thief" crucified alongside Christ.

JESUS

As an infant or young child, Jesus (Jesús) appears (1) supported or accompanied by Mary or Joseph (figure 12.4); (2) with Mary and Joseph and Anne and Joachim, the parents of Mary; (3) with John the Baptist as a child; (4) with certain other saints as he appeared to them in visions; and (5) alone in cult images such as the Lost Child (El Niño Perdido).[7] As a youth, Jesus is sometimes shown in Joseph's carpenter shop, at Joseph's deathbed, or in other scenes not described in the Bible but indirectly based on biblical allusions (see, for example, Mark 6:3) and developed in popular beliefs dating back to the Middle Ages. (The New Testament does not describe Jesus' adolescence.) The adult Jesus appears in scenes described in the Gospels: his Presentation in the Temple (see "Mary" below), his Baptism, miracles he performed, the stages of his Passion, and his Resurrection.

In northern New Spain, the most frequent viceregal depictions of a solitary Jesus portray scenes from his ministry or his Passion, starting with his entry into Jerusalem and ending with his Crucifixion. His arrest, trial, agony, and death—where Jesus is shown scourged, scorned, wounded, and crucified—are most graphically portrayed in baroque painting and sculpture.

Child Jesus or Christ Child (El Niño Jesús or El Niño Cristo)

The child Jesus, invariably sculpted and usually unclad, is shown standing, sitting, or lying in a manger, his right hand raised in benediction and an orb or globe, signifying his destined role as Savior of the world, in his left; if standing, the image is often referred to as the "Victorious Christ Child" (El Niño Victorioso) or the "Triumphant Christ Child" (El Niño Triunfante).

Startlingly lifelike (realistically carved and finely painted) and with a commanding presence (human, yet projecting an ineffable spiritual quality), the standing Niño images of the Sevillan sculptor Juan Martínez Montañés (1568–1648) were widely imitated. Although the intended message of such images was innocence, they often expressed a sensuousness as well, which may explain why most later images were clothed in miniature gowns and robes or (with anatomy much simplified) in what amounted to painted loincloths (New Mexico).

Jesus may be shown as an infant or very young child, alone or with Mary and Joseph or other saints in their arms or in a manger. In northern New Spain, a small standing image, clothed in what appears to be an infant's christening robe and cap, was revered as the "Lost Child" (El Niño Perdido) in the town of Cuencamé de Ceniceros (Durango) beginning in the early nineteenth century, although the cult has all but disappeared today. The "Lost Child" refers to an episode (regarded as one of the seven sorrows of Mary) described in Luke 2:41–50: separated from his family in Jerusalem, the child Jesus is found three days later, sitting in the temple listening to and questioning the elders. Although Saint Luke states that this occurred when Jesus was twelve, the "Lost Child" is frequently represented as much younger. Renderings of the Cuencamé image may include what appear to be gold coins or medallions pinned to Jesus' gown.[8]

The Franciscans played an especially important role in developing the cult of the Christ Child: Saint Francis used the nativity scene in the Christmas celebration in the town of Greccio, Italy; the Christ child appeared to Franciscan Saints Clare and Anthony of Padua. Revelations of Spanish and other mystics during the sixteenth and seventeenth centuries served to promote the cult.

Christ at the Column (El Cristo a la Columna)—see "Christ Scourged" below.

Christ of Esquipulas (El Cristo de Esquipulas)

Another significant image of a crucified Christ in eighteenth- and nineteenth-century New Spain, the Christ of Esquipulas is always represented with a black body. Originating in Guatemala in the town Esquipulas, it is often associated with curative hot springs or mineral baths. Although popular belief has it that the image was deliberately made dark to identify with the suffering Indians, it is more likely that the carryover of the indigenous custom of honoring cult images with burning incense and the Christian habit of burning candles discolored the image, and that subsequent images have faithfully reproduced the dark color. In northern New Spain, an image of the Christ of Esquipulas can be found at the Santuario de Chimayó (New Mexico), a second in San Pedro de Aconchi (Sonora), and a third (once housed at the Presidio de Tucson and now "insensitively restored") at Señor San José de Ímuris (also Sonora).

Christ in Limbo (El Cristo en Limbo)

Sometimes called the "Descent into Hell," this theme explains Jesus' absence from the time of his entombment until his Ascension. He was supposed to have spent that time in Limbo, the place between Heaven and Hell reserved for the righteous who, though they died before the coming of Christ, were worthy of joining him in Heaven.[9] The basis of this tradition may be found in the apocryphal Gospel of Nicodemus. Clad only in a loincloth, with his wounds clearly evident, Christ triumphantly holds in one hand a staff with a white banner and red cross signifying the Resurrection, while raising the other in benediction or assisting the soul of an Old Testament patriarch out of Hell.

Christ of Patience (El Cristo de Paciencia)—see "Christ Scourged" below.

Christ Scourged

Crowned with thorns, hands bound, draped in a scarlet robe or clad only in a loincloth, Jesus after his scourging is represented in his entirety or from the waist up. In northern New Spain, the image of Jesus seated, holding a reed (the false scepter he was given by his torturers) is often called "El Señor de la Caña" (Lord of the Reed; figure 12.5) or "El Señor de las Burlas" (Lord of Mockery). The image of Jesus seated on a rock, without the reed, wearily awaiting the Crucifixion is called "El Cristo de Paciencia" (Christ of Patience); that of Jesus tied to a column after his scourging, his back a mass of bleeding welts, "El Cristo a la Columna" (Christ at the Column).

Lost Child (El Niño Perdido)—see "Child Jesus or Christ Child (El Niño Jesús or El Niño Cristo)" above.

Crucifix (El Crucifijo)

Jesus is shown dead or dying, clothed only in a loincloth and nailed to the Cross, his side pierced, his knees cut, his back scourged, his scalp bleeding from the crown of thorns, and his cheek sometimes wounded. At the top of the Cross, a plaque or scroll bears the Latin initials "I N R I" (Jesus the Nazarene, King of the Jews). Articulated crucifix images serve during Holy Week to dramatize Jesus' scourging, his carrying the Cross on the road to Calvary, his Crucifixion, and his entombment.

The medieval addition of a footrest to the iconography of the Crucifixion is very likely due to Byzantine influences. (It was customary to show Eastern emperors with their feet elevated on a pedestal.) Some of the most significant images of a crucified Christ in northern New Spain are described following (see figure 10.6).

Ecce Homo (Behold the Man)

Said to have been uttered by Pontius Pilate when Jesus was presented to the mob, "Ecce Homo" is used to describe the mocking of Christ before his humiliation and punishment at the hands of guards.

Good Shepherd (El Buen Pastor)

This theme is prefigured in Psalm 23 and in Ezekiel 34:12–16. Early Christians equated Christ with the Good Shepherd, guarding his flock (humanity) and always ready to seek out lost sheep (sinners). Jesus' loving care for his flock is symbolized by his carrying a lamb over his shoulders or in his arms. He is shown as a youth, wearing a simple robe and a shepherd's hat and holding a staff, his head ringed by a halo. The Good Shepherd is an important Eucharistic theme, sometimes seen on tabernacle doors, such as on the Retablo de Nuestra Señora de la Merced at San José de Parral (Chihuahua; see figure 10.26).

Holy Christ of Mapimí (El Santo Cristo de Mapimí)

Particularly revered by miners throughout Chihuahua, Durango, and Sonora, this image of the crucified Christ is said to have rescued a village in the Bolsón de Mapimí from an Indian attack in 1715. Led by a light, a villager found the image and wanted to take it to Mapimí, but for some reason could not; the statue was instead placed in Cuencamé, where it remains.

Badly restored in recent years, the original image has carved locks of hair down its back and right shoulder; its combined crown of thorns and tres potencias is made from what appears to be gold. Dressed in a white satin loincloth with metallic gold thread, it is mounted within a beautifully carved, elaborate, recessed retablo crucifijo. This image is believed to be particularly powerful in warding off physical and moral evils.

Another image, very probably moved from a previous church on the same site, is revered in the Cathedral of Chihuahua, where it has had its own collateral chapel since 1762 (see figure 3.22). In this image, smaller than the original and darkened by candle soot, Christ wears a gold-embroidered and -fringed satin loincloth and a silver crown of thorns with tres potencias over a full, dark, human-hair wig. The image is also mounted within a carved and gilded retablo crucifijo, although with much less elaborate profiles than at Cuencamé. Whereas the head of the Cuencamé image is bent slightly forward and to the right, suggesting that Christ has already died, the head of the Chihuahuan image is erect, giving the impression of a Christ who is still alive and suffering.

12.5. Lord of the Reed, sculpture in the collateral retablo, El Santuario de Nuestra Señora de Guadalupe de Parras, Coahuila, 1996. A plastic flower has been substituted for a stalk of cane.

Jesus the Nazarene (Jesús Nazareno)

In this image, Jesus is shown crowned with thorns and dressed in a dark red or violet robe, with long matted hair and a beard. His hands bound and a rope around his neck, he usually supports a cross on one shoulder (figure 12.6).

Lord of the Reed (El Señor de la Caña)—see "Christ Scourged" above.

Lost Child (El Niño Perdido)—see "Child Jesus or Christ Child (El Niño Jesús or El Niño Cristo)" above.

Man of Sorrows

In this post-Crucifixion image, introduced into the Western from the Eastern Church in the thirteenth century, Christ is crowned with thorns and shown alone, clad only in a loincloth, standing or seated on a rough block of stone exhibiting his wounds, lost in thought over his profound and bitter role.

Sacred Heart of Jesus (La Sagrada Corazón de Jesús)

Christ's heart is portrayed in highly realistic detail, surrounded by flames, most often with a spear wound on either side and encircled by a crown of thorns, which later touched and sometimes pierced the heart (see figure 11.5). The image may either be superimposed on the chest of Christ as he pulls back his robe better to reveal his heart or be represented by itself in two or three dimensions.

Although visions of Christ's heart were reported during the Middle Ages, this devotion did not receive a widespread public following until the late sixteenth century, when Christ appeared to Saint Margaret Mary Alacoque a number of times, showed her his "Sacred Heart," and told her to promote devotions to it.[10] The belief that public devotions had worked against the plagues sweeping France in the early eighteenth century did much to promote the cult, which achieved its greatest popularity in the late nineteenth century. The coexisting devotion to the Sacred Heart of Mary (see below), though even older, did not enjoy the popular following of the Sacred Heart of Jesus.

Sepulchered Christ (El Cristo Sepultado)

Images of Christ in the sepulcher, also called "Christ in the Tomb," are found throughout northern New Spain. Several of these are articulated and were intended to be hung from a cross, taken down, and then placed in a wooden sepulcher for viewing during Easter observances. The loincloth and shroud are frequently made from fine materials, embroidered and trimmed with lace, created and donated as acts of respect and devotion by the parishioners. The shroud serves many times as a suitable item onto which to pin milagros or other testimonies of grace received.

Stations of the Cross (Vía Crucis)

Representations of the fourteen different incidents in the Passion of Christ accepted as a matter of faith among believers and commemorated by Catholic tradition most often appear along the inside walls of the nave or outer aisles of a church (occasionally along the outside walls of a cemetery, cloister, or church; see figure 5.1). Marking the Via Dolorosa in Jerusalem, the fourteen stations are (1) Jesus is condemned to death; (2) the Cross is laid upon him and he starts toward Calvary; (3) his first fall; (4) he meets Mary; (5) Simon of Cyrene is also made to bear the Cross; (6) Veronica wipes his face with a cloth; (7) his second fall; (8) he speaks to the women of Jerusalem; (9) his third fall; (10) he is stripped of his garments; (11) he is crucified; (12) he dies; (13) his body is taken down from the Cross; and (14) his body is laid in its tomb.[11]

At first simply marked by crosses, the Stations later evolved into figurative representations of each incident and the cross markers were eliminated, until the eighteenth century, when the representations were each required to be surmounted by a cross.[12] These images were to be arranged "such that those making the Way of the Cross [Vía Crucis] follow our Lord around the church rather than meet him."[13]

Of Flemish or German origin and emerging as a popular devotion in the latter half of the fifteenth century, the devotion and the appearance of representations of the stations as aids to meditation were spread through Franciscan influence in the fifteenth century and were promoted throughout southern Spain by the blessed Álvaro de Córdo upon his return from the Holy Land in 1420. In 1686, Pope Innocent XI granted the Franciscans (who, in 1342, were designated guardians of the Holy Land and charged with establishing an official route for pilgrims) the right to erect stations in churches elsewhere because so few

12.6. Jesus the Nazarene, sculpture, San Miguel Arcángel de los Ures, Sonora, 1979.

believers were able to make the pilgrimage. The present number of stations, fourteen, was fixed by Pope Clement XII in 1731, when he granted the same indulgence for those who devoutly made the Stations of the Cross as for those who visited the holy places in Jerusalem.[14]

Mary

The mother of Jesus and preeminent among the saints, the Virgin Mary (La Virgen María) has long been overwhelmingly the most popular sacred figure in the Catholic Church. Her solicitude has extended over the entire range of human needs.[15] Her attraction was strengthened by the belief that she was never judgmental; she appeared to lettered and illiterate, noble and humble alike; indeed, her miracles extended to thieves, prostitutes, and vagabonds.

Mary's widespread popularity among worshippers was almost inevitable: God was a king too infinitely high and awesome to be approached; the Holy Spirit was too abstract to be grasped by the human mind; and Christ, in spite of his infinite love and self-sacrifice, served too often as a judge and mediator to be considered wholly merciful. Mary, on the other hand, was the embodiment of unalloyed maternal tenderness, whose sufferings for her divine son had only rendered her more eagerly beneficent in her desire to aid and save the race for which he died.[16] With the proclamation by the Council of Ephesus (431) that Mary was "Mother of God" and the declaration by the Fourth Lateran Council (649) that her perpetual virginity was Church doctrine, Mary's importance in the Christian religion grew.

Mary is known by a number of titles that relate to particular manifestations, images, and devotions. Many of these refer to places in New Spain, Spain, or other countries (Nuestra Señora de San Juan de los Lagos, de Valvanera, and de Loreto); others refer to her as a refuge for sinners (Nuestra Señora, Refugio de Pecadores); or to her spiritual perfection (the Immaculate Conception or the Immaculate One—La Purísima Concepción or La Inmaculada).[17] Still others refer to her association with an event, whether sacred, such as the Crucifixion (the Pietà—La Piedad), or historical, such as the reconquest of New Mexico (The Conqueror—La Conquistadora); or with nature (Our Lady of the Oak or of the Thunderbolts—Nuestra Señora del Roble or de los Rayos); or to one of her beneficent qualities or attributes (Our Lady of Mercy or of the Rosary—Nuestra Señora de la Merced or del Rosario).[18] In New Spain, as in Europe, Mary was intentionally not associated with the earth, most likely to distance her from preexisting, indigenous beliefs in and cults of an Earth Mother.

Legends about Mary's life and specific images of her were given credibility by artists in drawings, paintings, and sculpture—influenced by local preferences, religious orders, cults, or personal interpretations, as well as political maneuvering.[19] Her miraculous appearance, assistance, or the proclamation of her protection for some group gave particular images national importance, such as the reported appearance of Our Lady of the Rosary during the battle of Lepanto or the invocation of Our Lady of Guadalupe in a battle cry during Mexico's War of Independence.

One of the richest sources of Marian texts was the Apocrypha, a body of sacred writings excluded from the canonical Testaments. In these, Mary's parents are given names—Anne and Joachim—and the story is told of Anne's conception of Mary, and the basis for the belief that Mary was born without original sin: the Immaculate Conception. Other stories include expanded versions of the flight into Egypt and Jesus' childhood. Another deeply influential source concerning Mary was the *Golden Legend*, a collection of the (legendary) lives of saints collected and compiled by the Dominican friar Jacobus de Voragine around 1260—after the invention of the movable type printing press it became one of the most popular books created.

Gradually, Mary evolved into the second Eve (also immaculately conceived); proclaimed the "Mother of God," she became the very image of incorruptibility and, at the moment of her Assumption, Queen of Heaven. As such, Mary is often shown crowned. She is always represented as young and beautiful, her moods ranging from serene and joyous to compassionate and sorrowful. Each element in her iconography aspired to add another dimension of superlatives and to provide spiritual and artistic inspiration.

Not until the last session of the Council of Trent in 1563 were certain Marian attributes considered orthodox and guidelines established for the "correct" representation of Mary. The narrative cycle referred to as "Scenes from the Life of the Virgin" includes Mary's birth; her Presentation at the Temple; scenes with her parents, Anne and Joachim;

her betrothal and marriage to Joseph; the Annunciation; her visit to her cousin Elizabeth; the Nativity; episodes with the child Jesus and Joseph; the Passion of Christ; the Pentecost; and Mary's death. She appears also with Jesus and Joseph representing the Holy Family (the earthly Trinity) and with various saints or as protectress of certain religious orders.

Following a Byzantine tradition, a number of Marian images in New Spain, such as Our Lady of Guadalupe and Our Lady of Solitude (Oaxaca), are crowned. Twelve stars may stud the ends of her *resplendor* (rays of metal signifying a blaze of light emanating from the crown), alluding to the honor given the Daughter of Zion over Israel and the twelve tribes, or to the birth of the Church as represented by the Twelve Apostles.

The Conqueror (La Conquistadora)

In 1625, an estofado image entitled "Our Lady of the Assumption" (Nuestra Señora de la Asunción) was brought to New Mexico by Fray Alonso de Benavides. For a short time referred to as "the Immaculate Conception" (La Purísima Concepción), after its arms and hands were removed in the seventeenth century and replaced by others on metal hooks so that it might be dressed in miniature clothing, the image was called "Our Lady of the Rosary" (Nuestra Señora del Rosario).[20] It was taken by Spaniards fleeing the Pueblo Rebellion in 1680 and presumed to have accompanied de Vargas in his successful reconquest of New Mexico eighteen years later, when it was named "The Conqueror" (La Conquistadora).[21] In the early eighteenth century, it was placed in a chapel later incorporated into the Cathedral at Santa Fe (New Mexico), where it remains.

Although the image is neither remarkably beautiful nor well fashioned (especially after at least two major alterations), its tortuous history and the changing devotions and confraternities associated with it offer fascinating insights into the lives of believers in viceregal New Mexico.[22] Devotion to La Conquistadora was always local and is so to this day.

The Divine Shepherdess (La Divina Pastora)

Dating from the early thirteenth century, the devotion of this manifestation of Mary was not popularized until the eighteenth, by the much-revered Capuchin Saint Isidore of Sevilla, to whom Mary appeared in 1703 in the dress and demeanor of a shepherdess. Perceived as a powerful means of converting pagans, the devotion was introduced by the Capuchins into New Spain, where it gained a wide following among believers and not only Capuchins, but Franciscans generally.

In images of the Divine Shepherdess, Mary is shown seated, sometimes with her son, paying peaceful and loving attention to the flock of sheep that surrounds her. She is simply dressed—with a broad-brimmed hat on her head, hanging on her shoulders, or at her feet—sometimes with a shepherd's staff and water bottle nearby. The sheep, which represent the souls Mary is guarding, often have roses in their mouths and appear to be offering them to her. An image of the Divine Shepherdess appears on the north side of the drum of San Xavier del Bac (Arizona; figure 12.7), opposite the image of the Franciscan Saint John of Capistrano or possibly of Juan Serrano or Antonio Margil de Jesús, both of the College of Santa Cruz in Querétaro (Querétaro), the first missionary college of the Franciscans.

La Dolorosa—see "Our Lady of Sorrows" below.

The Immaculate Conception (La Inmaculada, La Purísima Concepción)

Among the most frequently painted manifestations of Mary in the seventeenth- and eighteenth-century Hispanic world, reflecting the intensive campaign by Spaniards (particularly Sevillans) to elevate it to the status of dogma, the Immaculate Conception encapsulates the doctrine, officially defined by the Roman Catholic Church in 1854, that Mary was free from original sin from the moment of her conception in the womb of Anne, her mother.[23] Attention is entirely on Mary, who stands alone, her hands joined in prayer, her posture demure.

In his role as inspector of art for the Inquisition in Sevilla, Francisco Pacheco (1564–1654) carefully and extensively elaborated upon the rulings of the last session of the Council of Trent in 1563; his detailed instructions to Spanish artists on how to represent the Immaculate Conception served as a guide for centuries to come:

> [Although] some say that The Immaculate Conception should be painted with the Christ Child in her arms . . . we side with those who paint her without the Child. . . .

12.7. Divine Shepherdess, tempera painting on the drum of San Francisco Xavier del Bac, near Tucson, Arizona, 2005. (Photo by Meredith L. Milstead)

> In this most lovely mystery the Lady should be painted in the flower of her youth, twelve to thirteen years old, as the most beautiful young girl, with fine and serious eyes, a most perfect nose and mouth and rosy cheeks, wearing her beautiful golden hair loose, in short, with as much perfection as the human brush can achieve. . . .
>
> She should be painted with a white tunic and blue mantle . . . clothed in the sun . . . crowned by stars, twelve arranged in a light circle between rays coming from her sacred forehead. The stars should be painted as very light spots of dry pure white excelling all rays in brightness. . . . An imperial crown should adorn her head which should not hide the stars. Under her feet is the moon . . . luminous and transparent above the landscape . . . as a half moon with points turned downward. . . .[24]

Pacheco's instructions notwithstanding, the moon under Mary's feet was much more frequently depicted as a crescent with its points turned upward (figure 12.8)—held variously to symbolize Diana, Goddess of the Hunt (signifying Mary's triumph over paganism; see figure 10.13), or the Muslim Turks (signifying her divine intervention in defeating the Turks at the Battle of Lepanto).

A number of symbols and iconographic elements used in association with Mary as the Immaculate One (La Inmaculada) were reinforced with litanies celebrated in church services. Both Franciscans and Jesuits cham-

12.8. Immaculate Conception, sculpture, Santa Ana Vieja, Sonora, 1973.

pioned the Immaculate Conception. Most Franciscan churches in northern New Spain included at least one representation of Mary in this theological image, and each province had a church given that name and placed under her protection.

La Mater Dolorosa—see "Our Lady of Sorrows" below.

Most Holy Mother of Light (La Santísima Madre de la Luz)

Introduced into New Spain in 1732, the original image is said to have been painted by an Italian Jesuit under the direct guidance of Mary, who appeared to him in a vision asking that he create a representation of her to assist missionaries in their conversion of pagans. The Most Holy Mother of Light was made patron saint of León (Guanajuato), chosen by lot to receive the painting. The Most Holy Mother of Light is associated with the Jesuit missionaries, especially those who labored throughout northern New Spain in the eighteenth century.

As with the *tilma* bearing the likeness of Our Lady of Guadalupe and the Veil of Veronica (see "Veronica" below), all later renderings of the original, achiropoeic (made under divine intervention) image are exact copies, although the colors may vary. Mary is standing, usually robed in white with a blue mantle, her feet supported by cherubs. In her left arm, she holds the infant Jesus, to whom the hearts of the faithful are being offered from a basket held by a kneeling angel. In her right hand, she grasps the left wrist of a man to prevent him from falling into the flame-filled jaws of a hideous monster symbolizing Hell (figure 12.9).[25]

Our Lady of Guadalupe (Nuestra Señora de Guadalupe)

According to popular legends, in 1531 Mary appeared to Juan Diego, an Indian whom she charged with announcing her wish to have a church built for her on the hill of Tepeyac, north of the Aztec capital of Tenochtitlán (now Mexico City). After he had been rebuffed by the Church authorities several times, Juan Diego's rough woven cape (tilma) was miraculously imprinted with Mary's image, giving credence to his story. This tilma with its achiropoeic image constitutes the principal relic of this cult (see also "Most Holy Mother of Light" above and "Veronica" below). "Treated as an icon," Stratton tells us, it was "replicated in the smallest detail so as not to lose any degree of its venerability and power."[26]

In this "Immaculate Conception" image, Mary is surrounded by a mandorla of light rays emanating from her body. She is clothed in a dark, rose-colored robe cuffed with white fur and tied at the waist with a belt; her head and shoulders are draped with a blue mantle. Her robe is decorated with a flat, stylized floral pattern (probably imitating an estofado effect); her mantle is bordered in gold and covered with gold stars. She stands on a crescent moon supported by a cherub whose head, hands, and multicolored wings alone are visible (figure 12.10).

The cult of La Guadalupana (named after Guadalupe, Spain, where her image is enshrined) was well established by the early seventeenth century; the Franciscan missionaries of El Colegio de Nuestra Señora de Guadalupe were particularly active in spreading her fame and image into northern New Spain.[27] Pronounced patron saint of Mexico City and of all New Spain on February 11, 1737, Our Lady of Guadalupe gained special importance during Mexico's War of Independence. Mary's demure countenance, with hands clasped in prayer and her feet on a moon place the image of Our Lady of Guadalupe among those of the Immaculate Conception.

The dark skin of Mary's image has been explained as manifesting her willingness to identify with indigenous and mestizo races—an explanation tolerated and even encouraged, if not officially endorsed, by the Church. In this respect, the image stands virtually alone. Indeed, apart from the Christs of Esquipulas, Chalma, and Villa Seca; Saint Benedict, the Holy Black; and the Virgin of Montserrat, Our Lady of Guadalupe was the only dark-skinned sacred figure to be revered by the Catholics of New Spain, and certainly the most popular.[28]

Before Guadalupe, the heroes of the Catholic Church of Spain were light-skinned—or were so portrayed in New Spain. That Jesus, his family, and his Twelve Apostles were very likely dark-skinned Semites was never considered. To the contrary, the deep-seated cultural bias against darker skin tones throughout Europe meant that the Devil and his minions were virtually the only figures in church art to be portrayed as dark-skinned. This bias, together with the earnest desire of early Catholic clerics overseeing the production of church art in New Spain to separate their indigenous converts from their former beliefs in and devotion to dark-skinned deities, resulted in almost exclusively

12.9. "Most Holy Mother of Light," an atypical sculpture assembly of the them, collateral retablo, San Francisco de Asis, Chihuahua, Chihuahua, 2001.

12.10. Our Lady of Guadalupe, oil on canvas painting, private collection.

light-skinned religious images there (although for an exception, see the discussion of dark-skinned nuns and angels in "San Xavier del Bac" under "Religious Images" in chapter 10).[29]

Our Lady of Loreto (Nuestra Señora de Loreto)

Tradition has it that when the Saracens threatened Mary's birthplace (Nazareth) in 1294, a host of angels moved it first to the Dalmatian coast and then to a grove near Loreto, Italy. In this manifestation, Mary is most often shown seated with the infant Jesus on top of a house borne by four angels. Alternatively, she may be shown standing, crowned with a papal tiara, holding the infant Jesus, who wears an imperial crown, with his right hand raised in benediction and an orb in his left. Mary and Jesus, whose heads are at about the same level, are wrapped in a gathered full cape or skirt, usually decorated with bands of pearls or swags of jewelry, which conceals Mary's hands and arms, and which is draped over her right shoulder, dipping down to her left (figure 12.11). Especially active in promoting this devotion, the Jesuits established Our Lady of Loreto as the titular saint of churches and altars, and built several camarines in northern New Spain for her. Her image in the church bearing her name in Loreto (Baja California Sur) is also called "La Conquistadora."

12.11. Our Lady of Loreto, woodblock, private collection.

Our Lady of Mercy (Nuestra Señora de Merced)

Patron saint of the Mercedarians, a religious order founded in 1218 principally for the ransoming of Christians captured or enslaved by the Saracens, Our Lady of Mercy is dressed in a white habit with an insignia of the shield of the kingdom of Aragón on her robe, at her throat, or on her scapular. She is frequently seen holding the child Jesus in her left arm while she offers a miniature scapular of the Mercedarians with her right (see "Our Lady of Mount Carmel [Nuestra Señora de Carmen]" following and **Mercedarians** under **Heraldry** in chapter 11).

Our Lady of Mount Carmel (Nuestra Señora de Carmen)

As patron saint of the Carmelite Order, Mary is clothed in brown with the insignia of the order—a shield with a cross atop a small, stylized hill and a star on either side of the cross—on her habit's scapular. She holds the child Jesus in her left arm and a miniature scapular of the order in her right hand. Very similar to Our Lady of Mercy in pose and attitude, Our Lady of Mount Carmel differs in the color of her habit and in the insignia on her scapular. Her feast continues to be a popular devotion in the former Spanish territories (see upper image in figure 2.18).

Our Lady of the Oak (Nuestra Señora del Roble)

Revealing herself to a young Indian shepherdess, Mary asked that this small sculpture be removed from the trunk of an oak (where, tradition tells us, it had been hidden by the Franciscan Andrés de León in 1592) and that a sanctuary be built for it on that spot. Twice taken to the parochial church, the sculpture was twice miraculously returned to the oak tree before Mary's wishes were finally honored. Made from *pasta de Michoacán* (sometimes referred to as *titzingueni*),[30] it is clothed in a long-sleeved, full-length dress and robe embroidered and fringed with gold (only Mary's face and hands are visible). It has been given a human-hair wig and gold for its crown and radiating halo. Our Lady of the Oak is regarded as the patron saint of Monterrey (Nuevo León); the sculpture is prominently displayed behind the main altar of the cathedral there.

Our Lady of the Pillar of Zaragoza (Nuestra Señora del Pilar de Zaragoza)

This image of Mary is distinguished by the pillar on which she stands, which often has a cross on its shaft. Mary holds the child Jesus in her left arm and may hold a pear in her right hand. Saint James the Greater (Santiago), who is traditionally credited with founding this devotion, may be shown kneeling at her side. A retablo dedicated to Our Lady of the Pillar of Zaragoza in the Santuario de Guadalupe in Parras (Coahuila) also contains the images of four martyred Zaragoza bishop saints; her presence there very likely bespeaks the influence of Spanish priests or immigrants from the province of Aragón (see figure 10.27), as may also her presence on the south wall of the west transept of San Xavier del Bac near Tucson (Arizona).[31]

Our Lady, Refuge of Sinners (Nuestra Señora, Refugio de los Pecadores)

Closely adhering to established Marian iconography and almost always painted, this image shows Mary from the chest up, holding the child Jesus in her left arm, their heads nearly touching as he leans against her and grasps her right thumb with his left hand.[32] She is wearing a red dress and dark blue cape. Around her shoulders, a striped scarf falls forward on her right side; above her and also to her right, the names or monograms of Jesus and Mary are embroidered in gold. Clouds fill the bottom of the painting; stars surround the heads and aureolas of the two figures. Jesus may be clad in gauzy garments, Mary may also be wearing jewelry on her neck, ears, and hands, and her aureola may be surrounded by roses instead of stars. Sometimes both Jesus and Mary may wear similar crowns.

The original version of this image was inspired by a primitive image called Our Lady of the Oak in the province of Montepulciano and painted in Fascati, both in Italy, at the beginning of the eighteenth century. (This is a different manifestation of Our Lady of the Oak from that discussed previously.) It was introduced to New Spain in 1719 by a Jesuit missionary and is said to be located at the Colegio de Propaganda Fide de Nuestra Señora de Guadalupe, a center of Franciscan missionary activity, just outside the city of Zacatecas. In the late eighteenth century, after Pope Pius VI officially declared Our Lady, Refuge of Sinners, patron saint for the colegio, her cult spread to other parts of New Spain.

12.12. Our Lady of Regla, sculpture in the main retablo, Catedral de Chihuahua, 1992.

Our Lady of Regla (Nuestra Señora de la Regla)

Recognition of this sculpted image, especially revered at the Cathedral of León, Spain, was largely confined in New Spain to the congregants of the Cathedral of Chihuahua, where Our Lady of Regla is one of the patron saints.[33] In a manner suggesting Gothic sculpture, Mary stands stiffly erect and holds the infant Jesus directly in front of her; indeed, her posture, clothing, and outline strongly evoke medieval Catalán figures. Her head is covered in a white wimple worn by sixteenth-century Spanish women of noble birth (called a *toca* or, when ruffled and associated with Mary or the saints, especially the virgin saints from the sixteenth to the eighteenth centuries, a *rostrillo*) and a veil; she is clothed in a robe covered with asterisk-like stars in relief over an elaborately painted skirt and dress (figure 12.12). Jesus has both hands raised in benediction and is posed in the same way as his mother; he is dressed in a bell-like skirt, which simply ends with no indication of feet.

Our Lady of Remedies (Nuestra Señora de los Remedios)

More a reflection of Mary's all-encompassing compassion than a title assigned to a particular image of her, Our Lady of Remedies has been associated since the Conquest with the Spaniards and, in particular, with the sculpted images that accompanied Cortés and later explorers and missionaries. The image venerated by that name at the Santuario de Remedios, just north of Mexico City, is popularly believed to be the original, carried by one of Cortés's soldiers, Juan Rodríguez Villafuerte. During the retreat from Tenochtitlán (La Noche Triste: July 8, 1520), it was hidden under maguey plants; an Indian who found it later built a small shrine for it in front of his house. During the War of Mexican Independence, loyalist forces fought under the banner of Nuestra Señora de los Remedios; Mexican forces, under the banner of La Guadalupana.

Our Lady of Saint John of the Lakes (Nuestra Señora de San Juan de los Lagos)

In 1623, a primitive little image of the Virgin Mary called "Cihuapilli" and venerated by the Indians of San Juan de Lagos (Jalisco) was placed upon the chest of a child acrobat who had died in a tightrope accident, whereupon the child miraculously revived. Tradition has it that before the child's grateful father could have the image restored in Guadalajara, this was done miraculously. As more miracles were attributed to the image, devotion to Our Lady of Saint John of the Lakes spread; in 1623, a sanctuary was built, followed by a huge church in 1732 to accommodate the multitude of pilgrims. Made from pasta de Michoacán, the image is mounted on an elaborate gold base with a half moon of gold and jewels. Mary is garbed in a full-length satin dress trimmed with pearls and heavily embroidered with gold; only her head (with human-hair wig) and clasped hands are showing.

Our Lady of Solitude (Nuestra Señora de Soledad)

Jesus has been entombed and Mary is now alone with her grief, mourning her son, from the evening of Good Friday until the day of his Resurrection. Clothed either entirely in mourner's black or in a white dress and long black mantle, Mary clasps her hands, sometimes holding a lily, handkerchief, or rosary, and simply stands, head bowed slightly, radiating an air of quiet dignity. Its black-and-white color scheme and absence of piercing swords or daggers distinguish this image from that of Our Lady of Sorrows.

Our Lady of Sorrows (Nuestra Señora de los Dolores)

Also called "The Sorrowful" (La Dolorosa) or "The Sorrowful Mother" (La Mater Dolorosa) in this manifestation, Mary is portrayed as mourning the events of her son's Passion. Usually wearing a red tunic and dark blue mantle over her head in a painted or sculpted tableau, she may appear with the crucified Jesus and with John the Evangelist ("The Crucifixion") or alone, tearfully clasping her hands in grief (see figure 10.17a) and sometimes contemplating objects symbolic of the Passion, particularly the nails and crown of thorns.

The most significant attribute of Our Lady of Sorrows is a sword or dagger piercing her heart. This is sometimes expanded to seven swords or daggers piercing her heart, an allusion to Mary's Seven Sorrows: the Prophecy of Simeon at the Presentation in the Temple, the Flight into Egypt, the child Jesus Lost on the Way to Jerusalem, the Meeting of Jesus and Mary on the Road to Calvary, the Crucifixion, the Descent from the Cross, and the Entombment.

Our Lady of the Rosary (Nuestra Señora del Rosario)

Mary is portrayed holding the infant Jesus in her left arm and a rosary in her extended right hand. Derived from medieval terms meaning "garland of roses" (a frequent Marian attribute), "rosary" came to designate a chain of simple prayer beads, divided into groups of ten, although the beads could be carved from rosewood or in the shape of a rose.

Mary may be portrayed either standing or enthroned. Saint Dominic of Guzmán, who according to legend initiated the cult of the rosary around 1215, may be shown kneeling at her feet to accept the rosary.[34] Devotion to Our Lady of the Rosary gained momentum with the victory of the Christian League's fleet over the Turkish armada at the Battle of Lepanto (1571), attributed by Pope Pius V to the instrumentality of the rosary. In some of the many painted and sculpted versions of this image, Mary may also hold other items in her right hand, such as a scepter or candle (see figure 2.27).[35]

Our Lady of the Thunderbolts (Nuestra Señora de los Rayos)

This important sculpted pilgrimage image is located in Parral (Chihuahua) in a church by the same name. Mary is shown standing in a blue robe with a white veil, her hands extended downward, with rays of gold descending from her fingers. A violent electrical storm erupted as the image was being carried in a procession there. Lightning struck nearby buildings and individuals in the procession, but Our Lady of the Thunderbolts, as the image came to be called, was not damaged; indeed, Mary's presence appeared to still the tempest.[36] Because Mary was also believed to have helped subdue rebellious Indians in the area around Parral, again acting through the image, it is also known as the "General, Patron Saint of the Armed Forces" (La Generala, Patrona de las Armas).

Our Lady of Valvanera (Nuestra Señora de Valvanera)

Patron saint of Spaniards from the province of Rioja, Our Lady of Valvanera may be portrayed as richly robed and seated on a throne borne by four eagles. According to legend, the original image was sculpted by Saint Luke, who was popularly believed to have sculpted and painted a number of images of Mary from life. In northern New Spain, her face is encircled by a rostrillo. She is crowned, as is the infant Jesus, whom she holds in her left arm, sometimes holding an upright book and an apple (alluding to Mary's role as the second Eve), pear, or heart in her right hand. Near them stands an oak tree, with water flowing from its base. An image of Our Lady of Valvanera appears prominently in the third story of the stone retablo of La Castrense, the eighteenth-century military chapel of Santa Fe (New Mexico; see figure 2.26).[37]

Pietà (La Piedad)

In this image, also called the "Virgin of the Pietà" (La Virgen de la Piedad), Mary is shown alone, holding or embracing the body of Jesus after its Descent from the Cross. Because the emphasis is on her and her suffering, she may appear larger than Jesus, a popular artistic device used since the Middle Ages. The cult of the Pietà arose at the end of the eleventh century in northern Europe, Spain, and Italy and reached its full development in the fourteenth century, dates that roughly encompass the recapture of the Holy Land by the Christians.

Sacred Heart of Mary (La Sagrada Corazón de María)

Although it predates that of the Sacred Heart of Jesus (see earlier) by twenty years, this devotion, not officially recognized until 1648, was never as popular. In images of the Sacred Heart of Mary, she is usually shown from the chest up, pointing to or exposing her flaming heart.

The Sorrowful Mother (La Mater Dolorosa)—see "Our Lady of Sorrows" earlier.

Saints

Called "soldiers of God," saints (santos; from Latin *sanctus* or *sancta*, holy person) are individuals judged by God to be worthy of entering the Kingdom of Heaven immediately after their death. Gradually, "saint" acquired the status of a title; thus, although many Christians were considered holy, comparatively few were regarded as saints. Among the first Christians to be so honored were martyrs (from Greek *martus*, witness) "because in the manner of their deaths they bore the ultimate witness to the name of Jesus Christ."[38]

The defense of the saints, and especially of the Virgin Mary, played a crucial role in the sacred art of the Counter-Reformation.[39] The consolidation and aggressive defense of Catholic themes and dogmas called for by the last session of the Council of Trent in 1563 combined with a renewed interest in symbolism in the portrayals of the saints and other sacred figures. Painted and sculpted images of saints proliferated in Europe and the New World alike. In northern New Spain alone, it would be no exaggeration to say that, at some time or other, virtually all of the two hundred or so most commonly portrayed saints—including manifestations of Jesus and Mary—lent their names to or were represented in some church, chapel, retablo, sacred or liturgical object, painting, or sculpture.[40] As a consequence of the replacement of baroque with neoclassical retablos, however, the number of sacred figures represented was greatly reduced.

Patron saints, whose chief function was to provide special protection and who, in return, received special acknowledgment and honors, varied from town to town, district to district, or country to country. Many patron saints were chosen because they were born, died, or had their relics located in a particular place; because they belonged to a particular trade or profession; or because they occupied a particular station in life. Based on often miraculous incidents in their lives or deaths, they became protectors against illnesses, accidents, or other misfortunes, and were appealed to for health, good fortune, and success. Churches were placed under the protection of titular saints, who were especially venerated there and after whom the churches were named (as were their main altars, consecrated to these saints).[41] Throughout New Spain, almost every occupation, church, and town had one or more patron saint.

In 1630, Pope Urban VIII declared that saints must be canonized: those chosen by clergy and parishioners with the approval of their bishops had to be confirmed by the Sacred Congregation of Rites. This requirement, along with denying official recognition to doubtful and spurious saints, helped thin and regularize their ranks, although there are to this day saints popularly revered outside official recognition.

In Spanish, saints are given the title of "San" or "Santa" ("Santo" for saints whose names begin with a hard "d" or "t," such as Domingo, Toribio, and Tomás), or "Santísimo" or "Santísima" (most holy—commonly used only with the founders of religious orders and with the Virgin Mary). They may also be given the title "Señor" (Lord) or "Nuestro Padre" (Our Father), for example, "Señor San José" or "Nuestro Padre San Ignacio."

Central to their iconography, the attributes of saints are nearly always associated either with their legends or with the etymology of their names. Following, saints most commonly found in churches throughout northern New Spain are briefly described and their iconography and most distinguishing attributes identified, with remarks on how these sacred figures are typically portrayed there. Not surprisingly, the relatively large proportion of saints and devotions important to Franciscans and Jesuits is due to the dominant presence of these orders in northern New Spain. The preponderance of men over women among the saints reflects their relative numbers among all officially recognized saints and, specifically, among saints portrayed in northern New Spain.

Twelve Apostles

[Andrew (Andrés)] Brother to Peter and a Galilean fisherman, the Apostle Andrew was the first to follow Jesus. He is usually shown as an old man with curly hair. He was crucified on an X-shaped, or transverse (saltire), cross, his principal attribute, which he may hold.

[Bartholomew (Bartolomé)] According to tradition, the Apostle Bartholomew was an Egyptian prince who, on his conversion, evangeli zed in Arabia, Mesopotamia, and Armenia, where he was skinned alive and then crucified or decapitated. Commonly portrayed as a young man, he holds a large flaying knife, the instrument of his torture. He may be also seen with a demon on a chain leash at his feet, referring to the legend of his having rescued the daughter of an Armenian king from demonic possession. The patron saint of butchers and leather workers, Saint Bartholomew is invoked against skin diseases and nervous disorders.

[James the Greater (Santiago Matamoros; Jaime el Mayor)] "Greater" was used to indicate that this Apostle James was the first of two called by Jesus. Brother to John the Evangelist, James the Greater was the first Apostle to go forth to preach. Accounts of his trips to Spain, where he is said to have evangelized after Christ's Ascension, are based on legend, not Scripture—as are those of his vision of Our Lady of the Pillar at Zaragoza (see earlier); the return of his martyred body to Spain for burial; and the miraculous incidents leading to the discovery of his relics at Compostela (from Latin Campus Stellae, Field of the Star).[42]

Legend has it that Saint James the Greater (Santiago) appeared to King Ramiro of Asturias on the eve of a battle at Clavijo (ca. 844), promising victory against the Moors. When the saint appeared again the next day on a white horse, the inspired Spanish forces routed the infidels with the battle cry of "Santiago!" For this reason, he is also known as "Matamoros" (Killer or Conqueror of the Moors). The patron saint of Spain, soldiers, and horsemen, Saint James the Greater is also invoked to promote the fertility of mares.

During the Conquest, traditions sprang up of the warrior saint appearing at battles, each time so inspiring the Spanish soldiers that victory was assured. He is reported to have twice appeared on his white horse surrounded by a

12.13. Saint James the Greater, sculpture, San Pedro de Sombrerete, Zacatecas, 1984.

blinding light to (the soon to be victorious) Juan de Oñate during the battle of Ácoma (New Mexico) in 1595.

Saint James the Greater is most frequently portrayed as a mature, bearded soldier with armor, helmet, shield, and sword, riding a horse (see figure 12.13). When not shown as a soldier, he is distinguished by his pilgrim's staff, gourd, hat, and cape—the last two usually displaying a scallop shell, the symbol for Compostela, which in the Middle Ages rivaled Jerusalem and Rome as a pilgrimage center—and a sword, by which he was decapitated (see also figure 4.45, figure on the right).[43] The red fleurette cross, emblem of the Spanish military Order of Santiago, may appear on his costume or armor. The presence of his image in the eighteenth-century stone retablo of La Castrense, the military chapel in Santa Fe (New Mexico) is thus particularly appropriate.

[James the Less (Jaime el Menor)] Called to be an Apostle after James the Greater, James the Less (according to legend) so closely resembled Jesus, to whom he was first cousin, that it took the kiss of Judas to tell them apart. He is usually portrayed as a young, clean-shaven man. First bishop of Jerusalem, the Apostle James the Less was martyred there by being beaten to death with a fuller's club, his principal attribute.

[John the Evangelist (Juan el Evangelista)] A cousin to Jesus and "the disciple whom Jesus loved," the Apostle John was one of Jesus' earliest followers, sat beside him at the Last Supper, and stood beside the Cross when Jesus charged him to care for his mother, Mary. He placed Jesus' body in the sepulcher and witnessed the Transfiguration. The only Apostle not dying a martyr's death, John appears in scenes of the Crucifixion, standing with Mary at the foot of the Cross (figure 12.14; see also figure 10.17, lower left). He may be shown as either a clean-shaven young or a bearded older man. His traditional attribute is a chalice with a snake or dragon crawling out of it, alluding, Voragine tells us, to the poison placed in it for him to drink.[44] Accordingly, he is considered a Eucharistic saint, whose principal attribute is an eagle proclaiming the Word.

[Jude (Judas Tadeo)] Also known as Thaddeus (the brave one) or Lebbaeus (John 24:22; Matthew 10:3), the Apostle Jude is thought to be the author of the Epistle of Jude in the New Testament and the brother of James the Less. Martyred in Persia with Simon the Zealot, Saint Jude may appear with a lance, ax, club, or rocks in his hand—the instruments of his martyrdom—and a carpenter's square, denoting his trade. Because of the carpenter's square, he is sometimes confused with the Apostle Thomas. Saint Jude has become quite popular as a patron saint of desperate or hopeless causes.[45]

[Matthew (Mateo)] The author of the first Gospel, Matthew the Evangelist (Mateo el Evangelista) was martyred in Ethiopia. He is portrayed as a young man with curly hair and a short beard, sometimes with a pen in hand, looking over his left shoulder at an angel, who is inspiring him. His attributes includ e a money bag and an ax or sword, alluding to his earlier occupation as a tax collector and to the instrument of his martyrdom, although his principal attribute is a winged man, representing the soul or incarnation (see figure 2.17, lower left).

[Matthias (Matías)] Not one of the original Twelve Apostles, Saint Matthias was selected by lot to replace Judas Iscariot after the latter hanged himself.[46] His principal attribute is an ax or lance, the instrument of his martyrdom; he appears only with the other Apostles, never alone.

[Peter (Pedro)] Also called Simon or Simon Peter, the Apostle Peter was a fisherman whose brother Andrew introduced him to Jesus. When Peter acknowledged Jesus as the Savior, Jesus replied: "You are Peter and on this rock will I build my church. . . . And I will give you the keys to the kingdom of heaven" (Matthew 16:18,19). This text provides the basis for Catholics' belief in the primacy of the papacy and in Peter as their first pope. Peter and Paul are honored as founders and defenders of the Christian Church and as representing, respectively, the Jewish and Gentile branches of Christendom. A book or scroll indicates Peter's receiving the New Testament, which does away with the Old (Peter embodying the New Law, as Moses embodied the Old).

Present with Jesus during many of his miracles, Peter fulfilled Jesus' prophecy at the Last Supper by denying him three times before the cock crowed at dawn the next day. Although keys are his principal attribute, he may also be shown with a fish or a raised sword, alluding, respectively to his former trade (or his being a "fisher of men"), and to his having cut off the ear of the high priest's servant Malchus when Jesus was being seized. Since the baroque era, a papal tiara has also been included among Peter's attributes. Uniquely distinguished by his means of martyrdom, Peter was crucified upside down at his own request so as not to emulate Jesus' Crucifixion. Since the fourth century, Saint Peter has been portrayed as an elderly, sometimes bald, robust man with a short, trimmed, curly beard.

[Philip (Felipe)] Active in Syria, where he was martyred by being tied to a pillar or a tall cross, the Apostle Philip appears only with the other Apostles, never alone, and sometimes with a large serpent at his feet. He may hold a small cross or a crosier ending in a cross, or loaves of bread, alluding to his role in Jesus' feeding of the multitudes.

[Simon (Simón)] Known as "Simon the Zealot" and martyred in Persia with Jude, the Apostle Simon is usually portrayed as a bald old man; his principal attribute is a saw, the instrument of his martyrdom.

12.14. Saint John the Evangelist, west portal, Catedral de Durango, 2006.

[Thomas (Tomás)] Skeptical about the Resurrection until he touched Christ's wounds and, according to legend, also about the Assumption of the Virgin until she lowered her belt to him from Heaven, the Apostle Thomas is said to have established the Church in India.

Legend has it that the risen Christ appeared to Thomas, telling him to go to India to build a palace for King Gondoforus. After directing Thomas how the palace should be built and giving him an enormous amount of money to that end, the king left for two years. Thomas built nothing and instead distributed the king's money to the poor. Enraged at what Thomas had done, the king was on the verge of killing him when a dream made clear to him the difference between riches on earth and those in Heaven. On the basis of this legend, Saint Thomas is considered the patron saint of architects; his principal attribute is the carpenter's square. Other attributes include an ax, lance, or sword, the instruments of his martyrdom. He is shown as a mature, sometimes bearded man.

Other Saints

[Acacius (Acacio)] According to legend, this second-century martyr, also called "Acacius of Mount Ararat," converted to Christianity along with his troops; he retired with his soldiers to found a community for the contemplative life. Saint Acacius and all his men were captured and martyred. He is shown dressed in military garb, crucified (tied rather than nailed to a cross), and with a crown of thorns on his head. On either side of the cross, there may be flags, drums, cannons, rifles, or other military equipment, as well as small figures of soldiers. One of the Fourteen Holy Helpers (see below), Saint Acacius is invoked against headaches and is seen mostly in New Mexican retablos.

[Agnes (Inés)] This fourth-century Christian martyr chose death by beheading rather than life as a pagan Roman. Although her name derives from the Greek *agnos* (chaste or pure), the close resemblance of *agnos* to the Latin *agnus* (lamb) strongly encouraged an association with the mystic Lamb of God; a lamb became Saint Agnes's principal attribute.[47] As her parents and friends paid their devotions at her tomb, she appeared with a pure white lamb at her side, assured them of her perfect happiness, and then vanished. Portrayed as a young woman, dressed in a long tunic or in the manner colonial artists believed a Roman noblewoman would be dressed, Saint Agnes is the patron saint of maidens and the betrothed.

[Aloysius Gonzaga (Luis Gonzaga)] Member of a powerful and aristocratic Italian family, Saint Aloysius Gonzaga (1568–1591) joined the Jesuits at an early age. During an epidemic in which he tirelessly worked to relieve the suffering of the victims, he himself fell ill and died. He is usually shown as a young man dressed in a Jesuit habit with a surplice, in prayerful contemplation of symbols of penance, including a scourge (figure 12.15). Saint Aloysius is considered the patron saint of youths and their purity.

12.15. Saint Aloysius Gonzaga, woodblock, private collection.

[Ambrose (Ambrosio)] Bishop of Milan and one of the Four Doctors, or Fathers, of the Church, Saint Ambrose (ca. 334–397) was the first teacher in the West to popularize hymns for divine praise. His abilities as statesman, theologian, and administrator helped heal divisions within the new Christian Faith. He is usually portrayed as a bishop, distinguished from other sainted bishops by the presence of a beehive, alluding to the sweetness of his eloquence. Images of this Pillar of the Faith appear regularly in the pendentives of church crossings. Saint Ambrose may also carry or wield a knotted scourge as an emblem of his punishment of the Emperor Theodosius and the Arian heretics, or of his vigorous denunciation of sins committed by the congregants of his diocese.

[Anne (Ana)] According to the Apocrypha, Saint Anne was mother to the Virgin Mary and wife to the shepherd Joachim.[48] Portrayed as an older woman, usually in a red robe with a green mantle, Anne appears in scenes with Mary as a child or young woman, pointing out to her the prophecies about Jesus in an open book (Bible) or presenting her in the temple. Carved or painted images of Anne and Joachim oppose one another on the sides of altars dedicated to Mary throughout northern New Spain. Anne, who had been barren, was believed to have conceived Mary without original sin, albeit with man—the Immaculate Conception—prefiguring the immaculate conception of Jesus by Mary—without original sin *and* without man. To bolster respect for the Holy Family, the Vatican made Saint Anne's feast day a universal holiday in 1584, which did much to promote her cult. The patron saint of motherhood, Saint Anne is invoked against both barrenness and the pains and ailments associated with childbirth.

[Anthony of Padua (Antonio de Padua)] The "Evangelical Doctor," Saint Anthony (1195–1231) was a Portuguese Franciscan noted for his preaching. Based on legends and popular accounts of miracles he worked, this much beloved saint is invoked in helping single women secure husbands, married women conceive children, and all believers find lost articles.

In one account, a heretic in Toulouse told Anthony he would not believe in the Holy Sacrament unless his donkey knelt down before it. A few days later the animal did just that, as Saint Anthony passed by carrying the Sacred Host to a dying man. He is thus considered a Eucharistic saint.

In another, his host, seeing light beneath Anthony's bedroom door, peeked through the keyhole, only to see the infant Jesus in Anthony's arms. His principal attribute is thus the Christ Child, which, together with a book and a stalk of lilies, distinguishes him from other Franciscan saints. Saint Anthony is always portrayed as a young, clean-shaven, tonsured Franciscan friar with a sweet demeanor (figure 12.16).

[Apollonia of Alexandria (Apolonia de Alejandría)] This aged spinster Christian deaconess was martyred in Alexandria (ca. 250) during the reign of Emperor Philip. Attacked by a pagan mob because her home provided a refuge for Christians, Apollonia had all her teeth knocked out. Threatened with death by fire, she willingly leapt into the flames. According to popular accounts, however, it was Apollonia's father who demanded that she renounce her faith. When she refused to do so and to marry the man he had chosen to be her husband, he ordered that her teeth be pulled out with tongs and that she be killed. Despite her age, she is typically shown as, and sometimes together with, the other virgin martyrs: beautiful and young, crowned with flowers, and holding a palm frond in one hand. Her principal and distinguishing attribute is a pair of tongs gripping a tooth, which she holds in her other hand. The patron saint of dentists, Saint Apollonia is invoked against toothaches and other ailments of the mouth.

[Augustine (Agustín)] Called the "Doctor of Grace," founder of the monastic order bearing his name, and one of the Four Fathers of the Church, Saint Augustine (354–430) is honored as the greatest theologian of the Roman Catholic religion. He was appointed Bishop of Hippo in North Africa and is always portrayed in bishop's garb, holding a staff and wearing a miter. Shortly after the Reformation, images of Augustine widely emphasized his role as defender of orthodoxy. He may hold a heart—whole, in pieces, pierced, or aflame—alluding to his piety and love of God or simply to the Augustinian Order. He may also hold a book, pen, or model of a church (figure 12.17). His image is commonly seen in the pendentives of church crossings, along with images of the other Fathers of the Church: Saints Ambrose, Jerome, and Gregory (see above and below) or sometimes on the predella of retablos. His mother, Saint Monica (Santa Monica), is considered the first Augustinian nun.

[Barbara (Bárbara)] Born in Asia Minor, this exceptionally beautiful third-century virgin martyr secretly converted to Christianity. When she was forced to live in a tower built for her by her obsessively possessive father, she had three windows especially built as a symbol of the Trinity. Learning of her conversion, her father had her beheaded, but was himself immediately struck dead by lightning and turned to ashes. Just before her beheading, she proclaimed that all who called on her at the moment of their death would be absolved of their sins.

Dressed like other Roman virgin martyrs, Saint Barbara is distinguished from them by her principal attribute, a tower with three openings or stages. She holds the palm frond of martyrdom in one hand and a monstrance in the

12.16. Saint Anthony of Padua, sculpture, museum, San José de Tumacácori, Arizona, 1975. (Courtesy of National Park Service)

12.17. Saint Augustine, bas-relief sculpture on a pendentive, Catedral de Chihuahua, 1992.

other, and is thus included among the Eucharistic saints. She is often portrayed with Catherine of Alexandria to symbolize, respectively, the active and the contemplative Church life.

The patron saint of artillerymen, firework makers, architects, builders, armorers, and gunsmiths, Saint Barbara is invoked against lightning, fire, explosions, sudden disasters, and calamities (particularly those in mines), apoplexy, and unexpected or sudden death.[49] Like Catherine of Alexandria, she is considered one of the Fourteen Holy Helpers (see below; see also "Acacius" above and statue atop right corner buttress in figure 2.11).

[Bernardine of Siena (Bernardino de Siena)] An Italian Franciscan noted for his zeal, preaching, and missionary activity, Saint Bernardine (1380–1440) founded the Observants, a reformed order of Franciscans. He is usually portrayed as a tonsured, gaunt older man, wearing a Franciscan habit and holding a book. His image can be found in Franciscan mission churches throughout northern New Spain, sometimes with "I H S," the trigram for Jesus he used in his preaching and missionary work, on a banner or a plaque surrounded by flames. Sometimes Saint Bernadine also has three miters at his feet, alluding to his threefold renouncement of the bishopric.

[Blaise (Blas)] A fourth-century Armenian bishop, Saint Blaise fled Diocletian's persecutions of the Christians and took refuge in a cave, where, legend has it, he was fed by the birds and animals gathered to be healed by him. Attracted by the commotion, Diocletian's men found Blaise, who because Christ had appeared to him in a dream saying, "Arise, and offer sacrifice to Me!" allowed himself to be captured. In prison, he was cruelly tortured and finally beheaded. Because his body was racked by metal spikes, interpreted as the metal teeth of wool-carding brushes (his principal attribute), he is considered the patron saint of the wool industry. One of the Fourteen Holy Helpers (see below), he is commonly shown in bishop's vestments and miter, holding wool-carding brushes as emblems of his torture. Because he is said to have saved a child choking on a fishbone and to have willingly offered his neck for beheading, Saint Blaise is invoked against throat ailments (figure 12.18).

[Bonaventure (Buenaventura)] Healed by Saint Francis of Assisi when he was a child, Saint Bonaventure (1221–1274) entered the Franciscan Order as an adolescent. Known as the "Seraphic Doctor" and renowned for his teaching and writing, he is regarded as the greatest Friar Minor after Francis himself. Although usually shown as a young, clean-shaven Franciscan holding a book, he is sometimes portrayed as cardinal-bishop, having been made one a year before his death.

[Cajetan (Cayetano)] Italian cofounder of the Order of the Theatines, Saint Cajetan (1473–1547) is usually shown in the habit of the order, a simple black robe with a white collar, sometimes holding a lily or the infant Jesus, an allusion to his purity and devotion. His principal attribute, however, is a jeweled chain, perhaps referring to the leadership of his order; other attributes include the symbols of the Passion, referring to his love of the apostolic life and his extreme asceticism (figure 12.19; see also figure 10.9).

[Caspar, Balthazar, and Melchior (Caspar, Baltasar, and Melchor)] The Wise Men, or Magi, later called the "Three Kings" (Los Reyes Magos), came from the East to Bethlehem to adore the child Jesus and offer him frankincense, myrrh, and gold (Matthew 2:1–12). Included in scenes of the adoration of the Christ Child since the beginning of the third century, they are typically portrayed as follows: Saint Caspar, as a young, fair-skinned, clean-shaven man bringing frankincense; Saint Balthazar, as a mature, dark-skinned, bearded man bringing myrrh; and Saint Melchior, as an old, gray-haired man with a large beard bringing gold. Always shown together, they are generally crowned, as befits royalty, with the Star of Bethlehem shining overhead.

[Catherine of Alexandria (Catalina de Alejandría)] This fourth-century maiden of royal descent, when challenged on her Christian beliefs, was said to have demolished the arguments of fifty philosophers. When her torturers tried to break her on the wheel, it flew apart and injured bystanders instead. Finally beheaded (her veins spilling milk rather than blood), her body was taken away by angels.

Saint Catherine of Alexandria is shown as a young Roman noblewoman, dressed in a tunic and cape. Her principal attribute is the wheel, the implement of her torture. Other attributes include a crown, book, and palm frond, alluding, respectively, to her royalty, learning,

12.18. Saint Blaise, detail of a collateral retablo, Santo Tomás de Villanueva, Chihuahua, 2004.

Retrato de la imagen de S.r Caietano Fiene fundad.or
de los clerigos Regulares que venera la debocion En
la capilla de N. S. de la Antigua q̃ esta en la S.ta Yglesia Ca
thedral de Mexico.

12.19. *Saint Cajetan, engraving, private collection.*

12.20. Saint Catherine of Alexandria, detail of the frontispiece, Santo Domingo, Sombrerete, Zacatecas, 1983.

and martyrdom. At her feet may be the head or bust of a crowned or turbaned figure—the Emperor Majencio—her persecutor, whom she conquered by her wisdom and steadfastness (figure 12.20). Introduced from the Eastern Church into the West by the crusaders, and listed among the Fourteen Holy Helpers (see below), Saint Catherine of Alexandria is the patron saint of wheelwrights, potters, millers, and spinners, young girls, students, orators, lawyers, and philosophers (see also "Agnes" above).

[Catherine of Siena (Catalina de Siena)] This Italian mystic and Dominican was consulted by popes, princes, and republican heads of state, whom she strongly influenced through her visions, spiritual insight, and diplomatic correspondence. While in rapturous prayer, Saint Catherine of Siena (1347–1380) received the stigmata of Christ on her hands, heart, and feet, which serve as her principal attribute. She is usually shown as a handsome, mature woman wearing the Dominican habit, with a heart in her hand and a crown of thorns or roses on her head.

[Cecilia (Cecilia)] According to legend, this third-century virgin martyr was born of a noble Roman family. On her conversion to Christianity, Saint Cecilia took vows of chastity, vows her husband respected when she was wed. He and his brother became Christians; the three of them secretly buried Christian martyrs. Captured, Cecilia refused to renounce her faith and to worship idols; after several unsuccessful attempts, she was finally beheaded. Said to have excelled in music, written hymns, invented the organ, and put the birds to shame with her singing, Saint Cecilia has been considered the patron saint of church music since about the fifteenth century. Dressed like the other young Roman noblewomen saints, she may be shown seated at an organ or holding a wreath of flowers and a palm frond (see also "Agnes" above).

[Clare of Assisi (Clara de Asís)] Cofounder with Francis of Assisi of the Poor Clares (Clarisas), the order of Franciscan nuns, in 1215, Saint Clare (1194–1253) wears a Franciscan nun's habit. Her attributes include the book of rules of her order, an abbess's staff, and a monstrance or ciborium, placing her among the Eucharistic saints. Indeed, in an allusion to the miraculous turning away of Saracen mercenaries who had attacked her convent in 1241, she may be shown displaying the monstrance atop the ramparts of a building.

[Didacus of Alcalá (Diego de Alcalá)] A Spanish Capuchin brother noted for his tender care of the sick, Saint Didacus (d. 1463) is most often depicted in simple Franciscan habit, with a cross in his hand and a basket of roses, alluding to the legend where the bread he was taking from his monastery to feed the poor was turned to roses to avoid detection by his superior. Saint Didacus is invoked against ulcers of the skin.

12.21. Saint Dominic of Guzmán, engraving, private collection.

[Dominic of Guzmán (Domingo de Guzmán)] Born in Castilla, Saint Dominic (1170–1221) was the founder of the Dominican Order and a principal promoter of the devotion to the rosary. According to tradition, his pregnant mother dreamed she had given birth to a black-and-white dog with a torch in his jaws intent on setting the world on fire. The Latin name Dominicanes (Dominicans) was often taken as a pun on *domini canes* (the Lord's dogs or the watchdogs of God), an indication that Dominic and his order would defend the Church against heresy like guard dogs, as indeed they did.

Saint Dominic is shown as a tonsured cleric in the distinctive Dominican black-and-white habit. A star or moon appears on his forehead, referring to the star that appeared during his Baptism or to his destined role, which his mother saw as giving light to the benighted nations; a black-and-white dog with a torch in its mouth stands at his side. Saint Dominic may also be seen holding a monstrance (which places him among the Eucharistic saints) or a staff with the insignia of the Dominican Order, or receiving the rosary from the Virgin, sometimes in association with naval war vessels in an allusion to the Spanish success at the Battle of Lepanto (figure 12.21).

Although it is uncertain whether Dominic ever met Francis of Assisi, his contemporary, there are many instances where images of the two saints appear opposite each other in the same retablo or frontispiece, or where the coat of arms or emblems of one order are included among the other order's church decorations. Saint Dominic's mother, Joan of Aza, was beatified.

[Ferdinand (Fernando Rey)] Soldier king of Castilla and first cousin to Saint Louis, King of France, through Louis's mother, Blanche of Castilla, Ferdinand III (1199–1252) engaged in successful campaigns against the Moors. Distinguished from Saint Louis by the absence of French insignia, Saint Ferdinand is shown as a young man in a suit of armor and royal robe, with a crown and scepter. He may also hold an orb and a sword, signifying his regal sovereignty and role as a soldier.

[Fourteen Holy Helpers (Los Catorce Intercesores)] These saints were promised special intercessory powers after their deaths.[50] A company of saints working together was perceived as more effective than a single intercessor; their collective feast is observed August 8. Widely diffused through Bohemia, Italy, France, Moravia, and Hungary in the fifteenth century, the cult was attacked by Church reformers in the sixteenth century and discouraged by the last session of the Council of Trent in 1563.

At least twenty-three saints have been listed at one time or other under this heading, almost all martyrs. In northern New Spain, eleven of these saints were venerated—though as individual saints only: Acacius, Barbara, Blaise, Catherine of Alexandria, Christopher, George, Margaret of Antioch, Nicholas of Bari, Roch, Sebastian, and Wilgefortis.

[Francis of Assisi (Francisco de Asís)] Founder of the Order of Friars Minor, the largest of all Roman Catholic orders, Saint Francis (1181–1226) was the son of a wealthy Italian merchant and a Frenchwoman. As a young man, he became convinced he should devote his life to helping the poor. Disinherited by his father, he and others became wandering preachers; their example of simplicity and humility attracted still others. In 1224, while praying, he was marked with Christ's stigmata. The legend of Saint Francis continued to grow after his death, and accounts of his life became modeled on that of Christ.

He is shown as a tonsured, bearded, gaunt man of middle years, clothed in the Franciscans' brown, gray, or blue robe with knotted cord, bearing his principal attribute, the stigmata, on his hands, heart, and feet, with a skull and cross symbolizing introspection and asceticism (figure 12.22). Saint Francis is invoked against fierce animals and against gangrene and persistent ulcers. A miraculous statue of the seated saint is venerated at La Purísima Concepción in Real de Catorce (San Luis Potosí).

12.22. Saint Francis of Assisi, engraving, private collection.

[Francis Borgia (Francisco Borja)] Spanish aristocrat, great-grandson to a pope and king, and cousin to the Emperor Charles V, Saint Francis Borgia (1510–1572) is considered a principal promoter of the Society of Jesus, to which he dedicated his considerable intellect and energies. He is portrayed as a bald, bearded, older cleric dressed in the black cassock of the Jesuits, often with a miter and a crown at his feet, alluding to his renunciation of both honors, and sometimes with a crowned skull (Queen Isabella's), alluding to his decision, inspired by Isabella's death, never again to serve mortal masters. A Eucharistic saint, he may also be seen kneeling before the Host or holding a monstrance in his left hand.

[Francis Xavier (Francisco Javier)] As a student in Paris, Saint Francis Xavier (1506–1552) met Ignatius of Loyola, who became his friend and companion. After severe struggles with himself, Francis Xavier became one of the very first to join the newly founded Society of

Jesus; for his missionary zeal and success, he was named patron saint of the Propagation of the Faith. He is portrayed as a robust, tall young man with a short, full beard in a priest's black gown with a surplice over it, holding a crucifix, sometimes with a blazing heart exposed in his open chest (figure 12.23).

12.23. Saint Francis Xavier, woodcut, private collection.

Saint Francis Xavier is invoked for good health and for bringing rains and good crops. The abundance of silver ex-votos that surrounds his handsome estofado pilgrimage statue at San Francisco Javier de Vigge-Biaundó (Baja California Sur) testifies to the effectiveness of the saint in these regards. Called "the Apostle of the Indies," he died of a fever while trying to enter China.

[George (Jorge)] A Christian knight born in Asia Minor, this fourth-century martyr converted pagans to Christianity in the region of Cappadocia. In early depictions of Saint George, a dragon was often used to symbolize paganism, and a woman, Cappadocia. As time passed and the significance of these symbols was lost, stories were invented to explain them. In a tale popularized by Voragine, Saint George is said to have rescued a princess about to be sacrificed to a hideous dragon and to have converted her father, the king, and all his kingdom to Christianity. He is always shown as a young man, usually mounted on a white battle steed, from which he slays a dragon or monster.

Probably because of the association of his dragon with the stinging scorpions of the viceregal city of Durango, Saint George is invoked against scorpions there, and a chapel is dedicated to him in the Cathedral of Durango (figure 12.24). Traditionally considered the patron saint of soldiers and one of the Fourteen Holy Helpers (see above), he is also invoked against diseases of the liver.

[Gertrude the Great (Gertrudis la Magna)] A German Benedictine nun and author of mystical writings commonly called "Revelations," Saint Gertrude the Great (d. 1302) is often portrayed with a crosier to which a veil is sometimes attached, even though she was not an abbess. She is thus often confused with Saint Gertrude of Nivelles, who was indeed an abbess. Her principal attribute is a flaming heart on her chest or held in her hand, although she may also be portrayed with Christ's stigmata on her hands, heart, and feet. Although never formally canonized, she was officially recognized as a saint in 1677. Saint Gertrude the Great is invoked against heart ailments and epilepsy.

[Gregory the Great (Gregorio Magno)] A pope and Father of the Church, Saint Gregory the Great (d. 604) introduced the doctrine of Purgatory and instituted celibacy among the clergy Christianizing Britain. His considerable efforts helped shape the Roman Catholic liturgy, regulate the form of church services, and supervise the instruction of priests regarding their moral and spiritual responsibilities toward their parishioners. He is also credited with the revision and rearrangement of church music.

Gregory is shown as a patriarch, sometimes bearded, with papal tiara and cross, holding a model of a church or a pen and book. Sometimes a dove, representing the Holy Spirit, is also included. Gregory's image is often seen on the pendentives in the crossings of churches along with images of the other three Fathers of the Church. Legend has it that as he was celebrating the Eucharist, a congregant expressed doubt that Christ was really pres-

12.24. Saint George, sculpture on a collateral altar dedicated to him and recently canonized Cristero martyrs, Catedral de Durango, 1996.

ent. In response to the saint's prayer, the crucified figure of Christ appeared on the altar with all the instruments of the Passion. Saint Gregory the Great is thus included among the Eucharistic saints.

Holy Kings (Los Reyes Magos)—see "Caspar, Balthazar, and Melchior" earlier.

[Ignatius of Loyola (Ignacio de Loyola)] Founder of the Society of Jesus (Jesuits), Saint Ignatius (1491–1556) was the youngest son of a noble Spanish family. Wounded as a young soldier, he retired to a cave in Catalán, where he wrote his famous spiritual "Exercises." In 1531, he organized the Jesuits, whose principal purpose was to serve the papacy, along military lines. Active during the Counter-Reformation, the Society of Jesus concentrated its efforts on the education of youth, scholarship, and foreign missions.

Ignatius is typically portrayed as a middle-aged cleric with receding hairline, high-bridged, thin nose, and scant beard, garbed in the black cassock and white collar of his order, sometimes with alb, chasuble, and maniple.[51] On his breast, the hand he holds over a chalice, or somewhere near him is the trigram for Jesus, I H S. He may hold a book (his "Constitutions") inscribed with the order's motto "Ad majorem Dei gloriam" (To the greater glory of God) or its initials, A M D G, or a monstrance; he is thus included among the Eucharistic saints (see center image in figures 6.10 and 6.16).

[Isidore the Farm Worker (Isidro el Labrador)] A humble Spanish farmer, Saint Isidore (d. 1170) is said to have worked his fields even on Sundays when poor crop conditions warranted—this despite threats from God. Finally, God sent an angel to help Isidore plow so that he might attend Mass. He is portrayed as a bearded, vigorous rustic, sometimes holding an ox goad or staff and a rosary, with oxen beside him and an angel overhead, usually shown much smaller than he. He is readily distinguished by his archaic peasant attire: jacket, short pants, and broad-brimmed hat (see figure 2.28). The patron saint of farmers, Saint Isidore the Farm Worker is called on to ensure good crops.

[Jerome (Jerónimo)] Considered the most learned of the Four Fathers of the Church, the scholar Saint Jerome (ca. 340–420) is the author of the Vulgate, the first authoritative Latin translation of the Bible from the Greek. He may appear as a bearded, half-clothed hermit in the desert, mortifying his flesh by striking his chest with a rock or by scourging himself. Or, dressed as a cardinal, he may strike a simple didactic pose. In images from the Counter-Reformation on, he is more often shown writing or reading (an allusion to his translation of the Bible), interrupted by an angel sounding the trumpet of the Last Judgment. His carved or painted image—along with those of the other three Fathers of the Church—is often found on the pendentives in the crossings of churches. His principal attribute is a lion, which he is said to have tamed by removing a thorn from its paw (figure 12.25). From early Christianity, a lion has been a metaphor for humans' bestial instincts; its taming a metaphor for the victory of morality over passion and instinct, or of love, holiness, and grace over the sinfulness of an unredeemed and fallen nature. The thorn represents sin; its removal signifies the washing away of original sin.[52]

[Joachim (Joaquín)] According to the Apocrypha, the wealthy shepherd Joachim was husband to Anne, the mother of the Virgin Mary.[53] Like his wife, he is always seen in conjunction with Mary as a child or young woman. Portrayed as an older man with white hair and beard, dressed in red and green, and wearing a rabbinical tunic with a wide sash,[54] a distinctive cape trimmed in ermine around his shoulders, he may hold a shepherd's crook. Because the elderly Joachim and Anne were childless before Anne miraculously conceived Mary, Saint Joachim is invoked against sterility in men.

[John the Baptist (Juan Bautista)] Considered the last prophet of the Old Testament and the first saint of the New Testament, John the Baptist (d. ca. 30) was cousin and close friend to Jesus. He predicted the coming of the Christ and baptized Jesus in the River Jordan at the beginning of Jesus' ministry. In baptisteries throughout northern New Spain, he is portrayed as an unkempt, gaunt man of middle years draped in a shaggy tunic, "his raiment of camel's hair, a leathern girdle around his loins" (Matthew 3:4), often holding a long, slender staff with a banner and cross on it. Sculpted or painted images of John performing the rite of Baptism with Jesus commonly appear on walls or ceilings of baptisteries, or on keystones over their entrances.[55] Considered a Eucharistic saint, he may also hold a lamb, sometimes with the words "Ecce Agnus Dei" (Behold the Lamb of

12.25. Saint Jerome, bas-relief sculpture on a pendentive, Catedral de Chihuahua, 1992. (His principal attribute, the lion, as well as a trumpet, are to his right.)

God). He may also carry a scallop shell, signifying the Baptism of Jesus.

[John of Capistrano (Juan de Capistrano)] Lawyer and former governor of Perugia, Italy, Saint John of Capistrano (1386–1456) joined the Franciscan Order in 1415 and became a priest five years later. A powerful orator, he was friend and counselor to four popes, reforming his order, evangelizing most of Europe, and promoting his order's missionary activities as well as a crusade against the Turks, who had seized Constantinople in 1453.

He is portrayed as a clean-shaven, mature man in a Franciscan habit, holding a banner with the trigram of Jesus (I H S) and a picture of three nails in the center. Turbaned figures appear under his feet and a miter by his side, representing Turks and his rejection of the bishopric.

[John of God (Juan de Dios)] A Portuguese soldier, Saint John of God (1495–1550) founded the Congregation of Hospitaliers to provide hospitals for the needy. Portrayed in the plain habit of the Hospitaliers, he may carry a bag, alluding to the one he used when begging food for the hospital. His principal attribute, and that of his order, however, is a pomegranate, the Christian symbol for spiritual fecundity, eternal life, and charity.

The order established a number of hospitals for the poor and for miners in northern New Spain, particularly in Durango (Durango) and Parral (Chihuahua), where the order's churches and parts of their hospitals and convents still exist. He is the patron saint of nursing, the sick, and hospitals.

[John of Nepomuk (Juan Nepomuceno)] A canon regular of Saint Augustine, Saint John of Nepomuk (ca. 1345–1393) was confessor to Queen Sophia, wife of King Wenceslas IV of Bohemia. According to one popular account, when he refused to reveal the queen's confessions to the king, John was beaten, bound and gagged, and thrown into the Vltava River. His drowned body was miraculously revealed by a field of stars. Typically shown in a black cassock and white surplice with a short ermine cape over his shoulders, he wears a biretta and holds a cross or the palm frond of martyrdom. The patron saint of the confessional and lawyers, Saint John of Nepomuk is invoked against slander and to protect bridges (See central figure in El Cuerpo de Gloria, figure 10.32).

[Joseph (José)] Husband to the Virgin Mary and earthly father to Jesus, Saint Joseph may appear by himself, but is always in implicit association with Mary or Jesus or both. He is usually shown dressed in yellow and green, holding the infant Jesus in one arm and a lily or blooming staff in the other hand. He often wears a crown, the only male saint not a king to do so.

The last session of the Council of Trent in 1563 argued that, because Joseph had been selected to protect and sustain Mary, he must have been much younger than the elderly individual portrayed in previous centuries. He was rejuvenated as a young and forceful man in his prime. His handsomeness and sweetness in images throughout northern New Spain are largely the result of the influence of the celebrated and much imitated Spanish painter Bartolomé Esteban Murillo.

Saint Joseph's range of protection is wide and varied based on real and apocryphal aspects of his life. For his taking Mary and Jesus to Egypt, he is considered a patron saint of travelers; for his trade, the patron saint of carpenters; and based on deathbed portrayals with Jesus and Mary, the patron saint of dying, who is invoked for a holy death.

Devotions to Joseph arose and developed much later than those to Mary.[56] The first church dedicated to Saint Joseph was built in Bologna about 1130; devotions to him were espoused by several orders, including the Augustinians and Franciscans, but not until the fourteenth century. Writing in the sixteenth century, Saint Teresa of Ávila urged believers to turn to Saint Joseph above other saints intercessors for his "great power with God."[57] Indeed, the prominence of Saint Joseph in New Spain and Mexico appears to have flowed naturally from sixteenth-century Spain's being "the chosen land of Saint Joseph."[58] Like those of Mary and Jesus, his image is in nearly every church (see figure 12.4).

[Lawrence (Lorenzo)] A Spanish deacon of Pope Sixtus I, Saint Lawrence (d. 258), was administrator of the Church treasury. When ordered by the Roman prefect to hand over the Church's wealth, he distributed it among the poor, declaring, "Here is the Church's treasure!" He was martyred by being burned on a grill, which he may hold as his principal attribute. He is portrayed as a young, clean-shaven, tonsured cleric wearing a dalmatic. Patron saint of the poor, Saint Lawrence is invoked against burns and blindness.

[Louis, King of France (Luis Rey)] Founder of many monasteries and hospitals and leader of two crusades, Saint Louis (1214–1270), like King Ferdinand, may appear in armor. He is crowned and fleurs-de-lis are sometimes seen on his robe or topping his scepter. A Franciscan tertiary, he is sometimes portrayed in the habit of that order or holding a skull. His name was invoked against scrofula and arthritic tuberculosis.

[Lucy (Lucía)] According to legend, this fourth-century virgin saint was martyred on the order of the Emperor Diocletian. When the beauty of her eyes caused a suitor to become ill with longing, she is said to have plucked them out and sent them to him on a plate—her principal attribute—only to grow a new pair. Because of this legend and because her name is derived from Latin *lux* (light) and hence associated with sight (see also "Veronica" following), Saint Lucy is invoked against diseases of the eyes.

[Luke (Lucas)] Like Mark, Luke the Evangelist (Lucas el Evangelista)—"the beloved physician" (thus patron saint of physicians)—was a disciple of Paul, not of Jesus. A tenth-century Greek legend claims that Saint Luke was also an artist and was supposed to have painted and sculpted images of the Virgin Mary from life; thus, he is also considered the patron saint of artists. Several Marian images are attributed to him, including the sculpture of Our Lady of Valvanera (see earlier). He is shown as an older, wise-looking man, sometimes balding or with a beard. His principal attribute is a winged bull or ox, symbolizing the priesthood and sacrifice, about which he wrote (figure 12.26).

Magi—see "Caspar, Balthazar, and Melchior" earlier.

[Margaret of Antioch (Margarita)] A legendary third-century virgin martyr of noble birth, Saint Margaret was a secret convert to Christianity. After refusing to marry the local governor, she was denounced as a Christian, placed in prison, and confronted by a dragon, which either she forced to disappear with the sign of the cross or which split in two after swallowing her, leaving her unscathed. Through her faith and steadfastness, Margaret converted many who witnessed her trial and tortures before she was at last beheaded at Diocletian's order.

She is portrayed as a beautiful young noblewoman or shepherdess holding the palm frond of martyrdom and a cross. She may have a dragon by her side or be stepping out of the mouth of a dragon. The saint's emergence unscathed from the belly of the dragon was associated with childbirth, and through the other sense of *alumbramiento,* the Spanish word for childbirth, with light or illumination as well. She is thus considered the patron saint of women in childbirth and may be shown carrying a torch (bringing light). One of the Fourteen Holy Helpers (see earlier), Saint Margaret of Antioch is invoked against ailments of the breasts and kidneys.

[Mark (Marcos)] A disciple of Paul, and neither an Apostle nor even a Christian until after the death and Ascension of Christ, when he was converted by Peter, Mark the Evangelist (Marcos el Evangelista) is the author of the second Gospel of the New Testament, written at the behest of the Romans.[59] He is believed to have gone to Libya and to Egypt, where he established the Christian Church in Alexandria, becoming its first bishop. There he was martyred by being dragged and beaten to death. Traditionally, Mark is shown as a forceful man in his prime with dark hair, mustache, and trimmed beard. The book (Gospel) he carries may have "Vox clamantis in deserto" (The voice of one crying in the wilderness; Mark 1:3) written on it. His principal attribute is a lion, referring both to his Gospel and to the mystery of the Resurrection (see figures 4.44, 6.4, and 6.5).

[Martin, Bishop of Tours (Martín de Tours)] As a young soldier in the Roman army, Saint Martin converted to Christianity. While stationed at Amiens, he cut his cloak in two for a freezing beggar. When Christ appeared to him that night, saying, "Martin, thou hast covered me with this garment," he left the army and devoted himself to converting others. After extensive travels, he founded a community of hermits in Gaul and later, by popular acclaim, was made bishop of Tours. He was active in fighting not only paganism but also schisms within the Church.[60] Saint Martin is traditionally portrayed as a young Roman soldier on horseback, slicing his cloak in two for a beggar in rags. He is considered a patron saint for soldiers, beggars, innkeepers, and reformed drunkards.

[Mary Magdalen (María Magdalena)] Considered a "composite" saint, Mary Magdalen was the penitent sinner who washed Jesus' feet (Luke 8:36–50) and who was healed by him of seven devils; she was sister to Martha (Luke 10:38–42) and to Lazarus (John 11:1–45). She

12.26. Saint Luke, sculpture in the east frontispiece, Catedral de Saltillo, Coahuila, 2006. Notice the other figures above, a choir of martyrs encircling the crossing, an unusual feature.

may be shown (1) as one of the three Marys at the foot of the Cross; (2) richly gowned, gazing at jewels and combs in tearful contemplation of earthly vanities; or (3) dressed in tatters as a hermit, hair hanging loosely, with a skull and cross in a desolate landscape, representing the contrite dedication of her life to penitence. Her principal attribute is a jar of balm, recalling her anointment of Jesus' feet. Presumed to have been a prostitute, Saint Mary Magdalen is believed to intercede on behalf of "lost" or "fallen" women (see right-hand image in figure 10.17a).

[Nicholas of Bari (Nicolás)] Born in Asia Minor and appointed bishop of Myra, Saint Nicholas of Bari (ca. 270–342) was imprisoned for his beliefs but was liberated with Emperor Constantine's official acceptance of Christianity. In 1092, his relics were transported to Bari, Italy, which became an important center of pilgrimage.

In one popular account, he secretly gave three bags of gold to an impoverished father for the dowries of his three daughters, thus saving them from a life of prostitution.[61] In another, he is said to have restored to life three youngsters who had been cut up and pickled in brine, establishing him as a patron saint of children. In a third, he is said to have saved a crew by quieting the storm that threatened to sink their ship, thus making him a patron saint of sailors. One of the Fourteen Holy Helpers (see earlier), Saint Nicholas of Bari is usually shown standing in full bishop's regalia, with three gold bags or balls in his hand—his principal attribute—and with three small children in a brine barrel at his feet.

[Nicholas of Tolentino (Nicolás de Tolentino)] After miraculously receiving food from the Virgin Mary, Saint Nicholas of Tolentino (1249–1309) used this food to cure the ill. He is also said to have miraculously multiplied a loaf of bread to feed multitudes and to have brought back to life a pair of partridges that had been cooked and served to him as he lay dying. He is shown as a tonsured cleric in Augustinian habit, holding two birds on a plate, his principal attribute, and sometimes also a stalk of lilies. Saint Nicholas of Tolentino is invoked against fever, plague, and starvation.

[Paul (Pablo)] An Apostle, though not among the original twelve, Saint Paul is considered the second most important figure after Saint Peter in the history of Christianity. He is known chiefly through his Epistles and The Acts of the Apostles. Founder of the Christian Church with Peter, Paul separated Christianity from Judaism once and for all. Initially antagonistic to the teachings of Jesus, he persecuted the early Christians until his conversion on the road to Damascus, where he was first struck blind, then miraculously healed. Thereafter, he became an untiring missionary and zealot of the new Faith, traveling to all corners of the Greco-Roman world.

Paul is usually portrayed as a man of small stature and middle years, bald and bearded; his principal attribute is a sword, the instrument of his martyrdom in Rome, where he was most likely beheaded. When pointed downward, the sword symbolizes his martyrdom; when brandished, his intrepid warring for Christianity. Legend has it that as he was gathering wood for a fire, a snake bit him but caused no harm; Saint Paul is thus invoked against poisonous wounds or bites.

[Peter of Alcántara (Pedro de Alcántara)] Instrumental with Saint Teresa of Ávila in the Carmelite reform within the Franciscan Order, Saint Peter of Alcántara (1499–1562) was noted for his extreme austerity. He is shown as a gaunt, even emaciated, older cleric in the Franciscan habit, holding a book, crucifix, and scourge.

[Rita of Cascia (Rita de Cascia)] Admitted into an Augustinian convent after the death of her husband and sons, Saint Rita (1362–1456) is distinguished by her principal attribute, the thorn wound she received on her forehead from mystically sharing Jesus' crown of thorns and his sufferings during his Passion. She is shown as an older woman in the black habit of an Augustinian nun, holding a cross, skull, and scourge, often with her two sons kneeling on either side of her. Roses, which miraculously bloomed in her convent's garden in the middle of winter as she lay dying, may also be present; they account for her being considered a patron saint for impossible causes.

[Roch (Roque)] According to legend, the French nobleman Saint Roch (d. ca. 1330), while on his pilgrimage to Rome, aided victims of the plague that had broken out at Aguapendente, Cesena, and Rimini. When he himself contracted the disease, he retired to the woods, where a dog brought him a loaf of bread every day. He is portrayed as a pilgrim with cape, hat, staff, and leather pouch, lifting his robe to display plague spots, while a dog stands nearby with a loaf of bread in his mouth. One of the Fourteen

Holy Helpers (see earlier), Saint Roch, whose cult was promoted by the Franciscans, is invoked against both human and animal contagious diseases, plague, abscesses, tumors, and rabies.

[Rosalie of Palermo (Rosalía de Palermo)] A recluse from youth, Saint Rosalie died (1160) in a grotto near Palermo. The presence of her bones (whose location was revealed in a vision) carried in a procession miraculously quelled an outbreak of the plague in 1624. She is portrayed in a simple tunic, tied at the waist with a cord or rope, her hair unbound, her head crowned with a wreath of roses, sometimes beside a skull and crucifix, traditional symbols of penitence (figure 12.27).

12.27. Saint Rosalie of Palermo (minus attributes of skull and crucifix), sculpture by El Niño Santero, private collection.

[Rose of Lima (Rosa de Lima)] The first New World saint to be canonized by the Church, Saint Rose (1586–1617) was noted for her piety and extreme asceticism. Portrayed as a beautiful young woman dressed in the Dominican habit, Saint Rose lived most of her short life in a little hut by her parents' house. Wearing a wreath of roses (sometimes with thorns entwined) around her head, she may be seen holding or adoring the infant Jesus. Or she may hold an anchor, in an allusion to the port of El Callao, Peru, which is under her protection.

[Scholastica (Escolástica)] The twin sister of Saint Benedict and the founder of an order of Benedictine nuns, Saint Scholastica (ca. 480–543) was profoundly religious from her earliest years. The leading female saint of the Benedictines, she is shown in the Benedictine habit, holding an abbess's staff, a book of the rules of her order, a crucifix, and a lily. A dove can be seen hovering over her head or coming from her mouth, alluding to her brother's vision of a dove that ascended into Heaven three days after her death.

[Sebastian (Sebastián)] An officer in Emperor Diocletian's palace guards, this third-century martyr was tied to a stake and shot with arrows for refusing to worship pagan gods. When, after his miraculous recovery, he reproached the emperor for his cruelty and intolerance toward the Christians, Saint Sebastian was clubbed to death. He is usually portrayed as a half-clothed young man bound to a tree or pole, his body bristling with arrows, sometimes with an angel present, pulling the arrows out. One of the Fourteen Holy Helpers (see earlier), Saint Sebastian is traditionally invoked against plagues (from the ancient belief that these were caused by divine arrows), typhus, epidemics, and wounds in general (see image beneath the Virgin of Guadalupe in figure 2.11).

[Stephen (Esteban)] One of the seven deacons appointed by the Apostles to manage funds established for the relief of the poor, the protomartyr Saint Stephen (d. ca. 35) was brought before the Jewish council on trumped-up charges of blasphemy against Moses.[62] Boldly proclaiming that his accusers had resisted the Holy Spirit and killed Christ, as the Bible had prophesied, he was immediately stoned to

death. Four hundred years later, his miraculously revealed remains were transferred to Rome. As they were being placed alongside those of Saint Lawrence, the latter saint is said to have moved over and stretched out his hand to welcome his fellow martyr and deacon (earning Saint Lawrence the title of "the courteous Spaniard"). Because of their joint burial and their similar rank and status, the two saints are frequently portrayed together. Stephen is shown as a young tonsured cleric in a deacon's dalmatic over a white tunic, holding a martyr's palm frond and sometimes the Gospels. His principal attribute, however, are stones, which may appear on his head or shoulders or which may be hidden from view, gathered in the folds of his dalmatic.

[Teresa of Ávila (Teresa de Ávila)] Also known as "Teresa of Jesus" (Teresa de Jesús) and called "Spouse of Christ," Saint Teresa (1515–1582) was a brilliant Spanish Carmelite nun whose mystic visions led her to reform her order and to establish the Order of Unshod Carmelites, and whose writings are masterpieces of mystical insight. Enormously important in promulgating the cult of Saint Joseph, whom she extolled as a rescuer of souls in need and a protector of travelers, she is portrayed in the habit of the Unshod Carmelites, holding a book, pen, and pastoral staff. She may also be shown wearing a doctor's biretta, alluding to her scholarship, an attribute unique among female saints.

[Thomas Aquinas (Tomás de Aquino)] Called the "Angel of the Schools," "Doctor Angelicus," "Eagle of Divines," "Father of Moral Philosophy," and the "Great Synthesizer," the Italian Dominican Thomas Aquinas (1225–1278) is considered by some to be the most important theologian in the Roman Catholic Church. His *Summa theologiae* won him the title of "Doctor of the Church" in 1567 and the designation of patron saint of Catholic schools and universities. He is portrayed as an older cleric holding a pen (signifying authorship) in one hand and an open book in the other, with a chalice (referring to his devotion to and defense of the Blessed Sacrament in his writing—thereby making him a Eucharistic saint), a dove (representing divine inspiration), and a sun (symbolizing wisdom) emblazoned on his chest or hung around his neck. Patron saint for students and theologians, Saint Thomas Aquinas was also invoked against fistulas of the eyes.

[Veronica (Verónica)] According to legend, Saint Veronica wiped Jesus' blood and sweat from his face with a towel on his way to Calvary. His tortured face, crown of thorns, and wounds were miraculously imprinted upon this piece of cloth as if it were being held for display.[63] This imprint of Divinity itself, a radically new relic for contemplation, was introduced into the Western Church from the East during the thirteenth century. It is likely that "Veronica" (from Latin *vera iconica*, true image) was invented to fit the miraculous relic (see also "Lucy" above).

[Vincent Ferrer (Vicente Ferrer)] A Dominican noted for his eloquent sermons and his numerous miracles, Saint Vincent (1350–1419) is shown dressed in the habit of his order with a large pair of wings, representing his angelic role; he holds a book, representing his effectiveness as a preacher, and a lily, representing his purity. Images of him pointing upward to the words "Timete dominum et date illi honorem quia venit hora judicii eius" (Fear the Lord and give him honor because the hour of his judgment is come) inspired the popular account of his suspending in midair a bricklayer who had fallen from his scaffolding until such time as the saint received permission from his bishop to complete the miracle and save the worker's life. Saint Vincent Ferrer is thus the patron saint of bricklayers and is also invoked against epilepsy, headaches, and hiccoughs (see figure 6.16, bottom left corner).

[Wilgefortis (Liberata or Librada)] A purely legendary figure, Wilgefortis may have evolved from a popular tale according to which a young Christian woman took a vow of chastity despite her father's wishes that she marry. When, in answer to her prayers for protection, she miraculously grew a mustache and beard, her enraged father had her crucified.[64] This tale was in turn absorbed into a Spanish cult of another saint named Liberata, who had been martyred by beheading. Consequently, although Wilgefortis is portrayed as a crucified young woman, usually with a crown of roses, she has neither beard nor mustache. One of the Fourteen Holy Helpers (see earlier), Saint Wilgefortis is invoked in times of distress, physical suffering (particularly headaches), and death. She appears mostly in New Mexican bultos and retablos.

Wise Men—see "Caspar, Balthazar, and Melchior" earlier.

Select List of Churches in Northern New Spain

The following churches or church ruins I consider to be of special interest, having personally visited them or examined their plans, drawings, or photographs. Each church or church ruin is listed by its official name, followed in parentheses by either its former name if it had one or its local name where not just a shortened form of its official name and any comment on its status, and then by its location, unless this appears (after "de" or "del") at the end of its official or local name—or is exactly the same (less accent marks for U.S. place-names). Entries marked with an asterisk are discussed in the main text or notes, illustrated, or both.

Arizona

San Bernardo de Awátovi (ruin)*
San Francisco Xavier del Bac, near Tucson*
San José de Tumacácori (ruin; now National Park Service site)*
Los Santos Ángeles de Guévavi (ruin)

Baja California Norte

San Francisco de Borja de Adac*
Santa Gertrudis de Kadakaaman, Santa Gertrudis*

Baja California Sur

Nuestra Señora de Loreto de Concho, Loreto*
San Francisco Javier de Vigge-Biaundó, San Francisco*
San Ignacio de Loyola de Kadakaaman, San Ignacio*
San José de Comondú (ruin)*
San Luis Gonzaga la Magna, San Luis*
Santa Rosalía de Palermo de Mulegé*

California (Alta California)

La Capilla Real, Monterey
La Estancia de Misión San Luis Rey, Pala
La Exaltación de la Santa Cruz, Santa Cruz*
Nuestra Señora de la Soledad, Soledad
La Purísima Concepción (reconstructed), Lompoc*
San Antonio de Padua, Jolon*
San Buenaventura, Ventura
San Carlos Borromeo de Carmelo de Monterey, Carmel*
San Diego de Alcalá, San Diego*
San Fernando Rey de España, San Fernando Rey*
San Francisco de Asís (Mission Dolores), San Francisco*
San Francisco de Solano, Sonoma
San Gabriel Arcángel, San Gabriel*
San José de Guadalupe, Fremont
San Juan Bautista, San Juan*
San Juan Capistrano (ruin and Serra's chapel)*
San Luis Obispo de Tolosa, San Luis Obispo*
San Luis Rey de Francia, Oceanside*
San Miguel Arcángel de la Frontera, San Miguel (Paso Robles)*
San Rafael Arcángel, San Rafael*
Santa Bárbara*

Santa Clara de Asís, Santa Clara*
Santa Inés, Santa Ynez*

Chihuahua

La Asunción de la Virgen María, Los Álamos de Cerro Prieto
La Capilla, former hacienda of Corralitos, Nuevas Casas Grandes*
La Capilla, former hacienda of Laborcita o Chaveña
La Capilla de la Quinta Carolina (abandoned)
La Capilla de la Virgen Dolores, former hacienda of Dolores
La Capilla de Nuestra Señora de Guadalupe, municipality of Borja
La Capilla de Nuestra Señora de Guadalupe (ruin), former hacienda of Guadalupe de Bagues
La Capilla de Nuestra Señora de Guadalupe (abandoned), Janos
La Capilla de Nuestra Señora de Guadalupe, San Francisco de los Conchos
La Capilla de Nuestra Señora de Guadalupe, Villa de Allende
La Capilla de San Antonio de Padua, former hacienda of Enramada
La Capilla de Santa Gertrudis, Carrizal
La Capilla de Santa Rosa de Lima, Catedral de Chihuahua, Chihuahua City*
La Capilla de Santa Rosalía (Santa Rosalía Vieja)
La Catedral de Chihuahua, Chihuahua City*
La Congregación de San José de Bachíniva
La Corazón de Jesús de Guachóchic
El Dulce Nombre de María de Sisoguíchic
El Nombre de Jesús de Carichic*
Former hacienda church of Canutillo, Ejido Canutillo
Jesús Nazareno de Ojinaga
Nuestra Señora de Aranzazú de Cajuríchic
Nuestra Señora de Guadalupe (El Santuario de Guadalupe), Chihuahua City*
Nuestra Señora de Guadalupe, Ciudad Juárez*
Nuestra Señora de Guadalupe de Cuzárare (formerly, Los Cinco Señores de Cuzárare)*
Nuestra Señora de Guadalupe, Guerrero
Nuestra Señora de Guadalupe de Morís
Nuestra Señora de Loreto (destroyed), Chihuahua City*
Nuestra Señora de Loreto de Yoquibo
Nuestra Señora del Monserrate de Nonoava
Nuestra Señora del Pilar de Norogachic*
Nuestra Señora de los Rayos de Parral*
Nuestra Señora, Refugio de los Pecadores, La Cruz
Nuestra Señora, Refugio de los Pecadores, El Molino
Nuestra Señora, Refugio de los Pecadores, Palmarejo
Nuestra Señora de los Remedios, former hacienda of Los Remedios (near Chihuahua City)*
Nuestra Señora del Rosario, Valle del Rosario
Nuestro Padre San Ignacio de Humariza
Nuestro Padre San Ignacio de Papajíchic
La Purísima Concepción, Guerrero
San Andrés Apóstol, Riva Palacio
San Antonio de Padua (ruin), Casas Grandes*
San Antonio de Padua de Janos (ruin)
San Antonio de Padua, Julimes
San Antonio de Padua, Morelos
San Antonio de Padua, San Antonio de Chacones
San Antonio de Padua, El Tule
San Bonaventura, Bonaventura*
San Felipe de Jesús, southwest of Parral
San Felipe y Santiago de Janos (ruin)*
San Fernando, Rey de España, Carrizal
San Francisco de Asís, Chihuahua City*
San Francisco de Borja de Tajirachic
San Francisco de los Indios, Conchos
San Francisco Javier de Cajuríchic
San Francisco Javier de Satevó*
San Francisco Javier de Tomósachi
San Francisco Javier, Valle del Rosario
San Francisco Javier, Villa Coronado
San Gerónimo de Huejotitlan
San Ignacio de Loyola de Arareco, Bocoyna
San Ignacio de Loyola de Humariza*
San Isidro el Labrador, San Isidro
San Isidro el Labrador, Matamoros
San José de Baqueáchic
San José de la Gracia, between Satevó and Nonoava
San José de Olivos

San José de Parral*
San José de Yepáchic
San Juan Bautista, Llanos de San Juan
San Juan Bautista de Tonachi
San Juan de Dios, Parral
San Lorenzo, Doctor Belasario Domínguez
San Miguel Arcángel, San Miguel de los Achondos
San Miguel de las Bocas, Villa Ocampo
San Nicolás Tolentino de Carreta, Gran Morales
San Pablo de Balleza
San Pedro de Meoqui
San Pedro de Valle de San Bartolomé (La Parroquia), Valle de Allende
Santa Ana de Chinarras, Aldama
Santa Eulalia de Mérida, Santa Eulalia*
Santa Inés de Chínipas
Santa Isabel de los Tarahumares, General Trias
Santa María de las Cuevas*
Santa María de Natívitas, Bachíniva*
Santa María del Pópulo de Guaguáchic
Santa Rita de Cascia (partially reconstructed), Chihuahua City
Santa Rosa de Lima de Cusihuiriáchic*
Santa Rosa de Lima de Pachera
Santa Rosalía de las Cuevas (Nueva), Santa Rosalía
Santa Rosalía de las Cuevas (Vieja; ruin), Santa Rosalía
Santiago Apóstol de Babonoyaba
El Santo Ángel de la Guarda de Satevó, Batopilas*
El Santo Cristo de Burgos, Jiménez*
Santo Tomás de Villanueva de Tojorare*
Señor San José de Pamáchic
Señor Santiago de Yepáchic
La Virgen del Carmen de Batopilas
La Virgen de Guadalupe de Cabórachic
La Virgen de Guadalupe de Tetaguíchic*
La Virgen de Guadalupe de Tónachic

Coahuila

El Calvario, Saltillo
La Catedral de Saltillo*
La Parroquia de la Asunción de Parras (Santa María de Parras)*
San Esteban, Saltillo
San Felipe Neri, Saltillo
San Ignacio de Loyola de Parras (El Colegio)*
San Juan Nepomuceno, Saltillo*
Santa María, former hacienda of Santa María
Santiago Apóstol de Monclova
El Santuario de Nuestra Señora de Guadalupe de Parras*

Durango

La Catedral de Durango, city of Durango*
El Colegio de Guadalupe, city of Durango*
Former hacienda church (unnamed) on Highway 45, north of city of Durango
Former hacienda church (unnamed), Palmillas
La Hermita, Nombre de Dios
El Nombre de Jesús, Nombre de Dios*
Nuestra Señora de los Dolores de Pedreceña*
Nuestra Señora de los Remedios, La Cerrita, city of Durango
San Agustín, city of Durango
San Antonio de Padua de Cuencamé*
San José de Canelas
San Juan Bautista de Analco, city of Durango*
San Juan de Dios, city of Durango*
Santa Ana, city of Durango*
Santiago Apóstol de Mapimí
El Santuario de Guadalupe, Nombre de Dios

New Mexico

La Castrense, Santa Fe (destroyed)*
La Catedral de Santa Fe*
El Cristo Rey, Santa Fe*
Nuestra Señora de la Asunción de Zia
Nuestra Señora de los Ángeles de Porciúncula (ruin), Pecos*
Nuestra Señora de Guadalupe, Santa Fe*
La Purísima Concepción de Quari (ruin; Salinas National Monument, Mountainair)*
San Agustín de la Isleta
San Buenaventura (ruin; Salinas National Monument, Mountainair), Gran Quivira (formerly, Humanas or Tabirá)

San Buenaventura de Cochití*
San Esteban de Ácoma*
San Felipe Apóstol, San Felipe Pueblo*
San Felipe Neri, Albuquerque*
San Francisco de Asís de la Villa, Santa Fe*
San Gregorio de Abó (ruin; Salinas National Monument, Mountainair)*
San José de la Gracia, Las Trampas*
San José de la Laguna*
San Lorenzo de Picuries (reconstructed)
San Miguel Arcángel, Santa Fe*
San Miguel Arcángel (formerly Nuestra Señora de Socorro), Socorro
San Miguel Arcángel de Tajique (ruin)*
Santa Ana, Santa Ana Pueblo
Santa Cruz de la Cañada, Santa Cruz
Santo Domingo (reconstructed)*
Santo Tomás de Abiquiú (reconstructed)
El Santuario del Señor de Esquipulas de Chimayó*

Nuevo León

La Catedral de Monterrey*
Nuestra Señora de Guadalupe, Salina Victoria
El Palacio del Arzobispo, Monterrey
San Felipe de Jesús de China
San Miguel de Aguayo, Bustamonte
San Pedro, Villaldama (ruin)
El Señor de la Misericordia de Linares*

San Luis Potosí

Nuestra Señora de Guadalupe, Ojo de Agua*
Nuestra Señora del Rosario de Charcas (Santa María de Charcas)*
San Francisco de Asís, former hacienda of San Francisco
La Tercera Orden, city of San Luis Potosí*

Sinaloa

La Catedral de Sinaloa, Culiacán
Nuestra Señora del Rosario*
San José de Copala*
San Lorenzo de Tabalá (ruin)*
San Sebastián, Concordia*

Sonora

Los Dulces Nombres del Valle de Tacupeto
Nuestra Señora de Balbanera de la Aduana*
Nuestra Señora de la Asunción de Arizpe*
Nuestra Señora de la Asunción de Baserac
Nuestra Señora de la Asunción del Real de los Álamos*
Nuestra Señora de la Asunción de Opodepe*
Nuestra Señora de los Ángeles de Sahuaripa
Nuestra Señora de los Dolores de Cósari (destroyed)*
Nuestra Señora de los Dolores de Tépahui
Nuestra Señora de Guadalupe (La Reina), Los Ángeles
Nuestra Señora de Guadalupe de Mazatán
Nuestra Señora de la Purísima Concepción de Movas*
Nuestra Señora de Loreto del Real de Baroyeca (ruin)
Nuestra Señora de Loreto de Sátachi
Nuestra Señora del Pilar y Santiago de Cocóspera (ruin)*
Nuestra Señora de los Remedios de Banámichi
Nuestra Señora del Rosario de Nacámeri, Rayón
Nuestra Señora del Rosario de Nacozari
Nuestro Padre San Ignacio de Loyola de Bacanora*
Nuestro Padre San Ignacio de Loyola de Cabórica*
Nuestro Padre San Ignacio de Loyola de Cuquiárachi
Nuestro Padre San Ignacio de Loyola de Onavas (reconstructed)*
Nuestro Padre San Ignacio de Loyola de Oputo
Nuestro Padre San Ignacio de Loyola de Sinoquipe
Nuestro Padre San Ignacio de Loyola de Suaqui Grande
La Purísima Concepción de Baviácora
La Purísima Concepción de Nuestra Señora de Caborca*
San Antonio Paduano de Oquitoa*
San Bartolo de Batacosa
San Diego de Alcalá del Pitiquito*
San Francisco de Asís del Río Chico (ruin)
San Francisco de Borja de Tecoripa
San Francisco de Regis del Presidio Real de San Carlos de Buenavista (ruin)
San Francisco Javier de Arivechi*
San Francisco Javier de Batuc (façade at Pitic; side portal at Caborca)*

San Francisco Javier de Huásabas
San Ildefonso de Yécora*
San Joaquín y Santa Ana de Nuri*
San José de Soyopa
San Juan Evangelista de Huachinera
San Lorenzo de Huépac*
San Luis Gonzaga de Bacadéhuachi*
San Miguel Arcángel de Bavispe
San Miguel Arcángel de Horcasitas
San Miguel Arcángel de los Ures*
San Miguel Arcángel de Macoyahui (ruin)
San Miguel Arcángel de Oposura, Moctezuma*
San Miguelito, road to Carretas
San Pedro de Aconchi*
San Pedro y San Pablo de Tubutama*
Santa Ana, Santa Ana Vieja*
Santa Cruz de Nácori
Santa Gertrudis del Altar
Santa María, Santa Cruz (formerly, Santa María de Suamca)
Santa María del Pópulo de Tonichic
Santa María Magdalena de Buquivaba
Santa María, Nuestra Señora de Navojoa Vieja
La Santísima Trinidad de Pitic
Los Santos Reyes de Cucurpe (ruin)
Santo Tomás de Sehuadéhuachi (ruin)
Señor San José de Chínapa
Señor San José de Ímuris*
Señor San José de Mátape
Los Siete Ángeles de Taraichi

Tamaulipas

La Capilla de los Alamitos, former hacienda of los Alamitos
Nuestra Señora de las Nieves, Palmillas*
Nuestra Señora de Loreto de Burgos
Nuestra Señora del Rosario, Llera de Canales
San Antonio de Padua de Tula*
San Carlos Borromeo, San Carlos*
San Francisco Javier de Güemes
San Lorenzo de Jaumave
Santa Ana, Camargo
Santa Bárbara, Ocampo
Santiago Apóstol de Altamira*
Santo Domingo de Hoyos, Hidalgo
El Templo de los Cinco Señores, Santander Jiménez*

Texas

Corpus Cristi de la Isleta
Nuestra Señora de la Purísima Concepción de Acuña, San Antonio*
Presidio church of La Bahía (reconstructed), Goliad
San Antonio de Valero (Alamo; reconstructed), San Antonio*
San Elizario*
San Francisco de la Espada, San Antonio*
San José y San Miguel de Aguayo, San Antonio*
San Juan Capistrano, San Antonio*

Zacatecas

La Capilla de Nuestra Señora de Guadalupe de Sombrerete*
La Capilla de San Francisco de Asís de Sombrerete*
Nuestra Señora de la Candelaria de Sombrerete
Nuestra Señora de la Soledad de Sombrerete*
La Purísima Concepción de Sombrerete (La Parroquia)*
San José, former hacienda of San José (northwest of Sombrerete)
San Juan de Dios de Sombrerete
San Mateo de Sombrerete*
San Pedro de Sombrerete
Santa Rosa de Lima de Sombrerete*
La Santa Vera Cruz de Sombrerete*
Santo Domingo de Sombrerete*
La Tercera Orden de Sombrerete (San Juan Bautista)*

Notes

Chapter 1

1. Annexed by Spain in 1535, the Kingdom of New Spain was governed in the king's name by his appointed vice-regent. The argument continues that art and architecture produced by New Spain's indigenous and European peoples should therefore be called viceregal, not colonial. Although the issue is certainly more than one of semantics, and although Latin American historians increasingly prefer "viceregal" to "colonial," it remains an open question whether New Spain was, in truth, considered part of Spain, rather than a dependency or colony, and more important, whether New Spain's peoples—those of mixed blood as well as Spaniards born in the New World—were considered equal to Spanish-born individuals. I therefore use both terms, particularly with regard to Mexican art and architecture before 1821.

For maps and an excellent, succinct discussion of the various geographical, political, and ecclesiastical boundaries of northern New Spain, see Gerhard, *North Frontier of New Spain*.

2. To avoid conflicting ecclesiastical and nonecclesiastical senses of "secular" and "secularized" when referring to clergy not belonging to religious orders and to the churches they once served, I will instead use "diocesan" and "converted to diocesan use" throughout the book.

3. For a concise description of the replacement of Jesuits by Franciscans, their activities in Sonora, and intrigues within the various Franciscan missionary colleges after 1767, see McCarty, *Spanish Frontier in the Enlightened Age*.

4. For a clear-eyed, unbiased overview of the Spanish Conquest and civilization process in North America, see Weber, *Spanish Frontier in North America*.

The spelling of place-names, especially indigenous place-names, varies widely in the literature and written records for northern New Spain. To allow readers to find these sites in contemporary works and on contemporary maps of Mexico and the United States, I have chosen the most common spelling wherever possible. To this end, and for place-names of sites no longer in existence or so obscure as not to have a common, let alone most common, spelling, I have consulted a variety of authoritative sources, most notably, *Guía Roji por las carreteras de México* (Mexico City, 1999), and Gerhard, *North Frontier of New Spain*.

Chapter 2

1. Most significant for our purposes were the beliefs of the Counter-Reformation (sixteenth century). To help stem the flow of Catholics to the newly formed Anabaptist and other Protestant sects, the Catholic Church established a distinct religious iconography and set boundaries around artistic creation. The mythological themes of the Renaissance were to be avoided, art was to be consciously created in defense of religious dogma, and its style was to reflect the mood of religious intensity—the baroque—while architecture was to support (literally and figuratively) art and ritual.

2. Thus, among the Jesuit missionaries credited with planning, organizing, overseeing, and even building mission churches in Chihuahua, Sonora, Sinaloa, and Baja California were Italians, Bohemians, Czechs, Slovaks, Moravians, Croatians, and Silesians. González Rodríguez, *Etnología y misión en la Pimería Alta*, 17–30, and *El noroeste novohispano en el época colonial*, 21–32.

3. Although Francisco de Zurbarán is the best-known Spanish painter working extensively for the New World markets, many other artists did so as well. Duncan Kinkead calculates that in the last half of the seventeenth century at least 24,000 pictures, primarily of religious themes, were exported to the New World from Sevilla (presumably from the workshops of that city; Kinkead, "Juan de Luzón").

4. There are many excellent sources for information concerning the Spanish artists and their influence on Mexican art. See Angulo Íñiguez, "Academia de Bellas Artes de México"; Bottineau, *Iberian-American Baroque*; Chaunu and Chaunu, *Séville et l'Atlantique*; Charlot, *Mexican Art and the Academy of San Carlos*; J. Fernández, *Arte del siglo XIX en México*; Kubler and Soria, *Art and Architecture in Spain and Portugal*; Maza, *Pintor Martín de Vos en México*; and Toussaint, *Colonial Art in Mexico*.

5. For example, by 1790 in Nueva Vizcaya alone, there were 183 carpenters, 142 blacksmiths, 36 silversmiths, 24 masons, and 8 painters (Jones, *Nueva Vizcaya*, 188–89).

6. A notable exception to this generalization is the Cathedral of Chihuahua, with its twin, three-stage towers and extensive, exceptionally fine stone carving within and without. That the cathedral was completed in only thirty-five years greatly contributed to its symmetry and homogeneity.

7. See Goss, "Churches of San Xavier, Arizona, and Caborca, Sonora." Churches of northern New Spain will be referred to by their full formal names in Spanish at first mention (omitting only "Misión de," "Iglesia de," and the like)—and again at second mention when building dates are not given until then; thereafter, for the most part, I use their commonly accepted shorter names. Anglicized names and shorter names that do not follow logically from full formal names will be noted in parentheses at first mention. For a complete list of full formal names, see "Select List of Churches in Northern New Spain" at book's end.

8. Throughout this work, except where otherwise noted, photographs are mine, floor plans are by Harriet J. Mann, and line drawings are by Meredith L. Milstead, based on photographs (both historic and my own), classic architectural illustrations, published reproductions of paintings and sculptures, and Meredith's own observations.

9. See Giacomo Barozzio Vignola, *Canon of the Five Orders of Architecture* (Rome, 1562; first English trans., London, 1665; new English trans., New York, 1999); Sebastiano Serlio, *The Five Books of Architecture* (Venice, 1584; English trans., 1611; reprint, New York, 1963); Andrea Palladio, *The Four Books of Architecture* (Venice, 1570; English trans., 1738; reprint, New York, 1965); and Marcus Vitruvius [Pollio], "On Architecture," in *Vitruvius: The Ten Books on Architecture* (Leipzig, 1899; English trans., 1914; reprint, New York, 1960).

10. Stanislawski, "Origin and Spread of the Grid Pattern Town," and *Early Spanish Town Planning in the New World*, 104.

11. Nutall, "Royal Ordinances Concerning the Laying Out of New Towns"; and Crouch, Garr, and Mundigo, *Spanish City Planning in North America*. Underlying the ordinances' design principles was the belief in harmonic division into quarters, most likely based on the mandala—a symbolic shape (usually round or oval but sometimes square or polygonal) viewed by some Eastern religions as a mystical chart of the cosmos, but also inspired by the Heavenly Jerusalem (Revelation 21:12–22). Mandalas appear in European Christian art, not only as Gothic rose windows of cathedrals and halos of saints and Christ, but also in the architecture of particular buildings. See Jaffé, "Symbolism in the Visual Arts," 240–43.

12. Ramírez Montes, *La escuadra y el cincel*, 15.

13. For an account of Baltasar de Echave Orio and Luis Juárez, who were active in Spain in the late sixteenth century but soon emigrated to Mexico, where they were to intermarry and firmly establish artistic dynasties, see Toussaint, *Pintura colonial en México*, 87, 100, 105; and Kubler and Soria, *Art and Architecture in Spain and Portugal*, 308.

14. This practice appears to have continued into the twentieth century in Mexico. In our field research (1978–1980), Jorge Olvera and I found that daughters of potters in Aguascalientes (Aguascalientes) married other potters or soon-to-be potters; sons of *maestros* learned from other *maestros*; and in one case, a *maestro* was godfather to a competitor's son.

15. Masterpieces of the Italian Renaissance in the royal palaces of the Escorial and Madrid served as important impetuses for seventeenth-century Spanish art. The many Titians and other Venetians now in the Prado reflect the Spanish kings' tastes. For the effect these paintings had on a number of young Spanish painters given the opportunity to view and study them, see Carducho, *Diálogos de la pintura*.

16. Native pigments, binders, and techniques are discussed by Edith Buckland Webb in her treatment of the painting tradition of the California Indians (Webb, *Indian Life at the Old Missions*, 231–44); and by Watson Smith in his excellent analysis and interpretation of architectural painting and murals (reconstructed from fragments) at the mission church ruins at Awatovi (which includes brief comparisons with other churches in the Southwest), in Montgomery, Smith, and Brew, *Franciscan Awatovi*, 243–51, 291–312. See also Smith and Ewing, *Kiva Mural Decorations*; and "Pigments" under "Materials" in chapter 4 of this volume.

17. Islamic architecture, poetry, astronomy, music, medicine, agriculture, mathematics, textiles, and metallurgy were among the richest and most advanced in the world for their time. These were directly infused into Spain by conquest and occupation. To appreciate the pervasive influence of Islamic culture on Spain, consult any good Spanish etymological dictionary: words of Arabic derivation can be found in all areas of the arts, engineering, medicine, chemistry, metallurgy, and agriculture.

18. Sevilla and the area around it offer the largest number of examples considered prototypes of popular Andalusian architecture: churches and convents with patios, grillwork over windows, and projecting decorative moldings over windows and portals, to name a few features seen throughout northern New Spain.

19. The basis for the military appearance of the early convents in Mexico is succinctly discussed by Chanfón Olmos, "El supuesto carácter militar de los conventos."

20. Most notable of these Andalusian churches were three built in the thirteenth century, Santa Ana in Triana, San Pedro in San Lucas la Mayor, and San Isidro in Italica—all within twenty miles of Sevilla.

21. *Ajaraca* designated a mudéjar treatment of plaster whereby two different-colored layers of lime plaster were applied to the walls, with the top layer cut through, usually in a geometric design, to expose the bottom layer.

22. Gothic Survival is distinguished from Gothic Revival, which entails "a conscious romantic endeavor intended to arouse a particular emotional response through the evocation of a historical atmosphere" (Loth, *The Only Proper Style*), 4.

23. See Hamlin, *History of Ornament*, 82–84.

24. See discussion of herms, atlantes, and caryatids in "Human and Animal Shapes" under "Decorative Motifs" in chapter 6.

25. Indeed, a case can even be made for the influence of the Renaissance style on the eighteenth-century hide paintings of New Mexico. See, for example, Wroth, *Christian Images in Hispanic New Mexico*, 47–48.

26. Fabienne E. Hellendoorn (*Influencia de manierismo-nórdico*) argues that Nordic rather than Italian mannerism was the primary influence on decorative design in Spain and later in New Spain, beginning in the sixteenth century with the plateresque and continuing into the eighteenth century.

27. Manrique, "Reflexión sobre el manierismo en México."

28. Kubler, *Mexican Architecture in the Sixteenth Century*, vol. 2, p. 307.

29. Manuel González Galván synthesizes the differences between European and American baroque, arriving at ten categories based on plans, façades, walls, axis, volume, and perspective—all in exact opposition (González Galván, "El espacio en la arquitectura religiosa virreinal de México"). Anthony Blunt narrowly focuses on the baroque as it applies to time, area, and salient features, preferring to assign later architectural forms in Spain and Mexico to neo-mannerism because of the use of the *estípite*, common elements of northern mannerism, and the absence of a baroque plan or spatial development (Blunt, *Baroque and Rococo*, 16). And Martin Soria chooses to divide seventeenth-century Mexican baroque painting into three periods: Mannerist Early Baroque (1600–1640), High Baroque Interlude (1640–1660), and Mannerist Late Baroque (1660–1710; Kubler and Soria, *Art and Architecture in Spain and Portugal*, 307–13).

30. Stierlin, *Barroco en España y Portugal*, 44.

31. Blunt, *Baroque and Rococo*, 11–14.

32. Baird, *Churches of Mexico*, 35.

33. Vargas Lugo, *Portadas religiosas de México*, 305–28.

34. Toussaint, *Colonial Art in Mexico*, 190–211.

35. González Galván, "Modalidades del barroco mexicano," uses ten divisions. Based on their occurrence in northern New Spain, some of the column types on which his terminology depends are described in this chapter and in "Columns" under "Architectural Details" in chapter 6.

36. Maza, *La ciudad de México en el siglo XVII*, 41. See also Elisa Vargas Lugo's discussion of baroque classifications in "Diferentes aspectos del desarrollo ornamental del barroco novohispano."

37. On the role of *estípite* both as a column type and as a design element, see Villegas, *Gran signo formal del barroco*, esp. chap. 14.

38. *Ultrabarroco* was coined by Dr. Atl. See Atl, Toussaint, and Benitez, *Iglesias de México*, vol. 6, 11. On Churrigueresque (coined by Toussaint)—its origin, application, and inadequacies as an artistic term—see Fernández, *Retablo de los Reyes*.

39. For a discussion of the influence of German engravings and prints in spreading the rococo style to central and southern New Spain, as expressed in the interiors of Santa Rosa in Querétaro (Querétaro) and of Santa Prisca in Taxco (Guerrero) and the exteriors of the churches at Jalpan and Tilaco (Querétaro), see Boils Morales, *Arquitectura y sociedad en Querétaro*, 29–33.

40. Krell, *California Missions*, 193; Webb, *Indian Life at the Old Missions*, 143.

41. Finances, demographics, and politics hampered construction of neoclassical religious edifices before 1821, although northern New Spain came close to having a neoclassical cathedral at Linares (the present-day city of Monterrey). See Zapata Aguilar, *Monterrey*.

In their desire to modernize existing churches, nineteenth-century renovators removed or destroyed many examples of valid baroque art—retablos, sculpture, altars, paintings, furnishings, and sometimes complete interiors or façades—and replaced these with sometimes poorly understood examples of neoclassicism, or what might be termed "pseudo-neoclassicism." This was particularly true in large parish churches and cathedrals. A clear example is the nineteenth-century retablo constructed in front of the original eighteenth-century rococo retablo in the Cathedral of Chihuahua (Chihuahua). Complete or almost complete examples of the original baroque decoration and furnishings can occasionally be found, however, in an isolated or poor village, where tradition or economics prevented refurbishing the church's interior in the new style.

42. On Moreno Villa's introduction of *tequitqui* into the vocabulary of Mexican art and the various inadequacies of this term, see Reyes Valerio, chap. 12, "Esencia del arte indocristiano," in *Arte indocristiano*.

43. Justino Fernández characterizes a statue of Santo Domingo found in Monterrey as tequitqui, although it is probably eighteenth-century (Fernández, "Una escultura tequitqui en Monterrey"). Aline Ussel C. amplifies the basis for the use of *tequitqui*, with corresponding elements in Romanesque, Gothic, Renaissance, and baroque stages, and sees it continuing into the eighteenth century (Ussel C., *Esculturas de la Virgen María*, 26).

44. On specific design and material characteristics that establish subcategories specific to regions and time, see Vargas Lugo, *Portadas religiosas de México*, esp. 220–28. Unfortunately for our purposes, she confines her discussion to the territory of modern Mexico.

45. Anaya Larios, *Historia de la escultura queretana*. From my research in Querétaro and in various archives elsewhere, I became convinced that the Colegio de Misioneros de Propaganda Fide (founded in Querétaro in 1683) played a crucial role in the dispersal of religious paintings, sculpture, and even entire retablos, as well as of architects and maestros for church construction in the mission areas of northern New Spain. Unfortunately, other scholars have not turned their attention to this matter.

46. Ramírez Montes, *Pedro de Rojas*.

47. See Gustín, *Barroco en la Sierra Gorda*.

Chapter 3

1. By the seventeenth century, the liturgy was viewed largely as a devotional exercise performed by religious specialists—the priest and his assistants—before an audience of passive spectators, whose piety was expressed entirely by their private devotions, rather than as a public act of worship among the Catholic community. This is particularly evident in Spanish baroque churches, where "the division of the worshipping body into audience and actors is further emphasized by the spectacular and theatrical development of church building. . . . The altar . . . now becomes part of the elaborate sculptural group involving altar and reredos" (Rykwert, *Church Building*, 110).

2. Santo Ángel was begun in the mid-eighteenth century as a mission for the Tarahumaras by a Jesuit missionary from Parral, Father Luis Martín, who functioned as craftsman, laborer, painter, and artist (Decorme, *Obra de los jesuitas mexicanos*, 147–246). Although we might imagine that Father Martín or his architect (*maestro albañil*) had been influenced by European baroque floor plans by way of imported stylebooks, from the back, the church's massive rounded shapes strongly suggest the Romanesque.

3. Kubler (*Mexican Architecture in the Sixteenth Century*, vol. 2, p. 249) informs us that San Miguel de Chapultepec was the only sixteenth-century church of circular plan built in all of New Spain, probably by Claudio de Arciniega, "the only man then in Mexico capable of devising such a classic form."

4. Fernández, "Santa Brígida de México."

5. "Plan" is understood to mean a top or horizontal view of the partitions and walls of a building or group of buildings. The main altar and portal are indicated by a label and a broad arrow, respectively, for each church floor plan; other parts are labeled as deemed useful.

6. To make a particular historical or architectural point, I have included an occasional example from Europe as well.

7. Rectangular, no-aisle churches are often, but mistakenly, referred to as hall churches. For the correct architectural application of the term, see discussion of hall churches under "Multiple Aisles."

8. Liturgically, "basilica" is a title given to a church honored by the pope; among other honorific privileges, the basilica takes prominence over other churches in the diocese except for the cathedral. San Carlos Borromeo in Carmel (California) is a recent example.

9. See Swift, *Roman Sources of Christian Art*, 23–30, on the origin and evolution of the basilica plan.

10. Bargellini, *Arquitectura de la plata*, 28, points out that in 1640 the Cathedral of Durango was a basilica in floor plan only; the nave and two aisles of the early structure were covered with a flat roof, effectively creating a hall church. The cathedral would later be expanded in width and length, the nave raised, and both it and the side aisles vaulted, generating a basilica profile in the elevation.

11. There were several bishoprics in New Spain. Northern New Spain was divided differently at various times as boundaries of bishopric jurisdiction changed or shifted. Although in southern and central New Spain, the division of an area and the assignment of a bishop usually signaled the conversion of its missions to diocesan use, this was not the case for the bishoprics of the sparsely populated north, where missions and missionaries persevered (Kubler, *Mexican Architecture in the Sixteenth Century*, vol. 2, p. 308).

12. Sartor, *Arquitectura y urbanismo en Nueva España*, 132. Because San Agustín is a heavily restored structure, its cryptocollateral typology is not easily recognized. Sartor regards the Dominican Order as principals in cryptocollateral church design, citing as examples three significant Dominican structures in the cities of México, Puebla, and Oaxaca, all begun in the sixteenth century.

13. Kubler, *Portuguese Plain Architecture*, 56–57.

14. *Capilla*, most likely derived from the Latin *capella* (chapel or oratory), is said to come from *capa pequeña* (little cape), referring to the piece of cape that Saint Martin of Tours gave to a poor man (actually Christ) and to the chapel that was erected for this relic.

15. A church's tabernacle, however, could be used for devotions by viewing it from an auxiliary chapel through a squint or hagioscope, a medieval feature perhaps incorporated in at least one seventeenth-century northern Arizona church (Montgomery, Smith, and Brew, *Franciscan Awatovi*, 184–85, and fig. 43).

At San José y San Miguel de Aguayo (Texas) the second-story, head friar's office is still intact, with its window open to the nave. Although the altar is not visible from this opening, the friar could keep an eye on the congregation. Tribunes (*tribunas*), balcony-like appurtenances on the upper levels, may also have been intended for this purpose. Built near the altar and overlooking the nave, they were generally covered with an obscuring screen or latticework, which ensured privacy during services or permitted the occupant to hear and see what occurred in the nave without being observed.

16. Durandus (*Symbolism of Churches*, 177–79) gives a number of reasons—especially the association of Christ with the east—for the selection of east over other directions for church orientations. Reading from the Vulgate—the official Latin version of the Bible for the Roman Catholic Church, translated by Saint Jerome in the fourth century at the insistence of Pope Saint Damasus I—Durandus makes two particularly apt citations: "Behold the man, whose name is the East" (Zechariah 6:12) and "We ought to pray eastward, where the light ariseth" (Wisdom 16:28). Placing the altar in the east end of the church and orienting the church along an east-west axis also find their basis in the Old Testament, Ezekiel 43:4: "And the glory of the Lord came into the house by the way of the gate whose prospect is toward the east." According to John O'Connell, the east-west orientation was well established in Christian church building by the third century, and was based on the analogy that the sun's path symbolized the coming of the Messiah from the east and thence departing—an allusion to the risen Christ (O'Connell, *Church Building and Furnishing*, 16–17). See also Bingham, *Origines ecclesiasticae*, vol. 1, pp. 653–54.

17. McAndrew, *Open-Air Churches*, 504.

18. Schuetz-Miller, *Architectural Practice in Mexico City*, 7.

19. Kubler, *Religious Architecture of New Mexico*, 23.

20. See in this regard Pennick, *Sacred Geometry*.

21. The atrio at some mission sites also served as a burial ground, although most often this would not be its original purpose but would represent a later development.

22. The word *convento* translates into English as "convent" or "monastery," or occasionally as "rectory" or "priest's house." Because none of these translations adequately describes the term in its expanded sense in northern New Spain (to include workshops, schools, community storage of grain and other supplies, and dormitories for acolytes), I will use *convento* instead.

23. "De profundis" (out of the depths) are the opening words of Psalm 130, used on behalf of the dead—"Out of the depths have I cried unto thee, O Lord" (Psalms 130:1). The sala "de profundis" was a large room or separate space, generally next to the refectory, through which friars passed on their way to their meals. Before eating, they would pause here and say prayers for the dead.

24. On the other hand, archaeological evidence and the writings of Eusebius indicate that courtyards were a feature of Old World churches dating back to early Christianity. See, for example, Bingham, *Origines ecclesiasticae*, vol. 1, p. 289. On the courtyards and other architectural features of mosques, see Hoag, *Islamic Architecture*.

25. An account of an Indian revolt in 1616 at Santiago Papasquiaro in Nueva Vizcaya speaks not only of the church being destroyed, but of the cross (mostly likely an atrio variety) in the center of the plaza being knocked down as well (Jones, *Nueva Vizcaya*, 101).

26. Webb, *Indian Life at the Old Missions*, 38, reports that Alta California missions ordered sundials in 1771 and that San Carlos Borromeo in Carmel once had a sundial with symbols of the daily mission activities carved on its face.

27. The smaller congregations served by the missions of northern New Spain may account for the scarcity or nondevelopment of open chapels and capillas posas there.

28. Kubler, *Religious Architecture of New Mexico*, 72–75; Domínguez, *Missions of New Mexico*, 55.

29. Ellis, *Bishop Lamy's Santa Fe Cathedral*, 80–81. See also chapter 5 in this volume.

30. Conversation with architectural historian Miguel Celorio, San Antonio, Texas, October 1985.

31. McAndrew, *Open-Air Churches*, 343.

32. Morales, "Nuevo dato sobre capillas abiertas españoles." As yet two other antecedents (common in North Africa and Andalucía alike) of New Spain's open chapels, I propose the *musall*, a mosque open to the sky, and the *iwan*, an open porch surrounding the courtyard of a mosque where teachers and students of Islam would gather to confer, or the faithful to pray or hear services.

33. Castillo Utrilla, "La hospedería de indias." As a Moorish antecedent to New Spain's *capillas posas*, I propose the *qubbas*, open-sided, domed structures in the corners of mosque courtyards, which with the iwan were essential features of Moorish (and Islamic) religious architecture. See, in this regard, Zahar, "Transformed Geometry"; Grube, "What Is Islamic Architecture?"; and Dickey, "Allah and Eternity."

34. On the education of girls in northern New Spain, see Foz y Foz, *Revolución pedagógica en Nueva España*, 245–47, 250.

35. Locked in conflict with a new territorial governor over his building costs, Llanos y Valdés left Monterrey in 1795 on the pretext of a pastoral visit and never returned. What remained of the unfinished building was years later converted to other uses, including a jail. See Roel, *Nuevo León*, 64–66; and Alessio Robles, *Acapulco, Saltillo y Monterrey*, 331.

36. Sagel, *Iglesia de Santa Cruz de la Cañada*, 65. A 1768 plan of burials in Santa Cruz de la Cañada (New Mexico), includes a sketch showing locations and prices. The most expensive was burial in the crossing for 19 pesos; a location in the transept capilla cost 12 pesos, one in the nave nearest the crossing 8 pesos, mid-nave 4 pesos, and a spot in the nave near the choir loft or under it 2 pesos. One peso would get you an outside location near the wall.

37. The decree of Charles III was gradually enforced with the Laws of Reform (1834), the liberalization movement of Benito Juárez, and the official establishment of public burial grounds on July 31, 1859. Bodies no longer had to be buried in church grounds or consecrated areas. The title of the burial ground was also changed, from camposanto (holy ground) to *panteón* (the Greek pantheon was a temple sacred to all the gods, but the meaning here is "most sacred place"), perhaps as a reflection of the neopaganistic interests of Charles III.

38. Many of the prescriptions for architectural siting throughout New Spain are directly related to the Catholic Church's

interest in cosmology (the sweeping philosophy of the universe considered as a totality of parts and phenomena subject to laws), dating back to the sixth century and Justinian's Santa Sophia in Constantinople (built between 532 and 537; restored after an earthquake between 558 and 563).

The "Ordenanzas de descubrimiento, nueva población y pacificación," which prohibited founding a new settlement without a license to do so from the viceregal authorities—on penalty of death—instructed settlers on siting from economic, defensive, and sanitary perspectives. Thus, proximity to cleared land, firewood, building materials, water, and pasturage was deemed crucial to the success and prosperity of settlements; seacoast locations were to be avoided because of the danger of attack by pirates; and moderate elevations were preferable to higher or lower ones because they were less subject to winds or diseases.

39. Stanislawski, "Origin and Spread of the Grid Pattern Town," 105–20. See also "Renaissance" in chapter 2 of this volume.

40. Crouch, Garr, and Mundigo, *Spanish City Planning in North America,* 15.

Chapter 4

1. The Jesuit missionary Andrés Pérez de Ribas, in *My Life among the Savage Nations of New Spain,* 130, reported that mission priests served as architects, overseers, and laborers for the purpose of training others. Jesuit chronicler Ugarte is quoted as saying the priests also served as carpenters, stonemasons, and artisans of all kinds—even as bell founders. Ignacio del Río, *Conquista y aculturación en la California jesuita,* 124–25. See also Clavijero, *Historia de la antigua o Baja California,* 108; Díaz, *Arquitectura en el desierto,* 75 and 122; and Ivey, *In the Midst of a Loneliness,* esp. chaps. 5–7 and 9–11.

2. The proportions, dimensions, and architectural details of buildings had been formalized in the Latin texts of Vitruvius and others available in Spain in the mid-sixteenth century. See esp. Vitruvius, *Ten Books,* 5–13; see also Baez Macías, *Obras de Fray Andrés de San Miguel.*

3. Many of the original adobe brick structures built by the Jesuits in the Pimería Alta were replaced or remodeled by the Franciscans using fired brick. See Roca, *Paths of the Padres.*

4. Clara Bargellini has done excellent archival work on architects and craftsmen involved in building metropolitan churches, especially those near rich silver mines. See Bargellini, *Catedral de Chihuahua* and *Arquitectura de la plata.*

5. Pedro Corbalán, Pedro Taxalde, and Pedro Alcado, "1774 Contract for Suaqui Grande, San Marcial, Sonora," unpublished manuscript translation at San Xavier del Bac Library, Tucson; Kessell, *Friars, Soldiers and Reformers,* 202–3.

6. Franco Carrasco, *Nuevo Santander y su arquitectura,* vol. 1, pp. 212–13.

7. Schuetz-Miller, "Professional Artisans in the Hispanic Southwest"; Castañeda, *Our Catholic Heritage in Texas,* vol. 2, p. 8; Ocaranza, *Los franciscanos en las Provincias Internas,* 206–8, 214.

8. Salvatierra, *Selected Letters about Lower California,* 226–27. Apparently, there was a critical shortage of all skilled craftsmen. See Baegert, *Observations in Lower California,* 149; Engelhardt, *Missions and Missionaries of California,* 346.

9. Fernández, "El albañil, el arquitecto y el alarife." Bear in mind, however, that the designations for architects and skilled craftsmen were more fluid in sparsely settled northern New Spain than in the more populous—and more strongly regulated—regions to the south.

10. Sometimes rich and powerful, cofradías served the social and religious needs of the guild artisans. They also functioned as mutual benefit societies, occasionally providing assistance to widows and orphans of members. Each craft had a patron saint (whose mortal life or attributes usually had something to do with that craft), given special veneration by the members of the craft's cofradía, who supported an altar devoted to that saint and who participated in religious processions as a group (Bracho, *De los gremios al sindicalismo,* 37).

11. For detailed accounts of the obligations of master to apprentice and apprentice to master, see Ruiz Gomar, *Gremio de escultores y entalladores,* 32–33; González Franco, Olvera Calvo, and Reyes y Cabañas, *Artistas y artesanos,* vol. 1, pp. 35–36; and Guillot Carrotalá, *Temas españoles,* 25–26.

12. Castro Gutiérrez, *Extinción de la artesanía gremial,* 33, lists a wide range of guilds whose members or journeymen may well have helped build, decorate, or furnish northern New Spain's churches—from masons, painters, and silversmiths to carpenters, gilders, and instrument makers.

13. For a more detailed description of social and occupational divisions within the guilds, working conditions, and use of slave labor, see Castro Gutiérrez, *Extinción de la artesanía gremial,* 73–100.

14. Many natives of Baja California learned masonry from a missionary, carpenter, or competent soldier and worked under the supervision of a master builder. Jesuit missionary Johann Jakob Baegert writes that, using abundantly available building stones, they were able to construct churches comparable to any in Europe in a few years and with little expense (Baegert, *Observations in Lower California,* 127).

Blacksmiths, carpenters, and masons recruited for the military settlements of Alta California helped the friars build and maintain early mission churches there, training native workers to be blacksmiths, carpenters, and masons and often continuing to practice their professions as civilian settlers (Schuetz-Miller, *Building and Builders in Hispanic California,* 11–21).

15. Fray Alonso de Benavides (*Memorial of Fray Alonso de Benavides,* 33) speaks of the women of the Indian nations of New Mexico building the walls of the churches. Pedro de Castañeda, a private soldier in Coronado's expeditionary group writing around 1554, describes women making the walls of dwellings from a mixture of ash, charcoal, and mud in a village near present-day Taos (New Mexico) as part of the customary division of labor (Castañeda, "Narrative of the Expedition of Coronado"). Kubler (*Religious Architecture of New Mexico,* 33) suggests that arches and domes may not have been used in New Mexican churches

because of resistance by women to any increase in their share of the labor.

16. Engelhardt, *Missions and Missionaries of California,* vol. 2, pp. 560–61.

17. There were a few women's guilds (mostly for Indians and mixed bloods), organized like men's guilds with elected officers and written constitutions, but again these were only in central and southern New Spain (Castro Gutiérrez, *Extinción de la artesanía gremial,* 161–80).

18. Ibid., 33.

19. Baegert (*Observations in Lower California,* 109) relates that a tent served as a chapel in the first days of Salvatierra's expedition of 1697 to Baja California; Alonso de Benavides (*Fray Alonso de Benavides' Revised Memorial,* 214), tells how the first mass among the Zuni was celebrated in a house bought to lodge the friars.

20. Adobe bricks of various shapes and sizes were also molded by hand and laid in courses with adobe mortar, although this technique was not in general use.

21. The clay was sometimes also pulled into tall, slender, and slightly flaring "jars" on a potter's wheel, allowed to partly harden, then sliced lengthwise in two before firing. Potter's wheel *tejas de barro* are found on structures in Andalucía into the twentieth century and also in Morocco, where they are made in the same way to this day. I have seen them used as drain spouts in the churches of northern New Spain, but not as tiles on extant roofs, although they may once have been used in that capacity.

22. Loza blanca, Chinese, and Tonala (Jalisco) plates can still be found on the outside apse wall of San José de Copala. Of the sixty Chinese and English trade plates originally attached to the single, three-staged bell tower at Nuestra Señora de la Asunción del Real de los Álamos (begun around 1794; completed in the early nineteenth century), only one entire plate and fragments of two others remain in place.

The inspiration for these apparently unique examples in northern New Spain may have been eighteenth-century Aguascalientes (Aguascalientes), where entire pieces of Pueblan loza blanca were embedded in the cupola of the bell tower of San Marcos and in the dome and cupola of San José. Those at San José were attached both whole and deliberately broken to create decorative patterns and religious monograms as well as to accentuate the segmented dome's angularity. The use of plates as church decoration dates back to early-twelfth-century Pisa, where church walls were adorned with Moorish pottery as part of the spoils of a war with the Saracens.

23. Montgomery, Smith, and Brew, *Franciscan Awatovi,* 293–334. Reconstruction of geometric motifs from the painted plaster walls of several rooms discovered during the excavation of Awatovi made it clear "even [to] casual observation . . . that they were painted in attempted simulation of the glazed tiles so lavishly used at the time in both ecclesiastical and secular buildings in Spain and Mexico" (p. 303). Moreover, in Charles Lummis's 1886 photograph of the interior of the military chapel La Castrense in Santa Fe (New Mexico), both apse and walls were painted in a tilelike design, as was the dado of the interior walls of San Xavier del Bac (Arizona) and the lower parts of the exterior of the bell tower of San José y San Miguel de Aguayo, San Antonio (Texas).

24. Díaz, *Arquitectura en el desierto,* 98.

25. Santamaría, *Diccionario de mejicanismos,* 1017.

26. This according to Clavijero, *Historia de la antigua o Baja California,* 14, who identifies a source of especially fine alabaster on the island of San Marcos near the beach of Mulegé.

27. Vitruvius's *Ten Books,* which greatly influenced Renaissance architects, includes a variety of techniques and instructions for plaster preparation and application.

28. Montgomery, Smith, and Brew, *Franciscan Awatovi,* 158, quote Kubler to the effect that lime plaster was not used in northern Arizona or New Mexico until the nineteenth century. Montgomery notes, however, that the friars surely knew how to prepare it and that sources of lime were abundant. Adobe mortar, readily available and requiring no fuel to make, was simply more convenient.

29. "Possolan" (*puzolana*), which narrowly refers to hydraulic cement, once made from a volcanic tuff quarried near Puzzuoli, Italy, also refers to a natural cement used by many native builders in northern New Spain. Ground, mixed with water, and allowed to harden, it is still used on the flat roofs of dwellings in the modern states of Zacatecas and Durango and may well have been so used in early church structures.

30. In Nuevo Santander, for example, a shortage of limestone or lime and of fuel to incinerate it restricted the use of limestone and lime mortar to only the most important buildings (Franco Carrasco, *Nuevo Santander y su arquitectura* 222–24).

31. There is no evidence that lead was used on the roofs of churches in northern New Spain, as it was on many important sixteenth-century churches in Mexico City. Nor is there evidence that molten lead was poured in cut channels to join the vertical faces of stones, a technique used by both Roman and Islamic builders and in a number of central Mexico's fountains and walls. For additional information on the uses of brass, bronze, copper, iron, and tin in the churches of northern New Spain, see "Arches, Vaults, Half Domes" and "Drain Spouts" under "Architectural Details" in chapter 6; and "Belfry," "Baptistery," "Upper Choir," "Nave and Transepts," "Sanctuary," and "Sacristy" in chapter 7.

32. The iron cross on the cupola of the Cathedral of Mexico in Mexico City was considered necessary for protection against lightning storms, although whether this was a matter of faith or science is unknown. Angulo Iñiguez, *Planos de monumentos arquitectónicos,* vol. 1, p. 171.

33. For illustrations of other surviving examples of original crosses and weather vanes in the southwestern United States and northern Mexico, see Simmons and Turley, *Southwestern Colonial Ironwork.* For dramatic illustrations of Mexican ironwork generally, see Castro Morales, *Art of Ironworks in Mexico.*

34. Bunting, *Early Architecture in New Mexico,* 67–68.

35. Montgomery, Smith, and Brew, *Franciscan Awatovi,* 61–62; Scholes and Adams, *Inventories of Church Furnishings,* 30.

36. Romero de Terreros y Vinent, *Artes industriales en la Nueva España,* 199.

37. Telephone conversation with Charles W. Polzer, SJ, June 1985; Baegert, *Observations in Lower California*, 125; Bargellini, *Catedral de Chihuahua*, 87–88.

38. On the qualitative properties of colors found in several mission churches, see Gloria Fraser Giffords and Christopher Stavroudis, "Preliminary Investigations of Decorative Techniques and Materials Used in San Xavier del Bac," unpublished manuscript, 1978; Hageman and Ewing, *Archeological and Restoration Study*, apps. A and C; Montgomery, Smith, and Brew, *Franciscan Awatovi*, 293–313; Steen and Gettens, "Tumacacori Interior Decorations"; Webb, "Pigments Used by the Mission Indians." In "A Study of Some California Indian Rock Art Pigments," Scott and Hyder report on binders, methods of preparation, application, and dissemination of pigments among the Chumash in California.

39. Grant, *Rock Paintings of the Chumash*, 72, 75, 79, 82.

40. Webb, *Indian Life at the Old Missions*, 242; Montgomery, Smith, and Brew, *Franciscan Awatovi*, 243–51; Bishop and Derrick, "Use of Wild Cucumber Seeds"; Scott et al., "Blood as a Binding Medium."

41. To this day, in the U.S. Southwest and northern Mexico, native builders add the fermented juice of the prickly pear cactus (*nopal*) to lime plaster and whitewash to permit these to be applied more smoothly and firmly and to make them more durable. Anthony Crosby ("More Ways to Wash White," 11), suggests they did so for San Xavier del Bac (Arizona) and the former mission church of La Purísima Concepción in Caborca (Sonora). See also van Lengen, *Manual del arquitecto descalzo*, 148.

In the spring of 1989, a latex coating was removed from the exterior surfaces of the vault and domes of San Xavier del Bac. Applied only a few years before, the coating had, by sealing in moisture, inadvertently promoted the deterioration of the underlying brickwork. Directed by historian Jorge Olvera and architect Robert Vint, restorers replastered the thoroughly stripped surfaces using a traditional nopal juice formula and burnished the new plaster to a marble-like sheen. Reports have since confirmed the superiority of the cactus juice sealer, which resists weathering but also allows the plaster to breathe.

42. In New Mexico, sod blocks (*terrones*) cut from the marshy mud of the Rio Grande riverbed were used to build temporary shelters. Archaeological evidence from the Salinas missions indicates these were houses rather than churches, however.

43. For a rare, detailed view of eighteenth-century frontier mission buildings, costumes, and life in Baja California, see Nunis, *Drawings of Ignacio Tirsch: A Jesuit Missionary in Baja California*.

44. The façade of this building is a virtual copy of an engraving from Vitruvius's *Ten Books*, whose Spanish translation was published in Madrid in 1787 and widely disseminated among architects of the time.

45. See Ephesians 2:20: "And [ye] are built upon the foundation of the Apostles and prophets, Jesus Christ himself being the chief corner stone"; and Matthew 16:18: "And I say also unto thee, That thou art Peter, and upon this rock [punning on the name "Peter," which means "rock" or "stone" in Greek] I will build my church; and the gates of hell shall not prevail against it."

The tradition of placing and blessing church cornerstones dates back to before the ninth century. See O'Connell, *Church Building and Furnishing*, esp. 18–19. The apparent absence of cornerstones in some of the churches of northern New Spain may be due to the stones' having been incorporated within the foundations or later construction, or to their having been plastered over by uninformed repairmen.

46. Baegert (*Observations in Lower California*, 127) notes that, in the arid and unforested lands of Baja California, scaffolding was made of poles or rails in whatever lengths were available. If a piece was too short, two or three were lashed together with rawhide strips.

47. Found in masonry walls of almost every age, the holes for putlogs were called *columbaria* by Vitruvius from their resemblance to pigeon holes, which, when left unfilled, they very likely became.

48. On a system of centering and shoring that combines lumber, nails, and wire with earth fill placed on platforms, see Goss, "Problem of Erecting the Main Dome and Roof Vaults"; and Herreras, "Problems of Restoration of San Xavier."

49. In tapia, or "rammed earth," builders tamped moist earth with a suitably high clay content between rigid forms, which they could move to other locations when the resulting wall had dried sufficiently to hold its shape. Multistoried structures such as Casa Grande (Arizona) and Paquime, Casas Grandes (Chihuahua) were made using *tapia*.

50. Pedto de Castañeda, "Narrative of the Expedition of Coronado," 352–53.

51. Santa Gertrudis in Baja California is reported in Río, *Conquista y aculturación en la California jesuita*, 119, to have had walls made of brush and mud (*carrizo y lodo*).

52. Fray Palou describes Mission San Luis Obispo de Tolosa in 1773 as a "stockade [within which] there is a little church (24 x 60 feet) constructed of poles . . . which are driven into the ground close together, and covered with tules" (quoted in Kocker, *Mission San Luis Obispo*, 13). See also Engelhardt, *Missions and Missionaries of California*, vol. 2, 205, on the first presidio in San Francisco, erected in 1776.

53. For one account of why the side walls of some New Mexican churches varied in thickness, see Kubler, *Religious Architecture of New Mexico*, 127–28.

54. In perhaps a unique example of a similar decorative technique for rubble masonry walls meant to be left unplastered, the stonemasons of San José de Parral (Chihuahua) covered the entire surface of the outside walls in a repeated, flattened-rhomb pattern of small rocks embedded in mortar (see figure 2.14).

55. See chapter 2, n. 21.

56. In northern Mexico, "canales" refers both to drains or drain spouts and to ditches or canals in the earth—whereas in central Mexico it refers only to ditches or canals. The technically more correct term for drains or drain spouts is *canaleras*. Nowadays, it is common practice to insert a metal pipe into the end of a drain spout or gargoyle, casting the water even farther away from the walls.

57. A soffit, though viewed from below as a ceiling, refers to the *underside* of a building part or element (choir loft, archway, cornice, or staircase). Thus, the soffit of a choir loft is viewed, not from the loft itself, but from the lower choir or vestibule below it.

58. Attached towers were not considered buttresses, although they served much the same structural function.

59. Pillared buttresses came in many forms. One such form, the diagonal, or bias façade, buttress, used in central Mexico from the middle to the end of the sixteenth century, did not reach northern New Spain until the seventeenth century, and can be seen in the parochial church of San José de Parral (Chihuahua) and the Cathedral of Durango.

60. Buttresses were sometimes added to shore up stress-weakened areas after a building was completed (see figure 4.28). Not part of the original design, these were often made of a different material or used a different masonry technique.

61. The relatively flat roofs of the churches in northern New Mexico, areas subject to substantial rain and snow, are anomalies.

62. Ben Wittick's 1882–83 photograph of the interior of the Cathedral of Chihuahua (see figure 6.13) clearly shows a similar type of floor, which no longer exists, probably as the result of remodeling in the early part of this century. Domínguez, *Missions of New Mexico,* 14, calls attention to a plank floor in San Francisco de la Villa in Santa Fe (New Mexico).

63. Bargellini, *Catedral de Chihuahua,* 90–91.

64. Montgomery, Smith, and Brew, *Franciscan Awatovi,* 61.

65. Pfefferkorn, *Sonora,* 79–80. A mason was brought from Mexico City to build San Francisco Javier de Batuc (Sonora), one of the most finely proportioned and skillfully constructed churches in northern New Spain, now inundated by the waters of a dam constructed nearby. Fortunately, however, the church's façade was removed to a small park in Pitic, a suburb of Hermosillo (Sonora), and its side portal to a plaza facing the former mission church of La Purísima Concepción in Caborca (Sonora).

66. Mason's marks—small, brandlike engravings carved on stones in the finished edges and moldings of arches, windows, and drums of churches in northern New Spain—may also have served to guide the assembly of pieces. Bargellini (*Catedral de Chihuahua,* 65–67) illustrates a number of different mason's marks from the Cathedral of Chihuahua as well as from the nearby Church of Santa Eulalia.

67. The use of oil paints (pigments suspended in a drying oil binder) for murals was rare, not only in northern New Spain but also in central and southern New Spain.

68. Artesones (wooden troughs or panels) are recessed compartments with molding along the edges, the center panel frequently containing paintings or reliefs. This term may be applied to furniture, shutters, or doors as well as to ceilings and soffits.

69. Domínguez, *Missions of New Mexico,* 14.

70. Carried atop a litter on the shoulders of several men, these figures were life-sized, realistically carved, painted, and dressed. The tradition of carrying religious figures through the streets during Holy Week, Lent, saints' days and other festivals, or times of catastrophes dates from at least the fourteenth century in Spain. With the formation of cofradías and penitential brotherhoods in the sixteenth century and with the Counter-Reformation, the Spanish tradition of religious pageantry was carried to New Spain as well. As a result of Benito Juárez's secularization of public festivals in 1857 and related legislation in the twentieth century, however, the spectacles that may be seen in Spain to this day hardly exist in Mexico. See also "Processional Figures" under "Sculptors" in chapter 10.

Chapter 5

1. This tradition may have begun with Emperor Theodosius I (ca. AD 346–395), who commanded that crosses be placed on and within pagan temples to purify them.

2. Although "frontispiece" and "façade" are sometimes used interchangeably, in this work, "façade" refers to the main façade (unless otherwise indicated) and "frontispiece" to its decoratively developed central part.

On the relationship of the frontispiece of a church to its retablo, see Anderson, "Figural Arrangements of Eighteenth-Century Churches"; on the relationship of the main façade to a church's floor plan, see Schuetz-Miller, "Proportional Systems and Ancient Geometry." Both authors assert that if the schema of a church's retablo or floor plan is understood, lost elements can be reconstructed: the figures in the frontispiece (Anderson) or the intended dimensions of the main façade (Schuetz-Miller).

3. Note that *portada* means not only "portal" but also "frontispiece" and "façade." On the forms and iconography of portadas, see Vargas Lugo, *Portadas churriguerescas* and *Portadas religiosas de México.*

4. As an exception to the generalization about the prominence of the main portal, Anderson divides sixteenth-century façades into two principal types with subcategories: figural (with dedicatory figures only, with dedicatory and secondary figures, or with secondary figures only); and nonfigural (Anderson, "Figural Arrangements of Eighteenth-Century Churches," 44).

5. Borromeo, *Instrucciones de la fábrica y del ajuar eclesiásticos,* 7–8.

6. Vitruvius admonishes architects to make the upper columns one-fourth smaller than those below because the latter would be loaded with weight and ought to be stronger. If more than one order is to be used, the strongest should occupy the lower level, and the tiers of columns should not be the same. Gwilt, *Encyclopedia of Architecture,* 850–51.

7. But see also Domínguez, *Missions of New Mexico,* 64.

8. In central New Spain during the sixteenth century, the north door of a convent church was often ornamented, symbolizing the desire of the Church to convert barbarians. In large Franciscan convent churches, the north door was called *porciúncula,* referring to the "little portion" of land that was given to Saint Francis of Assisi when he began his religious life. This door was used only during the days of indulgences of Nuestra Señora de los Angeles de Porciúncula.

9. Espadañas appear throughout southern Spain, particularly in Andalucía, from the late fourteenth century on. See Calderón Quijano, *Espadañas de Sevilla*.

10. In some of the more primitive domed churches, such as San Antonio de Padua de Cuencamé (Durango), the builders used no drum, placing the main dome directly on the crossing walls.

11. All domes, whether main or lesser, were called cúpulas (cupolas).

12. Borromeo, *Instrucciones de la fábrica y del ajuar eclesiásticos*, 14.

13. Transverse clerestories were used as early as 1550 BC in the hypostyle halls of the Great Temple of Amon at Karnak.

14. Kubler, *Mexican Architecture in the Sixteenth Century*, vol. 2, p. 279.

15. Hulme, *Symbolism in Christian Art*, 78–80. See also commentary on the symbolism of parts of the church building in the introduction to chapter 11.

16. Kubler, *Religious Architecture of New Mexico*, 37, 69–70.

17. One such freestanding stoup is described in the 1820 inventory of San Miguel in Culiacán (Sonora; Church inventory 1).

18. O'Connell, *Church Building and Furnishing*, 83–84. Holy water stoups became permanent parts of the church building sometime in the eleventh or twelfth century.

19. Stoups made from Chinese trade porcelain bowls embedded within the wall of the Pueblo Chapel in Los Angeles (California) were removed during a renovation around 1950. Conversation with John Deware, Patagonia, Arizona, June 2001.

20. For the baptistery's possible derivation from the *frigidarium*, a pagan Roman bath, see Swift, *Roman Sources of Christian Art*, 41.

21. Several churches in New Mexico were known to have once had a baptismal font and basin in their sacristy (Domínguez, *Missions of New Mexico*, 77, 156, 157, and passim). The significance of this placement so close to the main altar has not yet been established, although it may have been to prevent the Indians from taking the sanctified water.

22. Bowyer, *Liturgy and Architecture*, 122. Borromeo (*Instrucciones de la fábrica y del ajuar eclesiásticos*, 46) states that the level of the floor should be three steps lower than the main floor, exhibiting "some similarity of a tomb."

23. Just as Jesus and the Apostles were considered fishers of men, so the church and therefore also the nave were considered the ship that transported the faithful to the true way and salvation. Early Christians saw the cross of that ship's mast or anchor as a powerful symbol of their faith.

24. For brief discussion of entirely separate aisles divided into rooms for altars, see "Disguised Aisles" in chapter 3.

25. Seventeenth-century writers tend to identify the area of the crossing, transept, and sanctuary in cruciform churches as the capilla mayor. "Sanctuary" also popularly refers to a pilgrimage church.

26. By the fifteenth century, the usual number of steps was three, possibly to reflect the rank of priest, deacon, and subdeacon as they stood at their respective levels during Mass. O'Connell, *Church Building and Furnishing*, 162–63.

27. Although Borromeo approved of two sacristies for great churches, as did canon law, for economic and practical reasons, even the cathedrals in northern New Spain had only one.

28. Such an extension may reflect the desire of the friar-builders to create an uninterrupted line of wall and roof—or simply to reproduce a structure familiar to these men from their native Mallorca.

29. The church's tabernacle could also be viewed from an auxiliary chapel through a squint or hagioscope, a medieval feature that appears to have been incorporated in at least one seventeenth-century church in northern Arizona, San Bernardo de Awátovi. Montgomery, Smith, and Brew, *Franciscan Awatovi*, 184–85 and fig. 43.

CHAPTER 6

1. Serlio, book 4, esp. folios 3–63; Vitruvius, book 3, pp. 78–97, and book 4, pp. 102–9.

2. Although Manuel González Galván has created three other categories for columns on colonial Mexican churches, only his third category, *estrías móviles* (undulating grooves)—characterized by geometrical ridges along the shafts of columns or pilasters that cause the shafts to lose their rigid characteristic and appear flexible—appears in northern New Spain, and then somewhat timidly. It can be seen on the elongated pyramidal pilasters flanking the window above the side portal of the former mission church of San Francisco Javier (Baja California Sur) and on the columns in the second story of the frontispiece of the Cathedral of Chihuahua. González Galván, "De los fustes barrocos latinoamericanos."

3. Note in figure 2.16b that whereas the columns of the left and central pairs spiral in opposite directions, those of the right pair do not (most likely because the shaft of the rightmost column was installed upside down).

4. For an excellent history of the development of the estípite, including its historical antecedents and its use in the architecture of New Spain, see Villegas, *Gran signo formal del barroco*, 156–57.

5. Durandus (*Symbolism of Churches*, 24) equates piers with bishops and Doctors of the Church, who sustain it by their doctrines: "Although the piers are more in number than seven, yet they are called seven, according to that saying, 'Wisdom hath builded her house, she hath hewn out her seven pillars'" (*Proverbs* 7:1) and "because bishops ought to be filled with sevenfold influences of the Holy Ghost." The capitals of the piers are the opinion of the bishops and Doctors, while the bases are apostolic bishops who support the frame of the whole Church.

6. Guadalupe Toscano considers "nicho" (niche) an unacceptable synonym for "hornacina." She reserves "nicho" for a nichelike form found above doorways on *civil* buildings, in their remates, or most effectively dramatic, on the corners of buildings, usually on the second or third floor or on the parapet. Containing sculpted religious figures, the hornacinas are decorated with columns and

elements inspired by whatever contemporaneous style of architecture was in use at the time. She traces their genesis to early sixteenth-century Spain, when plateresque ornamentation and delicacy of detail was coupled with religious fervor intensified by the Inquisition (Toscano, *Testigos de piedra*, 17–25).

7. Churches lacking pitched roofs and built outside the norms of either baroque or neoclassical architecture did not have pediments; this is especially true of seventeenth- and early-eighteenth-century mission churches such as Santa Rosa de Lima in Cusihuiriáchic and Santa María de las Cuevas (both Chihuahua).

8. Also in Parral, an estampa was once located above eye level on the apse at Nuestra Señora de los Rayos, but it has since been chipped off.

9. Occasionally, as over the choir loft of San Pedro y San Pablo in Tubutama (Sonora) or along the nave of San Javier de Vigge-Biaundó (Baja California Sur), corbels are placed at the spring line of a groin. This purely ornamental type of corbel derives from the Gothic, where it served as a support for ribbing.

10. Reeding and fluting treatments on column or pilaster shafts are also referred to as moldings.

11. William Flinders Petri (*Egyptian Decorative Art*, 10–11) breaks down decoration into four broad categories: (1) geometric ornamentation; (2) naturalistic rendering of plants and animals; (3) structural ornament developing from structural and technical necessities; and (4) symbolic ornament.

12. Whether as monograms, anagrams, or initials having religious significance, lettering was often included on retablos, frontispieces, and keystones (both inside and out). Because the symbolic function of lettering completely eclipsed its decorative role, however, I discuss it separately under the **Letters and monograms** entry in chapter 11.

13. Decorative motifs resembling the pineapple can be found elsewhere in northern New Spain, although the fruit was not introduced into Europe or New Spain until the seventeenth or eighteenth century. Thus "pineapple" motifs in early colonial reliefs or paintings may actually be attempts to depict corn or some other fruit or vegetable.

14. In a study of five Churrigueresque churches in Mexico City, Vargas Lugo divided guardamalletas into those (1) with plant ornamentation (predominant in the churches studied); (2) with geometric forms (present in all the churches studied): (3) with three dangles; (4) with five dangles; (5) with volutes; and (6) with two or more layers superimposed (found in all the churches studied; Vargas Lugo, *Portadas churriguerescas*, 49–51). Because some of the guardamalletas also contain faces of *angelitos* or are perfectly plain with a scalloped edge having only one lobe, I feel other categories such as "human-faced" and "plain" might be included.

CHAPTER 7

1. My special thanks to Federico McAninch, retired curator of the Arizona Historical Society, specialist in Spanish colonial Church matters, and a scholar intimately familiar with Catholic liturgical linens and objects, vestments, and rites in Latin, English, and Spanish, for his invaluable assistance with this and the following two chapters, especially in elucidating certain terms, articles, and vestments no longer in use since Vatican II.

Although Clara Bargellini's notable work *La arquitectura de la plata* considers all of northern New Spain, it focuses on significant, metropolitan, diocesan churches, such as the present-day Cathedrals of Durango, Chihuahua, and Saltillo, and on wealthy parochial churches such as San José in Parral (Chihuahua) and La Purísima Concepción in Sombrerete (Zacatecas).

2. In 1769, for example, Fray Junípero Serra visited eleven former Jesuit missions in Baja California and took with him for the Franciscan missions of Alta California, besides vestments and their accessories, silver chalices, candles, bells, consecrated altar stones, carpets, religious images, and various pieces of fabric to be made into canopies, vestments, altar and casket or catafalque coverings, and veils for an image of the Virgin Mary (Engelhardt, *Missions and Missionaries of California*, vol. 1, pp. 382–88). See also Baegert (*Observations in Lower California*, 124–28), for a description of church ornaments in Baja California. Such redistribution of church furnishings makes it difficult if not impossible to determine with any certainty whether articles found within a given church today were originally intended for that specific site, a situation further complicated by the custom on the part of well-meaning individuals and museums of giving or lending articles to churches, or of simply storing them there—activities about which there exists almost no record.

With the exception of work by Jacinto Quirarte, who used eighteenth- through twentieth-century descriptions and inventories to establish the provenance of furnishings and art objects in several mission churches around San Antonio (Texas), and the surveys by Baer (*Painting and Sculpture at Mission Santa Barbara*), Ivey (*In the Midst of a Loneliness*), and Kessell (*Missions of New Mexico*), very little has been done along these lines (Quirarte, "Decorative and Applied Arts at the Missions," unpublished manuscript, University of Texas at San Antonio, Research Center for the Arts, 1982).

3. Visiting archives, libraries, and research centers in the United States, Mexico, Spain, and England, I examined more than three hundred inventories for churches in every province of northern New Spain and several dozen for comparable churches elsewhere in New Spain. From these, I was able to arrive at a general description of church structures, furnishings, and accoutrements "typical" to northern New Spain; to clarify similarities and differences between the region's mission and diocesan churches; and to categorize the types and qualities of religious art, ecclesiastical garments, and liturgical linens and objects. I have cited specific inventories to illustrate points in chapters 5, 7, 8, and 10. These are listed under "Church Inventories Cited" in "Sources," along with an additional seven, particularly rich and illustrative inventories for churches across northern New Spain (Church inventories 16–22).

4. Tools and equipment listed in most mission inventories can give us a good idea of the range of labor skills (from stock raising and farming to carpentry and masonry, from weaving and spinning

to blacksmithing) available to a given mission complex and, where the inventoried items are described specifically and in detail, of the level of those skills as well (see Leutenegger, "Inventory of the Material Possessions of Mission San José"; see also Coronado, "Misión de San Francisco Xavier Biaundó," esp. 62–63).

5. The richness of Mission San Miguel Arcángel de los Ures before 1767 reflects the wealth of the Jesuit Order and the refined taste of many of its members (see Church inventory 2). After 1767, San Miguel would become the headquarters for Franciscan missionaries, retaining its former holdings and gaining others from former Jesuit mission churches elsewhere in Sonora.

6. Beyond our reach, however, is any real sense of the ephemeral elements that accompanied religious rites and celebrations in northern New Spain, elements such as processional arches (*arcos procesionales*); triumphal cars (*carrozas*); Lenten monuments (*monumentos cuaresmales*); funerary monuments (*túmulos, piras,* or *catafalcos;* sometimes also called *tumbas*); banners (*banderolas* or *estandartes*); floral arrangements; dances; masks; *luminarias* and fireworks; music; temporary and movable altar arrangements; and paper, straw, and tinsel decorations. What little we know comes to us in a few tantalizing written descriptions or an occasional illustration commemorating some extraordinary event or significant individual. On ephemeral religious art and decoration in colonial Mexico (outside of northern New Spain), see Anaya Larios, *Arquitectura efímera de Querétaro*; Díaz, "Fiesta religiosa"; and Martínez Marín, "Pirotecnia."

7. Books found in northern New Spain ranged in quality from inexpensive to luxurious, depending on the importance of the book. They could be covered in paper, parchment, leather, or velvet; their pages could be made from the best, watermarked rag papers (sixteenth through eighteenth centuries) or from the cheapest, most acidic wood pulp (nineteenth century and later). Pages with trimmed edges might be gilt or marbled; endpapers might be marbled as well. It was not uncommon for missal covers to have silver corners and hasps.

The sources of these books also varied. Some came from Spain, of course, but many of the missals and breviaries were produced by the Plantin Press in Antwerp, which had been granted the privilege of printing all the liturgical books for Philip II's realm, and which continued to supply Spanish America with printed material until the early part of the nineteenth century. The books were illustrated by important European artists and engravers, who also produced engravings—and later lithographs—intended for individual framing. These imports would greatly influence the direction of the visual arts in Mexico well into the nineteenth century. Other sources of books were Italy, France, and Germany. Spanish trade restrictions to protect monopolies and to bar the importing of heretical or unauthorized printed material into the New World were circumvented by contraband material from other presses and nations.

New Spain's first printing press, Casa de Juan Cromberger, was established in Mexico City around 1540 by Juan Pablos, a native of Brescia. Although the first publications were religious, these were soon joined by works on philosophy, medicine, and science. When Pablos's monopoly expired in 1558, a number of other printers set up shop in Mexico City, followed by still others in Puebla, which would play an important role in New Spain's printing industry (Woodbridge and Thompson, *Printing in Colonial Spanish America,* 1–12).

8. Despite viceregal rules that forbade galleons from Manila from off-loading any cargo before they reached the official port of entry, Acapulco, inventories of the Baja California missions (and Sonoran missions falling under the same jurisdiction) have a significant number of ceramic, ivory, and brass articles that must have been obtained in this manner. For an engaging look at the galleon trade between New Spain and the Philippines, China, and Japan, see Schurz, *Manila Galleon.*

9. Baegert, *Observations in Lower California,* 127. See Scholes and Adams, *Inventories of Church Furnishings,* 27–38, and Ivey, *In the Midst of a Loneliness,* 209–13, on size, form, and composition of church art imported into New Mexico.

10. Franciscan missionaries were given an annual stipend of 400 pesos, which in cases of extreme exigency might be increased to 500 or 600 pesos. Unlike the missions elsewhere (Jesuit or otherwise), the Jesuit missions of Baja California were financed by a "pious fund," given to the Jesuits for the Christianization of Baja California and begun with donations of money and property from a cofradía in central New Spain and a wealthy priest in Querétaro in 1697. From this fund, each mission was given an initial grant of 10,000 pesos to establish itself. With the Jesuit expulsion in 1767, all Jesuit properties became state property. The pious fund was later used by Franciscans, especially in Alta California (Engelhardt, *Missions and Missionaries of California,* vol. 1, p. 102; Baegert, *Observations in Lower California,* 118–20).

11. Baegert, *Observations in Lower California,* 124–25.

12. See García Sáiz, "Bridge of Imagination," 86–93, quotation on p. 86; see also illustrations on pp. 52–63 and 65.

13. It is at such churches that the greatest concentration of colonial silver in Spain may be found to this day: in western Andalucía (esp. Sevilla, Hueva, and Cádiz); in Cantabria (formerly Santander); in Castilla (esp. Burgos, Palencia, and Valladolid); in Baja Extremadura (esp. Badajoz); in La Rioja, Navarra, and Basque country; in Galicia (esp. Pontevedra); and in the Canary Islands (Esteras Martín, "Mexican Silverwork in Spain," 90–93; see also illustrations on pp. 40–51).

14. Besides the squilla, nola, campana, and signum, Durandus (*Symbolism of Churches,* 77) also lists the *cymbalum,* used in the cloister, and the *nolula* (or double campana), used in the church clock, among his six kinds of church bells.

15. On the origin of the Church tradition of not ringing bells during this part of Passion Week, see Durandus, *Symbolism of Churches,* 195–96.

16. A foundry at Altar (Sonora) that produced bells from the late eighteenth well into the nineteenth century was probably fairly typical for northern New Spain. Bells were being cast in Mexico City by 1531, and perfectly formed and cast bells in all sizes with good voice and tone were being produced by Indian bell founders by 1555 (Carrillo y Gariel, *Campanas de México,* 7–8). Mather (*Colonial Frontiers*) also describes bell making in New Mexico in the late eighteenth century.

17. Salvatierra, *Misión de la Baja California,* 216–17. According to Baegert (*Observations in Lower California,* 121), bells were rung several times a day: for Mass, at three in the afternoon on Friday in remembrance of the mortal agony of Christ, toward sunset for saying the Rosary, and "according to Spanish custom, at eight o'clock in the evening to remind everyone to pray for the dead."

18. See Webb, *Indian Life at the Old Missions,* 31–36; Márquez Morfín, *Sociedad colonial y enfermedad,* 46.

19. The tradition of "baptizing" bells may have begun as early as the seventh century, was certainly performed by the eighth century, and was common by the twelfth (O'Connell, *Church Building and Furnishing,* 127). According to the *Catholic Encyclopedia,* 420–421, such "baptisms," though tolerated, were never officially recognized by the Church.

20. To make it turn over without a bell rope, the bell must first be pushed by someone standing at its edge away from the outward direction of its swing. When the bell swings far enough outward, the yoke can be reached and pushed downward quickly, which causes yoke and bell to turn over. Sacristans and bell ringers using this type of ringing technique throughout Mexico impressed me with how dangerous it was, to say nothing of the discomfort and damage to their ears. Time and time again, I heard of ringers being knocked down or thrown off the tower by the bell or yoke. Bells can, of course, also be rung (or chimed) by means of a bell rope or cable threaded through or hanging alongside the bell tower. Where clappers or bell ropes are broken or missing, I have also seen bells being "rung" by boys standing below and throwing stones at them.

21. Indeed, perhaps as many as one-third of the Spanish colonial church bells I examined in what was once northern New Spain were split. First denied access to the bell towers of Nuestra Señora de Guadalupe in Ojo de Agua (San Luis Potosí) by a sacristan who insisted that the presence of women caused the bells to break, I was later able to examine the towers' bells: two of four were badly split, all had been crudely cast, and wear patterns suggested that all had been consistently clocked.

22. Arrowsmith, *Bells and Bell Founding,* 21–24.

23. Carrillo y Gariel, *Campanas de México,* 11–14. In September 1983 in Jiménez (Chihuahua), I interviewed itinerant bell makers from the state of Hidalgo who had just finished casting three bells at the church site of El Santo Cristo de Burgos. The techniques they, and at least two previous generations of their family, used are principally those described by Carrillo y Gariel and other works on bell founding.

24. Various sources give different proportions; other bells have been found to contain lead, zinc, iron, manganese, and nickel, as well as particles of sand or other impurities (Ramos et al., "Restauración de campanas antiguas").

25. According to the German Jesuit missionary Baegert (*Observations in Lower California,* 125–26), every church on the peninsula of Baja California had no less than three bells, and Loreto, San Javier, and San José de Comondú had seven to nine bells. These bells, he notes, "do not sound badly when they are rung, or to speak more correctly, when they are struck, according to Spanish custom."

26. The technology for casting cannons drew directly on bell founding. Because cannons required bronze of a different composition from that used for bells, however, when bells were melted down to make cannons, as frequently happened in colonial Mexico, unless the proportion of copper to tin was adjusted, the cannons were likely to explode—poetic justice or, to some, evidence of divine wrath.

27. By Church custom, holy liquids must not be disposed of in any manner that allows them to mix with the contents of common drains. Therefore, a separate system, a sacrarium, was developed in the walls or floors of churches whereby used baptismal water and water from washing sacred vessels and linens could be conveyed directly into the ground through special drains. Some baptisteries had drains in their corners. Other sacraria could be found in the font's pedestal, the sanctuary wall, or in a special sink (*piscina,* Latin for reservoir) in the sacristy.

28. Some scholars have traced the Catholic practice of using blessed salt with holy water to the second or third century. It derives from a Jewish purification custom. Salt is also held to symbolize wisdom (Christ called his Apostles "the salt of the earth" in Matthew 5:13 and Luke 14:35) (Sullivan, *Externals of the Catholic Church,* 160). The combination of water and salt symbolizes washing away the stains of sin, quenching the fires of passion, and preserving individuals from relapses into sin.

29. If, for example, an ignorant or careless sacristan were to add more unblessed water than 50 percent by volume, the blessed water would no longer be licit for baptisms according to the Roman Ritual; the priest would then have to prepare and bless more baptismal water (telephone conversation with Federico McAninch, March 1987).

30. An organ, to be made in Mexico City and costing 4,300 pesos, was ordered for the Cathedral of Durango in 1721 (Porras Muñoz, *Iglesia y estado en Nueva Vizcaya,* 174). The new organ may have replaced the one that had been there since at least 1616. Neither of Durango's present organs, however, dates from the viceregal period.

31. Archbishop Alonso de Montúfar, who had called the council, solemnly announced: "The great excess in our archdiocese of musical instruments, of chirimías, flutes, viols, trumpets, and the great number of Indians who spend their time in playing and singing obliges us to apply a remedy and to place a limit on all this superabundance." Trumpets were banned as accompaniment to the liturgy, not to be bought, and relegated to use in outdoor processions; shawms (*chirimías*) and flutes were to be stored and used only during festival days; and viols not to be used at all. The clergy were urged to install organs to establish the organ as the universally correct instrument for use in the churches of New Spain. "We charge all clergy in our archdiocese," the archbishop went on to say, "and all other clergy in [New Spain] . . . to limit the number of singers . . . so that no more than are necessary shall continue to spend the time simply in singing. . . . Those who are permitted to continue must be able to sing plainchant intelligently. They shall sing polyphonic music only when their singing conforms to standards which we consider acceptable." Apparently, these prohibitions and restrictions (promulgated, it seems to me,

more in the interests of freeing up the indigenous labor pool and increasing tax revenues than of propriety or Church dignity) had little effect. Philip II felt obliged to call for them once more in 1561 (Stevenson, *Music in Mexico*, 63–67).

32. Around 1555, the Franciscan friar Toribio de Benavente, known as "Motolinia," wrote of the natives' natural proclivity toward music, their remarkable rapidity in learning to sing and play instruments, and their adeptness at singing and playing. (Motolinia, *Historia de los indios*, 239–42). For a clear sense of the richness and complexity of music performed in the churches of northern New Spain (and elsewhere in colonial Mexico, for that matter), I urge readers to listen to Chanticleer's superb recreation, *Mexican Baroque* (1994), on compact disc.

33. Vetancurt, *Crónica de la provincia*, vol. 4, p. 137, cites an organ, although the Benavides memorials of 1630 and 1634 make no mention of it. But see also Spiess, "Church Music in 17th-Century New Mexico," esp. 15–16.

34. Scholes, "Supply Service of the New Mexico Missions," 103; Benavides, *Revised Memorial of 1634*, 100–3. On all early varieties of the trumpet, notes were produced by the player's lips or with finger holes; valves were not introduced until 1826.

35. On music in the daily life of a northern mission and on the musical role of the missionary, who had not only to supply the musicians with instruments but to repair them when necessary, see Leutenegger and Habig, *Guidelines for a Texas Mission*, 18.

Writing in 1777 on the high quality of the music in Sonora and the natural abilities of native musicians at his Jesuit mission in Cucurpe, Pfefferkorn (*Sonora*, 246–47), reported: "The Marqués de Rubí . . . was surprised by a Salve Regina which . . . two women sang together. Their singing so astonished him that he jumped up in church and told me that never had he heard such glorious voices, not even in Madrid." Baegert (*Observations in Lower California*, 126), found "creditable singing, like beautiful [Loretan] litanies" in some of the mission churches of Baja California, where two priests, one from Bohemia and the other from Italy, had successfully taught choral singing to native congregants.

Benavides, (*Revised Memorial of 1634*, 164), tells us that Father Escobar not only taught the indigenous New Mexicans how to play the instruments but how to make them. Nothing is mentioned concerning the process of making the instruments though. The music of the Californian missions, however, is some of the best documented of any in northern New Spain. Not only did their friars compose music, but in some places they translated church songs into local dialects. Some mission music teachers struck upon the ingenious device of using colored notes in choir books for separate voices. A combination of secular and religious music was played and sung during services; because of the shortage of instruments, guitars, flutes, and violins were made locally (see Ray and Engbeck, *Gloria Dei*, 14; Da Silva, *Mission Music of California*). On the recently discovered presence of highly sophisticated music, composed by outstanding Mexico City composers such as Manuel de Zumaya (ca. 1680–1755) and Ignacio de Jerusalem (ca. 1710–1770), in the missions of Alta California, see Russell, "Mexican Cathedral Music"; Koegel, "Spanish Mission Music from California"; and Summers, "Recently Recovered Manuscript Sources."

36. Because "flute," "horn," "guitar," and the like are about as specific as church inventories of northern New Spain get in describing the musical instruments they list, I also consulted catalogues of European musical instruments during the colonial era. Apart from organs scattered throughout Mexico, for the most part heavily restored or modified or in a very neglected state, pitifully few colonial instruments survive. Representations in colonial paintings and sculpture may be as close a view of these instruments as we are able to get.

37. In the early seventeenth century, Torquemada reported that, on their own, the Indians of New Spain were able to reproduce every instrument except the organ, which, because of its costliness, they were allowed to build only under Spanish supervision. From making instruments and playing them, they progressed to composing skillful music for both instruments and voice (Torquemada, as cited in Stevenson, *Music in Mexico*, 68).

38. Spiess, "Church Music in 17th-Century New Mexico," 16. Judging from Domínguez's 1776 inventories of the New Mexican churches, which list not a single organ, the organs once present there were very likely destroyed during the 1680 Pueblo Revolt and replaced with the other instruments he does list (e.g., violins, guitars, and trumpets).

39. Webb, *Indian Life at the Old Missions*, 251–52. The barrel organs in Alta California, acquired from English and French traders and explorers, are antedated by one inventoried in 1773 at Mission Nuestra Señora de Loreto (Baja California Sur; Díaz, *Arquitectura en el desierto*, 102).

40. "Vihuela" was sometimes used as a generic term for any stringed instrument with a neck, such as a lute, rebec, or guitar. Notwithstanding scant references in the church and mission records on the matter, we can safely assume that at least the more valuable portable instruments were stored under lock and key, very likely in sturdy chests, in church sacristies, or both.

41. Estrada, *Música y músicos de la época virreinal*, 143. Religious services, native celebrations, dances, and other observances at the missions of Alta California (both Christian and pre-Christian) included music made with indigenous whistles, split-stick clappers, rattles, and flutes, although it is uncertain which musical instruments were used.

42. Simple examples of misericords (from Latin, pity or compassion), small carved protuberances under the choir seats upon which weary choristers might rest when the seats were lifted up, may be seen just outside the southern boundary of northern New Spain in the Convento de Nuestra Señora de Guadalupe in Zacatecas (Zacatecas). Dating back to the Middle Ages and found throughout Europe, misericords took fanciful forms and may be seen in some Spanish churches through the Renaissance.

43. O'Connell, *Church Building and Furnishing*, 73. The tabella is probably attributable to Saint Charles Borromeo, who introduced it in 1565 during the first Council of Milan. Having a confessional with compartments on either side of the priest was especially helpful during the Lenten season, when Confession was obligatory and penitents could number in the hundreds. While

the priest was hearing a penitent on one side, a second could be collecting his thoughts on the other (conversation with Federico McAninch, Tucson, Arizona, March 1989).

44. Conversation with Federico McAninch, Tucson, Arizona, May 1988.

45. Matthew 5:1; Durandus, *Symbolism of Churches*, 187.

46. On Spanish court etiquette surrounding the catafalque, traditional symbols used in its design, and physical and economic considerations in its construction during colonial times, see esp. Orso, *Art and Death at the Spanish Habsburg Court*. New Spain most likely followed Spanish traditions.

47. See Kelemen, "Mexican Colonial Catafalque"; and Prado Núñez, *Los túmulos de Santa Prisca*.

48. Although balustrades or railings are also referred to as "rejas," this term should properly be reserved for iron window or door grilles.

49. The frailero, in use by the mid-sixteenth century, and the *barqueño* (an upright cabinet, sometimes portable and other times footed, which appeared at the end of the fifteenth and beginning of the sixteenth centuries (and whose form was influenced by certain pieces of Dutch furniture), are considered two of the most typical Spanish colonial pieces of furniture.

50. Woods available during the viceregal period included cedars, pines, olive, red beech (*haya roja*), oaks, walnut, cherry, ebony, American mahogany, *barbusano* (a member of the laurel family resembling mahogany, from the Canary Islands), *cocobolo* (a species of cocoa tree, much prized by cabinetmakers), *granadillo* (a plentiful, fine-grained red and yellow wood from Cuba, possibly *Dalbergia granadillo*), and jacaranda (Aguiló Paz, *Mueble en España*, 69–74.

51. Sheepskin cushions (*cojines de badana*) were included in the 1801 inventory of the Cathedral of Chihuahua's sanctuary (Bargellini, *Catedral de Chihuahua*, 91).

52. Some of the most frequently used woods were pine, mesquite, cypress, mahogany, and at least three different kinds of "cedar" (Martínez López and Sánchez Martínez, "Estudio sobre la madera"). For inlaying or marquetry, craftsmen used these woods, as well as tortoiseshell; mother-of-pearl; and orange, lime, olive, willow, poplar, oak, and sapodilla, among other woods, to provide different colors and grains for patterns (Loyzaga, "Taracea en México").

53. According to Rule 3576 in *The Congregation of Sacred Rites* (Paris, 1860), the steps of the altar should be covered with a "large and beautiful carpet." Baegert (*Observations in Lower California*, 126) speaks of different carpets in the Jesuit mission churches of Baja California, one for Sunday, one for ordinary days, and another for high holidays. One of the churches even had a rug for the choir.

Inventories of Pimería Alta and Tarahumara missions make frequent mention of *jergas* (literally, coarse woolen cloths) from New Mexico: checkered or twill wool carpets woven in long strips about 3½ feet wide, commonly sewn together to achieve greater widths. Colors were the natural whites and browns of the wool, sometimes with indigo blue. See Minge, "Efectos del País"; and Spillman, "Jergas."

Rugs and carpets imported into the Philippines via India were customary cargo on the Manila galleons, as were Chinese rugs (Schurz, *Manila Galleon*, 32). As used in church inventories, "Berber" (*berber*) or "Berberesque" (*berberisco*) most likely referred to carpets with a knotted and cut pile. Because of the Moorish occupation, Spain was the first European country to import and later to produce knotted rugs of quality, although it is generally felt that with the expulsion of the Moors from Spain during the late fifteenth and the sixteenth centuries, much of the craftsmanship departed with them. Early carpets were adaptations of Middle Eastern geometric motifs, arabesques, inscriptions, and *lacería* (interlacing). Later, carpet decor reflected the influence of velvet and brocade, and included heraldic devices and armorial bearings. Still later, into the seventeenth century, plant and bird motifs were crowded together against rich backgrounds. The largest customers for these carpets were the Church and the Spanish court.

54. Durandus, *Symbolism of Churches*, 60.

55. John 8:12 and Durandus, *Symbolism of Churches*, 27. Although not specifically identified as such, the small lamp in San Jerónimo de Taos that Domínguez (*Missions of New Mexico*, 104) describes as made of leather and sprinkled with mica, with a small basket of artificial flowers suspended from it, was very likely a sanctuary lamp.

56. Oil, representing strength and spiritual activity for the "anointment of the limbs of God's athletes" and symbolizing the priestly power of Christ, was burned in sanctuary lamps. If oil was not available as lamp oil, then the purest beeswax might be substituted.

57. In New Mexico, such sconces, if L-shaped and tin-plated, are called *pantallas*.

58. Durandus (*Symbolism of Churches*, 40–41) considers the steps to the altar as virtues and as stages of spiritual development toward Christ.

The word "Mass" is derived from the Latin words intoned by the priest at the close of the rite—"Ite, missa est" (Go, you are dismissed).

59. The tradition of using stone for the altar stems from the sayings of Saint Paul, who called Christ the "cornerstone" of the Church, and dates from the time of the catacombs, when Mass was said on the tombs of martyrs, which included their relics. By general decree of the Council of Epone (509), no altar could be consecrated except one made of stone. Bingham, *Origines ecclesiasticae*, vol. 1, pp. 301–2.

Although Borromeo (*Instrucciones de la fábrica y del ajuar eclesiásticos*, 32) suggests that an altar stone should be about 14 × 18 inches, my inspection of the empty recesses of portable altars in northern New Spain indicates that generally a smaller, square stone was used. By canon law, the altar stone (ara) is sacred: it must never be left in an open chapel where no priest is in attendance, and it must never be sold. And although the few extant aras with their traveling cases are reported to have neither incised crosses nor a sepulcro for holy relics (see McAndrew, *Open-Air Churches*, 353–59), the original incising, sometimes no more than tracing or light scratching, might well have worn away with years of use, and the sepulcros, which were quite small and could be sealed with rocklike cement, might easily have been overlooked. According to many sixteenth-century sources, hard stones not subject to cracking, scratching, or chipping—such as native onyx, obsidian, and nephrite—were considered the most appropriate candidates for altar stones. The church's main altar stone seldom contained holy relics of the titular saint, which, if present, were instead contained in reliquaries placed on the main altar for special occasions.

60. Mission inventories include numerous aras in various sizes, one for each altar in a given church and others for altars at remote sites served by the priest. The stones were sealed in a coarse linen envelope to keep them clean and unbroken, especially under primitive conditions of transport.

61. Borromeo, as cited in Michael Andrew Chapman, "Liturgical Directions of Saint Charles Borromeo," 64. Bingham, *Origines ecclesiasticae*, vol. 1, p. 303.

62. In Spain, the imposing manifestadores are also called *tabernáculos*, a term that in Mexico is used to describe the far smaller cubicles incorporated into retablos or altars in which the consecrated wafers were safeguarded.

Around the middle of the nineteenth century, Balbas's ciprés was replaced by a neoclassical horror, which subsequently disappeared. The figure of Mary was melted down in 1847 to pay for the new construction (see Toussaint, *Catedral de México*; and Berlin, "Artifices de la catedral de México"). The ciprés Balbas designed for the high altar in the Cathedral of Puebla is still intact, however.

A 1798 description of the Altar of the Kings in the Cathedral of Monterrey reports a "cypress" with twelve Ionic pillars, four on the corners and eight presumably on another, higher stage under the cupola (Zapata Aguilar, *Monterrey*, 58).

63. Also listed in some church inventories were small boxes covered with tortoiseshell (*caray*) and trimmed in silver; these, too, were most likely imported from the Orient and may have been used to store small, fragile valuables.

64. To keep consecrated material from being stepped on, Durandus (*Symbolism of Churches*, 70) suggests disposing of these ashes in the baptistery or in the walls of the church, but gives no indication as to how to accomplish this.

65. The 1739 inventory for San José de Teopari lists a "hostiario de palo" (Church inventory 3). Along with hostiarios, church inventories sometimes also list the scissors used to cut sacramental wafers into bite-sized pieces.

66. Derived from "Mozárabes," the name for Christians under Moorish rule who observed it, the (non-Roman) Mozarabic Rite arose in Spain and in what would later become Portugal in the eighth century; it all but died out in the eleventh century. The Mozarabic wedding rite was transplanted to the New World; and elements survive to this day in Mexico and in Hispanic communities in the United States (see Jenner, "Mozarabic").

67. If olive oil was not available for making holy oils, then another pure vegetable oil could be substituted. Pure oil blessed by a bishop on Holy Thursday was the principal ingredient of the three sacramental holy oils. Holy Chrism (*Sacro Chrismate*), which was mixed with aromatic balsam, was used for baptisms; confirmations; the ordination of priests; and the consecration of churches, chalices, patens, church bells, and other objects directly associated with worship. It signifies the fullness and diffusion of grace. Although Holy Chrism was supposed to be used within a year after its blessing, New Spain was granted a papal allowance extending the time to three years, to accommodate the need to transport it over long distances. And, by an allowance of Pope Paul III (pope 1534–1549), balsam from Peru and Brazil could be substituted for balsam originally imported from Jerusalem. Oil of the Sick (*Oleum Infirmorum*) was used for the Extreme Unction, while Oil of Catechumens (*Oleo Sancto* or *Oleo Catechumenorum*) was used for the blessing of baptismal water, for baptisms, and in ordinations. The initials of these oils were commonly inscribed on the flasks containing them: S.C. or S.Ch., O.I., and O.S. or O.Cat.

68. Although no longer in general use, tenacillos can still be found in a few church silver collections.

Chapter 8

1. According to Anastasius, Pope Silvester I (314–335) ordained that the Eucharist be offered only on a white linen cloth. The Church prescribed the use of bleached linen, partly because of its mystical symbolism and significance, for all white cloth items destined for use in the Eucharist, whether placed on the altar itself (altar cloths, purificator, etc.) or worn by the celebrant and attendant clerics (albs, amices, etc.).

2. Gihr, *Holy Sacrifice of the Mass*, 248. Durandus (*Symbolism of Churches*, 39–49) holds that the whiteness of the altar cloths signifies Christ's body and thus humanity, and their covering the altar, "the joining of the soul to an immortal and incorruptible body."

3. Although cloth, stone, or carved wood frontals were by far the most common, in some of the wealthier communities throughout New Spain, particularly those in important silver-mining and -working areas, such as Chihuahua, San Luis Potosí, and Zacatecas, altar frontals were also made from pieces of embossed, pounded, and engraved silver, sometimes with religious symbols included in the decoration. Thus, in 1730, the wealthy miner Baltasar de Chávez donated a silver frontal to Nuestra Señora del Rosario in Charcas; the Cathedral of Chihuahua had a silver frontal made in Mexico City and donated in 1742 to the altar of Nuestra Señora de los Dolores (Bargellini, *Catedral de Chihuahua*, 49); and the Cathedral of Saltillo has one made about 1750, which can be seen to this day.

Not all the silver frontals were associated with mining centers, however. In his retrospective comments after the Jesuit expulsion in 1767, Baegert (*Observations in Lower California*, 126) describes Nuestra Señora de Loreto (Baja California) as having a silver frontal and tabernacle, then adds ruefully, "if it hasn't been melted down." Indeed, most of the silver frontals and tabernacles and many ecclesiastical treasures would eventually be stripped from the churches in northern New Spain, most likely to be melted down and converted to other forms, probably currency or bullion.

Nineteenth-century photographs of the main altar at San José de la Laguna in New Mexico show a painted altar frontal, a device that may have been used in poorer and more remote churches throughout northern New Spain. Domínguez (*Missions of New Mexico*, 16) describes a frontal constructed on a cardboard framework with embossed paste decoration in San Francisco de la Villa de Santa Fe. Other materials included sculpted, painted, and gilded wood, plaster, and stone.

4. Durandus (*Symbolism of Churches*, 19) refers to the (presumably pink or red) vesperal covers as "Parthian" because "the Parthians first dyed them thus." Parthia was an empire established in the third century BC, lasting five centuries and stretching from India to the Tigris River. It is not known exactly who the Parthians were, although they may well have been Persians.

The badanas encarnadas found in colonial references were very likely red-colored pelts intended as vesperal coverings. One church inventory leaves no doubt, referring to its badana encarnada as a "gamuza [goatskin or chamois] para el altar" (Church inventory 4; see also Church inventory 5).

5. Palias in northern New Spain mission and church inventories included tabernacle veils and covers for caskets, catafalques, or sepulchered sacred figures.

6. Inventories from the Franciscan missions in Sonora after 1769 list large quantities of silver, including lamps, Bible stands, candlesticks, and other liturgical objects, reflecting their having been inherited from the often richly endowed Jesuit missions, which they took over upon the expulsion of the Jesuits in the late eighteenth century. For a beautifully illustrated and written catalogue of the extraordinary exhibition of Mexican silverwork by El Centro Cultural/Arte Contemporáneo, see Martínez Peñaloza et al., *El arte de la platería mexicana*.

7. Gihr, *Holy Sacrifice of the Mass*, 251–52. Although it appeared only on processional crosses and was not part of the altar furnishings until the fourteenth century, the crucifix became obligatory on the altar during Mass as a result of Spanish influence upon the Counter-Reformation movement.

8. The Christ figure underwent changes through the centuries. After the ninth century, Christ's full garment was exchanged for a loincloth. He was shown as a living figure through the tenth century, and in the twelfth, three nails replaced the four (Norris, *Church Vestments*, 131–32).

9. In viceregal documents, *candelabro*, *portacirio*, and *candelero* were used to designate any candleholder, whether single or multiple. Currently, *candelabro* and *candelero* signify "candelabrum" and (single) "candlestick," respectively.

10. Neither centilleros nor tenebrarios were listed in the two hundred-plus inventories of mission churches of northern New Spain that I examined, very likely because the missions could not afford them or, in the case of tenebrarios, because the Tenebrae service was not performed publicly.

11. The three most important silver-working cities of New Spain were Mexico City, Zacatecas, and Puebla, although there probably were silversmiths producing competent work in every major town, especially those associated with silver mining such as Chihuahua, Durango, San Luis Potosí, Sombrerete, Taxco, and Álamos. Silversmiths were also active in the far reaches of New Spain, such as at Santa Fe (New Mexico), during this period (Boylan, *Spanish Colonial Silver*, 22). Esteras Martín (*Mexican Silverwork in Spain*) considers several Mexican pieces from the sixteenth, seventeenth, eighteenth, and nineteenth centuries that were specially made for specific churches in Spain. These and other examples from throughout New Spain demonstrate the superior technique, workmanship, and artistic merit of silverwork in the region.

Although large quantities of liturgical objects made from silver are listed in church inventories, the provenance of their manufacture or donors is seldom mentioned. Not surprisingly, the greatest amounts were to be found in former Jesuit churches; articles were listed by weight in inventories after the Jesuit expulsion in 1767 (see, for example, Church inventory 6).

Two examples of enamelwork are a (no longer extant) chalice at San Felipe Neri in Albuquerque (New Mexico), described by Domínguez (*Missions of New Mexico*, 163), as "completely enameled and with twelve blue stones," and a particularly beautiful monstrance made in Zacatecas in 1662, enameled throughout in elliptical cabochons, illustrated by Esteras Martín, 40–51.

12. According to Gihr (*Holy Sacrifice of the Mass*, 260), the paten harked back to the Old Testament plates of precious metal, upon which, as directed by God, gifts of wheaten meal were to be brought to the altar; as the immediate and actual bearer of the Sacred Host, it represented the tree of the Cross upon which Christ was crucified.

13. Missals included church music along with liturgical materials; their engraved illustrations may have inspired local artists. The *Missale Romanum*, published by Saint Pius V in 1570 and revised a number of times since then, is the most frequently mentioned missal in northern New Spain's church inventories. The early Franciscans did much to spread its use at a time when a great many dioceses had their own missals.

14. The central and largest card usually contained the Gloria, the Credo, the Offertory prayers for both the bread and the wine, the solemn words of consecrations, and certain other parts of the Mass as well. The card on the Epistle side of the altar contained two prayers that were recited there, the first when a few drops of water were poured into the chalice and the second when the priest washed his fingers (the Lavabo prayer: "Among the innocent will I wash my hands" from Psalms 25:6). The card on the Gospel side presented words from the first chapter of John, the last Gospel reading of the Mass.

15. Fray Domínguez (*Missions of New Mexico*, 222–33) lists 256 different books, in Latin and Spanish, all religious, at Mission Santo Domingo (New Mexico). In inventories of Jesuit properties in Baja California, besides the expected missals; Bibles; and books of sermons, saints, and religious practices; there were books on medicinal plants and Indian languages and a "how to" book on surgery. The collection at Mission Loreto in the capital of the province contained 195 titles, together with a history of the mission from its founding until 1770 (see Church inventory 7). Among books of "the kind one likes to read several times, because they are important companions in such complete isola-

tion," Father Baegert (*Observations in Lower California*, xviii–xix) included books by Pierre Daniel Hurt, known for his writings on Descartes, and by "some good new French historians, Bossuet, and above all some poetry, comedies, dramas and the like."

16. La Purísima Concepción in Movas (Sonora) had a bronze lectern (Church inventory 8). San Ildefonso de Yécora (Sonora) had a lacquered missal stand from Michoacán. Other colonial lecterns of the ledger variety, made from gilded wood, tinplate, and silver, are scattered throughout northern New Spain, and may be seen in storage rooms or displayed in museums.

17. María del Pilar Bertos Herrera (*Tema de la eucaristía*, vol. 1, pp. 277–79) distinguishes eight different types of monstrances found in Spain: (1) tower-shaped (*turriforme*)—describing a large monstrance used in processionals from the earliest years of the Conquest or Reconquest; (2) reliquary (ciprés)—having a circular opening in the front and back and divided into two types: hand-carried tower and retablo reliquary, the principal difference being their decoration; (3) cross—being divided into two types: one placing the figure of Christ in the center of the cross and the other placing the glass enclosure for the Host in the upper part of the cross; (4) image—generally placing the glass enclosure (viril) within the torso of an image of Christ, Mary, angels, and the dove of the Holy Spirit; (5) ciborium—having, for reasons of economy in churches of modest means, the glass enclosure on top of the lid of the ciborium (this type quickly came to signify Christ's sepulcher); (6) chalice—being crowned on the upper part with the figure of Christ, similar to the ciborium monstrance but without its improvised character; (7) branched—having a two-branched, trunk-shaped handle to hold the glass enclosure, which was crowned with angels; and (8) sun (*custodia del sol* or *viril con rayas*)—having a radiating disk around two pieces of glass on a pedestal with a spreading base. Not every type of monstrance was imported into or imitated in northern New Spain, where church inventories most often listed monstrances of the sun type.

18. Bertos Herrera, *Tema de la eucaristía*, 279–80. Bertos Herrera refers to the pyx as "porta viático" rather than "pixide."

19. The exception being the archiepiscopal cross, whose crucifix was turned toward the archbishop following it.

20. The aspergillum derives its name from "Asperges me, Domine, hyssopo et mundabor" (Thou shalt sprinkle me with hyssop, O Lord, and I shall be cleaned), the Latin phrasing of Psalms 51:7.

21. Included among the Cathedral of Tucson's effects was a large, worn clamshell, said to have been used for baptisms for as long as anyone could remember. Conversation with Federico McAninch, Tucson, Arizona, December 1991.

22. The naveta ("little ship") form is derived from the *nef*, a ship-shaped container, usually made of silver, that was used in the later Middle Ages as a holder for the Lord's napkin, spoon, and knife. The size of the naveta and its nautical decoration were severely altered in order for it to serve as a liturgical item; while its body shape suggested a ship's hull, it was about the size of a large sugar bowl.

Chapter 9

1. All descriptions of vestments and accoutrements refer to the Spanish colonial era unless otherwise noted.

2. Other Church positions included various assistants to a bishop: provisor, vicar, visitor general, vicar general, and governor. Thus, a bishop might appoint a provisor to assist him in nonsacramental matters; a vicar, often a parish priest, to serve as judge in local ecclesiastical courts; a visitor general to visit and inspect churches in his diocese; a vicar general, who shared the bishop's judicial authority, and who, unlike the bishop, was supposed to have had advanced training in canon law and preferably also civil law, to enforce canon law; and a governor, to serve as acting bishop in his absence or if he were incapacitated. For a detailed description of the duties of these and other Church positions, see Schwaller, *Church and Clergy in Sixteenth-Century Mexico*.

3. In colonial mission documents, however, "acolytes" (*acólitos*) refers to choir or altar boys, who might be vested in robes similar to priests' cassocks.

4. The word from the New Testament translated as "priest" is *hiereus*, meaning "one whose function is to offer a sacrifice."

5. "Habit" refers to the distinctive clothing worn by religious orders and congregations of monks, friars, and nuns (illustrated in figs. 9.2–9.6). "Crosier" is often erroneously applied to the archiepiscopal cross, which surmounts the archbishop's pastoral staff.

6. Norris, *Church Vestments*, 5. In its original sense of "overseer," "bishop" appears several times in the New Testament. See, for example, 1 Peter 2:25 and 1 Timothy 3:1.

7. The habit of a given order could also vary from country to country, area to area, and even community to community, as can be clearly seen in paintings and engravings of contemporaneous subjects. Such variations arose chiefly from differences in climate, available material, and interpretation of the order's habit.

8. The tradition of wearing short hair dates from the earliest years of Christianity, the result of Saint Paul's enjoining Christians to austerity. In the early days of the Church, slaves' heads were shaven, as were the heads of Christians condemned to the mines, according to Saint Cyprian. Early monks, penitents, and the primitive hermits of Egypt therefore adopted the tonsure as a symbol of mourning and penance. Later, around the end of the fifth and beginning of the sixth centuries, the diocesan clergy adopted the custom. To distinguish themselves from penitents and monks, however, their tonsure was reduced to the size of a sacramental wafer (or even smaller). First bestowed at a ceremony presided over by a bishop or his delegate, the tonsure marked a layman's entrance into the clerical state. (Tixeront, *Holy Orders and Ordination*, 133–37).

9. Engelhardt, *Missions and Missionaries of California*, vol. 1, p. 81.

10. The collective name "brothers" refers to men belonging to religious orders. "Lay brothers" are members of religious orders or congregations who choose not to become ordained priests.

11. For a handsome and highly informative lithograph of nuns from different religious orders in New Spain, clearly show-

ing their respective habits, see Riva Palacio, *México a través de los siglos*, vol. 2, p. 712. (A similar lithograph showing men's habits appears on p. 710.) See also Muriel de la Torre and Romero de Terreros, *Retratos de monjas*; and Muriel de la Torre, "Role of Convents in Colonial Mexico," esp. illustration on p. 8. For women in religious life, see Arenal and Schlau, *Untold Sisters*, and Paz, *Sor Juana*. On particular convents and some of their illustrious members, see Muriel's classic *Conventos de monjas*.

12. On the hierarchy, duties, and career patterns of secular clergy during the first century of colonial Mexico, see esp. Schwaller, *Church and Clergy in Sixteenth-Century Mexico*. Also helpful in understanding the Church's hierarchy, property, and secular and regular priesthood, as well as its orders and episcopal organization, is Norrington, "Beginning of the Church in Mexico."

13. Rodríguez Flores, *Historia del real de minas de Sombrerete*, 130–32.

14. Basalenque and Moreno García, *Agustinos*, 244. The chapel, San Agustín, still stands and now serves as a parochial church.

15. Ray and Engbeck, *Gloria Dei*, 14.

16. According to Carrillo y Gariel (*Traje en la Nueva España*, 190), the insignia of the Dominicans also appears stamped in black on the habit, although I have never seen this in Spanish colonial engravings, paintings, or sculptures.

17. Saint Bernardine of Siena was reported to have observed, "Even as [Saint Francis] bore Christ Jesus crucified within his heart, so he wished to wear the Cross as his habit, for love of Him" (Origo, *World of San Bernardino*, 20).

18. In clearly noting the blue of the habits, Isidro Félix de Espinosa (*Crónica de los colegios*, vol. 2, p. 95) attributes it to difficulty in obtaining the correct materials. Other explanations range from the desire of New Spain's Franciscans to honor the Virgin by wearing her color to the more prosaic observation that indigo was the most common dye available to the sixteenth- and seventeenth-century missionaries of all orders in New Spain. (Franciscans rewove their robes from discarded cloth remnants and then ostensibly dyed the rewoven garments with indigo to give them an even appearance.)

The Franciscans were early promoters of devotion to the Virgin Mary and champions of the doctrine of the Immaculate Conception. Franciscans in Spain wore blue as early as the sixteenth century, perhaps as the outward symbol of their struggle with the Dominicans regarding this theological matter (see also Baird, *Retablos del siglo XVII*, 39).

19. Saravia, *Obras*, vol. 1, 176, 177.

20. Engelhardt, *Missions and Missionaries of California*, vol. 1, p. 83.

21. Muriel de la Torre, *Hospitales de la Nueva España*, pp. 69–77.

22. Personal communication, Charles W. Polzer, SJ, January 2002.

23. Ignatius's "twelfth rule of the discernment of spirits" reads: "The enemy [the Devil] conducts himself as a woman. He is a weakling before a show of strength, and a tyrant if he has his will. It is a characteristic of a woman in a quarrel with a man to lose courage and take to flight if the man shows that he is determined and fearless. However, if the man loses courage and begins to flee, the anger, vindictiveness, and rage of the woman surge up and know no bounds. In the same way, the enemy becomes weak, loses courage, and turns to flight with his seductions as soon as one leading a spiritual life faces his temptations boldly, and does exactly the opposite of what he suggests. However, if one begins to be afraid and to lose courage in temptation, no wild animal on earth can be more fierce than the enemy of our human nature. He will carry out his perverse intentions with consummate malice" (Ignatius of Loyola, *Spiritual Exercises of Saint Ignatius*, 145).

24. "The function of liturgical vestments is said to be twofold: to act as an insignia designating the diversity of liturgical ministries, and to contribute to the dignity of the rite itself" (Mayer-Thurman, *Raiment for the Lord's Service*, 13).

In church records of New Spain, *terno* (literally, suit of clothes) refers to the vestments worn by celebrants of a High or pontifical Mass—chasuble, two dalmatics, cope, humeral veil, three stoles, and two maniples—made from the same material, with matching trim.

25. The increasingly complex structure and internal organization of early Christianity and the subsequent development of complex rules and ritual ceremonies served to elevate the importance of vestments. This development, when combined with the universal belief in the mystical nature of kingship (Christ, the King), made it appropriate, indeed imperative, that assistants and administrators be dressed in garments that matched the solemnity and grandeur of their sovereign.

26. Uses of various articles of ecclesiastical clothing have changed since the early nineteenth century and may vary slightly from country to country.

27. Church inventories 9 and 10.

28. "Ornamentos" can also refer to other types of embroidered or worked pieces of fabric, including gremial veils and altar frontals.

29. Albs decorated with apparels began to disappear with the introduction of lace at the start of the sixteenth century, with lace completely replacing apparels in the seventeenth and eighteenth century (Mayer-Thurman, *Raiment for the Lord's Service*, 26).

30. Norris, *Church Vestments*, 18.

31. For beautiful illustrations and excellent text on the history and art of silk in Mexico, see María y Campos and Castelló Yturbide, *Historia y arte de la seda en México*, and Armella de Aspe and Tovar de Teresa, *Bordados y bordadores*.

32. "Cáligas" also refers to studded sandals used by the soldiers of ancient Rome, as well as to leather ankle-length boots used by monks in the Middle Ages.

33. Alternatively, "chasuble" may derive from Latin *casulla* (literally, little house), a large cape that completely covered the wearer, with an opening in the center for the head.

34. Ecclesiastical vestments and liturgical objects from the churches of northern New Spain are available for public viewing at San Luis Rey in Oceanside, San Gabriel Arcángel in San Gabriel, and San Carlos Borromeo in Carmel (all California); San Xavier

del Bac in Tucson (Arizona); Nuestra Señora de Loreto (Baja California Sur); and San Ignacio de Cabórica (Sonora).

35. Since about the middle of the last century, "scapular" also designates a devotional item consisting of small pieces of cloth, measured in inches, joined by strings front and back and worn under everyday clothes as badges of a confraternity with indulgences conferred on those wearing them. There are specific ecclesiastical regulations concerning their size, color, and manner of use and each has several indulgences granted to it (Sullivan, *Externals of the Catholic Church*, 191–204). See also Hilgers, "Scapular."

36. Underwear (*paños menores*) listed in accounts of mission supplies for San José y San Miguel de Aguayo in San Antonio (Texas), and assumed to be for the missionary, was apparently made from cotton or linen: it is described as "de Languin" (a medium-grade cotton fabric) and "bramante" (Brabant linen, a fabric from Brabant, now part of Belgium). Leutenegger and Habig, *Guidelines for a Texas Mission*, 16, 34.

37. The number of tassels on the cardinal's hat was finally fixed (on each side) by the Sacred Congregation of Ceremonies in 1823 (Heim, *Heraldry in the Catholic Church*, 69). Made part of the official vestments by Innocent IV in 1245, the cardinal's red hat with thirty tassels was abolished in 1969 and replaced by a simple red cap.

38. Norris, *Church Vestments*, 137. The right to wear a pectoral cross was granted to cardinals only at the beginning of the twentieth century; during the colonial era, cardinals properly should not be shown with one.

39. After the alleged discovery of the True Cross by Saint Helen in 326, the use of a pectoral cross spread to the laity, with men and women wearing crosses having purported fragments of the holy relic (Norris, *Church Vestments*, 135).

40. Called "the Fisherman's Ring," the pontifical ring worn by a pope was engraved with a scene of Peter pulling in nets, the pope's name, and his number of succession since Saint Peter; it was used as his seal and destroyed at his death.

Chapter 10

1. A recurrent theme throughout this book is the shameful loss of so much superb colonial artwork through heavy-handed restoration or remodeling, or what my friend and colleague Jorge Olvera has called "barbaric renewal," such as happened at the Cathedral of Durango (1841–44) and the Cathedral of Chihuahua (1930 and 1939–40). As with façades, only retablos in a few of the most remote churches would escape this process, often leaving us with little more than a casual mention of a painting or sculpture in a church inventory—and no mention at all of how a particular work was produced.

2. Durandus, *Symbolism of Churches*, 42.

3. Bingham, *Origines ecclesiasticae*, vol. 1, pp. 321–23.

4. *Catholic Encyclopedia*, vol. 14, p. 533. Even though the second Council of Nicaea in 787 had supported the use of religious images, they had been widely and vehemently opposed by members of the Church hierarchy in the ninth century. The Church officially found in favor of the images once again in 850, but it was not until seven centuries later, in 1563, that the use and type of images and their relationship to Catholic dogma were codified by the Council of Trent, largely in defense of Mary and the saints against attacks by the Protestant Reformation.

5. Rubial García, *Convento agustino y la sociedad novohispana*, 230.

6. Yvonne M. Lange and Richard E. Alhorn's *Mission San Xavier del Bac* offers the reader identification and analysis of their appearance and placement.

7. Because of the portability of the statues, their arrangement in niches may have been changed from their original and intended placement over the centuries. Care must therefore be taken in ascribing significance to their order or lack thereof.

8. Missing are scenes that depict the finding of Jesus in the temple (the fifth Joyful Mystery), his Resurrection (the first Glorious Mystery), and the Assumption of the Virgin Mary (the fourth Glorious Mystery).

9. For more on the significance of skin color in the church art of northern New Spain, see discussion of Juan Correa under "Painters" in this chapter and "Our Lady of Guadalupe (Nuestra Señora de Guadalupe)" in chapter 12.

10. Pacheco, *Arte de la pintura*, vol. 2, pp. 212–19, 236. Translation mine.

11. Ramírez Leyva, "Censura inquisitorial novohispana."

12. An earlier, short-lived academy to teach painting was begun in 1753 in Mexico City. Among its instructors were four of the most celebrated painters of the mid-eighteenth century, Miguel Cabrera, José de Ibarra, Fray Miguel de Herrera, and José de Alcíbar. The academy was chiefly intended to confer certain privileges on its members (only Spaniards were admitted) under hoped-for royal patronage rather than to improve viceregal painting; it expired with its prime mover, José de Ibarra, in 1756 (Moyssén, "Grabado en la Nueva España").

13. Charlot, *Mexican Art and the Academy of San Carlos*.

14. Carrera Stampa, *Gremios mexicanos*, 204, 233.

15. Cornelius, "Restoration Notes on Certain Spanish Colonial Paintings." Caution must be exercised in ascribing authorship in many cases, and particularly where Cabrera's works are involved. His style was widely imitated and his signature applied to perhaps hundreds of paintings not from his brush or even necessarily from his prolific workshop.

16. Armella de Aspe and Meade de Angulo, *Tesoros de la pinacoteca virreinal*, 107; Kino, *Kino's Historical Memoir of the Pimería Alta*, vol. 1, p. 272.

17. The Jesuit missionary Martin de Benavides ordered paintings of saints by Correa for Santa Teresa de Guazapares, a Tarahumara mission church (as was Los Cincos Señores de Cuzárare); it is not known whether he ever received them, and if he did, what became of them (Benavides, "Memorias," AGN, Jes. I-14).

18. Vargas Lugo and Victoria, *Juan Correa*, vol. 2, part 1, p. 114; see also Domínguez, *Missions of New Mexico*, 133, 210. Besides this painting, Domínguez specifies throughout his text other paintings paid for by the crown.

19. Vargas Lugo, "Niños de color 'quemado" en la pintura de Juan Correa," in *Estudio de pintura colonial hispanoamericana.* See also the discussion of medallion images of four nun saints under "San Xavier de Bac" in this chapter.

20. For illuminating and thoughtful looks at art from the traditional studios, see Vargas Lugo, "Expresión pictórico religiosa" and "Una aproximación al estudio del retrato" in *Estudio de pintura colonial Hispanoamérica.*

21. For a thorough discussion of oil and tempera paints, mediums, and varnishes, see Mayer, *Artist's Handbook,* 118–279.

22. In the buon fresco technique, paints were applied to a freshly plastered and damp wall laid up in sections only as large as the artist could paint before the plaster dried. Because pigments were absorbed into the wet plaster, the colors of buon fresco maintained their brilliance over a surprising length of time. Seldom used even in central and southern New Spain, the technique was apparently never used in northern New Spain.

Absent costly scientific analysis, it is impossible to say with any certainty which of the original (non-oil) wall paintings extant in northern New Spain are fresco secco and which are tempera. Although the paintings in the squinches and sanctuary of San José de Tumacácori (Arizona), in the naves of San Diego de Alcalá at Pitiquito and La Purísima Concepción at Caborca (both Sonora) and in the sacristy of La Purísima Concepción in San Antonio (Texas) appear to be fresco secco, their delicate appearance may instead be the result of deterioration of tempera paint over the centuries. On the other hand, where the colors of original wall paintings remain robust and seem to be opaque, as in the mission churches of Alta California, in San Pedro y San Pablo in Tubutama (Sonora), and in San Xavier del Bac in Tucson (Arizona), they are very likely tempera.

23. On wall paintings, see, for example, Artigas H., *Piel de la arquitectura;* Arrendondo, Gurría Lacroix, and Reyes Valerio, *Juan Gerson Tlacuilo de Tecamachalco;* and Reyes Valerio, *Pintor de conventos.*

24. Attributed to an individual known only as "the Laguna Santero," the painted dossal was completed between 1800 and 1808 (Kessell, *Missions of New Mexico,* 187–92).

25. Paintings on tinplate are largely a mid-nineteenth-century, central Mexican phenomenon; for more information, see Giffords, *Mexican Folk Retablos.*

26. See Huerta Carrillo, "Una técnica del siglo XVI en pintura sobre tabla."

27. Victoria, *Pintura y sociedad en Nueva España,* 58; Toussaint, *Pintura colonial en México,* 17.

28. The gilders' and painters' ordinances of 1557 stipulate that painted images for sale were to be painted on new linen, cut from the bolt, a requirement presumably intended to protect the public, but one that also ensured a demand for new, unused material (Barrio Lorenzot, *Ordenanzas de gremios de la Nueva España,* 20). However, despite ordinances mandating that they use only Castilian linen canvas, colonial artists not only reused old canvases, but they also painted on less expensive canvases made in New Spain from hemp or a mixture of hemp and linen. Handwoven until the arrival of mechanical looms in the late eighteenth century, domestic canvases were characterized by the unevenness of their threads.

29. The use of red-brown toning throughout Renaissance and baroque art may well be a carryover from the medieval and Gothic technique of gold leafing on a red bole background in panel paintings and the later technique of painting light on dark.

30. On varnishes in colonial paintings, see Arcelus de Diego, *Estudio de los barnices en la pintura colonial;* and Carrillo y Gariel, *Técnica de la pintura de Nueva España.*

31. Hackett, *Historical Documents Relating to New Mexico,* vol. 3, p. 264.

32. Boyd, *Popular Arts of Spanish New Mexico,* 122, 130–43. Although Domínguez tells us little of his feelings for these pieces, he certainly does not condemn them. In the nineteenth century, other churchmen would outright reject their crude or folksy quality. We can see this in the visitation reports of de Quevara y Zureria and in a pastoral letter of the bishop of Durango that ordered the removal of paintings on animal hides (as well as the locally made wooden retablos)—both in the early nineteenth century. During his tenure in the mid-nineteenth century, Bishop Lamy expressed his disapproval of all forms of religious folk art; his desire to infuse the aesthetic of European art traditions into the churches accounts for the removal and destruction of many pieces.

33. Wroth, *Images of Penance, Images of Mercy,* 47–50.

34. For an exhaustive study of oil painting on copper, see Phoenix Art Museum, *Copper as Canvas,* and esp. Horovitz's essay therein, "Materials and Techniques of European Paintings on Copper Supports." That European techniques were transplanted to New Spain via Spain is abundantly clear in the technical and aesthetic similarity of the many Mexican, Spanish, German, and Dutch paintings on copper I have examined.

The small images of Saint Vincent Ferrer and Saint Nicholas of Tolentino flanking a sculpted image of Christ crucified that once graced the retablo of the Calvary altar at the (now obliterated) mission church of Nuestra Señora del Refugio (Texas) were perhaps typical of religious images painted on yet another support—glass; as far as I can determine, however, such images were extremely rare throughout New Spain (see Church inventory 11).

35. Reyes Valerio, *Pintor de conventos;* Arrendondo, Gurría Lacroix, and Reyes Valerio, *Juan Gerson Tlacuilo de Tecamachalco;* and Kubler, *Mexican Architecture in the Sixteenth Century,* vol. 2, pp. 372–76. On estampas as carved stone decorations on the exterior of churches, see "Outside Walls" under "Architectural Details" in chapter 6.

36. Hackett, *Historical Documents Relating to New Mexico,* 264, documents the use of engraved materials in New Mexico, reporting that an Indian artist there stated in 1665 that he wished to borrow a Bible to copy some medallions and that he had done this before.

37. Lange, "Lithography"; Neuerburg, "Function of Prints in the California Missions." The fourteen estampas listed in the 1796 inventory of Nuestra Señora del Pilar de Norogachic

(Chihuahua) were very likely depictions of the Stations of the Cross (Church inventory 12).

38. In her *Sculpture in the Kingdom of Quito*, Gabrielle Palmer connects Spanish sculpture with its counterpart in Ecuador in ways that apply to the sculpture of New Spain as well.

39. For analyses of materials and techniques of specific pieces of gilded and polychrome statuary and ordinances pertinent to such statuary, see Maquivar's excellent *Imaginero novohispano y su obra*.

40. Alarcón Cedillo and Lutteroth, *Tecnología de la obra*, 48. On religious sculptures made from woods native to the north, see esp. Wroth, *Christian Images in Hispanic New Mexico*.

41. On New Mexican bultos, see José E. Espinosa, *Saints in the Valleys*, 52–60.

42. "Embón" (literally, sheath) is also used by Mexican authors to describe a sculpted skirt that appears hollow or fluffed out, as if there were a number of skirts or crinoline petticoats underneath.

43. González Tirado, "Tzauhtl," 15; Moyssén, "Escultura de pasta de caña," 23–24.

44. The Purépechas of Michoacán carried images of their gods into battle to protect and assure themselves of victory. Made of cane, the images were lightweight so the Purépechas could easily flee with them if needed. María del Consuelo Maquivar, "Escultura devocional," 308. The first Catholic image from the corn and orchid mixture, Nuestra Señora de la Salud de Patzcuaro, may have been made on the orders of Vasco de Quiroga in 1538. This figure has been revered in the Michoacán area since the early sixteenth century.

45. See Domínguez, *Missions of New Mexico*, 162, 205; and Scholes and Adams, *Inventories of Church Furnishings*, 32.

46. Estrada Jasso, *Imágenes en caña de maíz*, 26; Carrillo y Gariel, *Cristo de Mexicalzingo*, 16; and Araujo Suárez, Huerta Carrillo, and Guerrero Bolan, "Esculturas de papel."

47. In "The Cornstalk Images of Michoacán," Enrique Luft quotes a source that says a poisonous plant (*flor de tijerilla*) was included in these pith sculptures to make them resistant to insect damage.

48. Bonavit, "Esculturas tarascas de caña de maíz y orquídeas."

49. Considering that many important Marian images are clothed over their original sculptured garments, this order was apparently ignored. In a particular example from northern New Spain, the carved garments of the figure called "La Conquistadora" in the Cathedral of Santa Fe (New Mexico) were deliberately chiseled off and the image hinged at the arms, then dressed in cloth garments. The figure's wardrobe and jewelry were carefully listed in inventories for more than two centuries (Chávez, *Our Lady of Conquest*, 55–67). In his 1776 inventory, Domínguez includes the names of the donors of some of her clothing and jewelry (*Missions of New Mexico*, 24, 26).

50. Villar Movellán, "Santos travestidos."

51. Although we do not know what parishioners in San Xavier thought of this practice of changing the figure of Christ into the reclining figure of San Xavier, Francisco de la Maza relates how two mystic nuns were rebuked by Mary, who appeared to them as they attempted to transform a statue of her called "La Incorporada" into a figure of Saint Gertrude. "Cómo? Me dejas por Santa Gertrudis?" (What? You are leaving me for Saint Gertrude?), the obviously vexed Virgin was reported to have said (Maza, *Catarina de San Juan*, 24).

52. An ivory image of Saint Michael is listed in the 1743 inventory of San Miguel Arcángel de los Ures (Sonora; Church inventory 2); an ivory crucifix with silver caps, in a (ca. 1737) inventory of a church in Bacanora (also Sonora; Church inventory 13). Figures described as bone may actually have been ivory. On the ivory figures imported into New Spain from Spain and Portugal, see Sada de González and Estella Marcos, *Ivories from the Far Eastern Provinces*.

53. Sánchez Navarro de Pintado, *Marfiles cristianos del Oriente en México*, 119–21. Although there were no specific guilds or standards of quality for it, ivory was worked in New Spain from the sixteenth through the eighteenth centuries in association with the manufacture of inlaid furniture, frames, crosses, and the like. A few signed seventeenth-century religious sculptures testify to the presence there of ivory sculptors of great skill.

54. Willetts, *Chinese Art*, 32.

55. Sometimes called missionary crosses, these small crucifixes were thought to have been distributed among the Indians by missionaries; identical pieces with no missionary association, however, may be found throughout Mexico, dating into the early twentieth century.

56. For an appreciation of the charm and versatility of wax as an artistic medium and the artistry of Mexican wax workers, see Esparza Liberal and Fernández de García-Lascurain, *Cera en México*.

57. Thurston, "Agnus Dei"; and Quintana, *Agnus Dei de cera*, 12.

58. Pacheco, *Arte de la pintura*, see esp. vol. 2, pp. 99–121.

59. Alfaro, "Óyeme con los ojos."

60. A small ivory image of Mary described in a 1774 inventory of San José del Cabo (Baja California Sur) had been given a gold peso for a halo (Church inventory 14).

61. In particular, see the inventories of articles relating to La Conquistadora in Chávez, *Our Lady of Conquest*, 55–95.

62. In his 1783 inventory of San Miguel de Sahuaripa (Sonora), Fray Pedro de la Cueva lists necklaces, a rosary, and possibly a brooch or pin, all made from white pearls of different sizes, as among the ornaments and jewelry given a figure of the Christ Child (Church inventory 15).

63. Specifically, among other jewelry belonging to La Conquistadora, Domínguez (*Missions of New Mexico*, 26) records nine silver-gilt and fourteen plain silver reliquaries in his 1776 inventory. He not only describes the objects, but notes the names of some of the donors. Other examples abound in Baja California and Sonora. See also Egan, *Relicarios*, 41.

64. Also listed in church inventories as "relicarios," or more precisely as "relicarios auténticos," were actual relics. These were embedded in or mounted on various articles placed on gradines or altar shelves for display (see Church inventories 2, 4, 7).

65. See Egan, *Milagros*; Montenegro, *Retablos de México*; and Giffords, *Mexican Folk Retablos* and *Art of Private Devotion*.

66. *Retablos de culto callejeros* (or simply, *retablos callejeros*), two- and three-dimensional religious images mounted on exterior walls or corners or recessed in niches facing the street in Spain, particularly in Sevilla, created sacred spaces for passers-by, bearing witness to the presence of the Catholic Church (which they do to this day; see Fernández de Paz, *Religiosidad popular sevillana*). *Hornacinas*, small niches housing three-dimensional religious images and incorporated into cornices and corners of buildings high above the street, particularly in Mexico City, are a transplanted variant of the retablos callejeros and serve much the same purpose (see Toscano, *Testigos de piedra*).

67. Berg-Sobré (*Behind the Altar Table*, 3–5) traces the immediate antecedents of retablos to decorated altar frontals and painted apse murals; elsewhere in her text, she provides detailed descriptions of materials and techniques used in making retablos. On the background and history of the retablo, see Braun, *Der christliche Altar*, and Jungmann, *Mass of the Roman Rite*. See also discussion of retablos exteriores in "Façades, Frontispieces, Portals" under "Outer Body" in chapter 5.

68. Hardison clearly establishes the role of the retablo as a literal backdrop in his "Essay II."

69. After the expulsion of the Jesuits in 1767, their property was parceled out to other churches. To the poorer mission churches, even old, worn, and out-of-style items, which would otherwise be burned to avoid their being used for profane purposes, were welcome (Anderson, "Figural Arrangements of Eighteenth-Century Churches," 120–28). Thus San José de Tumacácori and San Pedro y San Pablo in Tubutama, for example, contain many items antedating their completion.

70. For a description of a neoclassical altar built in the Casa de Moneda in 1803 to "modernize" the institution, and of another such altar, location unknown, and for information on neoclassical altars generally, including the designers' sketches, see Maza, "Dibujos y proyectos de Tresguerra," and "Algunas obras desconocidas de Manuel Tolsá," figures 50, 51, and 63–67.

71. Bargellini, *Catedral de Chihuahua*, 45–58.

72. Palomero Páramo, *Retablo sevillano del renacimiento*, 93–97.

73. Ibid., 94.

74. Ibid.

75. Ibid., 96–106.

76. Numerous authors have categorized retablos mayores and retablos colaterales in a variety of distinct ways. For example, in considering retablos before the Renaissance, particularly in the provinces of Castilla and Aragón, Berg-Sobré (*Behind the Altar Table*, 167–204) creates two broad categories: "symbolic" and "narrative," based on the individual paintings within these particular retablos. In her system, images of saints, no matter where they are placed within the retablo are considered symbolic in and of themselves, whereas the episodes from the life of the titular figure of the retablo, which usually appear along the edges, are considered narrative elements.

77. Barbier de Montault, *Traité pratique*, vol. 1, p. 93. In 1745, Pope Benedict XIV banned placing minor altars (and, by extension, retablos) in such a location that the celebrant would be forced to turn his back on the main altar. Placing collateral altars under organs or attached to columns or pilasters was also banned.

78. Indeed, the tabernacle retablo remained popular into the twentieth century. I believe the single paintings, mostly framed and sometimes flanked by columns, that are referred to as "retablos marcos" in various inventories of altars in northern New Spain should be considered a distinct subcategory.

79. Relics are divided into three classes: first-class relics are body parts of a saint or beatified person; second-class relics are clothing or objects touched or used by a saint or beatified person; and third-class relics are materials that have touched first-class relics.

80. One church inventory specified two such curtains: one of gauze and the other of satin trimmed in gold (Church inventory 11).

81. Although victims of "barbaric renewal" during the nineteenth century, the two cypresses mentioned in church inventories of northern New Spain, one at the Cathedral of Durango and the other at the parochial church of Nuestra Señora de la Asunción in Álamos (Sonora), may both have contained expositorios.

82. Anderson, "Figural Arrangements of Eighteenth-Century Churches," 212–15. Anderson's research demonstrates that, while the selection of styles of ornament, color schemes, and the like might be left to the discretion of the local priest or maestro de obras, the placement of images was prescribed. She does not, however, specifically cite the rules for such selection and placement.

83. Locally produced religious images were present in New Mexico at least by the late eighteenth century, as is evident from comments by Domínguez. Sometime in the late eighteenth or early nineteenth century, local santeros began constructing retablos and religious images not only for churches, but also for individuals (see Boyd, *Popular Arts of Spanish New Mexico*; Wroth, *Christian Images in Hispanic New Mexico*).

84. Packing crates containing parts of a retablo for assembly in some unnamed New Mexican church (possibly Nuestra Señora de los Ángeles de Pecos) are listed, along with those containing the principal image and specific parts for its mounting and display in the retablo (Hodge, Hammond, and Rey, "Supplies for Benavides," 121). Commenting in 1772 on the need to import all religious articles of any quality from Mexico City, Baegert (*Observations in Lower California*, 172) noted that the retablo for the high altar of San Francisco Javier de Vigge-Biaundó came already gilded, disassembled, and packed in thirty-two crates.

85. A premier example is a contract between the archbishop of New Spain and a maestro de ensamblador y entallador and maestro de dorador y estafador for a since-destroyed retablo of the Virgin of Guadalupe in the Jesuit church of La Compañía in Querétaro (Querétaro) in 1696. The document tells us that the maestros were of Indian nobility and specifies the purpose of the retablo as well as methods and amounts of payment for

its construction; it notes the location and the design of the retablo, including the number and nature of its columns and niches, and the nature and placement of the figures desired, as well as the techniques to be used in their making. That packing and cartage expenses to Querétaro were to be assumed by the maestros indicates that the retablo was to be constructed in the workshops of Mexico City, broken down, and later reassembled in place. What is sadly missing—along with the actual retablo, of course—is the original plan (Curiel, "Nuevas noticias sobre un taller de artistas").

86. See Bargellini, *Catedral de Chihuahua* and "Esculturas y retablos coloniales de la ciudad en Durango."

87. Palomero Páramo, *Retablo sevillano del renacimiento*, 35.

88. For discussion of laws governing the painting of statuary and ordinances on the separation of tasks in the fabrication of religious statuary in sixteenth- and seventeenth-century Spain, see Pacheco, *A los profesores del arte de la pintura*, 267–74.

89. "Contracto para dos retablos," 24 March 1685, Archivo de Notarías de México, Not. 199, vol. 4, book 1, pp. 107r-111V.

90. What became of the retablo mariano is uncertain: it may have been replaced by a neoclassical retablo in the early nineteenth century, covered over during a neo-Gothic "restoration" in 1897, or even destroyed by dynamite when the forces of Francisco Madero attacked in 1911.

91. The other four stone retablos are at Nuestra Señora del Carmen in San Luis Potosí, San Pablo el Viejo in Mexico City, the Cathedral of Puebla (Retablo de los Reyes), and San José de Chiapa—the last two retablos being carved from tecali (Vargas Lugo, *México barroco*, 112–13; and Maza, *Capilla de San José Chiapa*, 51–59, and *El alabastro en el arte colonial*, 31–34).

92. Wuthenau, "Spanish Military Chapels in Santa Fe"; Kelemen, "Significance of the Stone Retable of Cristo Rey."

93. The precedents for painting retablos on church walls may be found in the large monastery churches of sixteenth-century central New Spain (the Augustinian convent church at Acolman, for example), and even earlier in frescoed triptychs and cycles of saints' lives in Spain and Italy. A fragment of a retablo lienzo can also be seen at San Francisco de Asís (late eighteenth century) in Sombrerete (Zacatecas).

94. Domínguez (*Missions of New Mexico*, 146) describes what is clearly a retablo lienzo behind the main altar of San Felipe Neri in Albuquerque: "Father Fray Rafael Benavides installed an altar screen in perspective on canvas. It is very seemly. . . . Near the middle of the second section (it is understood that all is painted), a crucifix and on either side of it Lord St. Joseph and St. Augustine."

Other such retablos, no longer extant, were once at the following Alta California missions: Santa Clara (received 1788), San Antonio de Padua and San Luis Obispo (both received 1791), La Purísima Concepción and Santa Cruz (both ordered 1810; Neuerburg, "Angel on the Cloud," 45).

95. In the Cathedral of Chihuahua, an inscription on the painting of La Mater Dolorosa in the Capilla del Cristo de Mapimí by an individual identified only as "Muñoz" indicates that the retablo was given by Alejandro Manuel de Quijano Calderón as an act of devotion in 1762. In San Francisco de Mapimí, the painting of Saint Joseph and the sleeping Christ Child, signed by the artist José de Paez, is inscribed as a gift from Pedro Nicolás de Cadrecha.

96. See esp. Herrerías de la Fuente, *Retablo de la iglesia conventual de Xochimilco*, for plans and diagrams detailing retablo construction and attachment methods. See also Ramírez Montes, *Retablos y retablistas*, esp. "Maestros, oficios y producción," 33–46.

97. Alonso Lutteroth, "La madera del retablo de San Bernardino de Siena."

Chapter 11

1. Jung, "Approaching the Unconscious," 20; Jaffé paraphrasing Jung, "Symbolism in the Visual Arts," 249.

2. The Good Shepherd, who cares for souls of mortals (equated with sheep) in the "green pastures" of the underworld, is one of the oldest roles played by savior gods, including the Babylonian god Tammuz (Sumerian god Dumuzi) and the Egyptian god Osiris.

Many signs and symbols incorporated into Christian iconography originally represented both male and female fertility at their most fundamental and graphic. "As civilization advanced, the gross symbols of creative power were cast aside, and priestly ingenuity was taxed to the utmost in inventing a crowd of less obvious emblems, which should represent the ancient ideas in a decorous manner. The old belief was retained, but in a mysterious or sublimated form" (Newton, "Assyrian 'Grove' and Other Emblems," 115).

3. Eliade, "Symbolism and History," 161–62.

4. Barbara G. Walker details the gender shift in supernatural beings as characterized by Europeans—from female (pre-Christian) to male (Christian); see esp. "Angel" and "Demon" in Walker, *Woman's Dictionary of Symbols and Sacred Objects*.

5. Ross and McLaughlin, *Portable Medieval Reader*, 19.

6. Nichols, *Romanesque Signs*, 7.

7. Durandus, *Symbolism of Churches*, 17–18.

8. Eliade, "Sacred Architecture and Symbolism."

9. Durandus, *Symbolism of Churches*, 42.

10. As affirmed by Cataneo in his 1554 thesis on architecture. Blunt, *Artistic Theory in Italy*, 130. See also Durandus, *Symbolism of Churches*, 19.

11. For symbolism of sculpted figures and motifs on portals, see Vargas Lugo, *Portadas churriguerescas*; also see Bargellini, *Catedral de Chihuahua*, which provides a thorough, thoughtful interpretation of particular images and symbols carved on the portals and in the interiors of the cathedral and surrounding churches.

12. The Church in Spain fought for the establishment of the dogma of the Eucharist since the Council of Zaragoza (380). When the Council of Trent (1545–1563) defined and confirmed Communion bread and wine as the true body and blood of Christ, the Eucharist became a principal dogmatic theme of the Coun-

ter-Reformation. Bertos Herrera (*Tema de la eucaristía*) presents an excellent history of the development of the Eucharist in the Catholic liturgy and religion.

13. Vigorously espoused by the Franciscans since 1621, and widely believed by Catholics even before then, the doctrine of the Immaculate Conception—that Mary was conceived without Original Sin, albeit with man—was not formally defined by the Church until 1854 (*Catholic Encyclopedia*, vol. 7, pp. 674–80).

14. Godwin, *Angels*, 7.

15. Although much of the original imagery is lost, the remaining angels and their attributes on the soffit of the dome of San Xavier near Tucson (Arizona) may represent each of the different choirs of angels.

16. Waters, *Angels in Art*, 197.

17. Borromeo, *Instrucciones de la fábrica y del ajuar eclesiásticos*, 39.

18. Support for Christ as the New Adam is found in 1 Corinthians 15:45–47. Mary's role as the New Eve was celebrated as early as the second century (Duchet-Suchaux and Pastoureau, *Bible and the Saints*, 233). The reversal of "Ave" (Hail; used uniquely in invocations of Mary) to "Eva" (Eve) appears in a vesper hymn in the Commons of the Feast of the Blessed Virgin Mary (Watts, *Myth and Ritual in Christianity*, 56).

19. Durandus dates a silver figure of John the Baptist holding a sculpted banner with the inscription "Ecce Agnus Dei" (Behold the Lamb of God) to the late thirteenth century (Bingham, *Origines ecclesiasticae*, vol. 1, p. 310).

20. Durandus, *Symbolism of Churches*, 72–73.

21. The liturgical use of *bugia* (from Bougie, Algeria, an early source for wax; an apparent catchall term in church inventories of northern New Spain for any small candlestick with a saucer base) was discontinued in 1968 (*Maryknoll Catholic Dictionary*, 87).

22. Apostolos-Cappadona, *Dictionary of Christian Art*, 71.

23. The Tenebrae service was suppressed after Vatican II.

24. Chains or fetters (and also the scallop shell) were also associated with the Holy Child of Atocha (Santo Niño de Atocha), who assumed enormous importance in Mexico from the mid-nineteenth century through today but whose portrayals did not appear in Mexico until after Independence.

25. Norris, *Church Vestments*, 70. By special papal dispensation, sky-blue vestments are however allowed in Spain for all the Masses of the Immaculate Conception (Gihr, *Holy Sacrifice of the Mass*, 298 n. 1). On the use of pink, see Schenone, *Iconografía del arte colonial*, vol. 2, p. 808.

26. "Of the Nativity of Our Lord Jesus Christ" (Meditation VII), in *Meditations on the Life of Christ*, 32. Once attributed to Saint Bonaventure, *Meditations* is now believed to have been written by John of Caulibus.

According to Fray Juan Ricci (1600–81), the orders of columns expressed Christian values: the Tuscan order, the simple humility of the anchorite saints such as Paul; the Doric, the valor of extraordinary saints such as Stephen and Lawrence; the Ionic, the celibacy of saints who eschewed marriage; the Corinthian, the purity of Christ, Mary, and sacred virgins other than Mary.

27. See Heim, *Heraldry in the Catholic Church*, 65.

28. Webber, *Church Symbolism*, 99.

29. Walker, *Woman's Dictionary of Symbols and Sacred Objects*, 102.

30. Eberlein, "Curtain in Raphael's Sistine Madonna."

31. *La gloria* signifies the end of Lent, when the priest sings "Gloria in excelsis Deo," bells that had been silenced are rung (sometimes accompanied by fireworks), and paintings and sculptures that had been covered are uncovered.

32. Barbier de Montault, *Traité pratique*, vol. 1, p. 50.

33. Smith, *Architectural Symbolism of Imperial Rome*, 59–67.

34. Smith, *Dome*, 96.

35. Judges 5:10, 10:4, and 12:13–14; I Samuel 9 and 10; Zechariah 9:9; and Isaiah 1:3.

36. Jim Clare once told me that this type of donkey was called a "Palestinian donkey"—which I never questioned because Jim was a former jockey and horse trainer.

37. According to Marita Martínez del Río de Redo, these figures represent the marques de Pánuco and his son, who contributed money for the church's construction, an assertion supported by the inscription over the door of the sacristy: "A devoción de los marqueses de Pánuco se hizo esta sacristía en el año de 1785" (Martínez del Río de Redo, "Dos iglesias barrocas").

38. "The gospel," Durandus (*Symbolism of Churches*, 187) tells us, "is read from an eagle, according to that saying, 'He came flying upon the wings of the winds.' Ps[alms] 28:10."

39. See Gihr, *Holy Sacrifice of the Mass*, 256.

40. Influenced by Pythagorean thinking on polyhedrons united by and related to the golden number, symbolic tradition assigned a specific polyhedron to each of the four elements: the cube (six faces) to earth; the icosahedron (twenty faces) to water; the octahedron (eight faces) to air; and the tetrahedron (four faces) to fire. The universe in its totality was envisioned as a dodecahedron (twelve faces).

41. Before Columbus, the banner read "non plus ultra," reflecting the ancient belief that the Pillars of Hercules marked the utmost limit of the civilized or habitable world.

42. Rice, *Saint Jerome in the Renaissance*, 172.

43. Charbonneau-Lassay, *Bestiary of Christ*, 94–105.

44. Díaz Vaquero, *Virgen en la escultura cordobesa*, 27.

45. For more on the Christian symbolism of seven, see Durandus, *Symbolism of Churches*, 120.

46. To give its young access to food carried in the pouch of its bill, a pelican presses its lower mandible against its breast, a habit that, together with the red-tipped bills of its ravenous offspring, may have given rise to the belief that pelicans feed their young from their own flesh.

47. The legend of Joseph's selection was embodied in the Protoevangelion, an apocryphal text once recognized by the Church and ascribed to James the Less.

48. Burckhardt, *Moorish Culture in Spain*, 13–14.

49. A number of other scapulars were in use at different times; José Buenaventura's list of those approved and in use in 1906 gives us some idea of their number and variety (Buenaventura, *Escapularios*, 14–15).

50. Charbonneau-Lassay, *Bestiary of Christ,* 153–54.

51. Kelemen, *Baroque and Rococo in Latin America,* vol. 1, p. 50. Diane Apostolos-Cappadona refers to this device as a "cruciform nimbus," a symbol of the resurrected Christ and states that it implies that if Christ's head were transparent, the fullness of the Cross would be revealed (Apostolos-Cappadona, *Dictionary of Christian Art,* 92).

52. Saint John the Baptist's birthday is traditionally celebrated on June 24, about the time the summer rains begin in the southwestern United States. Because he baptized Christ with water, Saint John is associated not only with baptism but also with water (rain and renewal). In the Tucson area, it was an act of devotion and faith to bathe on Saint John's day—devotion to the saint and faith that the summer rains would come, bringing welcome relief from the June heat, which could exceed 100 degrees Fahrenheit for weeks at a stretch.

53. Wittkower, *Eagle and Serpent,* 162–66.

CHAPTER 12

1. See Exodus 20:4, Leviticus 26:1, and Deuteronomy 16:22.

2. See Wilder and Breitenbach, *Santos,* plate 63; Giffords, *Mexico Folk Retablos,* 36–37, frontispiece, and plates 12 and 13.

3. Watts, *Myth and Ritual in Christianity,* 39 n 1.

4. Walsh, *Dictionary of Catholic Devotions,* 116.

5. Chorpenning, "Iconography of St. Joseph," 79–80.

6. Ibid., 79.

7. To Christians, Jesus Christ (from Greek *Christos,* meaning "messiah," a Hebrew transcription of the Aramaic, meaning "the Lord's anointed") is the Messiah, the fulfillment of the Messianic prophecies in the Old Testament. "Jesus" is the name of the historical man, whereas "Jesus Christ" or "Christ Jesus" is used when speaking of him as Savior, or after the Resurrection.

8. Very probably a mid-nineteenth-century Mexican manifestation, the most significant image of the child Jesus throughout Mexico is the "Holy Child of Atocha" (El Santo Niño de Atocha). Jesus is presented as a young pilgrim in a plumed hat, holding a basket in one hand and a traveler's staff and gourd in the other. He is seated in a chair, sometimes with a prisoner's leg irons on his ankles, held by him, or lying at his feet (see Lange, "Santo Niño de Atocha").

9. Limbo is traditionally divided into two sections: Limbus Infantium, for unbaptized infants, and Limbus Patrum, for righteous adults. A place of waiting without suffering, Limbo was distinguished from Purgatory, where souls were purged of their sins. Recently, the Catholic Church has officially declared Limbo "closed".

10. Carroll, *Catholic Cults and Devotions,* 134.

11. The stations originally numbered seven, referring to the "seven falls" of Jesus, the seven times Christ was prostrate or nearly so; included were two suppressed falls, his removal from the Cross, and his entombment. The version of the stations as they are now known appears to have been the result of a book of devotional meditations published in 1563 in Louvain by a Carmelite prior.

12. O'Connell, *Church Building and Furnishing,* 112–15.

13. Collins, *Church Edifice and its Appointments,* 38.

14. Walsh, *Dictionary of Catholic Devotions,* 250–52.

15. Flynn, *Sacred Charity,* 28.

16. Lea, *History of the Inquisition of the Middle Ages,* vol. 3, p. 597.

17. During the twelfth century, Mary was given the feudal title of "Our Lady" (Nuestra Señora). Although she had been referred to as "Lady" in the writings of Saint Jerome (420–430), the universal popularity of the title in different languages since the thirteenth century captures the high esteem in which Mary was held by Catholics the world over (Warner, *Alone of All Her Sex,* 153–54).

18. For more than 180 different titles of the Virgin Mary (although without locational designators), see Freze, *Making of Saints,* 144–46.

19. Stratton, *Immaculate Conception in Spanish Art,* provides an excellent description of the development and acceptance of the dogma of the Immaculate Conception, a doctrine initially supported by the Spanish monarchy and eventually also by the people, thanks largely to the effectiveness of religious painting and sculpture.

20. Chávez, *Conquistadora,* 40–41.

21. Chávez, *Our Lady of Conquest,* 11–17. Although two other sculpted images of the Holy Virgin in northern New Spain are called "La Conquistadora"—in Loreto (Baja California Sur) and in Monterey (California)—the title is used as an honorific there, not as a formal designation.

22. Insights meticulously documented by researchers such as Angélico Chávez (see Chávez, *Conquistadora*).

23. Enggass and Brown, *Italy and Spain,* 165.

24. Pacheco, *Arte de la pintura,* vol. 2, pp. 208–12. Translation mine.

25. Although almost all her images are two-dimensional, a sculpture of the Most Holy Mother of Light can be seen in the south transept of San Francisco de Asís in Chihuahua City.

26. Stratton, *Immaculate Conception in Spanish Art,* 55.

27. For a clear and unemotional approach to the iconography and history of the image and cult of Our Lady of Guadalupe, see Berndt León Mariscal, Caudriello, and Montserrat Robledo Galván, "Mosaic of Guadalupan Iconography"; see also illustrations on pp. 26–57.

28. The cults of the numerous other dark-skinned manifestations of Mary, scattered throughout Europe and confined for the most part to their areas of origin, were never exported to New Spain.

29. For more on the significance of skin color in the church art of northern New Spain, see discussion of medallion images of four nun saints under "Religious Images," "San Xavier del Bac" and of Juan Correa under "Painters" in chapter 10.

30. Joseph L. Cassidy, *Mexico: Land of Mary's Wonders* (Paterson, N.J., 1958), 85.

31. In Spain, every kingdom, province, or important community had its special Marian devotion and specific image that attracted pilgrims from the Middle Ages on. Some of these images immigrated to New Spain with their Spanish devotees. With Mexico's Independence, however, the importance of these devotions diminished, whereas that of locally venerated images such as La Guadalupana and Our Lady of San Juan de los Lagos and Zopopan, both in the state of Jalisco, increased.

32. One of the two extant sculpted images of Our Lady, Refuge of Sinners, in northern New Spain was created by a New Mexican *santero* and dated "1820." It currently resides in the Taylor Museum of the Colorado Springs Fine Arts Center (Colorado). The second, probably about the same age as the first, is at the Church of San Francisco in Chihuahua City.

33. Our Lady of Regla (Nuestra Señora de Regla) was once the titular image of perhaps the earliest church (1709) in what was formerly San Francisco de Cuellar, now Chihuahua City. The image of Our Lady of Regla prominently displayed in the main retablo of the Cathedral of Chihuahua is very likely the original from the 1709 church, whose successor the cathedral replaced. Despite the prominence of the image, however, the devotion to this Marian manifestation today enjoys only a limited following.

34. Modern scholars have determined that, although the Dominicans helped popularize the devotion to Our Lady of the Rosary, they did not initiate it, nor did Saint Dominic, who very likely used the prayer beads as they were traditionally used during his lifetime—and would be for another three centuries after him—to pray "Our Fathers" (hence the beads' original name "paternosters"). See, for example, Carroll, *Catholic Cults and Devotions*, 12–13.

35. Because it is common to find votive offerings draped on or added to sculpted images of Mary, the mere presence of a rosary is not enough for absolute iconographic identification; conversely, this attribute may have been lost and Mary's right hand filled with something else or simply left empty, fingers touching each other in a gesture of giving something.

36. This image closely resembles the one described by Saint Catherine Labouré (1806–1876) and later reproduced on a medallion popularly referred to as the "Miraculous Medal."

37. Kelemen, "Significance of the Stone Retable of Cristo Rey." Although Our Lady of Valvanera is the titular saint of the church in the tiny mining town of La Aduana (Sonora), which hosts a pilgrimage attracting thousands each November in her honor, the iconography of the painted Marian image behind the main altar of this church more closely resembles that of Our Lady, Refuge of Sinners.

38. Nobel and Head, *Soldiers of Christ*, xiv–xix.

39. Taves, *Household of Faith*, 107.

40. The Catholic Church officially recognizes some 4,500 saints.

41. In at least two instances, individuals other than recognized or popular saints who were influential in establishing mission churches have been "sainted" and had churches named after them: Santo Domingo de Hoyos (Tamaulipas), founded in 1752, was named after Don Domingo de Unzaga e Ibarrola and the "sainted" name of Miguel de Aguayo, a *marqués* and benefactor, was added to "San José" for the church San José y San Miguel de Aguayo (Texas). Franco Carrasco, *Nuevo Santander y su arquitectura*, vol. 2, p. 282.

42. The place-name Compostela has also been said to derive from the Latin *compostum* (burial place) or even from the Italian name Giacompostolo (James the Apostle).

43. See also Sebastián, "Iconografía de Santiago," 276–88.

44. Voragine, *Golden Legend*, 61.

45. Saint Jude's intercessory role in this regard has been actively promoted by the Church since the early part of the twentieth century.

46. As the Bible tells us, Judas Iscariot (Judas Iscariote) betrayed Jesus for thirty pieces of silver. Because of the betrayal money, a money bag is his principal attribute. Depicted as an ugly and evil-looking man, he is seen only in scenes of the Last Supper.

47. The sheep that provide the pope and his archbishops the wool for their pallia (singular, pallium—a white woolen band with pendants front and back worn over the chasuble) are blessed on Saint Agnes's feast day in the Convent of Santa Agnese in Rome.

48. Neither Anne nor Joachim appears in the canonical texts of the Bible. Luis Réau believes Anne (Hebrew for "Grace of God") to be purely symbolic (Réau, *Iconographie de l'art chrétien*, vol. 2, p. 156).

49. Storage caves for dynamite used in road construction in northern Mexico are to this day called "Santa Bárbaras."

50. See Thurston and Attwater, *Butler's Lives of the Saints*, vol. 3, pp. 287–88.

51. Images of Saint Ignatius's face are based on two portraits painted from his death mask (see Schamoni, *Face of the Saints*, 132–37).

52. The legend of Jerome's taming a lion by removing a thorn from its paw is a Christianized version of Aesop's fable "The Lion and the Shepherd." The theme was developed in the apocryphal Acts of Paul (second century) with regard to Saint Paul's baptizing a lion and the lion's subsequent rejection of his mate's desires. This accounts for the placement of lion images on early medieval baptismal fonts. The lion also appears in a sixth-century (legendary) life of Saint Sabas of Palestine (439–532) and again in a legend of yet another Palestine ascetic, Saint Gerasimus. Through a copyist's error, Jerome inherited the lion and acquired other episodes demonstrating the lion's tameness, humility, and loyalty.

53. Again, as with Anne, Réau believes Joachim (Hebrew for "Preparation of the Lord") to be purely symbolic (Réau, *Iconographie de l'art chrétien*, vol. 2, p. 617).

54. Ferrando Roig, *Iconografía de los santos*, 151.

55. Borromeo, *Instrucciones de la fábrica y del ajuar eclesiásticos*, 45.

56. According to Chorpenning ("Iconography of St. Joseph," 49), devotions to Joseph were late to develop out of reluctance

to detract from "the dogmas of Jesus' divine origin and Mary's virginal motherhood."

57. *Book of Catholic Quotations,* 495.

58. Mâle, *L'art religieux après le Concile de Trente,* 315.

59. Mark (Marcus) is the Apostle's Roman name; Luke calls him "John" in the Acts of the Apostles 12:12, 12:25, 13:5, 15:37.

60. For more on the promotion of Saint Martin's cult, see Van Dam, *Saints and Their Miracles,* 13–28.

61. This widely believed account is perhaps the basis for the gift-giving "Santa Claus," whose white beard and colorful garments were provided by the Greek Church. The three bags of gold later became the three golden balls displayed outside pawnshops.

62. As the first to "witness unto death" for his faith in Christ, Saint Stephen is called a protomartyr. Because he suffered death "both in will and deed," he also belongs to the highest class of martyrs.

63. This "Veil of Veronica" has been preserved in the Vatican since the early eighth century.

64. At a certain stage, anorexia is known to produce facial hair. One of the few methods women had of controlling their lives and fates was starving themselves, a practice not uncommon during the Middle Ages and one that might have encouraged devotion to Saint Wilgefortis/Liberata. Known in England as the "Uncumberer," she was popularly invoked by Englishwomen wishing to rid themselves of tiresome husbands (Bynum, *Holy Feast, Holy Fast,* 194).

Sources

Photography Collections

Arizona State Museum, Tucson: DeLong and Miller, 1935 Sonoran Expedition, and Pál Kelemen Collections

Harry Ransom Humanities Research Center, University of Texas, Austin

Huntington Library, Pasadena, California

Library of Congress, Washington, D.C.: U.S. National Park Service Historic American Building Survey

Museum of International Folk Art, Santa Fe, New Mexico

Museum of New Mexico, Santa Fe: Photo Archives

Museum of the Southwest, Los Angeles: "Missions" and Charles Lummis Collections

New Mexico State Records and Center for Archives, Santa Fe: Arthur Loy and "Religious Structures of Northern New Mexico" Collections

San Francisco Xavier del Bac, Tucson, Arizona

Southwest Museum, Pasadena, California

Texas State Library, Austin

University of Texas, Austin: Benson Latin American Collection, University of Texas Institute of Texas Culture, San Antonio

University of Texas Library, Austin

Western Archeological Center, Tucson, Arizona

Microfilm Collections

Bancroft Library, University of California, Berkeley

Documentary Relations of the Southwest, Office of Ethno-Historical Research, Arizona State Museum, University of Arizona, Tucson

Old Spanish Missions Historical Research Library, Our Lady of the Lakes University, San Antonio

University of Arizona Library, Tucson: Special Collections

University of Texas, Austin: Benson Latin American Collection

Blueprint and Drawing Collections

Library of Congress, Washington, D.C.: U.S. National Park Service Historic American Buildings Survey

Mission La Purísima Concepción, Lompoc, California

University of Texas, Austin: Architectural Drawing Collection

Manuscript Collections

Archivo de la Catedral de Durango, Durango

Archivo del Estado de Coahuila, Saltillo, Coahuila

Archivo de Notarías de México, Mexico City

Archivo General de las Indias, Sevilla

Archivo General y Público de la Nación, Mexico City

Archivo Histórico de Hacienda, Mexico City

Archivo de Parral, Chihuahua

Bancroft Library, University of California, Berkeley

Old Spanish Missions Historical Research Library, Our Lady of the Lakes University, San Antonio

University of Texas Library, Austin

Abbreviations

ACD Archivo de la Catedral de Durango, Durango

AGEC Archivo General del Estado de Coahuila, Saltillo

AGN Archivo General y Público de la Nación, Mexico City

AHH Archivo Histórico de Hacienda, Mexico City

AMS Archivo de la Mitra de Sonora

BL Bancroft Library, University of California, Berkeley

DRSW Documentary Relations of the Southwest, Office of Ethno-Historical Research, Arizona State Museum, University of Arizona, Tucson

IIE Instituto de Investigaciones Estéticas, Mexico City

IIS Instituto de Investigaciones Sociales, Mexico City

INAH Instituto Nacional de Antropología e Historia, Mexico City

OSMHRL Old Spanish Missions Historical Research Library, Our Lady of the Lakes University, San Antonio

SEP Secretaría de Educación Pública, Mexico City

UAMLSC University of Arizona Main Library, Special Collections, Tucson

UNAM Universidad Nacional Autónoma de México, Mexico City

WBS W. B. Stevens Collection, University of Texas Library, Austin

Church Inventories Cited

1. Parroquia de San Miguel de Culiacán (Sinaloa), 1820. AMS (Culiacán). UAMLSC, film 811, reel 24.
2. Misión de San Miguel Arcángel de los Ures (Sonora), 16 December 1743. WBS 1744, pp. 175–92. DRSW film V-A-7.
3. Misión de San José de Teopari (Sonora), 23 April 1721. WBS 1744, pp. 17–18. DRSW film V-A-7.
4. Misión de San Francisco Javier de Batuc (Sonora), 18 November 1735. AHH, Temp., Leg. 278, exp. 24.
5. Iglesia del Presidio de San Agustín de Tucson (Arizona), 21 January 1797. AMS (Hermosillo). UAMLSC, film 811, reel 2.
6. Misión de San Francisco Javier de Batuc (Sonora), August 1796. AMS (Hermosillo). UAMLSC, film 811, reel 2.
7. Misión de Nuestra Señora de Loreto de Concho (Baja California Sur), 1773. AGN, Misiones, vol. 12, pp. 216r-222v. DRSW, film MIS 338:12.
8. Misión de Nuestra Señora de la Purísima Concepción de Movas (Sonora), 25 May 1741. WBS 1744, p. 133. DRSW, film V-A-7.
9. Misión de Nuestra Señora del Pilar (Baja California Sur; Todos Santos), 1773. AGN, Misiones, vol. 12, pp. 308r–312v. DRSW, film MIS 338:12.
10. Misión de San Francisco de Borja de Adac (Baja California Norte), 15 June 1774. AGN, Misiones, vol. 12, pp. 77r–78r, 81r. DRSW, film MIS 338:12.
11. Misión de Nuestra Señora del Refugio (Texas), 8 September 1796. OSMHRL, Zacatecas, reel 3, frames 3861–3865.
12. Misión de Nuestra Señora del Pilar de Norogachic (Chihuahua), [ca. 1776]. AGN, Historia, vol. 298, pp. 56r–60r. DRSW, film V-A-2.
13. Misiones de San Francisco Javier de Arivechi and Nuestro Padre de San Ignacio de Bacanora (both Sonora; "Memoria de la misión de Aribechi [*sic*] y Bacanora"), [ca. 1737]. WBS 1744, pp. 103–7. DRSW, film V-A-7.

14. Misión de San José del Cabo de la Peninsula de California (Baja California Sur), 1774. AGN, Provincias Internas, vol. 166, pp. 87r–88r. DRSW, film MIS 338:12.
15. Misión de San Miguel de Saguaripa (Sonora), 30 October 1783. Private collection of Father Ernesto López, Santa Teresita parish, Ciudad Obregón (Sonora). UAMLSC, film 881, reel 26 [17 transcribed pages].
16. Misiones de San Diego del Alcalá, San Gabriel Arcángel, San Luis Obispo de Toloso, San Antonio de Padua, and San Carlos Borromeo de Carmelo de Monterey (all California; "Informe de las misiones de Monterrey [*sic*] del Año 1774"). AGN, Provincias Internas, vol. 166, folio 14.
17. Misión de Nuestra Señora de la Purísima Concepción del Rio Colorado (California) [formerly Misión de San Lorenzo de la Santa Cruz (Texas)], Account book ("Cuentas de San Lorenzo"), 1762–69, 1779–81. OSMHRL, Celaya, reel 15, frames 5009–41 [33 transcribed pages].
18. Misión de San Luis Gonzaga de Bacadéhuachi and Visitas de Nuestra Señora de Guadalupe de Nácori and de San Ignacio de Mochopa (all Sonora), 23 August 1766. WBS 1744, pp. 455–59. DRSW film V-A-8.
19. Misión de San Luis Gonzaga de Bacadéhuachi (Sonora), 15 November 1722. AHH, Leg. 972, pp. 279–89. DRSW film III-C-2.
20. Catedral de Durango (Durango; "Inventario de las alhajas de oro y plata, y de todo lo demás perteneciente a esta Santa Iglesia Catedral de Durango, y que debe estar al cuidado del Sacristán Mayor"), 2 August 1790. ACD, Libro CCXV.
21. Misión de San Ignacio Topia Piaola y Sierra (Nueva Vizcaya), 21 November 1753. AGN, Misiones, vol. 13-1-22, exp. 2-D-7, pp. 17–20. DRSW film 2-D-7.
22. Misiones de San Francisco de Tlaxcala, San Miguel de Aguayo, Nuestra Señora de Victoria de Nadadores, and San Carlos de la Candela (all Coahuila), 8 August 1794. AGEC, Fondo colonial, exp. 48, folio 33.

Compact Disk Recordings

A Choir of Angels: Mission Music. Zephyr. Topanga, Calif.: Civic Records Group, 1997.

Matins for the Virgin of Guadalupe. Chanticleer and Chanticleer Sinfonia. Directed by Joe Jennings. Hamburg: Teldec, 1998.

Mexican Baroque: Music from New Spain. Chanticleer and Chanticleer Sinfonia. Directed by Joseph Jennings. Das Alte Werke. Hamburg: Teldec, 1994.

México barroco: Schola Cantorum and Conjunto de Cámara de la Ciudad de México. Vol. 1, *Ignacio de Jerusalem: Navidad*. Directed by Benjamín Juárez Echenique. Mexico City: Urtext, 1994.

Books, Articles, and Unpublished Works

Aguiló Paz, Alonso María. *El mueble en España: Siglos XVI–XVII*. Madrid: Consejo Superior de Investigaciones Científicas, 1993.

Ahlborn, Richard E. *Saints of San Xavier*. Tucson, Ariz.: Southwestern Mission Research Center, 1974.

Alarcón Cedillo, Roberto, and Armida Alonso Lutteroth. *Tecnología de la obra*. Mexico City: Universidad Ibero Americana, n.d.

Alessio Robles, Vito. *Acapulco, Saltillo y Monterrey el la historia y en la leyenda*. Mexico City: Editorial Porrúa, 1978.

Alfaro, Alfonso. "Óyeme con los ojos." In *Corpus auraeum: Escultura religiosa*, 10–18. Mexico City: Museo Franz Mayer and Artes de México, 1995.

Alonso Lutteroth, Armida. "La madera del retablo de San Bernardino de Siena, en Xochimilco." INAH *Boletín*, no. 2 (1979): 5–10.

Anaya Larios, José Rodolfo. *Arquitectura efímera de Querétaro*. Querétaro: Gobierno de Estado de Querétaro, 1997.

———. *Historia de la escultura queretana*. Querétaro: Universidad Autónoma de Querétaro, 1987.

Anderson, Barbara Christine. "The Figural Arrangements of Eighteenth-Century Churches in Mexico." Ph.D. diss., Yale University, 1979.

Angulo Íñiguez, Diego. "La Academia de Bellas Artes de México y sus pintores españoles." *Artes en América y Filipinas* 1 (1936): 1–76.

———. *Planos de monumentos arquitectónicos de América y Filipinas existente en el Archivo de Indias*. Vol. 1. Sevilla: Laboratorio de Arte, 1939.

Apostolos-Cappadona, Diane. *Dictionary of Christian Art*. New York: Continuum, 1994.

Araujo Suárez, Rolando, Alejandro Huerta Carrillo, and Sergio Guerrero Bolan. "Esculturas de papel, amate, y caña de maíz." Museo Franz Mayer (Mexico City) *Cuadernos Técnicos*, no. 1 (1989): 9–10, 16.

Arcelus de Diego, María Soledad. *Estudio de los barnices en la pintura colonial.* Mexico City: INAH, 1995.

Arenal, Electra, and Stacey Schlau. *Untold Sisters.* Translated by Amanda Powell. Albuquerque: University of New Mexico, 1989.

Armella de Aspe, Virginia, and Mercedes Meade de Angulo. *Tesoros de la pinacoteca virreinal.* Mexico City: Mercantil de México, 1989.

Armella de Aspe, Virginia, and Guillermo Tovar de Teresa. *Bordados y bordadores.* Mexico City: Grupo Gutsa, 1992.

Arredondo, Rosa Camelo, Jorge Gurría Lacroix, and Constantino Reyes Valerio. *Juan Gerson Tlacuilo de Tecamachalco.* Mexico City: Departamento de Monumentos Coloniales/INAH, 1964.

Arrowsmith, J. W. *Bells and Bell Founding.* Bristol, 1879. Reprint, New York: Scribner's, 1959.

Artigas H., Juan Benito. *La piel de la arquitectura: Murales de Santa María Xoxoteco.* Mexico City: UNAM, 1984.

Atl, Dr. [Murillo, Gerardo], Manuel Toussaint, and J. R. Benitez. *Iglesias de México.* Vol. 6. Mexico City: SEP, 1927.

Baegert, Johann Jakob. *Observations in Lower California.* Translated by M. M. Brandenburg and Carl L. Baumann. Berkeley: University of California Press, 1979.

Baer, Kurt. *Painting and Sculpture at Mission Santa Barbara.* Washington, D.C.: Academy of American Franciscan History, 1955.

Baez Macías, Eduardo. *Obras de Fray Andrés de San Miguel.* Mexico City: IIE/UNAM, 1969.

Baird, Joseph A., Jr. *The Churches of Mexico, 1530–1810.* Berkeley: University of California Press, 1962.

———. *Los retablos del siglo XVII en el sur de España, Portugal, y México.* Translated by Rebeca Barrera de Fraga. Mexico City: IIE/UNAM, 1987.

Barbier de Montault, Xavier. *Traité pratique de la construction, de l'ameublement et de la décoration des églises, selon les règles canoniques et les traditions romaines, avec un appendice sur le costume ecclésiastique.* 2 vols. Paris: Vivès, 1878.

Bargellini, Clara. *La arquitectura de la plata: Iglesias monumentales del centro-norte de México, 1640–1750.* Mexico City: IIE/UNAM, 1991.

———. *La catedral de Chihuahua.* Mexico City: UNAM, 1984.

———. "Esculturas y retablos coloniales en la ciudad de Durango." In *Imaginería virreinal: Memorias de un seminario,* 47–58. Mexico City: IIE/UNAM and INAH/SEP, 1990.

Barrio Lorenzot, Francisco del. *Ordenanzas de gremios de la Nueva España.* Mexico City: Secretaría de Gobernación, Dirección de Talleres Gráficos, 1920.

Basalenque, Diego de, and Heriberto Moreno García. *Los augustinos: Aquellos misioneros hacendados.* Introduction, selection of texts, and notes by Heriberto Moreno García. Mexico City: SEP, 1985.

Benavides, Alonso de. *Fray Alonso de Benavides' Revised Memorial of 1634.* Translated by George P. Hammond and Agapito Rey. Annotated by Frederick W. Hodge. Coronado Cuarto Centennial Publications, 1540–1940, vol. 4. Albuquerque: University of New Mexico, 1945.

———. *The Memorial of Fray Alonso de Benavides, 1630.* Translated by Mrs. Edward E. Ayer. Annotated by Frederick Webb Hodge and Charles Fletcher Lummis. Chicago: n.p., 1916.

Benavides, Martín de. *Memorias.* AGN. Jes. I-14.

Berg-Sobré, Judith. *Behind the Altar Table: The Development of the Painted Retable in Spain, 1355–1500.* Columbia: University of Missouri Press, 1989.

Berlin, Heinrich. "Artifices de la catedral de México." *Anales del Instituto de Investigaciones Estéticas* 2 (1944): 19–39.

Berndt León Mariscal, Beatriz, Jaime Caudriello, and Carmen de Montserrat Robledo Galván. "Mosaic of Guadalupan Iconography." *Artes de Mexico,* no. 29 (1995): 69–80. (See also illustrations on pp. 26–87.)

Bertos Herrera, María del Pilar. *El tema de la eucaristía en el arte de Granada y sus provincias.* 2 vols. Granada: Universidad del Granada, 1985.

Bingham, Joseph. *Origines ecclesiasticae: The Antiquities of the Christian Church.* 2 vols. London: Henry G. Bohn, 1850.

Bishop, Mitchell Hearne, and Michele Derrick. "The Use of Wild Cucumber Seeds (*Marah acrocarpus*) in California Rock Art." Paper delivered before the annual meeting of the Western Association for Art Conservators. Asilomar, Calif., Sept. 25–27, 1995.

Blunt, Anthony. *Artistic Theory in Italy, 1450–1600.* Oxford: Clarendon Press, 1940.

———. , ed. *Baroque and Rococo.* London: Granada, 1982.

Boils Morales, Guillermo. *Arquitectura y sociedad en Querétaro, siglo XVIII.* Querétaro: Gobierno del Estado de Querétaro, 1994.

Bonavit, Julian. "Esculturas tarascas de caña de maíz y orquídeas." *Anales del Museo Michoacana* 2, no. 3 (1944): 64–78.

Book of Catholic Quotations. Edited by John Chapin. New York: Farrar, Straus and Cudahy, 1956.

Borah, Woodrow. *Silk Raising in Colonial Mexico.* Berkeley: University of California Press, 1943.

Borromeo, Charles. *Instrucciones de la fábrica y del ajuar eclesiásticos.* Translated by Bulmaro Reyes Coria. Mexico City: IIE/UNAM, 1985.

Bottineau, Yves. *Iberian-American Baroque.* New York: Gross and Dunlap, 1970.

Bowen, Dorothy Boyd, et al. *Spanish Textile Tradition of New Mexico and Colorado.* Santa Fe: Museum of New Mexico Press, 1979.

Bowyer, Louis. *Liturgy and Architecture.* Notre Dame, Ind.: University of Notre Dame Press, 1967.

Boyd, E. *Popular Arts of Spanish New Mexico,* Santa Fe: Museum of New Mexico Press, 1974.

Boylan, Leona Davis. *Spanish Colonial Silver.* Santa Fe: Museum of New Mexico, 1974.

Bracho, Julio. *De los gremios al sindicalismo.* Mexico City: IIS/UNAM, 1990.

Braun, Joseph. *Der christliche Altar in seiner geschichtlichen Entwicklung.* 2 vols. Munich: Alte Meister Guenther Koch, 1924.

Buenaventura, José. *Los escapularios: Manual teórico-práctico.* Barcelona: Herederos de Juan Gili, 1906.

Bunting, Bainbridge. *Early Architecture in New Mexico.* Albuquerque: University of New Mexico Press, 1976.

Burckhardt, Titus. *Moorish Culture in Spain.* Translated by Alisa Jaffa. New York: McGraw-Hill, 1972.

Bynum, Caroline Walker. *Holy Feast, Holy Fast: The Religious Significance of Food to Medieval Women.* Berkeley: University of California Press, 1987.

Calderón Quijano, José Antonio. *Las espadañas de Sevilla.* Sevilla: Diputación Provincial de Sevilla, 1982.

Carducho, Vincencio. *Diálogos de la pintura.* Madrid: D. G. Cruzada Villamil, 1865.

Carrera Stampa, Manuel. *Los gremios mexicanos.* Mexico City: Edición y Distribución Ibero Americana de Publicaciones, 1954.

Carrillo y Gariel, Abelardo. *Campanas de México.* Mexico City: IIE/UNAM, 1989.

______. *El Cristo de Mexicalzingo: Técnica de las esculturas en caña.* Mexico City: Dirección de Monumentos Coloniales, INAH, 1949.

______. *Técnica de la pintura de Nueva España.* Mexico City: Imprenta Universitaria, 1946.

______. *El traje en la Nueva España.* Mexico City: INAH, 1959.

Carroll, Michael P. *Catholic Cults and Devotions: A Psychological Inquiry.* Kingston, Ont.; Montreal, Que.: McGill-Queen's University Press, 1989.

Cassidy, Joseph L. *Mexico: Land of Mary's Wonders.* Paterson, N.J.: Saint Anthony Guild Press, 1958.

Castañeda, Carlos E. *Our Catholic Heritage in Texas, 1519–1935.* 7 vols. Austin, Tex.: Von Boechmann-Jones, 1936.

Castañeda, Pedro de. "The Narrative of the Expedition of Coronado by Castañeda." In *Spanish Explorers in the Southern United States, 1528–1543,* edited by Theodore H. Lewis and Frederick W. Hodge, 275–387. Austin: Texas State Historical Association, 1990.

Castillo Utrilla, María José del. "La hospedería de indias y el atrio del convento Casa Grande del San Francisco de Sevilla." In *Andalucía y América en el siglo XVI: Actas de las II Jornadas de Andalucía y América,* 393–98. Sevilla, Spain: Escuela de Estudio Hispano-Americanos de Sevilla, 1983.

Castro Gutiérrez, Felipe. *La extinción de la artesanía gremial.* Mexico City: UNAM, 1986.

Castro Morales, Efraín. *The Art of Ironworks in Mexico.* Introduction by Guillermo Tovar de Teresa. Mexico City: Grupo Financiero Bancomer, 1994.

Catholic Encyclopedia. Edited by Charles G. Herbermann et al. 15 vols. New York: Encyclopedia Press, 1913.

Chanfón Olmos, Carlos. "El supuesto carácter militar de los conventos." In *Conventos coloniales en Morelos,* 94–115. Mexico City: El Instituto de Cultura de Morelos, 1994.

Chapman, Michael Andrew. "The Liturgical Directions of Saint Charles Borromeo." *Liturgical Arts* 4 (1935): 60–118; 5 (1936): 60–63, 105–9; and 6 (1938): 91–94.

Charbonneau-Lassay, Louis. *The Bestiary of Christ.* Translated and abridged by D. M. Dooling. New York: Penguin, 1991.

Charlot, Jean. *Mexican Art and the Academy of San Carlos, 1785–1915.* Austin: University of Texas Press, 1962.

Chaunu, Pierre, and Huguette Chaunu. *Séville et l'Atlantique, 1504–1650.* 10 vols. Paris: Serpen, 1955–60.

Chávez, Angélico. *La Conquistadora: The Autobiography of an Ancient Statue.* Santa Fe, N.Mex.: Sunstone Press, 1975.

______. *Our Lady of Conquest.* Santa Fe: Historical Society of New Mexico, 1948.

Chorpenning, Joseph F. "The Iconography of St. Joseph in Mexican Devotional Retablos." In *Mexican Devotional Retablos from the Peters Collection,* 49–92. Philadelphia: Saint Joseph's University, 1994.

Clavijero, Francisco Javier. *Historia de la antigua o Baja California.* Mexico City: Editorial Porrúa, 1975.

Collins, Harold E. *The Church Edifice and Its Appointments.* Philadelphia: Dolphin Press, 1936.

Corbalán, Pedro, Pedro Taxalde, and Pedro Alcado. "1774 Contract for Suaqui Grande, San Marcial, Sonora." Unpublished manuscript translation at San Francisco Xavier del Bac Library, Tucson, Ariz., n.d.

Cornelius, F. Dupont. "Restoration Notes on Certain Spanish Colonial Paintings in Santa Fe." In *Hispanic Arts and Ethnohistory of the Southwest,* edited by Martha Weigle with Claudia Lanscombe and Samuel Lanscombe, 226–239. Santa Fe, N.Mex.: Ancient City Press, 1983.

Coronado, Eligio Moisés. "Misión de San Francisco Xavier Biaundó." In *Descripción e inventarios de las misiones de Baja California,* 46–65. La Paz, Mexico: Gobierno del Estado de Baja California Sur, 1992.

Crosby, Anthony. "More Ways to Wash White." *National Park Service Technical Bulletin* 8, no. 6 (1985): 11.

Crouch, Dora P., Daniel J. Garr, and Axel I. Mundigo. *Spanish City Planning in North America.* Cambridge, Mass.: MIT Press, 1982.

Crouch, Margaret, and William John Summers. "An Annotated Bibliography and Commentary Concerning Mission Music of Alta California, 1769–1834." *Current Musicology* 22 (1976): 66–99.

Curiel, Gustavo. "Nuevas noticias sobre un taller de artistas de la nobleza indígena." In *Imaginería virreinal: Memorias de un seminario,* 119–35. Mexico City: IIE/UNAM and INAH/SEP, 1990.

Da Silva, Owen. *Mission Music of California: A Collection of Old California Mission Hymns and Masses.* Los Angeles: Warren F. Lewis, 1941.

Decorme, Gerard. *La obra de los jesuitas mexicanos durante la época colonial, 1572–1767.* Mexico City: Antigua Librería Robredo de José Porrúa e Hijos, 1941.

Díaz, Marco. *Arquitectura en el desierto: Misiones jesuitas en Baja California.* Mexico City: UNAM, 1986.

______. "La fiesta religiosa come articulación de la vida citadina." In *El arte efímero en el mundo hispánico,* 109–22. Mexico City: IIE/UNAM, 1983.

Díaz Vaquero, María Dolores. *La Virgen en el escultura cordobesa del barroco.* Córdoba: Publicaciones del Monte de Piedad y Caja de Ahorros de Córdoba, 1987.

Dickey, James. "Allah and Eternity: Mosques, Madrasas and Tombs." In *Architecture of the Islamic World,* edited by George Mitchell, 15–47. London: Thames and Hudson, 1978.

Domínguez, Francisco Atanasio. *The Missions of New Mexico, 1776: A Description by Fray Francisco Atanasio Domínguez with Other Contemporary Documents.* Translated and annotated by Eleanor B. Adams and Fray Angélico Chávez. Albuquerque: University of New Mexico Press, 1956.

Dorta, Enrique Marco. *Arte en América y Filipinas.* Ars Hispaniae, vol. 21. Madrid: Editorial Plus-Ultra, 1973.

Duchet-Suchaux, Gaston, and Michel Pastoureau. *The Bible and the Saints.* Translated by David Radzinowicz Howell. Paris: Flammarion, 1994.

Durandus, William. *The Symbolism of Churches and Church Ornaments.* Latin original, Rome, ca. 1295. English translation, London: Gibbings, 1893.

Eberlein, Johann Konrad. "The Curtain in Raphael's Sistine Madonna." *Art Bulletin* 65, no. 1 (Mar. 1983): 61–77.

Egan, Martha J. *Milagros: Votive Offerings from the Americas.* Santa Fe: Museum of New Mexico Press, 1991.

______. *Relicarios: Devotional Miniatures from the Americas.* Santa Fe: Museum of New Mexico Press, 1991.

Eliade, Mircea. "Sacred Architecture and Symbolism." In *Symbolism, the Sacred, and the Arts,* 105–29. New York, Crossroad, 1985. Reprint, New York: Continuum, 1992.

______. "Symbolism and History." In *Images and Symbols,* 151–75. Princeton, N.J.: Princeton University Press, 1991.

______. "Symbolism of the 'Centre.'" In *Images and Symbols,* 27–56. Princeton, N.J.: Princeton University Press, 1991.

Ellis, Bruce. *Bishop Lamy's Santa Fe Cathedral.* Albuquerque: University of New Mexico Press, 1985.

Engelhardt, Zephyrin. *The Missions and Missionaries of California.* Vol. 1, *Lower California.* Santa Barbara, Calif.: Mission Santa Barbara, 1929.

______. *The Missions and Missionaries of California.* Vol. 2, *Upper California.* San Francisco: n.p., 1912.

Enggass, Robert, and Jonathan Brown. *Italy and Spain, 1600–1750.* Englewood Cliffs, N.J.: Prentice Hall, 1970.

Esparza Liberal, María José, and Isabel Fernández de García-Lascurain. *La cera en México: Arte e historia.* Mexico City: Fomento Cultural Banamex, 1994.

Espinosa, Isidro Félix de. *Crónica de los colegios de propaganda fide de la Nueva España.* Introduction and notes by Lino G. Canedo. Washington, D.C.: Academy of American Franciscan History, 1964.

Espinosa, José E. *Saints in the Valleys: Christian Sacred Images in the History, Life, and Folk Art of Spanish New Mexico.* Albuquerque: University of New Mexico Press, 1960.

Esteras Martín, Cristina. "Mexican Silverwork in Spain: Art, Devotion, and Social Status." *Artes de Mexico* 22 (Winter 1993–94): 90–93. (See also illustrations on pp. 40–51.)

Estrada, Julio, ed. *Música y músicos de la época virreinal.* Mexico City: SEP, 1973.

Estrada Jasso, Andrés. *Imágenes en caña de maíz.* San Luis Potosí: Universidad Autónoma de San Luis Potosí, 1966.

Fernández, Justino. *El arte del siglo XIX en México.* Mexico City: IIE/UNAM, 1967.

______. *El Retablo de los Reyes de la Nueva España.* Mexico City: IIE/UNAM, 1959.

______. "Santa Brígida de México." *Anales del Instituto de Investigaciones Estéticas* 9, no. 3 (1966): 15–25.

______. "Una escultura tequitqui en Monterrey." *Anales del Instituto de Investigaciones Estéticas* 3, no. 12 (1945): 15–17.

Fernández, Martha. "El albañil, el arquitecto y el alarife en la Nueva España." *Anales del Instituto de Investigaciones Estéticas* 14, no. 55 (1986): 49–68.

Fernández de Paz, Eva. *Religiosidad popular sevillana a través de los retablos de culto callejero.* Sevilla, Spain: Diputación Provincial de Sevilla, 1987.

Ferrando Roig, Juan. *Iconografía de los santos.* Barcelona, Spain: Ediciones Omega, 1950.

Flynn, Maureen. *Sacred Charity: Confraternities and Social Welfare in Spain, 1400–1700.* Ithaca, N.Y.: Cornell University Press, 1989.

Foz y Foz, Pilar. *La revolución pedagógica en Nueva España, 1754–1820: María Ignacia de Azlor y Echeverz y los Colegios de la Enseñanza.* 2 vols. Madrid: Instituto Gonzalo Fernández de Oviedo, 1981.

Franco Carrasco, Jesús. *El Nuevo Santander y su arquitectura.* 2 vols. Mexico City: IIE/UNAM, 1991.

Freze, Michael. *The Making of Saints.* Huntington, Ind.: Our Sunday Visitor, 1991.

García Sáiz, María Concepción. "A Bridge of Imagination: Mexican Colonial Art in Spain." *Artes de México* 22 (Winter 1993–94): 86–93. (See also illustrations on pp. 52–63, 65.)

Gerhard, Peter. *The North Frontier of New Spain.* Rev. ed. Norman: University of Oklahoma Press, 1993.

Giffords, Gloria Fraser. *The Art of Private Devotion: Retablo Painting of Mexico.* Fort Worth-Dallas, Tex.: InterCultura and Meadows Museum, Southern Methodist University, 1991.

______. *Mexican Folk Retablos.* Rev. ed. Albuquerque: University of New Mexico Press, 1992.

Giffords, Gloria Fraser, and Christopher Stavroudis. "Preliminary Investigations of Decorative Techniques and Materials Used in San Xavier del Bac." Unpublished manuscript, 1978.

Gihr, Nicholas. *The Holy Sacrifice of the Mass: Dogmatically, Liturgically and Ascetically Explained.* Saint Louis: B. Herder, 1918.

Godwin, Malcolm. *Angels: An Endangered Species.* New York: Simon and Schuster, 1990.

Göllner, Theodor. "Two Polyphonic Passions from California's Mission Period." *Yearbook for Inter-American Musical Research* 6 (1970): 67–89.

González Franco, Glorinela, María del Carmen Olvera Calvo, and Ana Eugenia Reyes y Cabañas. *Artistas y artesanos a través de fuentes documentales.* 2 vols. Mexico City: INAH, 1994.

González Galván, Manuel. "De los fustes barrocos latinoamericanos." In *Simpatías y diferencias,* 191–209. Mexico City: IIE/UNAM, 1988.

______. "El espacio en la arquitectura religiosa virreinal de México." *Anales del Instituto de Investigaciones Estéticas* 9, no. 35 (1966): 69–104.

______. "Modalidades del barroco mexicano." *Anales del Instituto de Investigaciones Estéticas* 8, no. 30 (1961): 39–68.

González Rodríguez, Luis. *Etnología y misión en la Pimería Alta, 1715–1740.* Mexico City: UNAM, 1977.

______. *El noroeste novohispano en el época colonial.* Mexico City: UNAM and Miguel Ángel Porrúa, 1993.

González Tirado, Carolusa. "El Tzauhtl: Adhesivo prehispánico obtenido a partir de orquídeas." *Imprimatura* 8 (Sept. 1994): 12–15.

Goss, Robert C. "The Churches of San Xavier, Arizona, and Caborca, Sonora: A Comparative Analysis." *Kiva* 40, no. 3 (Spring 1975): 165–79.

______. "The Problem of Erecting the Main Dome and Roof Vaults of the Church of San Xavier del Bac." *Kiva* 37, no. 3 (Spring 1972): 117–27.

Grant, Campbell. *The Rock Paintings of the Chumash.* Berkeley: University of California Press, 1965.

Grube, Ernst J. "What Is Islamic Architecture?" In *Architecture of the Islamic World,* edited by George Mitchell, 10–14. London: Thames and Hudson, 1978.

Guillot Carrotalá, José. *Temas españoles: Los gremios españoles.* Madrid: Publicaciones Españoles, 1954.

Gustín, Monique. *El barroco en la Sierra Gorda.* Mexico City: INAH, 1969.

Gwilt, John. *The Encyclopedia of Architecture, Historical, Theoretical, and Practical.* Rev. ed. New York: Bonanza, 1982.

Hackett, Charles W., ed. *Historical Documents Relating to New Mexico, Nueva Vizcaya and Approaches Thereto, 1773.* 3 vols. Washington, D.C.: Carnegie Institute, 1923–37.

Hageman, Fred C., and Russell C. Ewing. *An Archaeological and Restoration Study of Mission La Purísima Concepción.* Edited by Richard S. Whitehead. Santa Barbara, Calif.: Santa Barbara Trust for Historic Preservation, 1980.

Hamlin, A[lfred] D[wight] F[oster]. *A History of Ornament.* 2 vols. New York: Cooper Square, 1973.

Hardison, O. B. Jr. "Essay II: The Mass as Sacred Drama." In *Christian Rite and Christian Drama in the Middle Ages,* 35–79. Baltimore: Johns Hopkins University Press, 1965.

Heim, Bruno Bernard. *Heraldry in the Catholic Church.* Gerrards Cross, England: Van Duren, 1978.

Hellendoorn, Fabienne E. *Influencia del manierismo-nórdico en la arquitectura virreinal religiosa de México.* Mexico City: Technische Hogeschool, 1980.

Herreras, E. D. "Problems of Restoration of San Xavier." *Arizona Architect* 1, no. 9 (1958): 27–37.

Herrerías de la Fuente, Mónica. *El retablo de la iglesia conventual de Xochimilco.* Churubusco, Mexico: Escuela Nacional de Conservación, Restauración y Museografía, 1979.

Hilgers, Joseph. "Scapular." In *Catholic Encyclopedia,* edited by Charles G. Herbermann et al., vol. 13, p. 510. New York: Encyclopedia Press, 1913.

Hoag, John D. *Islamic Architecture.* New York: Rizzoli, 1987.

Hodge, Frederick Webb, George P. Hammond, and Agapito Rey. "Supplies for Benavides and Companions Going to New Mexico, 1624–1626." In *Fray Alonso de Benavides' Revised Memorial of 1634,* pp. 109–24. Albuquerque: University of New Mexico Press, 1948.

Horovitz, Isabel. "The Materials and Techniques of European Paintings on Copper Supports." In *Copper as Canvas: Two Centuries of Masterpiece Paintings on Copper, 1575–1775,* by Phoenix Art Museum, 63–92. New York: Oxford University Press, 1999.

Huerta Carrillo, Alejandro. "Una técnica del siglo XVI en pintura sobre tabla." *INAH Boletín* (ser. 2) no. 6 (July–Sept. 1973): 35–42.

Hulme, F. Edward. *Symbolism in Christian Art.* London: Swan Sonnerschein, 1909.

Ignatius of Loyola. *The Spiritual Exercises of Saint Ignatius.* Translated by Louis J. Puhl. Westminster, Md.: New Man Press, 1960.

Ivey, James E. *In the Midst of a Loneliness: The Architectural History of the Salinas Missions.* Prof. Paper no. 15. Santa Fe, N.M.: Southwest Cultural Resources Center, 1988.

Jaffé, Aniela. "Symbolism in the Visual Arts." In *Man and His Symbols,* by Carl G. Jung, Joseph L. Henderson, M[arie]-L[uise] von Franz, Aniela Jaffé, and Jolande Jacobi, 230–71. Garden City, N.Y.: Doubleday 1964.

Jenner, Henry. "Mozarabic." In *Catholic Encyclopedia,* edited by Charles G. Herbermann et al., vol. 10, pp. 611–22. New York: Encyclopedia Press, 1913.

Jones, Oakah L., Jr. *Nueva Vizcaya: Heartland of the Spanish Frontier.* Albuquerque: University of New Mexico Press, 1988.

Jung, Carl G[ustav] "Approaching the Unconscious." In *Man and His Symbols,* by Carl G. Jung, Joseph L. Henderson, M[arie]-L[uise] von Franz, Aniela Jaffé, and Jolande Jacobi, 18–103. Introduction by John Freeman. Garden City, N.Y.: Doubleday, 1964.

Jungmann, Joseph. *The Mass of the Roman Rite: Its Origins and Development.* 2 vols. 2d ed. New York: Benziger, 1951–55.

Kelemen, Pál. *Baroque and Rococo in Latin America.* 2d ed. 2 vols. New York: Macmillan, 1951.

______. "A Mexican Colonial Catafalque." *Art Quarterly* 28, no. 4 (1965): 277–92.

______. "The Significance of the Stone Retable of Cristo Rey." *Palacio* 61, no. 8 (Aug. 1954): 243–72.

Kessell, John L. *Friars, Soldiers and Reformers.* Tucson: University of Arizona Press, 1976.

______. *The Missions of New Mexico since 1776.* Albuquerque: University of New Mexico Press, 1980.

Kinkead, Duncan. "Juan de Luzón and the Sevillan Painting Trade with the New World in the Second Half of the Seventeenth Century." *Art Bulletin* 66, no. 2 (June 1984): 303–10.

Kino, Eusebio Francisco. *Kino's Historical Memoir of the Pimería Alta.* Translated, edited, and annotated by Herbert Eugene Bolton. 2 vols. in one. Berkeley: University of California Press, 1948.

Kocker, Paul H. *Mission San Luis Obispo de Tolosa.* San Luis Obispo, Calif.: Blake, 1972.

Koegel, John. "Sources of Hispanic Music of the Southwest (United States)." Paper delivered at the Fifty-Ninth Annual Meeting of the American Musicological Society in Montreal, Nov. 4–7, 1993.

______. "Spanish Mission Music from California: Past, Present and Future Research." *American Music Research Center Journal* 3 (1993): 78–111.

Krell, Dorothy, ed. *The California Missions.* Menlo Park, Calif.: Sunset Books, 1979.

Kubler, George. *Mexican Architecture in the Sixteenth Century.* 2 vols. Westport, Conn.: Greenwood, 1972.

______. *Portuguese Plain Architecture: Between Spices and Diamonds, 1521–1706.* Middletown, Conn.: Wesleyan University Press, 1972.

______. *Religious Architecture of New Mexico.* Albuquerque: University of New Mexico Press, 1972.

Kubler, George, and Martin Soria. *Art and Architecture in Spain and Portugal and Their American Dominions, 1500–1800.* Baltimore: Penguin, 1959.

Lange, Yvonne Marie. "Lithography, an Agent of Technological Change in Religious Folk Art: A Thesis." *Western Folklore* 33, no. 1 (Jan. 1974): 51–64.

______. "Santo Niño de Atocha: A Mexican Cult Is Transplanted to Spain." *Palacio* 84, no. 4 (Winter 1978): 2–7.

______. and Richard E. Ahlborn. *Mission San Xavier del Bac: A Guide to Its Iconography.* Tucson: University of Arizona Press.

Lea, Henry Charles. *A History of the Inquisition of the Middle Ages.* 4 vols. New York: Macmillan, 1922.

Leutenegger, Benedict, trans. "Inventory of the Material Possessions of Mission San José." In *The San José Papers: Edited Primary Manuscript Sources for the History of Mission San José y San Miguel de Aguayo,* edited by Benedict Leutenegger, Marion Habig, and M. Carmelita Casso, 93–104. San Antonio, Tex.: Old Spanish Missions Historical Research Library at San José Mission, 1983.

Leutenegger, Benedict, and Marion Habig, trans. and eds. *Guidelines for a Texas Mission: Instructions for the Missionary of Mission Concepción in San Antonio.* San Antonio, Tex.: Old Spanish Missions Historical Research Library at San José Mission, 1976.

Leutenegger, Benedict, Marion Habig, and M. Carmelita Casso, eds. *The San José Papers: Edited Primary Manuscript Sources for the History of Mission San José y San Miguel de Aguayo.* Translated by Benedict Leutenegger. San Antonio, Tex.: Old Spanish Missions Historical Research Library at San José Mission, 1983.

Lewis, Theodore H., and Frederick W. Hodge, eds. *Spanish Explorers in the Southern United States, 1528–1543,* Austin: Texas State Historical Association, 1985.

Loth, Calder. *The Only Proper Style.* Boston: New York Graphic Society, 1975.

Loyzaga, Jorge. "Taracea en México." In *El mueble mexicano,* 73–90. Mexico City: Fomento Cultural Banamex, 1985.

Luft, Enrique. "The Cornstalk Images of Michoacán." *Artes de Mexico* no. 153 (1972): 85–90. (See also illustrations on pp. 15–25.)

Mâle, Émile. *L'art religieux après le Concile de Trente: Étude sur l'iconographie de la fin du XVIe siècle, du XVIIIe siècle, Italie-France-Espagne-Flanders.* Paris: A. Colin, 1932.

Manrique, Jorge Alberto. "La estampa como fuente del arte en la Nueva España." *Anales del Instituto de Investigaciones Estéticas* no. 50 (1982).

______. "Reflexión sobre el manierismo en México." *Anales del Instituto de Investigaciones Estéticas,* no. 40 (1971): 21–42.

Maquivar, María del Consuelo. "La escultura devocional." In *Mexico en el mundo de las colecciones de arte*, vol. 1, pp. 301–27. Mexico City: Azabache, 1994.

———. *El imaginero novohispano y su obra: Las esculturas de Tepotzotlán*. Mexico City: INAH, 1995.

María y Campos, Teresa de, and Teresa Castelló Yturbide. *Historia y arte de la seda en México: Siglos XVI–XX*. Mexico City: Banamex, 1990.

Márquez Morfín, Lourdes. *Sociedad colonial y enfermedad*. Mexico City: INAH, 1984.

Martínez del Río de Redo, Marita. "Dos iglesias barrocas en la Sierra de Sinaloa." In José Guadalupe Victoria et al., *Estudios acerca del arte novohispano*, 73–75. Mexico City: UNAM, 1986.

Martínez López, María, and Fernando Sánchez Martínez. "Estudio sobre la madera." In *El mueble mexicano*, 135–49. Mexico City: Fomento Cultural Banamex, 1985.

Martínez Marín, Carlos. "La pirotecnia." In *El arte efímero en el mundo hispánico*, 201–23. Mexico City: IIE/UNAM, 1983.

Martínez Peñaloza, Porfirio, et al. *El arte de la platería mexicana: 500 años*. Mexico City: Fundación Cultural Televisa, 1989.

Maryknoll Catholic Dictionary. Edited by Albert J. Nevins. New York: Grossett and Dunlap, 1994.

Mather, Christine, ed. *Colonial Frontiers: Art and Life in Spanish New Mexico: The Fred Harvey Collection*. Santa Fe, N.Mex.: Ancient City Press, 1983.

Mayer, Ralph. *The Artist's Handbook*. 4th ed. New York: Viking Press, 1981.

Mayer-Thurman, Crista C. *Raiment for the Lord's Service*. Chicago: Art Institute of Chicago, 1975.

Maza, Francisco de la. *El alabastro en el arte colonial de México*. Mexico City: INAH, 1966.

———. "Algunas obras desconocidas de Manuel Tolsá." In *Obras escogidas*, edited by Elisa Vargas Lugo, 201–22. Mexico City: IIE/UNAM, 1992.

———. *La capilla de San José Chiapa*. Mexico City: INAH, 1960.

———. *Catarina de San Juan: Princesa de la India y visionaria de Puebla*. Edited by Elisa Vargas Lugo. Mexico City: Consejo Nacional para la Cultura y las Artes, 1990.

———. "La catedral de Chihuahua." *Anales del Instituto de Investigaciones Estéticas* 30 (1961): 21–30.

———. *La ciudad de México en el siglo XVII*. Mexico City: SEP, 1968.

———. "Dibujos y proyectos de Tresguerras." In *Obras escogidas*, edited by Elisa Vargas Lugo, 174–78, 192. Mexico City: IIE/UNAM, 1992.

———. *El pintor Martín de Vos en México*. Mexico City: IIE/UNAM, 1971.

McAndrew, John. *The Open-Air Churches of Sixteenth-Century Mexico: Atrios, Posas, Open Chapels, and Other Studies*. Cambridge, Mass: Harvard University Press, 1965.

McCarty, Kieran. *A Spanish Frontier in the Enlightened Age: Franciscan Beginnings in Sonora and Arizona, 1767–1770*. Washington, D.C.: Academy of American Franciscan History, 1981.

Medel Martínez, Vicente. *Vocabulario arquitectónico ilustrado*. Mexico City: Secretaría del Patrimonio Nacional, 1976.

Meditations on the Life of Christ: An Illustrated Manuscript of the Fourteenth Century. Translated by Isa Ragusa. Completed from the Latin and edited by Isa Ragusa and Rosalie B. Green. Princeton, N.J.: Princeton University Press, 1961.

Minge, Ward Alan. "Efectos del País: A History of Weaving along the Rio Grande." In Dorothy Boyd Bowen et al., *Spanish Textile Tradition of New Mexico and Colorado*, 8–28. Santa Fe: Museum of New Mexico Press, 1979.

Montenegro, Roberto. *Retablos de México: Ex-votos*. Mexico City: Ediciones Mexicanos, 1950.

Montgomery, Ross Gordon, Watson Smith, and John Otis Brew. *Franciscan Awatovi*. Cambridge, Mass.: Peabody Museum of American Archaeology and Ethnology, Harvard University, 1949.

Monumentos históricos inmuebles: Baja California, Baja California Sur, Coahuila, Tamaulipas and Chihuahua. 40 vols. Mexico City: SEP/INAH, Programa Cultural de las Fronteras, and Gobierno del Estado, 1986.

Morales, Alfredo J. "Nuevo dato sobre capillas abiertas españoles." In Bibiano Torres Ramírez and José Jesús Hernández Polomo, eds., *Andalucía y América en el siglo XVI: Actos de las II Jornadas de Andalucía y América*, vol. 2, pp. 453–63. Sevilla: Escuela de Estudios Hispano-Americanos de Sevilla, 1983.

Motolinia [Fray Toribio de Benavente, OFM]. *Historia de los indios de la Nueva España*. Mexico City: Salvador Chávez Hayhoe, 1941.

Moyssén, Xavier. "Escultura de pasta de caña y piedra." In *Imaginería virreinal: Memorias de un seminario,* 21–24. Mexico City: IIE/UNAM and INAH, 1990.

______. "El grabado en la Nueva España." INAH *Boletín* 18 (Dec. 1964): 15–17.

Muriel [de la Torre], Josefina. *Conventos de monjas en la Nueva España.* Mexico City: Editorial Jus, 1946.

______. *Hospitales de la Nueva España.* 2d ed. Vol. 2. Mexico City: UNAM and Cruz Roja Mexicana, 1990–91.

______. "Role of Convents in Colonial Mexico." *Artes de México* no. 198 (1979): 95–99. (See also illustrations on pp. 8–22.)

Muriel de la Torre, Josefina, and Manuel Romero de Terreros. *Retratos de monjas.* Mexico City: Editorial Jus, 1952.

Neuerburg, Norman. "The Angel on the Cloud, or 'Anglo-American Myopia' Revisited: A Discussion of the Writings of James L. Nolan." *Southern California Quarterly* 17, no. 1 (Spring 1980): 1–48.

______. "The Function of Prints in the California Missions." *Southern California Quarterly* 67, no. 3 (Fall 1985): 263–80.

Newton, John. "The Assyrian 'Grove' and Other Emblems." In *Ancient Pagan and Modern Christian Symbolism Exposed and Explained,* 107–35. New York: Peter Eckler, 1869.

Nichols, Stephen G., Jr. *Romanesque Signs.* New Haven, Conn.: Yale University Press, 1983.

Nobel, Thomas F. X., and Thomas Head. *Soldiers of Christ: Saints and Saints' Lives from Late Antiquity and the Early Middle Ages.* University Park: Penn State University Press, 1995.

Norrington, Edna. "The Beginning of the Church in Mexico, 1520–1600." Master's thesis, University of Kansas, Park College, 1920.

Norris, Herbert. *Church Vestments: Their Origin and Development.* New York: Dutton, 1950.

Nunis, Doyce B. *The Drawings of Ignacio Tirsch: A Jesuit Missionary in Baja California.* Original German captions translated by Elsbeth Schulz-Bischof. Baja California Travel Series, 27. Los Angeles: Dawson's Book Shop, 1972.

Nutall, Zelia. "Royal Ordinances Concerning the Laying Out of New Towns." *Hispanic American Historical Review* 4 (1921): 743–53.

Ocaranza, Fernando. *Los franciscanos en las Provincias Internas de Sonora y Ostimuri.* Mexico City: n.p., 1935.

O'Connell, John Berthram. *Church Building and Furnishing: The Church's Way.* Notre Dame, Ind.: University of Notre Dame Press, 1955.

Origo, Iris. *The World of San Bernardino.* New York: Harcourt, Brace and World, 1962.

Orso, Steven N. *Art and Death at the Spanish Habsburg Court: The Royal Exequies for Philip IV.* Columbia: University of Missouri Press, 1989.

Pacheco, Francisco. A los profesores del arte de la pintura. Sevilla, 1622. In *Fuente literarias para la historia del arte español,* vol. 5, translated and edited by F. J. Sánchez Cantón, 267–74. Reprint, Madrid: n.p., 1941.

______. *Arte de la pintura.* Sevilla: n.p., 1649. Introduction and notes by F. J. Sánchez Cantón. 2 vols. Reprint, Madrid: Instituto de Valencia de Don Juan, 1956.

Palladio, Andrea. *The Four Books of Architecture.* London, 1738. Reprint, New York: Dover, 1965.

Palmer, Gabrielle G. *Sculpture in the Kingdom of Quito.* Albuquerque: University of New Mexico Press, 1987.

Palomero Páramo, Jesús M. *El retablo sevillano del renacimiento.* Sevilla: Diputación Provincial de Sevilla, 1983.

Paz, Octavio. *Sor Juana: Her Life and World.* Translated by Margaret Sayers Peden. Boston: Faber, 1988.

Pennick, Nigel. *Sacred Geometry.* San Francisco: Harper and Row, 1980.

Pérez de Ribas, Andrés. *My Life among the Savage Nations of New Spain.* 1644. Translated by Tomás Antonio Robertson. Los Angeles: Ward Ritchie Press, 1968.

Petri, William Flinders. *Egyptian Decorative Art.* 2d ed. London: Methuen, 1920.

Pevsner, Nikolaus, John Fleming, and Hugh Honour. *A Dictionary of Architecture.* Woodstock, N.Y.: Overlook Press, 1978.

Pfefferkorn, Ignaz. *Sonora: A Description of the Province.* Cologne, 1794–95. Translated and edited by Theodore E. Treutlein. Albuquerque, N.Mex., 1949. Reprint, Tucson: University of Arizona Press, 1989.

Phoenix Art Museum. *Copper as Canvas: Two Centuries of Masterpiece Paintings on Copper, 1575–1775.* Oxford: Oxford University Press, 1999.

Porras Muñoz, Guillermo. *Iglesia y estado en Nueva Vizcaya, 1562–1821.* Mexico City: UNAM, 1980.

Prado Núñez, Ricardo. *Los túmulos de Santa Prisca.* Chilpancingo, Mexico: Instituto Guerrerense de la Cultura, 1991.

Quintana, José Miguel. *Agnus Dei de cera y otras noticias relativas.* Mexico City: Editorial Cultura, 1965.

Ramírez Leyva, Edelmira. "La censura inquisitorial novohispana sobre imágenes y objetos." In *Arte y coerción,* 149–62. Mexico City: IIE/UNAM, 1992.

Ramírez Montes, Mina. *La escuadra y el cincel: Documentos sobre la construcción de la catedral de Morelia.* Mexico City: IIE/UNAM, 1987.

———. *Pedro de Rojas y su taller de escultura en Querétaro.* Querétaro: Secretaría de Cultura y Bienestar Social del Gobierno del Estado de Querétaro, 1988.

———. *Retablos y retablistas: Querétaro en el siglo XVI.* Querétaro: Gobierno del Estado de Querétaro, 1998.

Ramírez, Torres, and José Jesús Hernández Polomo, eds. *Andalucía y América en el siglo XVI: Actas de las II Jornadas de Andalucía y América.* Sevilla: Escuela de Estudio Hispano-Americanos de Sevilla, 1983.

Ramos, I. G., et al. "Restauración de campanas antiguas: El estudio de un caso." *Imprimatura* no. 8 (Sept. 1940): 7–11.

Ray, Mary Dominic, and Joseph H. Engbeck Jr. *Gloria Dei: California Mission Music.* Sacramento: California Department of Parks and Recreation, 1974.

Réau, Louis. *Iconographie de l'art chrétien.* 6 vols. Paris: Presses Universitaires de France, 1955.

Reyes Valerio, Constantino. *Arte indocristiano: Escultura del siglo XVI en México.* Mexico City: INAH, 1978.

———. *El pintor de conventos: Los murales del siglo XVII en la Nueva España.* Mexico City: INAH, 1989.

Rice, Eugene F. Jr. *Saint Jerome in the Renaissance.* Baltimore: Johns Hopkins University Press, 1985.

Río, Ignacio del. *Conquista y aculturación en la California jesuita, 1697–1768.* Mexico City: UNAM, 1984.

Riva Palacio, Vicente, ed. *México a través de los siglos.* 5 vols. Mexico City: Ballescá, 1887.

Roca, Paul. *Paths of the Padres through Sonora.* Tucson: Arizona Historical Society, 1967.

Rodríguez Flores, Emilio. *Historia del real de minas de Sombrerete.* Sombrerete: H. Ayuntamiento de Sombrerete, 1990.

Roel, Santiago. *Nuevo León: Apuntes históricas en la historia y en la leyenda.* Monterrey: Impresor Bachiller, 1958.

Romero de Terreros y Vinent, Manuel. *Las artes industriales en la Nueva España.* Rev. ed. Mexico City: Banco Nacional de México, 1982.

Ross, James Bruce, and Mary Martin McLaughlin, eds. *The Portable Medieval Reader.* New York: Penguin, 1977.

Rubial García, Antonio. *El convento agustino y la sociedad novohispana (1533–1630).* Mexico City: UNAM, 1989.

Ruiz Gomar, José Rogelio. *El gremio de escultores y entalladores en Nueva España.* Mexico City: UNAM, 1990.

Russell, Craig H. "The Mexican Cathedral Music of Sumaya and Jerusalem: Lost Treasures, Royal Roads and New Worlds." In *Actas del XV congreso de la Sociedad Internacional de Musicología.* Madrid, Apr. 1992. Reprinted in *Revista de Musicología* 16, no. 1 (1993): 99–134.

———. "New Jewels in Old Boxes: Retrieving the Lost Musical Heritages of Colonial Mexico." *Ars Musica Denver* 5, no. 2 (Spring 1995): 13–38.

———. "Newly Discovered Treasures from Colonial California: The Masses at the San Fernando Mission." *Inter-American Music Review* 13, no. 1 (Fall–Winter 1992): 5–10.

Rykwert, Joseph. *Church Building.* New York: Hawthorn, 1956.

Sada de González, Lydia, and Margarita Mercedes Estella Marcos. *Ivories from the Far Eastern Provinces of Spain and Portugal.* Monterrey: Espejo de Obsidiana, 1977

Sagel, Jim, ed. *La iglesia de Santa Cruz de la Cañada.* Santa Cruz Parish, N.Mex.: 250th Anniversary Book Committee, 1983.

Salvatierra, Juan María de. *Misión de la Baja California.* Edited by Constantine Boyle. Madrid: La Editorial Católica S.A., 1946.

———. *Selected Letters about Lower California.* Translated and annotated by Earnest J. Burrus. Los Angeles: Dawson's Book Shop, 1971.

Sánchez Navarro de Pintado, Beatriz. *Marfiles cristianos del Oriente en México.* Mexico City: Fomento Cultural Banamex, 1986.

Santamaría, J[avier]. Francisco. *Diccionario de mejicanismos.* 2d ed. Mexico City: Porrúa, 1974.

Saravia, Atanasio G. *Obras.* Vol. 1, *Apuntas para la historia de la Nueva Vizcaya.* Mexico City: UNAM, 1978.

Sartor, Mario. *Arquitectura y urbanismo en Nueva España: Siglo XVI.* Mexico City: Azabache, 1992.

Schamoni, Wilhelm. *The Face of the Saints.* Translated by Anne Fremantle. New York: Pantheon, 1947.

Schenone, Héctor H. *Iconografía del arte colonial de los santos.* 2 vols. Buenos Aires: Fundación Tarea, 1992.

Scholes, France V. "The Supply Service of the New Mexico Missions in the Seventeenth Century." *New Mexico Historical Review* 5, no. 1 (1930): 93–115; no. 2 (1930): 186–210; and no. 4 (1930): 386–404.

Scholes, France V., and Eleanor B. Adams. *Inventories of Church Furnishings in Some of the New Mexico Missions, 1672*. Dargan Historical Essays. Edited by William M. Dabney and Josiah C. Russell. Albuquerque: University of New Mexico Press, 1952.

Schuetz-Miller, Mardith K. *Building and Builders in Hispanic California 1769–1850*. Tucson, Ariz.: Southwestern Mission Research Center and Santa Barbara, Calif.: A Santa Barbara Trust for Historic Preservation, 1994.

______. "Professional Artisans in the Hispanic Southwest." *Américas* 15, no. 1 (July 1983): 17–71.

______. "Proportional Systems and Ancient Geometry." *Southwest Mission Research Center Newsletter* 14, no. 48 (1980): 1–7.

______. , trans. *Architectural Practice in Mexico City: A Manual for Journeyman Architects of the Eighteenth Century*. Tucson: University of Arizona Press, 1987.

Schurz, William Lytle. *The Manila Galleon*. New York: Dutton, 1939.

Schwaller, John Frederick. *The Church and Clergy in Sixteenth-Century Mexico*. Albuquerque: University of New Mexico, 1987.

Scott, D. A., and W. D. Hyder. "A Study of Some California Indian Rock Art Pigments." *Studies in Conservation* 38, no. 3 (1993): 155–73.

Scott, D. A., et al. "Blood as a Binding Medium in a Chumash Indian Pigment Cake." *Archaeometry* 38, no. 1 (1996): 103–12.

Sebastián, Santiago. "La iconografía de Santiago en el arte hispanoamericano." In *Santiago y América*, 276–88. Santiago de Compostela: Xunta de Galicia and Arzobispado de Santiago de Compostela, 1993.

Serlio, Sebastiano. *The Five Books of Architecture*. Venice, 1584. English trans., London, 1611. Reprint, New York: Dover, 1963.

Sill, Gertrude Grace. *A Handbook of Symbols in Christian Art*. New York: Collier, 1975.

Simmons, Marc, and Frank Turley. *Southwestern Colonial Ironwork: The Spanish Blacksmithing Tradition from Texas to California*. Santa Fe: N.Mex.: Museum of New Mexico Press, 1980.

Smith, E. Baldwin. *Architectural Symbolism of Imperial Rome and the Middle Ages*. Princeton, N.J.: Princeton University Press, 1956.

______. *The Dome: A Study of Ideas*. Princeton, N.J.: Princeton University Press, 1978.

Smith, Watson, and Louie Ewing. *Kiva Mural Decorations: Awátovi and Kawaika*. Cambridge, Mass.: Peabody Museum of American Archaeology and Ethnology, Harvard University, 1952.

Spiess, Lincoln Bunce. "Church Music in 17th-Century New Mexico." *New Mexico Historical Review* 40, no. 1 (Jan. 1965): 5–21.

______. "Instruments in the Missions of New Mexico." In *Essays in Musicology: A Birthday Offering for Willi Apel*, edited by Hans Tischler, 131–36. Bloomington: Indiana University, School of Music, 1968.

Spillman, Trish. "Jergas." In Dorothy Boyd Bowen et al., *Spanish Textile Tradition of New Mexico and Colorado*, 146–52. Santa Fe: Museum of New Mexico Press, 1979.

Stanislawski, Dan. "Early Spanish Town Planning in the New World." *Geographical Review* 37, no. 1 (1947).

______. "The Origin and Spread of the Grid Pattern Town." *Geographical Review* 36, no. 1 (1946): 105–20.

Steen, Charlie R., and Rutherford J. Gettens. "Tumacacori Interior Decorations." *Arizoniana* 3, no. 3 (Fall 1962): 7–33.

Stevenson, Robert. *Music in Mexico: A Historical Study*. New York: Crowell, 1952.

Stierlin, Henri. *El barroco en España y Portugal. Saber Ver lo Contemporáneo del Arte*, no. 27 (1996).

Stratton, Suzanne L. *The Immaculate Conception in Spanish Art*. Cambridge: Cambridge University Press, 1994.

Sullivan, John. *The Externals of the Catholic Church*. 1917. 5th ed. New York: P. J. Kennedy, 1942.

Summers, William John. "New and Little Known Sources of California Mission Music." *Inter-American Music Review* 9 (1991): 13–24.

______. "Recently Recovered Manuscript Sources of Liturgical Polyphony from Hispanic California." *Ars Musica Denver* 7, no. 1 (Fall 1994): 13–30.

______. "Spanish Music in California, 1769–1840: A Reassessment." In *Report of the Twelfth Congress of the International Musicological Society*. Berkeley, 1977. Kassel, Germany: Bärenreiter, 1981.

Swift, Emerson H. *Roman Sources of Christian Art.* New York, 1951. Reprint, New York: Greenwood Press, 1970.

Taves, Ann. *The Household of Faith: Roman Catholic Devotions in Mid-Nineteenth-Century America.* Notre Dame, Ind.: University of Notre Dame Press, 1986.

Thurston, Herbert J. "Agnus Dei." In *Catholic Encyclopedia,* edited by Charles G. Herbermann et al., vol. 1, pp. 220–21. New York: Encyclopedia Press, 1913.

———. "Bells." In *Catholic Encyclopedia,* edited by Charles G. Herbermann et al., vol. 2, pp. 420–21. New York: Encyclopedia Press, 1913.

Thurston, Herbert J., and Donald Attwater. *Butler's Lives of the Saints.* 4 vols. Milltown, Md.: Christian Classics, 1981.

Tixeront, J. *Holy Orders and Ordination: A Study in the History of Dogma.* Translated by S. A. Raemers. Saint Louis: B. Herder, 1928.

Toscano, Guadalupe. *Testigos de piedra, las hornacinas del centro histórico de la ciudad de México.* Mexico City: Miguel Ángel Porrúa, 1988.

Toussaint, Manuel. *La Catedral de México y el Sagrario Metropolitano: Su historia, su tesoro, su arte.* Mexico City: Comisión Diocesana de Orden y Decoro, 1948.

———. *Colonial Art in Mexico.* Translated by Elizabeth Wilder Weismann. Austin: University of Texas Press, 1967.

———. *Pintura colonial en México.* Mexico City: 1965.

Tovar de Teresa, Guillermo. *Bibliografía novohispana de arte.* 2 vols. Mexico City: Fondo de Cultura Económica, 1988.

Ussel C., Aline. *Esculturas de la Virgen María en Nueva España, 1519–1821.* Colección Científica, vol. 24. Mexico City: INAH/SEP, 1975.

Van Dam, Raymond. *Saints and Their Miracles in Late Antique Gaul.* Princeton, N.J.: Princeton University Press, 1993.

Van Lengen, Johan. *Manual del arquitecto descalzo.* Mexico City: Editorial Concepto, 1980.

Vargas Lugo, Elisa. "Diferentes aspectos del desarrollo ornamental del barroco novohispano." In *Las portadas religiosas de México,* 311–28. Mexico City: IIE/UNAM, 1969.

———. "La expresión pictórica religiosa y la sociedad colonial" In *Estudio de pintura colonial hispanoamericana,* 9–27. Mexico City: UNAM, 1992.

———. *México barroco.* Mexico City: Hachette Latinoamérica, 1993.

———. "Niños de color 'quemado' en la pintura de Juan Correa." In *Estudio de pintura colonial hispanoamericana,* 55–63. Mexico City: UNAM, 1992.

———. *Portadas churriguerescas de la ciudad de México.* Mexico City: IIE/UNAM, 1986.

———. *Las portadas religiosas de México.* Mexico City: UNAM, 1969.

———. "Una aproximación al estudio del retrato en la pintura novohispana." In *Estudio de pintura colonial hispanoamericana,* 29–46. Mexico City: UNAM, 1992.

Vargas Lugo, Elisa, and José Guadalupe Victoria. *Juan Correa: Su vida y su obra: Catálogo.* Vol. 2, parts 1 and 2. Mexico City: UNAM, 1985.

Vargas Valdez, Jesús. *Catedral de testigo de la historia.* Chihuahua: Editorial Camino, 1993.

Vetancurt, Agustín de. Crónica de la provincia del Santo Evangélico de México. Part 4 of *Teatro mexicano.* Mexico City, 1698. Facsimile, Mexico City: Editorial Porrúa, 1971.

Victoria, José Guadalupe. *Pintura y sociedad en Nueva España: Siglo XVI.* Mexico City: IIE/UNAM, 1986.

Vignola, Giacomo Barozzio. *Canon of the Five Orders of Architecture.* Rome, 1562. First English translation, London, 1665. New English translation by Branko Mitrovic. New York: Acanthus Press, 1999.

Villar Movellán, Alberto, "Santos travestidos: Imágenes escondidas." Madrid: Fundación Universitaria Española. Reprinted in *Cuadernos de arte e iconografía* 2, no. 4 (1988): 183–91 and plates 68–71.

Villegas, Victor Manuel. *El gran signo formal del barroco.* Mexico City: IIE/UNAM, 1956.

Vitruvius, Marcus [Pollio]. "On Architecture." In *Vitruvius: The Ten Books of Architecture.* Leipzig, 1899. Translated by Morris Hicky Morgan. Cambridge, Mass., 1914. Reprint, New York: Dover, 1960.

Voragine, Jacobus de. *The Golden Legend.* Basel, 1470. Translated and adapted by Granger Ryan and Helmut Ripperger. London, 1941. Reprint, New York: Arno Press, 1969.

Walker, Barbara G. *Woman's Dictionary of Symbols and Sacred Objects.* New York: Harper Collins, 1988.

Walsh, Michael. *Dictionary of Catholic Devotions.* San Francisco: Harper, 1993.

Warner, Marina. *Alone of All Her Sex.* New York: Knopf, 1976.

Waters, Clara Erskine Clement. *Angels in Art*. Boston: L. C. Page, 1898.

Watts, Alan W. *Myth and Ritual in Christianity*. New York: Grove Press, 1954.

Webb, Edith Buckland. *Indian Life at the Old Missions*. 1952. Reprint, Lincoln: University of Nebraska Press, 1982.

______. "Pigments Used by the Mission Indians of California." *Américas* 2, no. 2 (Oct. 1945): 137–50.

Webber, Frederick Roth. *Church Symbolism*. 2d ed. Detroit: Gayle Research, 1971.

Weber, David J. *The Spanish Frontier in North America*. New Haven, Conn.: Yale University Press, 1992.

Weismann, Elizabeth Wilder. *Mexico in Sculpture*. Cambridge, Mass.: Harvard University Press, 1950.

Wilder, Mitchell A., and Edgar Breitenbach. *Santos: The Religious Folk Art of New Mexico*. Colorado Springs, Colo.: Taylor Museum, Colorado Springs Fine Arts Center, 1943.

Willetts, William. *Chinese Art*. Vol. 1. London: Richard Clay, 1958.

Wittkower, Rudolf. *Eagle and Serpent: Allegory and the Migration of Symbols*. London: Thames and Hudson, 1977.

Woodbridge, Hensley C., and Lawrence S. Thompson. *Printing in Colonial Spanish America*. Troy, N.Y.: Whiston, 1976.

Wroth, William. *Christian Images in Hispanic New Mexico*. Colorado Springs, Colo.: Taylor Museum, Colorado Springs Fine Arts Center, 1982.

______. *Images of Penance, Images of Mercy: Southwestern Santos in the Late Nineteenth Century*. Norman: University of Oklahoma Press, 1991.

Wuthenau, Alexander von. "The Spanish Military Chapels in Santa Fe and the Reredos of Our Lady of Light." *New Mexico Historical Review* 10, no. 3 (July 1935): 175–94.

Zahar, León R. "Transformed Geometry: Presences and Absences." *Artes de México* no. 54 (2001): 93–96. (See also illustrations on pp. 46–60.)

Zapata Aguilar, Gerardo. *Monterrey, siglo XVIII: Ciudad sin catedral*. Mexico City: Itnia, 1994.

INDEX

Pages with illustrations are indicated by *italics*. *Passim* is used for a cluster of references in close sequence.

B

C

J

K

L

M

Q

R

W

Z

The Southwest Center Series

Joseph C. Wilder, editor

Ignaz Pfefferkorn, *Sonora: A Description of the Province*

Carl Lumholtz, *New Trails in Mexico*

Buford Pickens, *The Missions of Northern Sonora: A 1935 Field Documentation*

Gary Paul Nabhan, editor, *Counting Sheep: Twenty Ways of Seeing Desert Bighorn*

Eileen Oktavec, *Answered Prayers: Miracles and Milagros along the Border*

Curtis M. Hinsley and David R. Wilcox, editors, *Frank Hamilton Cushing and the Hemenway Southwestern Archaeological Expedition, 1886–1889, volume 1: The Southwest in the American Imagination: The Writings of Sylvester Baxter, 1881–1899*

Lawrence J. Taylor and Maeve Hickey, *The Road to Mexico*

Donna J. Guy and Thomas E. Sheridan, editors, *Contested Ground: Comparative Frontiers on the Northern and Southern Edges of the Spanish Empire*

Julian D. Hayden, *The Sierra Pinacate*

Paul S. Martin, David Yetman, Mark Fishbein, Phil Jenkins, Thomas R. Van Devender, and Rebecca K. Wilson, editors, *Gentry's Rio Mayo Plants: The Tropical Deciduous Forest and Environs of Northwest Mexico*

W J McGee, *Trails to Tiburón: The 1894 and 1895 Field Diaries of W J McGee*, transcribed by Hazel McFeely Fontana, annotated and with an introduction by Bernard L. Fontana

Richard Stephen Felger, *Flora of the Gran Desierto and Río Colorado of Northwestern Mexico*

Donald Bahr, editor, *O'odham Creation and Related Events: As Told to Ruth Benedict in 1927 in Prose, Oratory, and Song by the Pimas William Blackwater, Thomas Vanyiko, Clara Ahiel, William Stevens, Oliver Wellington, and Kisto*

Dan L. Fischer, *Early Southwest Ornithologists, 1528–1900*

Thomas Bowen, editor, *Backcountry Pilot: Flying Adventures with Ike Russell*

Federico José María Ronstadt, *Borderman: Memoirs of Federico José María Ronstadt*, edited by Edward F. Ronstadt

Curtis M. Hinsley and David R. Wilcox, editors, Frank *Hamilton Cushing and the Hemenway Southwestern Archaeological Expedition, 1886–1889,* volume 2: *The Lost Itinerary of Frank Hamilton Cushing*

Neil Goodwin, *Like a Brother: Grenville Goodwin's Apache Years, 1928–1939*

Katherine G. Morrissey and Kirsten Jensen, editors, *Picturing Arizona: The Photographic Record of the 1930s*

Bill Broyles and Michael Berman, *Sunshot: Peril and Wonder in the Gran Desierto*

David W. Lazaroff, Philip C. Rosen, and Charles H. Lowe Jr., *Amphibians, Reptiles, and Their Habitats at Sabino Canyon*

David Yetman, *The Organ Pipe Cactus*

Gloria Fraser Giffords, *Sanctuaries of Earth, Stone, and Light: The Churches of Northern New Spain, 1530–1821*

David Yetman, *The Great Cacti: Ethnobotany and Biogeography*

About the Author

Conservator, historian, and author Gloria Fraser Giffords has studied the art and architecture of northern New Spain for more than thirty years. Her knowledge of the polychrome statuary and oil paintings of the region's Spanish churches and her wide experience in restoring artwork from the colonial period have given her a keen eye for the visual grammar of that time; she is considered to be among the foremost scholars of Spanish colonial art working today.

Giffords has served as curator, lecturer, and board member at the Los Angeles County Museum, the San Antonio Museum of Art, the Tucson Museum of Art, the Meadows Museum of Southern Methodist University, and the Millicent Rogers Museum. A fellow of the American Institute for Conservation, she maintains an art conservation practice while researching and writing on topics in Spanish colonial and nineteenth-century Mexican art history. She is the author of *Mexican Folk Retablos* (University of Arizona Press, 1974; revised edition, University of New Mexico Press, 1992) and *The Art of Private Devotion: Retablo Painting of Mexico* (InterCultura and Meadows Museum, 1991) and a contributor to *Artes de México, Native Peoples,* and other journals.